**Handbook of Human-Machine Systems**

# Handbook of Human-Machine Systems

*Edited by*

*Giancarlo Fortino*
University of Calabria
Italy

*David Kaber*
University of Florida
USA

*Andreas Nürnberger*
Otto-von-Guericke-Universität Magdeburg
Germany

*David Mendonça*
MITRE Corporation
USA

IEEE PRESS
WILEY

Published by John Wiley & Sons, Inc., Hoboken, New Jersey.
Published simultaneously in Canada.



***Library of Congress Cataloging-in-Publication Data applied for:***

Hardback ISBN: 9781119863632

Cover Design: Wiley
Cover Images: © bergamont/Shutterstock; SviatlanaLaza/Shutterstock; barleyman/Getty Images; 3alexd/Getty Images; Olemedia/Getty Images; Westend61/Getty Images; 3alexd/Getty Images; Monty Rakusen/Getty Images; Witthaya Prasongsin/Getty Images; Luca Sage/Getty Images; Nisian Hughes/Getty Images; Serhii Brovko/Getty Images

Set in 9.5/12.5pt STIXTwoText by Straive, Chennai, India

# Contents

**Editors Biography** *xxi*
**List of Contributors** *xxiii*
**Preface** *xxxiii*

1 **Introduction** *1*
*Giancarlo Fortino, David Kaber, Andreas Nürnberger, and David Mendonça*
1.1 Book Rationale *1*
1.2 Chapters Overview *2*
Acknowledgments *8*
References *8*

2 **Brain–Computer Interfaces: Recent Advances, Challenges, and Future Directions** *11*
*Tiago H. Falk, Christoph Guger, and Ivan Volosyak*
2.1 Introduction *11*
2.2 Background *12*
2.2.1 Active/Reactive BCIs *13*
2.2.2 Passive BCIs *14*
2.2.3 Hybrid BCIs *15*
2.3 Recent Advances and Applications *15*
2.3.1 Active/Reactive BCIs *15*
2.3.2 Passive BCIs *16*
2.3.3 Hybrid BCIs *16*
2.4 Future Research Challenges *16*
2.4.1 Current Research Issues *17*
2.4.2 Future Research Directions *17*
2.5 Conclusions *18*
References *18*

3 **Brain–Computer Interfaces for Affective Neurofeedback Applications** *23*
*Lucas R. Trambaiolli and Tiago H. Falk*
3.1 Introduction *23*
3.2 Background *23*
3.3 State-of-the-Art *24*
3.3.1 Depressive Disorder *25*
3.3.2 Posttraumatic Stress Disorder, PTSD *26*
3.4 Future Research Challenges *27*

3.4.1 Open Challenges *27*
3.4.2 Future Directions *28*
3.5 Conclusion *28*
References *29*

**4 Pediatric Brain–Computer Interfaces: An Unmet Need** *35*
*Eli Kinney-Lang, Erica D. Floreani, Niloufaralsadat Hashemi, Dion Kelly, Stefanie S. Bradley, Christine Horner, Brian Irvine, Zeanna Jadavji, Danette Rowley, Ilyas Sadybekov, Si Long Jenny Tou, Ephrem Zewdie, Tom Chau, and Adam Kirton*
4.1 Introduction *35*
4.1.1 Motivation *36*
4.2 Background *36*
4.2.1 Components of a BCI *36*
4.2.1.1 Signal Acquisition *36*
4.2.1.2 Signal Processing *36*
4.2.1.3 Feedback *36*
4.2.1.4 Paradigms *37*
4.2.2 Brain Anatomy and Physiology *37*
4.2.3 Developmental Neurophysiology *38*
4.2.4 Clinical Translation of BCI *38*
4.2.4.1 Assistive Technology (AT) *38*
4.2.4.2 Clinical Assessment *39*
4.3 Current Body of Knowledge *39*
4.4 Considerations for Pediatric BCI *40*
4.4.1 Developmental Impact on EEG-based BCI *40*
4.4.2 Hardware for Pediatric BCI *41*
4.4.3 Signal Processing for Pediatric BCI *41*
4.4.3.1 Feature Extraction, Selection and Classification *42*
4.4.3.2 Emerging Techniques *42*
4.4.4 Designing Experiments for Pediatric BCI *43*
4.4.5 Meaningful Applications for Pediatric BCI *43*
4.4.6 Clinical Translation of Pediatric BCI *44*
4.5 Conclusions *44*
References *45*

**5 Brain–Computer Interface-based Predator–Prey Drone Interactions** *49*
*Abdelkader Nasreddine Belkacem and Abderrahmane Lakas*
5.1 Introduction *49*
5.2 Related Work *50*
5.3 Predator–Prey Drone Interaction *51*
5.4 Conclusion and Future Challenges *57*
References *58*

**6 Levels of Cooperation in Human–Machine Systems: A Human–BCI–Robot Example** *61*
*Marie-Pierre Pacaux-Lemoine, Lydia Habib, and Tom Carlson*
6.1 Introduction *61*

6.2 Levels of Cooperation *61*
6.3 Application to the Control of a Robot by Thought *63*
6.3.1 Designing the System *64*
6.3.2 Experiments and Results *66*
6.4 Results from the Methodological Point of View *67*
6.5 Conclusion and Perspectives *68*
References *69*

**7 Human–Machine Social Systems: Test and Validation via Military Use Cases** *71*
*Charlene K. Stokes, Monika Lohani, Arwen H. DeCostanza, and Elliot Loh*
7.1 Introduction *71*
7.2 Background Summary: From Tools to Teammates *72*
7.2.1 Two Sides of the Equation *72*
7.2.2 Moving Beyond the Cognitive Revolution *73*
7.2.2.1 A Rediscovery of the Unconscious *74*
7.3 Future Research Directions *75*
7.3.1 Machine: Functional Designs *75*
7.3.2 Human: Ground Truth *76*
7.3.2.1 Physiological Computing *76*
7.3.3 Context: Tying It All Together *77*
7.3.3.1 Training and Team Models *77*
7.4 Conclusion *79*
References *79*

**8 The Role of Multimodal Data for Modeling Communication in Artificial Social Agents** *83*
*Stephanie Gross and Brigitte Krenn*
8.1 Introduction *83*
8.2 Background *84*
8.2.1 Context *84*
8.2.2 Basic Definitions *84*
8.3 Related Work *84*
8.3.1 HHI Data *85*
8.3.2 HRI Data *85*
8.3.2.1 Joint Attention and Robot Turn-Taking Capabilities *85*
8.3.3 Public Availability of the Data *87*
8.4 Datasets and Resulting Implications *87*
8.4.1 Human Communicative Signals *87*
8.4.1.1 Experimental Setup *87*
8.4.1.2 Data Analysis and Results *88*
8.4.2 Humans Reacting to Robot Signals *89*
8.4.2.1 Comparing Different Robotic Turn-Giving Signals *89*
8.4.2.2 Comparing Different Transparency Mechanisms *90*
8.5 Conclusions *91*
8.6 Future Research Challenges *91*
References *91*

9 **Modeling Interactions Happening in People-Driven Collaborative Processes** *95*
*Maximiliano Canche, Sergio F. Ochoa, Daniel Perovich, and Rodrigo Santos*
9.1 Introduction *95*
9.2 Background *97*
9.3 State-of-the-Art in Interaction Modeling Languages and Notations *98*
9.3.1 Visual Languages and Notations *99*
9.3.2 Comparison of Interaction Modeling Languages and Notations *100*
9.4 Challenges and Future Research Directions *101*
References *102*

10 **Transparent Communications for Human–Machine Teaming** *105*
*Jessie Y. C. Chen*
10.1 Introduction *105*
10.2 Definitions and Frameworks *105*
10.3 Implementation of Transparent Human–Machine Interfaces in Intelligent Systems *106*
10.3.1 Human–Robot Interaction *106*
10.3.2 Multiagent Systems and Human–Swarm Interaction *108*
10.3.3 Automated/Autonomous Driving *109*
10.3.4 Explainable AI-Based Systems *109*
10.3.5 Guidelines and Assessment Methods *109*
10.4 Future Research Directions *110*
References *111*

11 **Conversational Human–Machine Interfaces** *115*
*María Jesús Rodríguez-Sánchez, Kawtar Benghazi, David Griol, and Zoraida Callejas*
11.1 Introduction *115*
11.2 Background *115*
11.2.1 History of the Development of the Field *116*
11.2.2 Basic Definitions *117*
11.3 State-of-the-Art *117*
11.3.1 Discussion of the Most Important Scientific/Technical Contributions *117*
11.3.2 Comparison Table *119*
11.4 Future Research Challenges *121*
11.4.1 Current Research Issues *121*
11.4.2 Future Research Directions Dealing with the Current Issues *121*
References *122*

12 **Interaction-Centered Design: An Enduring Strategy and Methodology for Sociotechnical Systems** *125*
*Ming Hou, Scott Fang, Wenbi Wang, and Philip S. E. Farrell*
12.1 Introduction *125*
12.2 Evolution of HMS Design Strategy *126*
12.2.1 A HMS Technology: Intelligent Adaptive System *126*
12.2.2 Evolution of IAS Design Strategy *128*
12.3 State-of-the-Art: Interaction-Centered Design *130*

12.3.1 A Generic Agent-based ICD Framework *130*
12.3.2 IMPACTS: An Human–Machine Teaming Trust Model *132*
12.3.3 ICD Roadmap for IAS Design and Development *133*
12.3.4 ICD Validation, Adoption, and Contributions *134*
12.4 IAS Design Challenges and Future Work *135*
12.4.1 Challenges of HMS Technology *136*
12.4.2 Future Work in IAS Design and Validation *136*
References *137*

**13 Human–Machine Computing: Paradigm, Challenges, and Practices** *141*
*Zhiwen Yu, Qingyang Li, and Bin Guo*
13.1 Introduction *141*
13.2 Background *142*
13.2.1 History of the Development *142*
13.2.2 Basic Definitions *143*
13.3 State of the Art *144*
13.3.1 Technical Contributions *144*
13.3.2 Comparison Table *148*
13.4 Future Research Challenges *150*
13.4.1 Current Research Issues *150*
13.4.2 Future Research Directions *151*
References *152*

**14 Companion Technology** *155*
*Andreas Wendemuth*
14.1 Introduction *155*
14.2 Background *155*
14.2.1 History *156*
14.2.2 Basic Definitions *157*
14.3 State-of-the-Art *158*
14.3.1 Discussion of the Most Important Scientific/Technical Contributions *159*
14.4 Future Research Challenges *159*
14.4.1 Current Research Issues *159*
14.4.2 Future Research Directions Dealing with the Current Issues *160*
References *161*

**15 A Survey on Rollator-Type Mobility Assistance Robots** *165*
*Milad Geravand, Christian Werner, Klaus Hauer, and Angelika Peer*
15.1 Introduction *165*
15.2 Mobility Assistance Platforms *165*
15.2.1 Actuation *166*
15.2.2 Kinematics *166*
15.2.2.1 Locomotion Support *166*
15.2.2.2 STS Support *166*
15.2.3 Sensors *168*
15.2.4 Human–Machine Interfaces *168*
15.3 Functionalities *168*

15.3.1 STS Assistance *169*
15.3.2 Walking Assistance *169*
15.3.2.1 Maneuverability Improvement *169*
15.3.2.2 Gravity Compensation *170*
15.3.2.3 Obstacle Avoidance *170*
15.3.2.4 Falls Risk Prediction and Fall Prevention *170*
15.3.3 Localization and Navigation *170*
15.3.3.1 Map Building and Localization *171*
15.3.3.2 Path Planning *171*
15.3.3.3 Assisted Localization *171*
15.3.3.4 Assisted Navigation *171*
15.3.4 Further Functionalities *171*
15.3.4.1 Reminder Systems *171*
15.3.4.2 Health Monitoring *171*
15.3.4.3 Communication, Information, Entertainment, and Training *172*
15.4 Conclusion *172*
References *173*

**16 A Wearable Affective Robot** *181*
*Jia Liu, Jinfeng Xu, Min Chen, and Iztok Humar*
16.1 Introduction *181*
16.2 Architecture Design and Characteristics *183*
16.2.1 Architecture of a Wearable Affective Robot *183*
16.2.2 Characteristics of a Wearable Affective Robot *184*
16.3 Design of the Wearable, Affective Robot's Hardware *185*
16.3.1 AIWAC Box Hardware Design *185*
16.3.2 Hardware Design of the EEG Acquisition *185*
16.3.3 AIWAC Smart Tactile Device *185*
16.3.4 Prototype of the Wearable Affective Robot *186*
16.4 Algorithm for the Wearable Affective Robot *186*
16.4.1 Algorithm for Affective Recognition *186*
16.4.2 User-Behavior Perception based on a Brain-Wearable Device *186*
16.5 Life Modeling of the Wearable Affective Robot *187*
16.5.1 Data Set Labeling and Processing *188*
16.5.2 Multidimensional Data Integration *188*
16.5.3 Modeling of Associated Scenarios *188*
16.6 Challenges and Prospects *189*
16.6.1 Research Challenges of the Wearable Affective Robot *189*
16.6.2 Application Scenarios for the Wearable Affective Robot *189*
16.7 Conclusions *190*
References *190*

**17 Visual Human–Computer Interactions for Intelligent Vehicles** *193*
*Xumeng Wang, Wei Chen, and Fei-Yue Wang*
17.1 Introduction *193*
17.2 Background *193*

17.3 State-of-the-Art *194*
17.3.1 VHCI in Vehicles *194*
17.3.1.1 Information Feedback from Intelligent Vehicles *195*
17.3.1.2 Human-Guided Driving *195*
17.3.2 VHCI Among Vehicles *195*
17.3.3 VHCI Beyond Vehicles *195*
17.4 Future Research Challenges *196*
17.4.1 VHCI for Intelligent Vehicles *196*
17.4.1.1 Vehicle Development *196*
17.4.1.2 Vehicle Manufacture *197*
17.4.1.3 Preference Recording *197*
17.4.1.4 Vehicle Usage *197*
17.4.2 VHCI for Intelligent Transportation Systems *198*
17.4.2.1 Parallel World *198*
17.4.2.2 The Framework of Intelligent Transportation Systems *198*
References *199*

**18 Intelligent Collaboration Between Humans and Robots** *203*
*Andrea Maria Zanchettin*
18.1 Introduction *203*
18.2 Background *203*
18.2.1 Context *203*
18.2.2 Basic Definitions *204*
18.3 Related Work *205*
18.4 Validation Cases *206*
18.4.1 A Simple Verification Scenario *207*
18.4.2 Activity Recognition Based on Semantic Hand-Object Interaction *208*
18.5 Conclusions *210*
18.6 Future Research Challenges *210*
References *210*

**19 To Be Trustworthy and To Trust: The New Frontier of Intelligent Systems** *213*
*Rino Falcone, Alessandro Sapienza, Filippo Cantucci, and Cristiano Castelfranchi*
19.1 Introduction *213*
19.2 Background *214*
19.3 Basic Definitions *214*
19.4 State-of-the-Art *215*
19.4.1 Trust in Different Domains *215*
19.4.2 Selected Articles *215*
19.4.3 Differences in the Use of Trust *216*
19.4.4 Approaches to Model Trust *217*
19.4.5 Sources of Trust *218*
19.4.6 Different Computational Models of Trust *218*
19.5 Future Research Challenges *220*
References *221*

20 **Decoding Humans' and Virtual Agents' Emotional Expressions** *225*
*Terry Amorese, Gennaro Cordasco, Marialucia Cuciniello, Olga Shevaleva, Stefano Marrone, Carl Vogel, and Anna Esposito*
20.1 Introduction *225*
20.2 Related Work *226*
20.3 Materials and Methodology *227*
20.3.1 Participants *227*
20.3.2 Stimuli *228*
20.3.3 Tools and Procedures *228*
20.4 Descriptive Statistics *229*
20.5 Data Analysis and Results *230*
20.5.1 Comparison Synthetic vs. Naturalistic Experiment *234*
20.6 Discussion and Conclusions *235*
Acknowledgment *238*
References *238*

21 **Intelligent Computational Edge: From Pervasive Computing and Internet of Things to Computing Continuum** *241*
*Radmila Juric*
21.1 Introduction *241*
21.2 The Journey of Pervasive Computing *242*
21.3 The Power of the IoT *243*
21.3.1 Inherent Problems with the IoT *244*
21.4 IoT: The Journey from Cloud to Edge *245*
21.5 Toward Intelligent Computational Edge *246*
21.6 Is Computing Continuum the Answer? *247*
21.7 Do We Have More Questions than Answers? *248*
21.8 What Would our Vision Be? *249*
References *251*

22 **Implementing Context Awareness in Autonomous Vehicles** *257*
*Federico Faruffini, Alessandro Correa-Victorino, and Marie-Hélène Abel*
22.1 Introduction *257*
22.2 Background *258*
22.2.1 Ontologies *258*
22.2.2 Autonomous Driving *258*
22.2.3 Basic Definitions *259*
22.3 Related Works *260*
22.4 Implementation and Tests *261*
22.4.1 Implementing the Context of Navigation *261*
22.4.2 Control Loop Rule *262*
22.4.3 Simulations *263*
22.5 Conclusions *264*
22.6 Future Research Challenges *264*
References *264*

**23 The Augmented Workforce: A Systematic Review of Operator Assistance Systems** *267*
*Elisa Roth, Mirco Moencks, and Thomas Bohné*
23.1 Introduction *267*
23.2 Background *268*
23.2.1 Definitions *268*
23.3 State of the Art *269*
23.3.1 Empirical Considerations *270*
23.3.1.1 Application Areas *270*
23.3.2 Assistance Capabilities *270*
23.3.2.1 Task Guidance *271*
23.3.2.2 Knowledge Management *271*
23.3.2.3 Monitoring *273*
23.3.2.4 Communication *273*
23.3.2.5 Decision-Making *273*
23.3.3 Meta-capabilities *274*
23.3.3.1 Configuration Flexibility *274*
23.3.3.2 Interoperability *274*
23.3.3.3 Content Authoring *274*
23.3.3.4 Initiation *274*
23.3.3.5 Hardware *275*
23.3.3.6 User Interfaces *275*
23.4 Future Research Directions *275*
23.4.1 Empirical Evidence *275*
23.4.2 Collaborative Research *277*
23.4.3 Systemic Approaches *277*
23.4.4 Technology-Mediated Learning *277*
23.5 Conclusion *277*
References *278*

**24 Cognitive Performance Modeling** *281*
*Maryam Zahabi and Junho Park*
24.1 Introduction *281*
24.2 Background *281*
24.3 State-of-the-Art *282*
24.4 Current Research Issues *286*
24.5 Future Research Directions Dealing with the Current Issues *286*
References *287*

**25 Advanced Driver Assistance Systems: Transparency and Driver Performance Effects** *291*
*Yulin Deng and David B. Kaber*
25.1 Introduction *291*
25.2 Background *292*
25.2.1 Context *292*

25.2.2 Basic Definition *292*
25.3 Related Work *293*
25.4 Method *294*
25.4.1 Apparatus *295*
25.4.2 Participants *296*
25.4.3 Experiment Design *296*
25.4.4 Tasks *297*
25.4.5 Dependent Variables *297*
25.4.5.1 Hazard Negotiation Performance *297*
25.4.5.2 Vehicle Control Performance *298*
25.4.6 Procedure *298*
25.5 Results *299*
25.5.1 Hazard Reaction Performance *299*
25.5.2 Posthazard Manual Driving Performance *299*
25.5.3 Posttesting Usability Questionnaire *301*
25.6 Discussion *302*
25.7 Conclusion *303*
25.8 Future Research *304*
References *304*

**26 RGB-D Based Human Action Recognition: From Handcrafted to Deep Learning** *307*
*Bangli Liu and Honghai Liu*
26.1 Introduction *307*
26.2 RGB-D Sensors and 3D Data *307*
26.3 Human Action Recognition via Handcrafted Methods *308*
26.3.1 Skeleton-Based Methods *308*
26.3.2 Depth-Based Methods *309*
26.3.3 Hybrid Feature-Based Methods *309*
26.4 Human Action Recognition via Deep Learning Methods *310*
26.4.1 CNN-Based Methods *310*
26.4.2 RNN-Based Methods *311*
26.4.3 GCN-Based Methods *313*
26.5 Discussion *314*
26.6 RGB-D Datasets *314*
26.7 Conclusion and Future Directions *315*
References *316*

**27 Hybrid Intelligence: Augmenting Employees' Decision-Making with AI-Based Applications** *321*
*Ina Heine, Thomas Hellebrandt, Louis Huebser, and Marcos Padrón*
27.1 Introduction *321*
27.2 Background *321*
27.2.1 Context *321*
27.2.2 Basic Definitions *322*
27.3 Related Work *323*
27.4 Technical Part of the Chapter *324*

27.4.1 Description of the Use Case *324*
27.4.1.1 Business Model *324*
27.4.1.2 Process *324*
27.4.1.3 Use Case Objectives *325*
27.4.2 Description of the Envisioned Solution *325*
27.4.3 Development Approach of AI Application *326*
27.4.3.1 Development Process *326*
27.4.3.2 Process Analysis and Time Study *326*
27.4.3.3 Development and Deployment Data *327*
27.4.3.4 System Testing and Deployment *327*
27.4.3.5 Development Infrastructure and Development Cost Monitoring *327*
27.5 Conclusions *330*
27.6 Future Research Challenges *330*
References *330*

**28 Human Factors in Driving** *333*
*Birsen Donmez, Dengbo He, and Holland M. Vasquez*
28.1 Introduction *333*
28.2 Research Methodologies *334*
28.3 In-Vehicle Electronic Devices *335*
28.3.1 Distraction *335*
28.3.2 Interaction Modality *336*
28.3.2.1 Visual and Manual Modalities *336*
28.3.2.2 Auditory and Vocal Modalities *337*
28.3.2.3 Haptic Modality *338*
28.3.3 Wearable Devices *338*
28.4 Vehicle Automation *339*
28.4.1 Driver Support Features *339*
28.4.2 Automated Driving Features *341*
28.5 Driver Monitoring Systems *342*
28.6 Conclusion *343*
References *343*

**29 Wearable Computing Systems: State-of-the-Art and Research Challenges** *349*
*Giancarlo Fortino and Raffaele Gravina*
29.1 Introduction *349*
29.2 Wearable Devices *350*
29.2.1 A History of Wearables *350*
29.2.2 Sensor Types *351*
29.2.2.1 Physiological Sensors *352*
29.2.2.2 Inertial Sensors *352*
29.2.2.3 Visual Sensors *352*
29.2.2.4 Audio Sensors *355*
29.2.2.5 Other Sensors *355*
29.3 Body Sensor Networks-based Wearable Computing Systems *355*
29.3.1 Body Sensor Networks *355*

29.3.2 The SPINE Body-of-Knowledge *357*
29.3.2.1 The SPINE Framework *357*
29.3.2.2 The BodyCloud Framework *359*
29.4 Applications of Wearable Devices and BSNs *360*
29.4.1 Healthcare *360*
29.4.1.1 Cardiovascular Disease *362*
29.4.1.2 Parkinson's Disease *362*
29.4.1.3 Respiratory Disease *362*
29.4.1.4 Diabetes *363*
29.4.1.5 Rehabilitation *363*
29.4.2 Fitness *363*
29.4.2.1 Diet Monitoring *363*
29.4.2.2 Activity/Fitness Tracker *363*
29.4.3 Sports *364*
29.4.4 Entertainment *364*
29.5 Challenges and Prospects *364*
29.5.1 Materials and Wearability *364*
29.5.2 Power Supply *365*
29.5.3 Security and Privacy *365*
29.5.4 Communication *365*
29.5.5 Embedded Computing, Development Methodologies, and Edge AI *365*
29.6 Conclusions *365*
Acknowledgment *366*
References *366*

**30 Multisensor Wearable Device for Monitoring Vital Signs and Physical Activity** *373*
*Joshua Di Tocco, Luigi Raiano, Daniela lo Presti, Carlo Massaroni, Domenico Formica, and Emiliano Schena*
30.1 Introduction *373*
30.2 Background *373*
30.2.1 Context *373*
30.2.2 Basic Definitions *374*
30.3 Related Work *375*
30.4 Case Study: Multisensor Wearable Device for Monitoring RR and Physical Activity *376*
30.4.1 Wearable Device Description *376*
30.4.1.1 Module for the Estimation of RR *377*
30.4.1.2 Module for the Estimation of Physical Activity *377*
30.4.2 Experimental Setup and Protocol *378*
30.4.2.1 Experimental Setup *378*
30.4.2.2 Experimental Protocol *378*
30.4.3 Data Analysis *378*
30.4.4 Results *378*
30.5 Conclusions *379*
30.6 Future Research Challenges *380*
References *380*

**31 Integration of Machine Learning with Wearable Technologies** *383*
*Darius Nahavandi, Roohallah Alizadehsani, and Abbas Khosravi*
31.1 Introduction *383*
31.2 Background *384*
31.2.1 History of Wearables *384*
31.2.2 Supervised Learning *384*
31.2.3 Unsupervised Learning *386*
31.2.4 Deep Learning *386*
31.2.5 Deep Deterministic Policy Gradient *387*
31.2.6 Cloud Computing *388*
31.2.7 Edge Computing *388*
31.3 State of the Art *389*
31.4 Future Research Challenges *392*
References *393*

**32 Gesture-Based Computing** *397*
*Gennaro Costagliola, Mattia De Rosa, and Vittorio Fuccella*
32.1 Introduction *397*
32.2 Background *398*
32.2.1 History of the Development of Gesture-Based Computing *398*
32.2.2 Basic Definitions *399*
32.3 State of the Art *399*
32.4 Future Research Challenges *402*
32.4.1 Current Research Issues *402*
32.4.2 Future Research Directions Dealing with the Current Issues *403*
Acknowledgment *403*
References *403*

**33 EEG-based Affective Computing** *409*
*Xueliang Quan and Dongrui Wu*
33.1 Introduction *409*
33.2 Background *409*
33.2.1 Brief History *409*
33.2.2 Emotion Theory *410*
33.2.3 Emotion Representation *410*
33.2.4 EEG *410*
33.2.5 EEG-Based Emotion Recognition *411*
33.3 State-of-the-Art *411*
33.3.1 Public Datasets *411*
33.3.2 EEG Feature Extraction *411*
33.3.3 Feature Fusion *412*
33.3.4 Affective Computing Algorithms *413*
33.3.4.1 Transfer Learning *413*
33.3.4.2 Active Learning *413*
33.3.4.3 Deep Learning *413*
33.4 Challenges and Future Directions *414*
Acknowledgment *415*
References *415*

34 **Security of Human Machine Systems** *419*
*Francesco Flammini, Emanuele Bellini, Maria Stella de Biase, and Stefano Marrone*
34.1 Introduction *419*
34.2 Background *420*
34.2.1 An Historical Retrospective *420*
34.2.2 Foundations of Security Theory *421*
34.2.3 A Reference Model *421*
34.3 State of the Art *422*
34.3.1 Survey Methodology *422*
34.3.2 Research Trends *425*
34.4 Conclusions and Future Research *426*
References *428*

35 **Integrating Innovation: The Role of Standards in Promoting Responsible Development of Human–Machine Systems** *431*
*Zach McKinney, Martijn de Neeling, Luigi Bianchi, and Ricardo Chavarriaga*
35.1 Introduction to Standards in Human–Machine Systems *431*
35.1.1 What Are Standards? *431*
35.1.2 Standards in Context: Technology Governance, Best Practice, and Soft Law *432*
35.1.3 The Need for Standards in HMS *433*
35.1.4 Benefits of Standards *433*
35.1.5 What Makes an Effective Standard? *434*
35.2 The HMS Standards Landscape *435*
35.2.1 Standards in Neuroscience and Neurotechnology for Brain–Machine Interfaces *435*
35.2.2 IEEE P2731 – Unified Terminology for BCI *435*
35.2.2.1 The BCI Glossary *439*
35.2.2.2 The BCI Functional Model *439*
35.2.2.3 BCI Data Storage *439*
35.2.3 IEEE P2794 – Reporting Standard for *in vivo* Neural Interface Research (RSNIR) *441*
35.3 Standards Development Process *443*
35.3.1 Who Can Participate in Standards Development? *443*
35.3.2 Why Should I Participate in Standards Development? *444*
35.3.3 How Can I get Involved in Standards Development? *444*
35.4 Strategic Considerations and Discussion *444*
35.4.1 Challenges to Development and Barriers to Adoption of Standards *444*
35.4.2 Strategies to Promote Standards Development and Adoption *445*
35.4.3 Final Perspective: On Innovation *445*
Acknowledgements *446*
References *446*

36 **Situation Awareness in Human-Machine Systems** *451*
*Giuseppe D'Aniello and Matteo Gaeta*
36.1 Introduction *451*
36.2 Background *452*
36.3 State-of-the-Art *453*
36.3.1 Situation Identification Techniques in HMS *454*
36.3.2 Situation Evolution in HMS *455*

36.3.3 Situation-Aware Human Machine-Systems *455*
36.4 Discussion and Research Challenges *456*
36.5 Conclusion *458*
References *458*

**37 Modeling, Analyzing, and Fostering the Adoption of New Technologies: The Case of Electric Vehicles** *463*
*Valentina Breschi, Chiara Ravazzi, Silvia Strada, Fabrizio Dabbene, and Mara Tanelli*
37.1 Introduction *463*
37.2 Background *464*
37.2.1 An Agent-based Model for EV Transition *464*
37.2.2 Calibration Based on Real Mobility Patterns *466*
37.3 Fostering the EV Transition via Control over Networks *468*
37.3.1 Related Work: A Perspective Analysis *468*
37.3.2 A New Model for EV Transition with Incentive Policies *469*
37.3.2.1 Modeling Time-varying Thresholds *469*
37.3.2.2 Calibration of the Model *470*
37.4 Boosting EV Adoption with Feedback *470*
37.4.1 Formulation of the Optimal Control Problem *470*
37.4.2 Derivation of the Optimal Policies *471*
37.4.3 A Receding Horizon Strategy to Boost EV Adoption *472*
37.5 Experimental Results *473*
37.6 Conclusions *476*
37.7 Future Research Challenges *477*
Acknowlegments *477*
References *477*

**Index** *479*

# Editors Biography

Giancarlo Fortino (IEEE Fellow '22) is full professor of Computer Engineering in the Department of Informatics, Modeling, Electronics, and Systems at the University of Calabria (Unical), Italy. He has a PhD in Systems and Computer Engineering from University of Calabria in 2000. His research interests include wearable computing systems, Internet of Things, and cybersecurity. He is named Highly Cited Researcher 2002–2022 by Clarivate in Computer Science. He has authored more than 650 papers in international journals, conferences, and books. He is (founding) series editor of the IEEE Press Book Series on Human–Machine Systems and of the Springer Internet of Things series, and is Associate Editor of premier IEEE Transactions. He is cofounder and CEO of SenSysCal S.r.l., a Unical spinoff focused on innovative IoT systems, and cofounder of BigTech S.r.l., a startup focused on AI-driven systems and Big Data. Fortino is currently a member of the IEEE SMCS BoG and co-chair of the SMCS TC on IWCD.

David Kaber is currently the Dean's Leadership Professor and Chair of the Department of Industrial and Systems Engineering at the University of Florida (UF). Prior to joining UF, Kaber was a distinguished professor of industrial engineering at North Carolina State University where he also served as the Director of Research for the Ergonomics Center of North Carolina. Kaber's primary area of research interest is human-systems engineering with a focus on human–automaton interaction, including design and analysis for situation awareness in complex human in-the-loop systems. Domains of study for his research have included physical work systems, industrial safety systems, robotic systems, transportation systems, and healthcare. Kaber is a fellow of IEEE and previous editor-in-chief of the *IEEE Transactions on Human–Machine Systems*. He is a fellow of Institute of Industrial Engineers and a fellow of the Human Factors and Ergonomics Society. Kaber is also a Certified Human Factors Professional (BCPE) and a Certified Safety Professional (BCSP).

Andreas Nürnberger is professor of Data and Knowledge Engineering at the Otto-von-Guericke Universität Magdeburg (OVGU), Germany. His research focuses on adaptivity in human–machine systems, considering aspects such as user behavior analysis and intelligent user assistance. He was involved in the organization of many conferences and workshops in related areas and the development of new scientific events, among others, the IEEE SMCS sponsored international conference series on Human–Machine Systems (IEEE ICHMS). Andreas was visiting researcher at the University of Melbourne, Australia; postdoc at UC Berkeley, United States; and visiting professor at Université Pierre et Marie Curie, Paris. Andreas is an Emmy Noether Fellow of the German Science Foundation (DFG).

David Mendonça (Senior Member, 2012) is Senior Principal Decision Scientist at MITRE Corporation. He previously held the rank of professor in the Department of Industrial and Systems Engineering and in the Department of Cognitive Science at Rensselaer Polytechnic Institute. He served as a Program Director at the National Science Foundation from 2015 to 2017. He was a visiting scholar at the University of Lisbon (Portugal) and at Delft University of Technology (The Netherlands). He is currently a member of the Board of Governors of the IEEE Systems, Man and Cybernetics Society, and of the IEEE Boston (Massachusetts) Section. He holds a PhD in Decision Sciences and Engineering Systems from Rensselaer Polytechnic Institute, an MS from Carnegie Mellon University, and a BA from University of Massachusetts/Amherst.

# List of Contributors

**Marie-Hélène Abel**
Heudiasyc Laboratory
University of Technology of Compiègne
Compiègne
France

**Roohallah Alizadehsani**
Institute for Intelligent Systems Research and Innovation (IISRI)
Deakin University
Waurn Ponds, VIC
Australia

**Terry Amorese**
Department of Psychology
Università della Campania "L. Vanvitelli"
Caserta
Italy

**Abdelkader Nasreddine Belkacem**
Department of Computer and Network Engineering
College of Information Technology
United Arab Emirates University
Al Ain
UAE

**Emanuele Bellini**
Dipartimento di Matematica e Fisica
Universitá degli Studi della Campania "Luigi Vanvitelli"
Caserta
Italy

**Kawtar Benghazi**
Universidad de Granada
Granada
Spain

**Luigi Bianchi**
Department of Civil Engineering and Computer Science Engineering
"Tor Vergata" University of Rome
Rome
Italy

**Maria Stella De Biase**
Dipartimento di Matematica e Fisica
Universitá degli Studi della Campania "Luigi Vanvitelli"
Caserta
Italy

**Thomas Bohné**
Department of Engineering
Institute for Manufacturing
University of Cambridge
Cambridge
UK

**Stefanie S. Bradley**
III Bloorview Research Institute
Holland Bloorview Kids Rehabilitation Hospital
Toronto
Canada

**Valentina Breschi**
Department of Electrical Engineering
Eindhoven University of Technology
Eindhoven
Netherlands

**Zoraida Callejas**
Universidad de Granada
Granada
Spain

**Maximiliano Canche**
Faculty of Mathematics
Universidad Autónoma de Yucatán
Mérida, Yucatán
Mexico

**Filippo Cantucci**
Trust Theory and Technology Group
Institute of Cognitive Sciences and Technologies
National Research Council of Italy
Rome
Italy

**Tom Carlson**
Aspire Create
University College London
Stanmore, Middlesex
UK

**Cristiano Castelfranchi**
Trust Theory and Technology Group
Institute of Cognitive Sciences and Technologies
National Research Council of Italy
Rome
Italy

**Tom Chau**
III Bloorview Research Institute
Holland Bloorview Kids Rehabilitation Hospital
Toronto
Canada

**Ricardo Chavarriaga**
Centre for Artificial Intelligence
School of Engineering
Zurich University of Applied Sciences ZHAW
Winterthur
Switzerland

and

CLAIRE Office Switzerland, ZHAW digital
Zurich University of Applied Sciences
Winterthur
Zürich
Switzerland

**Jessie Y. C. Chen**
U.S. Army Research Laboratory
Aberdeen Proving Ground, Maryland
USA

**Min Chen**
School of Computer Science and Technology
Huazhong University of Science and Technology
Wuhan
China

**Wei Chen**
State Key Lab of CAD&CG
Zhejiang University
Hangzhou
China

**Gennaro Cordasco**
Department of Psychology
Università della Campania "L. Vanvitelli"
Caserta
Italy

**Alessandro Correa-Victorino**
Heudiasyc Laboratory
University of Technology of Compiègne
Compiègne
France

**Gennaro Costagliola**
Dipartimento di Informatica
Università di Salerno
Via Giovanni Paolo II, 132, 84084
Fisciano (SA)
Italy

**Marialucia Cuciniello**
Department of Psychology
Università della Campania "L. Vanvitelli"
Caserta
Italy

**Giuseppe D'Aniello**
Department of Information and Electrical
Engineering and Applied Mathematics
University of Salerno
Fisciano (SA)
Italy

**Fabrizio Dabbene**
Istituto di Elettronica e Ingegneria
dell'Informazione e delle
Telecomunicazioni – IEIIT
Centro Nazionale delle Ricerche
Torino
Italy

**Arwen H. DeCostanza**
U.S. DEVCOM
Army Research Laboratory
Aberdeen Proving Ground, MD
USA

**Yulin Deng**
Cepheid Human Factors and Engineering
Team
Sunnyvale, CA
USA

**Birsen Donmez**
Department of Mechanical and Industrial
Engineering
University of Toronto
Toronto, ON
Canada

**Anna Esposito**
Department of Psychology
Università della Campania "L. Vanvitelli"
Caserta
Italy

**Rino Falcone**
Trust Theory and Technology Group
Institute of Cognitive Sciences and
Technologies
National Research Council of Italy
Rome
Italy

**Tiago H. Falk**
Institut national de la recherche scientifique
University of Quebec
Montreal, Quebec
Canada

**Scott Fang**
Toronto Research Center
Defence Research and Development Canada
Toronto
Canada

**Philip S. E. Farrell**
Toronto Research Center
Defence Research and Development Canada
Toronto
Canada

**Federico Faruffini**
Heudiasyc Laboratory
University of Technology of Compiègne
Compiègne
France

and

DIBRIS
University of Genoa
Genoa
Italy

**Francesco Flammini**
School of Innovation, Design, and Engineering
Mälardalen University
Eskilstuna
Sweden

**Erica D. Floreani**
I BCI4Kids
University of Calgary
Calgary
Canada

and

II Department of Pediatrics
Alberta Children's Hospital
Calgary
Canada

**Domenico Formica**
School of Engineering
Newcastle University
UK

**Giancarlo Fortino**
Department of Informatics, Modeling
Electronics and Systems
University of Calabria
Rende
Italy

**Vittorio Fuccella**
Dipartimento di Informatica
Università di Salerno
Fisciano (SA)
Italy

**Matteo Gaeta**
Department of Information and Electrical
Engineering and Applied Mathematics
University of Salerno
Fisciano (SA)
Italy

**Milad Geravand**
Deep Care GmbH
Waiblingen
Germany

**Raffaele Gravina**
Department of Informatics, Modeling
Electronics and Systems
University of Calabria
Rende
Italy

**David Griol**
Universidad de Granada
Granada
Spain

**Stephanie Gross**
Austrian Research Institute for Artificial
Intelligence
Vienna
Austria

**Christoph Guger**
g.tec medical engineering GmbH
g.tec
Austria

**Bin Guo**
Department of intelligent computing system
School of Computer Science
Northwestern Polytechnical University
Xi'an
China

**Lydia Habib**
Department of Automation and Control
Univ. Polytechnique Hauts-de-France, CNRS
UMR 8201 – LAMIH
Valenciennes
France

**Niloufaralsadat Hashemi**
III Bloorview Research Institute
Holland Bloorview Kids Rehabilitation
Hospital
Toronto
Canada

**Klaus Hauer**
Agaplesion Bethanien-Hospital, Geriatric Centre
University of Heidelberg
Heidelberg
Germany

**Dengbo He**
Intelligent Transportation Thrust, Systems Hub
Hong Kong University of Science and Technology (Guangzhou)
Guangzhou
China

and

Department of Civil and Environmental Engineering
Hong Kong University of Science and Technology
Hong Kong SAR
China

**Ina Heine**
Organizational Development
Laboratory for Machine Tools and Production Engineering
RWTH Aachen University
Aachen, NRW
Germany

**Thomas Hellebrandt**
Organizational Development
Laboratory for Machine Tools and Production Engineering
RWTH Aachen University
Aachen, NRW
Germany

**Christine Horner**
III Bloorview Research Institute
Holland Bloorview Kids Rehabilitation Hospital
Toronto
Canada

**Ming Hou**
Toronto Research Center
Defence Research and Development Canada
Toronto
Canada

**Louis Huebser**
Organizational Development
Laboratory for Machine Tools and Production Engineering
RWTH Aachen University
Aachen, NRW
Germany

**Iztok Humar**
Faculty of Electrical Engineering
University of Ljubljana
Ljubljana
Slovenia

**Brian Irvine**
II Department of Pediatrics
Alberta Children's Hospital
Calgary
Canada

and

III Bloorview Research Institute
Holland Bloorview Kids Rehabilitation Hospital
Toronto
Canada

**Zeanna Jadavji**
I BCI4Kids
University of Calgary
Calgary
Canada

**Radmila Juric**
Independent Researcher London
UK

**David B. Kaber**
University of Florida
Department of Industrial and Systems Engineering
Gainesville, FL
USA

**Dion Kelly**
I BCI4Kids
University of Calgary
Calgary
Canada

and

II Department of Pediatrics
Alberta Children's Hospital
Calgary
Canada

**Abbas Khosravi**
Institute for Intelligent Systems Research and Innovation (IISRI)
Deakin University
Waurn Ponds, VIC
Australia

**Eli Kinney-Lang**
I BCI4Kids
University of Calgary
Calgary
Canada

and

II Department of Pediatrics
Alberta Children's Hospital
Calgary
Canada

**Adam Kirton**
I BCI4Kids
University of Calgary
Calgary
Canada

and

II Department of Pediatrics
Alberta Children's Hospital
Calgary
Canada

**Brigitte Krenn**
Austrian Research Institute for Artificial Intelligence
Vienna
Austria

**Abderrahmane Lakas**
Department of Computer and Network Engineering
College of Information Technology
United Arab Emirates University
Al Ain
UAE

**Qingyang Li**
Department of intelligent computing system
School of Computer Science
Northwestern Polytechnical University
Xi'an
China

**Bangli Liu**
School of Computer Science and Informatics
Faculty of Computing, Engineering, and Media
De Montfort University
Leicester, England
UK

**Honghai Liu**
School of Computing, Faculty of Technology
University of Portsmouth
Portsmouth, England
UK

**Jia Liu**
School of Computer Science and Technology
Huazhong University of Science and Technology
Wuhan
China

**Elliot Loh**
Defence Research and Development Canada
National Defence/Government of Canada
Ottawa, ON
Canada

**Monika Lohani**
University of Utah
Department of Psychology
Salt Lake City, UT
USA

**Stefano Marrone**
Department of Psychology
Università della Campania "L. Vanvitelli"
Caserta
Italy

and

Dipartimento di Matematica e Fisica
Universitá degli Studi della Campania "Luigi Vanvitelli"
Caserta
Italy

**Carlo Massaroni**
Departmental Faculty of Engineering
Università Campus Bio-Medico di Roma
Rome
Italy

**Zach McKinney**
IEEE Standards Association
Piscataway, NJ
USA

**David Mendonça**
MITRE Corporation
Bedford, MA
USA

**Mirco Moencks**
Department of Engineering
Institute for Manufacturing
University of Cambridge
Cambridge
UK

**Darius Nahavandi**
Institute for Intelligent Systems Research and Innovation (IISRI)
Deakin University
Waurn Ponds, VIC
Australia

**Martijn de Neeling**
Department of Neurology
Amsterdam University Medical Centers (UMC)
Amsterdam
Netherlands

**Andreas Nürnberger**
Faculty of Computer Science
Otto-von-Guericke-Universität Magdeburg
Magdeburg
Germany

**Sergio F. Ochoa**
Computer Science Department
University of Chile
Santiago, RM
Chile

**Marie-Pierre Pacaux-Lemoine**
Department of Automation and Control
Univ. Polytechnique Hauts-de-France, CNRS
UMR 8201 – LAMIH
Valenciennes
France

**Marcos Padrón**
Organizational Development
Laboratory for Machine Tools and Production Engineering
RWTH Aachen University
Aachen, NRW
Germany

**Junho Park**
Wm Michael Barnes '64 Department of Industrial and Systems Engineering
Texas A&M University
College Station, TX
USA

**Angelika Peer**
Faculty of Engineering
Free University of Bolzano
Bolzano
Italy

**Daniel Perovich**
Computer Science Department
University of Chile
Santiago, RM
Chile

**Daniela lo Presti**
Departmental Faculty of Engineering
Università Campus Bio-Medico di Roma
Rome
Italy

**Xueliang Quan**
School of Artificial Intelligence and Automation
Huazhong University of Science and Technology
Wuhan
China

**Luigi Raiano**
Departmental Faculty of Engineering
Università Campus Bio-Medico di Roma
Rome
Italy

**Chiara Ravazzi**
Istituto di Elettronica e Ingegneria dell'Informazione e delle Telecomunicazioni – IEIIT
Centro Nazionale delle Ricerche
Torino
Italy

**María Jesús Rodríguez-Sánchez**
Universidad de Granada
Granada
Spain

**Mattia De Rosa**
Dipartimento di Informatica
Università di Salerno
Fisciano (SA)
Italy

**Elisa Roth**
Department of Engineering
Institute for Manufacturing
University of Cambridge
Cambridge
UK

**Danette Rowley**
I BCI4Kids
University of Calgary
Calgary
Canada

and

II Department of Pediatrics
Alberta Children's Hospital
Calgary
Canada

**Ilyas Sadybekov**
I BCI4Kids
University of Calgary
Calgary
Canada

and

II Department of Pediatrics
Alberta Children's Hospital
Calgary
Canada

**Rodrigo Santos**
Electrical Engineering and Computers Department – ICIC
Universidad Nacional del Sur – CONICET
Bahia Blanca, Buenos Aires
Argentina

**Alessandro Sapienza**
Trust Theory and Technology Group
Institute of Cognitive Sciences and Technologies
National Research Council of Italy
Rome
Italy

**Emiliano Schena**
Departmental Faculty of Engineering
Università Campus Bio-Medico di Roma
Rome
Italy

**Olga Shevaleva**
Department of Psychology
Università della Campania "L. Vanvitelli"
Caserta
Italy

**Charlene K. Stokes**
U.S. Army Futures Command
DEVCOM
Aberdeen Proving Ground, MD
USA

**Silvia Strada**
Dipartimento di Elettronica
Informazione e Bioingegneria
Politecnico di Milano
Milano
Italy

**Mara Tanelli**
Istituto di Elettronica e Ingegneria dell'Informazione e delle Telecomunicazioni – IEIIT
Centro Nazionale delle Ricerche
Torino
Italy

and

Department of Electrical Engineering
Eindhoven University of Technology
Eindhoven
Netherlands

**Joshua Di Tocco**
Departmental Faculty of Engineering
Università Campus Bio-Medico di Roma
Rome
Italy

**Si Long Jenny Tou**
III Bloorview Research Institute
Holland Bloorview Kids Rehabilitation Hospital
Toronto
Canada

**Lucas R. Trambaiolli**
McLean Hospital
Harvard Medical School
Belmont, MA
USA

**Holland M. Vasquez**
Department of Mechanical and Industrial Engineering
University of Toronto
Toronto, ON
Canada

**Carl Vogel**
Trinity Centre for Computing and Language Studies
School of Computer Science and Statistics
Trinity College Dublin
The University of Dublin
Dublin
Ireland

**Ivan Volosyak**
Faculty of Technology and Bionics
Rhine-Waal University of Applied Sciences
Kleve
Germany

**Fei-Yue Wang**
The State Key Laboratory for Management and Control of Complex Systems
Institute of Automation
Chinese Academy of Sciences
Beijing
China

**Wenbi Wang**
Toronto Research Center
Defence Research and Development Canada
Toronto
Canada

**Xumeng Wang**
College of Computer Science
Nankai University
Tianjin
China

**Andreas Wendemuth**
Department of Electrical Engineering and Information Technology
Institute for Information Technology and Communications
Otto-von-Guericke-University
Magdeburg
Germany

**Christian Werner**
Agaplesion Bethanien-Hospital, Geriatric Centre
University of Heidelberg
Heidelberg
Germany

**Dongrui Wu**
School of Artificial Intelligence and Automation
Huazhong University of Science and Technology
Wuhan
China

**Jinfeng Xu**
School of Computer Science and Technology
Huazhong University of Science and Technology
Wuhan
China

**Zhiwen Yu**
Department of intelligent computing system
School of Computer Science
Northwestern Polytechnical University
Xi'an
China

**Maryam Zahabi**
Wm Michael Barnes '64 Department of Industrial and Systems Engineering
Texas A&M University
College Station, TX
USA

**Andrea Maria Zanchettin**
Politecnico di Milano
Dipartimento di Elettronica
Informazione e Bioningegneria
Milan
Italy

**Ephrem Zewdie**
I BCI4Kids
University of Calgary
Calgary
Canada

# Preface

Human-Machine Systems (HMS) refer to integrated systems where the functions of human operators and machines are combined. These systems can be seen as a unified entity that interacts with the external environment. In an HMS, humans and machines work together, leveraging their respective capabilities to achieve specific goals or perform tasks.

HMS can take various forms and exist in different domains. Examples include aircraft flight control systems, industrial automation systems, medical robotic systems, and even virtual assistants or chatbots. In these systems, humans contribute their cognitive abilities, decision-making skills, and expertise, while machines provide computational power, automation, and precision.

The integration of humans and machines in HMS can be achieved through different levels of automation. It can range from fully manual systems, where humans are responsible for all tasks, to partially automated systems, where machines assist humans in specific functions, to fully autonomous systems, where machines take over the majority of tasks with minimal human intervention.

The field of HMS engineering focuses on understanding, designing, and optimizing these integrated systems. It involves studying human capabilities, limitations, and interactions, as well as developing technologies and interfaces that facilitate effective collaboration between humans and machines. The goal is to create systems that enhance human performance, improve efficiency, and ensure safety and reliability in various operational contexts.

Overall, HMS represents the synergy between humans and machines, harnessing the strengths of both to create powerful and efficient systems that can tackle complex tasks and challenges across different domains.

This book aims to be a manifesto of HMS research and development, delineating the state-of-the-art in the field, also by means of representative use cases, as well as future research challenges.

It is organized in seven areas covering all aspects of HMS: Brain–machine interfaces and systems (BMIS), Collaborative intelligent systems and applications (CISA), Companion technology (CT), Human–AI interaction and cognitive computing & engineering (HAICCE),

Human factors engineering (HFE), Interactive and wearable computing and systems (IWCS), and Hybrid Technologies (HT). Apart from the introduction chapter, the book includes 36 chapters contextualized in the aforementioned areas.

The chapters 2–6 are related to BMIS and deal with BCI (Brain-Computer Interface) methods and technologies. In particular, chapter 2 provides a general background on BCIs, chapter 3 focuses on

BCI-enabled affective neurofeedback, chapter 4 introduces the adaptation of BCI techniques for children living with severe physical disability, chapter 5 proposes an application of BCI for controlling drones, and chapter 6 exploits BCI to allow people with disability to remotely control robots.

The chapters 7–13 refer to CISA and deal with advances on the development of scientific and engineering foundations, innovative technologies, and solutions for technology and data-driven collaborative intelligent systems. In particular, chapter 7 focuses on human–machine social systems such as human–machine teaming, chapter 8 introduces mechanisms for enabling human–robot interaction, chapter 9 explores people-driven collaborative processes enabled by human-machine units, chapter 10 reviews theoretical frameworks and recent advancements in human–machine transparency research and development, chapter 11 presents an overview of existing technology and methods for developing conversational human–machine interfaces, chapter 12 proposes an enduring strategy and methodology for complex socio-technical systems, and chapter 13 introduces a new computing paradigm of human–machine integration.

The chapters 14–17 belong to CT and deal with trans-disciplinary research in fields such as computer science and artificial intelligence, cognitive science, engineering, psychology, and neurobiology. In particular, chapter 14 overviews some background aspects of CT, chapter 15 focuses on mobility assistance robots of rollator-type and reviews their platforms and functionalities, chapter 16 focuses on the innovative concept of wearable affective robots, another instance of CT, and chapter 17 reviews the state-of-the-art on visual human–computer interaction in intelligent vehicles.

The chapters 18–22 focus on important topics in HAICCE and concern with human cognition in intelligent/AI system designs or/and development of AI algorithms, technology, methods for human beings. Specifically, chapter 18 addresses the problem of synchronization between human and robot actions, chapter 19 explores the new frontier of intelligent systems and their ability to enter into advanced collaboration with humans and other more or less intelligent artificial systems, chapter 20 focuses on decoding user emotional expressions as an important factor influencing interaction between humans and virtual assistants, chapter 21 reviews the intelligent computational edge, and chapter 22 addresses the important issue of implementing context awareness in autonomous vehicles.

The chapters 23–28 concern HFE and focus on the advancements in theory and practice related to human interaction with intelligent agents in a wide variety of environments. In particular, chapter 23 offers a systematic review on operator assistance systems, chapter 24 reviews cognitive performance modelling approaches in the human-systems engineering area, chapter 25 addresses advanced driver assistance systems, chapter 26 focuses on RGB-D based human action recognition, chapter 27 promotes the exploitation of AI in industry, and chapter 28 presents human factors in driving.

The chapters 29–33 are contextualized in IWCS and deal with advances and developments in interactive and/or wearable computing and systems. Specifically, chapter 29 presents a brief yet effective review of sensors, devices, and systems enabling wearable computing, chapter 30 concentrates on a technical use case about monitoring respiratory rate and activities using smart garments, chapter 31 highlights issues correlated with huge amounts of data generated by wearables, chapter 32 surveys the main methods and techniques for gesture-based computing, and chapter 33 reviews recent progress in EEG-based affective computing.

Finally, the chapters 34–37 deals with transversal topics related to HT. In particular, chapter 34 provides an overview of cyber-physical security applied to HMS, chapter 35 outlines the need and the role of standards in HMS, chapter 36 provide an overview of models, methods, and techniques of situation awareness measurement in the context of HMS, and chapter 37 defines a general and widely usable data-driven framework to perform human-centered service and process analysis.

# 1

# Introduction

*Giancarlo Fortino[1], David Kaber[2], Andreas Nürnberger[3], and David Mendonça[4]*

[1] *Department of Informatics, Modeling, Electronics and Systems, University of Calabria, Rende, Italy*
[2] *Department of Industrial and Systems Engineering, University of Florida, Gainesville, FL, USA*
[3] *Faculty of Computer Science, Otto-von-Guericke-Universität Magdeburg, Magdeburg, Germany*
[4] *MITRE Corporation, Bedford, MA, USA*

## 1.1 Book Rationale

Human–machine systems (HMS) [6] are systems in which the functions of a human operator (or a group of operators) and a machine are integrated. This terminology can also be used to identify a system as a single entity that interacts with an external environment. HMS engineering is different from the more general and well-known fields such as human–computer interaction (HCI) [3] and sociotechnical engineering in that it focuses on complex, dynamic control systems that often are partially automated (such as flying an airplane). It also studies human problem-solving in naturalistic settings or in high-fidelity simulation environments. HMS area therefore includes subareas such as human/machine interaction; cognitive ergonomics and engineering; assistive/companion technologies; human/machine system modeling, test and evaluation; and fundamental issues of measurement and modeling of human-centered phenomena in engineered systems. More specifically, HMS inform theory and improve engineering practice by Bass [1]:

1. Taking into account human sensory, motor, and cognitive capabilities, knowledge, skills, preferences, emotions, limitations, biases, learning, and adaptation;
2. Considering human synchronous and asynchronous interactions among humans and with intelligent agents, computational support, and assistive devices via associated input and output technologies within the person's operational, organizational, cultural, and regulatory contexts;
3. Developing, instantiating, testing, and refining measures, methods, models, and apparatus that address (i) and (ii) and that can provide insights given real world imprecision, uncertainty, and constraints that impact human characteristics, performance, behavior, and learning; and
4. Supporting operational concept development, architecture, design, implementation, and evaluation of dynamic, complex systems that include human participants in their multifaceted roles (such as analyst, decision-maker, operator, collaborator, communicator, and learner).

The aim of this handbook is to be a manifesto of HMS research and development, delineating the state-of-the-art in the field, also by means of representative use cases, as well as future research challenges. Thus, the main target is the worldwide scientific and technical communities of HMS,

*Handbook of Human-Machine Systems*, First Edition. Edited by Giancarlo Fortino, David Kaber, Andreas Nürnberger, and David Mendonça.

specifically those associated with technical committees as part of important scientific/technical societies such as IEEE [7], IFAC [8], HFES [12], etc.

The book is the first volume addressing all the main issues of HMS and, as such, is a comprehensive handbook. This handbook has therefore a scope broader than a vertical book, which is to provide the "big picture" of the state-of-the-art of research (and technology) of HMS. With this aim, the handbook is organized around the most important well-established six areas of HMS (listed here in alphabetical order):

- *Brain–machine interfaces and systems (BMIS)* include assistive technology and research allowing locked-in individuals to communicate and control exoskeletons/devices to improve locomotion [9].
- *Collaborative intelligent systems and applications (CISA)* address advances on the development of scientific and engineering foundations, innovative technologies, and solutions for technology- and data-driven collaborative intelligent systems [10].
- *Companion technology (CT)* covers and combines trans-disciplinary research in fields such as computer science and artificial intelligence, cognitive science, engineering, psychology, and neurobiology [2].
- *Human–AI interaction and cognitive computing & engineering (HAICCE)* encompasses human cognition in intelligent/AI system designs or/and development of AI algorithms, technology, methods for human beings [11].
- *Human factors engineering (HFE)* focus on the advancements in theory and practice related to human interaction with intelligent agents in a wide variety of environments [4].
- *Interactive and wearable computing and systems (IWCS)* focus on advances and developments in all aspects of interactive and/or wearable computing and systems [5].

Moreover, the handbook also includes the *Hybrid Technologies (HT)* area focusing on aspects that cut across the above six areas (e.g. security, interoperability, and awareness).

## 1.2 Chapters Overview

The chapters of the handbook, which are summarized in the following list, were purposely collected and organized according to the aforementioned HMS areas and are ordered as follows: BMIS, CISA, CT, HAICCE, HFE, IWCS, and HT. For each chapter, we detail title, author/s, and a brief summary. The first chapter/s of each HMS area will also provide a brief literature review to give a big picture of research in the area. The other chapters are either more vertical reviews or technical use cases.

- *Brain–machine interfaces and systems (BMIS)*:
  2. *"Brain–Computer Interfaces: Recent Advances, Challenges, and Future Directions," Tiago H. Falk, Christoph Guger, Ivan Volosyak.* In this chapter, the authors provide a general background on Brain–computer interfaces (BCIs), from their introduction to recent findings and beyond. Specifically, they focus on active, passive, and hybrid BCI configurations. Some representative BCI applications are also discussed.
  3. *"Brain–computer interfaces for affective neurofeedback applications," Lucas R. Trambaiolli, Tiago H. Falk.* Affective neurofeedback is a growing subfield of BCIs, as introduced in the second chapter. Participants are trained to achieve volitional control over neural patterns related to emotion regulation. The authors of this chapter present basic concepts necessary for neurofeedback protocols, including commonly used neuroimaging techniques and the

main differences in targeted features. Two interesting applications for neurofeedback in psychiatry are also discussed, including depressive disorder and posttraumatic stress disorder.

4. *"Pediatric Brain–Computer Interfaces: An Unmet Need," Eli Kinney-Lang et al.* In this chapter, the authors discuss the adaptation of BCI techniques (described in the Chapters 2 and 3) for children living with severe physical disability. The authors state that it involves understanding fundamental differences in the neurophysiology, signal processing, and task design among other considerations for adults versus pediatric cases. This chapter therefore provides the necessary context and considerations to help stakeholders drive forward the full realization of pediatric BCI.
5. *"Brain–Computer Interface-based Predator–Prey Drone Interactions," Abdelkader Nasreddine.* In this chapter, the author proposes an application of BCI (described in Chapter 2) for control of drones. Specifically, the BCI method determines the fight path in a predator–prey situation to seek enemy drones and track them. The applications were evaluated with different testbeds where subjects were equipped with EEG systems. The results show that BCI subjects were able to accurately generate near-optimal trajectories by reacting quickly to a target's movements.
6. *"Toward the Definition of Levels of Cooperation according to Human–Machine System Objectives and Constraints: example with Human-BCI-Robot cooperation," Marie-Pierre Pacaux-Lemoine, Lydia Habib, Tom Carlson.* In this chapter, the authors focus on the challenge of designing safe and efficient human–machine systems. Specifically, they introduce the concept of levels of cooperation, which is a generic and flexible approach to support the designers in identifying: human–machine common goals, individual and cooperative abilities, and criteria for dynamic task allocation. The proposed method is exemplified via a use case showing how people with a high level of disability might use only a BCI interface (see Chapters 2 and 5 for basics on BCI and BCI-controlled devices) to control a remote robot.

*Collaborative Intelligent Systems and Applications (CISA):*

7. *"Human–Machine Social Systems," Charlene K. Stokes, Arwen H. DeCostanza, Elliot Loh.* The focus of this chapter is on human–machine social systems (such as human–machine teaming) enabling intelligent, bidirectional interactions between humans and technologies that involve complex social interactions. The findings are applied in the military domain and examined in situ with real users in collaboration with the US military.
8. *"The Role of Multimodal Data for Modeling Communication in Artificial Social Agents," Stephanie Gross, Brigitte Krenn.* In this chapter, the authors introduce mechanisms for enabling human–robot interaction. The mechanisms are based on verbal and nonverbal communication cues that play a crucial role in interaction. In order to study human communication behavior in task-oriented scenarios, the authors present a selection of collected multimodal datasets and discuss the implications of their findings for modeling communicative behavior in artificial social agents.
9. *"Modeling Interactions Happening in People-Driven Collaborative Processes," Maximiliano Canche, Sergio F. Ochoa, Daniel Perovich, Rodrigo Santos.* This chapter explores people-driven collaborative processes, and the way to support interactions among participants using human–machine units. Specifically, the chapter surveys and analyzes the state-of-the-art on interaction (visual) modeling languages and techniques used to represent scenarios of interaction among human–machine units.
10. *"Transparent Communications for Human-Machine Teaming," Jessie Y.C. Chen.* This chapter reviews theoretical frameworks and recent advancements in human–machine

transparency research and development. The analysis covers implementation of transparent human–machine interfaces across a wide spectrum of human–machine systems involving human interactions; for example, small ground robots; multiagent systems and human–swarm interaction; automated/autonomous driving systems; and Explainable AI systems.

11. *"Conversational human–machine interfaces," Marıa Jesus Rodrıguez-Sanchez, Kawtar Benghazi, David Griol, Zoraida Callejas.* In this chapter, the authors present an overview of existing technology and methods for developing conversational human–machine interfaces. In specific, current approaches for the development of dialog systems are described along with a focus on the different objectives that dialogs may have, either to solve particular tasks or to hold open chit-chat conversations.
12. *"Interaction-Centered Design: An Enduring Strategy and Methodology for Complex Socio-Technical Systems," Ming Hou, Scott Fang, Wenbi Wang, Philip S. E. Farrell, and Renee Chow.* With collective human–machine intelligence, human–machine symbiosis technologies are prevalent in society and capable of solving complex problems. To provide guidance to understand and mitigate potential risks associated with employing such technologies, the evolution of design strategy and methodology for intelligent adaptive systems was reviewed in this chapter. In specific, an interaction-centered design (ICD) framework, an associated set of methodologies and roadmap and a related trust model called IMPACTS were then introduced as an enduring strategy and appropriate solution. The ICD approach was validated via experimental studies for utility and effectiveness involving real-world technology demonstrations and evaluation activities.
13. *"Human-Machine Computing: Paradigm, Challenges and Practices," Zhiwen Yu, Qingyang Li, Bin Guo.* This chapter introduces a new computing paradigm of human–machine integration, which is called Human-Machine Computing. It combines capabilities of humans and machines in the computing process. In specific, a general platform named hmOS is constructed for managing and scheduling humans and machines that interactively work together in a task in a continuous development environment. It is worth noting that during the human–machine cooperation and collaboration procedure, the performance of machines and humans may gradually improve through mutual influence.

*Companion technology (CT):*

14. *"Companion technology," Andreas Wendemuth.* The central concept of the contribution of this chapter is Companion technology that is fundamental to a new class of cognitive systems which are correspondingly called Companion systems. Such systems are characterized by capabilities to adapt to requirements of their users, which change with time and situation. In particular, companion systems respond appropriately to user capabilities, preferences, and current needs. Their technical functionalities reflect changes in the environment or users' disposition. This chapter therefore presents the concepts of companion technology and illustrates the wide spectrum of its concepts and applications.
15. *"A Survey on Rollator-Type Mobility Assistance Robots," Milad Geravand, Christian Werner, Klaus Hauer, Angelika Peer.* This review chapter focuses on mobility assistance robots of rollator-type (a companion technology, see Chapter 14) and reviews their platforms and functionalities. Specifically, the reviewed systems are grouped according to their actuation, kinematic structure as well as employed sensors and human–machine interfaces. Reviewed functionalities include the following categories: sit-to-stand and stand-to-sit assistance, walking assistance, locomotion, and navigation assistance.

16. *"Wearable Affective Robots," Jia Liu, Yingying Jiang, Min Chen, Iztok Humar.* In this chapter, the authors focus on the innovative concept of wearable affective robots, another instance of companion technology. Wearable robots are related to brain wearables in terms of hardware circuit design, electroencephalography data collection and analysis, user-behavior perception, algorithm deployment, and user-behavior recognition based on electroencephalography. A prototype emotional robot, named Fitbit, is shown in the chapter starting from its development to its analysis.
17. *"Visual Human–Computer Interactions for Intelligent Vehicles," Xumeng Wang, Wei Chen, Fei-Yue Wang.* In this chapter, the authors review the state-of-the-art on visual human–computer interaction (VHCI) in intelligent vehicles and discuss future directions. VHCI has been widely applied in intelligent vehicles. Technologies, such as route navigation, to allow drivers to take advantage of automatic approaches when driving intelligent vehicles. However, unreliable mechanics of VHCI may lead to frustrating driving experiences or traffic accidents.

*Human–AI Interaction and Cognitive Computing & Engineering (HAICCE)*:

18. *"Intelligent collaboration between humans and robots," Andrea Maria Zanchettin.* In future manufacturing environments, such as shop-floors, humans, and robots, not only will share the same workspace but will also collaborate, as dictated by collaborative robotics. Specifically, this chapter addresses the problem of synchronization between human and robot actions and proposes a semantic-based framework to classify and understand human behavior in collaborative robotics applications. Such a method is also validated on realistic collaborative assembly demonstrations.
19. *"To be Trustworthy and to Trust: the New Frontier of Intelligent Systems," Rino Falcone, Alessandro Sapienza, Filippo Cantucci, Cristiano Castelfranchi.* This chapter explores the new frontier of intelligent systems and their ability to enter into advanced collaboration with humans and other more or less intelligent artificial systems. Trust is a fundamental concept/dimension enabling collaboration. In this chapter, author introduces a systematic review of the state-of-the-art by providing a broad overview of the existing work on trust in intelligent systems, in the contexts of the Internet of Things, Multiagent Systems, and Human–Machine Systems.
20. *"Decoding humans' and virtual agents' emotional expressions," Terry Amorese et al.* In this chapter, the authors focus on decoding user emotional expressions as an important factor influencing interaction between humans and virtual assistants. In particular, they propose a study that involves a comparison between a naturalistic decoding task and a synthetic encoding task, with the synthetic encoding task realized through virtual agents expressing target emotions. Experimental results show the influence of emotional category, age, gender, and face typology on recognition of synthetic and naturalistic emotional expressions.
21. *"Intelligent Computational Edge From Pervasive Computing and Internet of Things to Computing Continuum," Rudmila Juric.* This chapter reviews the intelligent computational edge. The survey looks at a journey toward a pervasive and ubiquitous computing in which numerous physical elements (with variable computational powers) are interwoven with software and humans, delivering services and computational intelligence. The edge secures a computing continuum. Clouds/edge/fog/dust may be negotiated for the most suitable format of computational choices according to the context in which they are situated.
22. *"Implementing context awareness in autonomous vehicles," Federico Faruni, Alessandro Correa-Victorino, Marie-Helene Abel.* In this chapter, the authors address the important issue of implementing context awareness in autonomous vehicles, i.e. understanding

the surrounding context in which the navigation occurs. Besides recognizing the road components, potential obstacles, and vehicles, autonomous cars do not consider the integration of such information which is left to the human driver. The chapter therefore shows how an ontology-based architecture for the context of navigation could be sufficient to encode such information and to enable reasoning over it. How the control loop of the autonomous vehicle can be modified to adapt to the situation is also discussed.

*Human Factors Engineering (HFE)*:

23. *"The Augmented Workforce: A Systematic Review of Operator Assistance Systems," Elisa Roth, Mirco Moencks, Thomas Bohne.* This chapter is contextualized in the smart manufacturing area from the HMS-HFE perspective and focused on the following question, "How can human–machine systems augment the set of employee skills?" The answer is that Operator Assistance Systems (OAS) could be a potential solution. Therefore, the authors aim to sharpen the picture around OAS by contributing a systematic review. The review considered 201 papers to depict the field's most relevant aspects and highlight promising opportunities for future research.
24. *"Cognitive performance modeling," Maryam Zahabi, Junho Park.* In this chapter, the authors focus on cognitive performance models, which are computational models that represent human performance in the use of interfaces and provide information on user intentions and information processing. They review cognitive performance modeling approaches in the human-systems engineering area and some of the challenges and limitations of applying these methods. Specifically, the surveyed approaches include GOMS, EPIC, QN-MHP, and ACT-R models and their variants.
25. *"Advanced Driver Assistance Systems: Transparency and Driver Performance Effects," Yulin Deng, David B. Kaber.* This chapter addresses advanced driver assistance systems (ADAS) and aims at providing a method based on automation transparency to mitigate negative impacts of automation on driving performance. The method was experimentally evaluated, and the obtained results suggest that ADAS transparency could improve hazard negotiation performance. More importantly, the findings of this research may serve as an applicable guide for transparency in future ADAS systems.
26. *"RGB-D Sensing based Human Activity Analysis: A Survey," Bangli Liu, Honghai Liu.* The authors focus on RGB-D based human action recognition, which has been a hot research topic with the release of RGB-D devices. These are specific types of depth-sensing devices that work in association with a RGB (red, green and blue color) sensor camera. Many attempts have been made to achieve robust and effective action recognition. This chapter reviews human action recognition techniques, including handcrafted feature representations extracted from different data modality and various deep neural network architectures. Commonly used action datasets, performance comparison, and promising future directions are presented.
27. *"Hybrid Intelligence: Augmenting employees' decision-making with AI-based applications," Ina Heine, Thomas Hellebrandt, Louis Huebser, Marcos Padron.* In this chapter, the authors promote the exploitation of AI in industry as AI-based applications could have positive effects on employee decision-making and stress reduction. In particular, the authors propose and evaluate an approach to deal with such a challenge and a technical use case in the area of call center service that demonstrates human decision-making augmentation with AI-based applications.
28. *"Human Factors in Driving," Birsen Donmez, Dengbo He, Holland M. Vasquez.* The authors of this chapter present an overview of driver capabilities and limitations as they relate to

safety as well as vehicular and infrastructure design in the context of road transportation. A specific and larger focus is given to recent advancements in technology, including devices that are carried-in (e.g. smartphones) or built-into (e.g. on-board units) the vehicle, driver state monitoring, as well as higher levels of vehicle automation. Some of these advances raise safety concerns, yet others promise significant enhancement in safety.

*Interactive and Wearable Computing and Systems (IWCS)*:

29. *"Wearable Computing Systems: State-of the-art and Research Challenges," Giancarlo Fortino and Raffaele Gravina.* In this chapter, the authors present a brief yet effective review of sensors, devices, and systems enabling wearable computing. In particular, the Signal Processing In-Node Environment-Body of Knowledge (SPINE-BoK) is illustrated as one of the richest bodies of knowledge in this area. Finally, potential challenges to be faced to advance wearable computing systems are in terms of materials, wearability, electronics, power supply, communication, security, embedded computing, AI at the edge, and methodologies, are also discussed.
30. *"Multisensor wearable device for monitoring vital signs and physical activity," Joshua Di Tocco et al.* With wearable computing systems being introduced in Chapter 29, this chapter concentrates on a technical use case about monitoring respiratory rate and activities using a "smart garment" which embeds custom-made piezoresistive sensors and a magneto-inertial measurement unit. Respiratory rate is gaining interest in the scientific community as it can be useful to perform early detection of patient deterioration, retrieve information on cognitive load, analyze emotional stress, measure discomfort during working activities, and assess the physical effort and fatigue of the athletes during exercise.
31. *"Integration of Machine Learning with Wearable technologies," Darius Nahavandi, Roohallah Alizadehsani, Abbas Khosravi.* In this chapter, the authors highlight issues correlated with huge amounts of data generated by wearables, as described in the previous two chapters. First, the chapter focuses on a review of machine learning methods for wearable devices. Second, cloud, fog, and edge-computing technologies are introduced and discussed for supporting wearable systems.
32. *"Gesture-based computing," Gennaro Costagliola, Mattia De Rosa, Vittorio Fuccella.* This chapter surveys the main methods and techniques for gesture-based computing. The authors consider both mid-air and touch-based gestures. The survey includes hardware and software techniques for gesture recognition and the most widespread applications in the field. The authors summarize the state-of-the-art of the field, outline a brief history of its development, and identify future research challenges.
33. *"EEG-based Affective Computing," Xueliang Quan and Dongrui Wu.* This chapter reviews recent progress in EEG-based affective computing that aims to research and develop wearable systems and devices which can precisely recognize, interpret, synthesize, and/or simulate human affects. The authors first introduce the history and theories of EEG-based affective computing; then, they describe commonly used features and machine learning algorithms, focusing on transfer learning, active learning, and deep learning.

*Hybrid Technologies (HT)*:

34. *"Security of Human–Machine Systems," Francesco Flammini, Emanuele Bellini, Maria Stella de Biase, Stefano Marrone.* Secure human–machine systems are relevant in the context of future trustworthy autonomous systems. Such systems will be required to detect and counteract evolving threats through intelligent behaviors based on learning and adaptation. In this chapter, the authors provide an overview of cyber-physical security applied to HMSs, including a basic taxonomy, reference models, historical background, and state-of-the-art.

In particular, the chapter explores security paradigms integrating human-related factors, with a focus on data privacy, the Internet of Things, and computer security.

35. *"Integrating Innovation: the Role of Standards in Promoting Responsible Development of Human–Machine Systems," Zach McKinney, Martijn de Neeling, Luigi Bianchi, Ricardo Chavarriaga.* In HMSs, the immense diversity of technological modalities, data types, and use scenarios poses a big challenge on interoperability. Lack of interoperability in fact impedes large-scale distillation and communication of knowledge across many subfields, including wearables, neurotechnology, and robotics – and thus, the development and application of these technologies for maximum benefit. This chapter outlines the need and the role of standards in HMS. It provides an overview of key standards in the field of HMS, from well-established standards to those under current development, by also discussing a brief series of representative HMS case studies.
36. *"Situation Awareness in Human–Machine Systems," Giuseppe D'Aniello, Matteo Gaeta* In this chapter, the authors provide an overview of models, methods, and techniques of situation awareness measurement in the context of human–machine systems, ranging from the foundations of Endsley's model to the recent advancements in the field. Human–machine systems should be able to support human situation awareness, by leveraging computational methods and techniques for situation modeling, identification, prediction, reasoning, and control.
37. *"Modeling, Analyzing and Fostering the Adoption of New Technologies: the case of Electric Vehicles," Valentina Breschi et al.* In the context of service provisioning during environmental transition, the authors of this chapter define a general and widely usable data-driven framework to perform human-centered service and process analysis. The proposal is tested in the context of relevant technological transition from Internal Combustion Engine vehicles to Electrical Vehicles. Results validate the framework and pave the way to its application to many other technological transitions.

## Acknowledgments

We would like to thank the editorial team of IEEE Press/Wiley for their support, particularly Ekram Hossain, who was the IEEE Press Editor-In-Chief when this project was launched, and the editorial assistants/managers Vaishali Damle, Mary Hatcher, and Elke Morice-Atkinson. Our gratitude also goes to all authors (N. 118) of the 36 handbook chapters who committed their efforts and time in presenting their outcomes. Finally, we would like to also thank the IEEE Systems, Man and Cybernetics society for having endorsed and supported this endeavor, which took more than two years to complete.

## References

1 Bass, E.J. (2013). Editorial: IEEE systems, man, and cybernetics society's continuing legacy in human - machine systems. *IEEE Transactions on Human-Machine Systems* 43 (1): 1–7. https://doi.org/10.1109/THMS.2012.2234371.

2 Biundo, S., Höller, D., Schattenberg, B., and Bercher, P. (2016). Companion-technology: an overview. *KI-Künstliche Intelligenz* 30 (1): 11–20.

3 Cannan, J. and Hu, H. (2011). Human-Machine Interaction (HMI): A Survey. *Technical Report: CES-508*. University of Essex.

**4** Carayon, P. (2006). Human factors of complex sociotechnical systems. *Applied Ergonomics* 37 (4): 525–535.

**5** Fortino, G., Gravina, R., and Galzarano, S. (2018). *Wearable Computing: From Modeling to Implementation of Wearable Systems Based on Body Sensor Networks.* Wiley.

**6** Wikipedia. Human-Machine Systems. https://en.wikipedia.org/wiki/human%e2%80%93machine_system (last accessed July 2022).

**7** IEEE Technical Committees on Human-Machine Systems. https://www.ieeesmc.org/technical-activities/human-machine-systems (last accessed July 2022).

**8** IFAC TC 4.5 HMS, International Federation of Automatic Control, Technical Committee on Human Machine Systems. https://web.archive.org/web/20110928063045/http://www.uni-kl.de/pak/ifac/ (last accessed Jul 2022).

**9** Lebedev, M.A. and Nicolelis, M.A.L. (2006). Brain–machine interfaces: past, present and future. *TRENDS in Neurosciences* 29 (9): 536–546.

**10** Magnisalis, I., Demetriadis, S., and Karakostas, A. (2011). Adaptive and intelligent systems for collaborative learning support: a review of the field. *IEEE transactions on Learning Technologies* 4 (1): 5–20.

**11** Shergadwala, M.N. and El-Nasr, M.S. (2021). Human-centric design requirements and challenges for enabling human-AI interaction in engineering design: an interview study. *International Design Engineering Technical Conferences and Computers and Information in Engineering Conference*, volume 85420, V006T06A054. American Society of Mechanical Engineers.

**12** The Human Factors and Ergonomics Society. https://www.hfes.org/about-hfes (last accessed Jul 2022).

# 2

# Brain–Computer Interfaces: Recent Advances, Challenges, and Future Directions

*Tiago H. Falk[1], Christoph Guger[2], and Ivan Volosyak[3]*

[1] *Institut national de la recherche scientifique, University of Québec, Montréal, Canada*
[2] *g.tec medical engineering GmbH, g.tec, Austria*
[3] *Faculty of Technology and Bionics, Rhine-Waal University of Applied Sciences, Kleve, Germany*

## 2.1 Introduction

Brain–computer interfaces (BCIs), or more generally, brain–machine interfaces (BMIs), as the names suggest, are interfaces that connect brain-related data to/with computers or machines. As originally proposed in the late 1990s, early 2000s, BCIs/BMIs were targeted as assistive technologies that would bypass the human body's normal communication and control channels (i.e. peripheral nerves and muscles) and allow recordings from the brain to directly control an external actuator, such as a robotic arm. As will be shown in Section 2.2.1, BCIs that follow this scheme are called "active" or "reactive" BCIs, in the sense that the users are actively using/modulating their brain signals, either volitionally or via stimuli-evoked potentials, to control an external device. The block diagram included within the dash-dotted area of Figure 2.1 depicts such BCI configuration.

Signal acquisition originally relied on electroencephalography (EEG) signals, but as highlighted in [32], over the years, several other modalities have been explored, such as magnetoencephalography, functional near-infrared spectroscopy (fNIRS), functional magnetic resonance imaging (fMRI), and electrocorticography, to name a few (see [7] for a more complete list). As will be highlighted in Section 2.2.3, more recently, advances in sensor technologies have also allowed for hybrid systems to emerge, in which multiple of these modalities can be combined (e.g. EEG-fNIRS), including combinations with other physiological modalities (e.g. EEG and electromyography, EMG). A block diagram of such hybrid systems can be seen within the solid square in Figure 2.1. The work in [50] provides a review on signal modalities used for BCIs.

The next block in a BCI system consists of the signal processing and analysis module, in which signal artifacts are removed, relevant insights from the signals are extracted (and selected if many are extracted), and then mapped to a decision using a machine learning paradigm. The extracted parameters are often called "features," and they depend on the signal modality being used. The interested reader is referred to [37] and [36] for a review on signal processing and analysis modules typically used in BCIs, respectively. More recently, with the advances in deep learning and deep neural networks, these steps have been replaced by a deep neural network; a review can be found in [54].

*Handbook of Human-Machine Systems*, First Edition. Edited by Giancarlo Fortino, David Kaber, Andreas Nürnberger, and David Mendonça.

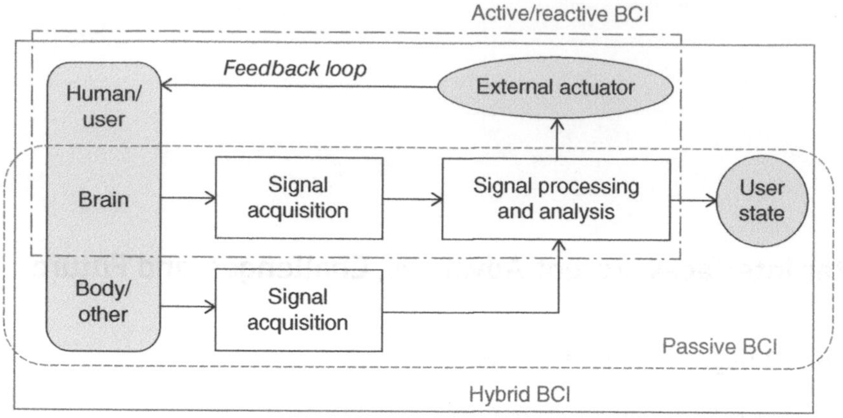


**Figure 2.1** Block diagram of the different BCI types, including active/reactive (dash-dot), passive (dashed), and hybrid (solid).

Lastly, the outputs from the classifier can serve multiple purposes. In the classic active/reactive BCIs, they are used to control actuators that serve as feedback to the user. These typically comprise robotic exoskeletons, computer cursors, robotic limbs, drones, wheelchairs [61], and with the assistance of functional electrical stimulation, even the user's muscles (see [32] for more details). As highlighted in [2], however, reliable control of a BCI is not for everyone, and the term "BCI illiterate" has been used to describe those who are unable to operate a BCI. This terminology has been criticized [59] as it assumes that the issue lies with the users not possessing the physiological or functional traits needed to operate the BCI. The more recent literature has shown that users and BCIs need to "learn" together [39], a concept termed mutual learning and described in detail in [48]. This has drastically improved the accuracy of reactive BCIs based on, e.g. visual-evoked potentials across a wide range of individuals [66].

In the early 2010s, the definition of a BCI was extended to include also so-called "passive BCIs." In this case, neural activity is monitored using the signal acquisition and the signal processing and analysis modules, but do not necessarily require real-time active feedback via actuators, but instead, a reading of the user's implicit mental state (e.g. attention level). The green dashed line in Figure 2.1 depicts the blocks involved in a passive BCI. The revised definition became "A brain-computer interface is a system that measures central nervous system (CNS) activity and converts it into artificial output that replaces, restores, enhances, supplements, or improves natural CNS output and thereby changes the ongoing interactions between the CNS and its external or internal environment" [69].

In this chapter, we will present a brief background on active/reactive, passive, and hybrid BCIs in Section 2.2, followed by a description of the state-of-the-art today in each of these areas (Section 2.3), as well as emerging applications and research challenges in Section 2.4. The purpose of the chapter is to provide the reader with a brief view of these topics and, where relevant, refer the interested reader to published works that provide a more in-depth view on the various concepts and ideas.

## 2.2 Background

The invention of the electroencephalogram (EEG) in the early twentieth century by Hans Berger [10] fired the human imagination of communication via brain activity. The expression

**Table 2.1** Representative examples, existing, and emerging applications of different BCI types.

| BCI type | Representative examples | Existing applications | Emerging applications |
|---|---|---|---|
| Active | Mental imagery: motor, word generation, mental rotation, subtraction, singing, navigation, and face imagery; ErrPs | Wheelchair control, stroke rehabilitation, gaming | Exoskeletons |
| Reactive | P300, SSVEP, SSMVEP, cVEP | BCI spellers, wheelchair/robot control, gaming | Consciousness disorders |
| Passive | Mental workload, stress, attention, fatigue, engagement, ErrP | Neuromarketing, quality assessment, neuroergonomics, arts, adaptive interfaces, BCI error correction | Affective neurofeedback, VR gaming |
| Hybrid | Pure (e.g. SSVEP and hemoglobin concentration), physiological (e.g. heart rate/P300), mixed (e.g. joystick/ERP) | Environment robustness, improved BCI accuracy, wheelchair control | Aviation, VR gaming |

"brain–computer interface" for a system that interconnects the human brain and a computer was introduced by Vidal in 1977, who presented the first BCI application – a cursor-object on a computer screen controlled by means of EEG [63]. Since then, EEG remains the main modality used for acquisitions of brain signals, despite the fact that EEG signals are noisy, nonstationary, complex, and of high dimensionality [35].

The earliest BCIs were mainly developed as communication tools for support of severely impaired patients, but modern BCI applications [52] may also be used to replace, restore, enhance, supplement, or improve natural central nervous system outputs [12, 70]. Modern BCI systems can be categorized in many different ways, e.g. dependent/independent, exogenous/endogenous, synchronous/asynchronous, or invasive/noninvasive, and the interested reader is referred to [44, 52] for more details. Here, we focus on the categorization of the type of modality used and targeted ap plication, making them either active/reactive, passive (as proposed in [71]), and/or hybrid. Table 2.1 summarizes some representative examples and application areas for these different BCI types.

### 2.2.1 Active/Reactive BCIs

An active BCI derives its outputs from brain activity which is directly and consciously controlled by the user, independent of external events, to control an application. The most common mental task used is motor imagery, where the person imagines moving their hands, feet, and/or tongue, and these imagined movements produce an event-related response (ERP) (can be either a synchronization, ERS, or a desychronization, ERD) over the sensorimotor cortex. The activation is detected by the BCI, and feedback is given to the user to acknowledge the decision. This principle has been used, for example in stroke rehabilitation by activating a functional electrical stimulator as soon as the movement imagination is detected, hence, providing direct feedback to the user via muscle stimulation [38]. Other types of mental imagery are also common, including word generation, mental rotation, subtraction, singing and navigation, and face imagery, to name a few [8].

A reactive BCI, in turn, derives its outputs from brain activity arising in reaction to external stimulation, which is indirectly modulated by the user to control an application. The P300 evoked potentials and the steady-state visual-evoked potentials (SSVEP), for example are the most widely used reactive BCI approaches [65]. The P300 principle refers to a spike seen in EEG activity approximately 300 milliseconds following the presentation of a target stimulus, which can be auditory, visual, and/or vibrotactile. The P300 brain speller, for example provides the user with a virtual keyboard on a computer screen with letters flashing randomly on the screen. If the user focuses their attention on a particular letter, when it flashes, it generates a P300 signal that is detected by the BCI and allows the user to type with fairly high accuracy [52].

SSVEP BCIs, in turn, rely on the principle that when the retina is excited by a visual stimulus flickering at a specific frequency, the brain generates electrical activity at the same frequency (and multiple thereof, termed harmonics), which can then be detected by a BCI [11]. By placing objects on a screen, each flickering at a different rate, one may translate the detection of different frequencies into different commands. For example, four arrows flashing at different rates could be used to steer a robot into one of four different directions [64]. More recently, steady-state motion visual-evoked potentials (SSMVEP) have also been explored as a BCI modality. Such BCIs work similarly to SSVEP ones, but with the main difference that the SSMVEP stimulus is smoothly changing in appearance with a continuous motion (as opposed to fast flashes), and this has shown to lead to lower user fatigue [58].

### 2.2.2 Passive BCIs

Passive BCIs monitor patterns of mental activity not related to volitional control, as in active BCIs, but instead to implicit mental states of the user to improve the human–machine interaction [71]. Such interfaces are also referred to as affective or cognitive BCIs and the interested reader is referred to [4, 43] for more details. Passive BCIs have gained popularity in recent years with the burgeoning of low-cost, portable devices. Such systems typically trade-off signal quality and temporal resolution for portability, thus hampering their use in active BCIs that require high signal-to-noise ratios and millisecond-order precision. Typically, such requirements are not as strict in passive BCIs; hence, mobile devices have gained popularity in, e.g. neuroergonomics applications (see [34] and references therein). Passive BCIs have been used to measure states such as mental workload [1], stress [47], attention [9], fatigue, patient engagement [3], and even human influential factors used in quality-of-experience models [28], to name a few. They have also found applications in the evaluation of products (e.g. neuromarketing [19]), in adaptive interfaces, such as an air-traffic controller display, which adapts to the user's current state [5], as well as in artistic applications [67].

Error-related potentials (ErrP), i.e. neural signatures representative of error processing (e.g. user perceiving an erroneous selection) have also been classified by some as a passive BCI modality when used to monitor, for example human states in human–robot interactions [24] or to predict auditory attentional errors in pilots during flights [22]. In other applications, however, they have been treated as an active BCI modality, as the detected ErrPs are used to automatically erase errors made by the active BCI [21] which can also lead to improvement in the information transfer rate of the BCI [72]. A review on the use of ErrPs for BCIs can be found in [18], and their use in active and passive applications can be found in [42].

While EEG still remains the main modality used for passive BCIs, the emergence of portable fNIRS devices has brought this modality into the spotlight, as it provides some advantages over EEG-based systems, such as reduced sensitivity to movement artifacts. Over the last few years, a number of fNIRS-based passive BCI systems have been proposed [23]. Oftentimes, however, given the poor temporal resolution of fNIRS systems (they offer the advantage of good spatial resolution), they are used in combination with EEG systems that offer good temporal resolution (but poor spatial). These combined systems are termed "hybrid" and are the focus of Section 2.2.3.

### 2.2.3 Hybrid BCIs

Hybrid BCIs (hBCI) rely on multiple modalities where at least one of them is a BCI [49]. Hybrid BCIs can be categorized based on what modalities are used [7], including (i) pure hBCI, where different modalities of a neural signal are used (e.g. SSVEP and ERP from EEG or P300 from EEG and oxygenated hemoglobin concentrations from fNIRS); (ii) physiological hBCI, where a neural modality is coupled with another nonneural modality (e.g. heart rate, EMG, and eye gaze); and (iii) mixed hBCI, where a nonpsychophysiological signal is coupled with a neural one (e.g. joystick response or an accelerometer signal). Hybrid BCIs are typically a combination of two active BCIs or one active and one passive, though passive–passive hBCIs do exist and have been proposed to improve the robustness of mental state monitoring by tapping into the complementarity of varying signal modalities (e.g. [46]).

Hybrid BCIs can combine the different signals and modalities at different stages of the signal processing and analysis pipelines. In "complementary" approaches, the signals are combined at the feature or decision levels to improve the accuracy and/or robustness of the BCI. For example, in [8], EEG and fNIRS features were combined to improve overall active BCI accuracy, hence, resulting in a pure hBCI. In [25], in turn, fNIRS signals were combined with cardiac and breathing signals to make the active BCI system more robust against distractions and environmental factors; this constituted a physiological hBCI. Moreover, in [1] and [47], physiological hBCIs were used for improved passive mental state monitoring of mental workload and stress, respectively. Lastly, in [33], P300-based EEG signals were used to control the direction of the movement of a wheelchair, while navigation sensors embedded into the chair itself were used for emergency stops and/or corrections; this constitutes a representative mixed hBCI.

Sequential approaches, on the other hand, act as "switches" or "selectors" and rely on one modality/BCI to activate/deactivate or select from the multiple choices from the other modalities, respectively. The work described in [61], for example, highlights many such methods that have been proposed for wheelchair control. As an example, the work in [51] proposed a sequential switch method in which P300 signals were used to trigger movement of the wheelchair followed by an ERP-based BCI which was used for speed control, hence, constituting a pure sequential hBCI. In turn, in [68], the ERD signal was used to control the direction of the wheelchair (forward or backward), which would then trigger one of the three possible complementary systems: ERD/ERS for left/right, P300 to accelerate/decelerate, and an eyeblink-based method to stop the wheelchair; hence, constituting a physiological hBCI.

## 2.3 Recent Advances and Applications

Advances in sensor technologies, machine-learning tools, and signal-processing pipelines have resulted in great advances in BCI technologies over the last decade. The last column of Table 2.1 lists some emerging applications. Here, more details are provided on a few of such innovations.

### 2.3.1 Active/Reactive BCIs

Motor imagery-based BCIs are often used for stroke rehabilitation of upper and lower limbs. In this case, the person is instructed to imagine a certain movement, and the BCI system detects it. Functional electrical stimulation or an exoskeleton movement is then triggered by the BCI system to provide feedback to the user. This process is repeated many times to produce brain plasticity, to reduce spasticity, and to restore movements of the patients [56]. In addition to the speller applications described previously, P300-based BCI systems are currently being used as an assessment tool for patients with disorders of consciousness. In this case, vibro-tactile stimulations on the left and right wrists are used. The patient is instructed to count the vibrations on the left or right wrist and a P300 signal is generated when the vibration happens on the target hand, whereas a standard event-related potential is seen for the nontarget hand. Depending on the outcomes, a BCI can then be developed for simple YES/NO questions and has shown to be successfully tested in patients with locked-in syndrome and patients with disorders of consciousness [26].

Moreover, among the different visual-evoked potentials (VEP)-based paradigms, BCIs based on code-modulated VEPs (cVEP) have achieved the most promising results, with an average transmission rate of approximately 96.9 bits/min, i.e. 19.5 characters/min [66]. Unlike conventional SSVEP, cVEP stimuli flicker following a pseudorandom pattern, with the m-sequence being the most commonly used pattern. Notwithstanding, Golay codes were recently investigated and shown to provide several advantages [60].

### 2.3.2 Passive BCIs

Passive BCIs have gained popularity over the last decade as wireless devices and has become more widespread. Today, we see applications in aviation, maritime, transportation, human performance monitoring, marketing, multimedia quality-of-experience modeling, and in workplace environments, to name a few. The interested reader is referred to [6, 31] for a more in-depth view of existing and emerging passive BCI applications. Moreover, EEG systems have remained the most popular due to their relative low cost, portability, and recent advances seen, e.g. in "dry electrode" technology. Notwithstanding, portable fNIRS systems have emerged over the last five years, so the modality has been gaining grounds recently, especially in situations where movement artifacts may hamper system performance. A review on the passive BCIs for affective neurofeedback can be seen in [62].

### 2.3.3 Hybrid BCIs

Building BCIs with a single modality has numerous limitations, including but not limited to lower accuracy, slower detection speeds, increased sensitivity to certain artifacts (e.g. movement or environment related), and greater influence of different confounds (e.g. activity and fatigue). Hybrid approaches attempt to overcome these limitations by taking a multifaceted view to the task at hand. As emphasized by Choi et al. [20], pure hBCIs based on two or more EEG modalities are still the most popular, especially for active/reactive BCIs. EEG and fNIRS, in turn, have shown to be the most popular when it comes to pure hybrid BCIs for both active and passive applications. In fact, some works have proposed to use EEG and fNIRS in a physiological hBCI passive approach where heart rate information derived from the fNIRS signal is used as a third modality showing improved accuracy in measuring user's emotional reactions [27]. Applications in aviation [13], out-of-the-lab active BCIs [25], wheelchair control [61], and virtual reality gaming [41] exemplify some recent applications of hBCIs.

## 2.4 Future Research Challenges

Brain–computer interfaces have been around for decades. Original applications were aimed at assistive technologies and typically relied on expensive, research-grade neuroimaging systems constrained to laboratory settings. As technologies have evolved, however, lower-cost dry electrodes have emerged, alongside multimodal wireless bioamplifiers, computational power has enabled the re-emergence of deep learning, and consumer-grade systems have enabled (big) data collection from many participants in everyday environments, including at home. On the one hand, these advances have enabled the development of state-of-the-art portable active/passive/hybrid BCIs. On the other hand, these innovations have also created some issues that need to be addressed as the field moves forward. Here, we place focus on only a handful of such limitations.

### 2.4.1 Current Research Issues

Regarding the emergence of new devices and neuroimaging technologies, this has led to issues concerning standardization, ranging from data representation to terminology used [17]. In February 2020, the IEEE Standards Association released a roadmap for neurotechnologies and BCIs [29], and, at the time of writing, three standardization projects were up and running, including IEEE P2725.1 (Standard for Microwave Structural, Vascular, or Functional Medical Imaging Device Safety), IEEE P2794 (Reporting of In Vivo Neural Interface Research), and IEEE P2731 (Standard for a Unified Terminology for Brain–Computer Interfaces). Regarding the burgeoning of deep learning models, while state-of-the-art performance is being reported [54], deep neural networks (DNN) are known to suffer from the so-called "adversarial attacks," where imperceptible, carefully crafted noise can be added to the network input and force it to make erroneous decisions. Recently, researchers have shown that DNN-based BCI systems are vulnerable to such attacks [73]. The reader should be able to quickly see the concern this can cause with DNN-based BCIs used to control, for example, wheelchairs where adversarial attacks could be life-threatening.

In turn, widespread recording of neural information in everyday settings raises a number of privacy and ethical issues that need to be addressed [30]. And as BCIs become plug-and-play devices that can be used at home, special attention will need to be placed when developing systems for patients with severe neuromuscular disabilities [45], including taking personhood into account [55]. As devices become ubiquitous and at-home/work BCI usage increases, we will reach the "big data" levels needed to truly benefit from data-hungry machine-learning methods. Models, however, will need to be trained carefully to compensate for the inter- and intrasubject variability that is known to hamper BCI performance. This will be a challenging step, but recent research is already showing promising results with cVEP-based BCIs [57].

### 2.4.2 Future Research Directions

As BCIs technologies become more mainstream, several doors for innovative research directions have opened. Here, we focus on a handful of directions being explored by the authors. For example, with portable BCIs (also termed mobile BCIs) new signal enhancement and artifact removal algorithms will be needed to remove artifacts related to gait, for example [53]. Moreover, virtual reality (VR) applications are also burgeoning. As these are applications that require the use of a head-mounted display, it becomes a prime location for the placement of a BCI. The work in [14], for example, describes the development of an hBCI-instrumented VR headset and in [40], its use for saccadic eye movement classification without the need for an eye tracker. Figure 2.2 depicts the developed wireless BCI-equipped VR headset composed of dry EEG electrodes placed directly on the foam and straps of the headset.

Moreover, with portable hBCIs, one can now more easily monitor multiple users, a method referred to as "hyperscanning." This will enable new knowledge to be gained, for example, on how users interact and socialize, work together as a team, and may lead to additional insights on how

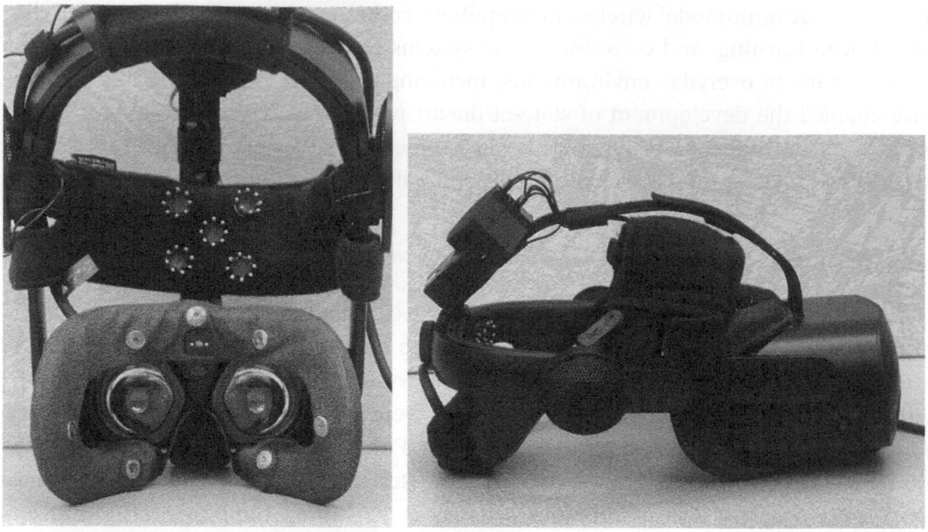

**Figure 2.2** A passive BCI-enabled VR headset for emerging applications with immersive media.

humans integrate multiple senses in the famous cocktail party problem. Passive hyperscanning, for example, has been proposed to track two Argentine tango dancers and detect when they reach a desirable flow state [16]. Lastly, with advances in, e.g. transcranial magnetic stimulation and transcranial direct current stimulation, future research directions can target bidirectional or brain-to-brain communications [32], as well as develop new VR-based clinical applications [15].

## 2.5 Conclusions

This chapter reviewed the recent advances in active, reactive, passive, and hybrid brain–computer interfaces (BCIs), showcased some existing and emerging applications, as well as highlighted challenges seen in the field, such as standardization, adversarial attacks, inter-/intrasubject variability, and patient usability. We conclude with an outlook of future research directions, including brain-to-brain communications and BCI-integrated extended reality headsets.

## References

1 Albuquerque, I., Tiwari, A., Parent, M. et al. (2020). WAUC: a multi-modal database for mental workload assessment under physical activity. *Frontiers in Neuroscience* 14: 549524.

2 Allison, B.Z. and Neuper, C. (2010). Could anyone use a BCI? In: *Brain-Computer Interfaces, Human-Computer Interaction Series* (ed. D. Tan and A. Nijholt), 35–54. London: Springer.

3 Angrisani, L., Arpaia, P., Esposito, A. et al. (2021). Passive and active brain-computer interfaces for rehabilitation in health 4.0. *Measurement: Sensors* 18: 100246.

4 Appriou, A., Cichocki, A., and Lotte, F. (2020). Modern machine-learning algorithms: for classifying cognitive and affective states from electroencephalography signals. *IEEE Systems, Man, and Cybernetics Magazine* 6 (3): 29–38.

**5** Aricò, P., Borghini, G., Di Flumeri, G. et al. (2016). Adaptive automation triggered by EEG-based mental workload index: a passive brain-computer interface application in realistic air traffic control environment. *Frontiers in Human Neuroscience* 10: 539.

**6** Aricò, P., Borghini, G., Di Flumeri, G. et al. (2018). Passive BCI beyond the lab: current trends and future directions. *Physiological Measurement* 39 (8): 08TR02.

**7** Banville, H. and Falk, T.H. (2016). Recent advances and open challenges in hybrid brain-computer interfacing: a technological review of non-invasive human research. *Brain-Computer Interfaces* 3 (1): 9–46.

**8** Banville, H., Gupta, R., and Falk, T.H. (2017). Mental task evaluation for hybrid NIRS-EEG brain-computer interfaces. *Computational Intelligence and Neuroscience* 2017: 3524208.

**9** Belo, J., Clerc, M., and Schön, D. (2021). EEG-based auditory attention detection and its possible future applications for passive BCI. *Frontiers in Computer Science* 3: 661178.

**10** Berger, H. (1929). Über das elektroenkephalogramm des menschen. *Archiv für psychiatrie und nervenkrankheiten* 87 (1): 527–570.

**11** Brennan, C., McCullagh, P., Lightbody, G. et al. (2020). Performance of a steady-state visual evoked potential and eye gaze hybrid brain-computer interface on participants with and without a brain injury. *IEEE Transactions on Human-Machine Systems* 50 (4): 277–286.

**12** Brunner, C., Birbaumer, N., Blankertz, B. et al. (2015). BNCI Horizon 2020: towards a roadmap for the BCI community. *Brain-Computer Interfaces* 2 (1): 1–10.

**13** Callan, D.E. and Dehais, F. (2019). Neuroergonomics for aviation. In: *Neuroergonomics*, 55–58. Elsevier.

**14** Cassani, R., Moinnereau, M.-A., Ivanescu, L. et al. (2020). Neural interface instrumented virtual reality headsets: toward next-generation immersive applications. *IEEE Systems, Man, and Cybernetics Magazine* 6 (3): 20–28.

**15** Cassani, R., Novak, G.S., Falk, T.H., and Oliveira, A.A. (2020). Virtual reality and non-invasive brain stimulation for rehabilitation applications: a systematic review. *Journal of Neuroengineering and Rehabilitation* 17 (1): 1–16.

**16** Cassani, R., Tiwari, A., Posner, I. et al. (2020). Initial investigation into neurophysiological correlates of argentine tango flow states: a case study. *2020 IEEE International Conference on Systems, Man, and Cybernetics (SMC)*, pages 3478–3483. IEEE.

**17** Chavarriaga, R. (2020). Standards for neurotechnologies and brain-machine interfacing. *IEEE Systems, Man, and Cybernetics Magazine* 6 (3): 50–51.

**18** Chavarriaga, R., Sobolewski, A., and Millán, J.R. (2014). Errare machinale est: the use of error-related potentials in brain-machine interfaces. *Frontiers in Neuroscience* 8: 208.

**19** Cherubino, P., Martinez-Levy, A.C., Caratu, M. et al. (2019). Consumer behavior through the eyes of neurophysiological measures: state-of-the-art and future trends. *Computational Intelligence and Neuroscience* 2019: 1976847.

**20** Choi, I., Rhiu, I., Lee, Y. et al. (2017). A systematic review of hybrid brain-computer interfaces: taxonomy and usability perspectives. *PLoS One* 12 (4): e0176674.

**21** Cruz, A., Pires, G., and Nunes, U.J. (2017). Double ErrP detection for automatic error correction in an ERP-based BCI speller. *IEEE Transactions on Neural Systems and Rehabilitation Engineering* 26 (1): 26–36.

**22** Dehais, F., Rida, I., Roy, R.N. et al. (2019). A pBCI to predict attentional error before it happens in real flight conditions. *2019 IEEE International Conference on Systems, Man and Cybernetics (SMC)*, 4155–4160. IEEE.

**23** Derosière, G., Mandrick, K., Dray, G. et al. (2013). NIRS-measured prefrontal cortex activity in neuroergonomics: strengths and weaknesses. *Frontiers in Human Neuroscience* 7: 583.

**24** Ehrlich, S.K. and Cheng, G. (2018). Human-agent co-adaptation using error-related potentials. *Journal of Neural Engineering* 15 (6): 066014.

**25** Falk, T.H., Guirgis, M., Power, S., and Chau, T.T. (2010). Taking NIRS-BCIs outside the lab: towards achieving robustness against environment noise. *IEEE Transactions on Neural Systems and Rehabilitation Engineering* 19 (2): 136–146.

**26** Guger, C., Spataro, R., Pellas, F. et al. (2018). Assessing command-following and communication with vibro-tactile P300 brain-computer interface tools in patients with unresponsive wakefulness syndrome. *Frontiers in Neuroscience* 12: 423.

**27** Gupta, R., Banville, H.J., and Falk, T.H. (2016). Multimodal physiological quality-of-experience assessment of text-to-speech systems. *IEEE Journal of Selected Topics in Signal Processing* 11 (1): 22–36.

**28** Gupta, R., Laghari, K., Banville, H., and Falk, T.H. (2016). Using affective brain-computer interfaces to characterize human influential factors for speech quality-of-experience perception modeling. *Human-Centric Computing and Information Sciences* 6 (1): 1–19.

**29** IEEE-SA (2020). Standards Roadmap: Neurotechnologies for Brain-Machine Interfacing. https://standards.ieee.org/content/dam/ieee-standards/standards/web/documents/presentations/ieee-neurotech-for-bmi-standards-roadmap.pdf (accessed 11 January 2023).

**30** Klein, E. (2020). Ethics and the emergence of brain-computer interface medicine. In: *Handbook of Clinical Neurology - Brain-Computer Interfaces*, Chapter 24, vol. 168 (ed. N. Ramsey and J.D.R. Millán), 329–340. Elsevier.

**31** Krol, L.R., Haselager, P., and Zander, T.O. (2020). Cognitive and affective probing: a tutorial and review of active learning for neuroadaptive technology. *Journal of Neural Engineering* 17 (1): 012001.

**32** Lebedev, M. and Nicolelis, M. (2017). Brain-machine interfaces: from basic science to neuroprostheses and neurorehabilitation. *Physiological Reviews* 97 (2): 767–837.

**33** Lopes, A., Rodrigues, J., Perdigao, J. et al. (2016). A new hybrid motion planner: applied in a brain-actuated robotic wheelchair. *IEEE Robotics & Automation Magazine* 23 (4): 82–93.

**34** Lotte, F. and Roy, R.N. (2019). Brain-computer interface contributions to neuroergonomics. In: *Neuroergonomics*, 43–48. Elsevier.

**35** Lotte, F., Congedo, M., Lécuyer, A. et al. (2007). A review of classification algorithms for EEG-based brain–computer interfaces. *Journal of Neural Engineering* 4 (2): R1.

**36** Lotte, F., Bougrain, L., Cichocki, A. et al. (2018). A review of classification algorithms for EEG-based brain-computer interfaces: a 10 year update. *Journal of Neural Engineering* 15 (3): 031005.

**37** Makeig, S., Kothe, C., Mullen, T. et al. (2012). Evolving signal processing for brain-computer interfaces. *Proceedings of the IEEE* 100 (Special Centennial Issue): 1567–1584.

**38** Marquez-Chin, C. and Popovic, M.R. (2020). Functional electrical stimulation therapy for restoration of motor function after spinal cord injury and stroke: a review. *Biomedical Engineering Online* 19: 1–25.

**39** McFarland, D.J. and Wolpaw, J.R. (2018). Brain-computer interface use is a skill that user and system acquire together. *PLoS Biology* 16 (7): e2006719.

**40** Moinnereau, M.-A., Oliveira, A., and Falk, T.H. (2020). Saccadic eye movement classification using ExG sensors embedded into a virtual reality headset. *2020 IEEE International Conference on Systems, Man, and Cybernetics (SMC)*, 3494–3498. IEEE.

**41** Monnereau, M.-A., Oliveira, A.A., and Falk, T.H. (2022). Measuring human influential factors during VR gaming at home: towards optimized per-user gaming experiences. *13th International Conference on Applied Human Factors and Ergonomics.*

**42** Mousavi, M. and de Sa, V.R. (2019). Spatio-temporal analysis of error-related brain activity in active and passive brain-computer interfaces. *Brain-Computer Interfaces* 6 (4): 118–127.

**43** Mühl, C., Allison, B., Nijholt, A., and Chanel, G. (2014). A survey of affective brain-computer interfaces: principles, state-of-the-art, and challenges. *Brain-Computer Interfaces* 1 (2): 66–84.

**44** Nicolas-Alonso, L.F. and Gomez-Gil, J. (2012). Brain computer interfaces, a review. *Sensors* 12 (2): 1211–1279.

**45** Nijboer, F., Plass-Oude Bos, D., Blokland, Y. et al. (2014). Design requirements and potential target users for brain-computer interfaces: recommendations from rehabilitation professionals. *Brain-Computer Interfaces* 1 (1): 50–61.

**46** Parent, M., Tiwari, A., Albuquerque, I. et al. (2019). A multimodal approach to improve the robustness of physiological stress prediction during physical activity. *2019 IEEE International Conference on Systems, Man and Cybernetics (SMC)*, 4131–4136. IEEE.

**47** Parent, M., Albuquerque, I., Tiwari, A. et al. (2020). PASS: a multimodal database of physical activity and stress for mobile passive body/brain-computer interface research. *Frontiers in Neuroscience* 14: 1274.

**48** Perdikis, S. and Millan, J.R. (2020). Brain-machine interfaces: a tale of two learners. *IEEE Systems, Man, and Cybernetics Magazine* 6 (3): 12–19.

**49** Pfurt-scheller, G., Allison, B.Z., Bauernfeind, G. et al. (2010). The hybrid BCI. *Frontiers in Neuroscience* 4: 3.

**50** Ramadan, R.A. and Vasilakos, A.V. (2017). Brain-computer interface: control signals review. *Neurocomputing* 223: 26–44.

**51** Rebsamen, B., Burdet, E., Zeng, Q. et al. (2008). Hybrid P300 and Mu-Beta brain computer interface to operate a brain controlled wheelchair. *Proceedings of the 2nd International Convention on Rehabilitation Engineering & Assistive Technology*, 51–55.

**52** Rezeika, A., Benda, M., Stawicki, P. et al. (2018). Brain–computer interface spellers: a review. *Brain Sciences* 8 (4): 57.

**53** Rosanne, O., Albuquerque, I., Cassani, R. et al. (2021). Adaptive filtering for improved EEG-based mental workload assessment of ambulant users. *Frontiers in Neuroscience* 15: 341.

**54** Roy, Y., Banville, H., Albuquerque, I. et al. (2019). Deep learning-based electroencephalography analysis: a systematic review. *Journal of Neural Engineering* 16 (5): 051001.

**55** Sample, M., Aunos, M., Blain-Moraes, S. et al. (2019). Brain-computer interfaces and personhood: interdisciplinary deliberations on neural technology. *Journal of Neural Engineering* 16 (6): 063001.

**56** Sebastián-Romagosa, M., Cho, W., Ortner, R. et al. (2020). Brain computer interface treatment for motor rehabilitation of upper extremity of stroke patients: a feasibility study. *Frontiers in Neuroscience* 14: 1056.

**57** Stawicki, P. and Volosyak, I. (2022). CVEP training data validation—towards optimal training set composition from multi-day data. *Brain Sciences* 12 (2): 234.

**58** Stawicki, P., Rezeika, A., and Volosyak, I. (2021). Effects of training on BCI accuracy in SSMVEP-based BCI. *International Work-Conference on Artificial Neural Networks*, 69–80. Springer.

**59** Thompson, M.C. (2019). Critiquing the concept of BCI illiteracy. *Science and Engineering Ethics* 25 (4): 1217–1233.

**60** J.A.R. Torres and Daly, I. (2021). How to build a fast and accurate code-modulated brain-computer interface. *Journal of Neural Engineering* 18 (4): 046052.

**61** Trambaiolli, L.R. and Falk, T.H. (2018). Hybrid brain-computer interfaces for wheelchair control: a review of existing solutions, their advantages and open challenges. In: *Smart Wheelchairs and Brain-Computer Interfaces*, 229–256. Elsevier.

**62** Trambaiolli, L.R., Tiwari, A., and Falk, T.H. (2021). Affective neurofeedback under naturalistic conditions: a mini-review of current achievements and open challenges. *Frontiers in Neuroergonomics* 2: 15.

**63** Vidal, J.J. (1977). Real-time detection of brain events in EEG. *Proceedings of the IEEE* 65 (5): 633–641.

**64** Volosyak, I. and Schmidt, M. (2019). Asynchronous control of a spherical robot by means of SSVEP-based brain-computer interface. *2019 E-Health and Bioengineering Conference (EHB)*, 1–4. IEEE.

**65** Volosyak, I., Guger, C., and Gräser, A. (2010). Toward BCI wizard-best BCI approach for each user. *2010 Annual International Conference of the IEEE Engineering in Medicine and Biology*, 4201–4204. IEEE.

**66** Volosyak, I., Rezeika, A., Benda, M. et al. (2020). Towards solving of the illiteracy phenomenon for VEP-based brain-computer interfaces. *Biomedical Physics & Engineering Express* 6 (3): 035034.

**67** Wadeson, A., Nijholt, A., and Nam, C.S. (2015). Artistic brain-computer interfaces: state-of-the-art control mechanisms. *Brain-Computer Interfaces* 2 (2–3): 70–75.

**68** Wang, H., Li, Y., Long, J. et al. (2014). An asynchronous wheelchair control by hybrid EEG-EOG brain-computer interface. *Cognitive Neurodynamics* 8 (5): 399–409.

**69** Wolpaw, J.R. and Wolpaw, E.W. (2012). Chapter 1: Brain-computer interfaces: something new under the sun. *Brain-Computer Interfaces: Principles and Practice*, Oxford University Press: NY, USA.

**70** Wolpaw, J.R., Birbaumer, N., McFarland, D.J. et al. (2002). Brain-computer interfaces for communication and control. *Clinical Neurophysiology* 113 (6): 767–791.

**71** Zander, T.O. and Kothe, C. (2011). Towards passive brain-computer interfaces: applying brain-computer interface technology to human-machine systems in general. *Journal of Neural Engineering* 8 (2): 025005.

**72** Zeyl, T., Yin, E., Keightley, M., and Chau, T. (2016). Improving bit rate in an auditory BCI: exploiting error-related potentials. *Brain-Computer Interfaces* 3 (2): 75–87.

**73** Zhang, X. and Wu, D. (2019). On the vulnerability of CNN classifiers in EEG-based BCIs. *IEEE Transactions on Neural Systems and Rehabilitation Engineering* 27 (5): 814–825.

# 3

# Brain–Computer Interfaces for Affective Neurofeedback Applications

*Lucas R. Trambaiolli[1] and Tiago H. Falk[2]*

[1] *McLean Hospital, Harvard Medical School, Belmont, MA, USA*
[2] *Institut national de la recherche scientifique, University of Quebec, Montreal, Quebec, Canada*

## 3.1 Introduction

In neurofeedback protocols, noninvasive brain–computer interface (BCIs) systems are used to train participants to voluntarily control their ongoing local neural activity [51]. This system provides real-time feedback related to the user's brain activity (Figure 3.1A), allowing them to create and improve self-regulation strategies to achieve the desired neuromodulatory control. Over the past decade, different clinical applications of neurofeedback have been tested, with special attention placed on those focusing on psychiatric disorders [27]. For these applications, the majority of existing protocols focus on putative circuits associated with emotion regulation [34], hence are termed "affective neurofeedback." The goal of this chapter is to provide a brief overview of basic concepts of affective neurofeedback research, the status of protocols for applications in psychiatry, current challenges, and future directions.

## 3.2 Background

Neurofeedback protocols can be initially grouped based on the imaging modality used during its experiments. The most common approach so far is the use of neuroeletric data to evaluate brain processes in real-time [51]. In fact, neurofeedback was first introduced with the idea of achieving voluntary control of electroencephalography (EEG) frequencies associated with electric potentials generated during neural activity of groups of neurons. Another modality focusing on electromagnetic oscillations is the magnetoencephalography (MEG), which uses a superconducting quantum interference device to record magnetic disturbances created during neuronal activity [51]. Examples of protocols focusing on neuroelectric signals include the self-regulation of single frequencies [12, 45, 61, 62] or of frequency ratios [10] over specific regions over the scalp.

Another group of protocols includes those focusing on features related to cerebral hemodynamics, i.e. the blood flow due to metabolic needs caused by neural activity. Functional magnetic resonance imaging (fMRI) is the most common method for hemodynamic-based neurofeedback [54], and focus has been placed on the evaluation of the local blood

*Handbook of Human-Machine Systems*, First Edition. Edited by Giancarlo Fortino, David Kaber, Andreas Nürnberger, and David Mendonça.

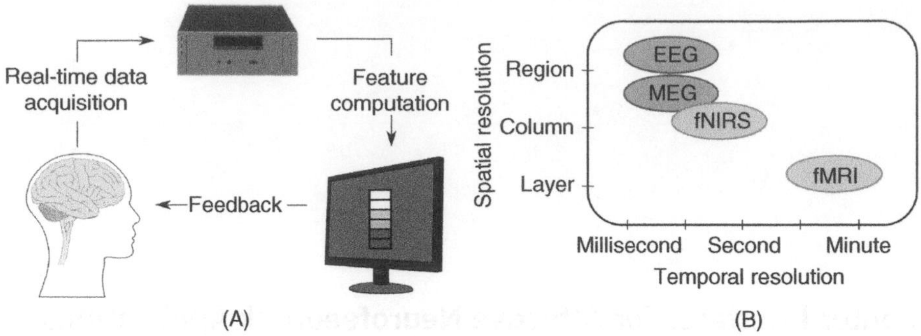


**Figure 3.1** (A) Example of a neurofeedback sequence with a regular thermometer feedback screen. (B) Comparison of spatial and temporal resolution of common neural imaging modalities used in neurofeedback protocols.

oxygenation-level-dependent (BOLD) signals associated with metabolic changes [51]. For instance, some studies showed that participants are able to self-regulate the BOLD signal in one [64, 69] or more brain regions [33, 37], or the functional connectivity between different regions [30]. Other studies have also proposed the use of decoding neurofeedback approaches, with multivariate pattern analysis algorithms being used to identify different hemodynamic patterns in groups of voxels [11]. An alternate hemodynamics-based approach which has been gaining attention recently for neurofeedback is functional near-infrared spectroscopy (fNIRS) [29]. This approach uses the infrared spectrum to measure alterations in the intensity of attenuated light resulting from changes in oxyhemoglobin and deoxyhemoglobin concentrations [51]. Experiments targeting single regions [66] or using brain decoding [56] have been reported using this technique, although not investigated within clinical populations yet.

Commonly, protocols using MEG and fMRI have higher spatial resolution (Figure 3.1B), thus allowing for targeting specific structures in the brain. For example, fMRI allows for deeper subcortical targets, such as the amygdala, thalamus, hippocampus, and nucleus accumbens [54]. However, the higher costs, low portability, and restrictions associated with magnetic fields reduce its potential outside of large research and clinical centers. The EEG, on the other hand, is limited by its reduced spatial resolution, but present higher temporal resolution allowing for the identification of faster neural events. In an attempt to bridge the advantages of these different imaging modalities, some authors have suggested the combination of two or more neuroimaging techniques in multimodal systems [36]. In fact, studies with simultaneous EEG-fMRI recordings showed that frontal EEG patterns present signatures of deep brain regions during neurofeedback protocols [26, 71, 72] and can be combined to provide real-time feedback [73]. Given this possibility of identifying signatures from deeper structures, combining EEG and fNIRS has allowed for systems that have lower cost and increased portability, thus enabling neurofeedback protocols for daily usage "in the wild," i.e. in everyday environments [58].

## 3.3 State-of-the-Art

The possibility of noninvasive manipulation of putative mechanisms underlying affective and anxiety disorders places affective neurofeedback protocols as a potential therapeutic approach for psychiatry [27]. In the following sessions, we will briefly discuss the state-of-the-art of affective

**Table 3.1** Examples of neurofeedback protocols for depression and PTSD.

| Illness | Imaging technique | Regulation target |
|---|---|---|
| Depressive disorder | EEG | Up-regulation of alpha asymmetry in F3 and F4 electrodes [12, 45, 61, 62] |
| | | Down-regulation of beta frequencies in AF3, AF4, T3, and T4 electrodes [43] |
| | | Self-regulation of SMR or beta band in F3, T3, or T4 electrodes (according to symptoms), followed by down-regulation of alpha/theta ratio in Pz [32] |
| | | Up-regulation of alpha frequencies in parietal-occipital electrodes [15] |
| | | Up-regulation of beta frequencies at F3 electrode and down-regulation of alpha/theta ratio in Pz electrode [10] |
| | fMRI | Up-regulation of BOLD signal in the left amygdala [63, 64] |
| | | Up-regulation of BOLD signal in the left dorsolateral PFC [53] |
| | | Up-regulation of BOLD signal in multiple regions at the same time [33, 37] |
| | | Up-regulation of correlations between the right superior anterior temporal lobe and the posterior subgenual cortex [23] |
| | fMRI + EEG | Up-regulation of BOLD signal in left ACC and amygdala and Up-regulation of alpha frequencies and beta asymmetry in F3 and F4 electrodes [73] |
| Posttraumatic stress disorder | EEG | Down-regulation of alpha frequencies in Pz electrode [28, 40, 48] |
| | | Down-regulation of multiple frequency bands in T4-P4 or T3-T4 electrodes (according to randomization) [17, 59] |
| | | Up-regulation of alpha–theta synchronization [46, 47] |
| | | Down-regulation of amygdala fingerprint activity in Pz electrode [16, 26] |
| | fMRI | Down-regulation of BOLD signal in the bilateral amygdala [18, 42] |
| | | Up-regulation of BOLD signal in the left amygdala [72] |
| | | Voxel-level decoding [11] |

*Abbreviations:* ACC = anterior cingulate cortex; BOLD = blood-oxygen-level-dependent; EEG = electroencephalography; fMRI = functional magnetic resonance imaging; PFC = prefrontal cortex; SMR = sensorymotor rhythm.

neurofeedback protocols in two major psychiatric illnesses: depressive disorder and posttraumatic stress disorder (PTSD). In Table 3.1, we list some of the significant studies for these applications.

### 3.3.1 Depressive Disorder

Depression was one of the first applications for neurofeedback protocols, with the first case reports using EEG neurofeedback published in the 1990s [7, 14, 50]. Nowadays, neurofeedback protocols for depression present more structured and controlled study designs, including randomized clinical trials, and consistent symptom improvement reported across studies [57].

Among the studies using EEG-based neurofeedback training, the majority of protocols focused on the self-regulation of the frontal alpha asymmetry [12, 45, 61, 62]. In these cases, researchers assume that differences in alpha frequencies in frontal hemispheres reflect the valence experienced during emotion regulation [21] and that this effect is affected in patients with depression [55]. Controlled experiments suggest significant effects in depressive and anxiety symptoms compared to control conditions [12, 62]. Other frequencies have also been explored in EEG protocols, including self-regulation of single frequencies in frontotemporal [32, 43] and parieto-occipital channels [15], or changes in frequency ratios from fronto-temporal channels [10].

Studies using fMRI-based protocols, on the other hand, have the power to target specific brain regions commonly described as potential biomarkers of depression. Examples include cortical regions, such as the medial or lateral portions of the prefrontal cortex (PFC), the anterior cingulate cortex (ACC), and deep structures, including the amygdala, and striatum [20, 25]. Thus, many neurofeedback studies for depression aim to directly or indirectly modulate the neural activity in these structures. For instance, studies can target single regions, such as the amygdala [63, 64] or the dorsolateral PFC [53], multiple regions at the same time [33, 37], or the functional connectivity between regions [23]. Controlled trials including patients with depression showed significant reduction of depressive symptoms in the experimental group compared to controls after up to five intervention sections [33, 37, 63, 64], as well as functional connectivity reorganization [65, 68]. Importantly, symptom improvement seems to be sustained for weeks after intervention [37].

Of interest, patterns identified during protocols based on EEG and fMRI show some level of interaction. For example, amygdala up-regulation involves top-down control from PFC structures [70]. As a consequence, protocols using EEG-fMRI recordings showed that frontal EEG frequencies are correlated with the amygdalar activity during neurofeedback training [71], and these features were later combined to provide real-time feedback from both modalities [73].

### 3.3.2 Posttraumatic Stress Disorder, PTSD

Neurofeedback protocols for PTSD have also been widely explored since the early 1990s [46, 47]. Among the studies using EEG-based protocols, the most common approach is the self-modulation of alpha frequencies [5, 17, 28, 40, 48, 59], as they are associated with relaxed mental states. Abnormal patterns in these frequencies have been commonly identified in patients with PTSD [11]. In a recent controlled study, the group receiving alpha neurofeedback presented reduced number of participants meeting criteria for PTSD after training when compared to the control group [59]. Importantly, plastic functional connectivity changes were also observed after alpha neurofeedback in patients with PTSD [28, 40]. Other EEG targets for neurofeedback have included sensorimotor rhythms [5] and alpha/theta ratios [46, 47].

Similar to studies for depression, many fMRI-based neurofeedback protocols for patients with PTSD have focused on the self-regulation of amygdala activity [18, 42, 72]. Patients in the neurofeedback group showed moderate symptoms improvement, although no statistically significant difference to control groups was observed [72]. However, changes in functional connectivity were observed postintervention in patients involved in amygdala neurofeedback [41, 42, 72]. Another approach explored in patients with PTSD has been the use of decoding neurofeedback for reduction in physiological fear responses, with studies involving small samples showing reduction in symptomatic scales [11].

Also similar to protocols for patients with depression, associations between fMRI amygdala activity and EEG frequencies have been reported in studies including patients with PTSD [72]. In fact, a recent innovative protocol identified the electrophysiological fingerprints from amygdalar activity during real-time neurofeedback to train amygdala self-regulation based only in EEG data [16, 26].

## 3.4 Future Research Challenges

### 3.4.1 Open Challenges

Despite promising results, state-of-the-art neurofeedback protocols are still limited by open challenges, which restrict applications in the broader clinical practice. Some essential aspects to advance neurofeedback technologies include:

- *Convenience* is an important usability factor in determining the patient engagement and continuity of a therapeutic approach. The physical limitations of fMRI neurofeedback, or the relatively long time for cap preparation and residual gel on the scalp after EEG- and fNIRS-based protocols, showcase these approaches' inconvenient aspects. An emerging alternative for this issue is the use of dry and active electrodes. Available headbands using dry electrodes were recently used for emotion classification [4] and stress monitoring [44], and should be further explored to shorten the preparation of affective neurofeedback setups.
- *Attention and workload variations* can be caused by different environmental distractions, leading to involuntary neural patterns driven by the constant information processing in the human brain. Moreover, reactive eye movements and muscular responses may generate abrupt signal variations (electrooculography and electromyography noises). In this context, hybrid protocols have the potential for combining multimodal recordings to differentiate the targeted neural data from undesired noises [8]. For example, these approaches have been shown effective in monitoring mental workload and stress levels [1, 44], and could be used to improve the neurofeedback algorithms.
- *Neurofeedback illiteracy*, or inefficiency, are terms used to describe the phenomenon that affects 10–50% of neurofeedback users. These participants are unable to achieve adequate control of local neural activity. Illiteracy can be associated with biological factors, such as functional and neuroanatomical differences across users [2], or other personal aspects such as control belief, concentration, and frustration [24]. One possible solution is the identification of potential illiteracy predictors [2], so patients could be allocated to different therapeutic approaches. Another possible solution is the use of multimodal methods to compensate for functional or anatomical limitations from different imaging modalities [8]. Another possibility that has been considered is the combination of neurofeedback with brain stimulation techniques in the so-called brain-state-dependent-stimulation [38].
- *Nonspecific effects* can drive the results from neurofeedback training, depending on the experimental design. For example, clinical response may be associated with placebo effects, environmental enrichment, trainer–participant interactions, among other factors [49]. In this context, to ensure its therapeutic efficacy, new neurofeedback studies must present adequate designs, including appropriate control groups and validated experimental measures. For example, groups receiving sham feedback from brain regions other than the targeted ones should be included in future studies [52].

- *Replicability and reproducibility* are essential for the potential translation of neurofeedback training into realistic therapeutic approaches. However, many neurofeedback studies have a poor or unclear description of real-time signal preprocessing, feature extraction, and feedback algorithms [22]. In addition, the definition of control success is inconsistent across studies, hampering direct comparisons of efficacy. In this context, recent checklists for proper study design and reporting and now available [49] and should be followed by researchers in the field to allow cross-studies evaluations.

### 3.4.2 Future Directions

Recent technological advances in data acquisition, signal processing methods, and feedback modalities set the stage for new opportunities in neurofeedback research. For example, virtual reality (VR) has emerged as a promising feedback approach for affective neurofeedback protocols. For instance, the experiment from Lorenzetti et al. [35] presented an fMRI-based protocol in which the VR scenario changed colors according to recalled complex emotions, such as tenderness and anguish. In a different experiment, participants were trained to modulate bilateral fNIRS oxyhemoglobin concentrations to cheer up a virtual agent [3, 9]. These protocols suggest that participants are receptive to VR feedback during affective neurofeedback training, allowing for a transitional step to evaluate how the learned strategies can be transferred to realistic scenarios [58].

Another interesting concept that has been explored recently is the idea of closed-loop brain-state-dependent stimulation (CL-BSDS). The idea is that if the feedback provides direct stimulation to the targeted brain region, the brain-feedback-brain loop would be closed, and the neurophysiological effects of neurofeedback reinforced [38]. Proof-of-concept studies reported increased excitability in the motor cortex after combined motor imagery BCI and transcranial magnetic stimulation over the same region [19]. In fact, controlled experiments demonstrated that participants receiving CL-BSDS presented higher corticospinal excitability in comparison with the control group [31].

Hyperscanning is a relatively recent concept that can also be explored for neurofeedback. In this approach, the neural activity of multiple brains is recorded simultaneously and demonstrates how brain regions, or large-scale networks, act in synchrony during social interactions [6]. In previous studies with collaborative BCIs, pairs of participants improved their control over the BCI system when their neural recordings were combined in real-time [60, 67]. More recently, this concept was extended to neurofeedback protocols based on EEG [39] and fNIRS data [13] from pairs of participants. In psychiatry, collaborative neurofeedback could increase clinical outcomes, for example due to the communication and social interactions to discuss strategies or mutual incentives.

## 3.5 Conclusion

Neurofeedback is a noninvasive intervention, where the patient learns to voluntarily modulate putative neural circuits associated with cognitive and affective symptoms. Although being relatively new, this approach has shown positive results in preliminary and rigorous controlled experiments in clinical psychiatry. Open challenges still should be addressed before its inclusion in the clinical armamentarium, but recent technological advances provide promising perspectives to improve these protocols and advance neurofeedback science.

## References


1 Albuquerque, I., Tiwari, A., Parent, M. et al. (2020). WAUC: A multi-modal database for mental workload assessment under physical activity. *Frontiers in Neuroscience* 14: 549524.

2 Alkoby, O., Abu-Rmileh, A., Shriki, O., and Todder, D. (2018). Can we predict who will respond to neurofeedback? A review of the inefficacy problem and existing predictors for successful EEG neurofeedback learning. *Neuroscience* 378: 155–164.

3 Aranyi, G., Pecune, F., Charles, F. et al. (2016). Affective interaction with a virtual character through an fNIRS brain-computer interface. *Frontiers in Computational Neuroscience* 10: 70.

4 Arsalan, A., Majid, M., Butt, A.R., and Anwar, S.M. (2019). Classification of perceived mental stress using a commercially available EEG headband. *IEEE Journal of Biomedical and Health Informatics* 23 (6): 2257–2264.

5 Askovic, M., Watters, A.J., Aroche, J., and Harris, A.W.F. (2017). Neurofeedback as an adjunct therapy for treatment of chronic posttraumatic stress disorder related to refugee trauma and torture experiences: two case studies. *Australasian Psychiatry* 25 (4): 358–363.

6 Babiloni, F. and Astolfi, L. (2014). Social neuroscience and hyperscanning techniques: past, present and future. *Neuroscience & Biobehavioral Reviews* 44: 76–93.

7 Baehr, E., Rosenfeld, J.P., and Baehr, R. (1997). The clinical use of an alpha asymmetry protocol in the neurofeedback treatment of depression: two case studies. *Journal of Neurotherapy* 2 (3): 10–23.

8 Banville, H. and Falk, T.H. (2016). Recent advances and open challenges in hybrid brain-computer interfacing: a technological review of non-invasive human research. *Brain-Computer Interfaces* 3 (1): 9–46.

9 Charles, F., De Castro Martins, C., and Cavazza, M. (2020). Prefrontal asymmetry BCI neurofeedback datasets. *Frontiers in Neuroscience* 14: 601402.

10 Cheon, E.-J., Koo, B.-H., and Choi, J.-H. (2016). The efficacy of neurofeedback in patients with major depressive disorder: an open labeled prospective study. *Applied Psychophysiology and Biofeedback* 41 (1): 103–110.

11 Chiba, T., Kanazawa, T., Koizumi, A. et al. (2019). Current status of neurofeedback for post-traumatic stress disorder: a systematic review and the possibility of decoded neurofeedback. *Frontiers in Human Neuroscience* 13: 233.

12 Choi, S.W., Chi, S.E., Chung, S.Y. et al. (2011). Is alpha wave neurofeedback effective with randomized clinical trials in depression? A pilot study. *Neuropsychobiology* 63 (1): 43–51.

13 Duan, L., Liu, W.-J., Dai, R.-N. et al. (2013). Cross-brain neurofeedback: scientific concept and experimental platform. *PLoS One* 8 (5): e64590.

14 Earnest, C. (1999). Single case study of EEG asymmetry biofeedback for depression: an independent replication in an adolescent. *Journal of Neurotherapy* 3 (2): 28–35.

15 Escolano, C., Navarro-Gil, M., Garcia-Campayo, J. et al. (2014). A controlled study on the cognitive effect of alpha neurofeedback training in patients with major depressive disorder. *Frontiers in Behavioral Neuroscience* 8: 296.

16 Fruchtman-Steinbok, T., Keynan, J.N., Cohen, A. et al. (2021). Amygdala electrical-finger-print (AmygEFP) NeuroFeedback guided by individually-tailored Trauma script for post-traumatic stress disorder: proof-of-concept. *NeuroImage: Clinical* 32: 102859.

17 Gapen, M., van der Kolk, B.A., Hamlin, E. et al. (2016). A pilot study of neurofeedback for chronic PTSD. *Applied Psychophysiology and Biofeedback* 41 (3): 251–261.

18 Gerin, M.I., Fichtenholtz, H., Roy, A. et al. (2016). Real-time fMRI neurofeedback with war veterans with chronic PTSD: a feasibility study. *Frontiers in Psychiatry* 7: 111.

19 Gharabaghi, A., Kraus, D., Leao, M.T. et al. (2014). Coupling brain-machine interfaces with cortical stimulation for brain-state dependent stimulation: enhancing motor cortex excitability for neurorehabilitation. *Frontiers in Human Neuroscience* 8: 122.

20 Groenewold, N.A., Opmeer, E.M., de Jonge, P. et al. (2013). Emotional valence modulates brain functional abnormalities in depression: evidence from a meta-analysis of fMRI studies. *Neuroscience & Biobehavioral Reviews* 37 (2): 152–163.

21 Harmon-Jones, E., Gable, P.A., and Peterson, C.K. (2010). The role of asymmetric frontal cortical activity in emotion-related phenomena: a review and update. *Biological Psychology* 84 (3): 451–462.

22 Heunis, S., Lamerichs, R., Zinger, S. et al. (2020). Quality and denoising in real-time functional magnetic resonance imaging neurofeedback: a methods review. *Human Brain Mapping* 41 (12): 3439–3467.

23 Jaeckle, T., Williams, S.C.R., Barker, G.J. et al. (2019). Self-blaming emotions in major depression: a randomized pilot trial comparing fMRI neurofeedback training with self-guided psychological strategies (NeuroMooD). *medRxiv*, 19004309.

24 Kadosh, K.C. and Staunton, G. (2019). A systematic review of the psychological factors that influence neurofeedback learning outcomes. *NeuroImage* 185: 545–555.

25 Kaiser, R.H., Andrews-Hanna, J.R., Wager, T.D., and Pizzagalli, D.A. (2015). Large-scale network dysfunction in major depressive disorder: a meta-analysis of resting-state functional connectivity. *JAMA Psychiatry* 72 (6): 603–611.

26 Keynan, J.N., Cohen, A., Jackont, G. et al. (2019). Electrical fingerprint of the amygdala guides neurofeedback training for stress resilience. *Nature Human Behaviour* 3 (1): 63–73.

27 Kim, S. and Birbaumer, N. (2014). Real-time functional MRI neurofeedback: a tool for psychiatry. *Current Opinion in Psychiatry* 27 (5): 332–336.

28 Kluetsch, R.C., Ros, T., Théberge, J. et al. (2014). Plastic modulation of PTSD resting-state networks and subjective wellbeing by EEG neurofeedback. *Acta Psychiatrica Scandinavica* 130 (2): 123–136.

29 Kohl, S.H., Mehler, D., Lührs, M. et al. (2020). The potential of functional near-infrared spectroscopy-based neurofeedback-a systematic review and recommendations for best practice. *Frontiers in Neuroscience* 14: 594.

30 Koush, Y., Meskaldji, D.-E., Pichon, S. et al. (2017). Learning control over emotion networks through connectivity-based neurofeedback. *Cerebral Cortex* 27 (2): 1193–1202.

31 Kraus, D., Naros, G., Bauer, R. et al. (2016). Brain state-dependent transcranial magnetic closed-loop stimulation controlled by sensorimotor desynchronization induces robust increase of corticospinal excitability. *Brain Stimulation* 9 (3): 415–424.

32 Lee, Y.-J., Lee, G.-W., Seo, W.-S. et al. (2019). Neurofeedback treatment on depressive symptoms and functional recovery in treatment-resistant patients with major depressive disorder: an open-label pilot study. *Journal of Korean Medical Science* 34 (42): e287.

33 Linden, D.E.J., Habes, I., Johnston, S.J. et al. (2012). Real-time self-regulation of emotion networks in patients with depression. *PLoS One* 7 (6): e38115.

34 Linhartová, P., Látalová, A., Kóša, B. et al. (2019). fMRI neurofeedback in emotion regulation: a literature review. *NeuroImage* 193: 75–92.

35 Lorenzetti, V., Melo, B., Basílio, R. et al. (2018). Emotion regulation using virtual environments and real-time fMRI neurofeedback. *Frontiers in Neurology* 9: 390.

36 Mano, M., Lécuyer, A., Bannier, E. et al. (2017). How to build a hybrid neurofeedback platform combining EEG and fMRI. *Frontiers in Neuroscience* 11: 140.

**37** Mehler, D.M.A., Sokunbi, M.O., Habes, I. et al. (2018). Targeting the affective brain-a randomized controlled trial of real-time fMRI neurofeedback in patients with depression. *Neuropsychopharmacology* 43 (13): 2578–2585.

**38** Moreno, J.G., Biazoli, C.E. Jr., Baptista, A.F., and Trambaiolli, L.R. (2021). Closed-loop neurostimulation for affective symptoms and disorders: an overview. *Biological Psychology* 161: 108081.

**39** Müller, V., Perdikis, D., Mende, M.A., and Lindenberger, U. (2021). Interacting brains coming in sync through their minds: an interbrain neurofeedback study. *Annals of the New York Academy of Sciences* 1500 (1): 48–68.

**40** Nicholson, A.A., Ros, T., Frewen, P.A. et al. (2016). Alpha oscillation neurofeedback modulates amygdala complex connectivity and arousal in posttraumatic stress disorder. *NeuroImage: Clinical* 12: 506–516.

**41** Nicholson, A.A., Friston, K.J., Zeidman, P. et al. (2017). Dynamic causal modeling in PTSD and its dissociative subtype: bottom–up versus top–down processing within fear and emotion regulation circuitry. *Human Brain Mapping* 38 (11): 5551–5561.

**42** Nicholson, A.A., Rabellino, D., Densmore, M. et al. (2017). The neurobiology of emotion regulation in posttraumatic stress disorder: amygdala downregulation via real-time fMRI neurofeedback. *Human Brain Mapping* 38 (1): 541–560.

**43** Paquette, V., Beauregard, M., and Beaulieu-Prévost, D. (2009). Effect of a psychoneurotherapy on brain electromagnetic tomography in individuals with major depressive disorder. *Psychiatry Research: Neuroimaging* 174 (3): 231–239.

**44** Parent, M., Albuquerque, I., Tiwari, A. et al. (2020). Pass: a multimodal database of physical activity and stress for mobile passive body/brain-computer interface research. *Frontiers in Neuroscience* 14: 1274.

**45** Peeters, F., Oehlen, M., Ronner, J. et al. (2014). Neurofeedback as a treatment for major depressive disorder–a pilot study. *PLoS One* 9 (3): e91837.

**46** Peniston, E.G. and Kulkosky, P.J. (1991). Alpha-theta brainwave neurofeedback for Vietnam veterans with combat-related post-traumatic stress disorder. *Medical Psychotherapy* 4 (1): 47–60.

**47** Peniston, E.G., Marrinan, D.A., Deming, W.A., and Kulkosky, P.J. (1993). EEG alpha-theta brainwave synchronization in Vietnam theater veterans with combat-related post-traumatic stress disorder and alcohol abuse. *Advances in Medical Psychotherapy* 6 (7): 37–50.

**48** Ros, T., Frewen, P., Theberge, J. et al. (2017). Neurofeedback tunes scale-free dynamics in spontaneous brain activity. *Cerebral Cortex* 27 (10): 4911–4922.

**49** Ros, T., Enriquez-Geppert, S., Zotev, V. et al. (2020). Consensus on the reporting and experimental design of clinical and cognitive-behavioural neurofeedback studies (CRED-nf checklist). *Brain* 143 (6): 1674–1685.

**50** Rosenfeld, J.P., Baehr, E., Baehr, R. et al. (1996). Preliminary evidence that daily changes in frontal alpha asymmetry correlate with changes in affect in therapy sessions. *International Journal of Psychophysiology* 23 (1–2): 137–141.

**51** Sitaram, R., Ros, T., Stoeckel, L. et al. (2017). Closed-loop brain training: the science of neurofeedback. *Nature Reviews Neuroscience* 18 (2): 86–100.

**52** Sorger, B., Scharnowski, F., Linden, D.E.J. et al. (2019). Control freaks: towards optimal selection of control conditions for fMRI neurofeedback studies. *Neuroimage* 186: 256–265.

**53** Takamura, M., Okamoto, Y., Shibasaki, C. et al. (2020). Antidepressive effect of left dorsolateral prefrontal cortex neurofeedback in patients with major depressive disorder: a preliminary report. *Journal of Affective Disorders* 271: 224–227.

**54** Thibault, R.T., MacPherson, A., Lifshitz, M. et al. (2018). Neurofeedback with fMRI: a critical systematic review. *Neuroimage* 172: 786–807.

**55** Thibodeau, R., Jorgensen, R.S., and Kim, S. (2006). Depression, anxiety, and resting frontal eeg asymmetry: a meta-analytic review. *Journal of Abnormal Psychology* 115 (4): 715.

**56** Trambaiolli, L.R., Biazoli, C.E., Cravo, A.M. et al. (2018). Functional near-infrared spectroscopy-based affective neurofeedback: feedback effect, illiteracy phenomena, and whole-connectivity profiles. *Neurophotonics* 5 (3): 035009.

**57** Trambaiolli, L.R., Kohl, S.H., Linden, D.E.J., and Mehler, D.M.A. (2021). Neurofeedback training in major depressive disorder: a systematic review of clinical efficacy, study quality and reporting practices. *Neuroscience & Biobehavioral Reviews* 125: 33–56.

**58** Trambaiolli, L.R., Tiwari, A., and Falk, T.H. (2021). Affective neurofeedback under naturalistic conditions: a mini-review of current achievements and open challenges. *Frontiers in Neuroergonomics* 2: 15.

**59** van der Kolk, B.A., Hodgdon, H., Gapen, M. et al. (2016). A randomized controlled study of neurofeedback for chronic PTSD. *PLoS One* 11 (12): e0166752.

**60** Wang, Y. and Jung, T.-P. (2011). A collaborative brain-computer interface for improving human performance. *PLoS One* 6 (5): e20422.

**61** Wang, S.-Y., Lin, I.-M., Peper, E. et al. (2016). The efficacy of neurofeedback among patients with major depressive disorder: preliminary study. *NeuroRegulation* 3 (3): 127.

**62** Wang, S.-Y., Lin, I.-M., Fan, S.-Y. et al. (2019). The effects of alpha asymmetry and high-beta down-training neurofeedback for patients with the major depressive disorder and anxiety symptoms. *Journal of Affective Disorders* 257: 287–296.

**63** Young, K.D., Zotev, V., Phillips, R. et al. (2014). Real-time fMRI neurofeedback training of amygdala activity in patients with major depressive disorder. *PLoS One* 9 (2): e88785.

**64** Young, K.D., Siegle, G.J., Zotev, V. et al. (2017). Randomized clinical trial of real-time fMRI amygdala neurofeedback for major depressive disorder: effects on symptoms and autobiographical memory recall. *American Journal of Psychiatry* 174 (8): 748–755.

**65** Young, K.D., Siegle, G.J., Misaki, M. et al. (2018). Altered task-based and resting-state amygdala functional connectivity following real-time fMRI amygdala neurofeedback training in major depressive disorder. *NeuroImage: Clinical* 17: 691–703.

**66** Yu, L., Long, Q., Tang, Y. et al. (2021). Improving emotion regulation through real-time neurofeedback training on the right dorsolateral prefrontal cortex: evidence from behavioral and brain network analyses. *Frontiers in Human Neuroscience* 15: 135.

**67** Yuan, P., Wang, Y., Gao, X. et al. (2013). A collaborative brain-computer interface for accelerating human decision making. *International Conference on Universal Access in Human-Computer Interaction*, 672–681. Springer.

**68** Yuan, H., Young, K.D., Phillips, R. et al. (2014). Resting-state functional connectivity modulation and sustained changes after real-time functional magnetic resonance imaging neurofeedback training in depression. *Brain Connectivity* 4 (9): 690–701.

**69** Zotev, V., Krueger, F., Phillips, R. et al. (2011). Self-regulation of amygdala activation using real-time fMRI neurofeedback. *PLoS One* 6 (9): e24522.

**70** Zotev, V., Phillips, R., Young, K.D. et al. (2013). Prefrontal control of the amygdala during real-time fMRI neurofeedback training of emotion regulation. *PLoS One* 8 (11): e79184.

**71** Zotev, V., Yuan, H., Misaki, M. et al. (2016). Correlation between amygdala bold activity and frontal EEG asymmetry during real-time fMRI neurofeedback training in patients with depression. *NeuroImage: Clinical* 11: 224–238.

**72** Zotev, V., Phillips, R., Misaki, M. et al. (2018). Real-time fMRI neurofeedback training of the amygdala activity with simultaneous EEG in veterans with combat-related ptsd. *NeuroImage: Clinical* 19: 106–121.

**73** Zotev, V., Mayeli, A., Misaki, M., and Bodurka, J. (2020). Emotion self-regulation training in major depressive disorder using simultaneous real-time fMRI and EEG neurofeedback. *NeuroImage: Clinical* 27: 102331.

# 4

# Pediatric Brain–Computer Interfaces: An Unmet Need

*Eli Kinney-Lang[1,2*], Erica D. Floreani[1,2*], Niloufaralsadat Hashemi[3], Dion Kelly[1,2], Stefanie S. Bradley[3], Christine Horner[3], Brian Irvine[1,2], Zeanna Jadavji[1], Danette Rowley[1,2], Ilyas Sadybekov[1,2], Si Long Jenny Tou[3], Ephrem Zewdie[1], Tom Chau[3], and Adam Kirton[1,2]*

[1] *BCI4Kids, University of Calgary, Calgary, Canada*
[2] *Department of Pediatrics, Alberta Children's Hospital, Calgary, Canada*
[3] *Bloorview Research Institute, Holland Bloorview Kids Rehabilitation Hospital, Toronto, Canada*

## 4.1 Introduction

*"I think it's given her, I don't want to say a sense of purpose, but I really do feel this [sense of] accomplishment of 'Hey, look what I can do'. [She] deserves to feel proud." – Parent in the BCI4Kids program, Calgary, AB., Canada (2019).*

Connection is the prevailing theme of the twenty-first century. From widespread availability of personal mobile phones to the advent of social media, connection has become a critical part of daily life. For many living with severe disabilities, the *ability to connect* in the ever-expanding network of available technology is limited, or even impossible. Despite monumental advancements making technology available across the socioeconomic spectrum, the *fundamental right to interact with the world* is still limited for thousands of individuals with severe disabilities due, in part, to limitations in accessibility design and user considerations. Children with severe physical disabilities are systematically being left behind and such neglect risks diverse aspects of child's physical and mental health, development, learning, social connectivity, and quality of life with life-long consequences. Brain–computer interfaces (BCIs) offer a promising new solution, but require additional development to be realized for children. This chapter explores how evolving BCI technology can be leveraged to best impact the lives of children with severe physical disabilities. Our hope is readers will gain the following:

- Understanding of the motivations driving pediatric BCI research, including who can benefit and how BCI can impact these individuals.
- Ability to identify key differences and considerations when designing, developing, and implementing BCI systems for children compared to adults.
- Awareness of present limitations and challenges facing pediatric BCI and open calls-to-action to tackle these barriers.

* Authors contributed equally to this work.

*Handbook of Human-Machine Systems*, First Edition. Edited by Giancarlo Fortino, David Kaber, Andreas Nürnberger, and David Mendonça.

### 4.1.1 Motivation

Early-life brain injuries and disorders can cause life-long neurological disability, such as quadriplegic cerebral palsy (CP), which affects at least 17 million persons globally [40]. Many such children are cognitively capable, but trapped in bodies that cannot move, deprived of their right to connect with the world. BCIs may be able to bridge this disconnect between a young mind full of hope, ambition, and potential and the world around them. BCIs equip the brain with the ability to manipulate external devices using thoughts alone, without requiring neuromuscular control.

The extent to which BCI technologies can currently enhance the quality of life of millions of children worldwide living with life-long disabilities has been demonstrated in adult populations, gaining popularity in media [14], industry, and academics [16]. Translating advancements in BCI research to the youngest and most vulnerable of those living with severe physical disability is a crucial next step. Despite significant potential, pediatric populations have been largely neglected in BCI research – studies exploring pediatric BCI still represent less than 2% [29] of all BCI publications. The time to focus on pediatric BCI is now, as addressing this gap offers pronounced returns for affected children and families as well as for the BCI field as a whole. Extending BCI access to children will also motivate solutions for human-factor barriers present in traditional adult BCI.

The remainder of this chapter aims to provide the necessary background, context, and technical frameworks needed to identify key considerations regarding pediatric BCI, describes major areas of limitations and challenges to the field, and presents trends and applications informed by end-users of pediatric BCI directly.

## 4.2 Background

### 4.2.1 Components of a BCI

Brain–computer interfaces (BCIs) decode intentions from the brain to control external devices in real-time. BCIs rely on three core steps to build a BCI paradigm: *signal acquisition*, *signal processing*, and interfacing to an output device for *feedback* [21] (Figure 4.1).

#### 4.2.1.1 Signal Acquisition

Existing pediatric BCI research has mostly utilized noninvasive recording technologies, like electroencephalography (EEG) for electrophysiological measurements, with emerging research looking into functional near-infrared spectroscopy (fNIRS) for hemodynamic measurements (see 4.4.3 for more details).

#### 4.2.1.2 Signal Processing

This stage aims to first remove unwanted artifacts and noise corrupting the signals of interest and to subsequently identify relevant features encoding the user's intent [21]. Through a series of operations, a statistical model is built to estimate and classify user intent into actions used to generate feedback in the BCI.

#### 4.2.1.3 Feedback

To close the BCI loop, feedback is provided to the user following classification of the signal. Feedback can be presented visually, audibly, or by other means, but it should be provided with meaningful timing and outputs to maintain engagement by the user.

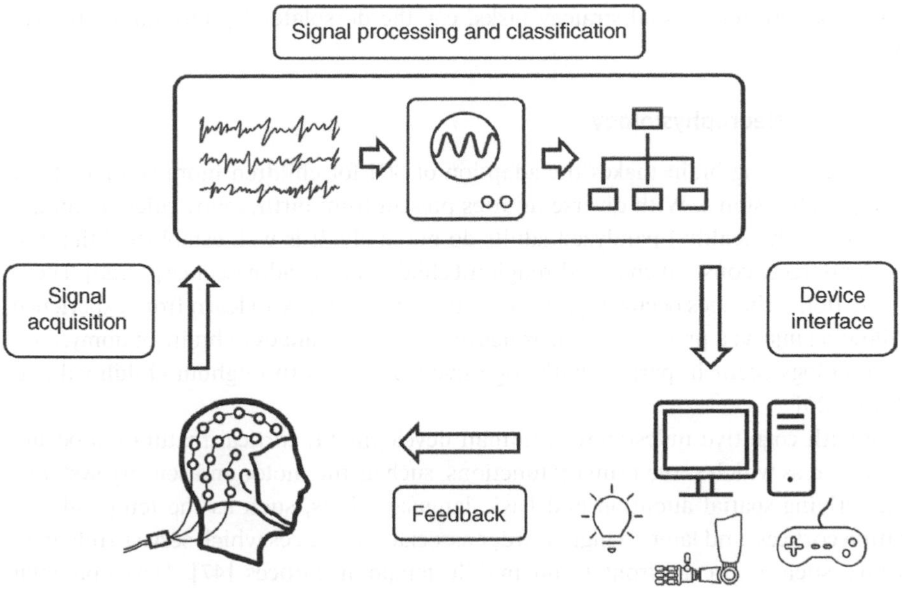


**Figure 4.1** Illustrated example of typical components in a BCI system. Each of these components are potential targets for alteration in adapting BCIs to pediatric populations.

#### 4.2.1.4 Paradigms

Combining the above steps creates the framework for a BCI paradigm – the complete structure in which a BCI operates. Commonly, BCI paradigms can be categorized into one of three groups based on user interaction with the BCI: passive, reactive, and active BCI. Passive BCIs operate and detect brain activity not voluntarily modulated by end-users; reactive (synchronous) BCIs measure brain activity responses to external sensory stimuli; and active (asynchronous) BCIs are initiated by the user's volition, e.g. using motor or visual imagery [21]. For a more in-depth review on BCI paradigms, please see Chapter 1.

### 4.2.2 Brain Anatomy and Physiology

Understanding of brain anatomy and function is essential for advancing pediatric BCI applications. The outermost layer of the brain, the cerebral cortex, is often divided into four main external lobes: frontal, parietal, occipital, and temporal lobes. Functional areas that are relevant for BCI control include the motor cortex (frontal lobe) and somatosensory cortex (parietal lobe) for planning, initiation, and execution of voluntary actions in asynchronous BCI control; visual cortex (occipital lobe) and auditory cortex (temporal lobe) for activation by external stimuli in synchronous BCI control [38]; among other cognitive regions, e.g. the dorolateral prefrontal cortex for BCI control through mental arithmetic [21, 42].

The motor and somatosensory cortices are involved in conveying one's intent through planning, initiation, and execution of voluntary actions, including reaching and speaking [42]. When an individual imagines performing movement without execution, referred to as motor imagery, specific brain signals are created over the sensorimotor cortex corresponding to the somatotopic location of the imagined body part which can then be decoded to control a BCI [38]. The somatosensory, visual, and auditory cortices can be activated by external stimuli to produce a specific, decodable, neural signals for BCI control [38]. Other cognitive regions can also be selectively activated for BCI control by performing mental strategy tasks, e.g. the dorsolateral prefrontal cortex via mental arithmetic [21].

### 4.2.3 Developmental Neurophysiology

The nature of the developing brain makes the adaption of BCI for children more complex than simply replicating adult systems. With diverse injuries present from birth, many rules stemming from brains of (previously healthy) paralyzed adults do not apply. It is well established that the developing brain undergoes constant change throughout childhood and adolescence [17, 20]. These structural and functional changes occur in part due to the brain's ability to learn from experience and to adapt following injury: a process known as neuroplasticity. Changes in brain anatomy, connectivity, and physiology occur in parallel with cognitive maturation throughout childhood and adolescence [17, 19, 20].

Corresponding with cognitive milestones in human development, cortical maturation occurs first in lower-order areas which serve primary functions, such as the motor and sensory systems; then regions underlying spatial attention and basic language skills, such as the temporal and parietal association cortices; and later, in higher-order association cortices which serve to integrate primary functions, such as the prefrontal and middle temporal cortices [47]. Developmental changes to subcortical regions, including those in which the association cortices project, occur simultaneously.

In the immature brain, subcortical areas which play a key role in motor function are enriched with excitatory neurons (e.g. thalamus and basal ganglia), making them more vulnerable to developmental injury [20]. Similarly, the prolonged plasticity demonstrated by late-maturing higher-order association cortices mediating higher cognitive abilities such as decision-making, language, and attention, may enhance their vulnerability to the effects of developmental injuries [47]. A common example of such a developmental injury is perinatal hypoxic-ischemic brain injury resulting in quadriplegic cerebral palsy. Selective injury to deep gray matter structures that modulate motor control while sparing the cortical neurons that dictate higher cognitive functions may manifest as a child who is essentially "locked-in," having no functional movement to interact despite retaining cognitive and intellectual function [4]. Such an individual stands to benefit enormously from BCI.

Enhanced plasticity of the developing brain also means children may have the ability to recover from early brain injuries. This is achieved through adaptive plasticity, where brain circuits reorganize to compensate for lost functionality due to damage. Recovery can be facilitated by tailored interventions; however, they must be introduced during the period of maximal plasticity for optimal developmental outcomes [20]. This, coupled with the potential for lifelong impact mandates the introduction of BCIs early in childhood to promote optimal outcomes for children with neurological injury.

### 4.2.4 Clinical Translation of BCI

BCIs are often developed with the intent to supplement or replace function for individuals living with physical disabilities. The primary role of BCIs for these individuals would be as an *alternative access technology* within the larger umbrella of *assistive technology*.

#### 4.2.4.1 Assistive Technology (AT)

AT refers to any device, equipment, or system used to increase, maintain, or improve functional capabilities of individuals living with disability [1]. Both the technology and the coupled services that support AT selection, procurement, and maintenance help ensure that AT can be successful

**Table 4.1** Summary table of background literature (Top Panel) & Current body of knowledge (Bottom Panel) for pediatric BCI.

| Author | References | Title |
|---|---|---|
| Bausch et al. 2005 | [1] | The Assistive Technology Act of 2004: What Does it Say and What Does It Mean? |
| Bruno et al. 2009 | [4] | Locked-in syndrome in children: report of five cases and review of the literature |
| Cook et al. 2020 | [11] | Delivering Assistive Technology Services to the Client |
| Federici and Scherer 2012 | [12] | Assistive Technology Assessment Handbook |
| Ismail et al. 2017 | [17] | Cerebral plasticity: Windows of opportunity in the developing brain |
| Jochumsen et al. 2018 | [19] | Movement intention detection in adolescents with cerebral palsy from single-trial EEG |
| Johnston 2004 | [20] | Clinical disorders of brain plasticity |
| Kawala-Sterniuk et al. 2021 | [21] | Summary of over Fifty Years with Brain-Computer Interfaces – A Review |
| Müller-Putz 2020 | [38] | Chapter 18 – Electroencephalography in *Handbook of Clinical Neurology* |
| Ramsey 2020 | [42] | Chapter 1 – Human brain function and brain-computer interfaces in *Handbook of Clinical Neurology* |
| Sydnor et al. 2021 | [47] | Neurodevelopment of the association cortices: Patterns, mechanisms, and implications for psychopathology |
| Kinney-Lang et al. 2016 | [23] | [E]xploring current literature trends for translating EEG based BCI for motor rehabilitation in children |
| Mikołajewska and Mikołajewski 2014 | [36] | The prospects of brain-computer interface applications in children |
| Orlandi et al. 2021 | [39] | BCI for Children with Complex Communication Needs and Limited Mobility: A Systematic Review |

and enable users to engage in personal, social, and economic occupations of their community [11]. Children with complex physical impairments are often not able to use available AT requiring touch or mechanical input, with other alternative access options (e.g. head-tracking or eye-gaze cameras) potentially not viable solutions for the most severely disabled individuals [11].

#### 4.2.4.2 Clinical Assessment

Various clinical measures (sensory, physical, etc.), functional assessments (language, cognitive skills), and psychosocioenvironmental evaluations (positioning, availability of AT devices and services, experience with technology) can support BCI provision, and improve performance and promote long-term adoption of the technology [12]. Tools specific to optimize the selection of pediatric users for BCI do not exist but are currently in development (Table 4.1).

## 4.3 Current Body of Knowledge

Despite the limited research of pediatric BCI compared to its adult counterpart, the last 10 years has seen increased attention and activity in the field. We recommend readers to direct their attention to a handful of scoping reviews that have characterized the state-of-the-art in pediatric BCI [23, 36, 39].

Mikołajewska and Mikołajewski [36] is the earliest review published on the prospects of pediatric BCI. They describe motivation and justification for BCI as a potential therapeutic approach for pediatric neurorehabilitation. Potential challenges and considerations were considered from reviewing four available publications investigating BCI in children using various BCI paradigms. Kinney-Lang et al. [23] conducted a systematic review to examine if BCI applications for motor rehabilitation held the potential for translation to pediatric populations. While BCI research for motor rehabilitation in children was essentially nonexistent, positive trends in comparable adult populations supported the exploration of BCI for children. A recent systematic review by Orlandi et al. [39] presents a comprehensive view of BCI publications for children with complex communication needs and limited mobility that report on BCI performance. They identified 12 publications matching their inclusion criteria, in which four involved invasive BCIs, five involved noninvasive reactive BCIs, and three explored noninvasive active BCIs.

All three reviews highlight that although pediatric BCI research is still under-represented, the existing work holds promise for large impact. This finding is supported by new collaborative efforts to realize pediatric BCI advancement through the BCI-CAN network [26] and a survey of physicians showing overall poor awareness of BCI but anticipated potential for its life-changing impact [29].

## 4.4 Considerations for Pediatric BCI

Pediatric BCI systems can be viewed as specialized cases of the principles and rules governing adult BCIs. However, operating tasks and methods used in adult BCIs may not translate to pediatric BCIs. For example, children may lack the neurophysiological biomarkers fundamental to some adult BCI systems, where such biomarkers may be absent or display different properties making them ineffective for BCI until the child matures (e.g. readiness potential; [8]). Similarly, children living with disabilities may not have acquired the necessary skills required to operate BCI tasks meant for adults, e.g. previous ability to physically hand-write letters [48]. Thus, from the genesis of brain activity patterns to how users are instructed to produce outputs, each step of a pediatric BCI system poses unique considerations for design, development, and implementation distinct from adults. To support and inspire the next generation of pediatric BCI developers, this chapter provides short, descriptive use cases exploring opportunities, challenges, and other considerations for child-focused BCI.

### 4.4.1 Developmental Impact on EEG-based BCI

EEG-based BCI relies on stable, predictable synchronized electric activity of the brain in EEG rhythms, often identified as the 'classical' frequency bands of: delta (0.5–3 Hz), theta (3.5–7 Hz), alpha (7.5–12 Hz), lower and upper beta (13–30 Hz), and gamma bands (> 30 Hz) [45]. However, developmental changes have profound effects on the frequency, predominance, and relative location of the precursor bands which mature into these classic EEG bands in adults [45], rendering some features from these bands impractical for pediatric BCI [24].

The developmental progression of resting-state early-life EEG correlates have been well characterized [35] and should be leveraged when designing pediatric BCI systems. For example, the posterior dominant rhythm (PDR) which is the precursor to classic alpha is known to transition from lower frequencies early in childhood (8 Hz at 5–8 years of age) before settling into expected ranges in adolescence [45]. Similarly, the posterior slow wave of youth promotes predominance delta and theta bands which can contribute to potential difficulty in identifying and extracting features for BCI [23, 24] before decreasing during adolescence [45]. Resting-state EEG settles toward expected adult classic bands throughout adolescence but does not "stabilize" until young adulthood [35, 45].

Task-driven EEG also varies throughout development and can affect many BCI paradigms. Significant age-related changes in magnitude and phase for visual-evoked potentials (VEPs) have been reported for adults compared to children (3–16 years) [3]. Visual acuity and flash VEP latency also show age-dependent factors that could have potential influence when designing BCIs for younger children [28]. The complex effects of these developmental differences in the EEG of typically developing children are likely to be amplified in children with early-life injury or impairment.

### 4.4.2 Hardware for Pediatric BCI

Many options exist for BCI acquisition hardware from high-cost, research-grade devices to low-cost, consumer-grade devices with a growing number of emerging systems targeting the latter [49]. Key factors to evaluate BCI hardware include cost, signal quality, artifact resistance, comfort and tolerance, ease of setup, number and locations of available sensors, flexibility to alter sensor locations, adaptable size and fit, and aesthetics [49]. For pediatric users, some of these factors are likely more salient than others. Children typically have a lower tolerance for uncomfortable sensors, tight-fitting headsets, and overall headset weight. Headsets must have dedicated pediatric sizes or adjustable mechanisms to ensure headsets stay firmly in place on the scalp and resist motion artifacts, particularly for children who may experience involuntary movements (e.g. dyskinetic cerebral palsy).

For children with disabilities, BCI hardware selection will be highly dependent on individual user needs and must accommodate their personal medical aids/supports (e.g. wheelchair supports, cochlear implants, feeding tubes, ventilators). A critical unmet design is BCI hardware that accommodates specialized seating supports, such as headrests with pads around the head/neck which can interfere with posterior BCI sensors. Many children with disabilities have limited head control and need their headrest to help them maintain an upright and centered position to view BCI stimulus, feedback, and meaningfully use an application over potentially prolonged periods. Headset aesthetics may also be important and support the child's desires to "fit in" with peers or minimize attention to disability. Future efforts should be made to ensure that BCI hardware fits such criteria and is usable in a variety of environments.

### 4.4.3 Signal Processing for Pediatric BCI

Relevant signal processing approaches for pediatric BCI are outlined with attention and consideration for where state-of the-art innovations could benefit.

***Preprocessing:*** Preprocessing typically involves both filtering and artifact rejection steps to boost SNR and eliminate spurious or destructive artifacts. There is currently no evidence in the literature that indicates significant differences in EEG filters used for children compared to adults [23, 39]. Since frequency bands vary as a function of age, filter banks or multiple passband selection should be adjusted accordingly to reflect the relevant neurodevelopmental changes. Poorly conceived passband selections (e.g. relying only on classical bands) may exclude or partially occlude features of interest. To more readily capture developmental differences researchers should consider adapting filters based on the individual alpha frequency [15] or employing overlapping narrow-bands (i.e. multiple bands < 4 Hz with over 25% overlap).

Artifacts (eye-blinks, muscle movement, etc.) contaminating signals must be removed. Similar approaches to adult BCI have been described for children [39], but advancements are needed to validate the effectiveness of these approaches for pediatric BCI, particularly for removing development-specific artifacts [23, 24]. Automated artifact component selection processes hold promise, but rely heavily on the generalizability of training data which may not hold true for children of different ages and disabilities.

#### 4.4.3.1 Feature Extraction, Selection and Classification

Due to developmental topological changes and potential atypical organization in neurodivergent children, optimal electrode locations identified for adults through various selection methods (filtering, wrapping, embedding, and hybrid) may not translate to children using BCI. Data-driven methods must acknowledge potential confounding features that will differ across age, development, and underlying brain abnormalities. For instance, cortical damage due to perinatal stroke can have profound impact on the underlying reorganization of the child's motor plan and network [7], thereby subsequently affecting areas of interest. This area needs substantial additional research to help shed light on how robust spatial optimization approaches are for children throughout and across development.

Classifiers reported in pediatric BCI literature have largely been similar to adult BCI [39], but shortened attention spans of children may limit both the quantity and quality of calibration data collected impacting classifiers reliant on large high-quality training sets, e.g. convolutional neural networks [32]. Classifiers that use smaller amounts of training data are thus potentially more attractive for BCI, e.g. shrinkage LDA (sLDA) or Riemannian geometry-based classifiers [32]. Developmental effects on the nonlinearity and nonstationarity of the signals may also influence classifier selection for pediatric BCI paradigms and require further research.

#### 4.4.3.2 Emerging Techniques

A number of emerging feature extraction, selection, and classification techniques to augment BCI performance that have been gaining traction in adult BCI literature [32] hold significant potential for pediatric use. Multiway tensor analysis, for example, exploits the high-dimensional nature of EEG to uncover latent factors underlying EEG [9]. Tensor approaches have potential for isolating and separating hidden factors related to noise and development in children [24] and may be leveraged for calibration-free pediatric BCI systems [25]. Similarly, Riemannian geometry techniques look to retain the inherent structural relationships of the EEG data through representing and processing the EEG data within the Riemannian geometric space (e.g. Riemannian manifold), rather than typical Euclidean space [10, 32]. This approach is of particular relevance to pediatric BCI as it retains the latent functional connections of the EEG supporting a potential framework robust to the potential amplifications of nonlinear properties in the developing and injured brain. Another emerging area relevant for pediatric BCI is transfer learning, where persistent sets of features are able to be co-opted to support improved feature identification, extraction, and classification between users or sessions [13, 18], e.g. between motor imagery tasks [18]. As inter-session and inter-subject variability is accentuated in children, efforts to adapt transfer learning protocols to longitudinal and cross-sectional data from children could be highly informative in deciphering common and persistent latent properties present throughout development.

Hemodynamic-based fNIRS BCIs hold potential for pediatric BCI, as fNIRS is relatively more tolerant to motion artifacts, easier to set up and more comfortable than EEG systems. Common tasks employed in fNIRS-BCI are similar to EEG-BCI, including cognitive tasks [37] and motor imagery. While the specific brain regions and networks driving these tasks have been elucidated in typically developing children [33, 37], they have not been observed in children with CP, thus requiring further research. Similar to EEG-BCIs, more work is needed to validate preprocessing, feature extraction, and classification techniques for fNIRS-BCIs for children.

### 4.4.4 Designing Experiments for Pediatric BCI

Careful design of the experimental protocol is an essential part of collecting high-quality training data for BCI use. BCI training protocols are often repetitive and uninteresting reducing the quality (and quantity) of training data in children who are more prone to fatigue, boredom, and distraction. Feedback should be meaningful and informative in telling the child what and how they can achieve a successful performance [31]. Gamification is one approach to be considered to support engagement [22]. In addition, pediatric BCI experimental sessions should be short (< 90 minutes) with frequent breaks, age-appropriate verbal instructions, and minimal equipment set-up time where possible. For children with disabilities, timing of medication, feeding, school, and other medical appointments can affect their motivation, alertness, and fatigue thereby affecting the BCI session. Where reasonable, early research designs should be co-developed and informed by the children, families and other key stakeholders to increase the relevance and translation of the research design.

BCI studies typically include small sample sizes, and the same has held true for pediatric BCI [39]. Efforts should be made to increase recruitment through community and science outreach, including BCI demonstrations at school events, such as science fairs and career days to achieve appropriate sample sizes and properly assess population-level effects. Stratification of participants into age groups may also help assess developmental differences [39]. BCI data is also limited; a fact further exacerbated in pediatrics. The principles of open science and open sharing of de-identified pediatric BCI data, including both neurophysiological activity and the surrounding experimental meta-data, are critical to amplify efforts of researchers driving pediatric BCI development.

### 4.4.5 Meaningful Applications for Pediatric BCI

BCI applications should strive to meet end-users' needs and wants [44]. Recent surveys of families and children with disabilities in the BCI4Kids program reveal that top priorities for BCI applications are those that support communication, independent movement, environmental control, play and interaction with peers, and participation in school activities. In each of these, BCI applications should aim to integrate into the educational and play activities typically developing peers that would participate in [46]. For example social media and online gaming are significant vectors for many children to interact with their peers, so BCI applications should aim to enable children with disabilities to access these same platforms natively. It is important to incorporate principles of user experience and user interaction (UX/UI) design in such digital applications for children (see [34] for a comprehensive review).

The broader field of AAC technology can help inform on the design pediatric BCI applications, prioritizing developmentally relevant and age-appropriate activities that adapt dynamically as the child matures and gains new skills, needs, and wants [30]. For example, rather than presenting all 26 characters of the [English] alphabet in a communication application (typical in adult BCIs [43]), the interface could utilize a limited number of on-screen symbols relevant to young children minimizing the cognitive demand [30]. The number and types of targets can be progressively incremented as the child develops, alongside increasingly complex language representations.

### 4.4.6 Clinical Translation of Pediatric BCI

BCI suffers from a translation gap between research conducted on healthy participants in laboratory settings and research involving adult and child end-users with disability in natural environments [27]. Complicating factors include lack of access to technology, amplified noise or distraction in natural environments, confidence in independent set-up and operation of BCI, and lack of meaningful BCI applications. If these issues are not addressed, BCIs will not meet performance expectations and may lead to device abandonment – a significant problem for many assistive technologies [41].

To enhance prospects of pediatric BCI use in daily life, researchers must carefully consider the needs and wants of child end-users. We recommended the adoption of a user-centered design (UCD) framework [27]. The UCD framework emphasizes the importance of understanding the user and context of use, engaging users early and often in the design process, and frequent user evaluation and iteration of design solutions. This framework is essential to address the ever-changing and diverse neurophysiology, cognitive abilities, and motivational needs of pediatric BCI end-users. For these children, BCI could be a lifelong assistive technology and as such must be able to adapt with them over time.

How children can learn to use BCI remains virtually unexplored. Learning to use new access methods is a complex juggle between physical, cognitive, sensory, and language demands. Allowing children to explore and learn the technology through play is crucial to facilitating success [2], as is flexibility in adapting to unique needs of each child and family. Proposed frameworks for other access methods could be adapted for BCI use, in which initial simple tasks (e.g. cause and effect) grow in complexity and progress until eventually achieving multi-functional control [5]. Goal-oriented opportunities can also facilitate this skill development and learning, with substantial opportunity for repetitive practice with intention and variation [6].

## 4.5 Conclusions

The road forward for pediatric BCI is wide open with significant opportunities to pioneer the next gold standards of BCI design. This chapter explored current approaches, considerations, and recommendations relevant for translating BCI systems for children with severe physical disability. The limited availability of pediatric BCI research, however, underscores a need to better understand and tackle the future research challenges facing its full realization. The authors stress the importance of including end-users and their families in the process of BCI design, development, and research. Children and families are experts in their own lives and will be crucial in the translation of BCI out of the lab into a life-changing access technology. We leave the reader with the following calls to action for pediatric BCI research:

- Design comfortable, simple-to-use, adaptable, BCI hardware that is compatible with medical equipment and personal supports.
- Adapt and design novel signal processing techniques appropriate for utilizing pediatric EEG (and fNIRS) for BCI control.
- Optimize protocols and develop meaningful applications to improve the quality of data collected for pediatric BCI training.

- Identify the features and functions important to real-world pediatric BCI users and their families.
- Implement BCI into existing clinical pathways for AT procurement and provision and identify optimal ways to teach, support BCI use in everyday life.

We hope this work inspires investment and engagement in the development of pediatric BCI and will help lead the realization of BCI into a technology that is accessible for everyone.

## References


1 Bausch, M.E., Mittler, J.E., Hasselbring, T.S., and Cross, D.P. (2005). The assistive technology act of 2004: what does it say and what does it mean? *Physical Disabilities: Education and Related Services* 23 (2): 59–67. Publisher: Division for Physical and Health Disabilities, Council for Exceptional Children.

2 Beauchamp, F., Bourke-Taylor, H., and Brown, T. (2018). Therapists' perspectives: supporting children to use switches and technology for accessing their environment, leisure, and communication. *Journal of Occupational Therapy, Schools, & Early Intervention* 11 (2): 133–147. https://doi.org/10.1080/19411243.2018.1432443.

3 Birca, A., Carmant, L., Lortie, A. et al. (2010). Maturational changes of 5Hz SSVEPs elicited by intermittent photic stimulation. *International Journal of Psychophysiology* 78 (3): 295–298. https://doi.org/10.1016/j.ijpsycho.2010.09.003.

4 Bruno, M.-A., Schnakers, C., Damas, F. et al. (2009). Locked-in syndrome in children: report of five cases and review of the literature. *Pediatric Neurology* 41 (4): 237–246. https://doi.org/10.1016/j.pediatrneurol.2009.05.001.

5 Burkhart, L. (2018). Stepping Stones to Switch Access. https://pubs.asha.org/doi/pdf/10.1044/persp3.SIG12.33.

6 Campbell, P.H., Milbourne, S., Dugan, L.M., and Wilcox, M.J. (2006). A review of evidence on practices for teaching young children to use assistive technology devices. *Topics in Early Childhood Special Education* 26 (1): 3–13. https://doi.org/10.1177/02711214060260010101.

7 Carlson, H.L., Craig, B.T., Hilderley, A.J. et al. (2020). Structural and functional connectivity of motor circuits after perinatal stroke: a machine learning study. *NeuroImage: Clinical* 28: 102508. https://doi.org/10.1016/j.nicl.2020.102508.

8 Chiarenza, G.A., Villa, M., and Vasile, G. (1995). Developmental aspects of bereitschaftspotential in children during goal-directed behaviour. *International Journal of Psychophysiology* 19 (2): 149–176. https://doi.org/10.1016/0167-8760(95)00002-A.

9 Cong, F., Lin, Q.-H., Kuang, L.-D. et al. (2015). Tensor decomposition of EEG signals: a brief review. *Journal of Neuroscience Methods* 248: 59–69. https://doi.org/10.1016/j.jneumeth.2015.03.018.

10 Congedo, M., Barachant, A., and Bhatia, R. (2017). Riemannian geometry for EEG-based brain–computer interfaces; a primer and a review. *Brain–Computer Interfaces* 4 (3): 155–174. https://doi.org/10.1080/2326263X.2017.1297192.

11 Cook, A.M., Polgar, J.M., and Encarnação, P. (2020). Delivering assistive technology services to the client. In: *Assistive Technologies*, Chapter 6, 5e (ed. A.M. Cook, J.M. Polgar, and P. Encarnação), 87–116. St. Louis, MO: Mosby. ISBN 978-0-323-52338-7. https://doi.org/10.1016/B978-0-323-52338-7.00006-8.

12 Federici, S. and Scherer, M (eds.) (2012). *Assistive Technology Assessment Handbook*. Boca Raton, FL: CRC Press. ISBN 978-0-429-15148-4. https://doi.org/10.1201/b11821.

**13** Gayraud, N.T.H., Rakotomamonjy, A., and Clerc, M. (2017). Optimal Transport Applied to Transfer Learning For P300 Detection, 7.

**14** Gilbert, F., Pham, C., Viaña, J.N.M., and Gillam, W. (2019). Increasing brain–computer interface media depictions: pressing ethical concerns. *Brain–Computer Interfaces* 6 (3): 49–70. https://doi.org/10.1080/2326263X.2019.1655837.

**15** Goljahani, A., D'Avanzo, C., Schiff, S. et al. (2012). A novel method for the determination of the EEG individual alpha frequency. *NeuroImage* 60 (1): 774–786. https://doi.org/10.1016/j.neuroimage.2011.12.001.

**16** Hu, K., Chen, C., Meng, Q. et al. (2016). Scientific profile of brain–computer interfaces: bibliometric analysis in a 10-year period. *Neuroscience Letters* 635: 61–66. https://doi.org/10.1016/j.neulet.2016.10.022.

**17** Ismail, F.Y., Fatemi, A., and Johnston, M.V. (2017). Cerebral plasticity: windows of opportunity in the developing brain. *European Journal of Paediatric Neurology* 21 (1): 23–48. https://doi.org/10.1016/j.ejpn.2016.07.007.

**18** Jayaram, V., Alamgir, M., Altun, Y. et al. (2016). Transfer learning in brain–computer interfaces. *IEEE Computational Intelligence Magazine*. https://doi.org/10.1109/MCI.2015.2501545.

**19** Jochumsen, M., Shafique, M., Hassan, A., and Niazi, I.K. (2018). Movement intention detection in adolescents with cerebral palsy from single-trial EEG. *Journal of Neural Engineering* 15 (6): 066030. https://doi.org/10.1088/1741-2552/aae4b8.

**20** Johnston, M.V. (2004). Clinical disorders of brain plasticity. *Brain and Development* 26 (2): 73–80. https://doi.org/10.1016/S0387-7604(03)00102-5.

**21** Kawala-Sterniuk, A., Browarska, N., Al-Bakri, A. et al. (2021). Summary of over fifty years with brain–computer interfaces-a review. *Brain Sciences* 11 (1): 43. https://doi.org/10.3390/brainsci11010043.

**22** Kelly, D., Jadavji, Z., Zewdie, E. et al. (2020). A child's right to play: results from the brain–computer interface game Jam 2019 (calgary competition). *2020 42nd Annual International Conference of the IEEE Engineering in Medicine Biology Society (EMBC)*, 6099–6102. https://doi.org/10.1109/EMBC44109.2020.9176272. ISSN: 2694-0604.

**23** Kinney-Lang, E., Auyeung, B., and Escudero, J. (2016). Expanding the (kaleido)scope: exploring current literature trends for translating electroencephalography (EEG) based brain–computer interfaces for motor rehabilitation in children. *Journal of Neural Engineering* 13 (6): 061002. https://doi.org/10.1088/1741-2560/13/6/061002.

**24** Kinney-Lang, E., Spyrou, L., Ebied, A. et al. (2018). Tensor-driven extraction of developmental features from varying paediatric EEG datasets. *Journal of Neural Engineering* 15 (4): 046024. https://doi.org/10.1088/1741-2552/aac664.

**25** Kinney-Lang, E., Ebied, A., and Escudero, J. (2018). Building a tensor framework for the analysis and classification of steady-state visual evoked potentials in children. *2018 26th European Signal Processing Conference (EUSIPCO)*, 296–300. https://doi.org/10.23919/EUSIPCO.2018.8553012. ISSN: 2076-1465.

**26** Kinney-Lang, E., Kelly, D., Floreani, E.D. et al. (2020). Advancing brain–computer interface applications for severely disabled children through a multidisciplinary national network: summary of the inaugural pediatric BCI Canada meeting. *Frontiers in Human Neuroscience* 14: 593883. https://doi.org/10.3389/fnhum.2020.593883.

**27** Kübler, A., Nijboer, F., and Kleih, S. (2020). Hearing the needs of clinical users. In: *Handbook of Clinical Neurology, Brain–Computer Interfaces*, Chapter 26, vol. 168 (ed. N.F. Ramsey and J.R. Millán), 353–368. Elsevier. https://doi.org/10.1016/B978-0-444-63934-9.00026-3.

28 Lenassi, E., Likar, K., Stirn-Kranjc, B., and Brecelj, J. (2008). VEP maturation and visual acuity in infants and preschool children. *Documenta Ophthalmologica* 117 (2): 111–120. https://doi.org/10.1007/s10633-007-9111-8.

29 Letourneau, S., Zewdie, E.T., Jadavji, Z. et al. (2020). Clinician awareness of brain computer interfaces: a Canadian national survey. *Journal of NeuroEngineering and Rehabilitation* 17 (1): Article number: 2. https://doi.org/10.1186/s12984-019-0624-7.

30 Light, J., McNaughton, D., Beukelman, D. et al. (2019). Challenges and opportunities in augmentative and alternative communication: research and technology development to enhance communication and participation for individuals with complex communication needs. *AAC: Augmentative and Alternative Communication* 35 (1): 1–12. https://doi.org/10.1080/07434618.2018.1556732.

31 Lotte, F., Larrue, F., and Mühl, C. (2013). Flaws in current human training protocols for spontaneous brain–computer interfaces: lessons learned from instructional design. *Frontiers in Human Neuroscience* 7: 1–11. https://doi.org/10.3389/fnhum.2013.00568.

32 Lotte, F., Bougrain, L., Cichocki, A. et al. (2018). A review of classification algorithms for EEG-based brain-computer interfaces: a 10 year update. *Journal of Neural Engineering* 15 (3): 031005. https://doi.org/10.1088/1741-2552/aab2f2.

33 Lust, J.M., Wilson, P.H., and Steenbergen, B. (2016). Motor imagery difficulties in children with Cerebral Palsy: a specific or general deficit? *Research in Developmental Disabilities* 57: 102–111. https://doi.org/10.1016/j.ridd.2016.06.010.

34 Markopoulos, P., Read, J.C., and Giannakos, M. (2021). Design of digital technologies for children. In: *Handbook of Human Factors and Ergonomics*, 5e, 1287–1304. https://doi.org/10.1002/9781119636113.ch49.

35 Matsuura, M., Yamamoto, K., Fukuzawa, H. et al. (1985). Age development and sex differences of various EEG elements in healthy children and adults - quantification by a computerized wave form recognition method. *Electroencephalography and Clinical Neurophysiology* 60 (5): 394–406. https://doi.org/10.1016/0013-4694(85)91013-2.

36 Mikołajewska, E. and Mikołajewski, D. (2014). The prospects of brain–computer interface applications in children. *Central European Journal of Medicine* 9 (1): 74–79. https://doi.org/10.2478/s11536-013-0249-3.

37 Moriguchi, Y. and Hiraki, K. (2013). Prefrontal cortex and executive function in young children: a review of NIRS studies. *Frontiers in Human Neuroscience* 7 (DEC): 1–9. https://doi.org/10.3389/fnhum.2013.00867.

38 Müller-Putz, G.R. (2020). Electroencephalography. *Handbook of Clinical Neurology* 168: 249–262. https://doi.org/10.1016/B978-0-444-63934-9.00018-4.

39 Orlandi, S., House, S.C., Karlsson, P. et al. (2021). Brain–computer interfaces for children with complex communication needs and limited mobility: a systematic review. *Frontiers in Human Neuroscience* 15 https://doi.org/10.3389/fnhum.2021.643294.

40 Oskoui, M., Coutinho, F., Dykeman, J. et al. (2013). An update on the prevalence of cerebral palsy: a systematic review and meta-analysis. *Developmental Medicine & Child Neurology* 55 (6): 509–519. https://doi.org/10.1111/dmcn.12080.

41 Petrie, H., Carmien, S., and Lewis, A. (2018). Assistive technology abandonment: research realities and potentials. In: *Computers Helping People with Special Needs, Lecture Notes in Computer Science* (ed. K. Miesenberger and G. Kouroupetroglou), 532–540. Cham: Springer International Publishing. ISBN 978-3-319-94274-2. https://doi.org/10.1007/978-3-319-94274-2_77.

**42** Ramsey, N.F. (2020). Human brain function and brain–computer interfaces. In: *Handbook of Clinical Neurology, Brain-Computer Interfaces*, Chapter 1, vol. 168 (ed. N.F. Ramsey and J.R. Millán), 1–13. Elsevier. https://doi.org/10.1016/B978-0-444-63934-9.00001-9.

**43** Rezeika, A., Benda, M., Stawicki, P. et al. (2018). Brain–computer interface spellers: a review. *Brain Sciences* 8 (4): 57. https://doi.org/10.3390/brainsci8040057.

**44** Shah, S.G.S. and Robinson, I. (2007). Benefits of and barriers to involving users in medical device technology development and evaluation. *International Journal of Technology Assessment in Health Care* 23 (1): 131–137. https://doi.org/10.1017/S0266462307051677.

**45** St. Louis, E.K., Frey, L.C., Britton, J.W. et al. (2016). Electroencephalography (EEG): an introductory text and atlas of normal and abnormal findings in adults, children, and infants. In: *The Developmental EEG: Premature, Neonatal, Infant, and Children*. American Epilepsy Society.

**46** Sturm, J.M., Erickson, K., and Yoder, D.E. (2002). Enhancing literacy development through AAC technologies. *Assistive Technology* 14 (1): 71–80. https://doi.org/10.1080/10400435.2002.10132056.

**47** Sydnor, V.J., Larsen, B., Bassett, D.S. et al. (2021). Neurodevelopment of the association cortices: patterns, mechanisms, and implications for psychopathology. *Neuron* 109 (18): 2820–2846. https://doi.org/10.1016/j.neuron.2021.06.016.

**48** Willett, F.R., Avansino, D.T., Hochberg, L.R. et al. (2021). High-performance brain-to-text communication via handwriting. *Nature* 593 (7858): 249–254. https://doi.org/10.1038/s41586-021-03506-2.

**49** Zerafa, R., Camilleri, T., Falzon, O., and Camilleri, K.P. (2018). A comparison of a broad range of EEG acquisition devices - is there any difference for SSVEP BCIs? *Brain–Computer Interfaces* 5 (4): 121–131. https://doi.org/10.1080/2326263X.2018.1550710.

# 5

# Brain–Computer Interface-based Predator–Prey Drone Interactions

*Abdelkader Nasreddine Belkacem and Abderrahmane Lakas*

*Department of Computer and Network Engineering, College of Information Technology, United Arab Emirates University, Alw Ain, UAE*

## 5.1 Introduction

Brain–computer interface (BCI) is an integrated system of hardware and software for connecting human brain to an external device. BCI is based on the principle of capturing some relevant signal patterns from the brain or from the scalp using invasive or noninvasive measurement techniques such as electrocorticography (EcoG) and electroencephalography (EEG), respectively. BCI is used for developing communication and control systems for medical and nonmedical applications. It has shown to be beneficial in many ways to the improvement of human condition by offering the ability to improve and boost the capabilities of human individuals by developing assistive, adaptive, and rehabilitative cognitive and neural motor prostheses. Indeed, many research projects have developed BCI applications which improve the health and well-being of users namely those who have psychiatric diseases or motor-control impairments caused by spinal cord injury, brain stroke, and amyotrophic lateral sclerosis [4, 7–9]. BCI can also be used for understanding brain functions and mechanisms and for exploring new brain-related features such as event-related desynchronization or synchronization extracted from motor imagery (MI). However, the benefits of BCI technology are not limited to improving the lives of disabled people but they also extend to able-bodied people including senior citizens. Indeed, there are currently many applications where BCI was used for brain-controlling augmentative and alternative communication systems (e.g. a swarm of drones and ground robots), and for entertainment where BCI users can play medical and nonmedical games. For instance, BCI can be used by soldiers to control simultaneously robots and drones using their EEG signals and enable them to perform successfully multitask missions at the same time (e.g. using drone-transmitted feedback of a scanning area, whereas the robot is engaged in a field battle. In such applications, BCI provides an additional power by enhancing the multitasking ability of the user.

There are two BCI application categories: medical and nonmedical BCIs. Medical BCIs are mainly used to enhance, assist, and improve human abilities by providing more autonomy and sometimes more mobility such as in the case of a brain-controlled wheelchair for motor-impaired users, or brain-controlled limb prosthesis for paralyzed people or senior citizens. Nonmedical BCIs applications are typically developed to provide users with better tools to enhance remote

*Handbook of Human-Machine Systems*, First Edition. Edited by Giancarlo Fortino, David Kaber, Andreas Nürnberger, and David Mendonça.

and faster control such as in communication and entertainment applications. In recent years, BCI researchers have successfully developed several medical and nonmedical applications that demonstrate the efficiency and robustness of BCI techniques, including brain-controlling a wheelchair, robotic arms, mobile robots, humanoid/human-like robots, and games to mention a few. Furthermore, some innovative BCIs methods have been proposed to improve the accuracy and the degree of freedom by combining two modalities or by adding nonbrain activity as an additional input. In addition, many techniques propose algorithms to gain reliable control over Unmanned Aerial Vehicles (UAVs, also known as drones) and to perform remote operations. However, UAV kinematics and autonomy are the only classification metrics considered in the existing studies. [2, 3, 5, 16, 18].

## 5.2 Related Work

The recent popularity of UAVs and their increasing deployment in various daily-life applications and services led many to view them as a strong candidate to benefit from the use of BCI. That is, many researchers have developed BCI-based systems for the control of UAV in various situations including monitoring and target tracking. Resorting to the use, BCI is dictated by the complexity of remotely controlling and executing multitasked aerial operations with no pilot on-board. The authors of [17] have developed a BCI-system capable of controlling the direction (2 degrees of freedom – DOF) of a virtual helicopter using motor imagery. Akce et al. [1] were able to control a fixed-wing aircraft using MI-based binary classifier for choosing trajectory. Doud et al. [6] controlled a virtual helicopter using MI and increased the number of freedom from two to three (he added forward–backward to right–left and up–down). In [14], the authors succeeded in controlling a real quadcopter using the same method (MI, ERD/ERS, 3-DOF) as Doud et al. Kosmyna et al. [12, 13] used hybrid BCI (a combination of MI and facial gesture) to control 2-DOF of a quadcopter using adaptive recurrent neural network (RNN) instead of using linear classifier. Kim et al. [11] have combined EEG data with eye movements (EOG) to control 3-DOF of a quadcopter using kernet-based Support Vector Machine (SVM) method. Shi et al. [19] have controlled 2-DOF of a hexacopter using MI and logistic regression (LR). Lin and Jiang [15] have controlled quadcopter (3-DOF) using hybrid BCI (combination between EEG and electromyography (EMG)) and Zhang and Jackson [20] have done the same thing using google glass and EEG to combine brain activity (MI and SSVEP) with head poster using RBF-based SVM classifier.

One of the most frequently used EEG's features in BCI is the P300 method, consists of a positive deflection that occurs around 300 ms after a unexpected stimulus has occurred. P300 method has many applications, and one of them is the P300 speller, which allows a user to enter thought-derived commands based on characters that are randomly flashing in a letter matrix.

In this chapter, we propose a P300-based method which allows a user to control a UAV maneuvering as a predator chasing after another drone as prey-controlled manually (see Figure 5.1). Predator–prey model refers to the interactions between two species where one species is the hunted food source for the other. This model is adapted to the interactions between two drones where one drone is the hunted target for the other. The control commands generated by the BCI reflect the behavior of a drone while tracking and/or closing on the target in a constrained environment. The system uses a wireless EEG interface based on the P300 and using Unicorn software, which has the potential to output EEG signals from the participant. Controlling an UAV in three-dimensional space (3D) using brain activity might be an optimal way compared to using joysticks, hand gestures, and voices for empowering pilots and de-risking missions. That is, the brain is notably faster

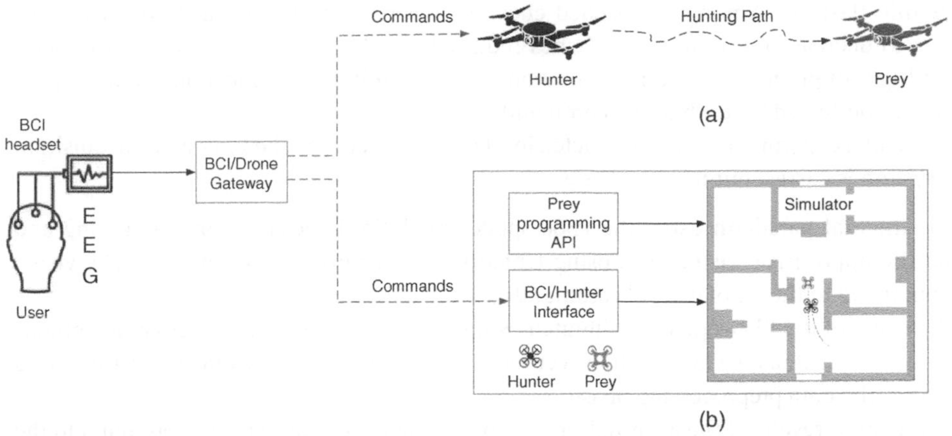


**Figure 5.1** System architecture of virtual and real EEG-based predator–prey chasing application. (a) Experimental test-bed and (b) software-based simulation platform.

in responding to an impending hazard that the hand is. In the future, people may be able to pilot aircraft using their brains just like they perform everyday activities like walking or running.

## 5.3 Predator–Prey Drone Interaction

In this section, we provide a description of the system setup. The validation of our system is done through two experimental settings. For the BCI component and the acquisition of the EEG signals, we use a noninvasive approach using a wireless portable EEG headset, which contains biosignal amplifier and an acquisition and processing system using Unicorn Hybrid Black from g.tec medical engineering GmbH (Austria). As for the number of participating subjects, we limited it to three given constraints imposed on us due to current pandemic situation caused by COVID-19. During the experiments, we asked the participants to learn the use of a P300 speller paradigm to control a drone using a cheap easy-to-use EEG but good signal quality Unicorn equipment. The electrodes were applied on the scalp at locations according to the international 10–20 system. Eight EEG electrodes were used in both experiments. The dry EEG electrodes were placed at Fz, Cz, P3, Pz, P4, PO7, Oz, and PO8 following common electrode setup for P300 speller paradigm. The ground electrode was mounted on the forehead at FPz, and the reference electrodes were attached to the right and left ears. The EEG signals, acquired using a Unicorn speller device, are processed using the system's Python application programming interface (API). For both experiments, the study was divided into three stages: (i) building the P300 experimental paradigm for drone control application, (ii) recording/processing the EEG signals, (iii) implementing/testing a real-time BCI system.

To reduce the muscle artifacts effect during the EEG experiments, the subject was instructed to minimize the head and eye movements. All subjects reported normal or corrected-to-normal vision. The setup consists of a participant seated on a chair watching a monitor at eye level around 50 cm away. The subject is instructed to focus on a $3 \times 4$ 12 images graphically laid out in $3 \times 4$ matrix denoting place destinations. The icons are flashed randomly where an icon's image is displayed for 100 ms and then replaced by a black icon for 75 ms. This experiment represents a paradigm which contains 12 visual cues each referring to a drone command (*Up*, *Down*, *Right*, *Left*, *Stop/Pause*, *Land-Emergency stop*, *Land*, *Takeoff*, *Take a picture*, *Move backward*, *Move forward*, and *Start video stream*) The participant subject is then asked to focus on only one of the cues at a time while flashing. Among the flashed cues, we inserted the images of faces of famous personalities to decrease the number of flashes required in P300-speller modality and to get a long-lasting high-amplitude positive ERP component to reach high classification accuracy [10]. Ten trials were conducted for each drone command.

In this study, BCI experiments were conducted in a laboratory setting. The EEG signal acquisition of the BCI system is carried out in four phases:

1. The experimental paradigm using the P300 speller modality is designed by identifying and selecting the appropriate visual cues using Unicorn Suite Hybrid Black software. The visual cues are mapped to the set of control commands accepted by the drone.
2. The acquisition of the EEG signal is calibrated using a set of predefined preprocessing methods for the improvement of the classification accuracy. The calibration and testing steps are started directly after the data preprocessing phase.
3. The classification results of the acquired signals for selected cues are sent as a command to the second laptop for further processing.
4. The commands received by the laptop are interpreted and processed by a Python-based control logic destined for the drone. Depending on whether we are in the virtual setting (simulation), or the experimental setting (testbed), the control logic will issue control commands to either the drone simulator or to the real drone itself.

As mentioned earlier and explained here, we use the same P300-based BCI to issue real-time control commands to both the simulator and the real drone. We instructed one participant (the predator) who wears the EEG cap, to sit in front of the P300-speller interface to synchronously send commands using his/her brainwaves. The second participant (the prey) was instructed to manually use either keyboard or joystick to control the movements of the drone. For BCI calibration, we start reading the predator's brainwaves while looking at the screen and carefully checking the quality of EEG signal. We use two decoding algorithms for calibration and testing phases. These algorithms are mainly based on Linear Discriminant Analysis (LDA) classifier to detect the presence or absence of P300 component (two-class classification problem), and accordingly, the decoding algorithm can predict which icon the subject was considering. The obtained prediction is sent to another computer to be further processed and converted into a set of commands to be executed either by a virtual or a real drone. The connection to the secondary computer is made through a unshielded twisted pair (UTP) cable using a local area network socket. Experiments using P300 paradigm require a calibration phase prior to training the classifier model.

In the calibration phase, we build a signal database using eight EEG channels from three subjects. We apply three different types of filters to the collected signals using Unicorn EEG recorder software. We used a scaling filter to display the amplitude ranges of all EEG channels (around $\pm$50 mV). In addition, we apply a predefined Infinite Impulse Response (IIR) bandpass filters on the raw data to remove high frequency information (i.e. we kept the low frequencies around 2–30 Hz). Finally, to suppress the power line noise, we apply a predefined IIR notch filter with a value of 60 Hz. The more we run calibrations for the user, the better the software is trained well, and the result accuracy might be increased.

After denoising the raw EEG data, we obtain the targeted cues by decoding the presence or absence of the P300 amplitude of each received EEG epoch. For the purpose of improving the accuracy of the machine learning methods used in this experiment, we opted for 90% of the prepared data for training and 10% for testing. We implemented a linear discriminant analysis (LDA) classifier as a technique for reducing the number of dimensions in the dataset while retaining as much

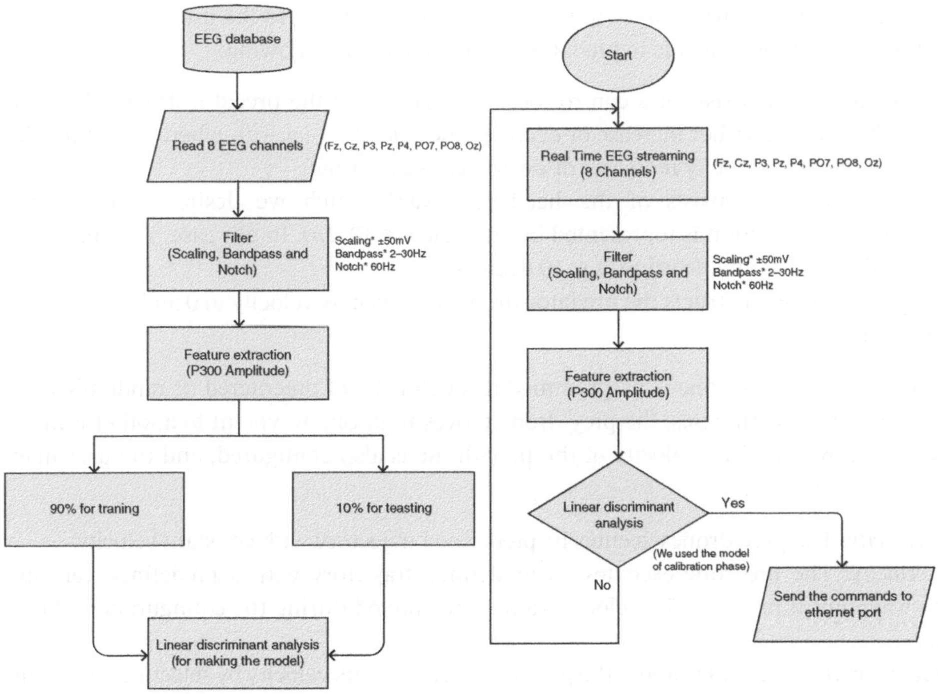


**Figure 5.2** A flowchart of the proposed calibration and real-time P300-based brain-drone control interface to chase another drone. In the left, the algorithm flowchart for calibration/training phase to build the classifier model. In the right, the algorithm flowchart for online decoding phase for the P300 proposed application.

information as possible (see Figure 5.2). The testing phase is different from the training phase with regards to LDA classification. If the software was able to receive and recognized the P300-wave amplitude for the selected drone command cue, the system directly sent the selected drone command function to the second laptop using UTP cable. After the training phase, we run the testing algorithm using the offline classification model. For instance, when the user selects takeoff icon by focusing on visual cue related to takeoff, the mapped function of the selected icon will be sent to the second laptop. The second laptop has a Python code which can translate the BCI results into commands and wirelessly send them to the drone. The drone executes the commands consecutively as they are received. In addition, the participant is provided with a video stream as a visual feedback to monitor the drone's movement while chasing the prey. and correct any miss-classification result.

The BCI-controlled predator–prey application is built so as to accommodate both experimental testing and simulation testing. Figure 5.4 provides a visual representation of the most important part of the architecture consists of the P300-based BCI system. This component is common to both the experimental testbed and to the software-based simulation platform. Further elaboration on the experimental testbed including the BCI component for both training and execution as well as the elements of the simulation platform will be provided in subsequent paragraphs.

The simulation platform for the BCI-controlled predator–prey application is initially used to test the accuracy and the efficiency of the implemented BCI training and execution algorithms. The simulation platform consists of a BCI/hunter interface which received and interpreted the commands from the BCI gateway. The commands are translated into motion and navigation directives which cause the predator-drone to move in its environment according to the user's control commands. That is, the controls available to predator-drone include the following:

- *Velocity*: This directive consists of a control over the velocity of the predator-drone. Through this control, the user can either increase or decrease the velocity: $\{+v, -v\}$, where $v$ is a tunable step-value by which the velocity increases or decreases at each time.
- *Direction*: This control consists of the heading toward which we desire to direct the predator-drone. The direction is represented by an angle $\theta \in [0, 2\pi]$. In our case, the value of $\theta$ has to be a multiple of a tunable value (e.g. 10 degrees).
- *Hover*: This controls and instructs the predator-drone to reduce its velocity to 0 and remain still in its current position.

The trajectory of the prey-drone is programmed through a set of preentered or randomly pregenerated waypoints. In both cases, the prey-drone moves from one waypoint to another until it reaches the final waypoint. The velocity of the prey-drone is also configured, and the user may select anyone of few options:

- *Constant velocity*: The prey-drone executes its predefined trajectory with constant velocity.
- *Variable velocity*: The predrone executes its predefined trajectory with a predefined velocity after each waypoint it reaches. The velocity values are entered during the configuration of the waypoints.
- *Random velocity*: In this configuration, the prey-drone changes its velocity by selecting a random value within a range or interval of values predefined by the user.

The simulation platform includes a BCI-Drone interface (see Figure 5.3) that receives as input control commands from the BCI and translates them into the drone controls mentioned above (*velocity*, *direction*). The 12 commands (i.e. 12 visual cues) generated by BCI were mapped with the control parameters of the virtual drone (e.g. the BCI cues such as *Forward* and *Backward* are mapped with the value of the velocity, and so on). In addition, the simulator provides *alert* messages indicating when either of the predator or the prey drones collides against an obstacle or into each other. This feature is necessary to address the effectiveness of the controls sent to the drone but also of the configuration of the simulation, that is, the simulation environment is modeled by

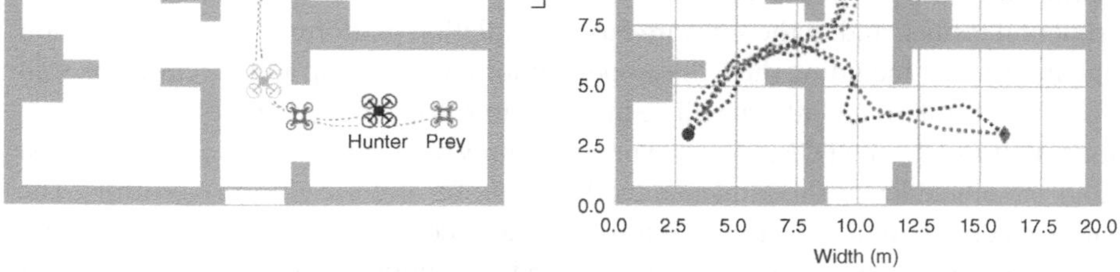

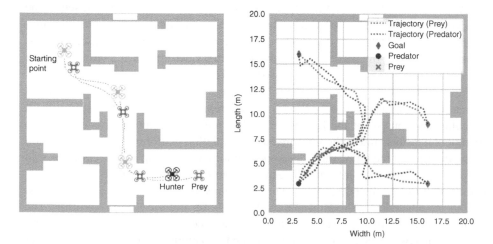


**Figure 5.3** P300-based simulation platform.

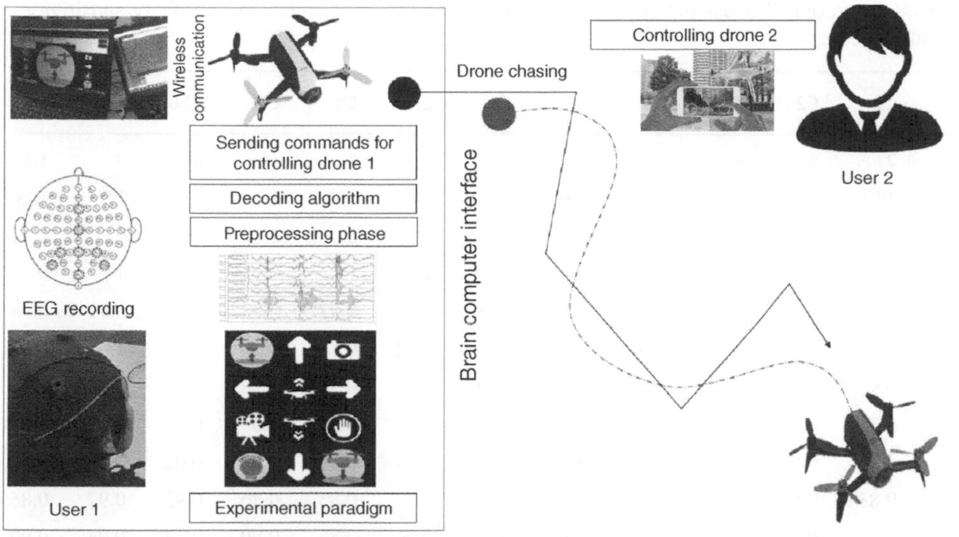


**Figure 5.4** Our proposed real-time P300-based brain-drone interface system to chase another drone. Source: © Stanisic Vladimir / Adobe Stock.

a map containing walls and obstacles. It is important to assess the accuracy of the BCI-generated commands as well as controls sent to or configured on the drones especially in tight environments such as corridors and sudden turns where it is hard to maneuvre the drones; therefore, the simulation platform allows for a flexible use of various maps and environments.

To implement EEG-based brain-controlled drone navigation and target tracking for indoor environment, we used Unicorn software. The P300 calibration phase requires few minutes prior to training the decoder model (see Figure 5.4). Each session of collecting EEG data comprises 120 trials, 10 trials for each visual cue. For drone control, we have instructed the EEG participants to choose any path for chasing the prey by selecting any visual cue from P300 speller interface. The BCI user should turn on the camera of predator drone to get the visual feedback (i.e. a video stream). Based on the feedback, the BCI user takes a quick decision to select the appropriate cue to keep the prey drone in the vision field. We use Python to implement the function that takes the predicted visual cue as input and translates it to its corresponding set of commands to be sent to the drone for execution. The communication between the laptop processing the code and the drone is done wirelessly and in real-time. A third laptop is used to control the movements of prey drone using preprogrammed Python code (we also used handed joystick or virtual joystick on Parrot's phone application) to evaluate the efficiency of chasing the prey-drone.

In both presented experiments, the users were able to control virtual or real predator-drone using a wireless EEG equipment, while the prey-drone was controlled using preprogrammed code or joystick. The flight and piloting settings (e.g. speed and velocity) were fixed during experiments for both predator and prey drones (e.g. the angular speed is 30 degrees per second and the vertical speed is 0.5 m/s). The BCI user can increase and/or decrease the speed by 0.1 m/s while choosing the visual cues *Move forward* and *Move backward*, respectively. In the first experiment, we showed that using high commends can be an effective way to control a drone if we have the map of the 2D virtual environment to avoid obstacles. In the second experiment, we succeeded to control the drone using brain activity in real-time 3D environment to chase another drone to demonstrate the potential of using another communication pathway for many special applications instead of using hand or voice.

**Table 5.1** Evaluation of multiclass BCI system: Online decoding accuracy, precision, specificity, sensitivity, error rate, and F1-score.

| | C1 | C2 | C3 | C4 | C5 | C6 | C7 | C8 | C9 | C10 | C11 | C12 |
|---|---|---|---|---|---|---|---|---|---|---|---|---|
| TP | 7 | 8 | 8 | 7 | 9 | 8 | 8 | 9 | 10 | 8 | 9 | 10 |
| TN | 109 | 108 | 107 | 110 | 108 | 108 | 107 | 108 | 108 | 110 | 110 | 108 |
| FP | 1 | 2 | 3 | 0 | 2 | 2 | 3 | 2 | 2 | 0 | 0 | 2 |
| FN | 3 | 2 | 2 | 3 | 1 | 2 | 2 | 1 | 0 | 2 | 1 | 0 |
| Accuracy | 0.96 | 0.96 | 0.96 | 0.97 | 0.97 | 0.96 | 0.95 | 0.97 | 0.98 | 0.98 | 0.99 | 0.98 |
| Precision | 0.87 | 0.8 | 0.72 | 1.0 | 0.81 | 0.8 | 0.72 | 0.81 | 0.83 | 1.0 | 1.0 | 0.83 |
| Specificity | 0.99 | 0.98 | 0.97 | 1.0 | 0.98 | 0.98 | 0.97 | 0.98 | 0.98 | 1.0 | 1.0 | 0.98 |
| Sensitivity | 0.7 | 0.8 | 0.8 | 0.7 | 0.9 | 0.8 | 0.8 | 0.9 | 1.0 | 0.8 | 0.9 | 1.0 |
| Error rate | 0.03 | 0.03 | 0.04 | 0.02 | 0.02 | 0.03 | 0.04 | 0.02 | 0.02 | 0.02 | 0.01 | 0.02 |
| F0.5 score | 0.83 | 0.8 | 0.74 | 0.92 | 0.83 | 0.8 | 0.74 | 0.83 | 0.86 | 0.95 | 0.97 | 0.86 |
| F1 score | 0.77 | 0.8 | 0.76 | 0.82 | 0.85 | 0.8 | 0.76 | 0.86 | 0.90 | 0.88 | 0.94 | 0.90 |
| F2 score | 0.72 | 0.8 | 0.78 | 0.74 | 0.88 | 0.8 | 0.78 | 0.88 | 0.96 | 0.83 | 0.91 | 0.96 |

TN: True negative, TP: True positive, FN: False negative, and FP: False positive.
In the table, the visual cues are abbreviated as the following: C1 (Cue1): *Takeoff*, C2 (Cue2): *Right*, C3 (Cue3): *Start video stream*, C4 (Cue4): *Emergency landing*, C5 (Cue5): *Up*, C6 (Cue6): *Forward*, C7 (Cue7): *Backward*, C8 (Cue8): *Down*, C9 (Cue9): *Take a picture*, C10 (Cue10): *Left*, C11 (Cue11): *Stop/Pause*, C12 (Cue12): *Land.*

For the purpose of online testing, an offline calibration is required, the BCI control system is run with a virtual drone where the participant is asked to select among the 12 visual cues to thought-control the virtual drone while chasing the prey-drone. For each of the executed 120 trials, we calculated the classification accuracy of the proposed system, along with the response time of the participant. In Table 5.1, we present statistics about the trials and per visual cue comprising the main metrics measurements such as accuracy, precision, sensitivity, and specificity. Are also included the recall and F1-Score which is the harmonic mean of the precision. The selected evaluation criteria in Table 5.1 are defined as follows:

$$Accuracy(Acc) = \frac{TP + TN}{TP + FP + FN + TN} \tag{5.1}$$

$$Precision(Prec) = \frac{TP}{TP + FP} \tag{5.2}$$

$$Sensitivity(Sens) = \frac{TP}{TP + FN} \tag{5.3}$$

$$Specificity(Sepc) = \frac{TN}{TN + FP} \tag{5.4}$$

$$F1\ Score = 2 \times \frac{Sens \times Prec}{Sens + Prec} \tag{5.5}$$

where $TP$ is the number of true positives, $TN$ is the number of true negatives, $FP$ is the number of false positives, and $FN$ is the number of false negatives.

The table shows an overall accuracy of 84.2% and Kappa of 0.827 for multiclass decoding. The main challenge in the proposed system is to include an emergency stop feature, which will allow the participant to immediately react to mis-classification by invoking a corrective control measure. The results of the conducted experiments show that all subjects were able to accurately generate

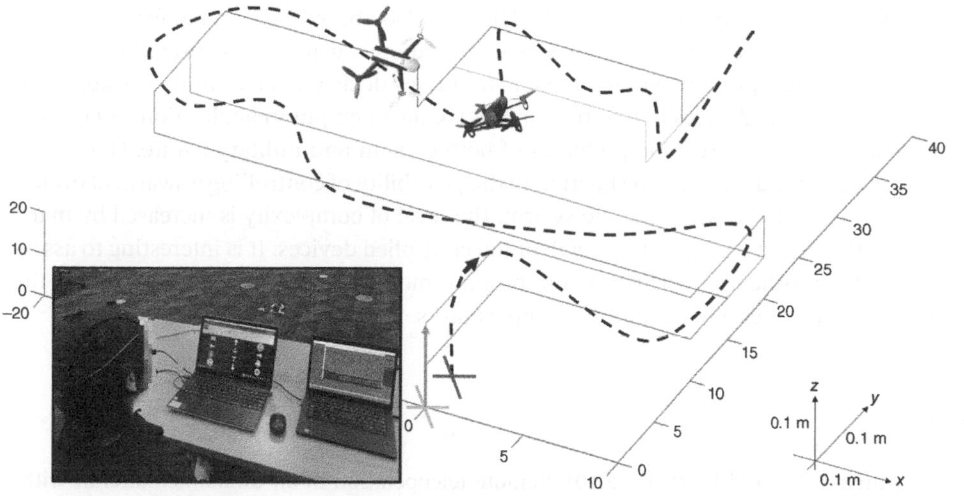


**Figure 5.5** The 3D trajectories of the predator/prey drones with the setup of real-time P300-based brain-drone interface system.

near-optimal solutions and reacting quickly to the target's movements by keeping the prey (target) as close as possible and within the vision field of the predator's camera. Given that the brain succeeds at performing a task, the best way possible based on the available visual information, Figure 5.5 does show a near-optimal BCI user's performance in finding drone trajectories. The BCI user kept the predator-prey distance less than 0.5 m. The P300-based BCI, at its best performance, selecting a visual cue takes around 0.03 s, while receiving the selected cue and processing it by Laptop 2 may take less than 0.001 s. In addition, generating the corresponding commands to the drone for execution will take around 0.02 s. It appears that controlling a drone using noninvasive BCI for this type of application can be relatively more efficient than the traditional tracking and control programming methods. Indeed, in the proposed system, the drone reacts instantly to the user's thoughts when deciding where to direct the drone to. This method prevents the drone from waiting too long to detect the prey, before it decides of its next move. This allows the predator to find a path for chasing any prey and/or discovering its surroundings using shortcut paths which may minimize time and energy. However, the proposed brain-controlled drone application has some limitations, notably because the BCI user must shift attention from the predator-prey scenario to the P300-speller matrix which may affect the quickness of the user's response. In addition, direct control using the traditional manual control system to fly the drone might be for now faster and more precise than using discretely selected brain commands. However, the usefulness and effectiveness of brain-based drone control with intensive training has been demonstrated for pursuit, hunting, and tracking, especially in modern military operations where managing multiple devices has a high priority.

## 5.4 Conclusion and Future Challenges

In this chapter, we described BCI-based control application for controlling drones operating in a predator-prey situation. In this application, the brain-generated signals are captured using P300 paradigm and translated into drone control commands using LDA classifier. We successfully validated our solution using two settings: simulated drone environment and experimental testbed with real drones. Both approaches rely on the use of a Unicorn P300-based BCI system for controlling drone predator while chasing another drone. Controlling drones using BCI is useful to enhance users' multitask ability and give them more freedom for taking decision in real-time. The approach of mind-controlling remote devices in real-time multitasking when put in application can be very beneficial for solving complex real-life problems of both civilian and military nature. One of the challenges might be expanding this investigation to the possibility of controlling a swarm of drones in various situations. In the case of a drone swarm, the level of complexity is increased by many factors including the multitasking and the DOF of the controlled devices. It is interesting to assess the accuracy of the classification algorithm and propose more robust methods for capturing the brain and nonbrain activities when handling complex tasks.

## References


1 Akce, A., Johnson, M., and Bretl, T. (2010). Remote teleoperation of an unmanned aircraft with a brain-machine interface: theory and preliminary results. *2010 IEEE International Conference on Robotics and Automation*, 5322–5327. IEEE.

2 Al-Nuaimi, F.A., Al-Nuaimi, R.J., Al-Dhaheri, S.S. et al. (2020). Mind drone chasing using EEG-based brain computer interface. *2020 16th International Conference on Intelligent Environments (IE)*, 74–79. IEEE.

3 Belkacem, A.N. and Lakas, A. (2021). A cooperative EEG-based BCI control system for robot–drone interaction. *2021 International Wireless Communications and Mobile Computing (IWCMC)*, 297–302. IEEE.

4 Belkacem, A.N., Jamil, N., Palmer, J.A. et al. (2020). Brain computer interfaces for improving the quality of life of older adults and elderly patients. *Frontiers in Neuroscience* 14: 692.

5 Chen, C., Zhou, P., Belkacem, A.N. et al. (2020). Quadcopter robot control based on hybrid brain–computer interface system. *Sensors and Materials* 32 (3): 991–1004.

6 Doud, A.J., Lucas, J.P., Pisansky, M.T., and He, B. (2011). Continuous three-dimensional control of a virtual helicopter using a motor imagery based brain-computer interface. *PLoS One* 6 (10): e26322.

7 Hireche, A., Zennaia, Y., Ayad, R., and Belkacem, A.N. (2021). A decoding algorithm for non-invasive SSVEP-based drone flight control. *2021 IEEE International Conference on Bioinformatics and Biomedicine (BIBM)*, 3616–3623. IEEE.

8 Jamil, N., Belkacem, A.N., Ouhbi, S., and Guger, C. (2021). Cognitive and affective brain–computer interfaces for improving learning strategies and enhancing student capabilities: a systematic literature review. *IEEE Access* 9: 134122–134147.

9 Jamil, N., Belkacem, A.N., Ouhbi, S., and Lakas, A. (2021). Noninvasive electroencephalography equipment for assistive, adaptive, and rehabilitative brain–computer interfaces: a systematic literature review. *Sensors* 21 (14): 4754.

10 Kaufmann, T., Schulz, S.M., Grünzinger, C., and Kübler, A. (2011). Flashing characters with famous faces improves ERP-based brain–computer interface performance. *Journal of Neural Engineering* 8 (5): 056016.

11 Kim, B.H., Kim, M., and Jo, S. (2014). Quadcopter flight control using a low-cost hybrid interface with EEG-based classification and eye tracking. *Computers in Biology and Medicine* 51: 82–92.

12 Kosmyna, N., Tarpin-Bernard, F., and Rivet, B. (2014). Drone, your brain, ring course: accept the challenge and prevail! *Proceedings of the 2014 ACM International Joint Conference on Pervasive and Ubiquitous Computing: Adjunct Publication*, 243–246.

**13** Kosmyna, N., Tarpin-Bernard, F., and Rivet, B. (2015). Towards brain computer interfaces for recreational activities: piloting a drone. *IFIP Conference on Human-Computer Interaction*, 506–522. Springer.

**14** LaFleur, K., Cassady, K., Doud, A. et al. (2013). Quadcopter control in three-dimensional space using a noninvasive motor imagery-based brain–computer interface. *Journal of Neural Engineering* 10 (4): 046003.

**15** Lin, J.-S. and Jiang, Z.-Y. (2015). Implementing remote presence using quadcopter control by a non-invasive BCI device. *Computer Science and Information Technology* 3 (4): 122–126.

**16** Nourmohammadi, A., Jafari, M., and Zander, T.O. (2018). A survey on unmanned aerial vehicle remote control using brain–computer interface. *IEEE Transactions on Human-Machine Systems* 48 (4): 337–348.

**17** Royer, A.S., Doud, A.J., Rose, M.L., and He, B. (2010). EEG control of a virtual helicopter in 3-dimensional space using intelligent control strategies. *IEEE Transactions on Neural Systems and Rehabilitation Engineering* 18 (6): 581–589.

**18** Shao, L., Zhang, L., Belkacem, A.N. et al. (2020). EEG-controlled wall-crawling cleaning robot using SSVEP-based brain-computer interface. *Journal of Healthcare Engineering* 2020: 6968713.

**19** Shi, T., Wang, H., and Zhang, C. (2015). Brain computer interface system based on indoor semi-autonomous navigation and motor imagery for unmanned aerial vehicle control. *Expert Systems with Applications* 42 (9): 4196–4206.

**20** Zhang, D. and Jackson, M.M. (2015). Quadcopter navigation using Google Glass and brain–computer interface. *Georgia Inst. Technol., Atlanta, GA, USA, Master Project*.

# 6

# Levels of Cooperation in Human–Machine Systems: A Human–BCI–Robot Example

*Marie-Pierre Pacaux-Lemoine*[1], *Lydia Habib*[1], *and Tom Carlson*[2]

[1] *Department of Automation and Control, Univ. Polytechnique Hauts-de-France, CNRS, UMR 8201 - LAMIH, Valenciennes, France*
[2] *Aspire Create, University College London, Stanmore, Middlesex, UK*

## 6.1 Introduction

Human–machine system (HMS) designs are, most of the time, based on existing concepts and tools. That is especially the case for the studies dealing with task-sharing, which normally use concepts such as levels (or degrees) of automation or levels of autonomy. These concepts are mainly oriented toward the ability for a new machine or a new system, to control an environment. New human–machine interfaces (HMIs) are also considered. Many kinds of "building blocks" have been proposed, but they are often not particularly useful for designers to reach the goal required by the new HMS. Moreover, cooperative adaptations between human and machine, while they perform tasks, are sometimes neglected. This is especially the case when considering the necessity for human and machine to build up a model of the other to adapt their behavior to the others' needs.

This chapter proposes a method to identify the abilities of an existing HMS. We consider not only the abilities to control environments, i.e. the *Know-How-to-Operate* (KHO) but also the competences agents have to cooperate with each other, which we term *Know-How-to-Cooperate* (KHC). The objective is to modify or extend both abilities (KHO and KHC) of both agents (human and machine) in order to design the future system. Several levels might be identified for each ability, and the mix of each agent's levels defines the levels of cooperation.

The first part of the chapter presents the concept of levels of cooperation and its links with literature, as well as the method that supports the identification of the most suitable levels regarding the new HMS. The second part illustrates an application of the method to implement cooperation between human, brain–computer interface, and robot. The third and final part assesses the method and proposes future perspectives.

## 6.2 Levels of Cooperation

The levels of cooperation have been defined to complement other scales proposed in the literature, such as the levels (or degrees) of automation, the modes of autonomy, or the scales defined in car driving or the railway. The analysis of those scales through the functions they tackle and criteria they use to manage function allocation highlights some shortcomings. It is almost impossible to find the exact levels that correspond to the needs of designers; adaptations are always required.

*Handbook of Human-Machine Systems*, First Edition. Edited by Giancarlo Fortino, David Kaber, Andreas Nürnberger, and David Mendonça.

Moreover, most of the time, function allocation criteria address many aspects separately when they could be combined. For example, time for negotiation between cooperative agents could be combined with time to incident event and so the capacity to anticipate. Capabilities of agents must be combined with responsibility, mainly allocated to human, as well as with authority sometimes allocated to the machine, even if the human is responsible [5].

The levels of cooperation answer the needs by proposing a method to identify the best levels of interaction between human and machine and by improving the way to define the levels, i.e. not only according to their abilities to control an environment, the so-called KHO, but also according to their competences to cooperate with other actors participating in manipulating the same environment and sharing the same objective, which we term KHC [6]. Then, the levels of cooperation are not predefined but designed according to the needs of the HMS [9]. Analysis of not only current but also possible future, human and machine functions led to the identification of these necessary levels [8], through grids [2] constructed from the model of a cooperative human, machine, or more generally, agent [7].

This model, presented in Figure 6.1, highlights the several possible interactions between human and machine (adapted with permission from Pacaux-Lemoine et al. [11]). KHO functions of agents interact through a *Common Work Space* to share not only information about the environment but also information about each agent concerned by the environment control. The Common Work Space is indicated by the light gray rectangle, which can mainly be described by four separate scales, sharing functions between human and machine. Information available in this Common Work Space is then used by each agent's KHC functions to first support the identification or the update of a model of the other agent (rectangles on the left part of the schema) and second to evaluate how this agent is involved in the control of the process. The comparison between this evaluation of their own involvement in the process and of the model of themselves leads to the detection and subsequent management of interference and to the adjustment of the position of sliders of the scales that describe the function's allocation. The levels of cooperation are defined according to the two scales; the one built for the KHO and the one built for the KHC.

The degree to which each function is shared between each agent is indicated by the position of the slider on the scale. Indeed, either machine or human can manage some functions alone not

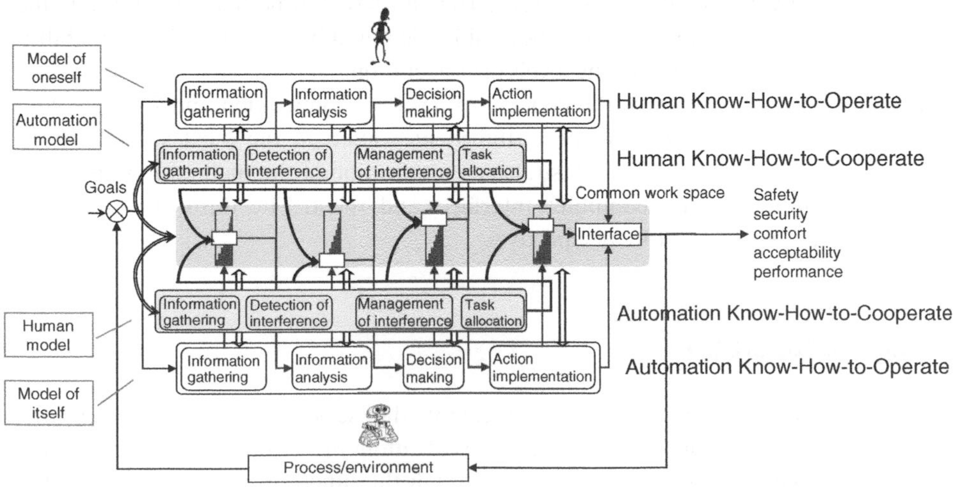


**Figure 6.1** Cooperative agents interactions. Source: © [2018] IEEE. Adapted, with permission, from Pacaux-Lemoine et al. [11].

only according to their competency and capacity (slider completely on one side) but also according to how they can take into account the activity of the other. Therefore, agents have to identify and implement adequate coordination of the four KHO functions. The grey rectangles with scale and thin grey straight arrows between each KHO function represent such a coordination. Human, machine, or both must define the best balance between each agent's involvement, and so find the right place for the slider on each scale for a specific situation. Such a representation may suggest a smooth shifting control authority; indeed, the control of the slider identifies who has the authority.

Section 6.3 presents the application of the method based on levels of cooperation and model of cooperative agents to a project where a human has to cooperate with a robot using a brain–computer interface (BCI).

## 6.3 Application to the Control of a Robot by Thought

One excellent example of a project that has applied this method is aimed to provide people who have severe motor impairments with assistance systems to enable them to communicate with others and interact with their environment. Some of these potential end-users may not be able to communicate using their impaired peripheral output pathways and may instead benefit from being able to directly exploit their brain signals. Imagine a scenario where someone is confined to their bed or wheelchair due to tetraplegia, but may have access to a remotely controlled telepresence robot, which could act as a proxy to enable many of their daily interactions. The overall interaction with the system is supported by two key components: a BCI [4] and a graphical interface, which provides the user with feedback about the state of their brain signals. The robot motion control is then shared between the human and the robot according to the situation and the human's goal. To share control is no easy task, so we further assist the user "emulated haptic supports," which modulate the effort required from the user according to the difficulty of the situation, and support to design shared control will be explained further in the following section.

Two objectives had to be reached. First, the user and the robot have to focus on avoiding any obstacles. A camera mounted on the robot, provided a live video feed of the environment for the human to perform their obstacle detection, and the robot is able to perceive obstacles using a scanning ultrasonic sensor (this represents both shared information gathering and shared information analysis). Both the human and the robot can make decisions (shared decision); however, only the robot can execute the decision in the sense that only it can modify the actual trajectory (cf. Figure 6.2). Second, the user manages modifications to the mission plan, i.e. if there is an unexpected obstacle, how should the trajectory be modified to arrive at the goal location? However, in this case of telepresence, the goal location could be moved at any point, as new opportunities appear: different people to meet and greet, new information to seek, etc. Moreover, the comparatively low fidelity and throughput (information transfer rate) of the BCI can make it difficult for the human to precisely indicate the target to the robot. Consequently, the robot would not explicitly know the target and therefore would be unable to satisfactorily replan to reach it.

Both human and robot are able to detect, then manage interference, both in terms of obstacle detection and subsequent decision-making through the Common Work Space that implements the "emulated shared control." The final decision concerning the command to be executed (e.g. turn left or right) is always made by the robot because the BCI inherently limits the human's capacity to react quickly, regardless of the situation. However, the idea is to compensate for this by *emulating* haptic behavior [1] through a graphical display. Unlike in real haptic situations, there will be no

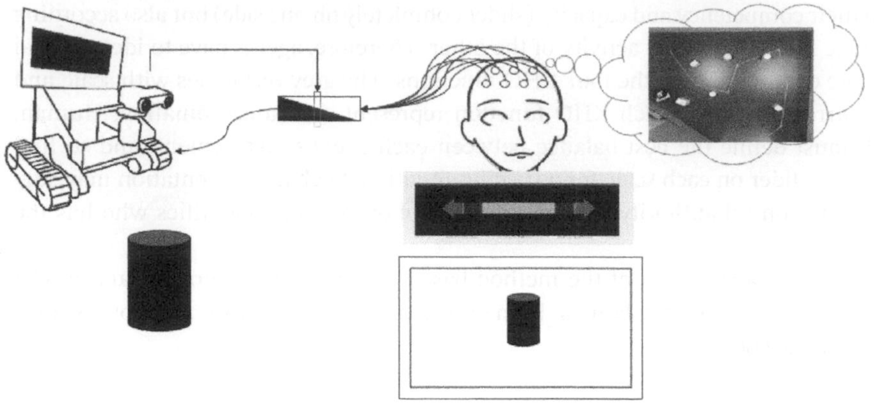

**Figure 6.2** A conceptual illustration of the brain-controlled telepresence robot setup, which indicates the different roles played by the human and the robot to implement successful shared control of the overall system.

force feedback; instead, the system modulates the difficulty – or (mental) effort required – for the human to deliver a command, according to where obstacles and potential targets are detected by the robot. The changes in difficulty are indicated to the user by adapting the visual feedback accordingly to help them understand why this is happening and thus maintain a good mental model of the system behavior.

### 6.3.1 Designing the System

The system has been designed according to the method based on the cooperative agent model briefly presented previously. For each function of the KHO and the KHC, the designers analyze the abilities of both agents. A "1" or "0" replaces each function name to indicate the functional abilities of each agent (i.e. "1" indicates the agent possesses the capability to perform that particular subfunction). The result of this process is presented in Figure 6.3. Each part of the array presents for each agent (Human and robot) their KHO (respectively dark gray and light gray rectangles) and their KHC (white rectangles).

Regarding the KHO, the Figure 6.3 indicates that only the robot is capable of gathering information in the environment, since the human is physically located in another place. In the condition with obstacle avoidance, both the human and the robot can analyze the situation and make a decision, but only the robot can *implement* the action because while it is physically in the environment, the human is not (c.f. light gray rectangle on the robot's KHO). Information analysis and decision-making can be considered as complementary functions between human and robot because they don't have the same experiences, or even the same information about the environment (the robot perceives more information than the remote human).

Concerning the KHC, Figure 6.3 underlines the fact that both the robot and the human can gather information about each other, but only in the condition with emulated haptic feedback; so in that case, both have the ability to detect and manage interference (light gray rectangle on the robot's KHC). The other difference is about the authority management; in the condition with obstacle avoidance, the control is not shared and the robot manages the modification of the trajectory alone (second rectangle on the human's KHC).

Part of the common workspace is composed of live streamed video of the environment from the robot's perspective. Here though, we focus on the other part of the workspace: the feedback of the

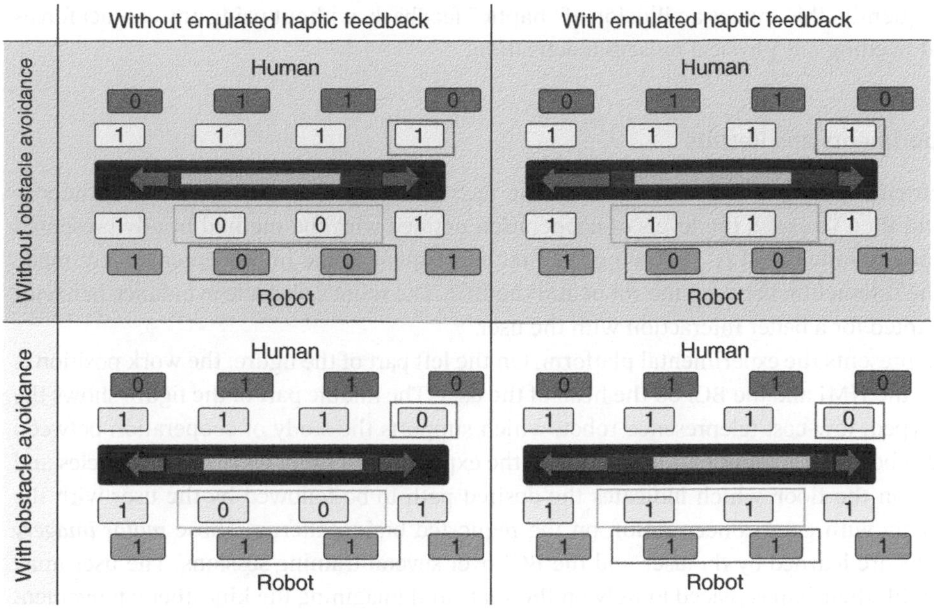


**Figure 6.3** Defined levels of cooperation. Source: © [2018] IEEE. Reprinted, with permission, from Pacaux-Lemoine et al. [11].

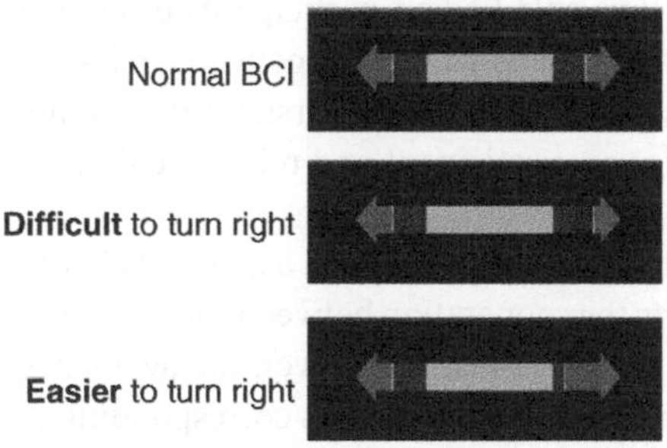


**Figure 6.4** Emulated haptic feedback. Source: © [2018] IEEE. Reprinted, with permission, from Pacaux-Lemoine et al. [11].

BCI in visual form. Figure 6.3 shows how the level of automation can be increased in terms of KHC (second rectangle on the horizontal axis) and on the KHO (second rectangle on the vertical axis).

Figure 6.3 also presents a part of the HMI proposed to simulate the emulated haptic feedback. A more detailed presentation is shown in Figure 6.4. This HMI represents the human's decoded brain signals and the possible actions, which are modulated by the robot's perception of the environment and hence represents the common workspace. The gray bar between the arrows is moved from side to side by the user with thought. Both arrows are managed by the robot: reducing or augmenting the size of the arrows according to the detection of any nearby obstacles. Then, the user is able to nudge the gray bar slightly to the right or left by imagining movement of their corresponding hand (motor imagery). A turn right or turn left command is issued to the robot only when the gray bar touches the corresponding arrow. The system is able to make it (mentally) more difficult (or easier) to turn in a particular direction by dynamically adjusting the size of the corresponding arrow; this essentially changes the BCI threshold the user has to reach for a particular class. Consequently, this creates an illusion of "haptic" feedback, without using any contact forces and without needing any physical muscular activation.

### 6.3.2 Experiments and Results

Two experiments were conducted to evaluate the technical feasibility and usability of the system [11], and then to assess the levels of cooperation defined with the method briefly presented previously and detailed in [12]. Following the first experiment, some improvements were made regarding the interaction between the robot and the BCI. The robot's obstacle avoidance behavior was also adapted for a better interaction with the user.

Figure 6.5 presents the experimental platform. On the left part of the figure, the work position is composed of the HMI and the BCI on the head of the user. The middle part of the figure shows the rapid-prototyped, low-cost telepresence robot, which supports the study of cooperation between human and robot. On the right part of the figure, the experimental room consists of obstacles and a white tape on the floor, which indicates the desired path to be followed by the user with the robot, remotely with good concentration on the requested brain patterns. Those *motor imagery* brain patterns are learned by the user and the BCI over several training sessions. The user must be relaxed, with their hands placed loosely on their lap, and imagining the kinesthetic movement of their right or the left hand to indicate the direction in which the robot should turn (cf. [12] for more details).

Four experimental conditions were tested, as presented in Figure 6.3: with/without obstacle avoidance and with/without emulated haptic feedback. Five able-bodied participants evaluated the cooperation with the robot, and we collected subjective data as well as objective metrics. To measure the global performance for every experimental condition and to understand the quality of cooperation, a coding was performed on the actions of every participant and robot. Qualitative results were obtained through questionnaires.

Overall, the emulated haptic support mode with no obstacle avoidance yielded a generally better cooperation. Indeed, the emulated haptic feedback supports the cooperation between the robot and the user by sharing the perception and the analysis of the environment. However, the avoidance of obstacles made by the robot, especially the selected direction, was not always corresponding to the intention of the user. In which case, the participants preferred to let the robot stop when an obstacle was detected, and then decide the direction to select with the BCI. More results can be found in [12], as the main objective of this chapter is to deal with methodological point of view, and in particular the benefits provided by the proposed method.

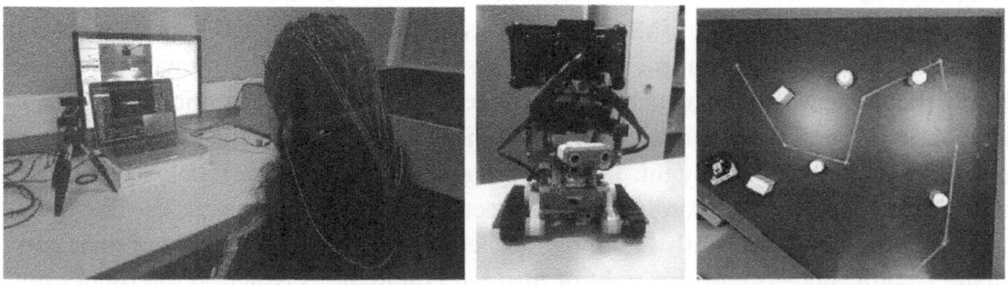

(a) (b) (c)

**Figure 6.5** Experimental platform: BCI and operator interface (a); teleoperated robot (b); top view of remote environment (c).

## 6.4 Results from the Methodological Point of View

The method based on the use of the cooperative agent model has been very useful to identify the functions that the agents (human and machine) must manage, if they are to achieve the task's goal together. The method allows designers to analyze step by step the current and future functions not only for each agent but also for the agent to be complementary in their activity. Instead of the designer needing to conduct several experiments that place a high demand on users' time, the method supports the cooperation between the designer and the future users, or experts who know about the user's activity, in order to question themselves about all the necessary points.

While most methods only focus on machine design, without taking into account humans and their cooperation with the machines, the proposed method encourages designers to fill a grid with the core questions. Figure 6.6 proposes such a grid. It is composed of four parts crossing the KHO and KHC of each agent. The interaction of each function is identified by a cell. A total of 32 cells can be studied but most of the time they can be assembled to define a more general function or task. This grid complements Figure 6.3 by providing a precise description of function instead of only "1" or "0." The objective is not to be sure to have the good answer to each cell, but using this grid, usually, forgotten aspects of the HMS are underlined.

Then, the main questions highlighted by the grid concern:

1. on the left and upper square, for the KHO functions for each agent, what are the individual and shared functions? What can the pathway be from one function to the other?
2. on the right and upper square, for human KHC, what are the abilities of human to evaluate robot's ability: (i) to control the situation with its KHO, (ii) to gather information about him/herself, to detect and manage interference with his/her own understanding of the situation, and to control cooperation?

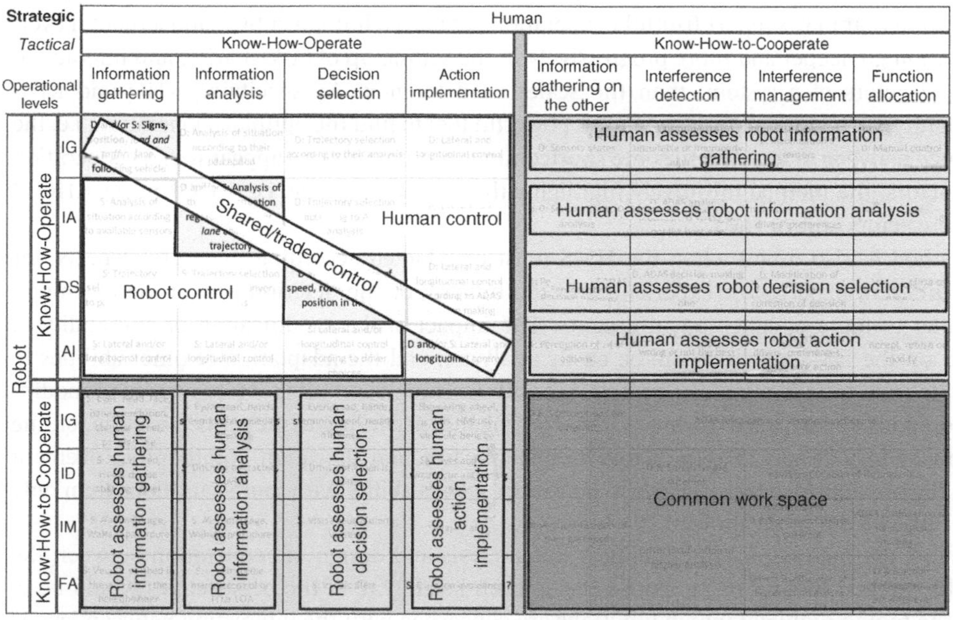


**Figure 6.6** Grid to analyze KHO and KHC functions and to define levels of cooperation.

3. on the left and lower square, for robot KHC, what are the abilities of robot to evaluate the human's ability: (i) to control the situation with his/her KHO, (ii) to gather information about itself, to detect and manage interference with its own understanding of the situation, and to control cooperation?
4. on the right and lower square, it is the HMI and how to support the communication between robot and human to present and manage all information handled by the functions of the three other scares.

This grid has been used to study human–BCI–robot cooperation that resulted in the experiments and conclusion presented in Section 6.3. However, for more details about the method, other examples can be found in other domains of application, for different human(s)–machine(s) cooperation scenarios:

- in crisis management, where humans and machines of three layers of cooperation cooperate to plan mission (strategic layer), to execute/update plan according to unexpected events (tactical layer), and to implement/modify actions like to move and to do reconnaissance in a hostile environment [3].
- in production manufacturing systems, where humans and machines of two layers of cooperation work to plan/modify production (tactical layer) and to implement/modify actions to manufacture products, to supply manufacturing robots and to unload finished products (operational layer) [10].
- in the railway domain, where one human tele-operates one train from a remote cabin, being involved into two layers (tactical and operational layers) [2].

## 6.5 Conclusion and Perspectives

The primary conclusion of this study is that the method has been useful in identifying the levels of cooperation that may support fruitful cooperation between a human, a BCI, and a robot. Levels of cooperation go deeper and more progressively in the setting up of task-sharing and interaction between all actors of a system, than the scales used for now. By specifying KHO and KHC independently, their combinations provide a powerful tool to find the optimal cooperation, i.e. the best balance between actors. When some shortcomings or interferences appear in the cooperation between actors, the method intuitively highlights the parts to improve, i.e. KHO and/or KHC of one or more actors and/or HMI.

The method is also useful when the HMS must be adapted according to several aspects, for example different expertise or experiences of the human, or the deterioration of the machine's abilities due to more complex environments. The impact of the modification of one ability of one agent on the HMS activities can be easily analyzed; and the adaptation of other abilities to compensate such modification can be updated with learning or training. Moreover, such modifications could also be detected during system control and, according to predefined criteria, online adaptation could be proposed to the actors for dynamic function allocation. Another improvement is to give the possibility to the designer to define an agent's ability with more variations than only "1" or "0" like we did in the project.

As of now, the method does not support the analysis and design of cooperation between the layers. The method focuses on functions inside each layer. One of the perspectives would be to improve the tool to highlight which functions are concerned with the interaction between layers, and how such interaction can be supported and be cooperative.

## References


1 Abbink, D.A., Mulder, M., and Boer, E.R. (2012). Haptic shared control: smoothly shifting control authority? *Cognition, Technology & Work* 14 (1): 19–28.

2 Gadmer, Q., Pacaux-Lemoine, M.-P., and Richard, P. (2021). Human-automation - railway remote control: how to define shared information and functions? *IFAC-PapersOnLine* 54 (2): 173–178. https://doi.org/10.1016/j.ifacol.2021.06.022.

3 Habib, L., Pacaux-Lemoine, M.-P., and Millot, P. (2017). Adaptation of the level of automation according to the type of cooperative partner. *2017 IEEE International Conference on Systems, Man, and Cybernetics, SMC 2017*, volume 2017-Janua, 864–869. ISBN 9781538616451.

4 Leeb, R., Tonin, L., Rohm, M. et al. (2015). Towards independence: a BCI telepresence robot for people with severe motor disabilities. *Proceedings of the IEEE* 103 (6): 969–982.

5 Pacaux, M.P., Debernard, S., Godin, A. et al. (2011). Levels of automation and human–machine cooperation: application to human–robot interaction. *IFAC Proceedings Volumes (IFAC-PapersOnline)* 18 (Part 1): 6484–6492. https://doi.org/10.3182/20110828-6-IT-1002.00312.

6 Pacaux-Lemoine, M.-P. (2020). *HUMAN–MACHINE COOPERATION: adaptability of shared functions between Humans and Machines - design and evaluation aspects*. Habilitation à diriger des recherches, Université Polytechnique Hauts-de-France, August 2020. https://hal.archives-ouvertes.fr/tel-02959402 (accessed 17 January 2023).

7 Pacaux-Lemoine, M.-P. and Flemisch, F. (2019). Layers of shared and cooperative control, assistance, and automation. *Cognition, Technology and Work* 21 (4): 579–591. https://doi.org/10.1007/s10111-018-0537-4.

8 Pacaux-Lemoine, M.-P. and Flemisch, F. (2021). Human-cyber-physical system integration (HSI) in industry 4.0: design and evaluation methods. *The 30th International Symposium on Industrial Electronics*, 6. Kyoto, Japan.

9 Pacaux-Lemoine, M.-P. and Vanderhaegen, F. (2013). Towards levels of cooperation. *2013 IEEE International Conference on Systems, Man, and Cybernetics*, 291–296. IEEE.

10 Pacaux-Lemoine, M.-P., Trentesaux, D., Rey, G.Z., and Millot, P. (2017). Designing intelligent manufacturing systems through Human–Machine Cooperation principles: a human-centered approach. *Computers and Industrial Engineering* 111: 581–595. https://doi.org/10.1016/j.cie.2017.05.014.

11 Pacaux-Lemoine, M.-P., Habib, L., and Carlson, T. (2018). Human-robot cooperation through brain–computer interaction and emulated haptic supports. *2018 IEEE International Conference on Industrial Technology (ICIT)*, 1973–1978. IEEE.

12 Pacaux-Lemoine, M.-P., Habib, L., Sciacca, N., and Carlson, T. (2020). Emulated haptic shared control for brain–computer interfaces improves human–robot cooperation. *2020 IEEE International Conference on Human-Machine Systems (ICHMS)*, 1–6. IEEE.

# 7

# Human–Machine Social Systems: Test and Validation via Military Use Cases

*Charlene K. Stokes[1], Monika Lohani[2], Arwen H. DeCostanza[3], and Elliot Loh[4]*

[1] *U.S. Army Futures Command, DEVCOM, Aberdeen Proving Ground, MD, USA*
[2] *University of Utah, Department of Psychology, Salt Lake City, UT, USA*
[3] *U.S. DEVCOM, Army Research Laboratory, Aberdeen Proving Ground, MD, USA*
[4] *Defence Research and Development Canada, National Defence / Government of Canada, Ottawa, ON, Canada*

## 7.1 Introduction

We are fully immersed in the current computing era, Industry 4.0, or digitalization, and well on our way to the next. Indeed, the circumstances thrust on society due to the COVID-19 pandemic are accelerating us toward the fifth industrial revolution or what some call Society 5.0 [55]. Anyone that looks attentively at society – the crowds standing at a bus stop; those dining in a restaurant; parents on a playground; practically any teen, preteen, or younger at nearly any point in the day or context; and nearly any person in a work context, particularly post–COVID – will notice a fundamental shift in our relationship with technology. We readily and often without conscious awareness, incorporate technology into nearly every aspect of our lives. Smartphones have opened the door to this intimate connection with technology. Semiintelligent home assistants such as Amazon's Alexa have opened the door further, and developments in AI/ML, sensing, and immersive technologies on the horizon (e.g. Metaverse) will solidify this gravitational shift in our social dynamics to Society 5.0.

Many of these new technologies are designed to learn and interact in a natural, humanized manner. As a special report in The Economist, Rise of the Robots [59] pointed out – as have many subsequent reports and studies – society is more ready than ever to integrate robots into their daily lives in large part due to the social-emotional aspects of newer designs. When technology adheres to human social expectations, people often find the interaction enjoyable, feeling empowered and competent [18]. However, with high expectations come greater risk of violating expectations [24]. Moreover, privacy and other ethical concerns are raised. As we have learned from the past, NSA scandal and more recently, the nuanced complexities of social media impact on our political system and social influence in general, and there are two parts to the technology equation: (i) the technology intended function and capability and (ii) the human use of the technology to include behavior and perceptions. There is a long history in *user interaction* or *user experience* research and design. However, the primary intent of much of that research is to increase use of a system, which can be strong enough to trigger addiction tendencies. There is relative scarce research on preparing the user by understanding, informing, or managing user behavior and expectations. These behaviors and expectations are often unconscious, socioemotional, context-driven, and nested, in other words, incredibly complex. If you build it, they will come, or in this case, they will use it… but should they? What do users need to know before they start relying on and trusting

*Handbook of Human-Machine Systems*, First Edition. Edited by Giancarlo Fortino, David Kaber, Andreas Nürnberger, and David Mendonça.

autonomous systems? To the extent possible, have the secondary and tertiary consequences or emergent dynamics considered, let alone empirically examined, documented, and clearly communicated to the user population?

## 7.2 Background Summary: From Tools to Teammates

There is fervent commercial and military interest in developing autonomous agent systems, not to replace humans, but to "extend and complement human capability in a number of ways" ([13], p. 1). Faced with expanding challenges of "big data" and the manpower demands of current and future autonomous systems, human capability will need to be supplemented or augmented in novel ways to confront the changing landscape of social interaction, warfare, and national security. In response to these trends, human–machine interfaces will be far more closely coupled [44]. Robotic platforms have long been incorporated as assistive tools in hostile environments such as search-and-rescue operations, casualty extraction, explosive detection and disposals, and reconnaissance, and surveillance [9, 42]. However, "future robotic systems are expected to transition from tools to teammates, characterized by increasingly autonomous, intelligent robots interacting with humans in a more naturalistic manner, approaching a relationship more akin to human–human teamwork" ([42], p. 60). The trend from tools to teammates operating in ever more complex environments applies not only to robotic systems but also to autonomous agent systems in general [12, 29].

Given the exponential rise in complexity and nuance with this shift toward autonomous agent systems, we can no longer rely on isolated, reductionist approaches for research in this area, particularly for the human side of the equation. Fully understanding the complexity of human–machine systems (HMS) dictates the need for greater examination of unconscious, socio-affective variables expressed by human users in situ. As with the development of assessment and selection [16], military use cases afford large-scale, in situ experimental environments with real users. In partnership with academia and commercial partners, collaboration on military use cases, such as Project Convergence [1], can generate the foundational empirical evidence underlying the shared problem of complexity in human–machine systems.

### 7.2.1 Two Sides of the Equation

On the technology side, improvements in computing power and algorithm sophistication such as AI/ML enable advanced human–agent teaming [9]. On the human side, there is growing recognition of and evidence for the implicit and explicit socio-affective connections we form with technology [9, 12, 25, 38–40, 52]. Although the increasing sophistication of technology design induces ever greater social responses and connections, the social dynamics of the human–machine system remain largely neglected in design, and rarely if ever make it into training or informed-user awareness considerations. As noted in a Defense Science Board Report: "For the operator, autonomy is experienced as human-machine collaboration, which is often overlooked during design" ([13], p. 21). To realize the full potential of future human–machine systems, science must move beyond Kipling's 1889 opening "Oh, East is East and West is West, and never the twain shall meet" [28] to the heart of his poem: East and West are one.

The human-centered design approach [53] and adherents of it such as human-centered automation [2] and human-automation cooperation [56], explicitly place the human at center stage in the design process. However, the human on this stage is often construed as a rational, information-processing machine, void of emotion, or unconscious bias. For example, Skjerve and Skraaning assert that the "distinctly social concept of cooperation should be transferred into the domain of human-automation transactions" ([56], p. 653). They also make an important distinction between a system's objective design characteristics and a user's subjective perception of those characteristics, with the latter being paramount in human–automation cooperation settings. Although this is certainly a step in the right direction, and it was reported that several useful findings for system design and the self-report survey used in the study were developed to focus on traditional cognitive aspects and excluded affective aspects of cooperation. We assert that what makes cooperation, teaming, partnership, relationships, and so forth, "distinctly social" is the affective component. If we are to truly understand human–agent teaming, more scientists and designers need to start acknowledging, investigating, and accounting for the nonrational, implicit, and socio-affective components that are integral and inseparable parts of human thinking and decision-making [43].

### 7.2.2 Moving Beyond the Cognitive Revolution

Decades of avoidance of the complex topic of affect in science is understandable given the firestorm set by the 1960s cognitive revolution, which spawned the cognitive sciences. In reaction to behaviorism and steadfast with philosophical tradition, the cognitive revolution's guiding metaphor was "the mind is like a computer" and cognitive scientists were focused on the software [10, 34]. Importantly, this computer metaphor led to a robust science of our inner life, neglected by behaviorism, and it led to the birth of artificial intelligence (AI). But as Lehrer [34] points out: "the computer metaphor was misleading, at least in one crucial respect. Computers don't have feelings." Feelings didn't fit into the preferred language of thought. As our emotions weren't reducible to bits of information or logical structures, cognitive psychologists diminished their importance.

This is not to say that significant research on emotion was not being produced at this time. Indeed, seminal theories of emotion and affective science are evident throughout the decades [19, 32, 33, 47, 54]. Theory and evidence clearly indicated that emotions were not a disorganized interruption of cognition that should be minimized and controlled; rather, they are the evolutionary advantage of higher organisms that fuels adaptability [14, 33, 54]. While lower organisms interpret and respond to their environment through rigid fixed action patterns, emotions, as part of the phylogenic expansion of the cerebral cortex, serve to decouple the rigid stimulus–response and allow flexibility in event interpretation and response choice [14]. Research has linked emotion and cognition, operationalized as judgment and decision-making, through the appraisal process where appraisals are direct, immediate, and intuitive evaluations of the environment that result in action tendencies [14]. Emotions play an integral role: appraisals are triggered to account for qualitative distinctions in emotions, and the resulting action tendencies are experienced as emotions.

The evolutionary adaptation of emotion may have arisen in line with the complex cooperation dynamics of social animals. Evidence of the biological aspects of empathy and emotion can be seen in primate studies. Frans de Waal [11] asserts that empathy and emotions are strong biological components that drive social dynamics, found that capuchin monkeys regularly display empathy and intuitively understand reciprocity. The monkeys would delay self-reward until the watching "friend" monkey also received a reward. The biological foundation of emotion provides evidence for a powerful innate and unconscious component underlying human decision-making. Emotion or affect is not a vestigial component on its way out the evolutionary door; it is what enables adaptable responses and decisions, particularly in social settings. In other words, we are not – and for good reason – computers operating on algorithms, explicit reason, and rational logic. And of course, human evidence of this departure from rationality in judgment and decision-making can be seen in the field of behavioral economics and a wealth of other areas [26].

#### 7.2.2.1 A Rediscovery of the Unconscious

Although the intertwined nature of affect and cognition has long been studied and recognized in commonsense and philosophy [19], the pure cognitive sciences continued to neglect it and compartmentalize emotion and cognition. Also as cognitive science gave birth to heavy hitters such as AI and systems control theory, much of the HCI and human-robot interaction fields have also neglected the role of affect. Ironically, although AI may not have developed without the exclusion of emotions in the computer metaphor, continued advances in AI and agent systems may not achieve their envisioned potential as teammates without accounting for the socio-affective aspects of humans. As quoted in [34], Marvin Minsky, a pioneer of AI, stated: "Because we subscribed to this false ideal of rational, logical thought, we diminished the importance of everything else. Seeing our emotions as distinct from thinking was really quite disastrous."

***Neuroscience to the Rescue*** As the influence of emotion and many socio-affective variables are largely unconscious, it is difficult to examine their effects. However, neuroscience advances and multimodal assessment techniques are leading to a rediscovery of the unconscious; functional neural imaging and real-time physiological assessment can monitor emotions as they unfold. Discoveries in these areas are giving the domain of socio-affective research its due and bringing it to center stage. Lerner et al. [36] published an excellent review on emotion and decision- making over the last three decades. Lerner et al. suggest the renewed vibrancy in the domain may lead to a much-needed paradigm shift in decision theories. Phelps et al. [49] provide a complementary review specific to the neuroscience of emotion and decision-making. As becomes evident in such reviews, neuroscience is confirming much of what previous emotion researchers have found. However, armed with the power of neural imaging technologies, the objectively gathered findings have underscored the thinking–feeling connection and are generating a new research enthusiasm for emotions and the unconscious [10].

Challenging the assumption that emotion interferes with rational thought and optimal decision-making, Damasio [10] tested patients with brain injuries that prevented them from perceiving their own feelings. He found repeated examples of ineffective decision-making such as investments leading to bankruptcy. Poignantly, most were unable to function effectively in life, spending hours deliberating over minor details such as where to eat lunch. Goel and Dolan's [23] fMRI results suggest that which emotional states influence which brain regions are recruited during decision-making. Although emotions are potent, pervasive, and importantly, predictable aspects of decision-making, they carry both beneficial and harmful effects; serving as a beneficial guide or negative bias [36].

**A Cautionary Tale of Neuroscience** Although neuroscience provides new tools and evidence for socio-affective variables, incorrectly used, it may inadvertently continue to fuel a reductionist fire. As Berrett [2] points out, the dominant conceptual framework for the study of emotion remains pre-Darwinian. In this typological view, emotions are construed as discrete mental types (e.g. anger, joy) with corresponding physical essences discoverable in reduced "patterns of peripheral nervous system response, facial muscle movements, and the structure or function of the mammalian brain" (p. 379). This reductionist approach brings us right back to a compartmentalized view of emotion, cognition, or perception domains.

Alternatively, Berrett [2] stresses the importance of a psychological construction framework for emotion, where emotions arise from a core system that is domain-general. Similar to ecological psychology's emphasis on behavior in situ [17, 22], emotions and socio-affective variables are situated affective states that vary in degree based on maximal utility in particular contexts. Following population-based thinking of the post-Darwinian type, there is more within-species variation than between, and that variation is meaningfully tied to variations in the environment. Emotions "reflect the structure of recurring situations that people find important and meaningful within our own cultural [and individual] context" ([2], p. 381).

Multimodal information from the environment and previous experience is recruited to produce a conceptual state or instance of emotion. As such, we strongly advocate that future research in socio-affective variables, emotion being one, move away from the reductionist approach and utilize a similar multimodal assessment technique and novel in situ designs to the greatest extent possible.

## 7.3 Future Research Directions

Obviously, in situ designs and unconscious, socio-affective variables are notoriously difficult to investigate given the added complexity. However, there are a diverse range of theories and approaches that can be leveraged. The following outlines several considerations that afford investigation of the more intimate, nuanced, and complex dynamics of human–machine teaming. Addressing both sides of the coin, various insights and recommendations are discussed for the agent system and for the human, as well as their interaction context in situ.

### 7.3.1 Machine: Functional Designs

The growing field of social robotics may have keen insights for the envisioned teammate role of autonomous systems. The ability to recognize, understand, and respond in a sociocultural and emotionally intelligent manner is recognized as a central concern for socially interactive robots [18, 35, 58]. Fong et al. [18] distinguish between two classes of socially interactive robots: biologically inspired vs. functionally designed. As with the biological mimicry found in anthropomorphic and zoomorphic external designs, biologically inspired social robots internally mimic the social intelligence of living creatures, to the extent possible. This approach poses some of the hardest problems in robotics and computational intelligence [57], as such developing an artificial theory of mind – although the AI community has made tremendous advances. The goal of a functionally designed social robot is to appear socially intelligent, regardless of the internal design basis in science or nature. We do not need to mimic the human mind, as it may be sufficient to incorporate designs that cue the basic socio-affective mechanisms and norms of human interaction. Similarly, we do not need to mimic the human or animal form to evoke socio-affective behavior.

Although true AI may be necessary in some instances, we assert that the functional design approach currently offers the greatest (cost-effective and untapped) potential for investigating and designing machines as teammates. Evidence for the pervasive readiness with which humans seek out and apply anthropomorphic assumptions and social norms to technology can be seen in the legacy of Clifford Nass' research and the theory of computers as social actors [40, 52]. Perceptions of system intelligence, autonomy, and capabilities are multifaceted and carry a strong implicit component [18].

Similar to the biological vs. functional distinction that Fong et al. [18] noted for embodied robots, Ni et al. [41] provided evidence indicating that reinforcement learning (RL) algorithms or rule-based methods of agent systems do not require human emulation. It was asserted that RL algorithms that reference an explicit learned human model for inferring human intent are often too rigid and fail in many real-world scenarios. As with the reductionist approaches of the cognitive revolution, the human model RL algorithms assume rational or logical human decision-making, which is not always the case. A novel human-model-free adaptive agent architecture was developed and proposed. The proposed model is not based on human data and has minimal assumptions of human behavior. Rather, the model is based on an adaptation strategy capable of responding to novel scenarios, which are far more characteristic of the complexities of human behavior, particularly in socio-affective laden situations.

## 7.3.2 Human: Ground Truth

The benefits of an agent system adaptively responding to novel scenarios require ground truth input from the target interaction source – the human teammate. As with human–human interaction, a successful teammate must be able to perceive various signals – explicit behavior and communication, implicit attitudes and intentions, fatigue, and so on – and do their best to respond accordingly based on their knowledge and past experience. Fortunately, advances in neuroscience, psychophysiology, sensor technologies, and other cutting-edge innovations provide a rich source of incoming signals to enhance the agent teammate's perceptual–response system.

### 7.3.2.1 Physiological Computing

The nascent capabilities of real-time physiological assessment and neuroscience is being employed in game-changing HMS advances such as physiological computing [15, 20, 21]. Physiological computing systems are being designed such that real-time assessment of users' physiological data are being captured to infer and communicate user psychological states to an adaptive system, such as was proposed by Ni et al. [41]. This approach opens the bandwidth of HMS enabling an implicit sense and perception channel of communication [15], affording bidirectional and individualized inferences on a spontaneous and unconscious level. Many HMS researchers [27, 48, 50] have recognized the value of physiological computing to address the socio-affective experiences of users. With the tremendous advances in sensor technologies for these domains, there are a wealth of multimodal factors that can now be empirically examined. An exhaustive review of these factors is beyond the scope of this chapter. Rather, the intent of this chapter is to highlight the interaction dynamics these advances enable for HMS understanding, assessment, development, and enhancement.

Several useful frameworks have been proposed to conceptualize the complex, bidirectional dynamics of HMS. For example, Galster and Johnson [20] have developed the sense-assess-augment framework. Developed to enhance mission effectiveness in military contexts, their taxonomy focuses primarily on cognitive and functional state sensing and assessment in order to augment human task performance. However, for any task-oriented augmentation to be successful, limiting factors such as poor acceptance, reliance, and trust – socio-affective factors, in other words – must be addressed. Parasuraman and Galster [44] note two primary concerns for augmentation: when to provide the augmentation and how to provide it. We argue that understanding the user's socio-affective context may assist in knowing when to provide augmentation, and imbuing a degree of socio-affective design in an agent system and interactive training to prepare for such may go a surprisingly long way to address how augmentation should be provided or communicated to the user.

Similar to the sense-assess-augment framework, Pope et al. [51], Fairclough [15] and many others have articulated and provided ample empirical evidence for the biocybernetic control system or loop. The focus of the biocybernetic loop "is to derive real-time adaptations to cognitions, motivations and emotions that appear both timely and intuitive from the users' perspective" ([15], p. 135). Given the relatively recent development of these models, much of the research is currently focused on the sensing or signal components. However, assessing and validating the neurocognitive or psychophysiological inference are of paramount concern [15]; augmentation is irrelevant if not detrimental if the inference it is based on is inaccurate.

Given the complexity of psychophysiological and neurocognitive inference, a multimodal approach that combines numerous assessments (e.g. physiology, neurocognitive, self-report, objective, or behavioral measures) will be required to establish a valid, real-time index of user state and intent [15]. Assuming that valid inferences can be derived from the multimodal signals available, Marathe et al. [37] proposed the Privileged Sensing Framework as a novel control systems framework to dynamically balance or "privilege" information based on the characteristics of the individual agent – human or machine – the task context, and the performance goals. The system develops a unique relationship with each user based on current and prior interactions.

### 7.3.3 Context: Tying It All Together

With both sides of the human–machine equation noted above, the overriding concern remains the environment or context: the task, the organizational demands and culture, the social context, and the physical environment. As Chen asserts: "There is no requirement for intellectual equality between human and artificial agents; the important issue is to understand what factors are necessary for partnership problem solving in truly complex real-world environments." ([9], p. 450). She argues that development of a true partnership is the missing element in current research. Thought leaders in the areas of ecological psychology, control systems, cognitive systems engineering, and the like [17] provide rich sources for a holistic systems design thinking approach that specifically account for emergent context dynamics and can be directly applied to HMS. When combined with these broader systems perspectives, the organizational science and teams literature [30] afford a contextualized view of key socio-affective, partnership variables grounded specifically in team dynamics. Figure 7.1 is an amalgamation of seminal theories and approaches tied together in a conceptual framework applied to HMS. Adhering to an ecological systems' perspective, all individual activity (human or machine; unconscious or overt) is grounded in and influenced by environmental dynamics and emergent team interactive dynamics in an ongoing cycle of influence. Although reducing the complexity of this ecological system for isolated study of variables has its uses, the emergent dynamics can only be realized in situ with natural variables present.

#### 7.3.3.1 Training and Team Models

If human–machine systems of the future are intended to be teammates as opposed to tools, a new approach to training with these systems must be considered. It will no longer be sufficient to simply show a user how the system works; the partnership must be fostered and managed from the start. In a review and comparison of human–machine teaming with human–animal teaming, Billings et al.'s [3] primary conclusion was that several training methods in human–animal teams should extend to human–machine teams, including training to foster shared mental models.

Shared mental models also play a preeminent role in human teams [7]. Hancock et al. suggest that training methods should be employed in human–machine systems to "adequately prepare an individual for the coming interaction" ([25], p. 525). The "partners" must be introduced and get

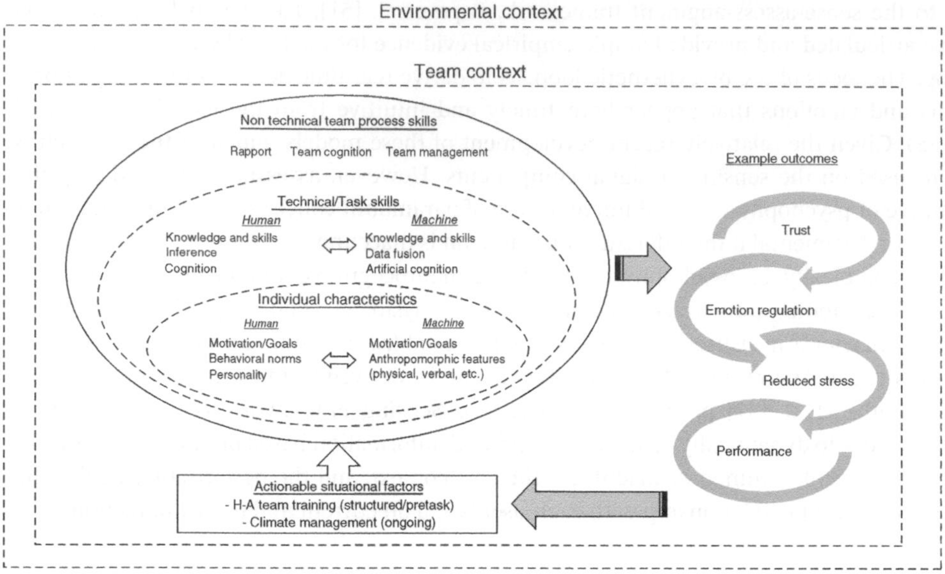


**Figure 7.1** Human–Machine Social Systems (HMSS) Framework. Example factors in a human–machine team context are depicted.

acquainted, possibly through team building exercises. Team building is one of the most effective group development interventions in organizations and sports [6, 7]. There is a strong socio-affective component to team building. Targeted social and emotional learning (SEL) programs have a rich history in the education domain [31]. Findings have shown SEL to improve academic performance, social interactions, classroom behavior, mental and physical health, and lifelong effectiveness [4]. Thus, beyond the task-focused or hard skill aspects, team-oriented training should include socio-affective soft skills and social normative factors such as fostering a team culture, establishing norms of communication, development of respect and transparency, and development of shared mental models for the task *and* the socio-affective partnership context [3, 4, 7, 9, 25].

Human models of teamwork and team effectiveness are complex, dynamic, multidimensional, and still expanding (see [46] for an applicable model). In other words, the transition of autonomous agents from tools to teammates will not be an easy task. Teamwork models, such as the model of collaborative creativity [46], highlight numerous socio-affective components manifesting explicitly or implicitly across individual, team, and context levels. Drawing from team models, empirical evidence exists for potential mirroring effects between human–human and human–machine teams. For example, conflict is a major player in human team models, and socio-affective elements of team building or soft skills development is the primary mitigation strategy [7, 46]. Similarly, evidence shows that the occurrence of conflict or disagreement between humans and automation is a robust predictor of disruption or failure in the human–machine system [8, 45]. However, to our knowledge, there is limited to no research investigating the benefits of socio-affective team building for mitigating or resolving conflict. Although human–human team and training models offer a good starting point to explore novel socio-affective and emergent dynamics (explicit or implicit) in HMS, direct analogy cannot be assumed and empirical research is needed to examine if, when, and how such models apply in HMS contexts. Of the empirical evidence for socio-affective factors that do exist in HMS research, rarely are the factors examined in the full context of a systems perspective or full emergent team processes model. Rather, the investigation is often focused on single, isolated factors (e.g. conflict, agent humanization) without the consideration of context or emergent dynamics over time that team training models and approaches afford.

**Multiplicative Benefits** Extending human team and training models to HMS contexts can provide multiplicative benefits. Beyond the potential translation of benefits on the human side, socio-affective team building and training programs provide increased opportunities for an intelligent system to learn and adapt to its user, and for customization by the user. Leveraging such social learning mechanisms, common to developmental psychology and training research, offers a more efficient and possibly a necessary way to build adaptable machines to establish true partnerships. As the machine partner acquires new knowledge (e.g. ML training data) of its human teammate autonomously, it "become[s] increasingly more complex and capable without requiring additional effort from human designers" ([5], p. 481). This iterative design strategy often improves human–machine system effectiveness [18]. It can be surmised, but remains to be tested, that the increased effectiveness is in part attributable to increased feelings (primarily implicit) of acceptance, trust, cohesion, transparency, and reduced feelings of conflict, competition, rejection, and the socio-affective list goes on.

## 7.4 Conclusion

As evidenced throughout this paper, socio-affective factors are neither random nor epiphenomenal, and they hold vast untapped potential for HMS. To fully understand and leverage their benefits for HMS, they must be examined in situ where the complex, emergent dynamics they are derived from are allowed to unfold. Indeed, understanding the impact of socio-affective factors from a systems level perspective and sufficiently informing, preparing/training human users/partners will not only be critical for the maximal effectiveness of future human–machine systems, but for the future well-being of our ever-increasing digital society.

## References


1 Army Futures Command (2020). Project convergence. http://www.armyfuturescommand.com/convergence (accessed 15 November 2021).

2 Berrett, L.F. (2013). Psychological construction: the Darwinian approach to the science of emotion. *Emotion Review* 5 (4): 379–389.

3 Billings, C.E. (1991). *Human-Centered Aircraft Automation: A Concept and Guidelines*, NASA Technical Memorandum 103885. Moffett Field, CA: NASA Ames Research Center.

4 Brackett, M.A., Patti, J., Stern, R. et al. (2009). A sustainable, skill-based approach to building emotionally literate schools. In: *Handbook for Developing Emotional and Social Intelligence: Best Practices, Case Studies, and Strategies* (ed. M. Hughes, H.L. Thompson, and J.B. Terrell), 329–358. New York: Pfeiffer.

5 Breazeal, C. and Scassellati, B. (2002). Robots that imitate humans. *Trends in Cognitive Sciences* 6 (11): 481–487.

6 Bruner, M.W., Eys, M.A., Beauchamp, M., and Côté, J. (2013). Examining the origins of team building in sport: a citation network and genealogical approach. *Group Dynamics: Theory, Research, and Practice* 17 (1): 30–42.

7 Cannon-Bowers, J.A., Salas, E., Tannenbaum, S.I., and Mathieu, J.E. (1995). Toward theoretically-based principles of training effectiveness: a model and initial empirical investigation. *Military Psychology* 7: 141–164.

8 Causse, M., Dehais, F., Péran, P. et al. (2013). The effects of emotion on pilot decision-making: a neuroergonomic approach to aviation safety. *Transportation Research Part C: Emerging Technologies* 33: 272–281.

9 Chen, J.Y.C. and Barnes, M.J. (2013). Human-Agent Teaming for Multi-Robot Control: A Literature Review. Army Research Laboratory. *Technical Report ARL-TR-6328*.

10 Damasio, A. (1994). *Descartes' Error: Emotion, Reason, and the Human Brain*. New York: Grosset/Putnam.

11 de Waal, F.B.M. (2000). Attitudinal reciprocity in food sharing among brown capuchins. *Animal Behavior* 60: 253–261.

12 DeCostanza, A.H., Marathe, A.R., Bohannon, A. et al. (2018). Enhancing Human-Agent Teaming with Individualized, Adaptive Technologies: A Discussion of Critical Scientific Questions. US Army Research Laboratory. Interactive Paper, *ARL-TR-8359*. https://doi.org/10.13140/RG.2.2.12666.39364.

13 Defense Science Board (July, 2012). *The Role of Autonomy in DoD Systems*. Washington DC: Office of the Under Secretary of Defense for Acquisition, Technology and Logistics.

14 Ellsworth, P.C. and Scherer, K.R. (2003). Appraisal processes in emotion. In: *Handbook of Affective Sciences* (ed. R.J. Davidson, K.R. Scherer, and H.H. Goldsmith), 572, 2003–595. Oxford: Oxford University Press.

15 Fairclough, S.H. (2009). Fundamentals of physiological computing. *Interacting with Computers* 21 (1–2): 133–145. https://doi.org/10.1016/j.intcom.2008.10.011.

16 Faunce, J. (2016). A history of assessment and selection. *Special Warfare; Fort Bragg* 29 (2): 12–18.

17 Flach, J.M., Hancock, P.A., Caird, J., and Vicente, K.J. (ed.) (1995). *Global Perspectives on the Ecology of Human–Machine Systems*, vol. 1. Lawrence Erlbaum Associates, Inc.

18 Fong, T., Nourbakhsh, I., and Dautenhahn, K. (2002). A Survey of socially Interactive Robots: Concepts, Design, and Applications. Carnegie Mellon University. *Technical Report CMU-RI-TR-02-29*.

19 Forgas, J.P. (1995). Mood and judgement: the affect infusion model (AIM). *Psychological Bulletin* 117 (1): 39–66.

20 Galster, S.M. and Johnson, E.M. (2013). *Sense-Assess-Augment: A Taxonomy for Human Effectiveness. Technical Report*. Wright-Patterson Air Force Base, OH: United States Air Force Research Laboratory.

21 Garcia, J.O., Brooks, J., Kerick, S. et al. (2017). Estimating direction in brain-behavior interactions: proactive and reactive brain states in driving. *NeuroImage* 150: 239–249.

22 Gibson, J.J. (1966). *The Senses Considered as Perceptual Systems*. Boston: Hughton Mifflin.

23 Goel, V. and Dolan, R. (2003). Reciprocal neural response within lateral and ventral medial prefrontal cortex during hot and cold reasoning. *NeuroImage* 20 (4): 2314–2321.

24 Groom, V. and Nass, C. (2007). Can robots be teammates? Benchmarks in human–robot teams. *Interaction Studies* 8 (3): 483–500.

25 Hancock, P.A., Billings, D.R., Schaefer, K.E. et al. (2011). A meta-analysis of factors affecting trust in human-robot interaction. *Human Factors: The Journal of the Human Factors and Ergonomics Society* 53: 517.

26 Kahneman, D., Slovic, P., and Tversky, A. (1982). *Judgment under Uncertainty: Heuristics and Biases*. Cambridge: Cambridge University Press.

**27** Keltner, D. and Lerner, J.S. (2010). Emotion. In: *The Handbook of Social Psychology* (ed. D.T. Gilbert, S.T. Fiske, and G. Lindzey), 317–352. New York: Wiley.

**28** Kipling, R. (1889). The Ballad of East and West. Retrieved 1 September 2014 from Wikipedia. http://en.wikipedia.org/wiki/The_Ballad_of_East_and_West.

**29** Klein, G., Woods, D.D., Bradshaw, J.M. et al. (2004). Ten challenges for making automation a "team player" in joint human-agent activity. *IEEE Intelligent Systems* 19 (6): 91–95.

**30** Kozlowski, S.W.J. and Ilgen, D.R. (2006). Enhancing the effectiveness of work groups and teams. *Psychological Science in the Public Interest* 7 (3): https://doi.org/10.1111/j.1529-1006.2006.00030.x.

**31** Kress, J.S. and Elias, M.J. (2006). School-based social and emotional learning programs. In: *Handbook of Child Psychology*, 6e, vol. 4 (ed. A. Renninger and I.E. Sigel), 592–618. Hoboken, NJ: Wiley.

**32** Lazarus, R.S. (1991). Progress on a cognitive-motivational-relational theory of emotion. *American Psychologist* 46: 819–834.

**33** Leeper, R.W. (1948). A motivational theory of emotion to replace "emotion as disorganized response". *Psychological Review* 5: 5–12.

**34** Lehrer, J. (2007). Hearts and minds. The Boston globe, 29 April 2007. Retrieved 1 September 2014, from http://Boston.com news. http://www.boston.com/news/globe/ideas/articles/2007/04/29/hearts__minds (accessed01 September 2014).

**35** Leite, I., Castellano, G., Pereira, A. et al. (2014). Empathic robots for long-term interaction: evaluating social presence, engagement and perceived support in children. *International Journal of Social Robotics* 6 (3): 329–341.

**36** Lerner, J.S., Valdesolo, P., and Kassam, K. (2014). Emotion and decision making. *Annual Review of Psychology* 66 (33): 1–33.

**37** Marathe, A., Metcalfe, J., Lance, B.J., and McDowell, K. (2017). The privileged sensing framework: a principled approach to improved human-autonomy integration. *Theoretical Issues in Ergonomics Science* 19 (3): 283–320.

**38** Merritt, S.M. (2011). Affective processes in human–automation interactions. *Human Factors* 53 (4): 356–370.

**39** Merritt, S.M., Huber, K., LaChapell-Unnerstall, J., and Lee, D. (2014). *Continuous Calibration of Trust in Automated Systems.* Air Force Research Laboratory: Technical Report.

**40** Nass, C. and Moon, Y. (2000). Machines and mindlessness: social responses to computers. *Journal of Social Issues* 56 (1): 81–103.

**41** Ni, T., Li, H., Agrawal, S. et al. (2021). Adaptive agent architecture for real-time human-agent teaming. arXiv:2103.04439 [cs.RO].

**42** Ososky, S., Schuster, D. Phillips, E., and Jentsch, F. (2013). Building appropriate trust in human-robot teams. *Trust and Autonomous Systems: Papers from the 2013 AAAI Spring Symposium*, Bellevue, Washington, USA (14–18 July 2013). Association for the Advancement of Artificial Intelligence. www.aaai.org.

**43** Pak, R., Fink, N., Price, M. et al. (2012). Decision support aids with anthropomorphic characteristics influence trust and performance in younger and older adults. *Ergonomics* 2012: 1–14.

**44** Parasuraman, R. and Galster, S. (2013). Sensing, assessing, and augmenting threat detection: behavioral, neuroimaging, and brain stimulation evidence for the critical role of attention. *Frontiers in Human Neuroscience* 7: 273. https://doi.org/10.3389/fnhum.2013.00273.

**45** Parasuraman, R. and Miller, C.A. (2004). Trust and etiquette in high-criticality automated systems. *The Communications of the ACM* 47: 51–55.

**46** Paulus, P.B., Dzindolet, M.T., and Kohn, N. (2011). Collaborative creativity-group creativity and team innovation. In: *Handbook of Organizational Creativity* (ed. M.D. Mumford), 327–357. New York: Elsevier.

**47** Petty, R.E. and Cacioppo, J.T. (1986). *Communication and Persuasion: Central and Peripheral Routes to Attitude Change*. New York: Springer-Verlag.

**48** Pfister, H.R., Wollstädter, S., and Peter, C. (2011). Affective responses to system messages in human–computer-interaction: effects of modality and message type. *Interacting with Computers* 23: 372–383.

**49** Phelps, E.A., Lempert, K.M., and Sokol-Hessner, P. (2014). Emotion and decision making: multiple modulatory neural circuits. *Annual Review of Neuroscience* 37: 263–288.

**50** Picard, R.W. (1997). *Affective Computing*. Cambridge, MA: The MIT Press.

**51** Pope, A.T., Bogart, E.H., and Bartolome, D.S. (1995). Biocybernetic system evaluates indices of operator engagement in automated task. *Biological Psychology* 40: 187–195.

**52** Reeves, B. and Nass, C. (1996). *The Media Equation: How People Treat Computers, Television, and New Media like Real People and Places*. New York: Cambridge University Press.

**53** Rouse, W.B. (1991). *Design for Success: A Human-Centered Approach to Designing Successful Products and Systems*. US: Wiley.

**54** Salovey, P. and Mayer, J.D. (1990). Emotional intelligence. *Imagination, Cognition and Personality* 9: 185–211.

**55** Sarfraz, Z., Sarfraz, A., Iftikar, H.M., and Akhund, R. (2021). Is COVID-19 pushing us to the fifth industrial revolution (society 5.0)? Pak. *Journal of Medical Sciences* 37 (2): 591–594. https://doi.org/10.12669/pjms.37.2.3387.

**56** Skjerve, A.B.M. and Skraaning, G. Jr., (2004). The quality of human-automation cooperation in human-system interface for nuclear power plants. *International Journal of Human Computer Studies* 61: 649–677.

**57** Steinberg, M. (2012). Moving from supervisory control of autonomous systems to human-machine teaming. *Keynote Presentation at the 7th ACM/IEEE International Conference on Human-Robot Interaction: 4th Annual Human-Agent-Robot Teamwork Workshop*. Boston, USA (March 5–8). Association for Computing Machinery, New York, NY, United States.

**58** Tapus, A., Matarić, M., and Scassellati, B. (2007). The grand challenges in socially assistive robotics. *IEEE Robotics and Automation Magazine: Special Issue on Grand Challenges in Robotics*.

**59** The Economist (2014). Retrieved 1 September 2014. From The Economist. http://www.economist.com/news/special-report/21599522-robots-offer-unique-insight-what-people-want-technology-makes-their (accessed 01 September 2014).

# 8

# The Role of Multimodal Data for Modeling Communication in Artificial Social Agents

*Stephanie Gross and Brigitte Krenn*

*Austrian Research Institute for Artificial Intelligence, Vienna, Austria*

## 8.1 Introduction

To successfully be employed in different application areas and undertake various tasks in coordination with their fellow humans, task-based interaction capabilities need to be modeled on the robots, so that a human may instruct a robot to do something or the human and the robot may collaborate on a certain task. Instructions need to be interpreted and actions coordinated, and accordingly, the robot needs to be equipped with adequate nonverbal and/or verbal communicative behavior. First, robots need to identify communicative cues generated by the human via different channels and merge this information. Second, robots (from humanoid to industrial) need to generate multimodal communicative behavior understandable for humans. If we want robots to communicate with us as naturally as possible, it is important to investigate how humans communicate with each other and which information they transmit via which modalities (language, gesture, eye gaze, etc.), see [3]. A common approach to do this is to collect and analyze data from relevant human–human interaction (HHI) scenarios. In Section 8.4.1, we present an example of such a data collection. The data illustrate which human communicative signals a robot should be able to identify and interpret in task-oriented situations. In Section 8.4.2, we focus on how humans interpret multimodal signals from their robotic interaction/ collaboration partner. An important aspect in human–robot interaction (HRI) is that humans tend to anthropomorphize nonhuman agents, i.e. they imbue the real or imagined behavior of nonhuman agents with human-like characteristics, motivations, intentions, or emotions [5]. Therefore, as soon as humans interact with a robot, robot actions are interpreted in a social way no matter whether they were designed for communication purposes or not. In this section, we present and discuss datasets which were designed to investigate in how far certain communicative signals of the robot were interpreted by humans as intended by us as robot behavior designers. The technical part of the chapter (Section 8.4) is preceded by a background section and related work. In Section 8.2, the range of scientific disciplines involved in modeling communication in artificial social agents is briefly listed and core concepts relevant to the chapter are defined. In Section 8.3, related work is presented, beginning with HHI data, followed by HRI. We will conclude the presentation of our work in Section 8.5 and identify future research challenges in Section 8.6.

*Handbook of Human-Machine Systems*, First Edition. Edited by Giancarlo Fortino, David Kaber, Andreas Nürnberger, and David Mendonça.

## 8.2 Background

### 8.2.1 Context

There are several disciplines involved in modeling aspects of communication in artificial social agents. Human communication is investigated, for example by linguists (e.g. the structuring of utterances and use of words), psychologists (e.g. the focus of attention during communication), and cognitive scientists (e.g. the relationship between words and the actual entity in the real word). How this knowledge can be best used to develop computational models, is then investigated by computer linguists (e.g. by developing language models) and computer scientists (e.g. the fusion of auditory and visual input, the development of machine learning models). Electrical engineers are for example concerned with the generation of robot movements and scientists working in the field of HRI investigate, e.g. how robot behavior is interpreted by humans, just to name a few examples. For all these disciplines, multimodal interaction data are of relevance. This includes the identification of relevant mechanisms in the data via qualitative and quantitative analyses, and the training and evaluation of the developed models.

### 8.2.2 Basic Definitions

Humans are able to transmit information via *multimodal interaction*, i.e. via a variety of modalities such as language, gestures, or other body movements. *Multimodal datasets* require recordings from different channels. Typically, the auditory and the visual channels are of interest when it comes to covering communicative behavior. Whereby recordings from the different channels need to be aligned on the same timeline to study the interplay of signals. Manual annotation of such datasets is time-consuming; therefore, such datasets are often rather small, limiting the applicability of machine learning algorithms. In *task-oriented, situated interaction* the communication focuses on structuring and accomplishing a task, and information from the visual scene is of great importance for communication, as well as joint attention. *Joint attention* is defined as "attention overtly focused by two or more people on the same object, person, or action at the same time, with each being aware of the other's interest."[1] *Transparency* in the context of this chapter refers to the issue of making artificial agents explainable to humans. When interacting with an artificial social agent, humans create their *mental models* of that agent. For successful HRI, it is necessary that these mental models approximate the robot's function, its plans and intentions. *Reference resolution* in linguistics is linking phrases that designate the same entity, e.g. "I like this book, can you hand it to me please?." In *multimodal reference resolution*, references to one entity in the real word need to be resolved, e.g. "the book" or "this" accompanied by a pointing gesture directed at a specific book.

## 8.3 Related Work

In the following, examples for multimodal HHI and HRI datasets will be given, and their application to investigate and model aspects of communication will be discussed. The collection of multimodal data is a highly resource intensive endeavor, and particular care must be given to the design of the data collection scenarios in view of the intended research goals.

1 APA Dictionary of Psychology, https://dictionary.apa.org/joint-attention.

### 8.3.1 HHI Data

There exist multimodal corpora, where a human teacher explains and conducts a task consisting of several subtasks, e.g. connecting a tube and mounting it in a box or assembling a piece of furniture. Most of these task descriptions last for a few minutes and another human might be present or not. The multimodal task description (MMTD) dataset [17] and the dataset collected by Kontogiorgos et al. [10] contain parallel data where all participants explain the same task(s) to another learner. Another example are datasets based on videos collected from the internet, such as the YouCook2 dataset comprising YouTube videos of people cooking different recipes [21]. The CHILDES corpus is a broad collection of datasets related to child speech. A subset of which comprises recordings of relatively unrestricted everyday interactions between adults and their toddlers/young infants [13].

HHI data serve well to investigate those aspects of HRI, where it is important for the robot to identify and interpret relevant human signals, for example which information humans provide when referring to objects and actions in task-related contexts, and how they structure a task. This is for instance important for computational models on **multimodal reference resolution**, where verbal information is combined with nonverbal signals, including pointing gestures, gaze of the person speaking, as well as objects which are in the joint visual field of the interlocutors [9, 19]. Foster et al. [6] also include objects currently being manipulated. In Section 8.4.1, the MMTD dataset [7, 17] is discussed. The dataset was collected by the authors of this chapter, among others, to systematically investigate via which modalities information relevant for reference resolution is transmitted and how reliable these modalities are.

### 8.3.2 HRI Data

In order to investigate how humans react to signals generated by a robot, multimodal HRI data are of relevance. Restricting factors of HRI are both the sensory capabilities of the robot, as well as its action generation capabilities, such as the degrees of freedom of the used robot and its appearance (humanoid vs. industrial, on a screen or in real life). In Sections 8.4.2.1 and 8.4.2.2 of this chapter, we will discuss two important aspects for successful HRI, namely the interpretation of robotic turn-taking signals, and the influence of different transparency mechanisms on human behavior.

#### 8.3.2.1 Joint Attention and Robot Turn-Taking Capabilities

It is fundamental that the human and the robot are able to coordinate their communicative interaction. In this context, joint attention is crucial, as it has the potential to make cooperation more efficient, e.g. by supporting disambiguation when cases of uncertainty occur (see [15]). Research on joint attention can be separated into initiating joint attention (IJA) and responding to others' joint attention (RJA) [14]. IJA is important for the robot to signal to the human what they are supposed to do, whereas RJA is relevant for the robot to react to the human's collaborative signals in an adequate way. Joint attention is also important for turn-taking in collaboration. In human–human task-oriented interaction, a number of nonverbal turn taking cues could be identified, such as eye gaze, step back, posture shifts, and hands on table (see [1, 7]). To facilitate smooth HRI, robots need to be able to both interpret and generate respective signals. Sheikholeslami et al. [18], for example, conducted a study where an industrial robot could effectively communicate instructional messages via gestures using its gripper in cooperative human–robot tasks.

**Transparency mechanisms** play a role when the user's mental model of the robot substantially differs from the robot's actual capabilities. In recent years, transparency methods receive increasing attention, often with the aim to foster trust and efficiency in HRI. Several social signals were investigated. Chao et al. [2] implemented an active learning strategy using shrugging gestures combined with uttering "yes" or "no" to indicate the robot's uncertainty. In a pilot study, the authors could show an increase of transparency, resulting in an increase of accuracy and efficiency of robot learning. De Greeff and Belpaeme [4] employed robot gaze and utterances to signal learning preference in a language game setting, which resulted in increased performance and better mental models of the human tutors. Another signal to convey information to the user is visualization on the computer screen, e.g. for identifying causes of interaction failure [16], or to display a robot's plans [20], both

**Table 8.1** Examples of publicly available, multimodal, task-based interaction data.

| | |
|---|---|
| | **Multimodal Task Description (MMTD) Corpus** |
| Topic: | Situated task descriptions |
| Setting: | Dyadic; human–human and human–robot interactions; laboratory; single encounters; instructor–learner roles |
| Nr. of participants: | Up to 26 participants |
| Media: | Videos from three positions, recorded speech (German) |
| Modalities: | Manually transcribed instructor utterances (text and parts-of-speech), instructor gaze, instructor gestures, objects touched or moved |
| Data link: | https://github.com/OFAI/MMTD-Corpus |
| | **Chinese Whispers** |
| Topic: | Furniture assembly (Ikea stool) |
| Setting: | Dyadic; human–human; laboratory; single encounters; instructor–builder roles |
| Nr. of participants: | 34 participants, 1 experimenter |
| Media: | Eye-tracking, recorded speech (English) from instructor and builder, motion capture (Optitrack) with markers on glasses, gloves, and stool, videos from two positions |
| Modalities: | Utterances from instructor and builder, gaze, actions and object movements, head orientation, pointing gestures, as well as manually annotated referring expressions |
| Data link: | https://www.kth.se/profile/diko/page/material |
| | **Childes Corpus** |
| Topic: | Child speech in a broad range of varieties regarding age group, mono- and bi-linguality, standard speech, clinical data |
| Nr. of participants: | From 1 participant to several 100 participants |
| Media: | Video and/or audio |
| Modalities: | Transcribed speech in various languages |
| Data link: | https://childes.talkbank.org/ |
| | **YouCook2 Dataset** |
| Topic: | Recipes with a large variety of cooking styles, methods, ingredients, and cookwares |
| Nr. of videos: | 2000 videos of recipes |
| Media: | YouTube videos |
| Modalities: | Temporally aligned procedure segments described by English sentences in imperative form (e.g. grill the tomatoes in a pan) |
| Data link: | http://youcook2.eecs.umich.edu/ |

improving the user's mental model of the respective robot. In the transparency study presented in this chapter, we used gaze, utterances, pointing, and a built-in tablet to increase the transparency of what the robot has already learned.

### 8.3.3 Public Availability of the Data

This is only given for a small subset of existing datasets (see Table 8.1 for the examples above) due to the reason that only some data were collected with the aim to cover different hypotheses and research questions. In general, existing datasets on multimodal communication vary greatly in their focus. This influences among others the setting, the number of participants, recorded media, and annotated modalities. The Childes Corpus [13] for example collects of a broad variety of corpora on child speech and is continuously growing. The MMTD dataset [17] on the other hand contains detailed manual annotations (e.g. eye gaze, gestures, referring expression) of a small set of simple manipulation tasks, see Section 8.4.1 for details. The Chinese Whispers dataset [10] focuses on one specific building task (assembly of an Ikea stool) and includes data from eye tracking and motion capture. Both the MMTD and the Chinese Whispers datasets comprise automatic as well as manual annotations and the publicly available versions of the datasets put a strong focus on protecting the privacy of the participants, i.e. no video or voice recording is publicized. In contrast, the YouCook2 dataset [21] is a collection of cooking videos from YouTube which were then manually annotated. Typically, these data are used for exploratory purposes, whereas data resulting from studies (e.g. [2, 4, 16, 18, 20]) are used to investigate concrete research questions. Accordingly, they are very specific and strongly depend on the respective research question. These data are typically not public.

## 8.4 Datasets and Resulting Implications

In the following, we will present selected examples of multimodal data we have collected in HHI and HRI experiments. We utilize the HHI data for investigating relevant communicative signals sent by the human (Section 8.4.1) and the HRI data for investigating how humans react to robot signals (Section 8.4.1). We describe the respective experimental setups and related research questions, and summarize the data analyses and related results.

### 8.4.1 Human Communicative Signals

The **OFAI MMTD dataset** is an example of HHI data to investigate human communicative signals occurring in situated task descriptions. By investigating how different people explain the same tasks, insights can be gained on how humans naturally present and structure information.

#### 8.4.1.1 Experimental Setup

A total of 22 people employed or studying at different universities in Munich explained and showed four different tasks to a human learner or toward a camera, (see Figure 8.1), resulting in 76 recordings. Each recording comprises an audio file and videos from three different perspectives. For details of the experimental setup and the data, see Schreitter and Krenn [17].

In Task 1, each of the 22 participants arranged wooden fruits and explained what they were doing toward a camera. This task has a focus on investigating the human structuring of a task where things have to be placed in a particular order. In tasks 2–4, each participant first was in the role of

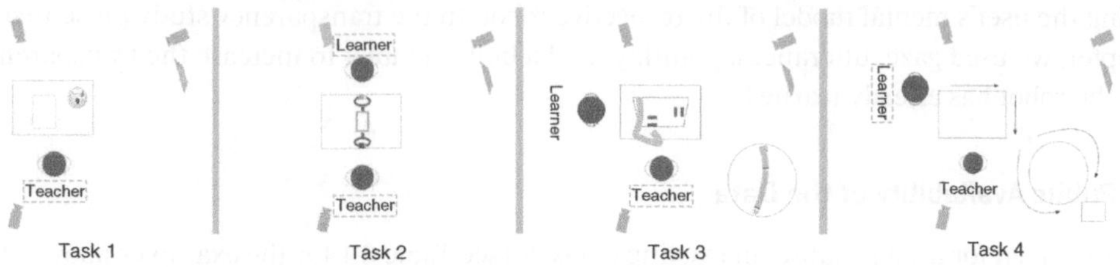


**Figure 8.1** Tasks 1–4 of the MMTD dataset. The teacher is describing the task, the person/s (dashed line) is/are conducting the task in parallel to the descriptions.

the learner who got information from a teacher how to conduct a task. The learner then became a teacher and passed on the information to a new learner. In Task 2, the instructor and the learner had to collaboratively lift a board and move it to a particular location. The focus of this task was on communicative signals in a collaborative task where both partners had at least one hand at the object they were moving together. In Task 3, a teacher explained and showed to another human how to combine two parts of a tube and mount the connected tube in a box. This task focused on communicative signals in task descriptions in which the learner is only observing while the teacher is explaining and conducting the task. In Task 4, the teacher instructed the learner to move to a certain location via a certain path. The focus of this task was on interactions where the teacher is instructing the learner to conduct a task on their own. A path correction is inbuilt into this scenario, where the instructor corrects and redirects the learner along a slightly different path.

#### 8.4.1.2 Data Analysis and Results

For synchronizing and annotating the data, the audio and video annotation tool ELAN[2] was employed. **Annotations of the data contain** (i) transcriptions of teacher utterances including disfluencies, dialectal utterances, and concatenations of words, (ii) transliterations in standard German, (iii) part-of-speech (POS) tags, (iv) gestures of the teacher comprise pointing gestures and where they are directed at, iconic gestures and the actions they depict, emblem gestures including the meaning of the emblem (e.g. "ok" for thumbs up), poising and exhibiting gestures including the object emphasized by the gesture, (v) the location where the teacher's eye is directed at continuously over time, (vi) salient objects playing a role in the current task description scene. Annotations of the data are published,[3] whereas the videos and sound files are subject to protection of data privacy, see also [17].

An important aspect in modeling communication in artificial agents is **multimodal reference resolution**, i.e. via which modalities (language, gesture, eye gaze, etc.) humans refer to objects and actions in an ongoing task. An analysis of the MMTD dataset revealed that only 50% of verbal references to objects by all participants in all four tasks could be resolved via language, pointing gestures, and eye gaze. Therefore, we extracted other cues which turned out to be necessary for reference resolution and investigated their reliability (for details, see [7]). **Linguistic references** to objects, actions, etc., in the MMTD dataset always intended to refer to task-relevant entities. However, in many cases, the lexical content was not enough to uniquely identify the reference object. In the MMTD dataset, only 23.19% of all verbal references to objects could be resolved via language. With regards to **gestures**, not only pointing gestures were valuable for multimodal reference resolution, but also exhibiting and poising gestures. **Eye gaze** turned out to be an unreliable cue for automatic

2 https://tla.mpi.nl/tools/tla-tools/elan/.
3 https://www.ofai.at/resources/mmtd.

reference resolution, as human gaze has a variety of functions, including directing the interlocutor's attention, checking what the interlocutor just did, whether the learner is still on track. Other visual cues could be identified and the analyses showed that their relevance for reference resolution was interlinked with the linguistic form of the accompanying verbal reference: For underspecified noun phrases (e.g. "this thing"), the object the teacher grasped last and was still holding was most relevant. To resolve pronouns (e.g. "it"), however, the object grasped before the last one by the instructor is of higher relevance. For spatial indexicals (e.g. "here" in "I put the tube here"), it is important toward which object or location the instructor moves the object they are currently holding. Based on these visual cues and their interlinkage with verbal referring expressions, lessons for designing natural language understanding capabilities of robots were formulated, see [7].

Additionally, the MMTD dataset was employed to evaluate a computational model for situated open world reference resolution [19]. It was also used to develop a mechanism which sets different objects or actions in focus when an artificial agent learns new words or actions from a human tutor (see e.g. [11]). This also emphasizes the importance of multimodal interaction data for different aspects in communication modeling.

### 8.4.2 Humans Reacting to Robot Signals

This chapter focuses on how a robot's behavior may influence human behavior. We will present results from two HRI studies we conducted. In the first one, different robotic turn-giving signals were compared and differences in human behavior were investigated. The focus of the second study was on the influence of a robot's transparency mechanism on human communicative behavior.

#### 8.4.2.1 Comparing Different Robotic Turn-Giving Signals

The goal of this study was to investigate how different robotic turn-giving signals were interpreted by humans. First, the robot conducted an action and then signaled to the human to proceed with the task (for details see [12]). The study is part of the CoBot Studio project.[4]

***Experimental Setup.*** A total of 124 participants took part in the study collaborating with a virtual UR10 industrial robot in a virtual reality (VR) environment, see Figure 8.2. A human and a robot stand opposite of each other at a conveyor belt where the robot performs a pick-and-place task taking parcels from the belt and putting them into a cardboard box. The human was instructed to support the robot when needed. Nonverbal behavior was implemented to signal the user that it is now their turn to proceed with the task. The robot's turn-giving was realized in four ways: (i) the robot simply stopped working, (ii) the robot arm pointed at the human and then at the parcel on the conveyor belt, (iii) a light projection of downward running arrows appeared on the gripper, (iv) the robot displayed a combination of both pointing gesture and light signal.

***Data Analysis and Results.*** In a qualitative analysis of the VR videos, we identified different behavior by the participants after the robot had stopped working, e.g. they rearranged the objects, gestured the robot to proceed, or looked at the robot or the object. Comparing the different signals, we found evidence that humans interpreted the light signal as a request by the robot to hand over a certain object. For the robot's deictic gesture, we found evidence to be helpful for humans to identify what to do next, and it was also a strong trigger for the participants to look at the object.

---

4 https://www.cobotstudio.at/.

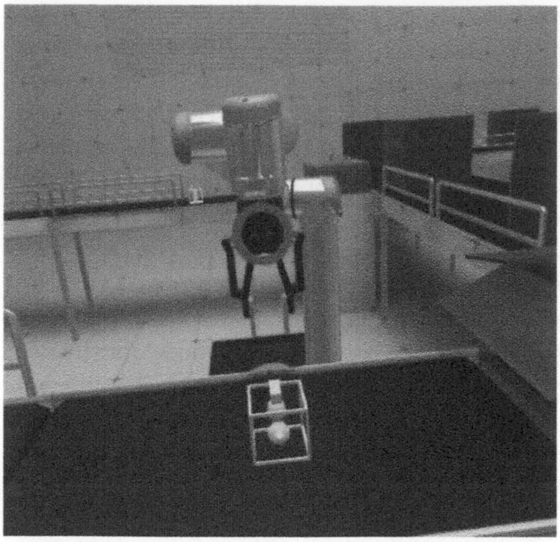

**Figure 8.2** A screenshot from the VR environment of the turn-taking study. The robot points at the human to indicate that it is now the human's turn to handle the object. The circle above the gripper indicates human eye gaze.

#### 8.4.2.2 Comparing Different Transparency Mechanisms

We conducted a user study where a Pepper robot learned object and action labels from a human tutor, see Figure 8.3, as part of the RALLI project.[5] The goal of the study was to investigate the effects of different robot transparency mechanisms on human teaching behavior, (for details see [8]).

***Experimental Setup.*** In total, 32 participants took part in the tutoring sessions. Indicators to which words the robot had already learned were varied in three experimental conditions. As base condition, the robot uttered the names of objects and actions whenever it observed them in the tutoring scene. In one extension, the robot also used pointing and gaze to communicate its knowledge about object names and to further request new object labels. In another extension, the current state of the lexicon was shown on the robot's tablet.

***Data Analysis and Results.*** In a qualitative analysis of participants' teaching behavior based on audio and video recordings of the tutoring sessions two major factors influencing human communication behavior could be observed: When the robot used pointing gestures and asked for object

**Figure 8.3** A participant is manipulating objects on a table and describing to a Pepper robot what she is doing.

5 https://ralli.ofai.at/.

labels or uttered them, the humans tended to increase their interactive behavior. This behavior, however, had a potential to impair the robot's learning success, as the system could not adequately process the extended input. Furthermore, over time participants simplified their utterances in order to adapt to the robot's perceived capabilities. In addition, the analysis of a questionnaire showed that the tablet was considered by the users to be most helpful to gain insights in what the robot had already learned. When the human input deviated substantially from the input required by the system, learning was impaired in all conditions.

## 8.5 Conclusions

In this chapter, HHI data were presented to investigate human communicative signals. Based on the MMTD dataset, the interplay between verbal and nonverbal cues in multimodal reference resolution was discussed.

The dataset also played a role for developing a model where a system learned from parallel input (linguistic and visual) and for the evaluation of a computational reference-resolution model. The HRI data presented in the chapter were used to investigate communicative signals sent by the robot and how humans reacted to them. Data including robotic turn-giving signals and how these signals were interpreted by humans were investigated. The data emphasize the importance of transparency and explainability. Based on a second HRI dataset, effects of different transparency mechanisms on human teaching behavior were presented. In general, multimodal data collections can be used to (i) identify human behavior which needs to be considered by the artificial system, (ii) identify how humans react to robot signals and investigate resulting consequences, and (iii) evaluate computational models covering aspects of communication in artificial social agents.

## 8.6 Future Research Challenges

While there is a range of studies investigating how certain robotic signals influence, e.g. the efficiency of HRI and the self-efficacy of humans, there exist not many studies on human social signals in HRI. These signals need to be further investigated, to identify what the robot needs to consider as relevant information. A general challenge is that comprehensive multimodal data collections are costly with regards to human resources for collecting and annotating the data. They are well suited for qualitative analyses and evaluation tasks and may be used in semisupervised machine learning. Main future research challenges derived from our analyses include the implementation of a references resolution algorithm based on the extracted relevant modalities. In turn-taking, it must be further investigated why some people were immediately successful, while others needed more time or even failed. The results from the transparency study showed that the interactivity of human multimodal behavior increases, when the robot generates more social signals. A future research challenge therefore is how the system then deals with this additional multimodal behavior.

## References

1 Calisgan, E., Haddadi, A., Van der Loos, M. et al. (2012). Identifying nonverbal cues for automated human–robot turn-taking. *International Symposium on Robot and Human Interactive Communication (RO-MAN)*, 418–423.

2 Chao, C., Cakmak, M., and Thomaz, A.L. (2010). Transparent active learning for robots. *IEEE International Conference on Human-Robot Interaction (HRI)*, 317–324.

3 Clark, H.H. and Krych, M.A. (2004). Speaking while monitoring addressees for understanding. *Journal of Memory and Language* 50 (1): 62–81.

4 De Greeff, J. and Belpaeme, T. (2015). Why robots should be social: enhancing machine learning through social human–robot interaction. *PLoS One* 10 (9): e0138061.

5 Epley, N., Waytz, A., and Cacioppo, J.T. (2007). On seeing human: a three-factor theory of anthropomorphism. *Psychological Review* 114 (4): 864–886.

6 Foster, M.E., Bard, E., Guhe, M. et al. (2008). The roles of haptic-ostensive referring expressions in cooperative, task-based human–robot dialogue. *IEEE International Conference on Human-Robot Interaction (HRI)*, 295–302.

7 Gross, S., Krenn, B., and Scheutz, M. (2017). The reliability of non-verbal cues for situated reference resolution and their interplay with language: implications for human robot interaction. *ACM International Conference on Multimodal Interaction (ICMI)*, 189–196.

8 Hirschmanner, M., Gross, S., Zafari, S. et al. (2021). Investigating transparency methods in a robot word-learning system and their effects on human teaching behaviors. *IEEE International Conference on Robot & Human Interactive Communication (RO-MAN)*, 175–182.

9 Kontogiorgos, D., Sibirtseva, E., Pereira, A. et al. (2018). Multimodal reference resolution in collaborative assembly tasks. *Proceedings of the International WS on Multimodal Analyses Enabling Artificial Agents in Human–Machine Interaction*, 38–42.

10 Kontogiorgos, D., Sibirtseva, E., and Gustafson, J. (2020). Chinese whispers: a multimodal dataset for embodied language grounding. *Language Resources and Evaluation Conference (LREC)*, 743–749.

11 Krenn, B., Sadeghi, S., Neubarth, F. et al. (2020). Models of cross-situational and crossmodal word learning in task-oriented scenarios. *IEEE Transactions on Cognitive and Developmental Systems* 12 (3): 658–668.

12 Krenn, B., Reinboth, T., Gross, S. et al. (2021). It's your turn!–A collaborative human–robot pick-and-place scenario in a virtual industrial setting. *International WS on Virtual, Augmented, and Mixed-Reality for Human–Robot Interactions (at HRI)*.

13 McWhinney, B. (2000). The childes project: the database.

14 Meindl, J. and Cannella-Malone, H. (2011). Initiating and responding to joint attention bids in children with autism: a review of the literature. *Research in Developmental Disabilities* 32 (5): 1441–1454.

15 Pereira, A., Oertel, C., Fermoselle, L. et al. (2019). Responsive joint attention in human–robot interaction. *International Conference on Intelligent Robots and Systems*, 1080–1087.

16 Ramaraj, P., Sahay, S., Kumar, S. et al. (2019). Towards using transparency mechanisms to build better mental models. *Advances in Cognitive Systems: Goal Reasoning WS*, 1–6.

17 Schreitter, S. and Krenn, B. (2016). The OFAI multi-modal task description corpus. *International Conference on Language Resources and Evaluation (LREC)*, 1408–1414.

18 Sheikholeslami, S., Moon, A.J., and Croft, E.A. (2017). Cooperative gestures for industry: exploring the efficacy of robot hand configurations in expression of instructional gestures for human–robot interaction. *International Journal of Robotics Research* 36 (5–7): 699–720.

19 Williams, T., Acharya, S., Schreitter, S., and Scheutz, M. (2016). Situated open world reference resolution for human–robot dialogue. *IEEE International Conference on Human–Robot Interaction (HRI)*, 311–318.

**20** Wortham, R., Theodorou, A., and Bryson, J. (2017). Improving robot transparency: real-time visualisation of robot AI substantially improves understanding in naive observers. *International Symposium on Human & Robot Interactive Communication (RO-MAN)*, 1424–1431.

**21** Zhou, L., Xu, C., and Corso, J. (2018). Towards automatic learning of procedures from web instructional videos. *AAAI Conference on AI*.

# 9

# Modeling Interactions Happening in People-Driven Collaborative Processes

*Maximiliano Canche*[1], *Sergio F. Ochoa*[2], *Daniel Perovich*[2], *and Rodrigo Santos*[3]

[1] *Faculty of Mathematics, Universidad Autónoma de Yucatán, Mérida, Yucatán, Mexico*
[2] *Computer Science Department, University of Chile, Santiago, RM, Chile*
[3] *Electrical Engineering and Computers Department - ICIC, Universidad Nacional del Sur - CONICET, Bahia Blanca, Buenos Aires, Argentina*

## 9.1 Introduction

According to [7], people-driven collaborative process (PDCP) involves the participants playing several roles, but there is no preestablished workflow that coordinates their actions. The participants decide their next action on-the-fly considering the status of context variables, such as their to-do list, the priority of their pending activities, or the availability of the counterpart. Examples of PDCPs are global software development [20], disaster relief efforts [1], hospital work [19], construction inspections [18], and elderly caregiving [6].

The PDCPs usually involve individual and group goals. The former are related to the roles played by the participants, and the latter are linked to the outcome these people have to reach as a team. Typically, the goals and work context of the participants establish the dynamic of the process, and also their needs of collaboration.

When the work in PDCPs is addressed using technology, the participants and their supporting application (usually a mobile collaborative system) become a human–machine unit (HMU). These units interact with others to perform the process, trying to reach individual and group goals.

Figure 9.1 shows two interaction scenarios where the participants (i.e., the HMUs) perform activities of a PDCP. In the first one, the inspectors (i.e., HMUs playing a particular role) are deployed into a construction site, for instance, to check the status of the facilities in a particular area. As mentioned in [18], during these inspections, the participants (i.e. the inspector-in-chief, the inspectors, and the foreman) work individually and collaborate on-demand when required. Once finished the information gathering, the participants met to cross-check their diagnosis, solve discrepancies, and communicate the results to the foreman and the inspector-in-chief.

A similar dynamic is followed by nurses, physicians, and paramedics when they take care of hospitalized patients (Figure 9.1b). These HMUs are responsible for different aspects of the healthcare process, and in almost any PDCP, they have to address individual and group goals.

The capability and flexibility to perform interactions among HMUs make a difference in the effectiveness of the PDCPs. Therefore, identifying and modeling interaction capabilities of each unit type (i.e., each role) is mandatory to design effective human–machine systems.

*Handbook of Human-Machine Systems*, First Edition. Edited by Giancarlo Fortino, David Kaber, Andreas Nürnberger, and David Mendonça.

**Figure 9.1** Examples of HMUs performing (a) construction inspection activities, and (b) hospital work. Source: © goodluz / Adobe Stock.

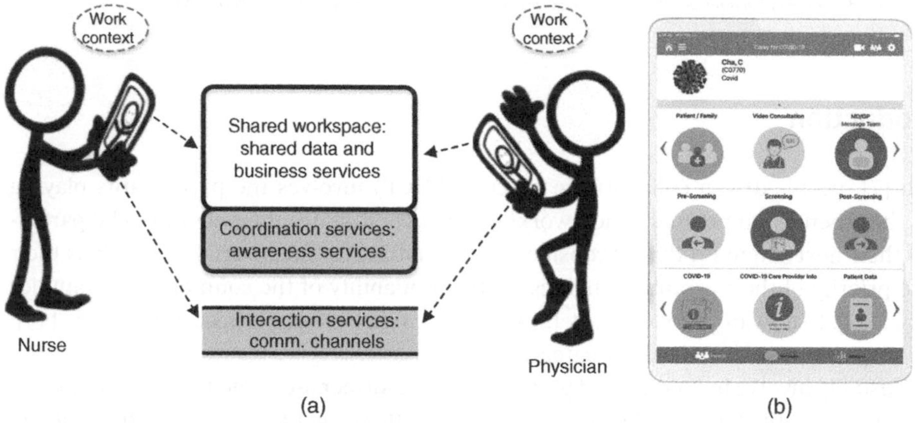


**Figure 9.2** (a) Structure of a mobile collaborative system that supports the work of two HMUs and (b) workspace example of a healthcare application.

Figure 9.2a shows two participants, a nurse and a physician, using a mobile collaborative application to perform hospital work. As mentioned before, the combination of user role and mobile application represents a HMU. Typically, the architecture of a mobile collaborative system involves three main components (Figure 9.2): a shared workspace (or collaboration environment), and coordination and interaction services. The higher layer provides the user interface and allows users to consume business services. Figure 9.2b shows an example of a workspace of a healthcare application to monitor the evolution of Covid-19 hospitalized patients.

The second layer corresponds to coordination services that allow the system to provide visual awareness to the users; for instance, information about actions performed by other participants or the status of the joint work and the user's context. This layer usually implements the workflow of activities that participants perform to reach group goals. However, in case of PDCP such a workflow cannot be pre-established at the application design time; therefore, only requirements of awareness services can be identified during the system design process.

Finally, the lower layer provides the services that allow the users, and also autonomous services, to exchange files and messages. These services implement the several communication channels that allow the HMUs to interact among them.

Regardless of the PDCP and business domain to be supported by the mobile application, the design of the interaction and awareness services (i.e., the two lower layers of the architecture) is central in the effectiveness of these systems. Although there is no clear recipe to address this design activity, the research community tends to prefer the use of a co-design approach to deal with it. This approach considers the joint work of developers and stakeholders to determine the interaction scenarios and services at analysis and design time of the system.

Next section presents the background in modeling the interaction scenarios involved in PDCPs. We also show the challenges to address by the interaction modeling languages and notations to allow stakeholders and engineers to codesign the interaction scenarios to be supported. Section 9.3 reviews the state-of-the-art on these modeling languages and notations, and presents a comparison among them considering the challenges stated in Section 9.2. Section 9.4 discusses the open issues and directions for future research.

## 9.2 Background

Figure 9.3 shows a typical interaction design process of a mobile collaborative application, which supports the interactions among the HMUs participating in a PDCP. During the first step of the design process, stakeholders and requirement engineers agree on the interaction scenarios to be supported; this includes the identification of roles participating in the PDCP (i.e., the type of HMU to be supported) and the interactions among them. The second step involves the joint work between stakeholders and the provider to characterize the roles and the interactions between every pair of user roles. In the third step, the participants decide the awareness and interaction services the system should provide to every HMU type.

The interaction scenarios, and also the services, must be specified in a visual representation that can be understood and validated by all parties. In order to do that, several modeling languages

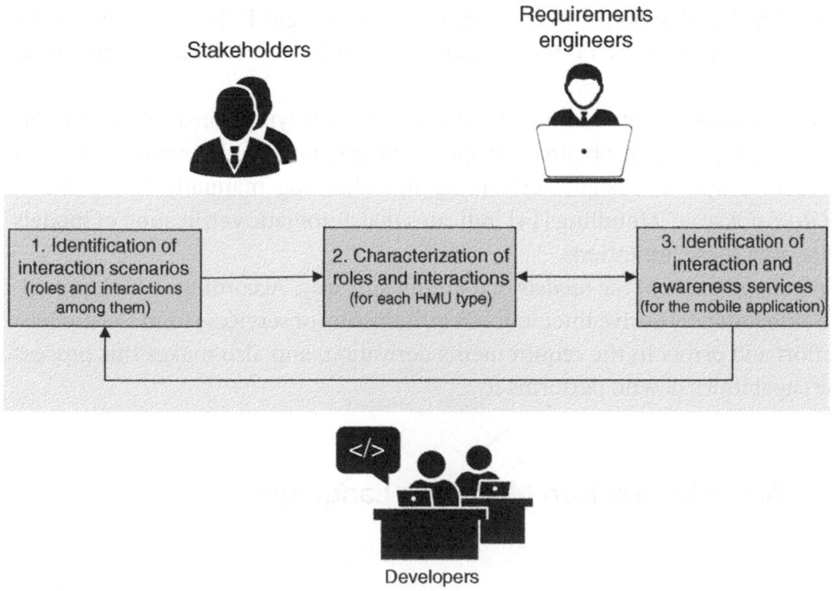


**Figure 9.3** Interaction design process of mobile collaborative systems.

and notations have been proposed; most of them specify the roles of participants in a PDCP, and the interactions among them. Canche et al. [5] report that languages and notations used to specify interaction scenarios should address various modeling challenges, mainly due to the diversity of people involved in the design and validation of these artifacts. Particularly, these representations should:

1. *Specify and characterize the roles participating in a PDCP, and also the interactions between them.* Zhu and Zhou [26] indicate that specifying and characterizing these roles and interactions allow designers to build, validate, and improve these scenarios and also identify the interaction services required to support them.
2. *Be understandable for stakeholders.* According to [16], the interpretation of technical representations for nonexperts is slower, error-prone, and requires more conscious effort, as opposed to technical experts. Therefore, if nontechnical people (e.g. regular stakeholders) are going to make design decisions on the product, then the design representations should be understandable for them.
3. *Ease the building of a shared understanding between stakeholders and developers about the scenarios to be supported.* Hoffmann et al. [13] state that building a shared understanding between both parts is a prerequisite to successfully develop, validate, and deploy a software system. Therefore, the symbols used to represent the interaction scenarios should ease the building of such a shared understanding.
4. *Allow representing interactions at different abstraction levels.* The cognitive fit theory, proposed by Vessey [24], indicates that different tasks and audiences usually require different information representations. Given the diversity of the audiences participating in the interaction design process, it is recommended to count on representations that specify the interaction scenarios at different abstraction levels.
5. *Manage the complexity and size of the interaction processes specifications.* When models are large or complex (e.g. interaction scenarios), they should be modularized to make them addressable for designers. According to the ontological theory proposed by Weber [25], managing these aspects of the models is essential for software engineering notations.
6. *Provide mechanisms for automatic model consistency checking.* Verifying consistency of interaction models is mandatory to then obtain appropriate interaction requirements that helps perform the collaborative system design. Performing this checking manually is expensive, error-prone, and it does not scale. Mendling [14] indicates that automatic verification of models usually allows addressing these limitations.
7. *Derive interaction requirements from the models in an automatic way.* According to [21], providing mechanisms to automatically derive interaction requirements (or services) from the models, allows to reduce effort and errors in the requirements derivation, and also makes this process independent of the capabilities of who performs it.

## 9.3 State-of-the-Art in Interaction Modeling Languages and Notations

The computer-supported collaborative work and process engineering research communities have proposed several modeling languages and notations. Some of them can be used to represent the interactions happening in PDCPs.

### 9.3.1 Visual Languages and Notations

Next, we briefly describe the main proposals, and then we compare them considering the challenges presented in the previous section.

1. The Object Management Group developed the *Case Management Model and Notation (CMMN)* [17], based on the Case Handling paradigm proposed by van der Aalst et al. [22], and adapted for modeling business processes that involve activities that depend on real-time evolving circumstances. The notation specifies interaction scenarios intertwining roles, interactions, and process activities, resulting in complex visual models. This aspect limits the understanding of these models by nontechnical people (e.g. the stakeholders). On the other hand, CMMN is well prepared to deal with large or complex processes, but their representations need to count on external software tools to check models consistency and derive interaction requirements from these models.
2. Bukhsh et al. [2] present a BPMN extension to specify people-driven processes. This notation, named *BPMN Plus*, includes several modeling concepts, like optional and undo activities, events, and performers (HMU types). The notation allows specifying business rules to orchestrate activities and actions envisioned for the HMUs, and thus manage the size and complexity of the models. The notation also takes advantage of capabilities provided by BPMN to deal with this design aspect. On the other hand, the resulting visual models are complex, since the notation was conceived for being used by technical people. This limits the participation of stakeholders. Checking models consistency or deriving interaction services from the models is feasible, but using third-party software.
3. Hanssen et al. [10] proposed *BPMN for Sensitive Business Process (BPMN-4SBP)* that integrates six modeling dimensions in order to represent the dynamic, interaction and knowledge aspects of a PDCP. Its graphical notation considers several design concepts, e.g. (individual) human and collective roles, tacit and explicit knowledge, and distinct kinds of knowledge flow. Although BPMN4SBP provides various elements that help model PDCPs, it has limitations similar to the previous one regarding to usability for stakeholders, automatic model checking, and interaction services derivation.
4. Dorn et al. [8] recommend to combine two human-centric languages designed to specify interaction intensive processes. These languages are *Little-JIL* that provides process-centric specifications, and *human Architecture Description Language (hADL)* that is focused on structure-centric human interaction specifications. Although this combined proposal has important advantages over other languages, using two different notations increases the complexity of the modeling process; particularly, it strongly limits the participation of stakeholders in the specification, analysis, and validation of the models. Moreover, third-party software is required to integrate the models, perform consistency checking, and derive interaction services from them.
5. Herskovic et al. [12] present the *Mobile Collaboration Modeling (MCM)* notation that allows designers to specify interaction scenarios using a directed graph, where the nodes represent the roles of the participants and the edges indicate the potential interactions among roles. The concepts included in this notation are few and simple, which favor the understandability of the models. However, the characterization of interactions between HMUs is difficult to understand for stakeholders. On the other hand, MCM allows designers to perform automatic model checking and derive interaction requirements from the models, but it does not include mechanisms to address large and complex PDCPs.

6. Based on MCM, Monares et al. [15] define the *IoT Modeling notation* to represent interactions in human-centric wireless sensor networks. The strengths and weaknesses of this notation are similar to MCM, except that IoT modeling does not provide mechanisms for model checking and interaction services derivation; therefore, third-party software are required for doing that.
7. Hawryszkiewycz [11] proposes an approach based on *collaboration graphs* that extends the social network diagrams and adapts them to specify integrated business activities. This notation represents roles and interactions and uses a combination of business activities, interaction graphs, and knowledge requirements to deal with the size and complexity of the interaction models. However, the meaning of the symbols and diagrams is not evident, particularly for stakeholders. Moreover, the model consistency checking and the interaction services derivation can be done only manually by the designers.
8. Canche et al. [4] defined *the Computer-mediated Interaction Modeling Language (CIMoL)* that is the evolution of the notation presented in [3]. Similar to MCM, this visual language defines a graph for each interaction scenario considered in a PDCP. These graphs specify roles (HMUs' types) and interactions in a simple way, easing the participation of stakeholders in the modeling process. However, the evaluation results indicate that some symbols of CIMoL need improvements, particularly to enhance reaching a shared understanding between stakeholders and developers, and also to address the modeling of large and complex PDCPs.

### 9.3.2 Comparison of Interaction Modeling Languages and Notations

Figure 9.4 shows a table that compares the capabilities of the already presented languages and notations, considering the items presented in Section 9.2. This evaluation used as input the results of the study reported in [5], but in this case, it considered the opinion of three researchers experienced in the design and use of interaction modeling languages. Using a process similar to Wideband–Delphi, these researchers reached agreements about how well a certain language or notation addresses a particular modeling challenge.

| Aspect \ Notation | CMMN | BPMN Plus | BPMN4SBP | Little-JIL and hADL | MCM | IoT Modeling | Collaboration Graphs | CIMoL |
|---|---|---|---|---|---|---|---|---|
| (1) Capability to specify and characterize roles and interactions between them | Limited | Yes | Yes | Yes | Yes | Yes | Yes | Yes |
| (2) Capability to be understandable for stakeholders | Limited | Limited | Limited | Limited | Limited | Limited | Limited | Yes |
| (3) Capability to represent the specifications at different abstraction levels | Limited | Limited | Limited | Limited | Limited | Limited | Limited | Limited |
| (4) Capability to manage the size and complexity of the specifications | Yes | Yes | Yes | Yes | No | No | Yes | Limited |
| (5) Capability to achieve a shared understanding of the specifications | Yes | No | Yes | Limited | No | No | Yes | Yes |
| (6) Capability for automatic model consistency checking | Limited | Limited | Limited | Limited | Yes | Limited | No | Yes |
| (7) Capability for automatic derivation of software requirements | Limited | Limited | Limited | Limited | Yes | Limited | No | Yes |

**Figure 9.4** Comparison of interaction modeling languages and notations.

The results show that there is no proposal able to deal with all stated challenges. Most of these languages and notations represent properly roles and interactions (item 1 of the table), and these representations have several levels of understandability for stakeholders (item 2). Therefore, the representations are diverse in terms of the capabilities to help engineers and stakeholders reach a shared understanding about the interaction scenarios to be supported (item 5). Usually, the understandability of these representations is influenced by the "physics of the notation" [16] and also by the capability of the language to express these models at different abstraction levels (item 3).

Mainly notations based on standards, like CMMN, BPMN Plus, and BPMN4SBP, are able to properly deal with large and complex representations (item 4), and this capability is usually inherited from their source modeling language. Most of the proposals have the potential of checking the models consistency and derive interaction services from them. However, only MCM and CIMoL provide these services through a software modeling tool that is available with the language.

Regardless of the advances in this study domain, these proposals represent just a first step toward the integral modeling of interactive systems, particularly, for those supporting PDCPs.

## 9.4 Challenges and Future Research Directions

In this study domain, there still are several open issues. Some of them became evident after the analysis presented in Section 9.3. For instance, the usability of the visual representations must be improved to ease the participation of stakeholders during the interaction modeling and evaluation processes. Moreover, providing effective mechanisms to help designers deal with large and complex representations seems to be a still pending issue. Something similar happens with the mechanisms to perform automatic processing of interaction models, in order to check their consistency and derive interaction requirements from them. Concerning these issues, more than modeling languages are required. In this sense, novel collaborative modeling tools must be conceived to address the interaction design, particularly when various designers and stakeholders should work together in a common model. The use of these tools should also help address the distributed work of these people.

On the other hand, the reviewed languages and notations were conceived to be used during the analysis and design stages of development projects, i.e. when the participants have time enough to perform a co-design process that involves various iterations. However, the interaction design is an aspect that should also be clear enough even at precontract time, i.e. when the provider is trying to identify the required interaction services to embed in the application, and based on that, to deliver a project bid to the customer.

As shown by Vera et al. [23], this definition at precontract time must be done quickly, involving a low application effort and having low dependence of key people (e.g. experts). Therefore, the interaction modeling languages and notations must considerably improve, not only their usability but also their usefulness and effectiveness for being used at project preselling time. Once again, novel collaborative modeling tools are required to help providers address these challenges.

There are also some quality aspects that are not considered in the previous proposals, and that are relevant for the interaction design of the applications; for instance, interaction security, privacy, and personalization.

Considering these open issues, the HCI, CSCW, and software engineering communities have many opportunities to advance the state-of-the-art in interaction design. In addition, and as indicated in [9], the advances in mobile and wearable technology will bring new challenges to researchers and technology designers.

## References

1 Aldunate, R., Ochoa, S.F., Peña-Mora, F., and Nussbaum, M. (2006). Robust mobile ad hoc space for collaboration to support disaster relief efforts involving critical physical infrastructure. *Journal of Computing in Civil Engineering* 20 (1): 13–27. https://doi.org/10.1061/(ASCE)0887-3801(2006)20:1(13).

2 Bukhsh, Z., van Sinderen, M., Sikkel, K., and Quartel, D. (2019). *How to Manage and Model Unstructured Business Processes: A Proposed List of Representational Requirements*, 81–103. Cham: Springer International Publishing. ISBN 978-3-030-11039-0.

3 Canche, M., Ochoa, S.F., Perovich, D., and Gutierrez, F.J. (2019). Analysis of notations for modeling user interaction scenarios in ubiquitous collaborative systems. *Journal of Ambient Intelligence and Humanized Computing* 13: 5321–5333.

4 Canche, M., Ochoa, S.F., and Perovich, D. (2021). CIMoL: A Language for Modeling Interactions in People-Driven Collaborative Processes. *Technical Report TR/DCC-2021-3*. Computer Science Department, University of Chile.

5 Canche, M., Ochoa, S.F., and Perovich, D. (2022). Understanding the suitability of modeling languages and notations to represent computer-mediated interaction scenario. In: *Advances in Intelligent Systems and Computing* (ed. Á Rocha, C. Ferrás, A. Méndez Porras, E. Jimenez Delgado). Cham: Springer.

6 Cruz, W., Isotani, S., Carrico, L., and Guerreiro, T. (2016). Interface to support caregivers in daily record and information visualization of patients with dementia. *Proceedings of the 15th Brazilian Symposium on Human Factors in Computing Systems*, 1–13. SBC.

7 Dorn, C. and Dustdar, S. (2011). Supporting dynamic, people-driven processes through self-learning of message flows. In: *Advanced Information Systems Engineering - 23rd International Conference, CAiSE 2011, London, UK, June 20–24, 2011. Proceedings, Lecture Notes in Computer Science*, vol. 6741 (ed. H. Mouratidis and C. Rolland), 657–671. Springer. ISBN 978-3-642-21639-8. http://dx.doi.org/10.1007/978-3-642-21640-4_48.

8 Dorn, C., Dustdar, S., and Osterweil, L.J. (2014). Specifying flexible human behavior in interaction-intensive process environments. In: *Business Process Management - 12th International Conference, BPM 2014, Haifa, Israel, September 7–11, 2014. Proceedings, Lecture Notes in Computer Science*, vol. 8659 (ed. S.W. Sadiq, P. Soffer, and H. Völzer), 366–373. Springer. ISBN 978-3-319-10171-2. http://dx.doi.org/10.1007/978-3-319-10172-9_24.

9 Gravina, R. and Fortino, G. (2021). Wearable body sensor networks: state-of-the-art and research directions. *IEEE Sensors Journal* 21 (11): 12511–12522. https://doi.org/10.1109/JSEN.2020.3044447.

10 Hassen, M., Turki, M., and Gargouri, F. (2019). A multi-criteria evaluation approach for selecting a sensitive business process modeling language for knowledge management. *Journal on Data Semantics* 8: 1–46.

11 Hawryszkiewycz, I.T. (2009). Modeling complex adaptive systems. In: *Information Systems: Modeling, Development, and Integration*. UNISCON 2009. *Lecture Notes in Business Information Processing*, vol. 20 (ed. J. Yang, A. Ginige, H.C. Mayr, and R.D. Kutsche), 458–468. Berlin, Heidelberg: Springer-Verlag.

12 Herskovic, V., Ochoa, S.F., and Pino, J.A. (2019). Identifying groupware requirements in people-driven mobile collaborative processes. *Journal of Universal Computer Science* 25 (8): 988–1017.

13 Hoffmann, A., Bittner, E.A.C., and Leimeister, J.M. (2013). The emergence of mutual and shared understanding in the system development process. In: *Requirements*

*Engineering: Foundation for Software Quality* (ed. J. Doerr and A.L. Opdahl), 174–189. Berlin, Heidelberg: Springer-Verlag. ISBN 978-3-642-37422-7.

**14** Mendling, J. (2009). *Empirical Studies in Process Model Verification*, 208–224. Berlin, Heidelberg: Springer-Verlag. ISBN 9783642008986.

**15** Monares, Á., Ochoa, S.F., Herskovic, V. et al. (2014). Modeling interactions in human-centric wireless sensor networks. *Proceedings of the 2014 IEEE 18th International Conference on Computer Supported Cooperative Work in Design (CSCWD)*, 661–666.

**16** Moody, D. (2009). The "physics" of notations: toward a scientific basis for constructing visual notations in software engineering. *IEEE Transactions on Software Engineering* 35 (6): 756–779. https://doi.org/10.1109/TSE.2009.67.

**17** Object Management Group (2016). The case management model and notation, specification v. 1.1. https://www.omg.org/spec/CMMN (accessed 01 April 2022).

**18** Ochoa, S.F., Bravo, G., Pino, J.A., and Rodriguez-Covili, J. (2011). Coordinating loosely-coupled work in construction inspection activities. *Group Decision and Negotiation* 20: 39–56.

**19** Pinelle, D. and Gutwin, C. (2006). Loose coupling and healthcare organizations: deployment strategies for groupware. *Computer-Supported Cooperative Work* 15 (5–6): 537–572. https://doi.org/10.1007/s10606-006-9031-2.

**20** Portillo-Rodríguez, J., Vizcaíno, A., Piattini, M., and Beecham, S. (2012). Tools used in global software engineering: a systematic mapping review. *Information and Software Technology* 54 (7): 663–685. https://doi.org/10.1016/j.infsof.2012.02.006.

**21** Turkman, S. and Taweel, A. (2019). Business process model driven automatic software requirements generation. In: *Business Modeling and Software Design*. BMSD 2019. *Lecture Notes in Business Information Processing*, vol 356 (ed. B. Shishkov), 270–278. Cham: Springer International Publishing. ISBN 978-3-030-24854-3.

**22** van der Aalst, W.M.P., Weske, M., and Grunbauer, D. (2005). Case handling: a new paradigm for business process support. *Data & Knowledge Engineering* 53 (2): 129–162.

**23** Vera, T., Perovich, D., and Ochoa, S.F. (2021). An instrument to define the product scope at preselling time. *2021 IEEE 24th International Conference on Computer Supported Cooperative Work in Design (CSCWD)*, 604–608.

**24** Vessey, I. (1991). Cognitive fit: a theory-based analysis of the graphs versus tables literature. *Decision Sciences* 22: 219–240.

**25** Weber, R. (1997). *Ontological Foundations of Information Systems, Coopers & Lybrand Accounting Research Methodology Monograph*. Coopers & Lybrand and the Accounting Association of Australia and New Zealand. https://books.google.cl/books?id=zmaVMQEACAAJ.

**26** Zhu, H. and Zhou, M. (2006). Role-based collaboration and its kernel mechanisms. *IEEE Transactions on Systems, Man, and Cybernetics, Part C: Appl. and Reviews* 36: 578–589.

# 10

# Transparent Communications for Human–Machine Teaming

*Jessie Y. C. Chen*

*U.S. Army Research Laboratory, Aberdeen Proving Ground, MD, USA*

## 10.1 Introduction

Due to tremendous advancements in artificial intelligence (AI) and autonomy-related technologies in recent decades, machines have become more intelligent and sophisticated; their complex decision-making and actions, while beneficial and useful in many cases, also pose challenges to the human–machine systems community when it comes to effective human–machine teaming [7, 32, 39]. Among the numerous challenges identified by various technical organizations and expert groups [1, 17, 20–22, 33, 49, 52], agent transparency has been raised consistently as a key topic and an area of research that is critical to achieving effective teaming between human and machine agents. Additionally, as intelligent systems continue to learn and evolve, their predictability may be compromised – as a result, the human partner's mental model of the system may be incorrect if the system's new capabilities are not explained to the human in a transparent manner. However, transparent human–agent interaction poses significant challenges to interface designers, as transparency contents may not be easily generated in real time, and too much information may overburden the human and be counterproductive [50].

There have been a number of high-profile research programs on transparency-related topics funded by the US government in recent years, and one of these programs is DARPA's eXplainable AI (XAI) [14]. Tech industry is also keenly aware of the importance of system transparency to the overall user-system interaction experience and effectiveness. Increasingly, tech companies have invested in transparency-related research, sometimes in collaboration with government agencies such as the National Science Foundation (e.g. NSF Program on Fairness in Artificial Intelligence in collaboration with Amazon, 2020–2023). A major milestone of transparency research is the recent publication of a special issue on Agent and System Transparency published in *IEEE Transactions on Human-Machine Systems*, which examines the transparency issue in a variety of human-machine teaming contexts [10].

## 10.2 Definitions and Frameworks

An often-cited definition of agent transparency in the context of human-agent interaction is "the quality of an interface to support a human operator's comprehension of an intelligent agent's intent, performance, future plans, and reasoning process," with a focus on the information recipient's

*Handbook of Human-Machine Systems*, First Edition. Edited by Giancarlo Fortino, David Kaber, Andreas Nürnberger, and David Mendonça.

situation awareness [8]. The High-Level Expert Group on AI (an advisory group for the European Commission) defines the transparency requirements for trustworthy AI as follows: traceability, explainability, and open communication about the system's limitations [17]. In the proposed IEEE P7001 Standard on Transparency [21], transparency is defined more broadly – addressing different stakeholders' needs – as "the transfer of information from an autonomous system or its designers to a stakeholder, which is honest, contains information relevant to the causes of some action, decision or behavior and is presented at a level of abstraction and in a form meaningful to the stakeholder" ([52], p. 2). In the context of recommender systems, Vorm [50] defines transparency as "a measure of observability, accessibility, ease, and completeness of explanations of system functions and outputs," particularly addressing the usability-related aspects of transparency (p. 22).

While system transparency has been a prominent research topic in the human–automation interaction community since the 1990s [13], transparency frameworks intended for intelligent systems (e.g. robots, AI-based systems) have only started to appear in the 2010s. Lyons [31] proposes the Human-Robot Transparency Model that covers two categories of transparency-related information: robot-*to*-human and robot-*of*-human. The former includes information that the robot needs to convey to the human about the *intentional* aspects (e.g. purpose of the system), *task*-related information, *analytical* processes, and *environmental* conditions. The latter deals with the information that the robot needs to communicate to the human to convey its awareness of the *teamwork* that the human–robot team is trying to achieve as well as the *human state* (e.g. cognitive, physical, and emotional aspects) as perceived by the robot.

Johnson et al. [23] developed the Coactive System Model to address human–machine shared understanding and joint activity. Particularly, the framework focuses on agent (both machine and human) Observability, Predictability, and Directability. Johnson et al. stress the importance of bidirectional communications between humans and machines to support the interdependence aspect of the human–machine team performance.

Chen and her colleagues develop the situation awareness-based agent transparency (SAT) framework [8] – influenced by concepts from the situation awareness (SA) model by Endsley [13], the belief–desire–intention (BDI) framework by Rao and Georgeff [41], and 3 Ps (automation's purpose, process, and performance) identified by Lee and See [29]. The SAT framework consists of three levels of information requirements from one agent (e.g. a robot) to its partner (e.g. a human operator) to support the partner's *perception* of the agent's current actions and plans (Level 1), *comprehension* of its underlying logic (Level 2), and *projections* of future outcomes based on the agent's predicted end-states of current actions and plans (e.g. likelihood of success/failure), and any uncertainty associated with the projections (Level 3). The SAT framework, after its initial introduction in 2014 [8], was updated in 2018 [9] to incorporate bidirectional communications and teaming-related aspects between human and machine agents. The SAT framework has been adopted by numerous research groups with their own modifications and additions such as "what if" simulation as a Level 3 item [4, 16, 46].

## 10.3 Implementation of Transparent Human–Machine Interfaces in Intelligent Systems

### 10.3.1 Human–Robot Interaction

Agent transparency has significant implications for a wide variety of human-agent systems, which require appropriate human trust calibration and effective joint decision-making. Transparent

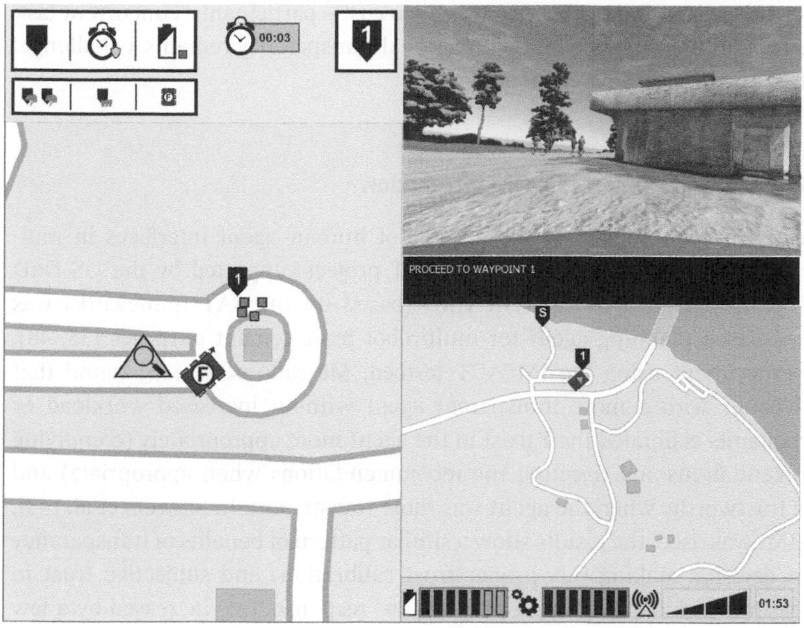


**Figure 10.1** "At-a-glance" transparency module (upper left corner) [53].

interfaces for human–robot interaction (HRI) have been implemented in various contexts – from military robotic teammates to assistive robots for older adults. For example, the SAT framework was used to guide the human–machine interface (HMI) designs for the Autonomous Squad Member (ASM) project supported by the U.S. Department of Defense's Autonomous Research Pilot Initiative [47, 53]. The ASM's HMI features an "at a glance" transparency module (Figure 10.1), where iconographic representations are used to indicate the ASM's current actions and plans (SAT Level 1), top motivators (SAT Level 2), and projected outcomes and uncertainties (SAT Level 3). Simulation-based studies on the ASM's transparent interface show that research participants had greater SA and trust in the ASM when it was more transparent [47]. The additional information required for higher levels of transparency did increase participants' fixations on the transparency module but no increase in subjective workload. However, when the ASM was unreliable, even with a high level of transparency, participants' trust and perceptions of the robot degraded [53]. In contrast to the findings of Wright et al. [53], Pynadath et al. [40] found that robot transparency (about the reasoning process behind its recommendations) had a positive effect on the human–robot team performance (in a military reconnaissance context) *especially* when robots were not perfectly reliable, as it enabled human teammates to identify robots' incorrect input or assumptions.

In the context of assistive robots, Olatunji et al. [38] developed transparent HMIs for person-following and table-setting robots to support older adults. Olatunji et al. found that the participants (aged 62 years and older) were more engaged in HRI activities when interacting with robots with a lower level of automation and a higher level of transparency (information about the human, the robot, HRI task, and the environment).

Recent efforts have started to examine ways to promote bidirectional/mutual transparency in human–agent teams [9]. For example, in a simulated human–robot collaboration study, Lakhmani [28] found that participants perceived the more interactive robot (both pushing and pulling information) – compared with the less interactive one (push only) – to be more animate, likeable, and intelligent. However, the greater interactivity came with a cost – participants' concurrent task performance degraded. This finding suggests that bidirectional transparency remains a challenge, particularly in highly dynamic tasking environments.

### 10.3.2 Multiagent Systems and Human–Swarm Interaction

Transparency principles have been applied to the designs of human–agent interfaces in multiagent management contexts. For example, in the IMPACT project supported by the US DoD Autonomy Research Pilot Initiative, a transparent HMI (based on the SAT framework) was developed for a *Playbook*-based planning agent for multirobot management purposes [35, 48]. In a simulation-based experiment using the IMPACT testbed, Mercado et al. [35] found that participants performed better with a more transparent agent without increased workload or response time. The participants calibrated their trust in the agent more appropriately (complying with the agent's recommendations and rejecting the recommendations when appropriate) and rated the agent as more trustworthy when the agent was more transparent. In Stowers et al. [48], in which a redesigned HMI was used, the results show a similar pattern of benefits of transparency for supporting operator decision-making (i.e. proper trust calibration) and subjective trust in the agent without increasing workload (although participants' response time increased by a few seconds in the most transparent condition). An Australian group of military researchers developed a multiagent management HMI based on the SAT framework and evaluated the interface's efficacy in an experimental paradigm similar to the IMPACT's [3]. The results are largely consistent with those reported in Mercado et al. in terms of task performance and workload. Participants performed better with SAT Level 1 + 2 information compared with the SAT Level 1 information only. However, when the Level 3 (projections) information was added to the interface, participants had a tendency to overtrust the agent when it was incorrect.

In the context of helicopter cockpit environments, Roth et al. [43] applied transparency principles based on the SAT framework to design the HMI of an adaptive cognitive agent to support human pilots' SA and comprehension of the agent's actions (e.g. interventions based on pilots' workload levels) in multiagent management tasks. Roth et al. found that, in a simulation-based human subject experiment, transparent interfaces enhanced participants' task performance, SA, and perceptions of the agent, although the workload results were less conclusive.

Transparent human–swarm interaction presents unique challenges as uncertainties due to latency and asynchrony between human input and swarm responses may affect humans' assessments of swarm's states and dynamics as well as predictions of emergent swarm behaviors based on human input. Empirical studies show that humans' trust in swarm systems are often based on swarms' visually available patterns rather than their task performance, which tends to be less perceivable due to the nonlinear dynamics of swarms [37]. To better support transparency, Hepworth et al. [16] develop a human–swarm interaction and management architecture (Human–Swarm-Teaming Transparency and Trust), with all three SAT levels (i.e. interpretability, explainability, and predictability) embedded. In Ref. [44], Roundtree et al. identify several key HMI design challenges associated with transparency principles based on the SAT model. In a follow-on study on visualization techniques in a human–swarm interaction context (managing a swarm of 200 agents), Roundtree et al. [45] demonstrate that transparency-based visualizations that showed the agents collectively supported better human performance (situation awareness) than did those that showed the agents individually. Detailed design guidelines on transparent human–swarm interface visualizations are available in Roundtree et al. [45].

### 10.3.3 Automated/Autonomous Driving

In the area of automated and autonomous driving, transparency principles have been applied to HMI designs. For example, Kridalukmana [26] develops the HMI for an advanced driving assistance system, based on the agent's Artificial SA States to generate the three levels of SA-based transparency items. Time constraints are considered to determine when and what items to convey to the human driver. A number of studies empirically tested the effects of transparency in automated and autonomous driving situations. Kraus et al. [25] found that agent transparency (e.g. information about system malfunctions) supported the participants' understanding of the functioning of the automated driving system (SAE Level 3) and mitigated their trust degradations following system malfunctions. Korber et al. [24], on the other hand, found that posthoc explanations (regarding takeover requests) had no overall effect on drivers' trust in the automated system although their perceived understanding of the system increased significantly. In a study in the context of a conditionally automated driving simulation environment [27], uncertainty visualizations supported drivers' performance (SA, trust calibration and appropriate takeovers, and attention allocation); however, operator workload became elevated when frequent visual monitoring was required. Lee et al. [30] suggest that the presence of nondriving-related tasks may make a difference in the utility of transparent interfaces in the context of automated driving – with the effects of transparency being *more* pronounced when the drivers have to engage in nondriving-related tasks.

### 10.3.4 Explainable AI-Based Systems

An emerging area of research related to transparency is eXplainable AI (XAI), defined by Gunning and Aha [14] as "AI systems that can explain their rationale to a human user, characterize their strengths and weaknesses, and convey an understanding of how they will behave in the future." It is interesting to note the striking similarity between this statement (which describes the DARPA XAI program's vision) and the SAT framework [8, 9] – explanations should not only support communication recipients' Level 2 SA (comprehension) but also Level 3 SA (projection).

XAI systems can be delivered via various techniques (e.g. feature- or policy-based explanation, causal link, contrastive explanation, simplification, and local explanation techniques such as LIME, "what if" simulation) and modalities (e.g. visual, language/dialogue, and multimodal) (see review articles by Ref. [5, 36, 42]). For example, Han et al. [15] embedded their XAI agent within an augmented reality system, which projected visual explanations directly into the HRI environment. Recent advances in natural language processing show promising results in enabling bidirectional communications and queries between human and machine agents [40]. Cabour et al. [4] propose the Abstracted Explanation Space framework – with all three SAT [8] levels embedded in the architecture – and present a case study of a HMI-design for an aircraft anomaly detection agent based on the architecture. In the cyber domain, Holder and Wang [19] apply the SAT model in the HMI design of a "junior cyber analyst," which is an XAI-based agent that can assist human analysts in military intelligence analysis. The SAT model was also used to design the XAI-based HMI of a fake news detection agent [12]. In such environments such as military intelligence analysis and fake news detection, transparent HMIs capable of justifying recommendations are particularly beneficial for humans to determine whether to accept the agent's input.

### 10.3.5 Guidelines and Assessment Methods

A number of organizations have published their guidance on designs of systems with transparent HMIs. Some are high-level guidelines on AI systems in general [1, 20], while some are more

**Table 10.1** Guidelines and assessment methods on transparency.

| Author | Domain | References |
|---|---|---|
| ACM | Algorithms | [1] |
| IBM | AI systems | [20] |
| IEEE | Autonomous systems | [52] |
| Hoffman et al. | XAI-based systems | [18] |
| Sanneman and Shah | HRI | [46] |
| van der Waa et al. | XAI/decision support | [51] |
| Vorm | Recommender systems | [50] |

focused on autonomous systems [21, 52]. Specific assessment methods have also been proposed to evaluate system transparency levels. For example, multiple sets of metrics have been proposed by XAI researchers to assess the effectiveness of XAI systems [42]. The metrics largely focus on four aspects of the XAI systems: correctness and robustness; usefulness, understandability, and processing difficulty for the human; congruity (congruence between human's and machine's mental models); generalizability, adaptability, and versatility [36]. A survey, the Explanation Satisfaction Scale, has been developed to evaluate XAI users' experience [18] with a focus on assessing congruence between the AI systems output and the human's mental model of the problem space. Sanneman and Shah [46] propose the SA-Framework for XAI (SAFE-AI) to assess transparency of robots' XAI-based explainer and how well it supports humans' SA. Another assessment method for XAI-based systems is developed by van der Waa et al. [51], particularly for decision support systems. Vorm [50] developed a System Transparency Evaluation Method that is based on his Explanation Vector Framework for recommender systems, focused particularly on system usability-related aspects. These guidelines and assessment methods are summarized in Table 10.1.

## 10.4 Future Research Directions

Transparency research has been primarily focused on two areas: developing transparent HMIs and assessing the effects of transparency on human (or human–machine joint) performance [2]. Sections 10.2 and 10.3 have discussed some examples of the former. Studies on human performance have largely focused on humans' task performance (including SA and calibration of trust in the machine agent), workload (based on self-assessments and physiological measures), and subjective perceptions of the machine agents (e.g. perceived trust, anthropomorphism, intelligence). Effects of agent transparency have also been examined in the contexts of individual and cultural differences [11, 34]. Matthews et al. [34] found that individual differences in humans' attitudes toward robots (e.g. unreasonable expectations of robot capability or negative attitudes toward humanlike robots) may impact their trust calibration and SA. Chien et al. [11] found that there were cultural differences in how people interact with transparent agents, which may impact the degree to which they are willing to accept recommendations from an opaque agent. These results suggest that individual and cultural differences need to be considered when designing transparent HMIs and transitioning systems across cultures. User interface modifications and training interventions may be required to ensure human–machine system effectiveness.

There remain some key challenges that will require further research and development to advance the capabilities of transparent human–machine interfaces. For example, information architectures of agent transparency could be developed to support real-time bidirectional transparency between human and machine agents [9]. Several papers in a recently published *International Journal of Human-Computer Interaction* special issue on Transparent Human-Agent Communications present promising approaches to such architectures [6]. Longitudinal research on long-term effects of transparent interfaces can also be informative. Real-time and dynamic generation of transparency content requires interdisciplinary research and can benefit from advancements in XAI and its subfields such as XAI Planning [5, 36]. Multimodal communications are also promising research areas to keep humans engaged and maintain situation awareness. Finally, issues related to ethics (e.g. privacy and biases) and security (e.g. transparent counter-adversarial manipulations or perturbations) remain challenges and require multidisciplinary collaboration to advance the capabilities.

## References


1 ACM (2017). Statement on algorithmic transparency and accountability. Retrieved 17 March 2021, from https://www.acm.org/binaries/content/assets/public-policy/2017_usacm_statement_algorithms.pdf.

2 Bhaskara, A., Skinner, M., and Loft, S. (2020). Agent transparency: a review of current theory and evidence. *IEEE Transactions on Human-Machine Systems* 50: 215–224.

3 Bhaskara, A., Duong, L., Brooks, J. et al. (2021). Effect of automation transparency in the management of multiple unmanned vehicles. *Applied Ergonomics* 90: 103243.

4 Cabour, G., Morales, A., Ledoux, E., and Bassetto S. (2021). Towards an explanation space to align humans and explainable-AI teamwork. arXiv:2106.01503.

5 Chakraborti, T., Sreedharan, S., and Kambhampati, S. (2020). The emerging landscape of explainable automated planning & decision making. In: *Proceedings of the International Joint Conference on Artificial Intelligence (IJCAI-20)*, vol. 29 (ed. C. Bessiere), 4803–4811. International Joint Conferences on Artificial Intelligence.

6 Chen, J.Y.C. (2022). Transparent human-agent communications. *International Journal of Human Computer Interaction* 38: 1737–1738.

7 Chen, J.Y.C. and Barnes, M.J. (2014). Human-agent teaming for multirobot control: a review of human factors issues. *IEEE Transactions on Human-Machine Systems* 44: 13–29.

8 Chen, J.Y.C., Procci, K., Boyce, M. et al. (2014). *Situation Awareness-Based Agent Transparency (ARL-TR-6905)*. Aberdeen Proving Ground, MD: U.S. Army Research Laboratory.

9 Chen, J.Y.C., Lakhmani, S.G., Stowers, K. et al. (2018). Situation awareness-based agent transparency and human–autonomy teaming effectiveness. *Theoretical Issues in Ergonomics Science* 19: 259–282.

10 Chen, J.Y.C., Flemisch, F., Lyons, J. et al. (2020). Guest editorial: agent and system transparency. *IEEE Transactions on Human-Machine Systems* 50: 189–193.

11 Chien, S., Lewis, M., Sycara, K. et al. (2020). Influence of culture, transparency, trust, and degree of automation on automation use. *IEEE Transactions on Human-Machine Systems* 50: 205–214.

12 Chien, S., Yang, C., and Yu, F. (2022). XFlag: explainable fake news detection model on social media. *International Journal of Human Computer Interaction* 38: 1808–1827.

13 Endsley, M. (1995). Toward a theory of situation awareness in dynamic systems. *Human Factors* 37: 32–64.

14 Gunning, D. and Aha, D. (2019). DARPA explainable AI program. *AI Magazine* 40: 4–53.

15 Han, Z., Allspaw, A., Norton, A., et al. (2019). Towards A robot explanation system: a survey and our approach to state summarization, storage and querying, and human interface. *Proceedings of the AI-HRI Symposium at AAAI-FSS*.

16 Hepworth, A., Baxter, D., Hussein, A. et al. (2021). Human-swarm-teaming transparency and trust architecture. *IEEE/CAA Journal of Automatica Sinica* 8: 1281–1295.

17 High-Level Expert Group on Artificial Intelligence (HLEG AI) (2020). Assessment list for trustworthy AI (ALTAI).

18 Hoffman, R., Mueller, S., Klein, G., et al. (2018). Metrics for explainable AI: challenges and prospects. arXiv preprint arXiv:1812.04608.

19 Holder, E. and Wang, N. (2021). Explainable artificial intelligence (XAI) interactively working with humans as a junior cyber analyst. *Human-Intelligent Systems Integration* 3: 139–153.

20 IBM (2018). IBM's Principles for trust and transparency. Retrieved 17 March 2021, from IBM'S Principles for Data Trust and Transparency.

21 IEEE (2020). IEEE Draft Standard for Transparency of Autonomous Systems. *Technical Report IEEE P7001/D1*, pp. 1–76. Piscataway, NJ: IEEE.

22 International Organization for Standardization (2020). Ergonomics of Human-System Interaction – Part 810: Robotic, Intelligent and Autonomous Systems. *Technical Report ISO/TR 9241-810:2020(E)*. Geneva, Switzerland: ISO.

23 Johnson, M., Bradshaw, J., Feltovich, P. et al. (2014). Coactive design: designing support for interdependence in joint activity. *Journal of Human-Robot Interaction* 3: 43–69.

24 Korber, M., Prasch, L., and Bengler, K. (2018). Why do I have to drive now? Post hoc explanations of takeover requests. *Human Factors* 60: 305–323.

25 Kraus, J., Scholz, D., Stiegemeier, D. et al. (2020). The more you know: trust dynamics and calibration in highly automated driving and the effects of take-overs, system malfunction, and system transparency. *Human Factors* 62: 718–736.

26 Kridalukmana, R. (2021). Human-anatomy teaming with a supportive situation awareness model. PhD dissertation. University of Technology Sydney. Sydney, Australia.

27 Kunze, A., Summerskill, S., Marshall, R. et al. (2019). Automation transparency: implications of uncertainty communication for human-automation interaction and interfaces. *Ergonomics* 62: 345–360.

28 Lakhmani, S. (2019). Transparency and communication patterns in human-robot teaming. PhD dissertation. University of Central Florida. Orlando, Florida, USA.

29 Lee, J. and See, K. (2004). Trust in automation: designing for appropriate reliance. *Human Factors* 46: 50–80.

30 Lee, J., Abe, G., Sato, K. et al. (2020). Impacts of system transparency and system failure on driver trust during partially automated driving. *2020 IEEE International Conference on Human-Machine Systems* (paper #115), Rome, Italy (07–09 September 2020): IEEE.

31 Lyons, J. (2013). Being transparent about transparency: a model for human–robot interaction. In: *Trust and Autonomous Systems* (ed. D. Sofge, G. Kruijff, and W. Lawless), 48–53. Menlo Park, CA: AAAI Press.

32 Lyons, J., Sycara, K., Lewis, M., and Capiola, A. (2021). Human–autonomy teaming: definitions, debates, and directions. *Frontiers in Psychology* 12: 589585.

**33** Matheny, M., Israni, S., Ahmed, M. et al. (2019). *Artificial Intelligence in Health Care: The hope, the Hype, the Promise, the Peril*. Washington, DC: National Academy of Medicine.

**34** Matthews, G., Lin, J., Panganiban, A. et al. (2020). Individual differences in trust in autonomous robots: Implications for transparency. *IEEE Transactions on Human-Machine Systems* 50: 234–244.

**35** Mercado, J., Rupp, M., Chen, J. et al. (2016). Intelligent agent transparency in human-agent teaming for multi-UxV management. *Human Factors* 58: 401–415.

**36** Miller, T. (2019). Explanation in artificial intelligence: Insights from the social sciences. *Artificial Intelligence* 267: 1–38.

**37** Nam, C., Walker, P., Li, H. et al. (2020). Models of trust in human control of swarms with varied levels of autonomy. *IEEE Transactions on Human-Machine Systems* 50: 194–204.

**38** Olatunji, S., Oron-Gilad, T., Markfeld, N. et al. (2021). Levels of automation and transparency: interaction design considerations in assistive robots for older adults. *IEEE Transactions on Human-Machine Systems* 51: 673–683.

**39** O'Neill, T., McNeese, N., Barron, A., and Schelble, B. (2020). Human–autonomy teaming: a review and analysis of the empirical literature. *Human Factors* 64 (5): 1–35.

**40** Pynadath, D., Barnes, M., Wang, N., and Chen, J. (2018). Transparency communication for machine learning in human-automation interaction. In: *Human and Machine Learning. Human–Computer Interaction Series* (ed. J. Zhou and F. Chen), 75–90. Cham: Springer.

**41** Rao, A. and Georgeff, M. (1995). BDI agents: from theory to practice. *Proceedings of the 1st International Conference on Multiagent Systems* 1: 312–319.

**42** Rawal, A., McCoy, J., Rawat, D., and Sadler, B. Recent advances in trustworthy explainable artificial intelligence: status, challenges and perspectives. *IEEE Transactions on Artificial Intelligence* 3 (6): 852–866.

**43** Roth, G., Schulte, A., Schmitt, F. et al. (2020). Transparency for a workload-adaptive cognitive agent in a manned–unmanned teaming application. *IEEE Transactions on Human-Machine Systems* 50: 225–233.

**44** Roundtree, K., Goodrich, M., and Adams, J. (2019). Transparency: transitioning from human–machine systems to human-swarm systems. *Journal of Cognitive Engineering and Decision Making* 13: 171–195.

**45** Roundtree, K., Cody, J., Leaf, J. et al. (2021). Human-collective visualization transparency. *Swarm Intelligence* 15: 237–286.

**46** Sanneman, L. and Shah, J. (2022). The Situation awareness framework for explainable AI (SAFE-AI) and human factors considerations for XAI systems. *International Journal of Human Computer Interaction* 38: 1772–1788.

**47** Selkowitz, A., Lakhmani, S., and Chen, J. (2017). Using agent transparency to support situation awareness of the Autonomous Squad Member. *Cognitive Systems Research* 46: 13–25.

**48** Stowers, K., Kasdaglis, N., Rupp, M. et al. (2020). The IMPACT of agent transparency on human performance. *IEEE Transactions on Human-Machine Systems* 50: 245–253.

**49** Topcu, U., Bliss, N., Cooke, N. et al. (2020). *Assured Autonomy: Path Toward a Transformation Fueled by Autonomous Systems*, 2020. Washington DC: Computing Research Association.

**50** Vorm, E.S. (2019). Into the black box: designing for transparency in artificial intelligence. PhD dissertation. Indiana University. Bloomington, Indiana, USA.

**51** van der Waa, J., Nieuwburg, E., Cremers, A., and Neerincx, M. (2021). Evaluating XAI: a comparison of rule-based and example-based explanations. *Artificial Intelligence* 291: 103404.

**52** Winfield, A., Booth, S., Dennis, L. et al. (2021). IEEE P7001: a proposed standard on transparency. *Frontiers in Robotics and AI* 8: 665729.

**53** Wright, J., Chen, J., and Lakhmani, S. (2020). Agent transparency and reliability in human-robot interaction: the influence on user confidence and perceived reliability. *IEEE Transactions on Human-Machine Systems* 50: 254–263.

# 11

# Conversational Human–Machine Interfaces*

*María Jesús Rodríguez-Sánchez, Kawtar Benghazi, David Griol, and Zoraida Callejas*

*Universidad de Granada, Cuesta del Hospicio sn. 18071, Granada, Spain*

## 11.1 Introduction

According to McTear [13], a dialog or conversational system may be defined as "a computer program that supports spoken, text-based, or multimodal conversation interactions with humans." Thus, these systems support a great variety of input and output modes including, but not limited to, text or spoken interaction [15, 31].

As the underlying technology develops and becomes more robust, conversational interfaces have gained mainstream popularity, and a plethora of new application scenarios have appeared. Personal digital assistants such as Apple Siri or Amazon Alexa are becoming widespread, and many stakeholders are interested in developing voice content for smart speakers as a more direct company–customer communication means [24]. Similarly, chatbots as web-based assistants or on messaging applications (e.g. WhatsApp or Telegram) are also being adopted by companies as part of their customer relationship management protocols.

Natural language conversation is also very well-suited for communication with embodied virtual agents and robots,[1] in car, when the user's hands and eyes are busy [27], or as an intuitive interface that hides the complexity of the services from the user. For example in *ambient intelligence* settings [16], where multiple systems, sensors, devices, and external services are interconnected, while the user can control everything easily by posing voice commands to an assistant. These benefits are even more relevant when accessibility and usability are key, for example, for users that face difficulties employing traditional human–machine interfaces.

## 11.2 Background

There is a long trajectory in research in dialog systems. In Section 11.2.1, we provide a brief historical perspective of the main advances that have promoted the current flourishing of conversational interfaces.

* The research leading to these results has received funding from the Spanish *R&D&i* projects financed by MCIN/AEI/10.13039/501100011033 GOMINOLA (PID2020-118112RB-C21 and PID2020-118112RB-C22) and CAVIAR (TEC2017-84593-C2-1-R), the European Union's Horizon 2020 research and innovation program under grant agreement No. 823907 (MENHIR project: https://menhir-project.eu), and the Andalusian *R&D&i* project BonAppPetit (P18-RT-4550).

1 See, for example the interesting results from the EU-Japan Virtual Coach for Smart Ageing (e-VITA) project: www.e-vita.coach/.

*Handbook of Human-Machine Systems*, First Edition. Edited by Giancarlo Fortino, David Kaber, Andreas Nürnberger, and David Mendonça.

Fuelled by the appearance of big data and the promising results of the use of neural networks and machine learning in dialog systems, the field is becoming more and more attractive for researchers and practitioners in different areas and sectors. These multidisciplinary and cross-sector efforts have led to a rich variety of terminology and sometimes different terms are coined by different communities to refer to the same concept. Section 11.2.2 presents some basic definitions to familiarize the reader with the most relevant vocabulary.

### 11.2.1 History of the Development of the Field

The Turing test in 1950 during the early days of artificial intelligence, linked the intelligence of machine with its ability to make a human believe that it is interacting with another human. Conversational capabilities are essential to achieve a high degree of human-likeliness. The first attempts to build such systems were the chatbots Eliza [29] and Parry [6], text-based systems based in hand-crafted rules that achieved surprising acceptability despite their limited language understanding capabilities.

Rule-based systems have been used since then, mostly to develop systems that solve specific tasks. In fact, it was in the late 1980s when research in dialog systems was established more solidly, with some key projects such as SUNDIAL and DARPA. The Speech Understanding and Dialog (SUNDIAL) project [17] was a conversational agent that can talk with the user about trains and flights timetables in different languages. The DARPA project [9] was in the domain of flights reservation (with ATIS – Air Travel Information Services – corpus data).

Throughout decades commercial systems have been developed using these approaches, with some standardization attempts, for example the W3C VoiceXML markup language,[2] which allows to build rule-based, slot-filling dialogs that are accessible over the phone.

Rule-based approaches have been also used to build more open-ended dialogs. Scripting languages such as AIML have been used to build successful chatbots, e.g. ALICE, which won the Loebner Prize to human-likeliness several times in the early 2000s [28].

Many of the current development tools are to some extent based on crafted rules and state machines to control dialog. However, as will be described in Section 11.3, rule-based systems are difficult to scale and port to new application domains. To address these issues, corpus-based approaches were developed in the 2000s and 2010s to train dialog systems from datasets of human–human conversations [3, 20, 21].

In 2010, IBM Watson set a milestone when their system was able to defeat the human champions in the TV show Jeopardy! answering questions using deep natural language processing [7]. The ability to exploit a massive amount of data and computational resources has made it possible to obtain more human-like chatbot systems, for example Google's Meena (2020) or Facebook's Blender (2020) [14], and favored that personal assistants become mainstream, e.g. Apple's Siri, Amazon's Alexa, or Microsoft Cortana. Big technology companies have organized challenges related to conversational systems. For example, the Alexa Prize,[3] was the competition series that was used by the selected teams to build conversational systems that solve a relevant state-of-the-art challenge.

Despite big technological companies becoming players in the area, academic research continues to explore new opportunities and address the many challenges of current dialog systems (see Section 11.4). For a more complete survey, see [1, 18].

2 https://www.w3.org/TR/voicexml30/ (Last access: January 2022)
3 https://developer.amazon.com/alexaprize (Last access: January 2021)

### 11.2.2 Basic Definitions

Possible names for the conversational interface:

- *Dialog system*. It is a computer program that can hold a conversation with human users.
- *Conversational system/interface*. We consider it as a synonym of *dialog system*.
- *Conversational AI*. It is similar to a *conversational system*, but has the additional connotation that the system exploits artificial intelligence methods, so it is usually employed for systems developed using a corpus-based approach (see Section 11.3).
- *Chatbot*. Sometimes used interchangeably with *dialog/conversational system*, it usually refers to nontask-oriented systems, that is, a system with which the user converses without a specific purpose (see Section 11.3).
- *Voice user interface (VUI)*. It can be used as a synonym of *dialog / conversational system*, although the term VUI is more frequent within the industrial sphere, compared to dialog system, which is more widespread in academia.

Relevant components of conversational interfaces:

- *Automatic speech recognizer (ASR)*. It is the part of the dialog system that recognizes the user's utterance converting voice into text.
- *Natural language understanding (NLU)*. This module transforms the textual representation of the user input into a semantic representation, that is, it determines the meaning of the user input.
- *Dialog manager (DM)*. This provided an understanding of the user input, the previous history of the dialog and other sources of information, it determines the next action to be taken. According to [13], it can be further subdivided into a dialog context model and a dialog decision/policy model.
- *Natural language generation (NLG)*. This module generates the response to the user in text format.
- *Text-to-speech synthesis (TTS)*. It transforms a textual system prompt into synthesized speech (reads the output aloud).

For an illustrative review of these technologies through the lens of a virtual conversational assistant check [31].

Deep learning has brought its own terminology into the dialog systems. The most widespread approach is **Transfer Learning**, which leverages prior knowledge in a certain task, domain, or language into a different task, usually to take advantage of models trained with a massive amount of data. The most popular approaches to transfer learning in conversational systems are **sequence-to-sequence (Seq2Seq)** models, where the deep network automatizes all the intermediate processing steps and maps a dialog context into a learned distributed representation and then generates the next system response using an **encoder/decoder** structure (more details in [2]).

## 11.3 State-of-the-Art

This section presents a review of the most relevant state-of-the-art in conversational/dialog systems, with a comparison of the advantages and disadvantages of the current development alternatives.

### 11.3.1 Discussion of the Most Important Scientific/Technical Contributions

Dialog systems can be classified into two big groups: task-oriented (goal-oriented) and nontask-oriented (chat-oriented, open domain).

Task-oriented systems aim to assist the user in completing certain tasks (e.g. book a flight, respond to questions about a specific topic, or control an appliance). They can be single or multidomain according to their knowledge base and the topic/s in which the system is expert in. Most dialog systems are experts in only one specific domain and are difficult to port to another, so current research efforts are addressed to developing multidomain conversational systems or transferring knowledge and conversational abilities between domains.

Nontask-oriented systems engage in chit-chat dialogs with users usually with no specific purpose, that is, the social aspect is more relevant than achieving a particular objective. Open-domain systems are aimed at establishing a conversation with the user, but do not necessarily have a particular expertise in specific topics.

Both types of systems can be developed with a pipelined or end-to-end architecture, although the end-to-end architecture is more frequent with nontask-oriented dialogs.

The traditional approach is a pipelined modular architecture which typically contains five modules that are sequentially connected as shown in Figure 11.1, see Section 11.2.2 for a definition of each module.

The components of the pipeline can be implemented following a rule-based (handcrafted), corpus-based (statistical), or hybrid approach. Thus, it is possible to implement a dialog system following the traditional modular architecture and at the same time develop some of its components using a corpus-based approach.

In the rule-based approach, the responses of the dialog system to the varying user inputs must be anticipated by the designer considering multiple variables, including the "persona" that the system will render. These aspects are studied under the area of *voice user experience (VUX) design*. In contrast, with a corpus-based approach, the different modules can be trained using existing conversation corpora.

The current trend is to embrace an end-to-end paradigm using deep neuronal networks. As shown in Figure 11.2, the aim of end-to-end approaches is to directly take a natural language input and output a natural language response without engaging in the intermediate steps of the pipeline [30]. This approach was introduced in the late 2010s [4] exploiting the encoder–decoder model [26] (see Section 11.2.2).

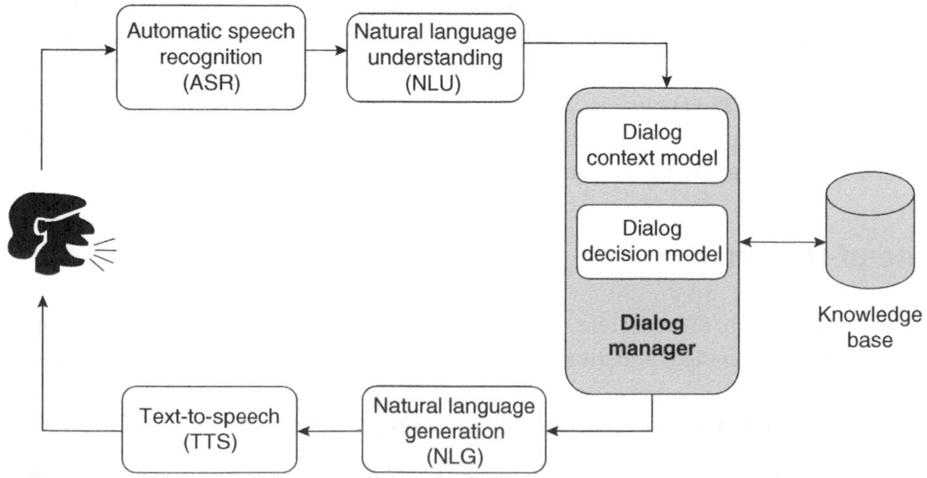


**Figure 11.1** Pipeline classic approach for Dialog Systems.

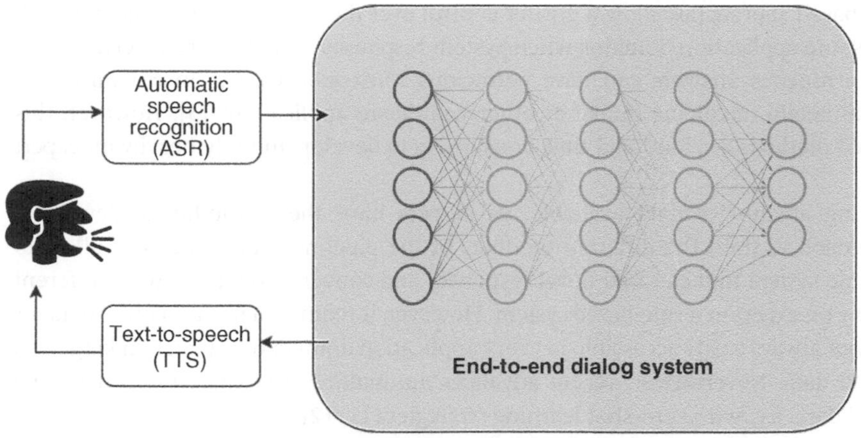


**Figure 11.2** End-to-end approach for dialog systems.

This way, the advances in end-to-end dialog systems come hand to hand with the advances in artificial intelligence, and in particular, with novel approaches to transfer learning in natural language processing and dialog management. These have facilitated to move from recurrent neural network (RNN) architectures to for long short-term memory (LSTM) [23], to extract conversational models from noisy datasets, or to build multidomain systems that capture the conversational dynamics in each domain [19].

As stated in [13], until the 2000s, dialog systems were developed following the rule-based approach with a pipeline architecture. Although neural and end-to-end approaches are becoming the state-of-the-art research trend, pipeline systems and even rule-based approaches are still in force, as they offer several advantages that will be described in Section 11.3.2.

### 11.3.2 Comparison Table

In Section 11.3.1, we, classified dialog systems according to different criteria. Next, we compare the different types identified, highlighting their benefits and potential limitations.

Table 11.1 refers to the classification according to the development approach (pipeline vs. end-to-end). The pipeline approach is further subdivided into rule-based and corpus-based

**Table 11.1** Comparison of the main dialog system development approaches.

| | | Advantages | Limitations |
|---|---|---|---|
| Pipeline | Rule-based | Predictable, controllable | Costly, difficult to maintain, lacks portability to other application domains |
| | Corpus-based | Flexible, unlike end-to-end it is more easily infused with semantic knowledge | Data and training are required for the different stages of the pipeline |
| End-to-End | Corpus-based | No need for intermediate steps, less human intervention required, less need for expert knowledge in language/dialog for its development | Possible incoherent answers, restricted explainability, and reduced control over system answers |

approaches. Rule-based approaches allow a greater control over the outputs of the system, which can be crucial in some application domains when system responses must be very precise and/or unpredictable or erroneous answers can have pernicious consequences, e.g. in certain dialog systems for mental-health, medicine intake or other healthcare applications [5]. However, this kind of handcrafted methods are hard and time-consuming to develop and rely heavily on expert knowledge.

With the growing amount of data available, developers have the possibility to develop a corpus-based approach to train the different modules of the pipeline. These methods allow to build a more flexible system that can find novel responses and conversational pathways different from the ones set by an expert in a rule-based system. However, it requires a big amount of data for training which is not always easily accessible in every application domain or interaction language, specially annotated data. Nevertheless, recent advances are making it possible to decrease the reliance on labeled data, e.g. with zero-shot learning strategies [11, 12].

On the other hand, end-to-end approaches ease development, as they require less expert knowledge in language/dialog technologies, and it is not necessary to implement the modules in the pipeline. This makes it possible to work on tasks for which domain knowledge may not be readily available. Although these systems can be generalized to new domains and may learn to produce system responses not observed during training, they may as well generate trivial or at times illogical responses [25]. Additionally, the black-box nature of these systems makes their decisions less explainable.

Table 11.2 presents the classification of conversational systems according to the type of task addressed, and we distinguish them as task-oriented and nontask-oriented systems. As can be observed, each type of conversational system poses different challenges for its development. Task-oriented systems are based on more structured knowledge. Although the domain is restricted, it is crucial to be able to perform strong semantic understanding and dialog management to identify key entities, predict the user's intention, provide responses that are consistent with the previous dialog history, and be able to recover from recognition errors, as correct task completion is key.

For open-domain systems, the social aspect of interaction is crucial. As there is no particular conversation domain, the system must deal with unstructured data and proceed with the dialog on the basis of users' interests. In this case, it is not necessary to fully understand the user inputs and data-driven methods that are more widespread. For chat applications, timely completion or

**Table 11.2** Comparison of the main types of dialog systems.

| | | Advantages | Limitations |
|---|---|---|---|
| Task-oriented | Single-domain | High success rate in the domain, training data necessary in only one domain | Can only engage successfully in a conversation about the specific domain |
| | Multidomain | Conversations in multiple domains | Potential conflicts among domains (e.g. same words or expressions may belong to multiple topics), need to detect topic change, data required in multiple domains |
| Nontask-oriented | Open-domain | Favors user engagement and interactiveness | Based in less structured knowledge, need to establish a guiding thread in the conversation, social cue processing is key |

minimization of the number of dialog turns is not relevant and sometimes even not desirable. In this case, the objective is to foster engagement and interactiveness.

We provide the previous classifications to present a more structured overview of the topic. However, practical applications often demand multiple dialog capabilities (chat, task completion, and social engagement) within the same system.

## 11.4 Future Research Challenges

In this section, we identify the main research trends, challenges, and limitations of current dialog systems. Then, we provide our personal view of the future directions of the research field.

### 11.4.1 Current Research Issues

Several open research issues are currently being addressed by the dialog systems community, from which we highlight:

- Enhancing human likeliness.
- Rendering consistent and coherent behavior.
- Dealing with data scarcity.
- Fostering multidomain, multiobjective dialogs.
- Enhance data approaches with knowledge infusion.
- Ensuring explainability.
- Ethic assurance, bias avoidance, data security, and privacy.

### 11.4.2 Future Research Directions Dealing with the Current Issues

There is a great interest in making dialog systems more human-like. To do so, future task and nontask-oriented systems must be endowed with better social capabilities, the ability to process social and emotional cues, show affective and empathetic behavior, and a consistent personality.

A particularly challenging aspect of task-based systems, specially in multidomain scenarios, is achieving consistency in the dynamics of the conversation, i.e. that the different turns are in accordance with the history of conversation. With this aim, it is necessary to predict and manage changing user intents and goals. Failure to recognize users' intents is probably the most important cause of frustration and unpleasant experiences when interacting with these systems.

For corpus-based approaches, the insufficient availability of labeled data for dialog manager training is a great limitation. To solve this issue, several avenues are being explored to optimize data collection, use pretrained dialog models, exploit unlabeled data, and transfer resources available for specific domains into different ones. See a review of recent advances and challenges in task-oriented dialog systems in [32].

As chat-based systems gain popularity, there is an increasing interest in infusing commonsense knowledge into these systems and making responses coherent with the previous information provided during the interaction. Another key aspect is to foster model explainability, making the system able to provide justifications to its decisions/recommendations. For a survey of current challenges of neural approaches, see [8, 10].

It is also important that end-to-end systems are able to overcome the biases in the training data, e.g. gender or ethnicity biases, as well as to avoid offensive language. Not only the system should avoid selecting inappropriate answers, but it should ideally be able to protect itself from destructive user behaviors, e.g. sexually explicit content [22].

Data security and privacy are also significant concerns for both providers and users when interacting with conversational systems, specially when confidential, personal, sensitive, or financial data must be transmitted.[4]

## References


1 Adamopoulou, E. and Moussiades, L. (2020). Chatbots: History, technology, and applications. *Machine Learning with Applications* 2: 100006.

2 Azunre, P. (2021). *Transfer Learning for Natural Language Processing*. Manning.

3 Bengio, Y., Ducharme, R., Vincent, P., and Jauvin, C. (2003). A neural probabilistic language model. *Journal of Machine Learning Research* 3: 1137–1155.

4 Bordes, A., Boureau, Y.-L., and Weston, J. (2017). Learning end-to-end goal-oriented dialog. *Proceedings of the 5th International Conference on Learning Representations, ICLR 2017*, Toulon, France.

5 Callejas, Z. and Griol, D. (2021). Conversational agents for mental health and wellbeing. In: *Dialog Systems: A Perspective from Language, Logic and Computation* (ed. T. Lopez-Soto), 219–244. Springer.

6 Colby, K.M. (1975). *Artificial Paranoia: A Computer Simulation of Paranoid Process*. Pergamon Press.

7 Ferrucci, D., Brown, E., Chu-Carroll, J. et al. (2010). Building Watson: an overview of the DeepQA project. *AI Magazine* 31 (3): 59–79.

8 Gao, J., Galley, M., and Li, L. (2019). *Neural Approaches to Conversational AI: Question Answering, Task-oriented Dialogues and Social Chatbots*. Now Foundations and Trends.

9 Hirshman, L. (1989). Overview of the DARPA speech and natural language workshop. *Proceedings of the Speech and Natural Language Workshop*, Philadelphia, USA.

10 Huang, M., Zhu, X., and Gao, J. (2020). Challenges in building intelligent open-domain dialog systems. *ACM Transactions on Information Systems* 38 (3): 21:1–21:32.

11 Lin, Z., Liu, B., Madotto, A. et al. (2021). Zero-shot dialogue state tracking via cross-task transfer.

12 Liu, Z., Winata, G.I., Lin, Z. et al. (2020). Attention-informed mixed-language training for zero-shot cross-lingual task-oriented dialogue systems. *Proceedings of AAAI Conference on Artificial Intelligence*, 8433–8440, New York, USA.

13 McTear, M. (2021). *Conversational AI: Dialogue Systems, Conversational Agents, and Chatbots*. Morgan & Claypool Publishers.

14 McTear, M. and Bond, R. (2020). The conversational user interface: a brief history and futurology of chatbots. *History of Human Computer Interaction*.

15 McTear, M., Callejas, Z., and Griol, D. (2016). *The Conversational Interface. Talking to Smart Devices*. Springer.

16 Merdivan, E., Singh, D., Hanke, S., and Holzinger, A. (2019). Dialogue systems for intelligent human computer interactions. *Electronic Notes in Theoretical Computer Science* 343: 57–71.

17 Peckham, J. (1993). A new generation of spoken dialogue systems: results and lessons from the sundial project. *Proceedings of Eurospeech*, Berlin, Germany.

18 Pieraccini, R. (2021). *AI Assistants*. The MIT Press.


4 e.g. See: https://www.lorentzcenter.nl/speech-as-personal-identifiable-information.html.

**19** Rastogi, A., Zang, X., Sunkara, S. et al. (2020). Towards scalable multi-domain conversational agents: the schema-guided dialogue dataset. *Proceedings of AAAI Conference on Artificial Intelligence*, volume 34, 8689–8696, New York, USA.

**20** Ritter, A., Cherry, C., and Dolan, B. (2010). Unsupervised modeling of Twitter conversations. *Proceedings of the 2010 Annual Conference of the North American Chapter of the ACL*, 172–180. Los Angeles, USA.

**21** Roller, S., Dinan, E., Goyal, N. et al. (2021). Recipes for building an open-domain chatbot. *Proceedings of the 16th Conference of EACL*, 300–325, Virtual Meeting, ACL.

**22** Ruane, E., Birhane, A., and Ventresque, A. (2019). Conversational AI: social and ethical considerations. *Proceedings of AICS - 27th AIAI Irish Conference on Artificial Intelligence and Cognitive Science*, 104–115. Galway, Ireland.

**23** Sherstinsky, A. (2020). Fundamentals of recurrent neural network (RNN) and long short-term memory (LSTM) network. *Physica D: Nonlinear Phenomena* 404: 32306.

**24** Smith, K.T. (2020). Marketing via smart speakers: what should Alexa say? *Journal of Strategic Marketing* 28 (4): 350–365.

**25** Sordoni, A., Galley, M., Auli, M. et al. (2015). A neural network approach to context-sensitive generation of conversational responses.

**26** Sutskever, I., Vinyals, O., and Le, Q.V. (2014). Sequence to sequence learning with neural networks. *Advances in Neural Information Processing Systems*, 3104–3112.

**27** Vernuccio, M., Patrizi, M., and Pastore, A. (2021). Developing voice-based branding: insights from the Mercedes case. *Journal of Product & Brand Management* 30 (5): 726–739.

**28** Wallace, R.S. (2009). The anatomy of A.L.I.C.E.. In: *Parsing the Turing Test: Philosophical and Methodological Issues in the Quest for the Thinking Computer* (ed. R. Epstein, G. Roberts, and G. Beber), 181–210. Springer.

**29** Weizenbaum, J. (1966). Eliza-a computer program for the study of natural language communication between man and machine. *Communications of the ACM* 9 (1): 36–45.

**30** Wen, T.-H., Vandyke, D., Mrksic, N. et al. (2016). A network-based end-to-end trainable task-oriented dialogue system.

**31** Young, S. (2021). *Hey Cyba. The Inner Working of a Virtual Personal Assistant*. Cambridge University Press.

**32** Zhang, Z., Takanobu, R., Zhu, Q. et al. (2020). Recent advances and challenges in task-oriented dialog systems. *Science China Technological Sciences* 63: 2011–2027.

# 12

# Interaction-Centered Design: An Enduring Strategy and Methodology for Sociotechnical Systems

*Ming Hou, Scott Fang, Wenbi Wang, and Philip S. E. Farrell*

*Toronto Research Center, Defence Research and Development Canada, Toronto, Canada*

## 12.1 Introduction

Artificial intelligence (AI) and robotics as two emerging and disruptive technologies (EDTs) of the Fourth Industrial Revolution evolve rapidly and become ubiquitous in our society. These EDTs enable the transformation of machines from simple automation to complex autonomy (i.e. systems with autonomous functions) that replace human physical tasks with improved productivity, augment human cognitive functions (e.g. information processing) with increased mental capacity, and enhance human decision-making capabilities with collective human–machine intelligence. The merge of biology-based human intelligence with technology-based machine intelligence has fostered the advance of twenty-first century human–machine symbiosis (HMS) technologies that are becoming ubiquitous to many domains of human activity. The trend introduces important issues about the limitations, liabilities, privacy, risks, and trust associated with growing autonomy in safety-critical sociotechnical applications such as self-driving vehicles, homecare robots, Industry 4.0 smart manufacturing, or remotely piloted combat drones. Society is confronting major challenges to assure the safety and trustworthiness of HMS technologies that manifest aggregate intelligence empowered by optimized human–machine teaming (HMT) equipped with their united capabilities and strengths to attain shared objectives.

While these HMS technologies can provide solutions to a wide range of human needs, capability gaps, and challenges, the digitization of our society is not intended to replace human involvement completely. The use of AI and robotics involves complex legal, ethical, moral, social, and cultural issues that may impede their development, evaluation, and exploitation [2, 5, 21]. However, currently there is a lack of guidance to support the design, development, and validation of these HMS technologies while keeping benefits, as well as limitations and potential harm, in mind. Errors caused by actions or faulty advice from AI systems can put human lives at risk and may even lead to unintended conflicts or catastrophic consequences. For example, one of the five main reasons for the two fatal crashes of the Boeing 737 Max in 2018 and 2019 is a faulty assumption about the system design and performance of human pilots [7, 8]. The faulty assumption and disregard for design principles and regulations made the two Boeing 737 Max flight crews confused, lost control, and failed with the AI-enabled but uncontrollable maneuvering characteristics augmentation system (MCAS). It reiterates that the design of HMS sociotechnical systems needs to seriously consider the capacity and capability limitations of both human intelligence and machine intelligence. It reaffirms that the human needs to have the authority to be in control during

*Handbook of Human-Machine Systems*, First Edition. Edited by Giancarlo Fortino, David Kaber, Andreas Nürnberger, and David Mendonça.

emergencies with sufficient situation awareness (SA) about the status of the task, environment, and what the machine is doing and intends to do. These principles are crucial when considering technical, institutional, legal, regulatory, and human factors (e.g. misuse, abuse, and adversarial use) for the development of an AI/Autonomy Code of Ethics [23, 24].

With so much at stake, it calls for the imperative needs of appropriate enduring strategy, science-based design methodologies, and evidence-based process standards to ensure that these HMS technologies can be trusted and employed effectively, safely, legally, and ethically before AI or autonomy is exploited more broadly across domains in multiple ways. This chapter introduces intelligent adaptive system (IAS) first as an emerging HMS technological solution to address the aforementioned issues. It then reviews the evolution of IAS design strategies followed with an interaction-centered design (ICD) methodology, a trust model for developing trustworthy IASs, and associated IAS development roadmap that have been validated through mission-critical system designs and applications. The systemic and structured ICD approach as an enduring strategy and guiding principle has been validated and adopted by North Atlantic Treaty Organization (NATO) standards for human systems integration with autonomy. Future work on their broader integration with systems engineering processes for ethics and trustworthiness validation is recommended.

## 12.2 Evolution of HMS Design Strategy

Since World War II, the technological breakthroughs have been focusing on solving problems related to environmental forces such as space travel in the 1950s. With the advance of high-performance computing, the focus has evolved into solutions of information processing and decision-making problems in the 1980s. Recent technological progresses in AI and augmented cognition offer new possibilities for enhancing human capabilities that have accelerated the development of adaptive automation aids and intelligent human–machine interfaces (HMIs) for cognitively complex and challenging applications [21, 35]. These automation and interface technologies become essential components of an IAS with the capabilities of changing their behavior and displays in real-time as a function of the user cognitive state and the status of task, machine, and world (i.e. working environment). IASs are HMS technologies with collective human–machine intelligence that can intelligently adapt to the competency, capacities, limitations and requirements of the user and the machine in real-time to attain and maintain safety, trust, effectiveness, and efficiency with which humans perform various cognitively challenging tasks in complex and dynamic environments [21].

### 12.2.1 A HMS Technology: Intelligent Adaptive System

To achieve IAS objectives discussed above for its broad range of applications, the system needs to exhibit at least five fundamental characteristics: (i) tracking goals, plans, or intents, and the progress toward them; (ii) monitoring and inferring the internal state of the user (e.g. behavioral, physical, cognitive, and emotional); (iii) monitoring and inferring the external status of the world (e.g. environmental conditions, entities, and domain constraints); (iv) monitoring the effects of machine status, automation, advice, and adaptation on user and world status (i.e. closed-loop feedback); and (v) customizing HMI to handle the interaction between the user and the machine [21]. With this understanding, a comprehensive review on both theoretical concepts and practical design approaches over the past few decades for constructing knowledge-based IASs, a generic and integrated framework and associated design methodologies were developed to provide

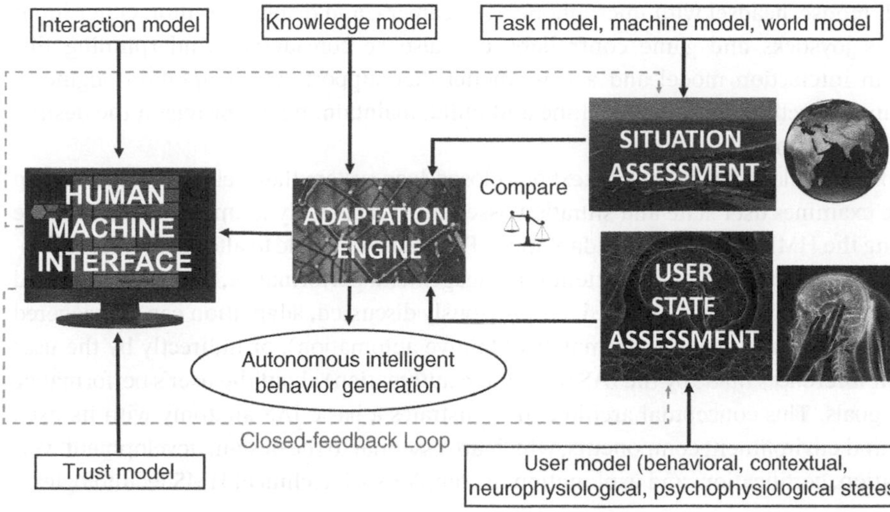


**Figure 12.1** A generic conceptual architecture of an IAS with critical modules and supporting models [21].

guidance for systems designers to gain a high-level technical understanding of the scope and capabilities of IAS components and how they interact with each other to achieve common goals [17, 21]. Accordingly, a conceptual architecture was developed as a basic IAS anatomy with critical components that are common to all knowledge-based IASs. As illustrated in Figure 12.1, a generic IAS includes four modules regarding situation assessment, user state assessment, adaptation engine, and HMI. There are also a number of knowledge models to support each of these modules.

**Situation assessment** is concerned with the assessment of the external world, or the "situation," and comprises functionality relating to the real-time analysis of the activities (to achieve a specific goal), automation, and decision support. Underpinning this module are task, machine, and world models that monitor and track the current progress toward a specific activity, goal, or status through the sensing and fusion of internal (i.e. machine status) and external data sources by using task, goal, and situational knowledge. This knowledge supports the adaptation engine module to decide appropriate strategies to assist the user through decision support, automation, or by adapting what information is presented to the user through the HMI.

**User state assessment** provides information and knowledge about user state within the context of a specific work activity. The module comprises functionality relating to real-time analysis of the user's behavioral, contextual, neurophysiological, and psychophysiological states. Underpinning this component is a user model that supports the continuous monitoring of user workload and making inferences about the current focus of the user's attention, engagement with the tasks, ongoing cognition (e.g. visual and verbal processing load), emotion, and intentions. This information is used to optimize user performance and safety and provides a basis for the implementation of user assistance and trust calibration.

**Adaptation engine** uses high-level outputs from the user state assessment and situation assessment modules. Underpinning this component is a knowledge model that has abstract representations of the context knowledge about application domain, task, user, machine, and world. The knowledge supports the module to maximize the fit of the user state provided by the user state assessment module to the machine status and situational assessments provided by the situation assessment module.

**Human–machine interface** is the means by which the user interacts with the machine to satisfy common goals. There are many ways that a user can interact with the system through the

HMI: keyboard, mouse, headset with microphone, web camera, and display monitor. Other input devices, such as joysticks and game controllers, can also be considered. Underpinning this component is an interaction model and a trust model that supports the adaptation engine to optimize human interactions with the machine and build, maintain, repair, or regain the desired trust (i.e. trust calibration and assurance).

Overall, all four modules work in the context of a closed-loop system that a closed-feedback loop in each module examines user state and situation assessment repeatedly to update all knowledge models following the HMI or automation adaptation. Thus, an IAS is able to alter the level of adaptation such that optimal user states (e.g. attention, engagement, performance, and workload) and trust are achieved, maintained, and assured. As previously discussed, adaptation can be triggered directly by the user through explicit commands (adaptive automation), or indirectly by the user through implicit inferences made by the IAS (adaptable automation) about the user's performance against system goals. This conceptual architecture illustrates a basic IAS anatomy with its user, machine, task, and environment components, which are essential to the design, development, verification, validation, certification, and exploitation of complex sociotechnical HMS technologies.

### 12.2.2 Evolution of IAS Design Strategy

As humans play more and more supervisory roles (e.g. controlling a self-driving car using an autopilot) during interactions with machine partners, appropriate design strategy and methods are needed to understand what needs to be done when humans switch from supervisory control to manual control or verse visa. This helps foresee and mitigate potential risks or accidents that humanity often recollects important lessons learned from historical incidents. It will also provide a means to understand and mitigate potential risks associated with the exploitation of the HMS technologies and thus offer methodological foundations to the development of relevant legal, social, and ethical frameworks. Therefore, it is critical to understand the evolution of design strategy based on established principles and methodologies first.

**Technology-centered design (TCD):** the development of traditional automation and HMI usually follow a TCD strategy that started in the 1950s and mostly based on a task model [9]. As

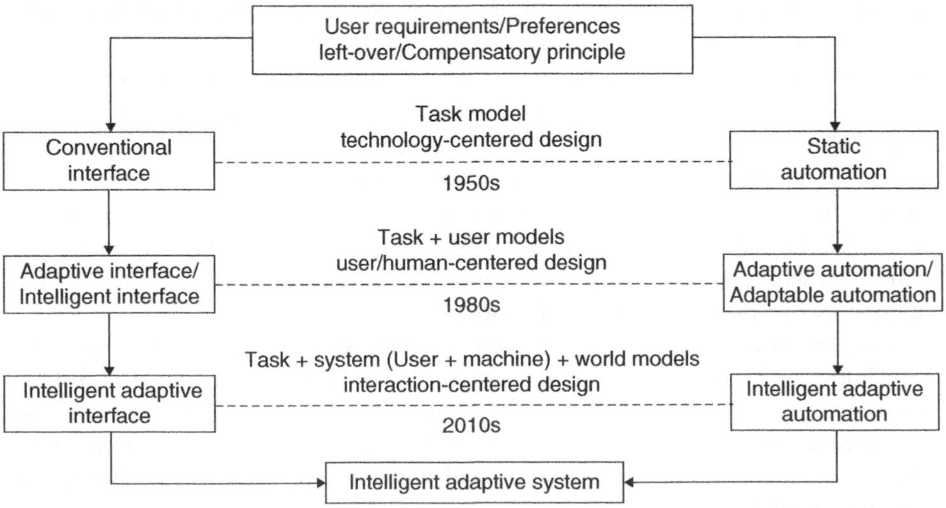


**Figure 12.2** Evolution of design strategy for interface and automation technologies as two critical components of an IAS from TCD to UCD/HCD and then to ICD principles [21].

depicted in Figure 12.2, they incorporate a combination of user requirements and preferences and emphasize on how to allocate more tasks to automation. The goal is to reduce user workload and increase productivity, efficiency, or convenience. Designers can use a task model to preplan and predesign all automation functions. With basic situational knowledge and task requirements, technology acts as an assistant to the human through a HMI and the user does not take over the automation's tasks [21]. Automation capability is derived from the leftover and compensatory principles. The leftover principle states that humans are left with functions that have not been automated or that could not be automated. The compensatory principle states that function allocation is based on the strengths and limitations of the human and of the machine.

The desire to support the human more flexibly has cultivated the birth of adaptive or adaptable automation, and adaptive or intelligent interface technologies [21]. To help the user, the technology initiates automation supports based on one or more of the following triggering conditions: (i) assessment of task status; (ii) user attention and engagement status; and (iii) user stress or workload levels. Understanding and updating of the related information requires a user model that contains the system's knowledge of the capabilities, limitations, and needs of the user. This then advanced the evolution of design strategy from a TCD to a user-centered design (UCD) or human-centered design (HCD) approach in the 1980s with the shift of focus onto human elements of the system from technology capabilities.

**User-centered design (UCD) and human-centered design (HCD):** HCD covers a broader group of people impacted by the design (i.e. stakeholders), whereas UCD refers only to those who directly use the system. Both UCD and HCD take the problem-solving approach that begins with the understanding of the users involved in a human–machine system and applies this understanding to the design of the system [31, 33]. The underlying goal of UCD and HCD is to ultimately create designs with improved usability and performance such that the users will adopt and embrace. Thus, it requires the knowledge of both task and user models [32, 33], as shown in Figure 12.2. As a critical component of an IAS shown in Figure 12.1, the user model may incorporate physiological, psychological, and emotional preferences as well as perception mechanisms and limitations into the characteristics of human behavior and performance. The focus is to understand the user such that automation and HMI technologies can adapt to the human needs and demands. With both task and user models, human–machine interactions can be active such that the machine can take over user's tasks if given permission and then the user can play a supervisory role and maintain "on-the-loop" [21].

Since the human is just one of the many attributes of the broader human–machine system and design should emphasize the system as a whole. Early in the 1990s, Vicente posited that the UCD approach is not always ideal, arguing that for certain domains, a systems design perspective is more advantageous [38]. An issue with HCD has been further identified as local optimization that fails to consider the big picture and system's perspective. This is because designers might tend to focus on a specific person or group without having proper support for the entire activity or they may listen to the users too much and end up with a design that lacks cohesion and vision [32]. From a systems' perspective, knowledge of user and task models only is not sufficient for designing the entire system. Designers should also be equipped with models of the intended machine and the world (i.e. working environment of the anticipated system) [21]. Further, as technologies turn into independent entities, issues about human–machine interactions come to the forefront [34]. Meanwhile, as the frontiers between human and technologies blur, systems HMS technology designers need to realize that they are developing not only technologies but also relationships [36]. Thus, IAS design strategy has naturally evolved into an ICD phase with the focus on interactions of all system components (i.e. task, user, machine, and environment).

**Interaction-centered design (ICD):** since UCD or HCD is insufficient to address issues for domain applications of safety-critical systems with sociotechnical complexities [32], the knowledge of task and user models need to be expanded to include models of machine and the world, as illustrated in Figure 12.2. These models enable system intelligence as functional integration, rather than function allocation (between human and machine) that is a key characteristic of IASs [21]. With functional integration, the task execution and performance required by the application domain are shared across multiple functional components, including the user and automation through interactions via HMI. Thus, the same task can be performed by one of several components like effective human–human collaborative partnerships that maintain shared SA toward achieving system common goals. At this stage, functional integration with collective human–machine intelligence creates robust systems that are better able to handle unexpected events. This is extremely important in emergency situations. For example, safety redundancies should be built into the aircraft control systems to allow an alternate course of action if a key component fails. If this strategy had been followed by the Boeing 737 Max design, the two catastrophic accidents in 2018 and 2019 could have been avoided even though MCAS failed as essential IAS characteristics, functional integration.

An IAS then exhibits humanlike behaviors of both intelligence and adaptability to dynamically and intelligently optimize task integrations based on the needs, strengths, and limitations of both the user and the technology. Therefore, an IAS is essentially the unified evolution of an intelligent and adaptive interface and intelligent adaptive automation into a hybrid system that features the state-of-the-art automation and HMI technologies. Figure 12.2 illustrates the parallel evolution of design principles for interface and automation technologies from TCD to UCD/HCD, and then to ICD. It also demonstrates their consistent evolution and eventual amalgamation into the IAS.

## 12.3 State-of-the-Art: Interaction-Centered Design

Unlike conventional automation systems that rely on discrete control centers, IASs are fully integrated systems that adopt agent-like properties. Although various system components, such as machine hardware or software entities, can be agents, the term "agent" here specially refers to AI software agents. Agent-based concepts offer a significant benefit to human–machine interactions [39]. Agent-based IAS design demonstrates a paradigm shift in automation and HMI technologies from being tools that are used to complete a specific job to entities that collaborate with users or work independently on behalf of users. Following an ICD approach, IAS design emphasizes augmenting human judgment (e.g. decision-making) and responsibilities with the knowledge about task processes and user interactions. An IAS contains many agents to understand users, act for users, and explain and specify adaptations to users. Human–machine interaction is then essentially human–agent interaction. With assistance from various agents, an IAS provides flexible task allocation between users and agents while maintaining overall human authority.

### 12.3.1 A Generic Agent-based ICD Framework

To optimize human–agent interactions, agents need to explain the system status and suggest next steps if necessary. Agents have the intelligence of user' intentions, task performance, stress and resource level, and attention and engagement with tasks. They are also adaptive to the changes in the status of task, machine, environment, and user states. Further, agents communicate and

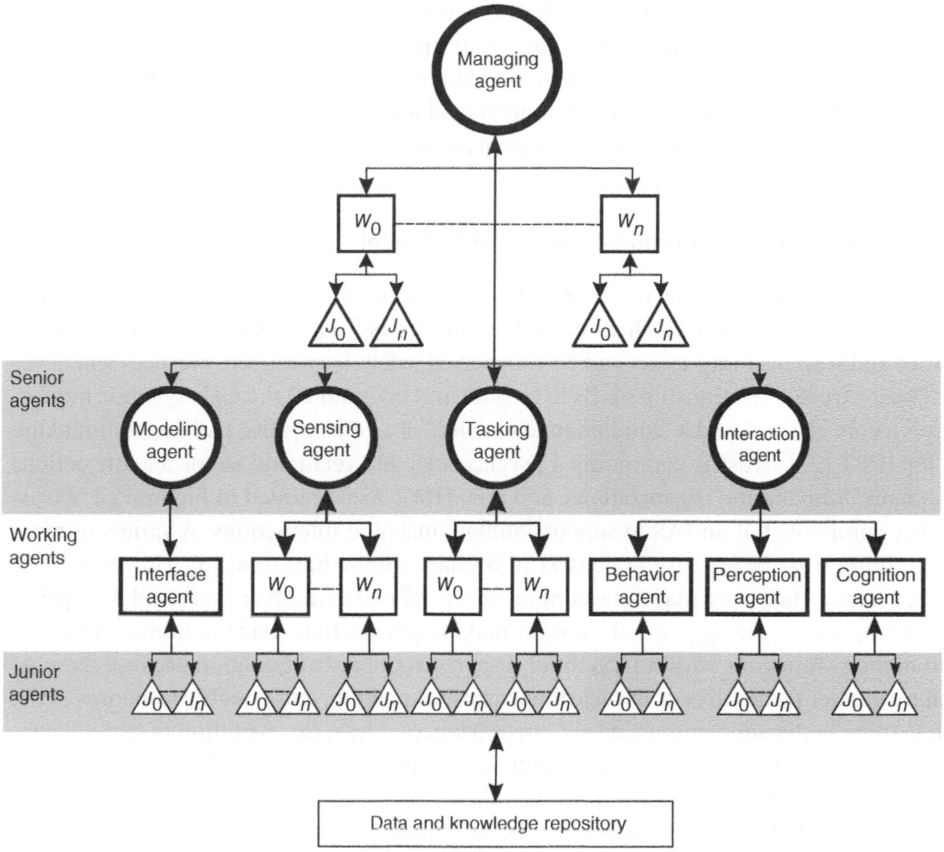


**Figure 12.3** A conceptual agent-based framework for the design of an IAI where four levels of agent groups working together to facilitate interactions among themselves and with human partners toward IAS system common goals [21].

cooperate among themselves to achieve their common goals. Thus, an IAS contains multiple AI agents that are not only intelligent and adaptive but also cooperative. As an IAS example, Figure 12.3 illustrates a generic conceptual agent-based architecture for an intelligent adaptive interface (IAI) to address human cognitive limitations in attention, memory, learning, and decision-making. This type of IASs extends human information management capacity through AI and computing technologies. An IAS computational capability monitors the state of the user, through behavioral, psychophysiological, and/or neurophysiological data in real-time to generate system intelligence adaptation strategy to augment the computational HMI for improved system performance (see user model in Figure 12.1). The IAI conceptual framework typically includes four different function groups (i.e. managing, senior, working, and junior agents) of hierarchically managed agents that work collaboratively with the user for increased SA and maximized IAS performance. The IAI framework is then a cooperative multiagent architecture that track of all system resources. As such, this architecture plays a crucial role in facilitating human–agent interactions [19].

The agent-based hierarchical architecture shown in Figure 12.3 represents a typical translation of ICD methodology into IAS functional design to facilitate human–machine interactions with the capabilities of perceiving, reasoning, interpreting, and projecting the current and future status of the user, the task, the machine, and the environment. It can also predict user's attention, intention, and performance. The prescriptive aiding capability supports decision-making on task integration and execution, automation adaptation and management strategy, system behaviors, and transfer of responsibilities, etc. Thus, this approach offers a foundation for AI agents to adapt simultaneously and in real-time to the user, the working environment, and to the task context in order to assist the user in effectively performing tasks, achieving system goals, ensuring safety, and enabling trust.

### 12.3.2 IMPACTS: An Human–Machine Teaming Trust Model

IAS requires active human–machine collaborations where both human and machine act and support each other proactively toward achieving system objectives [21]. Active collaboration means that authority and responsibility to act can be transferred safely between the partners whenever necessary. Thus, a trusted relationship needs to be built and maintained through dynamic interactions. Trust is a core element and a "fundamental enabler" of a collaborative IAS decision-making capability for HMT [22]. Trust is commonly a psychosocial and relational factor for interactions between humans, humans and organizations, and now HMT. As illustrated in Figure 12.1, a trust model is a key component of an IAS to support human–machine interactions. A variety of models exist examining trust factors in the context of human–automation trust [6]. However, these trust models, whereas thorough, may not examine aspects related to the ever-increased AI capabilities and their impacts on the aggregated decision-making powers that reside in human–machine teams. Autonomous functions within IASs differ from conventional automation because these AI functions have greater flexibilities of self-learning, decision-making, and possibly responses to the requests in extremely dynamic and uncertain circumstances. Thus, the evolution of technologies from conventional automation to intelligent adaptive automation (see Figure 12.2) influences the trust relationship between the human and the technology [22].

As machines and IASs exhibit higher levels of autonomy and intelligence, Hou et al. [21] and Sheridan [37] suggest that the human–autonomy trust relationship mirror that of human-to-human trust to reflect dynamic and complex HMT nature. For human relationships, trust is concerned with capability and integrity. Human trust in autonomy cannot exist without these two attributes. Capabilitywise, IASs with AI-enabled autonomous functions are more competent than their human partners in certain areas. To build up humanlike integrity, a model of IMPACTS has been developed for IASs to exhibit seven characteristics to gain actual trust from

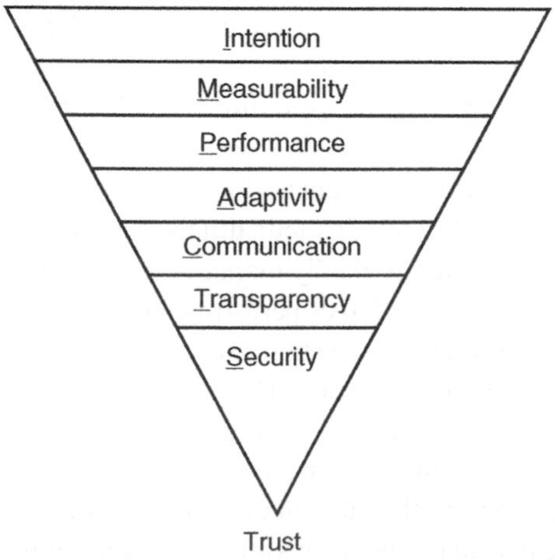


**Figure 12.4** IMPACTS: a trust model with seven integrity characteristics [22].

humans [22]. As illustrated in Figure 12.4, the essential characteristics of the IMPACTS model are intention, measurability, performance, adaptivity, communication, transparency, and security.

The design of IASs should enable a machine with associated AI agents to exhibit its shared intention to achieve common goals with its human partner. These AI agents' behaviors, actions, and patterns need to be measurable to gauge their supportive intentions. The performance of these AI agents needs to be valid, reliable, dependable, and predictable. AI agents also need to be adaptive to the changes of the status of user, task, machine, and working environment. Bi-directional communications are required between agents and their human partners as a key to team success. Transparency about AI agents' critical decision-making tasks and intentions are critically required to build mutual understanding of the collaborative relationship. AI agents should also protect an IAS from accidents or deliberate threats (e.g. cyberattack) and thus build human trust. Namely, they should be truly trustworthy, predictable, and reliable. AI agents should demonstrate humanlike integrity with shared goals through their agile and measurable performance, intuitive and transparent communications, and secured protection. As such, researchers and practitioners need to design them properly to build confidence and develop trust, and the IMPACTS is a conceptually practical model as guidance for the design and development of collaborative and trusted human–machine symbiotic partnerships.

### 12.3.3 ICD Roadmap for IAS Design and Development

ICD approach follows systems engineering principles, and systems design methodologies differ from domain to domain. Issues can arise because design methodologies are often loosely used and there exist differences among these methodologies (e.g. TCD vs. UCD/HCD vs. ICD). If systems designers apply unclear design methodologies, it can lead to poor design and potential accidents [21, 28, 38]. To mitigate this risk, an ICD roadmap, as shown in Figure 12.5, has been developed as a systematic and structured process for IAS design and development activities to follow [21]. Basically, the roadmap includes activities at six stages: taxonomic analysis, systems design framework selection, analytical technique selection, design methodology selection, user monitoring techniques selection, and selection of appropriate domain standards.

First, designers need to conduct taxonomic analysis to understand the intended use of a new or upgraded system, task, working environment, roles, and responsibilities of intended users and technologies, and the consequences of system failures or unexpected events. Generally, through stakeholder analysis, operational concepts and context constraints can be analyzed and understood. Then, appropriate domain taxonomies can be chosen as guidance to understand the nature and scope of human–machine interactions for the design. Second, a specific design

**Figure 12.5** ICD roadmap as guidance for the design and development of IASs [21].

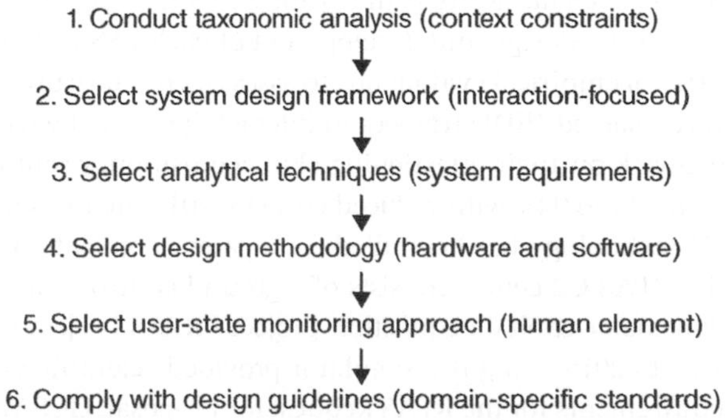
1. Conduct taxonomic analysis (context constraints)
2. Select system design framework (interaction-focused)
3. Select analytical techniques (system requirements)
4. Select design methodology (hardware and software)
5. Select user-state monitoring approach (human element)
6. Comply with design guidelines (domain-specific standards)

framework needs to be chosen pertaining to operational concepts and context constraints. Technology maturity then needs to be assessed to determine suitability for design methodology for the envisioned system design. Given the growing AI capabilities, ICD approach is desired to design HMS technologies for safety and/or mission-critical IASs in complex sociotechnical applications. Third, appropriate analytical techniques need to be chosen to analyze tasks and goals such that systems and functional requirements can be created to satisfy system operational requirements. These techniques are used to decompose high-level operational goals into more detailed IAS implementation strategies and extract the information necessary to populate various IAS models to a sufficient level of detail. The analysis focuses on identifying the components of required cognitive work and decision-making to understand the information required, the decisions, and the actions that must take place. Fourth, designers and developers can then decide what tasks, functions, and decisions are the best candidates for technology or human or both. They can then start choosing different mature methodologies to design and develop system hardware and software. The selection of a particular design methodology (e.g. software engineering and/or agent-based approaches) should fit best with the contextual design problem and the type of solution being designed. Fifth, the design also needs to consider what user-monitoring techniques are available and feasible for the system. Based on the decisions about what user state measurements can be successfully monitored, proper techniques need to be chosen for learning and understanding human cognitive state, workload, attention, and engagement.

The last, but not the least, design, development, implementation, validation, certification, and exploitation of IASs need to comply with policies and guidelines. Based on operational context and constraints, domain-specific standards, validated processes, principles, standards, and best practices need to be followed thoroughly. Special considerations need to be given to legal, ethical, social, moral, and cultural issues as more and more decision-making tasks and responsibilities are being assigned to AI agents. Safety, security, and privacy should all be the concerns of the designer [21].

### 12.3.4 ICD Validation, Adoption, and Contributions

As an enduring strategy and methodology for designing an effective and trustworthy HMS technologies, the IAS framework, IAI architecture, IMPACTS trust model, and associated ICD roadmap have been applied and validated through a series of defense concept development and experimentation (CD&E) activities. A few example of IAS technologies include the first Canadian intelligent tutoring system (ITS) for the Canadian Armed Forces (CAF) improvised explosive device disposal (IEDD) operator training, the first CAF command and control (C2) center for remotely piloted aircraft systems (RPAS), and the first CAF intelligent adaptive decision aid system that is called authority pathway for weapon engagement (APWE).

After the design and development of each IAS technology, the system was evaluated through a series of empirical evaluations to assess its military utility and effectiveness. The ITS-based courseware enabled IEDD trainees to interact dynamically with training scenarios and receive real-time feedback on their questioning skill acquisition, resulting in a course success rate that increased from 60% to 94% with reduced cost [18, 20]. Due to its novel concepts based on ICD approach, this ITS technology has been filed for a patent application in Canada and the United States [10, 15]. The RPAS C2 center consists of a ground control station (GCS) simulator for supporting a Canadian major capital acquisition project – RPAS [11]. A series of empirical studies conducted from 2016 to 2018 using the simulator provided scientific evidence that informed the development of requirements for the RPAS Request for Proposal, GCS Workspace Optimization and Airworthiness

Certification, and Operator Training Technology and Strategy [1, 16, 27]. The second GCS simulator has been transferred to the CAF as the new training system for the Joint RPAS operator training for Canadian Army, Navy, and Special Operations Forces.

To address complex, lengthy, and error-prone issues during target engagement processes, APWE automatically streamlines engagement processes and enables the operator to visualize the dynamic engagement status intuitively through its intelligent, adaptive "state broad" interface, thereby reducing engagement times and errors while enhancing the operator' SA [25, 26]. APWE was integrated into a joint C2 system which consists of a variety of highly emerging and disruptive technologies that were then demonstrated and assessed through a large-scale and complex international exercise in controlling multiple heterogeneous unmanned vehicles [4]. The evaluation results revealed that military participants identify APWE as one of the top three strengths of the joint C2 system and a significant contributor to the success of the exercise. The implementation of APWE within the C2 system is considered "exemplary, with major enhancements" because it "could seriously benefit future operations." In particular, APWE "takes a lot of stress away from the operator," and most importantly, it demonstrates "the most trustworthy aspect of the whole thing (the joint C2 system) because the increased SA and reduced workload and potential human error…" [4, 22].

These defense CD&E activities provided real-world validation evidence of the ICD approach, IAS framework, and IMPACTS principles as an enduring strategy and methodology for designing an effective and trustworthy HMS technology. The innovative IAS framework and ICD approach are praised by academic experts, industrial practitioners, government authorities, and users from operational communities for their novelty and trend-setting initiative of the human–AI symbiotic partnership. The ICD strategy is noted for setting "… the agenda for the coming years as human factors practitioners grapple with the demands that IAS will make on its operators," where "outlining how collaboration and partnership between human and AI can be achieved through interaction (-centered) design …" [3]. The ICD paradigm was also recognized by NATO that adopted the IAS framework and ICD strategy as guiding principles for the development of NATO Standard Recommendations: "Guidance on Sense and Avoid for UAS" and "Human Systems Integration (HSI) Guidance for UAS" to support the efforts of integrating RPASs into the nonsegregated civilian airspace [29, 30]. The related IAS design and development processes have been regarded as the best practices and advocated through the invited NATO Lecture Series on UAS technical challenges, concepts of operations, and regulatory issues [12–14].

## 12.4 IAS Design Challenges and Future Work

As systems with autonomous functions become more intelligent and sophisticated due to advances in AI and robotics technologies, machines are able to perform more cognitive tasks (e.g. decision-making) once performed by humans. This triggers the change of humans' roles and responsibilities or even authorities in the human–machine symbiotic partnership. Humans are playing more supervisory roles, while more contextual decisions are taken by automation [21, 37]. Unsurprisingly, this change in roles and responsibilities has the potential to create issues for humans interacting with automation. Systems designers must apply appropriate methodologies to understand the challenges and then capitalize on validated strategies and established principles to develop these trustworthy HMS technologies for their safe and effective employment.

### 12.4.1 Challenges of HMS Technology

Primarily, technological, human performance, validation, and certification (for application) issues are the challenges for designers to address when developing and employing HMS technologies. First, technology limitations introduce potential issues to systems design. AI algorithms need big data to learn and train. Due to the lack of computational theory behind the development of both computing capability and new algorithms, current AI capabilities still cannot provide timely support in decisions on what, where, when, who, and how to act when being challenged by insufficient or biased data and in, indeterministic conditions. Second, human performance issues occur when interacting with machine partners who take more system roles and responsibilities, especially considering limited human attention span due to limited cognitive resources [21]. Third, the broad integration of AI and autonomy in our society increases system complexity and thus invites new challenges that can influence user trust and acceptance. Further, the complexity and opacity of AI algorithms and models usually make AI decisions and actions unexplainable that their intentions might not transparent or logical to humans [22]. Fourth, legal, ethical, moral, social, and cultural issues are also challenges to systems designers for systems with fully autonomous functions. Systems practitioners must seriously assess "should we?" vs. "can we?" Constraints associated with possibility, acceptability, and integrity require careful assessments on societal and political impacts.

### 12.4.2 Future Work in IAS Design and Validation

Evidently, appropriate strategy and methodology are imperative to address all these issues for the design, development, validation, and certification of the HMS technologies. Compared to the technology-centered design strategy started off in the 1950s or UCD and HCD approach popularized in the 1980s, ICD principles are more suitable for providing solutions, especially for various issues during the dynamic transitions of human interactions with machine from "on-the-loop" to "in-the-loop." Specifically, real-world HMS design examples and NATO standards discussed in Section 12.3 demonstrate the effectiveness of the validated IAS technologies and ICD paradigm as technological and methodological solutions address these issues. However, there is still more work to do for ensuring the safety and trustworthiness of the HMS technologies before they are exploited into broad application domains and our society.

First, the ICD approach addresses a key challenge of systems design: the need to elucidate, develop, and validate operational requirements that are obscured by the complexity of human–machine interactions and of the intelligent system itself. It needs to be incorporated into the formal systems engineering processes to guide IAS design and development activities for the team to ensure maximum effectiveness under uncertainty from such a symbiotic partnership. Second, a trust model is a critical component supporting the HMI module in the IAS architecture as shown in Figure 12.1. It is an integral part of the ICD approach and needs to be integrated and used as a system engineering analysis and design tool, such as a trust management system. Third, the focus of human–machine trust relationship thus far has mostly been on the human's trust in the machine. But to fully consider the safety property of human–machine partnerships, additional components of the partnership must be considered [22]. This should include machine-to-machine and machine-to-human (i.e. does the machine trust the human's decision-making and performance) trust relationships. These mutual trust relationships are therefore well suited for representing a more comprehensive and complete trust partnership. Further, legal and ethical issues concerning the use of highly automated systems were identified from the literatures [5, 21], especially sensitive when considering autonomous weapon systems.

These issues include the possibility that an HMS system may purposely and deliberately withhold information concerning a system failure, malfunction, or error. The question has been raised as to whether certain trust repair strategies are ethical. There is inarguably more work to address these issues. Therefore, a framework for understanding trust and ethics in the context of verification regimes needs to be identified or developed to guide the implementation of the measure of trust and ethical design review in the verification and certification processes. The IAS framework and associated ICD approach and IMPACTS model have provided a sophisticated architecture, systematic methodology, and structured process to support this endeavor.

## References

1 Arrabito, R., Hou, M., Banbury, S. et al. (2020). A review of human factors research performed from 2014 to 2017 in support of the royal Canadian air force remotely piloted aircraft system project. *Journal of Unmanned Vehicle Systems* 9 (1): 1–20.

2 Awad, E., Dsouza, S., Kim, R. et al. (2018). The moral machine experiment. *Nature* 563: 59–64.

3 Baber, C. (2017). Book Review: Intelligent Adaptive Systems: an interaction-centered design perspective. *Ergonomics* 60 (10): 1458–1459.

4 Bartik, J., Wark, S., Thorpe, A., and Hou, M. (2020). TTCP Autonomy Strategic Challenge (ASC) Allied IMPACT Final Report. *Technical Report DRDC-RDDC-2021-N062*. Defence Research and Development Canada.

5 Bonnefon, J.-F., Shariff, A., and Rahwan, I. (2016). The social dilemma of autonomous vehicles. *Science (American Association for the Advancement of Science)* 352 (6293): 1573–1576.

6 Cho, J.H., Chan, K., and Adali, S. (2015). A survey on trust modeling. *ACM Computing Surveys* 48 (2): 1–40.

7 Defazio, P. (2009). Loss of Thrust in Both Engines After Encountering a Flock of Birds and Subsequent Ditching on the Hudson River, Us Airways Flight 1549, Airbus A320?214, N106us. *Technical Report Accident Report NTSB/AAR-10/03*. National Transportation Safety Board.

8 Defazio, P. (2020). Final Committee Report: The Design, Development, and Certification of the Boeing 737 Max. *Technical report*. The United States House Committee on Transportation and Infrastructure.

9 Fitts, P., Viteles, M., Barr, N. et al. (1951). *Human Engineering for an Effective Air-Navigation and Traffic-Control System*. National Research Council: Washington, DC.

10 Hou, M. (2014). QuestionIT (Intelligent Tutor for Questioning Technique). *Technical Report 1416-12/016CA*. Defence Research and Development Canada.

11 Hou, M. (2015). Report on the Development of Testbed for Integrated GCS Experimentation and Rehearsal (TIGER). *Technical Report DRDC-RDDC-2015-L282*. Defence Research and Development Canada.

12 Hou, M. (2017). Context-Based and Interaction-Centred Design for UAS GCS, NATO Lecture Series AVT-274 on Unmanned Air Vehicles: Technological Challenge, Concepts of Operations, and Regulatory Issues. *Technical Report DRDC-RDDC-2022-N063*. Defence Research and Development Canada.

13 Hou, M. (2017). Training Needs Analysis for UAS Operators, NATO Lecture Series AVT-274 on Unmanned Air Vehicles: Technological Challenge, Concepts of Operations, and Regulatory Issues. *Technical Report DRDC-RDDC-2022-N062*. Defence Research and Development Canada.

14 Hou, M. (2017). Human Systems Integration and its Guidance for UAS GCS Certification, NATO Lecture Series AVT-274 on Unmanned Air Vehicles: Technological Challenge,

Concepts of Operations, and Regulatory Issues. *Technical Report DRDC-RDDC-2022-N064.* Defence Research and Development Canada.

**15** Hou, M. and Fidopiastis, C.M. (2016). A generic framework of intelligent adaptive learning systems: from learning effectiveness to training transfer. *Theoretical Issues of Ergonomics Science* 18 (2): 167–183.

**16** Hou, M. and Sarnalata, J. (2018). Human Factors Considerations for Unmanned Aircraft System Ground Control System (UAS GCS) Airworthiness Certification. *Technical Report DRDC-RDDC-2018-L277*. Defence Research and Development Canada.

**17** Hou, M., Gauthier, M., and Banbury, S. (2007). Development of a generic design framework for intelligent adaptive systems. In: *Human–Computer Interaction. HCI Intelligent Multimodal Interaction Environments*. HCI 2007. *Lecture Notes in Computer Science*, vol. 4552 (ed. J.A. Jacko), 313–320. Berlin, Heidelberg: Springer-Verlag.

**18** Hou, M., Kramer, C., Banbury, S., and Osgoode, K. (2010). Suitable Adaptation Mechanisms for Intelligent Tutoring Technologies. *Technical Report TR 2010-074*. Defence Research and Development Canada.

**19** Hou, M., Zhu, H., Zhou, M.C., and Arrabito, R. (2011). Optimizing operator-agent interaction in intelligent adaptive interface design: a conceptual framework. *IEEE Transactions on Systems, Man, and Cybernetics - Part C: Applications and Reviews* 41 (2): 161–178.

**20** Hou, M., Kramer, C., Banbury, C. et al. (2013). Questioning Technique Review and Scenario Specification for the CF Counter-IED Operator Training Course. *Technical Report TR 2013-061*. Defence Research and Development Canada.

**21** Hou, M., Banbury, S., and Burns, C. (2014). *Intelligent Adaptive Systems - An Interaction-Centered Design Perspective*. Boca Raton, FL: CRC Press.

**22** Hou, M., Ho, G., and Dunwoody, D. (2021). Impacts: a trust model for human–autonomy teaming. *Human-Intelligent Systems Integration* 3: 79–97.

**23** IEEE Standard 7000-2021 (2021). *IEEE Standard Model Process for Addressing Ethical Concerns during System Design*. IEEE.

**24** Lee, J.D. (2008). Review of a pivotal human factors article: "humans and automation: use, misuse, disuse, abuse". *Human factors* 50 (3): 404–410.

**25** McColl, D., Banbury, S., and Hou, M. (2016). Test-bed for integrated ground control station experimentation and rehearsal: crew performance and authority pathway concept development. In: *Virtual, Augmented and Mixed Reality* (ed. S. Lackey and R. Shumaker), 433–445. Cham: Springer International Publishing.

**26** McColl, D., Heffner, K., Banbury, S. et al. (2017). Authority pathway: intelligent adaptive automation for a UAS ground control station. In: *Engineering Psychology and Cognitive Ergonomics: Performance, Emotion and Situation Awareness* (ed. D. Harris), 329–342. Cham: Springer International Publishing.

**27** McColl, D., Hou, M., Arrabito, R., and Pavlovic, N. (2017). UAS Workstation Layout Evaluation of the Testbed for Integrated GCS Experimentation and Rehearsal. *Technical Report DRDC-RDDC-2017-L302*. Defence Research and Development Canada.

**28** Miller, C., Mitchell, C., Lakinsmith, P. et al. (2000). Intelligent user interfaces for correspondence domains (panel session): moving IUIs off the desktop. *Proceedings of the 5th International Conference on Intelligent User Interfaces*, IUI '00, 181–186. ACM.

**29** NATO STANREC 4811 (2018). *Guidance on Sense and Avoid for Unmanned Aircraft Systems.* NATO Standardization Office.

**30** NATO STANREC 4685 (2022). *Human Systems Integration Guidance for Unmanned Aircraft Systems.* NATO Standardization Office.

**31** Norman, D.A. (1986). Cognitive engineering. In: *User Centered System Design: New Perspectives on Human–Computer Interaction*, 31–61. Lawrence Erlbaum Association.

**32** Norman, D.A. (2005). Human-centered design considered harmful. *Interactions* 12 (4): 14–19.

**33** Norman, D.A. and Draper, S.W. (1986). In: *User Centered System Design: New Perspectives on Human–Computer Interaction*. Lawrence Erlbaum Associates.

**34** Rasmussen, J. (1986). *Information Processing and Human–Machine Interaction: An Approach to Cognitive Engineering*. New York: Elsevier Science Publishers B.

**35** Schmorrow, D.D. and Kruse, A.A. (2004). Augmented cognition. In: *Berkshire Encyclopedia of Human–Computer Interaction*, 54–59. Berkshire Publishing Group.

**36** Sheridan, T.B. (2002). *Humans and Automation: System Design and Research Issues*. Santa Monica, CA: Wiley-Interscience.

**37** Sheridan, T.B. (2019). Individual differences in attributes of trust in automation: measurement and application to system design. *Frontiers in Psychology* 10: 1117.

**38** Vicente, K.J. (1990). Coherence- and correspondence-driven work domains: implications for systems design. *Behaviour & Information Technology* 9 (6): 493–502.

**39** Wooldridge, M.J. (2002). *An Introduction to Multiagent Systems*. West Sussex: Wiley.

# 13

# Human–Machine Computing: Paradigm, Challenges, and Practices

*Zhiwen Yu, Qingyang Li, and Bin Guo*

*Department of Intelligent Computing System, School of Computer Science, Northwestern Polytechnical University, Xi'an, China*

## 13.1 Introduction

Initially, the invention of machines is to make human beings effectively complete the task. Nowadays, the development trend of machines is to make them more intelligent, imitating unique ability of human beings, such as learning, thinking, perceiving emotions, and so on. With the help of some intelligent machines, humans can solve more complex, uncertain, and flexible problems and tasks in various applications. For instance, pattern recognition techniques such as image recognition are widely used in human identification [20], autonomous driving [17], and so on. The accuracy and effectiveness of the recognition are usually affected by the complexity of models and calculations, so it is necessary to use intelligent machines when solving these problems. However, the intelligence of the machine depends primarily on the learning algorithm and model, so intelligent machines cannot be applied to each problem facing humanity. Due to the uncertain and flexible environment humans are living in, as well as the openness of issues faced by humans, regardless of how machines are intelligent, they cannot completely replace human beings [21].

During the development of computer architecture, guidelines always focus on boosting enhancement and extending communication and collaboration between devices. To take full advantage of the machines' computing power and storage ability and maximize the implementation efficiency, a variety of computing concepts and paradigms have been designed, such as grid computing [5], cloud computing [12], edge computing [16]. The computing paradigms of computer architecture improve machines mainly from the structure or organization of the machine. The significance of human beings is neglected during the computing process by most of the existing computing architectures.

Machines and humans are essential in solving problems because both of them have their own strengths. Machines have excellent calculation and memory capabilities, while human beings are more expert in subjective judgment and accumulation of experience. At the same time, machines and humans also have their own disadvantages. From the perspective of machines, adaptation to the growing environment can be realized by altering and updating the leveraged hardwares or embedded algorithms. However, machines usually cannot determine the direction of the change. In this situation, humans with knowledge can be employed to offer assistance to devices. However, from the perspective of humans, handing all tasks over to humans are labor-intensive, impractical, and unscientific. In fact, the advantages of machines and humans have complementarity. The previous study has confirmed that human being is the

*Handbook of Human-Machine Systems*, First Edition. Edited by Giancarlo Fortino, David Kaber, Andreas Nürnberger, and David Mendonça.

most proper choice that ensures the adaptability of a human–machine system [7]. It is believed that human–machine combination computing is a meaningful future development trend under exploration.

Although there are already some research fields to consider the participation of humans in a computing architecture, such as human–computer interaction (HCI) [13], collective intelligence [11], mobile crowd sensing and computing (MCSC) [6], and so on, the existing concepts of human–machine combination are usually guided by case-orientation. In the continuous development environment, the demand and the degree of attention for humans and machines will vary in different stages of computing tasks. At the same time, the allocation strategy of computing resources including humans and machines should be dynamically changed to fit the growing task and environment. Thus, a universal computing paradigm should be proposed in which combinations of humans and machines are used to model the complex computing mode between humans and machines.

In this chapter, we conceive a new paradigm for human–machine collaboration and cooperation called human–machine computing (HMC). This paradigm is intended to define and demonstrate the concept of human–machine hybrid computing and construct a generic framework for different categories of tasks with human–machine interaction and cooperation.

## 13.2 Background

### 13.2.1 History of the Development

In the previous studies, there are a series of approaches and frameworks to incorporate importance of humans and machines during the process of performing tasks. HCI [13] studies the communication patterns and interaction medium between users and computing machines. With the prosperity and popularity of HCI technology, users can more intuitively and succinctly input and output through machines. However, HCI mainly emphasizes interactive interfaces and processes between humans and machines and pays attention to the convenience and legibility of machine usage for users. Interactive Machine Learning [4] proposes a framework for regulating classifiers, which can be adopted by users for training and visualizing data and correcting the classified results. The human worker mainly focuses on selecting informative samples and creating training data in order to rectify errors and mistakes of the classifier. Human-centered computing (HCC) [8] discusses the design, development, and deployment of the human–machine hybrid system. It appears from a fusion of multiple disciplines that are related to understanding humans and computational artifacts. HCC is related to information science and HCI, but it has differences compared to HCI. HCC usually pays attention to technology and practice, while HCI focuses more on ergonomics. Human-in-the-loop (HITL) [9] is defined as a framework that takes human interaction into consideration. During the event or the process, the user is allowed to change the outcome and determine the final design of the intelligent system based on his judgments and experience. Correspondingly, human-in-the-loop cyber-physical systems (HiLCPSs) [15] are proposed by leveraging HITL, consisting of a human participant, an intelligent system, and the natural physical environment. HilCPSs measure human cognitive activities through various wearable sensors to collect data that can infer users' intention. The intelligent system analyzes users' intention and translates it into signals to control robotic actuators acting like human beings in the physical environment. Human-engaged computing (HEC) [14] is a new conceptual framework based on HCI to keep an appropriate balance between users and devices, and finally it can make users and machines reach a true synergistic interaction. The concept of HEC considers practitioners from several perspectives, such as religion, philosophy, habits, culture. which contain special significance to the users. HEC pays more attention to the importance of personal differences during human–machine collaboration and interaction.

Besides humans with domain knowledge, common crowd people can provide useful knowledge when participating in tasks. Collective intelligence [11] is widely defined to accomplish a complex and laborious task by accumulating knowledge or wisdom of each individual in the group. Wikipedia is an appropriate example to explain collective intelligence. Contributors from all over the world have access to create and revise records in the online encyclopedia, which can be constantly improved by collaboration among contributors. In this way, more comprehensive knowledge can be constructed by merging thousands of personal knowledge. Hybrid Crowd-Machine Learning [2] employs common crowd people to select informative features and annotate labels of data, then, it leverages machine learning approaches to change weights of these chosen features. Finally, models with higher accuracy and more human-understandable features are proposed. In recent years, MCSC [6] is becoming a popular concept that taking advantage of devices from crowds to collaboratively complete a task in a conscious or unconscious way. By active participation or passive arrangement, every participant is responsible for one of the part of the task, and obtains the corresponding reward after completion. Currently, MCSC is mostly leveraged for abundant data collection and information supplement.

Although mentioned existing research works involve human–machine combination computational systems or methodologies, most of them explore certain aspects of human–machine collaboration or cooperation, such as interactive interface design, human participation incentives, and so on. Unlike existing works, HMC is proposed as a general paradigm for human–machine combination in a dynamically changed environment. HMC considers humans as computing components and designs a framework for modeling different patterns and modes of human–machine collaboration. The machine can be gradually increased through human guidance and participation.

### 13.2.2 Basic Definitions

The main idea of HMC is the organic integration of human and machine advantages during the completion of the task. In the dynamic environment, performance of machines can be enhanced by borrowing human wisdom which can indicate the direction of optimization. In turn, the computing power and storage capacity of machines are used to make up for the deficiencies of humanity, and machines even produce expected products that can expand human cognition. Figure 13.1 shows the concept and core idea of HMC. In HMC, humans and machines implement the task in a complementary relationship by collaborating or cooperating with each other, and both of them achieve an improvement during the process. However, if the collaboration process requires participants to consume a lot of energy and time, it violates the original intention of machine design. Thus, in the HMC system, most of the tasks are completed by machines, and humans supply the necessary guidance and assistance.

To meet the requirements mentioned before, the definition of HMC in natural language is as follows: *In a dynamically evolved environment, machines and humans interactively collaborate with some kind of cooperation, in which the machine implements optimized performance under appropriate amount of human guidance.*

In the definition, the dynamically evolved environment means that status and characteristics of tasks and computing participants (including machines and humans) might dynamically change over time. For example, when identifying person in a dynamic environment, if the application

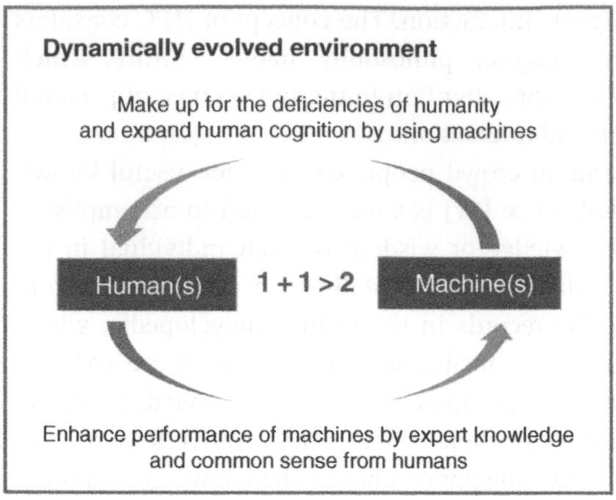


**Figure 13.1** The concept and core idea of HMC. Humans and machines establish a complementary relationship in interactive cooperation and collaboration process.

scenario changes, the requirements of the identification accuracy will be different. Intuitively, the high-precision recognition is required in the security preservation scenario, while the limitation on recognition accuracy can be properly broadened in the daily monitoring scenario. Additionally, changes in dressing, weather, or season can result in the characteristics of the same identification subject to change over time.

From the view of users who use HMC, the whole calculation process is the same as a "black box." Only paying attention to the interaction with the interface is sufficient for the user. The user proposes the requirements of the task through the interface and receives the result of the corresponding task completion from the interface. By combining humans (including an expert and common people) and machines (including immobile and mobile ones), the final computing is completed. During the computing procedure, users do not need to know the specific location and information of individuals and machines for completing tasks, which ensure that users lacking computer knowledge can use HMC conveniently. The detailed framework and computing process will be described in the following part of the chapter.

## 13.3 State of the Art

### 13.3.1 Technical Contributions

Figure 13.2 indicates the abstract computing process of HMC. A kernel is designed in HMC, as a coordinator of the HMC system. The kernel is considered the "brain" of the proposed framework due to its coordination of the operation of different components and computing units of the system. Specifically, the kernel needs to schedule computing resources, and several important functions should be embedded to implement the scheduling procedure. Users propose tasks through the interface to HMC system. Before allocating computing resources to the task, the kernel first analyzes the category of the task to preliminary estimate the number and attributes of computing resources required. Then, computing resources are allocated to the different parts and phases of the task. During the computing process, humans mainly give guidance according to their knowledge to improve performance of machines. By observing and analyzing results produced from machines, cognition of humans can probably be broadened. To achieve the final results of the task, the kernel needs to merge or aggregate the intermediate results from machines and humans. Finally, to confirm the validity and practicability of the HMC system during completing tasks with human–machine combination, evaluation methods and metrics should be designed in the kernel.

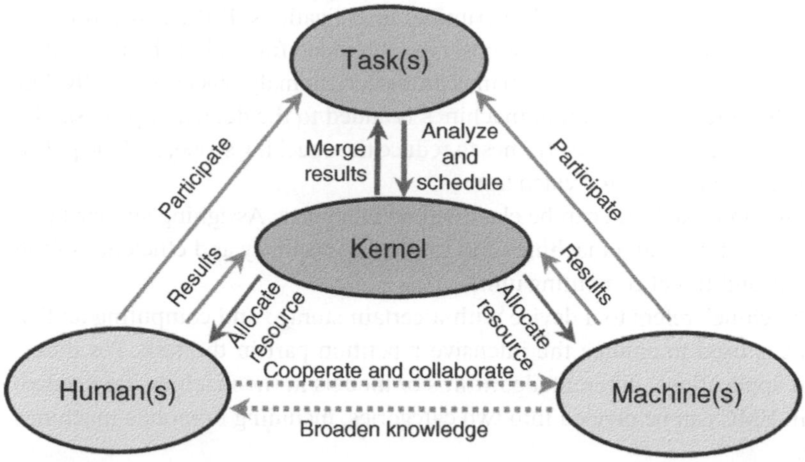


**Figure 13.2** Abstract computing process of HMC, containing four main composition elements: tasks, humans, machines, and kernel.

Please note that users and humans have different definitions in HMC. The user is an individual that publishes the task and uses the HMC system to complete the task and obtain the final result. Humans are considered as a kind of computing resource in HMC, and both humans and machines participating in the computing process are regarded as computing units. The task published by a user is completed under cooperation of multiple computing units.

To clarify HMC better, composition elements involved in the computing process are described in detail as follows: containing task, human, machine, and kernel.

- *Task*. HMC is primarily designed for complex and continuous development tasks, which require machines and humans to complete together. The way of combination and cooperation between humans and machines depends on the category and characteristics of the task.

  If the task is performing a workflow that focuses on representative and quality of the dataset, humans are usually employed to collect more informative data in the initial phase of the task. Then, machines solve the calculation and learning issue during the task implementation. In this case, the combination way between humans and machines is cascade. For example, in identity recognition application, machines recognize people by leveraging local historical data and algorithms designed in the device. Different from machines, humans identify people according to common sense and experience. However, identification models typically do not effectively adjust and update their own structures with the dynamic changes in the evolved environment. Therefore, the recognition accuracy is reduced, and the availability of the entire identification system is lowered. Obviously, even if human beings with domain knowledge can quickly and accurately identify a certain number of person, continuously identifying all users are wasteful and unrealistic. Thus, human–machine combination is necessary for more accurately and efficiently enforcing tasks. In the HMC system, human experts (such as guards) can dynamically provide quality feedback during machine recognition to boost the performance of the recognition system.

  If the task focuses on the calculation and modeling, humans and machines are required to simultaneously deal with corresponding parts of the task, and the final result is obtained by integrating or merging the results of the respective implementations. This combination way is considered parallel, taking an anomaly detection of video objects as an example. Detecting suspicious people in a video is usually related to criminal investigations. If the detection only relies on the manpower of policemen, they must observe each video frame, but the amount of frames may exceed one thousand. In short, humans can detect anomaly objects carefully, but the efficiency is low. After the participation of machines is added to the detection process, the computer first selects and removes unrelated frames to reduce the checking scope, and the police conduct detection detailed on the selected video frames.

In HMC, tasks, humans, and machines can be classified on attributes. Assigning similar tasks to the appropriate type of humans and machines and improving accuracy and efficiency of the system by combining capabilities of computing units.

- *Machine*. In HMC, "Machine" refers to a device with a certain storage and computing ability. Typically, the machine is used to enforce the intensive repetition part in the task. For different kinds of tasks and applications, different algorithms or models in the machine are needed. Machines leveraged in HMC can be divided into two categories, including immobile machines and mobile machines.

  The immobile machine mainly represents a computing device that is fixed to a location, such as PCs, servers, fixed sensors, and so on. Immobile machine uses its embedded algorithms and storage space to perform a large amount of calculations. Obviously, the method of cooperation between these machines and humans is limited, which denotes that this type of machine is more susceptible to human beings.

  The mobile machine mainly represents a device with a certain mobility, such as removable sensors, mobile phones, robots. Mobile machines have higher scalability and operability because of its flexibility. Therefore, besides updating algorithms under human guidance, the methods of cooperation between humans and this kind of machines are diverse. For instance, humans can contribute their physical signals and activity data in different places with a wearable sensor or a mobile phone, which allows the machine to get more types of data to improve the robustness of itself. In addition, robots and humans can complete collaborative mandates under intelligent perception and commands from humans, making robots to achieve higher intelligence. At the same time, continuously improved robots can better help human beings reach the goals that are difficult to achieve only by humans. However, the flexibility and mobility of this type of machine is a double-edged sword, which will increase the difficulty of cooperation between humans and machines. More aspects need to be considered during the cooperation, including ways of collaboration, cooperative timing, cooperative interface, communication methods, and so on.

- *Human*. In HMC, "Human" refers to people with knowledge and normal cognition who taking part in tasks with machines. Users and humans participating in the computing process have different concepts. Users release tasks, use HMC, and resolve tasks with computing resources in the system. Humans in HMC serve as part of the computing resource and collaborate with the machine. For users, individual and groups participating in the calculation process are considered as virtualized computational units. The most important role of humans in HMC is to provide a certain assistance for machines to enhance the intelligence of them. In HMC, humans are divided into two categories based on their authority: experts and ordinary people.

  For the first type, the corresponding person is usually an expert improving the machines by his expertise in professional fields. According to the human knowledge and valuable experience, mistakes and faults can be found and corrected timely, then components of machines such as hardware, algorithms, interfaces, can be further adjusted and updated. Professional knowledge provided by experts is considered to be an explicit assistance, which is a kind of active participation.

  For another type, the ordinary people usually indicate those who do not have specific professional knowledge, and they participate in the task in groups in HMC. Ordinary people have normal awareness and can provide useful information including common sense, interest, habits, cultures, regularity. Although the data and information provided by a single person looks negligible, the information has become rich after accumulating data from crowd of people. By accumulating a large amount of data, it is possible to help the machine get information in a wider coverage. Assistance from ordinary people is considered to be an implicit guidance, which is a kind of passive participation.

- *Kernel.* In HMC system, the kernel is the most important component to implement the task relying on human–machine collaboration, as it is not only responsible for analyzing and assigning tasks but also responsible for scheduling the computing resources including machines and humans based on the condition of the task. The role of the kernel for the whole HMC system is equivalent to the importance of the brain for human beings. The kernel controls and monitors the computing process to ensure the success of the task completion.

  Since the kernel needs to focus on both the machine and human computing resources and it cannot affect the original use of the machine, the kernel is usually placed between the original operating system and the application platforms and designed as a middleware or virtual operating system. The kernel can deploy on the local computer, remote server, or a cloud server based on the complexity of the task, the required storage space and computing power and the application scenario. Figure 13.3 shows the framework of HMC kernel, named **human–machine operating system (hmOS)**, to illustrate the interaction between the various components and the corresponding design on functions.

  The interfaces of interaction between every component should be designed in hmOS. For user convenient utilization, the interactive interface and operation should be as simple and concise as possible. Interfaces for computing units should be connectors not only between different categories of units but also between the same kinds of units. Unlike the user's interface, the interface for human computing resources should learn more about the computing process and intermediate results, enabling people to provide appropriate guidance during this process while receiving new knowledge generated by the machine. In order to select the appropriate computing units to perform the corresponding task module, the properties of machines and

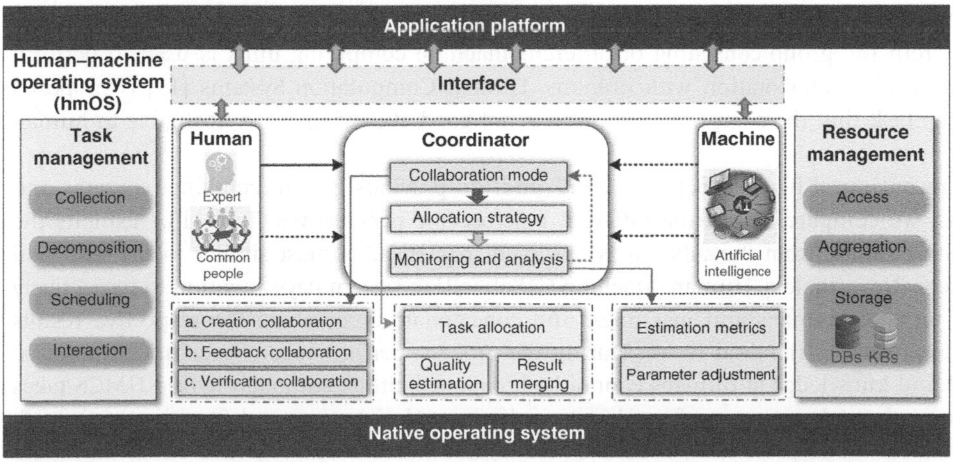


**Figure 13.3** Framework of the hmOS. The hmOS denotes the kernel of HMC system, which is placed between the original operating system and the application platforms. It is designed for analyzing and assigning tasks and scheduling the computing resources including machines and humans.

humans need to be recorded through interfaces before registering the machine resources and virtualizing the human computing resources, such as the machine's storage space and computing power, human's preference and capability, and so on.

The coordinator is center of the kernel, which manages the operations of humans and machines. Specifically, the coordinator first analyzes the complexity and features of the task to decide the collaboration mode before computing resources are allocated to the task. Collaboration mode is designed as three categories according to the effect and method of the collaboration in the task. The three collaboration modes include creation collaboration, feedback collaboration, and verification collaboration. Then, the task is allocated to the appropriate computing units, including humans and machines. At the same time, the coordinator monitors and analyzes the process of the task completion, to adjust the allocation and estimate parameters. Besides, the coordinator is responsible for estimation metric selection for the HMC system, including task completion quality, effectiveness of the system, resource consumption, user satisfaction, and so on.

Besides, the kernel designs management modules for task and resource, respectively. The task management module contains strategies and algorithms for task collection, task decomposition, task scheduling, and interaction method between humans and machines. The resource management module pays attention to computing units, communication, and storage capability of the system. Before employing the computing resource, information of the related devices and person needs to be recorded. The resource management module provides access to the virtualized computing resources and aggregation approaches to integrate distributed computing units. Besides, database and knowledge base are conducted in the resource management module.

### 13.3.2 Comparison Table

In addition to HCI [13], HCC [8], MCSC [6], and HEC [14] mentioned in Section 13.2.1, there are other previous systems or paradigms involved in combining humans with machines. Human–Machine Collaboration [3] has put forward a continuous learning circle, which is knowledge exchange between humans and machines. Works can be completed by humans more efficiently and accurately with the assistance of artificial intelligence. Hybrid human–machine computing systems (hybrid HMCS) [1] put forward a general framework for performing distributed tasks, wherein the group consisting of different machine computing units is used to perform tasks that require collaboration with humans. Human Computation Systems [19] is proposed to solve the task that the computing machine is not good at solving but is negligible to human beings.

To figure out the difference between HMC and the previous human combined systems and paradigms, we compare them from different macroscopic perspectives. Table 13.1 exhibits the comparison results. From the table, it is observed that HMC is most similar to the fifth and sixth system. Nevertheless, Human–Machine Collaboration system pays attention to respectively schedule tasks to humans and machines, and concatenate or combine the respective results together to consist of the final result. During the process, performance of machines cannot be improved and knowledge of humans cannot be broadened either. Although hybrid HMCS takes into account the enhancement of machines, it does not design a general framework. Overall, HMC considers the improvement of both machines and humans and regards humans as a kind of computing resource, which is more comprehensive and general compared to most previous human–machine combination systems and paradigms.

**Table 13.1** The differences between HMC and the previous human-combined systems and paradigms on macroperspectives.

| Systems/paradigms | Application scenario | | Role of humans | | Machine improvement | | Human enhancement | | General platform | |
|---|---|---|---|---|---|---|---|---|---|---|
| | Human-oriented | Machine-oriented | User | Computing unit | Yes | No | Yes | No | Yes | No |
| HCI | √ | | √ | | | √ | | √ | | √ |
| HCC | √ | | √ | | | √ | √ | | | √ |
| MCSC | √ | √ | √ | √ | | √ | | √ | | √ |
| HEC | √ | | √ | | | √ | | √ | | √ |
| Human–Machine Collaboration | √ | √ | √ | √ | √ | | | √ | | √ |
| Hybrid HMCS | √ | √ | √ | √ | | √ | | √ | √ | |
| Human Computation System | √ | √ | √ | √ | | √ | | √ | | √ |
| HMC (ours) | √ | √ | √ | √ | √ | | √ | | √ | |

## 13.4 Future Research Challenges

### 13.4.1 Current Research Issues

We first introduce current research issues and case studies on HMC. There are three problems that need to be addressed during our recent preliminary studies.

- *How to design task assignment mechanism for human–machine combination.* There exists sufficient necessity to design distinct allocation methods in the HMC system based on the category of the task and the form of human–machine combination. For some types of tasks, such as identity recognition, employing a few people and recognition devices are sufficient to realize online identification in high quality and efficiency. For other types of tasks, such as data collection and annotation, there is usually a number of people involved to mitigate the amount of task for individuals. Due to the large amount of data that needs to be processed, the performance requirements of the device used in the task are high.
- *How to determine the timing and form of human–machine combination.* During the entire task implementation, humans provide guidance in different forms at different stages of the task, to ensure the way of human–machine collaboration is appropriate for the task. For machine learning-based tasks, humans can assist machines by annotating unlabeled data or selecting informative features for training phase. Different from the training phase, for the testing phase, humans can guide machines by providing feedback to the intermediate results from machines, and models and algorithms embedded in machines can be improved. Adding human participation in the correct stage and the correct time, the performance of machines can be maximized by a low cost.
- *How to design the evaluation metrics of the task completion quality and the performance of the HMC system.* In order to illustrate the effectiveness of HMC system, some important factors should be considered when evaluating the performance. First, since the core idea of HMC is combining capabilities of machines with abilities of humans, and designing human–machine collaboration during the task completion procedure, it is necessary to consider the reliability of participants. In addition, the proficiency of humans is one of the factors affecting the correctness and time cost of the system. In addition, designing simulation experimental environments, especially for human participation is important. Because human resources are relatively expensive, it is necessary to simulate the process of human–machine collaboration before practical application, to design optimal collaborative mechanisms and resource allocation strategies.
- *How to determine the type and quantity of the appropriate computing resources.* The computing resources contain humans and devices, which should be selected from resource pool based on the type of task and collaboration form between participants. Types of the task decide characteristics of humans and machines that take part in the task. For machine selection, the computing power and storage space are important factors need to consider. For human employment, the professional knowledge level and cognitive ability determine the type of work that people can be competent. Meanwhile, incentives for both humans and machines should be considered as well. There may be a variety of selection strategies for humans and machines, depending on the performance requirements and budget restrictions on the task. A well-designed policy helps to accomplish the task with relative great quality and effectiveness and relatively little price.

To prove the usability of HMC, preliminary practices have been conducted in two application scenarios: interactive identity recognition and interactive video anomaly detection.

Most of the existing machine-learning-based identification methods follow traditional workflows, that is, the model is trained on a limited training set. In the identification process, the participation of end users is limited, and the dynamic changes of the learning process are ignored. In practical applications, high-quality observations are usually provided with expert assistance. Therefore, the HMC is suitable for adjusting recognition model by using human assistance. The detailed workflow and methodology are introduced in paper [10].

From a large number of monitoring video, how to automatically and effectively find objects that may be abnormal or needed to be concerned is a challenging task. In order to improve the accuracy of the detection, more representative training samples need to collect to re-train or update model, but some abnormal objects like the eye-catching target is still difficult to detect directly by the device, and human beings with knowledge are more easier to identify such objects. Based on the above consideration, HMC can be used to solve problems on video anomaly detection. The detailed framework and algorithm are introduced in paper [18].

### 13.4.2 Future Research Directions

In order to make the HMC system make full play in practice, we summarize the three important future research directions in HMC.

- *Task analysis and decomposition.* The core idea of HMC is to complete complex tasks by combining machines and humans capabilities. In order to determine the way and timing of human–machine collaboration, the characteristics of the task are needed to be analyzed, and the task requires to be appropriately decomposed into several stages. The calculation resources are arranged to execute corresponding part of task in different stages. The unreasonable decomposition will lead to insufficient utilization of machines and humans, such as generating redundant work or consuming unnecessary resources in unimportant components of the task. Tasks are typically heterogeneous in the case where multiple tasks require HMC to solve. Since these tasks are published by users with different requirements, the required human resources and machine resources exist various quantities and characteristics. A good decomposition method and allocation strategy will help the HMC system to address tasks in high quality and efficiency in an acceptable time period.
- *Distributed computing resources management and dispatch.* As mentioned before, the HMC system consists of a variety of machines (involving mobile machines and immobile machines) and humans (including expert and ordinary people). At the same time, the computing resources are large scale, and the machines and humans involved in a task are usually located in different physical spaces. Therefore, the distributed computing resources ought to be managed reasonably and scientifically. During the management process, information of the candidate machines and humans should be registered and recorded. After analyzing and decomposing the task, proper devices and humans can be selected to conduct the corresponding works in various combinations. Resource dispatch is also one of the important issues. Different categories of tasks are different from the demands of computing resources. Therefore, a reasonable resource dispatch strategy can ensure that the number and capability of the selected computing resources are applicable to the current task. At the same time, waste or lack of resources can be avoided by designing dynamic dispatch algorithms.
- *HMC pattern design.* In the HMC system, the task is accomplished by human–machine combination. Due to the type of task and requirements of users that are different, the combination patterns are usually diverse, so that the HMC system should select the appropriate human–machine combination pattern based on the time limitation and the existing computing resources. Considering

the reality, the combination pattern and the number of resources required should be constantly evolving according to the current task condition. For instance, in the initial phase of the task, there exists the high frequency of human assistance, but the capacity of the machine achieved enough guidance has improved over time, so the number and frequency of human participation can be appropriately reduced. In addition, as the degree of task completion is constantly increasing, it is also possible to reduce the usage of human resources and machine resources so that the combination pattern can be gradually simplified.

## References


**1** Candra, M.Z.C. (2016). Hybrid human–machine computing systems: provisioning, monitoring, and reliability analysis. PhD thesis. Wien University.

**2** Cheng, J. and Bernstein, M.S. (2015). Flock: hybrid crowd-machine learning classifiers. *Proceedings of the 18th ACM Conference on Computer Supported Cooperative Work & Social Computing*, 600–611.

**3** Daugherty, P.R. and Wilson, H.J. (2018). *Human + Machine: Reimagining Work in the Age of AI*. Harvard Business Press.

**4** Fails, J.A. and Olsen, D.R. Jr. (2003). Interactive machine learning. *Proceedings of the 8th International Conference on Intelligent User Interfaces*, 39–45.

**5** Foster, I. and Kesselman, C. (2003). *The Grid 2: Blueprint for a New Computing Infrastructure*. Elsevier.

**6** Guo, B., Chen, C., Zhang, D. et al. (2016). Mobile crowd sensing and computing: when participatory sensing meets participatory social media. *IEEE Communications Magazine* 54 (2): 131–137.

**7** Hoc, J.-M. (2001). Towards a cognitive approach to human–machine cooperation in dynamic situations. *International Journal of Human–Computer Studies* 54 (4): 509–540.

**8** Jaimes, A., Sebe, N., and Gatica-Perez, D. (2006). Human-centered computing: a multimedia perspective. *Proceedings of the 14th ACM International Conference on Multimedia*, 855–864.

**9** Karwowski, W. (2006). *International Encyclopedia of Ergonomics and Human Factors, -3 Volume Set*. Crc Press.

**10** Li, Q., Yu, Z., Yao, L., and Guo, B. (2021). RLTIR: activity-based interactive person identification via reinforcement learning tree. *IEEE Internet of Things Journal* 9 (6): 4464–4475.

**11** Malone, T.W., Laubacher, R., and Dellarocas, C. (2009). Harnessing crowds: mapping the genome of collective intelligence.

**12** Mell, P. and Grance, T. (2011). The NIST definition of cloud computing.

**13** Myers, B.A. (1998). A brief history of human–computer interaction technology. *Interactions* 5 (2): 44–54.

**14** Ren, X., Silpasuwanchai, C., and Cahill, J. (2019). Human-engaged computing: the future of human–computer interaction. *CCF Transactions on Pervasive Computing and Interaction* 1 (1): 47–68.

**15** Schirner, G., Erdogmus, D., Chowdhury, K., and Padir, T. (2013). The future of human-in-the-loop cyber-physical systems. *Computer* 46 (1): 36–45.

**16** Shi, W., Cao, J., Zhang, Q. et al. (2016). Edge computing: vision and challenges. *IEEE Internet of Things Journal* 3 (5): 637–646.

**17** Wei, J., Snider, J.M., Kim, J. et al. (2013). Towards a viable autonomous driving research platform. *2013 IEEE Intelligent Vehicles Symposium (IV)*, 763–770. IEEE.

**18** Yang, F., Yu, Z., Chen, L. et al. (2021). Human–machine cooperative video anomaly detection. *Proceedings of the ACM on Human-Computer Interaction* 4 (CSCW3): 1–18.

**19** Yuen, M.-C., Chen, L.-J., and King, I. (2009). A survey of human computation systems. *2009 International Conference on Computational Science and Engineering*, volume 4, 723–728. IEEE.

**20** Zhang, Q., Zhou, D., and Zeng, X. (2017). HeartID: a multiresolution convolutional neural network for ECG-based biometric human identification in smart health applications. *IEEE Access* 5: 11805–11816.

**21** Zheng, N.-n., Liu, Z.-y., Ren, P.-j. et al. (2017). Hybrid-augmented intelligence: collaboration and cognition. *Frontiers of Information Technology & Electronic Engineering* 18 (2): 153–179.

# 14

# Companion Technology*

*Andreas Wendemuth*

*Department of Electrical Engineering and Information Technology, Institute for Information Technology and Communications, Otto-von-Guericke-University, Magdeburg, Germany*

## 14.1 Introduction

Technical assistant systems which are tailored to the specific needs of their user are called *Companions* – and they exhibit a functionality which appears responsive, competent, adaptable, and reliable. *Companion technology* as a technical discipline will therefore bridge the gap between complex technical functionality of modern systems and the users' demand for an easy-to-use, customized deployment of this functionality. To do so, technical systems are realized as cognitive systems featuring *Companion* characteristics: adaptability, availability, cooperativeness, competence, individuality, and trustworthiness. By merging perception, planning, dialog, reasoning, and interaction, cognitive processes exhibit those characteristics.

*Companion* technology R & D balances cognitive technical systems and human users of such systems. Companion technology is therefore cross-disciplinary and encompasses basic and methodological research in engineering, informatics, and life sciences. It deals with implementation issues sufficient to enable behavior-like performance on the user side, empirical research footing on psychological behavioral models, and likewise, on analyses of brain activity in human-system interplay.

## 14.2 Background

Common technical systems used on a daily basis have increasingly complex functionality which is often termed "intelligent." However, on the usage side, a considerable shortcoming of convenience and comfort is often observed. Especially when the promise of "self-explainability" reaches its limits, users are prompted to refer to online operating manuals with lengthy menu processes. These barriers may lead to frustration and inability to use, ultimately causing the user to lose interest in such systems or a least show heavy reluctancy.

Summarizing, we experience a huge discrepancy between the alleged functional intelligence of technical systems and the stunning absence of intelligence in delivering this functionality to the users. As can be seen in Figure 14.1, a typical cause for such frustration is uniformity of technical

* Some contents and figures of this chapter have been presented, in modified form, by the author and coauthors in [6] and [25].

*Handbook of Human-Machine Systems*, First Edition. Edited by Giancarlo Fortino, David Kaber, Andreas Nürnberger, and David Mendonça.

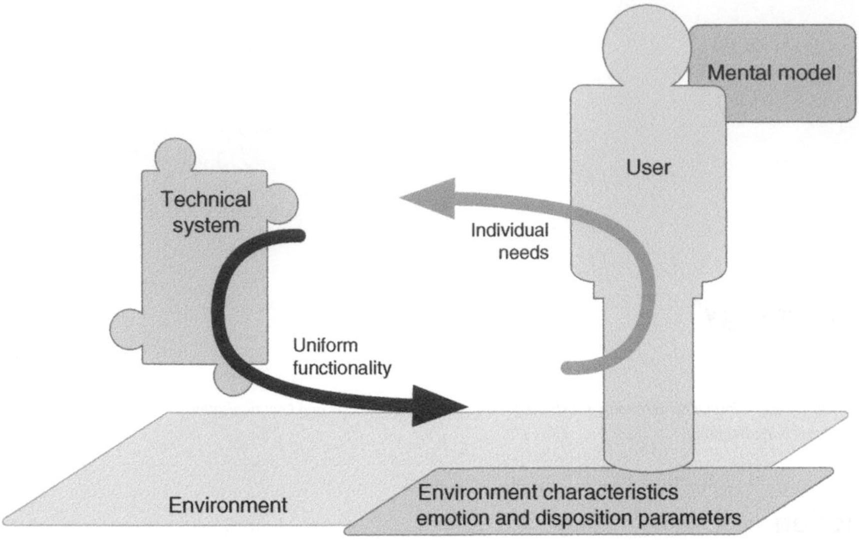


**Figure 14.1** Present-day human–technology Interaction. Source: Adopted from [6].

performance. User types or individual users remain unconsidered, as well as level of experience or explainability.

At this point, *Companion* technology comes into play. It balances the growing functional intelligence of technical systems with a rivaling intelligence in user interaction. Ultimately, any technical system has to be realized as a *Companion* system. This reflects the user's emotional and dispositional state and the current personal situation. The *Companion* systems will be available, reliable, and cooperative and function as competent and trustworthy users' partners. The core *Companion characteristics* of *Companion* systems are *competence*, *adaptability*, *individuality*, *availability*, *cooperativeness*, and *trustworthiness*. On the implementation side, this requires an interplay of cognitive processes of advanced perception, reasoning, planning, and interaction features.

### 14.2.1 History

The concept of *Companions* yet is being described in only a few contexts. On the forefront, Wilks [29] describes *Companions* as conversational software agents, accompanying users over a (life-)long span. Instead of "just" giving assistance, they issue companionship by personalization. Lately, *Robot Companions* emerged in the field of cognitive robotics as a paradigm [2, 11, 18]. Those *Robot Companions* are envisaged as autonomous embodied systems, as partners of humans in everyday situations. Research in this field centers about advanced learning and training processes which are designed to continuously improve the robot's capabilities through assessing novel skills and knowledge.

*Companion* technology advances on that concept by including cognitive abilities of technical systems. The research field of *cognitive systems* has, since the turn of the millennium, focused on the realization of merging environment perception, emotion recognition, reasoning, planning, and learning, with novel human–computer interaction. Vernon et al. [23] give an early overview. Putze and Schultz [19] provide more recent trends.

Here, we aim at giving a systemic approach to *Companion* technology through the interdisciplinary Transregional Collaborative Research Centre "*Companion* Technology for Cognitive Technical Systems" [4, 5, 24].

### 14.2.2 Basic Definitions

As shown in Figure 14.1, individualized and context-sensitive functionality of technical systems requires particular prerequisites. This starts with environmental embedding. Based on perception capabilities, a *Companion* system recognizes context parameters relevant for its proper functioning and its interaction with the user. The system further knows its user's contentment and emotional and dispositional state from perceived parameters. Moreover, the user's expectations regarding the system's functionality is encoded in a mental model.

The cognitive processes that form the *Companion* technology are based on these prerequisites, exhibiting components as shown in Figure 14.2. The knowledge base of the *Companion* system parallels the user's mental model. It encompasses knowledge about the system itself, including declarative descriptions of the operation conditions and technical functionality, yet also about the user's preferences, abilities, and requirements. On the basis of this knowledge, technical functionality is provided through advanced planning and reasoning capabilities. The user's profile is the basis for automatically generated plans of action which directly control the system, or recommend actions matching the current task.

On the sensory end, context is provided through the emotional and dispositional state of the user. This is obtained through multiple modalities as facial expressions, hand and body gestures, speech, as well as physiological measurements. These user states enable the correct dynamical adaptation to the system's functionality, reacting on novel conditions of the world and the user's internal condition.

Interaction is based to a huge part on the system's knowledge base. *Companion* technology provides technical systems with the ability to choose appropriate communication modalities and devices through employing proper motoric and cognitive skills. At a second stage, cognitive competences such as a robust recognition of the environmental situation and the user's dispositional state enable individualized user–system interaction with corresponding technical functionality through continuous consideration of time, location, and behavioral context, plan execution

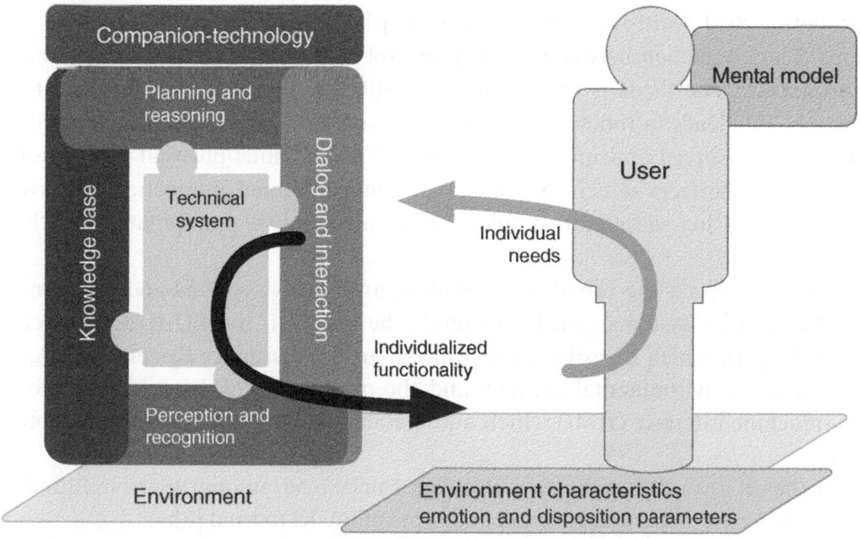


**Figure 14.2** Future human–technology interaction. Source: Adopted from [6].

monitoring and robust activity recognition. Lastly, in a third stage, building on these capabilities, a number of meta-functions manifest the *Companion* characteristics:

- recognition of a user's intentions;
- support to the user with motivating comments and confirmation;
- detection of erroneous situations and appropriate reactions;
- sustaining the dialog with the user and conducting metadialogs;
- explanation of the system's recommendations and behavior;
- generation and presentation of alternatives for action;
- convincing the user of overarching goals;
- recognition of changes in users' behavioral strategies;
- clarification of ambiguous user reactions through appropriate system intervention.

All sorts of technical systems will be equipped with *Companion*-characteristics, for example digital cameras, ticket vending machines, (semi-)autonomous cars, and autonomous robots; electronic support systems such as fitness-apps or navigation systems; complex application systems or services like booking agents or planning assistants for everyday tasks.

## 14.3 State-of-the-Art

Collaborative systems have been documented since B. Grosz's seminal keynote on AAAI-94 [12]. On the focus were shared plans for collaboration, with a mutual belief of a recipe, individual or group plans for subacts, as well as the commitment and intention for the group's success. This required research in agent-action assignment, plan construction, modeling commitment, negotiation, communication, constraints, and tradeoffs, as well as intention–conflict resolution. Group decision-making [17] as an ability to plan and act together therefore was, at the time, at the forefront of the construction of collaboration, which was understood as an a-priori negotiation of strategies among the actors. At the time of execution, this was merely adapted.

Likewise, collaborative robotics defined goals and abilities. The US Robotics Roadmap 2016 [22] and the EU Robotics 2020 Multi-Annual Roadmap [14] both envisage robotic systems as collaborative systems. The interaction between human and robot is seen as a safe and dependable in a shared workspace. The focus is on human-compatibility which is the guideline for robot design. Ultimately, this leads to robots which sense, reason, and act in close contact with humans in an imperfectly observed and understood world. This demands physical interaction and proper conversational interfaces which exhibit social context-defined interaction patterns between humans and robots for adaptation of plans and collaborative manipulation of the environment.

This entails intent estimation on the robot's side, leading to proactive actions and reactions. Parallels to technical assistance systems can, for example, be found in the EU-H2020 project ADAS & Me (2017–2020, [3]), which investigates Advanced Driver Assistance Systems (ADAS) that incorporate situational/ environmental context, and the observation of driver/rider states, for adaptive human–machine interface (HMI) which automatically hands over control at various levels of automation.

The current state-of-the-art toward *Companion* technology can be read, among others, in Biundo et al. [9] in the special issue on *Companion Technology* as part of the KI journal [8].

### 14.3.1 Discussion of the Most Important Scientific/Technical Contributions

Nowadays, we face the inclusion of "A.I. sidekicks" which aim at understanding the linked issues of understanding what human collaborator's intentions are and identifying and planning actions to support these intentions [13]. Likewise, increasingly open plot situations demand a design of supportive cooperative processes for technical assistance with a deep understanding of user states and an ability to negotiate between system and user. Again, this is the core of *Companion* technology [6] with the capabilities described above. Research issues in this field are conducted by various actors and concerted research initiatives. As examples for the latter, we see the EU-FP6 project COMPANIONS (2006–2010, [28]), the German Collaborative Research Centre "Companion-Technology for Cognitive Technical Systems" (2009–2017, [7]), and the EU-EFRE project "Intention-based anticipatory interactive systems" [26]. Accompanying this we first see steps for industrial roll-outs, like an emotion-based, supportive high-quality dialog in real-world conditions in call-centers, providing feedback and assessment of the call-center agent with respect to his emotional state and the adequacy of his interaction with the caller [20].

## 14.4 Future Research Challenges

Where underspecified prerequisites for classical planning are observed, *Companion* technology comes to play since it aims at conceptual improvement of human–machine interaction.

As classical planning models normally require fixed targets, operating with loops of planning and acting, this works in an environment of set allocation of spheres of activity, where centralized or decentralized monitoring comes handy in multiagent systems. This can be realized through process-related or parametric variables which are typically adapted only, causing monitoring to be run through cyclically. The paradigm which is proposed here, contrasts this by defining interacting levels of cooperation where the actors dynamically coordinate their activities. This happens on three levels: the operational level, the negotiation level, and the level of reflection.

### 14.4.1 Current Research Issues

Let us consider three equally ranked classes of actors (where in each class it is possible that one or many actors are present): user, technical agent, and external resource [25]. These classes of actors interplay in the processes of goal finding and strategy change through proper technically assisted processes. As an example, take a robot with mounting skills as an agent. It must coordinate and negotiate with actors of other classes on questions on the operational level (which tool is to be used), on the negotiation level (when and by whom is the tool offered), and lastly on the reflection level (is this tool appropriate for the joint mounting process). These levels may lead to small adaptations of the procedures, but possibly also to a selection of completely different tools or workpieces, which may even change the original target. These coordinations and negotiations can be performed by any proper-deeming combination of multimodal object-related and communicative actions. The outcome then defines the currently observed state of the joint system. When interacting, the actors take into account external resources as a third – equally determining – active partner. This must lead to an open system description of the interaction between human and artificial agents.

The mentioned active external resources are defined by their characteristic as being not (inherently) available to the human and artificial agents. Not only classical external information sources (WWW, databases, ...) apply here but also tele-assistants (technical or medical remote diagnostics, writing office, ...) or external experts (helpline, consultants). These external resources have no immediate sensory access to the current environment where the action takes place. Hence, it is impossible for them to participate directly in actions or to manipulate the action environment. Still, external resources are clearly a determinant actor, since their influence in the decision and execution processes codefines the problem area.

Let us advance on the above example to illustrate the interaction between local agents and external resource: suppose the user requires and obtains a functional description of a particular tool (operational level). On inspection of the description, it becomes clear that the tool is inappropriate for the purpose at hand. This is confirmed by advice from a helpline (negotiation level). Consequently, there is demand for alternative tools. If these turn out to be unavailable or unmanageable, the original target functionality has to be given up (reflection level). At this point, it should be noticed that the external resource has had potential access to all involved levels and could have intervened; hence, it can be understood as an equal actor. Over time and depending on the actions of other actors, the external influence can change and must be cooperatively managed. Unlike in usual models of interaction where external resources are seen as (passive, static) support instances, here it is seen as an active determining factor.

The competences of the actors determine their degree of influence at the three levels. It is thinkable in the above example that a technical agent can only clarify at the specification level. In a different setting, where internal technical process data are obtainable, a technical agent may analyze the full train of processing steps, related not only to the tools at hand but also to other available and suitable tools. In the same vein, the external resource should not be understood as a mere database, but rather as an active assistant system which is being configured by the robot's manufacturer. Equipped with this knowledge, it can assess entire processing procedures and advance necessary or potential configurations with complex usage of tools. As a preemptive measure, alternative modi of operation can already be proposed in an early stage at the negotiation level.

### 14.4.2 Future Research Directions Dealing with the Current Issues

If we want to take advantage of the open plot situations with action processes defined by the three levels above, we require cognitive systems which support all involved processes efficiently. This entails a number of research questions:

- How do we recognize the appropriate states and traits of the involved human actors (perceptual, dispositional, motoric, and cognitive)? Which particular multimodal sensory information as well as inferential processes are useful? How do we infer on the state of interaction process and possible conflicts?
- How do we find a description for tasks, goals, and strategies? Which ontologies and semantics should be used? How will the dynamic goal finding and exploitation of alternative strategies be supported by anticipatory and predictive planning? When and on the basis of which recognizable markers are these strategies altered, initiated, or even given up?
- Which are the mechanisms of interactive coordination and negotiation at the three described levels? How are they realized in technical cognitive systems?
- How do we create and transcribe datasets based on empirical interaction studies which support automatic training strategies?

- How do we find solutions or compromises in the complex interplay of teams of human and artificial actors? How do we implant efficiency, transparency, autonomy, and fairness in such hybrid systems?

Obviously, a high level of interdisciplinarity and transdisciplinarity is required to come up with answers to these questions. Let us report on recent avenues and findings.

The process of acquiring information gets dialogical to an ever-increasing extent. In problem-solving, the identification of technologies which are appropriate for a given industry is known as technology scouting [30]. Technical assistance is limited by the level of complexity of the problem at hand. Utilizing exploratory search [27] aims at defining search spaces for a user, in contrast to fixed item searches. Such information seeking approaches are reviewed, for example by Al-Suqri and Al-Aufi [1]. One way of organizing these search processes is behavioral modeling through Markov chains. Often, the efficiency of strategies is impeded by user dispositions and traits. The effect of this in collaborative search is reviewed by Steichen et al. [21]. The concept of good-enough ("satisficing") models has been introduced to manage a trade-off between accuracy and efficiency [15].

In the arena of negotiating, co-operative activities are required as outcomes. Here, flexibility is required and achieved through multimodal communication and adaptive dialogs. This type of situated communication has to consider shared action contexts, where communication is sustained through gestural or verbal references or direct actions related to the task. These signals are interpreted both operationally and socially, changing the actors' task models and user models. This type of effect has been investigated, e.g. by Buschmeier and Kopp [10]. Lastly, the level of cooperation has to be learned smoothly, proceeding in incremental steps which are assured by operational and social feedback. Cognitive systems which are capable of such behavioral learning have been described by Kopp et al. [16].

## References


**1** Al-Suqri, M. and Al-Aufi, A. (2015). *Information Seeking Behavior and Technology Adoption: Theories and Trends*. Springer. 01ISBN 9781466681576. https://doi.org/10.4018/978-1-4666-8156-9.

**2** Albrecht, S., Ramirez-Amaro, K., Ruiz-Ugalde, F. et al. (2011). Imitating human reaching motions using physically inspired optimization principles. *Proceedings of the 11th IEEE-RAS International Conference on Humanoid Robots*.

**3** Anund, A. (2020). Advanced driver assistance systems incorporate driver/rider state, situational/ environmental context, and adaptive HMI to automatically hand over control at different levels of automation (ADAS & ME),. URL http://www.adasandme.com (accessed 14 November 2021).

**4** Biundo, S. and Wendemuth, A. (2010). Von kognitiven technischen Systemen zu Companion-Systemen. *Künstliche Intelligenz* 24 (4): 335–339. https://doi.org/10.1007/s13218-010-0056-9.

**5** Biundo, S. and Wendemuth, A. (2016). *Companion*-technology for cognitive technical systems. *Künstliche Intelligenz* 30 (1): 71–75. https://doi.org/10.1007/s13218-015-0414-8.

**6** Susanne, B. and Andreas, W. (eds.) (2017). *Companion Technology: A Paradigm Shift in Human–Technology Interaction*. Cognitive Technologies. Cham: Springer. ISBN 978-3-319-43664-7. https://doi.org/10.1007/978-3-319-43665-4.

**7** Biundo, S. and Wendemuth, A. (2018). Eine Companion-Technologie für kognitive technische Systeme. http://www.sfb-trr-62.de (accessed 14 November 2021).

8 Biundo, S., Höller, D., and Bercher, P. (2016). Special issue on companion technologies. *Künstliche Intelligenz* 30 (1): 5–9. https://doi.org/10.1007/s13218-015-0421-9. Editorial.

9 Biundo, S., Höller, D., Schattenberg, B., and Bercher, P. (2016). Companion-technology: an overview. *Künstliche Intelligenz* 30 (1): 11–20. https://doi.org/10.1007/s13218-015-0419-3.

10 Buschmeier, H. and Kopp, S. (2018). Communicative listener feedback in human–agent interaction: artificial speakers need to be attentive and adaptive. *AAMAS 2018*.

11 Dautenhahn, K., Woods, S., Kaouri, C. et al. (2005). What is a robot companion - friend, assistant or butler. *Proceedings of IEEE IROS*, 1488–1493.

12 Grosz, B.J. (1996). Collaborative systems (AAAI-94 presidential address). *AI Magazine* 17 (2): 67. https://doi.org/10.1609/aimag.v17i2.1223.

13 Grosz, B.J., Hunsberger, L., and Kraus, S. (1999). Planning and acting together. *AI Magazine* 20 (4): 23. https://doi.org/10.1609/aimag.v20i4.1476.

14 Horizon (2020). Robotics 2020 Multi-Annual Roadmap for Robotics in Europe. *Call 2 ICT24, Release B*.

15 Kopp, S. and Pöppel, J. (2018). Satisficing models of Bayesian theory of mind for explaining behavior of differently uncertain agents. *AAMAS 2018*.

16 Kopp, S., Welbergen, H., Torky, R.Y., and Buschmeier, H. (2013). An architecture for fluid real-time conversational agents: integrating incremental output generation and input processing. *Journal on Multimodal User Interfaces* 8: 11. https://doi.org/10.1007/s12193-013-0130-3.

17 Macindoe, O. (2014). Sidekick agents for sequential planning problems. PhD thesis. Massachusetts Institute of Technology.

18 Matthews, J.T., Engberg, S.J., Glover, J. et al. (2004). Robotic assistants for the elderly: designing and conducting field studies. *Proceedings of the 10th IASTED International Conference on Robotics and Applications*.

19 Putze, F. and Schultz, T. (2014). Adaptive cognitive technical systems. *Journal of Neuroscience Methods* 234: 108–115. https://doi.org/10.1016/j.jneumeth.2014.06.029.

20 Siegert, I. and Ohnemus, K. (2015). A new dataset of telephone-based human–human call-center interaction with emotional evaluation. *ISCT 2015*, 143–148.

21 Steichen, B., Ashman, H., and Wade, V. (2012). A comparative survey of personalized information retrieval and adaptive hypermedia techniques. *Information Processing Management* 48: 698–724. https://doi.org/10.1016/j.ipm.2011.12.004.

22 University of California San Diego (2016). A Roadmap for US Robotics - From Internet to Robotics. *Call 2 ICT24, Release B*.

23 Vernon, D., Metta, G., and Sandini, G. (2007). A survey of artificial cognitive systems: implications for the autonomous development of mental capabilities in computational agents. *Transactions on Evolutionary Computation* 11 (2): 151–180. https://doi.org/10.1109/TEVC.2006.890274.

24 Wendemuth, A. and Biundo, S. (2012). A companion technology for cognitive technical systems. In: *Cognitive Behavioural Systems, Lecture Notes in Computer Science*, vol. 7403 (ed. A. Esposito, A.M. Esposito, A. Vinciarelli et al.), 89–103. Berlin, Heidelberg: Springer-Verlag.

25 Wendemuth, A. and Kopp, S. (2019). Towards cognitive systems for assisted cooperative processes of goal finding and strategy change*. *2019 IEEE International Conference on Systems, Man and Cybernetics (SMC)*, 4302–4307. https://doi.org/10.1109/SMC.2019.8914179.

26 Wendemuth, A., Böck, R., Nürnberger, A. et al. (2018). Intention-based anticipatory interactive systems. *2018 IEEE International Conference on Systems, Man, and Cybernetics (SMC)*, 2583–2588. https://doi.org/10.1109/SMC.2018.00442.

**27** White, R. and Roth, R. (2009). *Exploratory Search: Beyond the Query-Response Paradigm*, vol. 1, Springer. https://doi.org/10.2200/S00174ED1V01Y200901ICR003.

**28** Wilks, Y. (2001). Companions (EU-project). http://cordis.europa.eu/project/rcn/96289_en.html (accessed 14 November 2021).

**29** Wilks, Y. (2010). *Close Engagements with Artificial Companions: Key Social, Psychological, Ethical and Design Issues, Natural Language Processing*, vol. 8. John Benjamins Publishing.

**30** Wolff, M. (1992). Scouting for technology. *Research Technology Management* 35: 10–12. https://doi.org/10.1080/08956308.1992.11670801.

# 15

## A Survey on Rollator-Type Mobility Assistance Robots

*Milad Geravand[1], Christian Werner[2], Klaus Hauer[2], and Angelika Peer[3]*

[1] *Deep Care GmbH, Waiblingen, Germany*
[2] *Agaplesion Bethanien-Hospital, Geriatric Centre, University of Heidelberg, Heidelberg, Germany*
[3] *Faculty of Engineering, Free University of Bolzano, Bolzano, Italy*

## 15.1 Introduction

Many activities of daily living involve walking and transfers, making mobility an important human ability. Low-physical activity is a known risk factor for age-associated health decline [20] and is often associated with reduced independence, quality of life, and self-esteem.

The demand for mobility assistance of the population aged 60 or over (who is predicted to nearly represent a quarter of the world's population by 2050 [96]), however, is endangered by an increasing lack of qualified workforce, decrease in social support systems (family members), and the costs for care.

Mobility assistance robots have potential to cover parts of this demand and thus, their development has received significant attention over the last decades. In this chapter, we review rollator-type mobility assistance robots according to their platforms and functionalities, see Figure 15.1. We start with comparing the platforms in terms of their kinematics, actuation systems, sensors, and human-machine interfaces (HMI) in Section 15.2. We then discuss different implementations of provided functionalities like sit-to-stand and stand-to-sit (STS) assistance (Section 15.3.1), walking assistance (Section 15.3.2), localization, and navigation assistance (Section 15.3.3) as well as further functionalities that don't fall into the aforementioned categories (Section 15.3.4). We conclude with a critical discussion and a list of potential future research directions. It should be noted that the intention of this chapter (which represents an updated and condensed version of the state-of-the-art overview of [26]) is to review functionalities from an engineering perspective and not from a user or clinical point of view as available literature shows a lack of formal evaluation studies with final end-users and thus, does not allow taking strong conclusions about the benefits of developed systems and functionalities from a clinical or user perspective. Our findings and recommendations in terms of user evaluation are summarized in a separate survey paper, see [100].

## 15.2 Mobility Assistance Platforms

We start with reviewing mobility assistance platforms with focus on their kinematics and actuation systems, sensors as well as human–system interfaces used for 31 mobility assistance robots of rollator type, see Table 15.1 for an overview.

*Handbook of Human-Machine Systems*, First Edition. Edited by Giancarlo Fortino, David Kaber, Andreas Nürnberger, and David Mendonça.

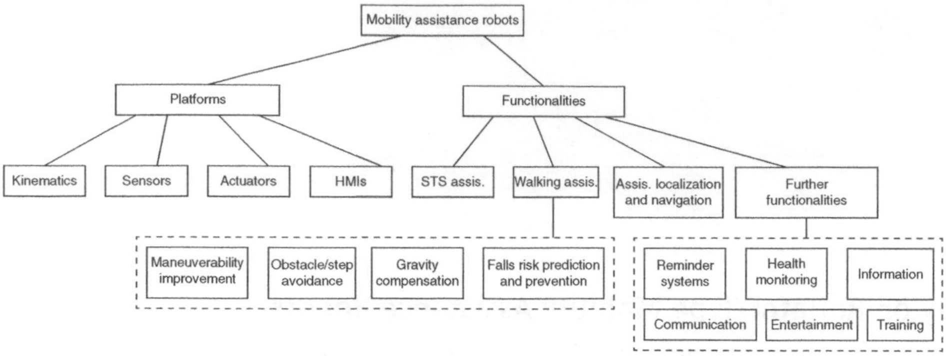


**Figure 15.1** Overview of mobility assistance robots.

### 15.2.1 Actuation

Mobility assistants can be of passive and active types. *Passive* mobility assistants are typically established with brakes to guide and decelerate and only move if the user applies forces onto them, while *active* mobility assistants have inbuilt motors that allow their motion and interaction behavior to be actively controlled. Thus, safety is inherently guaranteed for passive mobility assistants. While poor maneuvering capabilities and rather high inertia are considered disadvantages of passive systems, active-type robots allow carrying additional weight and thus, the mobility assistants can be featured with further components. Active mobility assistants dominate the field as out of the 31 mobility assistant robots reviewed, only 7 devices belong to the passive category, while 24 devices belong to the active category.

### 15.2.2 Kinematics

Mobility assistant platforms provide mechanisms for locomotion and/or sit-to-stand support.

#### 15.2.2.1 Locomotion Support

Systems for locomotion support can be categorized into three or four wheel systems. A typical configuration of a four-wheel system consists of a support frame, two actuated rear wheels, and two castors at the front. Literature is dominated by systems that foresee motorized wheels at the rear as only few prototypes consider them at the front (e.g. [55]), have all wheels motorized (e.g. [31]), or are totally operating without motors (e.g. [42, 53]). Three-wheel systems are mostly build on commercial frames equipped with additional sensors and typically have an automated braking and steering system for the front wheel (e.g. [44, 98]).

Of the reviewed mobility assistants, most prototypes (24 systems) are nonholonomic. Systems based on holonomic bases use four omnidirectional wheels (see, e.g. "CMU walker" and "walbot"), two omnidirectional wheels plus castors (see, e.g. "PAMM"), or three omnidirectional wheels (see, e.g. "JARoW" and the "Walking Aid Robots").

#### 15.2.2.2 STS Support

From the reviewed systems only seven mobility assistance robots foresee mechanisms to provide STS assistance. In "MONIMAD" and its predecessor "robuWalker" parallel actuated arms with 2 DoFs are foreseen. A similar idea is followed for the "Mobot" platform, but with independently controlled spindle drives for each arm. In both devices, the handles are designed to remain horizontal irrespective of the commanded height of the handles. The Chugo group developed a 3 DoF

**Table 15.1** Comparison of hardware and sensing systems as well as functionalities of different rollator-type mobility assistants.

| Mobility assistant | Hardware and sensing systems | | | | | | | | | | | | | | | | | Functionalities | | | | | | | | | |
|---|---|---|---|---|---|---|---|---|---|---|---|---|---|---|---|---|---|---|---|---|---|---|---|---|---|---|---|
| | Actuation | | Kinematics | | | | Sensors | | | | | | | | | Interfaces | | | Walking assistance | | | | Loc./Nav. | | Further functionalities | | |
| | Active | Passive | Three Wheels | Four Wheels | Holonomic | Non-holonomic | LRF | Sonar | Cameras | GPS | Kinect | F/T | Tactile | Slope Detectors | Heart Rate | Touch Screen | Speech Interface | STS assistance | Maneuverability improvement | Fall prevention | Gravity comp. | Obstacle/step avoidance | Assis. localization | Assis. navigation | Reminder systems | Health monitoring | Comm., information, entertain. & training |
| **Kosuge walkers** [17, 18, 36, 37, 38, 39, 41, 42, 72] | ∘ | √ | – | √ | √ | ∘ | √ | √ | √ | – | √ | √ | – | √ | – | – | – | ∘ | √ | √ | √ | √ | – | – | – | – | – |
| **MARC** [97, 98, 99] | – | √ | √ | – | – | √ | √ | √ | – | – | – | √ | – | – | – | – | – | – | √ | – | – | ∘ | – | – | – | – | – |
| **iWalker (US)** [53] | – | √ | – | √ | – | √ | – | √ | – | – | – | – | – | – | – | – | – | – | – | – | – | – | √ | √ | – | – | – |
| **i-Walker (EU)** [19] | – | √ | – | √ | – | √ | – | – | √ | – | – | √ | – | – | – | – | – | – | – | – | – | – | ∘ | ∘ | – | – | – |
| **i-Walker (Japan)** [49] | – | √ | – | √ | – | √ | – | – | √ | – | – | – | – | – | – | – | – | – | √ | √ | – | – | – | – | – | – | – |
| **COOL Aide** [44] | – | √ | √ | – | – | √ | √ | – | – | – | – | √ | – | – | – | – | – | – | √ | – | – | √ | – | – | – | – | – |
| **Care-O-bot I-II** [33, 34, 61, 87] | √ | – | – | √ | √ | – | – | √ | √ | – | – | √ | – | – | – | √ | √ | – | – | – | – | – | – | √ | | – | – |
| **Guido** [55, 83] | √ | – | – | √ | – | √ | √ | √ | – | – | – | √ | – | – | – | – | √ | – | √ | – | – | √ | √ | √ | | – | – |
| **CMU walker** [31, 69] | √ | – | – | √ | √ | – | √ | √ | – | – | – | √ | – | – | – | – | – | – | – | – | – | √ | √ | √ | – | – | – |
| **Pearl and FLO** [67, 80, 84] | √ | – | – | √ | – | √ | √ | √ | √ | – | – | – | – | – | – | √ | √ | – | – | – | – | √ | – | √ | √ | √ | √ |
| **PAMM** [21, 94, 103] | √ | – | – | √ | √ | – | – | √ | √ | – | – | √ | – | – | √ | – | – | – | √ | √ | – | √ | – | √ | – | √ | – |
| **i-go** [45, 51, 52, 60] | √ | – | – | √ | – | √ | – | – | – | – | – | √ | √ | √ | – | – | – | – | √ | – | √ | – | – | √ | – | – | – |
| **Johnnie - CAIROW** [70, 104] | √ | – | – | √ | – | √ | √ | √ | – | – | – | √ | – | – | – | √ | – | – | – | √ | – | √ | – | – | – | √ | √ |
| **Walkmate** [88] | √ | – | – | √ | – | √ | √ | – | √ | – | – | √ | – | – | – | – | – | – | √ | – | – | – | – | – | – | – | – |
| **walbot** [92, 93] | √ | – | – | √ | √ | – | √ | – | – | – | – | – | – | – | – | – | – | – | √ | – | – | √ | – | √ | – | – | – |
| **JARoW** [57, 58, 74] | √ | – | √ | – | √ | – | √ | – | – | – | – | – | – | – | – | – | – | – | √ | – | – | √ | – | – | – | – | – |
| **UTS** [62] | √ | – | – | √ | – | √ | √ | – | – | – | – | √ | – | – | – | – | – | – | – | – | – | √ | – | – | – | – | – |
| **HITOMI** [68] | √ | – | – | √ | – | √ | – | √ | √ | ∘ | – | – | √ | – | – | – | – | – | – | – | – | √ | √ | √ | – | – | – |
| **NeoASAS** [25, 73] | √ | – | – | √ | – | √ | – | √ | – | – | – | √ | – | – | – | – | – | – | √ | – | – | – | – | – | – | – | – |
| **PAM-AID** [56] | √ | – | – | √ | – | √ | – | √ | – | – | – | √ | – | – | – | – | √ | – | √ | – | – | – | – | – | – | – | – |
| **MONIMAD - robuwalker** [63, 64, 77, 78, 86] | √ | – | – | √ | – | √ | √ | – | – | – | – | √ | – | – | – | – | – | √ | – | – | – | – | – | – | – | – | – |
| **Chugo group walker** [13, 14, 15, 16] | √ | – | – | √ | – | √ | √ | – | – | – | – | √ | – | – | – | – | – | √ | – | – | – | – | – | – | – | – | – |
| **Standing assistive walker** [48, 75] | √ | – | – | 6W | – | √ | – | – | – | – | – | √ | √ | – | – | – | – | √ | – | √ | – | – | – | – | – | – | – |
| **WAR** [89, 90] | √ | – | – | √ | – | √ | √ | √ | – | √ | – | √ | – | √ | – | √ | – | √ | – | – | – | √ | – | √ | – | – | – |
| **SMW** [47, 50] | √ | – | – | √ | – | √ | – | – | – | – | – | √ | – | – | – | – | – | √ | – | – | – | – | – | – | – | – | – |
| **MOBIL** [85] | √ | – | – | √ | – | √ | – | √ | – | – | – | √ | – | – | – | – | – | √ | – | – | – | √ | – | – | – | – | – |
| **MOBOT** [9, 10, 11, 27, 28, 29, 30, 43] | √ | – | – | √ | – | √ | √ | – | √ | – | – | √ | – | – | – | √ | √ | √ | √ | √ | – | √ | √ | √ | – | – | – |
| **FriWalk** [2, 3, 4] | √ | – | – | √ | – | √ | – | – | √ | – | √ | – | – | – | – | – | – | – | √ | – | – | √ | – | √ | – | – | – |
| **IRO** [35] | – | √ | – | √ | – | √ | – | – | – | – | – | – | – | – | – | – | – | – | – | – | – | √ | – | – | – | – | – |
| **UFES' Smart walker** [46] | √ | – | √ | – | – | √ | √ | – | – | – | – | √ | – | – | – | – | – | – | – | – | – | – | – | √ | – | – | – |
| **ISR-AIWALKER** [79] | √ | – | – | √ | – | √ | – | – | √ | – | – | √ | – | – | – | – | – | – | – | √ | – | – | – | – | – | – | √ |
| **Nagoya Smart Walker** [59] | √ | – | – | √ | – | √ | – | – | – | – | – | √ | – | – | – | – | – | – | – | – | – | – | – | – | – | – | √ |
| **ANG II** [65] | √ | – | – | √ | – | √ | – | – | √ | √ | – | √ | – | – | – | – | – | – | – | – | – | – | – | – | – | – | – |
| **Walking-Aid Robot** [102] | √ | – | √ | – | √ | – | √ | – | – | – | – | √ | – | – | – | – | – | – | √ | √ | – | – | – | – | – | – | – |
| **Walking-Aid Robot** [101] | √ | – | √ | – | √ | – | – | √ | – | – | √ | – | – | – | – | – | – | – | √ | – | – | – | – | – | – | – | – |
| **AGoRA Smart Walker** [91] | √ | – | – | √ | – | √ | √ | √ | √ | – | – | √ | – | – | – | – | – | – | √ | – | – | √ | √ | √ | – | – | √ |

√: *full support*, ∘: *partial support*, –: *no support*

support pad manipulated by four parallel linkages mounted on an active mobile base. Finally, vertically moving support mechanisms are proposed for the "WAR," and the "Standing assistive walker." It is remarkable that only the "MOBOT" platform foresees independent movement of left and right handles.

### 15.2.3 Sensors

Laser range finders, sonar, and force torque sensors can be found on most developed prototypes, while color and depth cameras as well as GPS play a more minor role. Some platforms are equipped with very specific sensors, e.g. a slope detection sensor [45, 51], heart-rate sensors [21, 94], and tactile sensors [68].

To support navigation and obstacle avoidance, laser range finders or sonar sensors are typically adopted. Cheaper IR sensors represent the exception [35]. Laser range finders are sometimes also used to distinguish user states (walking, stopped, and emergency) [41], or to measure lower-limb positions and speed [57, 74] as well as walking patterns [9, 10, 22, 23, 76].

To measure the interaction forces applied by the user, force torque sensors or specially positioned strain gauges are typically adopted.

Cameras are employed for localization [21, 53, 68, 94], obstacle avoidance [89, 90], or in case of rehabilitation also for documentation of the user behavior [49].

Self-localization with the help of global positioning systems/geographical information system (GPS/GIS) is analyzed, e.g. in [89, 90].

### 15.2.4 Human–Machine Interfaces

HMIs that are studied in the context of mobility assistant robots are manifold. Very basic HMIs consider manual switches or buttons to accept control inputs from the user and loudspeakers to communicate the robot state [31, 55]. Also hand-held remote controls [31] have been investigated to pass commands over distance. More advanced systems involving displays and touchscreens are used, e.g. in [82, 84, 89, 104] for switching robot control modes [82] and walking characteristics [104] or to set a destination [84, 89]. These displays are also used to provide information of, for example front cameras, the current location, and to communicate guiding messages [84, 89].

As the interaction through keyboards and computer screens may be difficult for elderly people, also verbal communication has been investigated. To this end, speakers and microphones are installed, see, e.g. [82] and speech analysis/synthesis modules that process verbal commands as well as provide spoken feedback have been tested in Care-O-Bot 3 [82] and Pearl and Flo [80, 84].

Widely missing so far are HMIs based on nonverbal communication, especially the recognition of gesture and facial expressions. The benefit of such HMIs for mobility assistance robots, however, has to be further investigated as the ability of elderly to communicate via gesture and mimics may be limited due to cognitive disabilities.

## 15.3 Functionalities

We review and classify functionalities of robot mobility assistants into STS assistance, walking assistance, localization, and navigation assistance, and further functionalities not covered by the aforementioned categories. Walking, localization, and navigation assistance are intensively studied in literature, while other functionalities are less focused on so far.

### 15.3.1 STS Assistance

Surveyed implementations for assisted-STS transfers can be assigned to three categories: force control, motion control, and switching control.

Considering force control, basic optimization approaches minimizing interaction forces with posture stability as side criterion [64] can be found in literature.

Robot motion control approaches include not only passive approaches to assist in STS transfers that activate brakes once the system is properly positioned in front of the user [38] but also more sophisticated approaches implementing guiding trajectories [46, 47, 50]. Trajectories approximate recorded hand paths with cubic splines [63], minimize jerk along the path [77], mimic specific assistance movements (e.g. Kamiya motions) [46] or are the result of a more general optimization problem [30, 63]. Also, online approaches that follow an admittance control law to move the support system instead of offline pre-calculating the entire trajectory have been reported [17].

Approaches based on switching controllers consider switching position/damping control as a function of the actual human postural state [13], threshold-based switching of control modes depending on real-time estimated pelvis, knee, and ankle torques determined with the help of a biomechanical model [16] or switching between different variations of admittance control based on fuzzy logic to ensure stability of the patient during assisted STS transfers [86]. Also stand-to-sit transfers have been studied and involved changing of the reference trajectories [15] and adjusting the seating position based on sensor readings [14].

Some of the aforementioned approaches differentiate between different postural phases when providing assistance. Fuzzy logic [86] and force-threshold-based algorithms [13] are employed for distinguishing from four to seven phases. Interestingly, no study could be found that analyzed how many and which of the various phases are essential for realizing a proper robot-supported STS functionality.

### 15.3.2 Walking Assistance

Walking assistance aims at the human-adaptive or environment-adaptive alteration of control inputs or parameters to achieve maneuverability improvement and gravity compensation or to handle safety-critical situations like the avoidance of collisions with the environment or human falls.

#### 15.3.2.1 Maneuverability Improvement

Variable admittance control dominates the field of maneuverability improvement, whereby admittance parameters for mass and damping, transformation matrices, weighting factors or additional forces/torques generated based on information extracted from the environment are adopted to alter the behavior of the system actively or passively. Variable admittance control concepts combined with intelligent force filtering techniques [25, 73] have been adopted for maneuverability improvement by reducing the inertia of the overall system [29, 91], implementing force-velocity or force-acceleration modes [88], applying transformations that alter the center of rotation of the mobility assistant [18], and implementing variable damping [93, 103]. Also, artificial potential fields were employed for passive path following realized through the activation of brakes [37, 40, 49, 72] and for active path following [55, 83, 92], whereby the active support in case of path and wall following only alters the angular velocity, and the support is triggered by intentional forces applied by the human.

An alternative to variable admittance control for maneuverability improvement is direct control of the position/velocity of the mobility assistant robot based on algorithms that estimate the human intention either directly from input devices like buttons combined with local intelligence to avoid erroneous inputs [56] or indirectly from sensor signals and context. The latter requires the estimation of the human intention, which can be accomplished from force signals [79, 101], detected human walking behavior [9, 10, 22, 23, 76] or a combination of the two [102]. This intention can be used to adjust the motion of the platform [57, 74, 79] or control the human–robot formation [12].

Again, an alternative way consists in using a visual feedback device to assist the human in keeping the optimal position with respect to the robot [32].

#### 15.3.2.2 Gravity Compensation

Assistance on slopes can be provided through gravity compensation. For passive mobility, assistance robots brake torques [37] have been implemented, while for active robots, e.g. model-predictive control has been adopted to estimate the slope height required to calculate the assistance torques [52].

#### 15.3.2.3 Obstacle Avoidance

Another often realized functionality is obstacle avoidance. With the help of artificial potential fields force components for passive [37, 40, 72] as well as active obstacle avoidance [36] are determined and compared to state-based constraints in [1]. Dangerous situations resulting from active approaches are, e.g. overcome by "conflict indexes" [44]. Beside aforementioned approaches that realize mainly fixed strategies for combining human and robot inputs or switch between the two extremes of a fully autonomous system and direct control, also adaptive shared control strategies have been proposed exploring the proximity to obstacles to shift the authority between autonomous system and human [97, 103] or by realizing a context-dependent, on-line adaptation of the support level by gain-scheduling of controller parameters inspired by human decision-making models [29]. Alternative approaches to variable admittance control adjust the platform translational and/or rotational velocity depending on the distance to obstacles [57, 70, 74, 91, 92] or use algorithms to realize obstacle avoidance and local path planning functionalities in full autonomous mode [55, 83] or in combination with, e.g. fuzzy logic to combine velocity inputs of the human and the autonomous agent [62]. Again, a different approach determines steering actions based on the estimation of the human intended walking path by combining sensor information, user input, history, and the position and orientation of the device by means of a dynamical path-weighting scheme [99] or a combination of Dempster–Shafer theory and a specially defined conflict index [44].

#### 15.3.2.4 Falls Risk Prediction and Fall Prevention

Finally, an important, but less focused on assistance function is falls risk prediction and fall prevention. Approaches for falls risk prediction use the estimation of feet positions, body posture, and/or forces applied to the rollator [5, 6, 8, 11, 79, 95, 102]. In terms of fall prevention, approaches like abruptly stopping the walker [49, 102], increasing damping in the desired admittance [39, 42, 103], as well as auditory cues paired with locking the platform [70] have been explored in literature. Controllers that aim for a more sophisticated approach by actively moving the robotic platform/arms for human posture stabilization have been studied in [27, 28, 75].

### 15.3.3 Localization and Navigation

For the realization of functionalities such as assisted localization and navigation software modules for map building, localization, and path planning are required.

#### 15.3.3.1 Map Building and Localization

Early approaches combine local information from odometry and gyroscopes with global information derived from a comparison of a given map and features with laser scan data and natural environment features, see [34]. Later, simultaneous localization and mapping (SLAM) algorithms and map-based navigation have been adopted [55, 83, 91], also featuring implementations for highly populated areas [67].

#### 15.3.3.2 Path Planning

In terms of path planning, graph-based methods [55, 83] with elastic path deformation for obstacle avoidance, rapidly exploring random trees, potential grids with wavefront expansion, quad trees, and visibility graphs [33, 34] for holonomic and nonholonomic platforms [33] assuming a given map and a desired target have been proposed and/or implemented. Advanced methods for dynamic path planning also allow for dynamic obstacles and support the planning of smooth paths and their alteration by user inputs by adopting approaches based on elastic bands as presented in [33, 61], dynamic via point calculations (Carnegie Mellon's Navigation Toolkit), or dynamic windowing [7, 91].

#### 15.3.3.3 Assisted Localization

While several mobility assistance robots have the ability to localize themselves, only few foresee a localization assistance for cognitively impaired users. Information about the specific location is found to be provided either by marking the user position visually on a map displayed via a screen [31, 53, 69] or via Braille [68]. Alternatively, also automatic verbal feedback has been tested to inform about the current location, navigation events, or selected goals [55, 83].

#### 15.3.3.4 Assisted Navigation

Assisted navigation functionalities typically foresee that users either manually mark desired targets on a given map [29], select from a given list visualized on a screen with the help of buttons [31, 69, 90], use physical buttons to select a labeled target location [55, 83], send voice commands or use a remote connected via Bluetooth, or Wi-fi [94]. Alternatively, the system employs a full speech dialog system [67]. In terms of user guidance, it is either provided by controlling the robot motion directly [91] or indirectly by adjusting the admittance parameters [46] or activating brakes [2, 3, 24, 29, 52, 60, 67, 92, 103], providing visual, auditory or tactile cues [31, 53], or by mixed versions of the above [4, 69].

### 15.3.4 Further Functionalities

#### 15.3.4.1 Reminder Systems

Reminding about routine activities is an assistance function that has been only rarely explored. In [80] a higher-level reasoning software is introduced that reminds people about activities such as eating, drinking, taking medicine, and using the bathroom.

#### 15.3.4.2 Health Monitoring

Also health-monitoring functionalities are available only in very few mobility assistance robots. Implementations of continuous health monitoring systems foresee the supervision of speed and applied forces of the user, heart rate, and gait patterns [94]. A more advanced gait analysis is realized in [70] with the aim of helping therapists in the rehabilitation process. Others again suggest collecting statistical data on medication and daily activities or aim for predicting medical risks by evaluating, e.g. blood sugar and leg diameter [80] (functionalities only partially implemented).

#### 15.3.4.3 Communication, Information, Entertainment, and Training

Occasionally, functionalities for phone and Skype call [104], inquiries related to the television program and the weather forecast [80, 81, 84], online information retrieval systems [84], music players [104] as well as social interaction and telepresence functions have been realized [84]. Another functionality rarely found is related to physical training [59].

## 15.4 Conclusion

Future rollator-type mobility assistant robots will have to be advanced in terms of platforms and functionalities.

In terms of platforms, sensing systems such as GPS, depth cameras, 3D lasers, IR sensors, and tactile sensors are less explored. The same holds for not only advanced platforms with independent handle actuation systems but also low-cost solutions.

When it comes to functionalities, STS transfer support, fall prevention, health monitoring, training, and extra functionalities involving more advanced human–system interfaces are candidates that could deserve more attention.

Human–machine interfaces explored so far involve mainly touch-screens and speech interfaces giving little attention to nonverbal interaction based on gesture and mimics. The benefit of such HMIs for mobility assistance robots, however, has to be further investigated as the ability of elderly to communicate via gesture and mimics may be limited due to cognitive disabilities.

Analyzing human-assisted STS transfers and posture stability mechanisms may help identifying underlying principles and developing computational models that can be exploited in robot assistance controllers. Currently, only few computational models for unassisted STS transfers could be found in literature, see [54, 66, 71] exploiting optimization-based approaches, while models for assisted STS transfers are still limited to offline optimizations [30, 66]. Different target groups would need to be examined to provide optimal and user-adapted assistance.

Different human movements require also the activation of appropriate robot controllers and the switching between them. Literature is dominated by hard switching mechanisms that evaluate predefined thresholds in measurement data or user inputs obtained via touch screens or voice interfaces. More advanced mechanisms for switching the robot controller were hardly investigated, despite of few approaches using Fuzzy control and with focus on STS assistance. Literature also misses control-theoretic investigations to proof the overall stability of the resulting hybrid and switched systems.

Further, safety is considered a crucial aspect when aiming for bringing systems on the market. For STS, transfer assistance safety is evaluated mainly in terms of posture stability and analyzed offline. Resulting safe robot force profiles and trajectories are then replayed online without taking into consideration eventual differences of offline and online situations. Safety during walking mainly concentrates on detecting discrete safety-critical states and the manipulation of the inertia/mass of the robot. Online posture analysis and control, however, has so far only rarely been explored. A more advanced safety analysis aiming for the definition of posture-dependent safe states and safe robot behaviors is still lacking. The analysis of reachable sets and allowed energy exchange between user and robot could be explored in this context.

Shared control plays an important role in mobility assistance robots. While fixed scheduling strategies dominate literature, research involving more context-dependent and dynamic authority sharing mechanism for combining user and autonomous robot inputs, exploiting, for example also methods of decision-making, have so far only received little attention. This also holds for advanced methods of human navigational intent recognition based on history and environment information.

While assisted navigation has been researched intensively, reminder and recommender systems for mobility assistant robots have hardly been investigated.

In terms of health monitoring only very basic features have been explored. More intelligent and especially long-term health monitoring functionalities could not be found. Such functionalities could also help building a training system to gradually enhance or keep the actual health status.

One of the main shortcomings observed in the preparation of this review was the lack of formal evaluation studies involving patients that investigate and compare developed systems and functionalities based on clinical measures and by taking the user perspective into consideration. User acceptance studies are widely missing making it difficult to judge the benefit of one functionality over another or comparing different implementations of one and the same functionality with each other. Also, the identification of the minimal or optimal set of provided functionalities can hardly be identified without such studies. Our findings and recommendations for future evaluation studies tackling these challenges are summarized in a separate survey article, see [100].

Finally, although a large amount of research and development has already been performed on mobility assistance robots, only very few prototypes have resulted in commercially available products. We believe that next to outlined technical and functional advancements and the availability of low-cost solutions, especially formal evaluation studies may help identifying essential functionalities and their benefits for users and with this help convincing users, engineering and leasing companies as well as health insurances to invest into mobility assistance robots.

## References


1 Aigner, P. and McCarragher, B. (1997). Contrasting potential fields and constraints in a shared control task. *IEEE International Conference on Intelligent Robots and Systems*, 140–146.

2 Andreetto, M., Divan, S., Fontanelli, D., and Palopoli, L. (2017). Path following with authority sharing between humans and passive robotic walkers equipped with low-cost actuators. *IEEE Robotics and Automation Letters* 2 (4): 2271–2278.

3 Andreetto, M., Divan, S., Ferrari, F. et al. (2018). Simulating passivity for robotic walkers via authority-sharing. *IEEE Robotics and Automation Letters* 3 (2): 1306–1313.

4 Andreetto, M., Divan, S., Ferrari, F. et al. (2019). Combining haptic and bang-bang braking actions for passive robotic walker path following. *IEEE Transactions on Haptics* 12 (4): 542–553.

5 Ballesteros, J., Urdiales, C., Martinez, A.B., and Van Dieën, J.H. (2016). On gait analysis estimation errors using force sensors on a smart rollator. *Sensors* 16 (11): 1896.

6 Ballesteros, J., Urdiales, C., Martinez, A.B., and Tirado, M. (2017). Automatic assessment of a rollator-user's condition rehabilitation using the i-Walker platform. *IEEE Transactions on Neural Systems and Rehabilitation Engineering* 25 (11): 2009–2017.

7 Ballesteros, J., Urdiales, C., Velasco, A.B.M., and Ramos-Jiménez, G. (2017). A biomimetical dynamic window approach to navigation for collaborative control. *IEEE Transactions on Human–Machine Systems* 47 (6): 1123–1133.

8 Ballesteros, J., Peula J.M., Martinez, A.B., and Urdiales, C. (2018). Automatic fall risk assessment for challenged users obtained from a rollator equipped with force sensors and a RGB-D camera. *2018 IEEE/RSJ International Conference on Intelligent Robots and Systems*, 7356–7361.

9 Chalvatzaki, G., Papageorgiou, X.S., Tzafestas, C.S., and Maragos, P. (2017). Comparative experimental validation of human gait tracking algorithms for an intelligent robotic rollator. *IEEE International Conference on Robotics and Automation*, 6026–6031.

10 Chalvatzaki, G., Papageorgiou, X.S., Tzafestas, C.S., and Maragos, P. (2017). Estimating double support in pathological gaits using an HMM-based analyzer for an intelligent robotic walker. *26th IEEE International Symposium on Robot and Human Interactive Communication*, 101–106.

11 Chalvatzaki, G., Koutras, P., Hadfield, J. et al. (2019). LSTM-based network for human gait stability prediction in an intelligent robotic rollator. *International Conference on Robotics and Automation*, 4225–4232.

12 Chalvatzaki, G., Papageorgiou, X.S., Maragos, P., and Tzafestas, C.S. (2019). Learn to adapt to human walking: a model-based reinforcement learning approach for a robotic assistant rollator. *IEEE Robotics and Automation Letters* 44 (4): 3774–3781.

13 Chugo, D., Kawabata, K., Okamoto, H. et al. (2007). Force assistance system for standing-up motion. *Industrial Robot: The International Journal of Industrial and Service Robotics* 34 (2): 128–134.

14 Chugo, D., Asawa, T., Kitamura, T. et al. (2009). A motion control of a robotic walker for continuous assistance during standing, walking and seating operation. *IEEE/RSJ International Conference on Intelligent Robots and Systems*, St. Louis, MO, USA.

15 Chugo, D., Sakaida, Y., Yokota, S., and Takase, K. (2011). Sitting motion assistance on a rehabitation robotics walker. *IEEE International Conference on Robotics and Biomimetics*, Phuket, Thailand.

16 Chugo, D., Morita, Y., Sakaida, Y. et al. (2012). A robotic walker for standing assistance with realtime estimation of patient's load. *12th IEEE International Workshop on Advanced Motion Control*, Sarajevo, Bosnia and Herzegovina.

17 Chuy, O. Jr., Hirata, Y., Wang, Z., and Kosuge, K. (2006). Approach in assisting a sit-to-stand movement using robotic walking support system. *IEEE/RSJ International Conference on Intelligent Robots and Systems*, Beijing, China.

18 Chuy, O. Jr., Hirata, Y., Wang, Z., and Kosuge, K. (2006). A new control approach for a robotic walking support system in adapting user characteristics. *IEEE Transactions on Systems, Man, and Cybernetics, Part C (Applications and Reviews)* 36 (6): 725–733.

19 Cortés, U., Martínez-Velasco, A., Barrué, C. et al. (2008). A SHARE-it service to elders' mobility using the i-Walker. *Gerontechnology* 7 (2): 95.

20 Delbaere, K., Close, J.C., Heim, J. et al. (2010). A multifactorial approach to understanding fall risk in older people. *American Geriatrics Society* 9 (58): 1679–1685.

21 Dubowsky, S., Genot, F., Godding, S. et al. (2000). PAMM - a robotic aid to the elderly for mobility assistance and monitoring: a "helping-hand" for the elderly. *IEEE International Conference on Robotics and Automation.*

22 Duong, H.T. and Suh, Y.S. (2017). Walking parameters estimation based on a wrist-mounted inertial sensor for a walker user. *IEEE Sensors Journal* 17 (7): 2100–2108.

23 Duong, H.T. and Suh, Y.S. (2020). Human gait tracking for normal people and walker users using a 2D LiDAR. *IEEE Sensors Journal* 20 (11): 6191–6199.

24 Ferrari, F., Divan, S., Guerrero, C. et al. (2020). Human–robot interaction analysis for a smart walker for elderly: the ACANTO interactive guidance system. *International Journal of Social Robotics* 12 (2): 479–492.

25 Frizera-Neto, A., Ceres, R., Rocon, E., and Pons, J.L. (2011). Empowering and assisting natural human mobility: the simbiosis walker. *INTECH: International Journal of Advanced Robotics, Special Issue Assistive Robotics* 8 (3): 34–50.

26 Geravand, M. (2017). Safe and adaptive control approaches for mobility assistance robots. PhD thesis. Technical University of Munich.

27 Geravand, M. and Peer, A. (2014). Safety constrained motion control of mobility assistive robots. *IEEE/RAS-EMBS International Conference on Biomedical Robotics and Biomechatronics*, Brazil.

28 Geravand, M., Rampeltshammer, W., and Peer, A. (2015). Control of mobility assistive robot for human fall prevention. *IEEE International Conference on Rehabilitation Robotics*, 882–887.

29 Geravand, M., Werner, C., Hauer, K., and Peer, A. (2016). An integrated decision making approach for adaptive shared control of mobility assistive robots. *International Journal of Social Robotics* 8: 631–648.

30 Geravand, M., Korondi, P.Z., Werner, C. et al. (2016). Human sit-to-stand transfer modeling towards intuitive and biologically-inspired robot assistance. *Autonomous Robots* 41: 575–592.

31 Glover, J., Holstius, D., Manojlovich, M. et al. (2003). A Robotically-Augmented Walker for Older Adults. *Technical report*. CMU-CS-03-170. Pittsburgh, PA: Carnegie Mellon University, Computer Science Department.

32 Golembiewski, C., Schultz, J., Reissman, T. et al. (2019). The effects of a positional feedback device on rollator walker use: a validation study. *Assistive Technology* 33 (6): 318–325.

33 Graf, B. (2009). An adaptive guidance system for robotic walking aids. *Journal of Computing and Information Technology - CIT* 17 (1): 109–120.

34 Graf, B., Hans, M., and Schraft, R.D. (2004). Mobile robot assistants - issues for dependable operation in direct cooperation with humans. *IEEE Robotics and Automation Magazine* 11 (2): 67–77.

35 Hellström, T., Lindahl, O., Bäcklund, T. et al. (2016). An intelligent rollator for mobility impaired persons, especially stroke patients. *Journal of Medical Engineering & Technology* 40 (5): 270–279.

36 Hirata, Y., Chuy, O. Jr., Hara, A., and Kosuge, K. (2005). Human-adaptive motion control of active and passive type walking support system. *IEEE Workshop on Advanced Robotics and its Social Impacts*.

37 Hirata, Y., Hara, A., and Kosuge, K. (2005). Motion control of passive-type walking support system based on environment information. *IEEE International Conference on Robotics and Automation*, Barcelona, Spain.

38 Hirata, Y., Muraki, A., and Kosuge, K. (2006). Standing up and sitting down support using intelligent walker based on estimation of user states. *IEEE International Conference on Mechatronics and Automation*, Luoyang, China.

39 Hirata, Y., Muraki, A., and Kosuge, K. (2006). Motion control of intelligent passive-type walker for fall-prevention function based on estimation of user state. *IEEE International Conference on Robotics and Automation*, Orlando, USA.

40 Hirata, Y., Hara, A., and Kosuge, K. (2007). Motion control of passive intelligent walker using servo brakes. *IEEE Transactions on Robotics* 23 (5): 981–990.

41 Hirata, Y., Hara, A., and Kosuge, K. (2008). Passive-type intelligent walking support system "RT walker". *IEEE/RSJ International Conference on Intelligent Robots and Systems*, Nice, France.

42 Hirata, Y., Komatsuda, S., and Kosuge, K. (2008). Fall prevention control of passive intelligent walker based on human model. *IEEE/RSJ International Conference on Intelligent Robots and Systems*, Nice, France.

43 Hoang, K.L.H. and Mombaur, K.D. (2015). Optimal design of a physical assistive device to support sit-to-stand motions. *IEEE International Conference on Robotics and Automation*, 5891–5897.

44 Huang, C., Wasson, G., Alwan, M. et al. (2005). Shared navigational control and user intent detection in an intelligent walker. *AAAI Fall 2005 Symposium*.

45 Huang, Y.-C., Yang, H.-P., Ko, C.-H., and Young, K.-Y. (2011). Human intention recognition for robot walking helper using ANFIS. *8th Asian Control Conference*, Kaohsiung, Taiwan.

46 Jiménez, M.F., Monllor, M., Frizera, A. et al. (2019). Admittance controller with spatial modulation for assisted locomotion using a smart walker. *Journal of Intelligent & Robotic Systems* 94 (3): 621–637.

47 Jun, H.-G., Chang, Y.-Y., Dan, B.-J. et al. (2011). Walking and sit-to-stand support system for elderly and disabled. *IEEE International Conference on Rehabilitation Robotics*, ETH Zurich, Switzerland.

48 Kawazoe, S., Chugo, D., Yokota, S. et al. (2017). Development of standing assistive walker for domestic use. *IEEE International Conference on Industrial Technology*, 1455–1460.

49 Kikuchi, T., Tanaka, T., Tanida, S. et al. (2010). Basic study on gait rehabilitation system with intelligently controllable walker (i-Walker). *IEEE International Conference on Robotics and Biomimetics*.

50 Kim, I., Cho, W., Yuk, G. et al. (2011). Kinematic analysis of sit-to-stand assistive device for the elderly and disabled. *IEEE International Conference on Rehabilitation Robotics*, ETH Zurich, Switzerland.

51 Ko, C.-H. and Agrawal, S.K. (2010). Walk-assist robot: a novel approach to gain selection of a braking controller using differential flatness. *American Control Conference*, Baltimore, MD, USA.

52 Ko, C.-H., Young, K.-Y., Huang, Y.-C., and Agrawal, S.K. (2012). Active and passive control of walk-assist robot for outdoor guidance. *IEEE/ASME Transactions on Mechatronics* 18 (3): 1211–1220.

53 Kulyukin, V., Kutiyanawala, A., LoPresti, E. et al. (2008). iWalker: toward a rollator-mounted wayfinding system for the elderly. *International Conference on RFID*.

54 Kuzelicki, J., Zefran, M., Burger, H., and Bajd, T. (2005). Synthesis of standig-up trajectories using dynamic optimization. *Gait and Posture* 21 (1): 1–11.

55 Lacey, G. and Rodriguez-Losada, D. (2008). The evolution of guido. *IEEE Robotics and Automation Magazine* 15: 75–83.

56 Lacy, G. and MacNamara, S. (2000). Context-aware shared control of a robot mobility aid for the elderly blind. *International Journal of Robotics Research* 19 (11): 1054–1065.

57 Lee, G., Ohnuma, T., and Chong, N.Y. (2010). Design and control of JAIST active robotic walker. *Journal of Intelligent Service Robotics* 3 (3): 125–135.

58 Lee, G., Jung, E.-J., Ohnuma, T. et al. (2011). JAIST robotic walker control based on a two-layered Kalman filter. *IEEE International Conference on Robotics and Automation*, Shanghai, China.

59 Li, P., Yamada, Y., Wan, X. et al. (2019). Gait-phase dependent control using a smart walker for physical training. *IEEE 16th International Conference on Rehabilitation Robotics*, 843–848.

60 Lu, C., Huang, Y., and Lee, C.J. (2015). Adaptive guidance system design for the assistive robotic walker. *Neurocomputing* 170: 152–160.

61 Manuel, J., Wandosell, H., and Graf, B. (2002). Non-holonomic navigation system of a walking-aid robot. *IEEE International Workshop on Robot and Human Interactive Communication*, Berlin, Germany.

**62** McLachlan, S., Arblaster, J., Liu, D.K. et al. (2005). A multi-stage shared control method for an intelligent mobility assistant. *9th Internatinal Conference on Rehabilitation Robotics*, Chicago, IL, USA.

**63** Médéric, P., Pasqui, V., Plumet, F., and Bidaud, P. (2004). Sit to stand transfer assisting by an intelligent walking-aid. *7th International Conference on Climbing and Walking Robots*, Madrid, Espagne.

**64** Médéric, P., Pasqui, V., Plumet, F. et al. (2005). Elderly people sit to stand transfer experimental analysis. *8th International Conference on Climbing and Walking Robots (Clawar'05)*, 953–960, Londres,Royaume-Uni.

**65** Merlet, J.-P. (2012). ANG, a family of multi-mode, low cost walking aid. *IEEE International Conference on Intelligent Robots and Systems, Workshop Assistance and Service Robotics in a Human Environment*.

**66** Mombaur, K. (2014). Optimization of sit to stand motions of elderly people for the design and control of physical assistive devices. In: *Proceedings in Applied Mathematics & Mechanics*, vol. 14 (ed. P. Steinmann and G. Leugering), 805–806. Wiley-VCH.

**67** Montemerlo, M., Pineau, J., Roy, N. et al. (2002). Experiences with a mobile robotic guide for the elderly. *Proceedings of the AAAI National Conference on Artificial Intelligence*, 587–592.

**68** Mori, H., Kotani, S., and Kiyohiro, N. (1994). A robotic travel aid "HITOMI". *IEEE/RSJ/GI International Conference on Intelligent Robots and Systems, 'Advanced Robotic Systems and the Real World'*, Volume 3, 1716–1723.

**69** Morris, A. (2003). A robotic walker that provides guidance. *IEEE International Conference on Robotics and Automation*, Taipei, Taiwan.

**70** Mou, W.-H., Chang, M.-F., Liao, C.-K. et al. (2012). Context-aware assisted interactive robotic walker for parkinson's disease patients. *IEEE/RSJ International Conference on Intelligent Robots and Systems*, Vilamoura, Portugal.

**71** Mughal, A.M. (2009). *Analytical Biomechanics - Modeling and Optimal Controller Designs*. VDM Verlag Dr. Müller.

**72** Nejatbakhsh, N. and Kosuge, K. (2005). User-environment based navigation algorithm for an omnidirectional passive walking aid system. *International Conference on Rehabilitation Robotics*, Chicago, USA.

**73** Neto, A.F., Gallego, J.A., Rocon, E. et al. (2010). Extraction of user's navigation commands from upper body force interaction in walker assisted gait. *Biomedical Engineering online* 9: 37.

**74** Ohnuma, T., Lee, G., and Chong, N.Y. (2011). Particle filter based feedback control of JAIST active robotic walker. *20th IEEE International Symposium on Robot and Human Interactive Communication*, Atlanta, GA, USA.

**75** Oigawa, K., Chugo, D., Muramatsu, S. et al. (2019). An assitive walker considering with its user's gait difference of both feet. *12th International Conference on Human System Interaction*.

**76** Papageorgiou, X.S., Chalvatzaki, G., Lianos, K. et al. (2016). Experimental validation of human pathological gait analysis for an assisted living intelligent robotic walker. *6th IEEE International Conference on Biomedical Robotics and Biomechatronics*.

**77** Pasqui, V., Saint-Bauzel, L., and Sigaud, O. (2010). Characterization of a least effort user-centered trajectory for sit-to-stand assistance user-centered trajectory for sit-to-stand assistance. *Symposium on Dynamics Modeling and Interaction Control in Virtual and Real Environments*, 197–204. IUTAM.

**78** Pasqui, V., Marin, D., Saint-Bauzel, L. et al. (2013). Description of robuWALKER. *Technical report*. Institut des Systemes Intelligent et de Robotique. https://www.yumpu.com/en/document/view/15822303/domeo-project-description-of-robuwalker-roboso-robosoft.

**79** Paulo, J., Peixoto, P., and Nunes, U.J. (2017). ISR-AIWALKER: robotic walker for intuitive and safe mobility assistance and gait analysis. *IEEE Transactions on Human–Machine Systems* 47 (6): 1110–1122.

**80** Pineau, J., Montemerlo, M., Pollak, M. et al. (2003). Towards robotic assistants in nursing homes: challenge and results. *Robotics and Autonomous Systems* 42 (3–4): 271–281.

**81** Pollack, M.E., Engberg, S., Matthews, J.T. et al. (2002). Pearl: a mobile robotic assistant for the elderly. *AAAI Workshop on Automation as Eldercare.*

**82** Reiser, U., Jacobs, T., Arbeiter, G. et al. (2013). Care-O-bot® 3 – vision of a robot butler. In: *Your Virtual Butler*, Lecture Notes in Computer Science, vol. 7407 (ed. R. Trappl), 97–116. Berlin, Heidelberg: Springer-Verlag.

**83** Rodriguez-Losada, D., Matia, F., Jimenez, A. et al. (2005). Implementing map based navigation in guido, the robotic SmartWalker. *IEEE International Conference on Robotics and Automation*, Barcelona, Spain.

**84** Roy, N., Baltus, G., Fox, D. et al. (2000). Towards personal service robots for the elderly. *Workshop on Interactive Robots and Entertainment.*

**85** Sabatini, A.M., Genovese, V., and Pacchierotti, E. (2002). A mobility aid for the support to walking and object transportation of people with motor impairments. *IEEE/RSJ Internatioal Conference on Intelligent Robots and Systems.*

**86** Saint-Bauzel, L., Pasqui, V., and Monteil, I. (2009). A reactive robotized interface for lower limb rehabilitation: clinical results. *IEEE Transaction on Robotics* 25 (3): 583–592.

**87** Schraft, R., Schaeffer, C., and May, T. (1998). Care-O-bot: the concept of a system for assisting elderly or disabled persons in home environments. *IECON: IEEE 24th Annual Conference.*

**88** Shi, F., Cao, Q., Leng, C., and Tan, H. (2010). Based on force sensing-controlled human-machine interaction system for walking assistant robot. *8th World Congress on Intelligent Control and Automation*, Jinan, China.

**89** Shim, H.-M., Lee, E.-H., Shim, J.-H. et al. (2005). Implementation of an intelligent walking assistant robot for the elderly in outdoor environment. *IEEE 9th International Conference on Rehabilitation Robotics*, Chicago, IL, USA.

**90** Shim, H.-M., Chung, C.Y., Lee, E.-H. et al. (2006). Silbo: development walking assistant robot for the elderly based on shared control strategy. *IJCSNS Int Journal of Computer Science and Network Security* 6 (9A): 189–195.

**91** Sierra M, S.D., Garzón, M., Munera, M., and Cifuentes, C.A. (2019). Human–robot–environment interaction interface for smart walker assisted gait: AGoRA walker. *Sensors* 9 (13): 2897.

**92** Song, K.-T. and Jiang, S.-Y. (2011). Force-cooperative guidance design of an omni-directional walking assistive robot. *IEEE International Conference on Mechatronics and Automation*, Beijing, China.

**93** Song, K.-T. and Lin, C.-Y. (2009). A new compliant motion control design of a walking-help robot based on motor current and speed measurement. *IEEE International Conference on Intelligent Robots and Systems*, St. Louis, MO, USA.

**94** Spenko, M., Yu, H., and Dubowsky, S. (2006). Robotic personal aids for mobility and monitoring for the elderly. *IEEE Transactions on Neural Systems and Rehabilitation Engineering* 14 (3): 344–351.

**95** Taghvaei, S., Jahanandish, M.H., and Kosuge, K. (2017). Autoregressive-moving-average hidden Markov model for vision-based fall prediction – an application for walker robot. *Assistive Technology* 29 (1): 19–27.

**96** UN Report (2015). United Nations Report: World Population Prospects, The 2015 Revision. http://esa.un.org/unpd/wpp/publications/files/key_findings_wpp_2015.pdf (accessed 17 February 2023).

**97** Wasson, G. and Gunderson, J. (2001). Variable autonomy in a shared control pedestrian mobility aid for the elderly. *Proceedings of the IJCAI'01 Workshop on Autonomy, Delegation, and Control.*

**98** Wasson, G., Gunderson, J., Graves, S., and Felder, R. (2000). Effective shared contol in cooperative mobility aids. *American Association for Artificial Intelligence.*

**99** Wasson, G., Gunderson, J., Graves, S., and Felder, R. (2001). An assistive robotic agent for pedestrian mobility. *International Conference on Autonomous Agents.*

**100** Werner, P., Koepp, C., Geravand, M. et al. (2016). Evaluation studies of robotic rollators by the user perspective: a systematic review. *Gerontology - Int Journal of Experimental, Clinical, Behavioural and Technological Gerontology* 62: 644–653.

**101** Xu, W., Huang, J., Wang, J. et al. (2015). Reinforcement learning-based shared control for walking-aid robot and its experimental verification. *Advanced Robotics* 29 (22): 1463–1481.

**102** Xu, W., Huang, J., and Cheng, L. (2018). A novel coordinated motion fusion-based walking-aid robot system. *Sensors* 18 (9): 2761.

**103** Yu, H., Spenko, M., and Dubowsky, S. (2003). An adaptive shared control system for an intelligent mobility aid for the elderly. *Autonomous Robots* 15 (1): 53–66.

**104** Yu, K.-T., Lam, C.-P., Chang, M.-F. et al. (2010). An interactive robotic walker for assisting elderly mobility in senior care unit. *IEEE Workshop on Advanced Robotics and its Social Impact.*

# 16

# A Wearable Affective Robot

*Jia Liu[1], Jinfeng Xu[1], Min Chen[1], and Iztok Humar[2]*

[1] *School of Computer Science and Technology, Huazhong University of Science and Technology, Wuhan, China*
[2] *Faculty of Electrical Engineering, University of Ljubljana, Ljubljana, Slovenia*

## 16.1 Introduction

Mental health is an important factor in people's physical health, happiness, and well-being. Research based on emotion perception can play an important role in the field of physical- and mental-health monitoring related to a national economy and people's livelihoods. Affective disorder refers to a group of diseases that are characterized by long-term changes in someone's emotion or mood for various reasons, which include depression, bipolar disorder, and other psychiatric problems. The cure rate for such diseases is low, whereas the death rate is high. According to statistics, suicide caused by depression is the second-leading cause of death among people aged 15 to 29, and it is also the main cause of disability in the world [24]. It has been shown that, on the one hand, affective disorders seriously threaten many people's health. On the other, there is a lack of timely and effective medical resources for people with emotional disorders.

With the development of artificial intelligence, cloud computing, and robot technology, intelligent robots provide the possibility for emotional interactions between human and machine, so that users can have an immersive, emotional, social experience. Common robots can be divided into social robots, emotional robots, and wearable robots. The social robot combines a service robot and a virtual robot, and has the capabilities of mechanical movement and basic voice interactions [2, 26]. Social robots are widely used in medical care, public services, and other fields [3, 13, 23]. The term "emotional robot" refers to a robot that can perceive the emotional state of users and provide the corresponding interaction strategies. It is often located in the environment of human activities in a fixed way to recognize the emotional state of people from a third-person perspective. The concept of the wearable robot has been applied to the field of medicine. The robot acts as an exoskeleton to assist the physical activities of the disabled and improve their quality of life. Later, with the concept of the body area network [4, 6, 14, 16, 17] the wearable robot can also include a variety of sensors to collect the required physiological indicators and the relevant multimodal information about the person's activities.

However, the common robots mentioned above have limitations when dealing with the need for emotional services. For example, the interaction design of a social robot is oriented toward the public and cannot carry out personalized modeling for specific users and interactive feedback according to emotional needs. The movement, which is limited by the surrounding environment of emotional robots, means they cannot obtain information about users in multiple locations and provide people

*Handbook of Human-Machine Systems*, First Edition. Edited by Giancarlo Fortino, David Kaber, Andreas Nürnberger, and David Mendonça.

with long-term company. Wearable robots have been able to effectively obtain physiological index information, but they are not intelligent enough in terms of emotion recognition and interactive feedback. In general, robotics research that combines social, emotional, and wearables is still in its infancy. The difficulties are related to the high costs, limited human–computer interactions, difficulties with movements over large areas, low levels of comfort, and acting as a single-service object.

Our proposed, wearable and emotional robot (Fitbot) closely integrates wearable equipment with emotional interaction and provides lasting, multimodal information collection and emotional interaction services for various groups of people. Collecting multimodal data (such as video and audio) from wearable devices and mobile phones for the early diagnosis and cognition of depression, for example, has become an effective auxiliary method of diagnosis [28]. It integrates visual, auditory, tactile, and electro-encephalography (EEG) perception [5]. On the basis of continuous interaction, the long-term, in-depth data collection of a single user is realized to achieve multimodal perception and the analysis of a user's emotion and behavior. Finally, we must establish a personalized cognitive model, and then understand the behavioral motivation behind the user's emotions, achieve a satisfactory emotional interaction experience, and achieve the goal of universal mental health care.

Fitbot has the following outstanding features:

- *Flexible switching between the first- and third-person perspectives.* Third-person information refers to the user's multimodal physiological indicators and the behavioral action information obtained in an objective manner, and is used to guide the modeling and analysis of the user. The first-person perspective refers to transmitting emotional information to the outside world by means of audio, video, and text on behalf of the users.
- *Human–machine–environment integration.* "Integration" means that the robot can naturally interact with the working environment, people, and other robots, and has the ability to independently adapt to the complex dynamic environment and work together with people. Robots and humans complement each other and have complementary advantages, which can make the perceptual, cognitive, and behavioral decision-making ability of human and machine co-evolve in the process of interaction and lead to an improvement in intelligence.
- *Undisturbed long-term company.* Taking smart clothes as the carrier and using flexible fibers to combine emotional and tactile interactions, as well as brain-wearable devices, multimodal data from multiscenes in the long time scale of users can be obtained. The goal of in-depth personalized modeling and long-term accompaniment for users is achieved.

The evolution process of Fitbot is shown in Figure 16.1. Virtual assistants refer to puresoftware applications with language-interaction capabilities, and service robots are hardwareinteraction platforms that can move autonomously. First, we combine the above two into a robot with

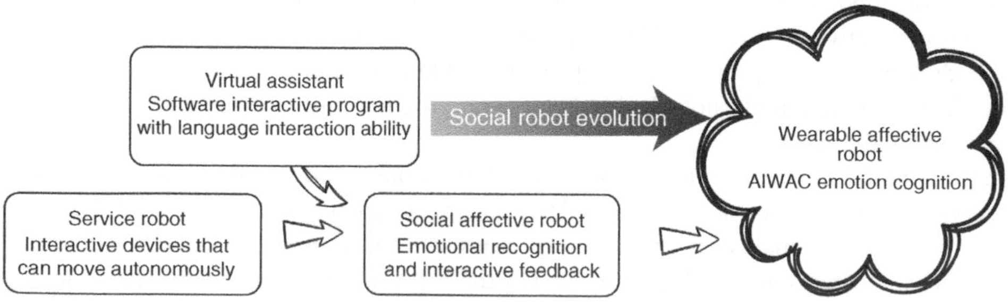


**Figure 16.1** The evolution of social robot.

social communication capabilities. Next, to improve the intelligence and service quality of social robots, it is necessary to be able to perceive the emotional state of the users and provide the corresponding feedback, which means social, emotional robots. Finally, we introduce the flexible, wearable technology and cognitivecomputing model to obtain the wearable, emotional robot known as Fitbot. Based on the cognitivecomputing model, the humanthinking process is simulated, and the working mode of the human brain is simulated by data mining and pattern recognition so that the robot can complete a complex interaction. Fitbot obtains data with both the breadth and depth of specific users and uses unlabeled emotion recognition and interactive algorithms to improve the accuracy of its user-emotion recognition. Fitbot is portable, stylish, and nondisturbing, and can provide services to a wider range of people. Its cognitive–emotional ability can be continuously improved through long-term interactions with its users.

## 16.2 Architecture Design and Characteristics

### 16.2.1 Architecture of a Wearable Affective Robot

Fitbot integrates three modules: an intelligent, emotional, interactive robot (Affective Interaction through Wearable Computing and Cloud Technology (AIWAC) box, AIWAC), an intelligent, tactile, interactive device [8], and a brain-wearable device. It represents a new type of wearable robot with emotional cognition in the form of smart clothing. Based on the abovethree modules, through continuous data collection in depth and breadth, a personalized cognitive model is established for the users, as shown in Figure 16.2.

In terms of appearance, the intelligent robot is integrated into the clothing in a wearable way, making it both comfortable and fashionable. The smart tactile device is integrated into the hooded clothing, the brain-wearable device is integrated into the hood, and we also design an isolation

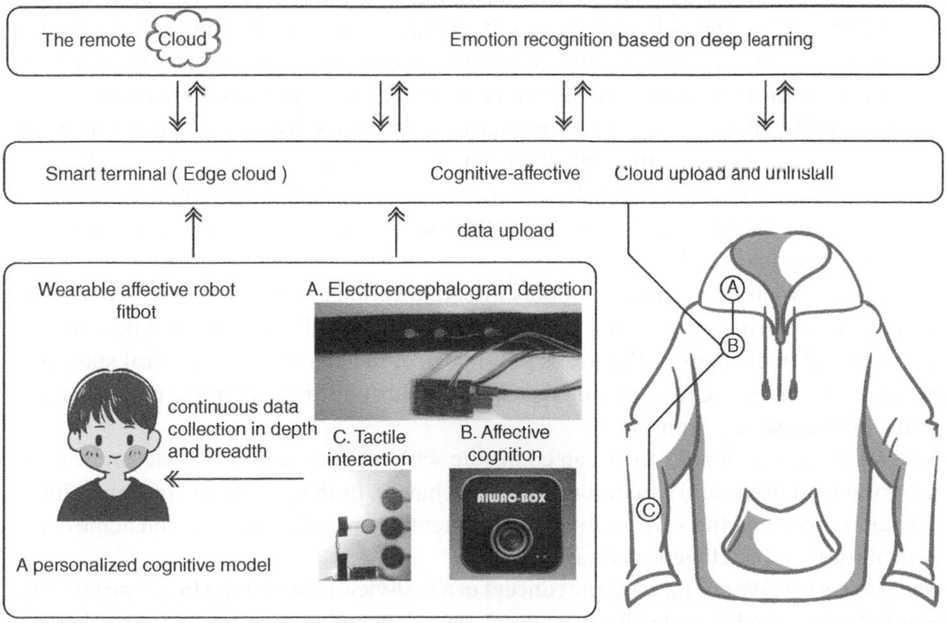


**Figure 16.2** Architecture design of a wearable affective robot.

layer for storing smart terminals. The AIWAC intelligent tactile system refers to the physical connection of intelligent, tactile devices, the AIWAC box, and smart phones through a USB I/O mode. It can perform simple control operations and tactile perception to complete tactile-based perception and interaction. This concept comes from the design concept of Wearable 2.0. As an edge server, intelligent terminals provide computing support for emotional cognition in different application scenarios [1, 7, 15, 21, 22]. Brain-wearable devices can collect EEG data and realize the perception of users' subtle expressions. In addition, we also deploy external mic devices for voice communication and provide visual interaction services through connected smartphones.

AIWAC integrates the emotion-recognition algorithms and can provide basic emotionrecognition and interaction services in offline conditions. For some tasks with high demands on the algorithms, data access, and service quality, such as user portraits and personalized emotional services, the AIWAC box can skip the smart terminal and directly communicate wirelessly with the remote cloud to meet the requirements of multimodal emotional communication [9, 18, 19, 25].

### 16.2.2 Characteristics of a Wearable Affective Robot

Compared with social robots, a wearable affective robot has the following characteristics:

- *Context-awareness*. To understand the intrinsic characteristics of perceptual information and give different responses in different scenarios [11]. Fitbot uses smartphones and wearable equipment to collect the user data and the scene data to facilitate personalized modeling for the users. Scene data provides a third-person perspective, shared with other users in the same scene. Context-aware computing pays attention to information such as user identity, scene, adjacent users, and environmental resources, providing a guarantee of understanding the complex behavior patterns of users.
- *Autonomy*. To adapt to complex and dynamically changing environments, taking into account the rising costs of managing perception systems, wearable affective robots should satisfy the characteristics of the autonomic system, including self-management, self-optimization, self-configuration, self-healing, self-protection, self-adaptation, self-scaling, and self-integration [27]. The system we designed has the ability to reject unreasonable requests from users and has a fault-tolerant mechanism to satisfy the requirements of self-healing and self-organization.
- *Portability*. A wearable, affective robot based on smart clothing can satisfy users' requirements for comfort and esthetics, and expand the limited movement capabilities of social robots. Portability also provides a guarantee that the user will be wearing the clothing, from time to time, so that it can effectively collect multimodal information of the user in multiple scenarios and realize the context-awareness mentioned above.
- *Interactive diversity*. Wearable emotional robots integrate various interaction methods such as voice, tactile, and EEG. The user can also issue control commands through the mobile terminal. After detecting sudden changes in the user's physiological indicators, psychological state, and behavioral characteristics, the system can also spontaneously initiate interactive behaviors to give feedback on the user's current state.
- *Integration*. Wearable emotional robots can cooperate with users to complete tasks and coexist with users, grow with users, and can imitate human behavior. In the process of constantly interacting with each other and the surrounding environment, users and machines can achieve the goal of co-evolution and intelligence enhancement.
- *First-person perspective*. We put forward the concept of a first-view robot for the first time [10].The first-person-perspective robot can collect the user's own data and communicate with others on behalf of the user, present the user's emotions, and transmit information by means of audio and video.

## 16.3 Design of the Wearable, Affective Robot's Hardware

As mentioned above, Fitbot is composed of an AIWAC box, brain-wearable devices, and intelligent tactile devices.

- *AIWAC box.* As the brain of the hardware, it performs data reception, storage, and transmission, and deploys emotion-recognition algorithms. The main chip of the AIWAC box is planned to adopt the ARM Cortex-A7 core with a quad core and a 1.2G main frequency
- *Brain-wearable device.* Close to the prefrontal lobe, we detect the EEG information of the user and upload it to the cloud platform through the AIWAC box for centralized processing and analysis of the data. The current robot prototype selects the AP6210 module, integrating the Wi-Fi and Bluetooth as the communication module, OV5640 as the image-acquisition module, collects audio through the mic, and performs voice interaction through a power amplifier and a player.
- *AIWAC intelligent tactile device.* It is flexibly integrated into the Fitbot's plug-and-play mode to provide a comfortable interaction. A smart, tactile device uses CH559T as the main control chip to realize efficient sensing-information transmission between the tactile sensor and the AIWAC box.

### 16.3.1 AIWAC Box Hardware Design

AIWAC's full name is Affective Interaction through Wide learning and Cognitive Computing (Affective interaction based on breadth learning and cognitive computing). The AIWAC emotional interaction robot takes the AIWAC box as the hardware core and connects the corresponding peripherals. The AIWAC box is capable of visual perception, tactile perception, and voice interaction. In addition, the AIWAC box integrates local emotion-recognition algorithms and has off-line emotion recognition and interaction functions. Relying on this powerful function, the AIWAC emotional interaction robot can show nine personality qualities and the behavior characteristics of courage, steadiness, kindness, foresight, self-confidence, optimism, tenacity, and sincerity, and recognize 21 emotions in others. It is the key to realizing a user's emotional comfort and regulating health.

### 16.3.2 Hardware Design of the EEG Acquisition

The weak electrical signal generated by a human's cerebral cortex can provide a variety of information, including the human's mental state, physiological indicators, and so on. From such electrical signals, it is a complex problem to remove excess noise and complete a humanemotion analysis. We use CH599T as the main control chip to realize the SPI communication and a USB mobile phone communication; ADS1299-x is used as the EEG signal acquisition chip, which is low noise and multichannel. Considering the influence of the power-supply design on the acquisition of a weak electrical signal, strict area division during the printedcircuitboard (PCB) wiring can weaken the signal's interference.

### 16.3.3 AIWAC Smart Tactile Device

To achieve a better service experience, we use a smart tactile device to expand the ability of tactile control and interaction, and design the extension of the smart tactile device for tactile interaction. The traditional interaction mode with the robot is extended, so that the human–computer interaction mode is not limited to traditional voice interactions. It is proposed to design a plug-and-play way to integrate the smart tactile device into a wearable emotional robot and realize convenient human–computer interaction with the help of a smart tactile device.

### 16.3.4 Prototype of the Wearable Affective Robot

Based on the above hardware modules, we designed a wearable emotional robot prototype system, and built a network test platform to test the feasibility of the system. In terms of network structure, Fitbot, as a data source, sends signals to intelligent terminals, i.e., edge servers, for data preprocessing and simple information processing. The intelligent terminal sends the preliminary calculation results to the remote cloud server, and Fitbot can also send data directly to the remote cloud. We designed the brain-wearable device in the hat to collect the EEG signals and assist with the emotional reasoning. The tactile sensing module is integrated into the clothing. The wearable emotional robot can continuously collect the depth and breadth data of users and establish a cognitive model based on long-term behavior perception and emotional analysis for the users, which can give the wearable, emotional robot a deeper cognition of users and give users a better interactive experience.

We will test the acquisition, analysis, and interaction capabilities of the system. In the experiment, we collect voice-emotion data through the external mic, and then the connected Fitbot transmits the data to the edge server for preliminary processing, and then transmits it to the remote cloud to realize emotion recognition based on deep learning. Then we test whether the system can meet the requirements of emotion recognition and interaction with high accuracy and ultra-low delay.

## 16.4 Algorithm for the Wearable Affective Robot

### 16.4.1 Algorithm for Affective Recognition

Fitbot can collect multimodal data such as audio, video, and EEG so that users interact with the system and other users in their daily life. We take speech data as an example to illustrate the algorithm flow of emotion recognition. Based on the temporal characteristics of speech data, we use an attention-based recurrent neural network (RNN) algorithm to realize the analysis of emotion. There are two reasons for using this algorithm. First, the cyclic neural network can remember the timeseries data for a long time and effectively extract the context-related feature information over a long time scale. In addition, the attention mechanism is introduced into the framework of the RNN algorithm, which makes the network introduce a new, weight-pooling strategy to focus on the parts of the perceptual data that show strong emotion. Specifically, the model allocates the corresponding weight by measuring the similarity between the current input and the expected output. By introducing a new, weight-pooling strategy we focus on the parts of speech with strong emotional characteristics. The contribution of the speech frame data to emotion recognition is measured and scored. Finally, the trained model can map continuous acoustic information into discrete emotion tags to complete the speech-emotion recognition.

### 16.4.2 User-Behavior Perception based on a Brain-Wearable Device

To realize the perception of microemotional changes, assist emotional analysis, and improve the human–computer interaction mode, it is particularly critical to have correct processing of the EEG

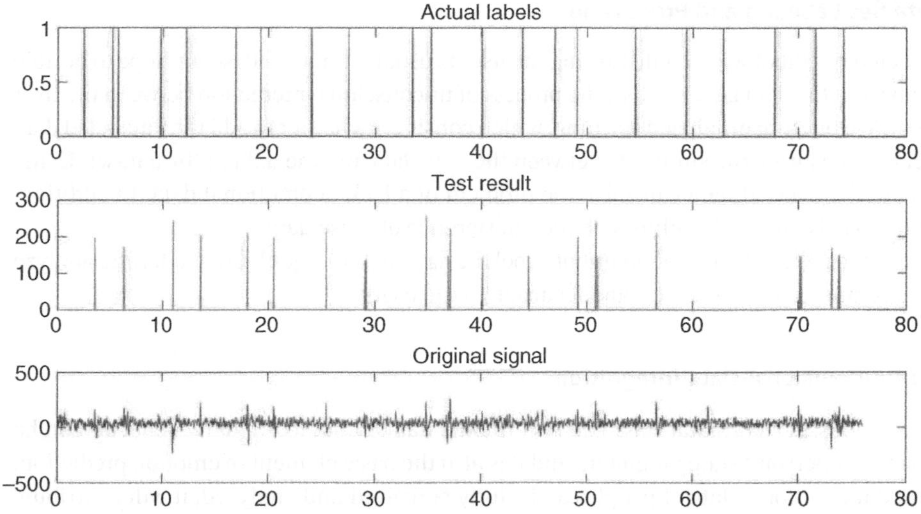


**Figure 16.3** The EEG-based eyeblink detection test.

data. We designed blink detection to measure the Fitbot's ability to recognize microexpressions. We used a public dataset as the benchmark dataset and used the device to sample the EEG data for users. By guiding the user to imagine the behavior according to the voice prompt, the multi-channel microcurrent signals generated by the brain in this process are collected. It is very necessary to use the collected exclusive data to modify and fine tune the algorithm model, which can reduce the judgment of individual physiological differences in the final emotional-analysis results. However, we also need to consider the possible psychological exclusion of users when using the system.

For the processing of a brain-wearable device's perception data, preprocessing, feature extraction, and classification are carried out first, and the modeling of the tester's motion imagination model is completed on this basis. We implement the blink-detection task based on the peak coefficient. The filtered EEG signal is detected by the amplitude of the positive and negative peaks, and kurtosis is introduced to measure the fluctuation of the signal. First, low-pass filtering is performed on the original EEG signal, then the timedomain signal is divided into short time-domain signals and framed by a sliding window. Finally, the existence of blinking is determined by calculating the crest coefficient. The test results are shown in Figure 16.3. In addition, we extract the characteristics of the game from the timedomain EEG and the frequencydomain EEG, and then analyze the characteristics of the game.

## 16.5 Life Modeling of the Wearable Affective Robot

Fitbot realizes the portrait of group behavior and personalized modeling of specific users by continuously collecting data with both depth and breadth. Breadth data refers to the data coming from a wide range of people with similar characteristics, from which the common features can be mined. The data obtained from a user's long-term tracking is called depth data. Using such data for analysis and mining will help to improve Fitbot's cognitive level and give users a better emotional interaction experience.

### 16.5.1 Data Set Labeling and Processing

The data collected by Fitbot without disturbing the user is usually unlabeled, so we hope to be able to label and analyze the data generated in the process of unconscious interaction between the user and the system. We propose unlabeled learning, which considers whether to add the unlabeled data to the dataset by measuring the similarity between the new data and the data in the dataset. Using a large number of unlabeled data can solve the problem of a lack of emotional data. In addition, data purification is also needed to eliminate the interference of noise data.

In this system, we collect data through Fitbot, label the data on the edge cloud, model and analyze the data using remote cloud resources, and feedback to the users.

### 16.5.2 Multidimensional Data Integration

Human behavior has rich connotations. The multimodal data embodied in daily behavior can be used as the basis for person's state judgment, and it is also the basic element of emotion prediction. If the multimodal emotional data of people can be fully perceived and analyzed, it will contribute to the subsequent prediction, diagnosis, and treatment of emotional disorders, and make the application of people's emotional experiences more intelligent.

Using the above equipment, users' emotional and social data can be collected in complex scenes, including multimodal data such as video, audio, text, EEG, tactile interaction, and so on. We combine these data with the public dataset and the experimental text, audio, video, and EEG data to form the dataset of the algorithm. Compared with the diagnosis based on single-mode data, the fusion of multiple information sources can more accurately capture rich emotional information and significantly improve the accuracy of an emotional diagnosis.

First, we carry out feature cleaning and feature screening based on feature engineering. Different machine-learning models are used for each modal data to extract the spatio-temporal features, obtain deeper patient-feature information, and obtain decision-making results. For example, for unstructured data, a convolutional neural network is used to the extract features. For structured data, a robust recognition effect can be obtained by integrating multiple machine-learning models. Finally, the final affective disorder diagnosis label can be obtained by fusing the decision results of different models. We will continuously optimize the algorithm according to the diagnosis results, so as to further improve the performance of the affective disorder diagnosis.

### 16.5.3 Modeling of Associated Scenarios

We must consider that emotional problems are closely related to behavioral events experienced by people and real-time emotions. Therefore, how to mine user-behavior events, design a cognitive model of coupling events and emotions, and realize the traceability analysis of emotions are the key problems to be solved. In the face of rich and diverse data sources, data scenarios are very important for emotion judgment and the motivation reasoning behind emotions. Therefore, scenes and events should be extracted for emotional judgment and relevance reasoning.

The processing flow includes the following: (i) extract the multimodal data of a user and label it; (ii) mark other users in the same scene as the user; (iii) further explore and analyze the correlation among users, scenes, and events, and finally realize the analysis of the causes of users' deep emotional changes.

## 16.6 Challenges and Prospects

### 16.6.1 Research Challenges of the Wearable Affective Robot

In a variety of application-service scenarios, research on wearable emotional robots faces a series of challenges:

- *Privacy disclosure.* The range of physiological and emotional information obtained using wearable devices is often sensitive data. During the use and interaction of the system, the user's information security needs to be guaranteed [21, 22]. On the one hand, we need to reduce the acquisition of easily identifiable information, such as face data, from the data source. Data leakage with identity identification will bring some potential legal security risks to users. Relatively speaking, using the device to obtain human behavior and action label data will not make the user psychologically resist, so the system can interact with the user for a long time. On the other hand, encryption measures are required to ensure that a user's data will not be stolen during the process of perception, transmission, and storage. For example, the wearable emotional robot is connected by flexible wires, which can reduce the hidden privacy leakage caused by wireless communication.
- *Battery life.* How to provide users with a long-term power guarantee is one of the difficulties in research during the continuous monitoring of users over many days. The weight of the power supply and the form and frequency of charging will be for the user to choose. Wearable emotional robots can use only one battery to power sensory and interactive devices all over the body, simplifying the tedious process of charging. In addition, we must consider setting a trigger mechanism to activate the corresponding sensor-interaction device when the user needs it.
- *Network reliability.* During use, there may be situations in which network interruption makes it difficult to provide cloudresource support to the user in a timely manner. In the event of network outages, we need to consider the reliability of cloud services. On the one hand, it is possible to provide users with continuous and effective services by setting flexible processing logic, such as combining localization with cloud intelligence; on the other hand, the miniaturization of machine-learning chips is also a solution.

### 16.6.2 Application Scenarios for the Wearable Affective Robot

The AI wearable emotional robot can be used in a wide range of intelligent interaction situations. It generates active intelligent interaction behavior, while also achieving emotional judgment and feedback intelligence. At the same time, wearable devices' operation portability, low-power consumption, and long use times, as well as a strong perception of various environments, strong data analysis and processing ability, and different devices corresponding to different application scenarios, make human–computer emotional interaction closer and more natural, and create a harmonious scene of integration of science and technology with human feelings.

- *Family*: A wearable affective robot can be used as a smart home to help provide company for children left at home, intelligent assistance for "empty nesters", and an intelligent dialog system for people living alone, make up for the lack of emotional support, accurately identify the emotions of people in a closed environment, and prevent mental abnormalities, and safety problems without supervision. Simultaneously, it will lower the rate of cognitive deterioration in vulnerable groups living alone and provide emotional warmth, similar to having a close housekeeper who follows and accompanies them 24 hours a day.

- *Hospital*: A wearable, affective robot can be used in outpatient and emergency departments, operating rooms, inpatient units, and other scenarios to provide personalized assisted diagnosis, companionship services, and emotional regulation through the emotional recognition of patients, doctors, and family members, and continuous recording and insight into patients' personal situations to reduce the occurrence of sudden illness or medical incidents [12]. AIWAC is an intelligent assistant for doctors and a "guardian angel" for patients, which cannot only create a more humane medical environment but also ease the tense doctor–patient relationship, thus establishing a useful complement to the emotional trust between doctors and patients.
- *Education system*: A wearable affective robot can continuously, in real-time, remotely and without contact, accurately identify students' emotions and lecturers' professional mental state in the case of examination-room monitoring, campus-security monitoring, distance learning and other connection-less, long-distance interactions, assist in good curriculum planning and resource allocation, help improve education and teaching efficiency, and at the same time, reduce campus AIWAC not only helps to achieve the triple purpose of expanding educational opportunities, improving education quality, and reducing education costs, but also promotes the deep integration of information technology and education teaching, thus forming a new model of multimedia, interactive, personalized, adaptive, and learner-centered talent training.
- *Other public places*: A wearable affective robot is also suitable for high-risk industries, crowded places, and areas with a high incidence of crime, such as tourist attractions, shops, hotels, entertainment, and commercial centers. A good security-management environment in public places helps with the civilization of a city or even a country and combined with video, there is a plenty of security-monitoring system data, providing intelligent emotion-recognition algorithms, and intervention strategies to achieve real-time analysis of the emotional validity and psychological changes of the target object, which can improve our ability to intervene in emergencies and effectively intervene beforehand, dispose of during the incident and trace afterward. We can improve security efficiency and reduce the occurrence of accidents.

## 16.7 Conclusions

This chapter review the application scenarios of common robots and designs a wearable, emotional robot Fitbot with emotional cognition ability and long-term learning ability. It consists of an AIWAC box, a tactile interactive device, and a brain-wearable device and integrates algorithms such as emotional cognition, multimodal data fusion, and scene-aided modeling. It can identify the user's emotion, excavate the motivation behind the emotion, and complete the interactive feedback with the user. Finally, its application scenarios and limitations are discussed. Future research will be focused on human–robot group-activity recognition [20].

## References

1 Andreoli, A., Gravina, R., Giannantonio, R. et al. (2010). SPINE-HRV: A BSN-based toolkit for heart rate variability analysis in the time-domain. In: *Wearable and Autonomous Biomedical Devices and Systems for Smart Environment, Lecture Notes in Electrical Engineering*, vol. 75

(ed. A. Lay-Ekuakille and S.C. Mukhopadhyay), 369–389. Berlin, Heidelberg: Springer-Verlag. ISBN 978-3-642-15687-8. https://doi.org/10.1007/978-3-642-15687-8_19.

2 Baker, S.B., Xiang, W., and Atkinson, I. (2017). Internet of Things for smart healthcare: technologies, challenges, and opportunities. *IEEE Access* 5: 26521–26544.

3 Barbera, M.V., Kosta, S., Mei, A., and Stefa, J. (2013). To offload or not to offload? The bandwidth and energy costs of mobile cloud computing. *2013 Proceedings IEEE INFOCOM*, 1285–1293. IEEE.

4 Bellifemine, F.L., Fortino, G., Guerrieri, A., and Giannantonio, R. (2009). Platform-independent development of collaborative wireless body sensor network applications: SPINE2. *Proceedings of the IEEE International Conference on Systems, Man and Cybernetics*, San Antonio, TX, USA (11–14 October 2009), 3144–3150. IEEE. https://doi.org/10.1109/ICSMC.2009.5346155.

5 Chatterjee, R., Maitra, T., Islam, S.K.H. et al. (2019). A novel machine learning based feature selection for motor imagery EEG signal classification in internet of medical things environment. *Future Generation Computer Systems* 98: 419–434. https://doi.org/10.1016/j.future.2019.01.048.

6 Chen, M., Gonzalez, S., Vasilakos, A. et al. (2011). Body area networks: a survey. *Mobile Networks and Applications* 16 (2): 171–193.

7 Chen, X., Jiao, L., Li, W., and Fu, X. (2015). Efficient multi-user computation offloading for mobile-edge cloud computing. *IEEE/ACM Transactions on Networking* 24 (5): 2795–2808.

8 Chen, M., Ma, Y., Li, Y. et al. (2017). Wearable 2.0: enabling human-cloud integration in next generation healthcare systems. *IEEE Communications Magazine* 55 (1): 54–61.

9 Chen, M., Zhou, P., and Fortino, G. (2017). Emotion communication system. *IEEE Access* 5: 326–337. https://doi.org/10.1109/ACCESS.2016.2641480.

10 Chen, M., Xiao, W., Hu, L. et al. (2021). Cognitive wearable robotics for autism perception enhancement. *ACM Transactions on Internet Technology* 21 (4). https://doi.org/10.1145/3450630.

11 Chen, M., Li, P., Wang, R., and Xiang, Y. (2022). Multifunctional fiber-enabled intelligent health agents. *Advanced Materials* 34 (52): https://doi.org/10.1002/adma.202200985.

12 Chen, M., Wang, R., Zhou, Y. et al. (2022). Digital medical education empowered by intelligent fabric space. In: *28 National Science Open.*

13 Chun, B.-G., Ihm, S., Maniatis, P. et al. (2011). CloneCloud: elastic execution between mobile device and cloud. *Proceedings of the 6th Conference on Computer Systems*, 301–314.

14 Fortino, G., Guerrieri, A., Bellifemine, F.L., and Giannantonio, R. (2009). SPINE2: developing BSN applications on heterogeneous sensor nodes. *IEEE 4th International Symposium on Industrial Embedded Systems, SIES 2009*, Switzerland: Ecole Polytechnique Federale de Lausanne (8–10 July 2009), 128–131. IEEE. https://doi.org/10.1109/SIES.2009.5196205.

15 Fortino, G., Guzzo, A., Ianni, M. et al. (2021). Predicting activities of daily living via temporal point processes: approaches and experimental results. *Computers and Electrical Engineering* 96 (Part B): 107567. https://doi.org/10.1016/j.compeleceng.2021.107567.

16 Ghasemzadeh, H., Panuccio, P., Trovato, S. et al. (2014). Power-aware activity monitoring using distributed wearable sensors. *IEEE Transactions on Human–Machine Systems* 44 (4): 537–544. https://doi.org/10.1109/THMS.2014.2320277.

17 Gravina, R. and Fortino, G. (2021). Wearable body sensor networks: state-of-the-art and research directions. *IEEE Sensors Journal* 21 (11): 12511–12522. https://doi.org/10.1109/JSEN.2020.3044447.

18 Hu, L., Li, W., Yang, J. et al. (2022). A sustainable multi-modal multi-layer emotion-aware service at the edge. *IEEE Transactions on Sustainable Computing* 7 (2): 324–333. https://doi.org/10.1109/TSUSC.2019.2928316.

19 Li, Y. and Wang, W. (2014). Can mobile cloudlets support mobile applications? *IEEE INFOCOM 2014-IEEE Conference on Computer Communications*, 1060–1068. IEEE.

20 Li, Q., Gravina, R., Li, Y. et al. (2020). Multi-user activity recognition: challenges and opportunities. *Information Fusion* 63: 121–135. https://doi.org/10.1016/j.inffus.2020.06.004.

21 Mao, Y., You, C., Zhang, J. et al. (2017). A survey on mobile edge computing: the communication perspective. *IEEE Communications Surveys & Tutorials* 19 (4): 2322–2358.

22 Tong, L., Li, Y., and Gao, W. (2016). A hierarchical edge cloud architecture for mobile computing. *IEEE INFOCOM 2016-The 35th Annual IEEE International Conference on Computer Communications*, 1–9. IEEE.

23 Truong-Huu, T., Tham, C.-K., and Niyato, D. (2014). A stochastic workload distribution approach for an ad hoc mobile cloud. *2014 IEEE 6th International Conference on Cloud Computing Technology and Science*, 174–181. IEEE.

24 Vos, T., Abajobir, A.A., Abate, K.H. et al. (2017). Global, regional, and national incidence, prevalence, and years lived with disability for 328 diseases and injuries for 195 countries, 1990–2016: a systematic analysis for the global burden of disease study 2016. *The Lancet* 390 (10100): 1211–1259.

25 Wang, D., Peng, Y., Ma, X. et al. (2018). Adaptive wireless video streaming based on edge computing: opportunities and approaches. *IEEE Transactions on Services Computing* 12 (5): 685–697.

26 Xiang, W., Wang, N., and Zhou, Y. (2016). An energy-efficient routing algorithm for software-defined wireless sensor networks. *IEEE Sensors Journal* 16 (20): 7393–7400.

27 Yang, G.-Z. and Yang, G. (2006). *Body Sensor Networks*, vol. 1, Springer.

28 Yang, L., Jiang, D., and Sahli, H. (2018). Integrating deep and shallow models for multi-modal depression analysis-hybrid architectures. *IEEE Transactions on Affective Computing* 12 (1): 239–253.

# 17

# Visual Human–Computer Interactions for Intelligent Vehicles

*Xumeng Wang*[1], *Wei Chen*[2], *and Fei-Yue Wang*[3]

[1] *College of Computer Science, Nankai University, Tianjin, China*
[2] *State Key Lab of CAD&CG, Zhejiang University, Hangzhou, China*
[3] *The State Key Laboratory for Management and Control of Complex Systems, Institute of Automation, Chinese Academy of Sciences, Beijing, China*

## 17.1 Introduction

Intelligent vehicles provide drivers with assistance from multiple aspects, including pedestrian avoidance and traffic signs identification. Advanced techniques, such as artificial intelligence [46] and block chain [34], have been applied to optimize the automatic service of intelligent vehicles and replace human labors. However, the increase of autonomy level is a double-edged sword. High automation may relax drivers' vigilance and cause accidents. To address this issue, it is necessary to support communication between intelligent vehicles and humans (e.g. researchers, developers, and drivers).

Visual human–computer interactions (VHCI) can facilitate effective and efficient interactions by taking advantage of the visual cognition channel of humans. Currently, VHCI has penetrated application and research on intelligent vehicles.

## 17.2 Background

Human involvement and autonomy of intelligent vehicles were first considered as antonyms – as automation increases, the role of humans will be gradually replaced [9, 23]. This perspective was refuted in 2020. Shneiderman [33] proposed a new possibility that human participations and computer autonomy can coexist in a two-dimensional framework, as shown in Figure 17.1. Especially, a *reliable, safe, and trustworthy* intelligent vehicle requires both high-level control from humans and high-level automation powered by computers [33] because humans and computers have complementary strengths. For instance, radar can facilitate obstacle avoidance by accurate measurement of distances, while humans can notice the intent of others, such as warnings of bad weather or requesting a shared ride.

*Handbook of Human-Machine Systems*, First Edition. Edited by Giancarlo Fortino, David Kaber, Andreas Nürnberger, and David Mendonça.

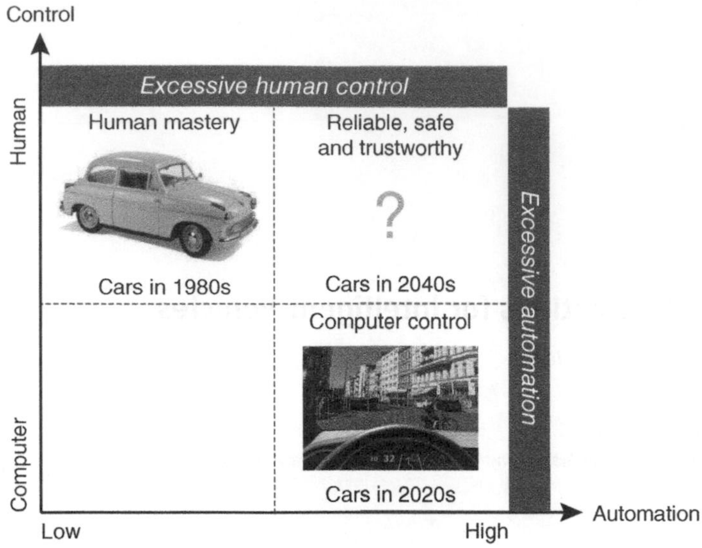


**Figure 17.1** The two-dimensional framework [33, 41].

**Table 17.1** Summary of existing technologies on VHCI for intelligent vehicles.

| **Perspectives** | **Visual techniques** | **Interaction techniques** |
|---|---|---|
| In-vehicle | Showing labels in a small screen [15, 16], providing contextual understandings [13], extending in-car infotainment [5] | Responding to ambiguous voice queries [19], understanding gesture interactions [1, 32], and capturing eye movements [3, 20] |
| Among-vehicles | Analyzing traffic congestion [22, 29], representing traffic predictions [47], and summarizing trajectory patterns [18, 31, 36] | Supporting traffic planning [7] and supporting visual query of trajectories [2, 11, 26, 39] |
| Beyond-vehicle | Exploring and analyzing high-dimensional log data [8, 28, 44], inspecting image collection data [12, 45], comparing and assessing clustering results [10, 27], comparing and assessing the performance of classification models [14, 30, 48], and explaining a traffic light detection [17] | Improving data quality [4, 6, 24], selecting features [21], construction decision tree [35], designing neural networks [42, 43], and improving model structure [25] |

## 17.3 State-of-the-Art

Intelligent vehicles can benefit from VHCI from various perspectives (see Table 17.1). In this section, we introduce latest studies on VHCI for intelligent vehicles.

### 17.3.1 VHCI in Vehicles

Drivers and passengers in vehicles have limited vision. Intelligent vehicles need to assist them in perceiving the world outside vehicles. Also, intelligent vehicles need to receive instructions from humans and satisfy their demands.

#### 17.3.1.1 Information Feedback from Intelligent Vehicles

Intelligent vehicles can feedback information to humans through multiple channels, such as images, sounds, and temperature. Among them, images are the most efficient way to represent complicated information like dynamic traffic scenarios. Therefore, it is necessary for intelligent vehicles to provide visualizations.

Currently, dashboards are widely applied in vehicles. For instance, speedometers visualize the change of speed by angles, and indicator lights warn drivers by red. Besides, navigation applications employ map visualizations to show available paths and places of interest (POIs). Gedicke et al. [15] propose an external labeling method to optimize the representation of POIs on a small screen. As for passengers, augmented reality is leveraged to provide infotainment without space limitations [5].

#### 17.3.1.2 Human-Guided Driving

With a low level of automation, drivers need to control vehicles by specific instructions, such as turning the steering wheel and stepping on the accelerator pedals. However, instructions from humans could be incorrect, especially when humans are intoxicated or panicked. As the automation level enhances, assistant services are leveraged to avoid such mistakes. Such services also come with problems – assistant features may work against driver intention. For example, steering functions, which aim to stay the vehicle in a lane, may impede drivers from changing lanes.

To provide appropriate assistance, intelligent vehicles must understand drivers' intentions. Existing intelligent vehicles can understand simple instructions expressed by voice or body language [1, 32]. When drivers are not able to give instruction actively (e.g. lethargy), intelligent vehicles need to take control promptly. Researchers have attempted to infer the status of drivers by monitoring their eye movements [3, 20].

### 17.3.2 VHCI Among Vehicles

As participants in the transportation system, intelligent vehicles should be considered as communities. Each intelligent vehicle can benefit from a well-organized intelligent transportation system (ITS).

Massive traffic data collected by various sensors are employed to construct an intelligent transportation system. Perceiving and analyzing such data needs the support of visualization techniques. For example, Lee et al. [22] proposed a visual analysis approach to monitor traffic congestion and seek corresponding solutions. Bi et al. [7] developed a visual interface that supports traffic planning based on which real-time deployment of intelligent vehicles can be implemented from the macrolevel.

### 17.3.3 VHCI Beyond Vehicles

Beyond vehicles, artificial intelligence (AI) approaches are applied to various vehicle-related tasks, including traffic light detection, obstacle avoidance, and route planning.

However, a majority of AI approaches are considered as black boxes, which are difficult to understand. To assess model performance and understand model mechanics, VHCI approaches are employed to interpret AI approaches. Squares [30] summarize the output of multiclass classification models, which allow humans to compare model performance and identify their weaknesses.

Seeking performance improvement, humans need to optimize model architecture. To support humans inspecting complicated architectures of neural networks, TensorFlow Graph Visualizer [43] develops an interface that employs advanced techniques for graph layout. CNN Explainer [42] further describes how data transform in a convolutional neural network.

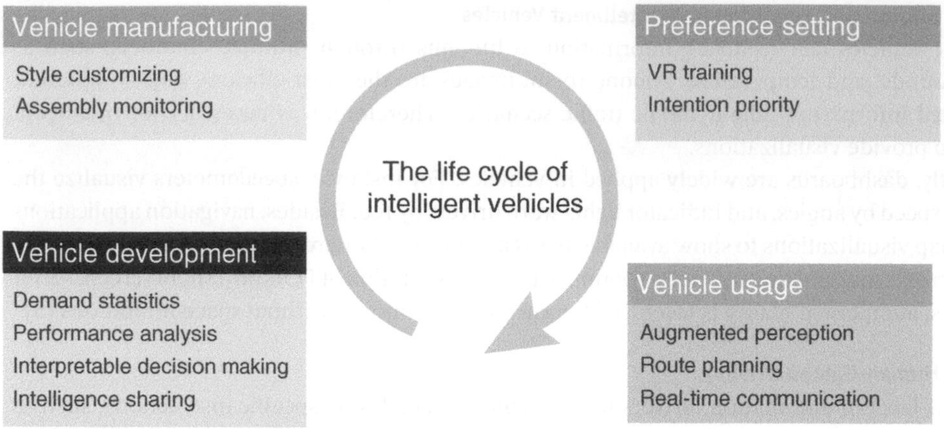


**Figure 17.2** VHCI can participate in the four stages of intelligent vehicles [41].

## 17.4 Future Research Challenges

In this section, we discuss future directions from the aspects of intelligent vehicles and intelligent transport systems, respectively.

### 17.4.1 VHCI for Intelligent Vehicles

The life cycle of intelligent vehicles can be split into four stages: vehicle development, vehicle manufacturing, preference setting, and vehicle usage (see Figure 17.2). Seeking reliable, safe, and trustworthy intelligent vehicles, visual human–computer interactions should be employed to support each stage.

#### 17.4.1.1 Vehicle Development

Intelligent vehicles integrate multiple models to support vehicle usage. In the stage of development, developers need to design, construct, and optimize various models, which can be facilitated by VHCI.

***Requirement Analysis*** According to the driving logs and user feedback collected from vehicle usage, developers can identify new requirements to perfect intelligent vehicles. For example, the performance of the features frequently utilized by users may need to be improved, while the features failing to satisfy users wait for updating. Considering that either driving logs or user feedback could mix important clues with massive irrelevant records, developers need an efficient visual analysis approach to explore data and refine significant requirements.

***Explainable AI*** Norman's principles mentioned that humans need to figure out the potential effect before making a decision. However, in the age of AI, it is challenging for developers to understand how a tiny tweak (e.g. adjusting a parameter) can affect the entire model and how it can further change the driving experience. Existing tools allow developers to adjust AI models and inspect model performance but provide no explanation of the correlation between performance and driving experience. Developers still need effective VHCI to explore the impacts on real-world vehicle usage.

***Experience Sharing*** Various scenarios can be met by different intelligent vehicles, in which vehicle status and obstacles could be unfamiliar. It is necessary for intelligent vehicles to share experiences and store important intelligence in their knowledge base. Developers should monitor the process of experience sharing to resist malicious attacks.

#### 17.4.1.2 Vehicle Manufacture

As vehicles become intelligent, vehicle manufactures need the corresponding improvement.

***Style Customization*** The styles (e.g. appearance, assistant service) of intelligent vehicles will be more diverse. VHCI should allow drivers to customize their own intelligent vehicles. Especially, multiple customization processes should be supported. For example, drivers with clear needs can specify features through detailed descriptions. As for other drivers, they need to explore available features and make comparison. It is necessary to leverage user-friendly VHCI to satisfy the above requirements.

***Production Monitoring*** According to the styles customized by drivers, the manufacture of intelligent vehicles needs to be implemented. However, the production lines of intelligent vehicles could be intricate due to style diversity. An appropriate schedule is significant to efficient production. Thus, humans need VHCI to arrange schedules and track the progress of vehicle production.

#### 17.4.1.3 Preference Recording

Intelligent vehicles can learn human preferences from interaction provenance. For example, intelligent vehicles can identify behavior patterns, like a driver always keeping the speed consistent with the speed limit; then, intelligent vehicles can understand how to set speed in autopilot mode.

***Provenance Analysis*** Intelligent vehicles can learn human preference from interaction provenance. For example, intelligent vehicles can identify behavior patterns, like as a driver always keep the speed consistent with the speed limit; then, intelligent vehicles can understand how to set speed in the autopilot mode.

***VR Training*** Preferences, like how to drive on a snowy road, are significant but difficult to collect. Intelligent vehicles should ask humans to describe their preferences. To avoid misunderstanding, intelligent vehicles can simulate various scenarios by virtual reality (VR) techniques and capture human reactions to record preferences.

#### 17.4.1.4 Vehicle Usage

Usage experience of intelligent vehicles can also benefit from VHCI.

***Augmented Perception*** Drivers dislike checking auxiliary information (e.g. interior temperature) displayed on a small screen when they have to focus on road conditions ahead. Intelligent vehicles should show auxiliary information in a manner that will not interfere with driving. To achieve this goal, intelligent vehicles can identify an unimportant area in the drivers' view and display auxiliary information in the area based on augmented reality (AR) techniques. Especially, AR can provide clearer route navigation than screen-based displays.

***Route Recommendation*** Recommending routes is one of the most used features of intelligent vehicles. Numerous approaches have been proposed to calculate feasible routes and select the best one efficiently. Certain advanced approaches take dynamic traffic congestion and collision risk into considerations. However, there is no effective means to summarize multiple considerations and provide real-time feedback to humans. Drivers may feel confused when the recommended route is updated. Intelligent vehicles should provide recommendations with visual explanation.

***Real-Time Communication*** Intelligent vehicles with advanced communication techniques can receive/send messages from/to multiple devices. When reliable high-level automation can provide security, humans are allowed to divert their attention from driving and utilize the communication feature. With communication permission, the passengers driving on the same road can form a social group. Restaurants nearby and congestion traffic could be popular topics among the group.

Besides, real-time communication can support negotiation of lane usages. When the passengers in an intelligent vehicle are in emergencies (e.g. sudden illness), surrounding intelligent vehicles should be notified and provide assistance.

### 17.4.2 VHCI for Intelligent Transportation Systems

As intelligent vehicles develop, the corresponding intelligent transportation systems need to be upgraded synchronously.

#### 17.4.2.1 Parallel World

Wang et al. [37, 38, 40] proposed the concept of parallel transportation and parallel driving to promote the development of intelligent transportation systems. The architecture of parallel driving consists of three coexisting worlds: the physical world, the mental world, and the artificial world. Artificial drivers and artificial vehicles (ADAV) simulate cognitive behaviors and physical behaviors of humans and generate driving data in the parallel artificial world. The driving data from the parallel artificial world and the physical world can be used to train parallel learning models and solve real-world problems.

#### 17.4.2.2 The Framework of Intelligent Transportation Systems

Inspired by parallel driving, we describe the framework of intelligent transportation systems integrating VHCI. As shown in Figure 17.3, transportation systems in physical world can interact with those in the parallel artificial world through three modules.

***Abstraction*** The first module aims at abstracting data from the physical world. Intelligent vehicles can be connected by communication techniques and construct the Internet of vehicles. The Internet of vehicles can collect real-time driving data in the physical world, which contributes to environment perception of the entire transportation system. To manage massive real-time data, information of different blocks can be stored by blockchain. VHCI techniques, like visual query, can facilitate humans to learn about the data and optimize data management.

***Simulation*** The second module simulates the transportation systems in the physical world by training models in the parallel artificial world. AI approaches can be employed to simulate traffic flows and special accidents. Considering the training data are massive, edge-computing techniques can be used to improve efficiency. Also, visual approaches can provide AI with explainability, which is necessary to model assessment and model optimization.

***Management*** The third model manages the transportation system in the physical world according to the simulation results in the parallel artificial world. To improve the efficiency of a transportation

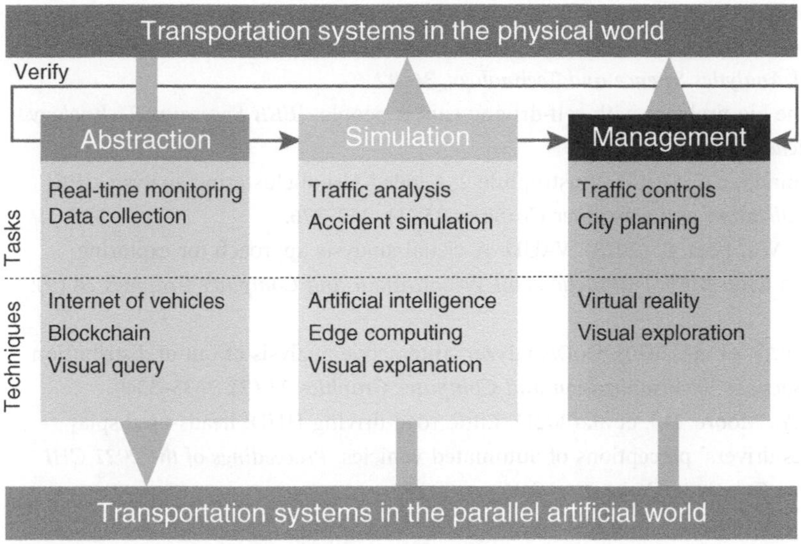


**Figure 17.3** The framework of intelligent transportation systems.

system, humans need to manage not only vehicles but also the traffic environment (e.g. road networks, traffic laws). When humans come up with a new scheme, virtual reality techniques can help users verify the effectiveness. Further, humans can leverage visual exploration to customize new schemes and make comparison.

## References


**1** Ackad, C., Tomitsch, M., and Kay, J. (2016). Skeletons and silhouettes: comparing user representations at a gesture-based large display. *Proceedings of the 2016 CHI Conference on Human Factors in Computing Systems*, 2343–2347.

**2** Al-Dohuki, S., Wu, Y., Kamw, F. et al. (2016). SemanticTraj: A new approach to interacting with massive taxi trajectories. *IEEE Transactions on Visualization and Computer Graphics* 23 (1): 11–20.

**3** Allsop, J., Gray, R., Bülthoff, H.H., and Chuang, L. (2017). Eye movement planning on single-sensor-single-indicator displays is vulnerable to user anxiety and cognitive load. *Journal of Eye Movement Research* 10 (5): 8, 1–15.

**4** Bäuerle, A., Neumann, H., and Ropinski, T. (2020). Classifier-guided visual correction of noisy labels for image classification tasks. *Computer Graphics Forum* 39: 195–205.

**5** Berger, M., Dandekar, A., Bernhaupt, R., and Pfleging, B. (2021). An AR-enabled interactive car door to extend in-car infotainment systems for rear seat passengers. *Extended Abstracts of the 2021 CHI Conference on Human Factors in Computing Systems*, 1–6.

**6** Bernard, J., Hutter, M., Reinemuth, H. et al. (2019). Visual-interactive preprocessing of multivariate time series data. *Computer Graphics Forum* 38 (3): 401–412.

**7** Bi, H., Mao, T., Wang, Z., and Deng, Z. (2019). A deep learning-based framework for intersectional traffic simulation and editing. *IEEE Transactions on Visualization and Computer Graphics* 26 (7): 2335–2348.

**8** Blumenschein, M., Behrisch, M., Schmid, S. et al. (2018). SMARTexplore: Simplifying high-dimensional data analysis through a table-based visual analytics approach. *2018 IEEE Conference on Visual Analytics Science and Technology*, 36–47.

**9** Brooks, R. (2017). The big problem with self-driving cars is people. *IEEE Spectrum: Technology, Engineering, and Science News.*

**10** Cavallo, M. and Demiralp, c.C. (2018). Clustrophile 2: Guided visual clustering analysis. *IEEE Transactions on Visualization and Computer Graphics* 25 (1): 267–276.

**11** Chen, W., Huang, Z., Wu, F. et al. (2018). VAUD: A visual analysis approach for exploring spatio-temporal urban data. *IEEE Transactions on Visualization and Computer Graphics* 24 (9): 2636–2648.

**12** Chen, C., Yuan, J., Lu, Y. et al. (2020). OoDAnalyzer: Interactive analysis of out-of-distribution samples. *IEEE Transactions on Visualization and Computer Graphics* 27 (7): 3335–3349.

**13** Currano, R., Park, S.Y., Moore, D.J. et al. (2021). Little road driving HUD: heads-up display complexity influences drivers' perceptions of automated vehicles. *Proceedings of the 2021 CHI Conference on Human Factors in Computing Systems*, 1–15.

**14** Filipov, V., Arleo, A., Federico, P., and Miksch, S. (2019). CV3: Visual exploration, assessment, and comparison of CVS. *Computer Graphics Forum* 38: 107–118.

**15** Gedicke, S., Bonerath, A., Niedermann, B., and Haunert, J.-H. (2020). Zoomless maps: external labeling methods for the interactive exploration of dense point sets at a fixed map scale. *IEEE Transactions on Visualization and Computer Graphics* 27 (2): 1247–1256.

**16** Gedicke, S., Jabrayilov, A., Niedermann, B. et al. (2021). Point feature label placement for multi-page maps on small-screen devices. *Computers & Graphics* 100: 66–80.

**17** Gou, L., Zou, L., Li, N. et al. (2020). *VATLD*: A visual analytics system to assess, understand and improve traffic light detection. *IEEE Transactions on Visualization and Computer Graphics* 27 (2): 261–271.

**18** Huang, X., Zhao, Y., Ma, C. et al. (2015). TrajGraph: A graph-based visual analytics approach to studying urban network centralities using taxi trajectory data. *IEEE Transactions on Visualization and Computer Graphics* 22 (1): 160–169.

**19** Huang, Z., Zhao, Y., Chen, W. et al. (2019). A natural-language-based visual query approach of uncertain human trajectories. *IEEE Transactions on Visualization and Computer Graphics* 26 (1): 1256–1266.

**20** Kang, Z. and Landry, S.J. (2015). An eye movement analysis algorithm for a multielement target tracking task: maximum transition-based agglomerative hierarchical clustering. *IEEE Transactions on Human–Machine Systems* 45 (1): 13–24.

**21** Krause, J., Perer, A., and Bertini, E. (2014). INFUSE: Interactive feature selection for predictive modeling of high dimensional data. *IEEE Transactions on Visualization and Computer Graphics* 20 (12): 1614–1623.

**22** Lee, C., Kim, Y., Jin, S. et al. (2019). A visual analytics system for exploring, monitoring, and forecasting road traffic congestion. *IEEE Transactions on Visualization and Computer Graphics* 26 (11): 3133–3146.

**23** Li, L. and Wang, F.-Y. (2007). *Advanced Motion Control and Sensing for Intelligent Vehicles.* Springer Science & Business Media.

**24** Liu, S., Chen, C., Lu, Y. et al. (2018). An interactive method to improve crowdsourced annotations. *IEEE Transactions on Visualization and Computer Graphics* 25 (1): 235–245.

**25** Ming, Y., Xu, P., Cheng, F. et al. (2019). ProtoSteer: Steering deep sequence model with prototypes. *IEEE Transactions on Visualization and Computer Graphics* 26 (1): 238–248.

26 Miranda, F., Doraiswamy, H., Lage, M. et al. (2016). Urban pulse: capturing the rhythm of cities. *IEEE Transactions on Visualization and Computer Graphics* 23 (1): 791–800.

27 Packer, E., Bak, P., Nikkilä, M. et al. (2013). Visual analytics for spatial clustering: using a heuristic approach for guided exploration. *IEEE Transactions on Visualization and Computer Graphics* 19 (12): 2179–2188.

28 Pezzotti, N., Lelieveldt, B.P.F., Van Der Maaten, L. et al. (2016). Approximated and user steerable tSNE for progressive visual analytics. *IEEE Transactions on Visualization and Computer Graphics* 23 (7): 1739–1752.

29 Pi, M., Yeon, H., Son, H., and Jang, Y. (2019). Visual cause analytics for traffic congestion. *IEEE Transactions on Visualization and Computer Graphics* 27 (3): 2186–2201.

30 Ren, D., Amershi, S., Lee, B. et al. (2016). Squares: supporting interactive performance analysis for multiclass classifiers. *IEEE Transactions on Visualization and Computer Graphics* 23 (1): 61–70.

31 Scheepens, R., Hurter, C., Van De Wetering, H., and Van Wijk, J.J. (2015). Visualization, selection, and analysis of traffic flows. *IEEE Transactions on Visualization and Computer Graphics* 22 (1): 379–388.

32 Shen, C., Chen, Y., Yang, G., and Guan, X. (2020). Toward hand-dominated activity recognition systems with wristband-interaction behavior analysis. *IEEE Transactions on Systems, Man, and Cybernetics: Systems* 50 (7): 2501–2511.

33 Shneiderman, B. (2020). Human-centered artificial intelligence: reliable, safe & trustworthy. *International Journal of Human–Computer Interaction* 36 (6): 495–504.

34 Singh, M. and Kim, S. (2018). Branch based blockchain technology in intelligent vehicle. *Computer Networks* 145: 219–231.

35 Van Den Elzen, S. and Van Wijk, J.J. (2011). BaobabView: Interactive construction and analysis of decision trees. *2011 IEEE Conference on Visual Analytics Science and Technology*, 151–160.

36 Von Landesberger, T., Brodkorb, F., Roskosch, P. et al. (2015). MobilityGraphs: Visual analysis of mass mobility dynamics via spatio-temporal graphs and clustering. *IEEE Transactions on Visualization and Computer Graphics* 22 (1): 11–20.

37 Wang, F.-Y. (2008). Toward a revolution in transportation operations: AI for complex systems. *IEEE Intelligent Systems* 23 (6): 8–13.

38 Wang, F.-Y. (2010). Parallel control and management for intelligent transportation systems: concepts, architectures, and applications. *IEEE Transactions on Intelligent Transportation Systems* 11 (3): 630–638.

39 Wang, F., Chen, W., Wu, F. et al. (2014). A visual reasoning approach for data-driven transport assessment on urban roads. *2014 IEEE Conference on Visual Analytics Science and Technology (VAST)*, 103–112. IEEE.

40 Wang, F.-Y., Zheng, N.-N., Cao, D. et al. (2017). Parallel driving in CPSS: a unified approach for transport automation and vehicle intelligence. *IEEE/CAA Journal of Automatica Sinica* 4 (4): 577–587.

41 Wang, X., Zheng, X., Chen, W., and Wang, F.-Y. (2020). Visual human–computer interactions for intelligent vehicles and intelligent transportation systems: the state of the art and future directions. *IEEE Transactions on Systems, Man, and Cybernetics: Systems* 51 (1): 253–265.

42 Wang, Z.J., Turko, R., Shaikh, O. et al. (2020). CNN explainer: learning convolutional neural networks with interactive visualization. *IEEE Transactions on Visualization and Computer Graphics* 27 (2): 1396–1406.

**43** Wongsuphasawat, K., Smilkov, D., Wexler, J. et al. (2017). Visualizing dataflow graphs of deep learning models in tensorflow. *IEEE Transactions on Visualization and Computer Graphics* 24 (1): 1–12.

**44** Xia, J., Ye, F., Chen, W. et al. (2017). LDSScanner: Exploratory analysis of low-dimensional structures in high-dimensional datasets. *IEEE Transactions on Visualization and Computer Graphics* 24 (1): 236–245.

**45** Xie, X., Cai, X., Zhou, J. et al. (2018). A semantic-based method for visualizing large image collections. *IEEE Transactions on Visualization and Computer Graphics* 25 (7): 2362–2377.

**46** Xing, Y., Lv, C., Wang, H. et al. (2019). Driver lane change intention inference for intelligent vehicles: framework, survey, and challenges. *IEEE Transactions on Vehicular Technology* 68 (5): 4377–4390.

**47** Zeng, W., Lin, C., Lin, J. et al. (2020). Revisiting the modifiable areal unit problem in deep traffic prediction with visual analytics. *IEEE Transactions on Visualization and Computer Graphics* 27 (2): 839–848.

**48** Zhang, J., Wang, Y., Molino, P. et al. (2018). Manifold: a model-agnostic framework for interpretation and diagnosis of machine learning models. *IEEE Transactions on Visualization and Computer Graphics* 25 (1): 364–373.

# 18

# Intelligent Collaboration Between Humans and Robots

*Andrea Maria Zanchettin*

*Politecnico di Milano, Dipartimento di Elettronica, Informazione e Bioningegneria, Milan, Italy*

## 18.1 Introduction

There is a fundamental difference between *looking* and *watching*. The former relates to the activity of directing the eyes in a particular direction, while the latter is rather referring to paying attention to what is happening.

Although the adoption of computer vision in automation has been growing during the last decades, it has been used for relatively simple tasks, such as recognizing defects or computing the position of the parts to be picked-up by the robot.

The increasing interest in collaborative robotics, which stands for the adoption of industrial robots operating side-by-side to human workers, might have gradually changed the perspective. To *look*, e.g. to recognize defects, is still an important technology in automation. On the other hand, *watching* the human, and more in general the collaborative workspace, to understand the context will be even more relevant in future manufacturing paradigms. Perceiving the presence of humans, or their position, is just a prerequisite for a safe coexistence. Understanding, in turn, might constitute a game changer toward a real and effective collaboration.

In the view of the discussion above, this chapter documents the research carried out in this field, as well as some novel results. It will be shown how collaborative robotics applications can benefit from a reasoning layer, allowing the robot to take conscious decisions based on the understanding of humans.

## 18.2 Background

### 18.2.1 Context

The first mathematical tools adopted to represent a certain scene are the so-called *Semantic Networks* or *Labeled Graphs*, see Winston [17] and [10]. Semantic networks are essentially graphs consisting of nodes, denoting objects or concepts, directed arcs, denoting the existence of relationship between them, and arc labels that further specify these relations. Their first use in robotics was described in Agarwal [2] as a reasoning framework to find plans to solve generic problems.

*Handbook of Human-Machine Systems*, First Edition. Edited by Giancarlo Fortino, David Kaber, Andreas Nürnberger, and David Mendonça.

Nowadays, semantic networks are primarily adopted in search engines, map localization problems in domestic scenarios, Galindo et al. [8], as well as in image captioning, Farhadi et al. [7], or question answering, Johnson et al. [9].

While the localization application is surely tailored to robotics, the latter two are not necessarily as such. The former, i.e. image captioning, consists in the automatic generation of text to describe, in natural language, the content of an image. The latter, in turn, addresses the problem of understanding whether or not a given image is consistent with a textual description.

When it comes to applying this technology to robotics, there are two relevant aspects to consider. First, the workspace is typically perceived through a 3D sensor. It follows that the robotic agent has no need to infer spatial relations between objects, as their 3D position can be directly estimated or measured. Moreover, textual representations of the semantic networks are not needed, as computing systems can leverage efficient algorithms to directly manipulate graphs, while simple boolean, Andrews [5], or fuzzy predicates, Ross [14] can be introduced to understand whether a certain relation exists between two objects in the network.

### 18.2.2 Basic Definitions

In this work, we will make use of *spatio-temporal semantic networks* (STSN) to describe the knowledge a robotic agent has on its workspace and to allow the robot to reason on it. *First-order logic*, and specifically predicates, will be adopted to retrieve information from the STSN. In the following, a formal mathematical description of both is given.

**Definition 18.1** ***(Spatiotemporal Semantic Network, STSN)*** A STSN is a dynamic (time-varying) oriented graph $G_k = \left(N_k, A_k, L, f_k\right)$, where at every discrete time $k$, $N_k$ is the set of nodes, $A_k$ is the set of arcs, $L$ is a set of labels (or signifiers), and $f_k$ is a function. The set of nodes $N_k$ is partitioned into classes. The set of arcs is simply $A_k \subseteq \{(x,y) \mid (x,y) \in N_k^2, x \neq y\}$. The set of labels $L$ further specifies the (semantic) meaning of arcs, through function $f_k$. One arc might have many labels, but at least one. Hence, function $f_k : A_k \to L$ is a one-to-many relation.

Furthermore, at every time instant $k$, each node $n \in N_k$ is characterized by its spatial representation in terms of position, $\boldsymbol{p}_{n,k} \in \mathbb{R}^3$, and its derivative $\dot{\boldsymbol{p}}_{n,k} \in \mathbb{R}^3$, or position and orientation, $\boldsymbol{R}_{n,k} \in \mathbb{R}^3 \times SO(3)$ together with $\dot{\boldsymbol{p}}_{n,k}, \boldsymbol{\omega}_{n,k} \in \mathbb{R}^3$.

The STSN just introduced is a generalization of the semantic networks described in [17], allowing for both spatial and temporal inference on the state of the workspace, Blumenthal et al. [6]. In fact, nodes, arcs and their labels are not necessarily static, as they might change according to the dynamics of the environment.

**Definition 18.2** ***(Update function)*** At any discrete time instant $k$, the network $G_k$ is updated through a suitable *Update function* $h : G \times \mathcal{U} \to G$, that maps the current network $G_k$ to the one at the next time instant $G_{k+1}$ based on current sensing data $u_k \in \mathcal{U}$, i.e. $G_{k+1} = h\left(G_k, u_k\right)$.

Once the concept of STSN has been introduced as a tool used by the robotic agent to store and maintain its knowledge of the world, we need a method to query such a knowledge.

**Definition 18.3** ***(Output function)*** Given a SSN $G$, an output function $g : G \to \mathbb{B} = \{0, 1\}$ is essentially a boolean function that, for the given net $G$, returns whether a certain condition is true or not.

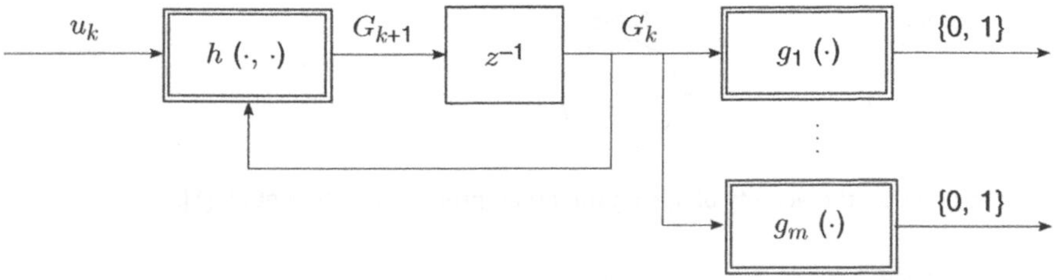


**Figure 18.1** Architectural diagram of the update dynamics of the STSN that transforms raw perception data $u_k$ into boolean signals.

As already stated, textual queries are not needed to retrieve information from the STSN. In turn, the output functions just introduced still allow the robotic agent to search and select relevant knowledge through, e.g. graph search algorithms, Thulasiraman and Swamy [15], embedded in one or many *output functions*.

The overall spatiotemporal dynamics of the workspace is then described by means of the following equations (algorithms):

$$G_{k+1} = h\left(G_k, u_k\right), \; y_k = \left[g_1\left(G_k\right), \ldots, g_m\left(G_k\right)\right]^T$$

where $h$ is the *Update function*, while $g_i$ are *Output functions* (see Figure 18.1).

This approach, that is based on systems dynamics, differs substantially from the ones in the literature proposing to derive the graph from measurements only, i.e. $G_{k+1} = h\left(u_k\right)$, Ziaeetabar et al. [20].

The values returned by output functions, if interpreted as digital signals, can be used to feed traditional PLC[1]-like control logics as explained in Zanchettin et al. [19]. This way, thanks to STSN and output functions, it is possible to link state-of-the-art *Artificial Intelligence* methods, like those to detect and track humans or objects, to traditional logical control architectures that are common in industrial automation.

## 18.3 Related Work

This work is focused on the recognition of human actions or activities based on relations between objects, or in general nodes, present in the semantic description of the workspace. As already stated, in collaborative robotics application, the understanding of human behavior can be beneficial to increase the flow of the application, reduce the frequency of errors, etc.

The problem of recognizing and labeling human activities can be tackled by searching for specific patterns (or subgraphs) in the STSN. The work in Yao and Fei-Fei [18] adopts both human pose (mutual relation between body parts) and object detection to model and classify human activities. Aksoy et al. [3] introduced spatial semantic networks to classify actions and categorize objects. A library of object-action complexes has been developed in Wächter et al. [16] to model actions in terms of their preconditions and effects on the manipulated objects, thus exploiting the temporal characteristics of the semantic network.

Aein et al. [1] proposed a classification of actions based on two or three nodes: the tool used, the place where the action takes place, and possibly what they called "indirect object" to indicate the one on which the action is performed, see Figure 18.2 for an example. A similar modeling

1 PLC stands for programmable logic controller.

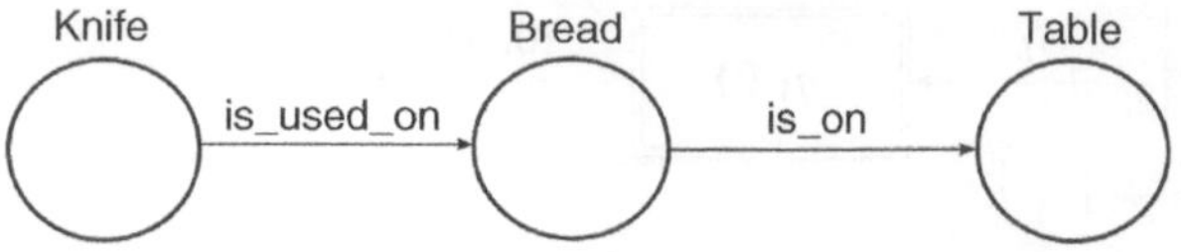


**Figure 18.2** Subgraph to describe the activity of slicing the bread proposed in Aein et al. [1].

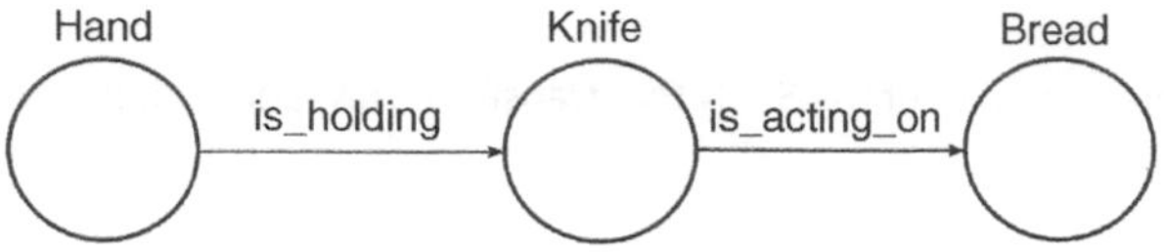


**Figure 18.3** Subgraph to describe the activity of cutting the bread proposed in Ramirez-Amaro et al. [13].

strategy has been also proposed in Ramirez-Amaro et al. [13] to classify human activities, see Figure 18.3. The work in Pieropan et al. [12] somehow combines the two previous methods, proposing to describe an activity based on the mutual spatial relations of the hand, the tool used, the object, and the position where the action is taking place. Finally, the work in Aksoy et al. [4] reports a method for the classifications of long and complex actions, point out the need for complete (i.e. 3D) spatial cues, that are not directly available within standard 2D computer vision techniques. Table below summarizes relevant features of state-of-the-art methods.

In this work, the classification of the ongoing action is based on proper logical combination of the values returned by the *output functions* $g_1(\cdot), \ldots, g_5(\cdot)$ (see again Figure 18.1). Specific examples will be given in Section 18.4.

| Paper | Perception | Dynamics | Action identified by... |
|---|---|---|---|
| Yao and Fei-Fei [18] | 2D | no | human pose, object |
| Askoy et al. [3] | 3D | no | hand, object |
| Wätcher et al. [16] | 3D | no | matching library |
| Aein et al. [1] | 3D | no | tool, object(s), place, see Figure 18.2 |
| Ramirez et al. [13] | 2D | no | hand, tool, object, see Figure 18.3 |
| Pieropan et al. [12] | 3D | no | hand, tool, object, place |
| Askoy et al. [4] | 3D | no | hand, object(s), library from [16] |
| **Proposed method** | 3D | yes | values returned by *Output functions* |

## 18.4 Validation Cases

In Messeri et al. [11], it has been shown that adapting the behavior of the robot to the one of the human is way better in terms of cumulated cognitive stress of the worker, with respect to forcing the human to follow the pace of the robot.

In this section, two validation experimental use cases are presented. In both the two demonstrations, a surveillance camera provided by Smart Robots,[2] a spin-off company of Politecnico

2 For further information, please refer to http://www.smartrobots.it/.

**Table 18.1** Set of arc labels $L$, and corresponding meaning.

| Label (or Signifier) | From | To | Meaning |
|---|---|---|---|
| has | human | hand | hands belong to humans |
| is_inside | hand, object, gripper | ROI | check if inside |
| is_holding | hand, gripper | object | hand/gripper holding an object |
| is_close_to | *any* | *any* | things close to each other |
| is_approaching | *any* | *any* | negative relative velocity |
| is_going_away_from | *any* | *any* | positive relative velocity |

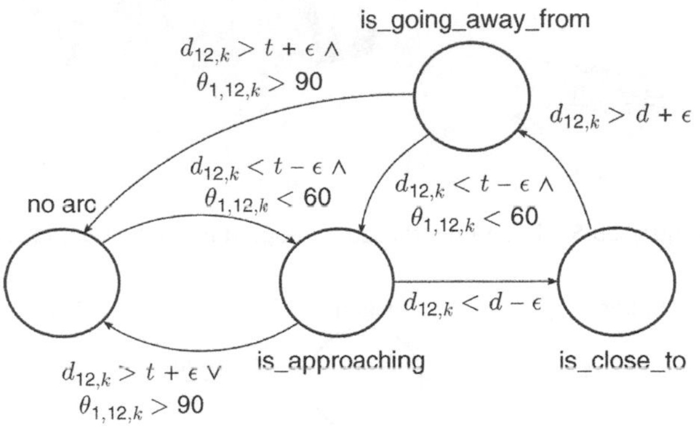


**Figure 18.4** Example of update dynamics for labels *is_close_to, is_approaching,* and *is_going_away_from*, $d_{12,k}$ is the distance between two objects, $\theta_{1,12,k}$ is the angle between the velocity of the first object, $\dot{\boldsymbol{p}}_{\mathcal{O}_1,k}$, and the segment connecting the two, $\boldsymbol{p}_{\mathcal{O}_2,k} - \boldsymbol{p}_{\mathcal{O}_1,k}$, while $0 < \epsilon \lll d \lll t$ are three parameters.

di Milano, will be adopted. Custom code has been developed to implement the architecture of Figure 18.1 apart from basic functionalities, such as human/object detection and tracking which are regarded as source of measurement data $u_k$.

The following classes are introduced to distinguish nodes: *human, hand, object, ROI* (Region of Interest), *robot, gripper,* while the set of labels $L$ is shown in Table 18.1 together with their meanings. Spatiotemporal semantic networks will be exploited to infer human behavior and to command the robot accordingly.

The need for dynamics to specify the evolution of a STSN should be evident from the labels of Table 18.1. Considering two objects, $\mathcal{O}_1$ and $\mathcal{O}_2$, it is clear that the relation between them is typically evolving from $\mathcal{O}_1$ *is approaching* $\mathcal{O}_2$, to $\mathcal{O}_1$ *is close to* $\mathcal{O}_2$, and not vice-versa. As an example, the dynamics governing the last three labels in Table 18.1 is shown in Figure 18.4.

### 18.4.1 A Simple Verification Scenario

The first verification scenario, taken from Zanchettin et al. [19], consists in the collaborative assembly of the head of a thermostatic valve for radiators, performed with an ABB YuMi dual-arm robot. The valve is composed of 6 elements. The components to be manipulated by the human are stored in four boxes, two on his/her right and two on the left. The outcome of the assembly consists in a pallet hosting the parts partially assembled and ready to feed a filling machine. The pallet that will host the subassemblies is placed in the middle between the human and the robot, see Figure 18.5.

For each of the four boxes and for the pallet, a corresponding ROI has been defined. The recognition of worker activity is simply rendered by looking whether his/her hand is inside the ROI.

**Figure 18.5** Experimental setup adopted in the first demonstration.

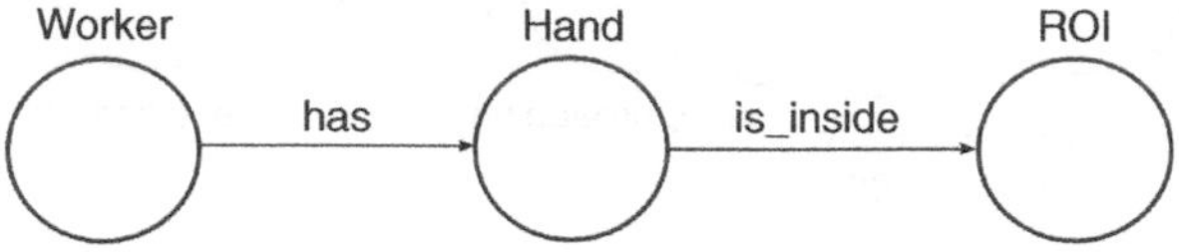


**Figure 18.6** Sub-graph describing a picking action.

In terms of STSN, the pattern in Figure 18.6 has to be discovered in the graph. This functionality, one per each of the four boxes and for the pallet, has been implemented and made available in terms of output functions $g_1(\cdot), \ldots, g_5(\cdot)$.

Based on the understanding on which part the human picks, the robot reacts accordingly. If the human starts picking items from any of the upper boxes, the left arm of the robot takes another part, awaits for the human to deposit the assembly on the pallets and complete the operation. In turn, if the human begins picking from any of the two lower boxes, the robot accommodates a ring on the pallet, and the human completes the assembly. Finally, the robot prepares the new pallet, after the human has removed the previous one from the corresponding area.[3]

### 18.4.2 Activity Recognition Based on Semantic Hand-Object Interaction

The second demonstration consists in the collaborative assembly of the rear braking system of a motorbike. The worker is taking part in the assembly of the oil tank and its securing to the pump. A collaborative robot, again the YuMi from ABB, is responsible for the preassembly of the oil tube connection from the caliper to the pump. The operator is finally responsible for the tightening of three screws, one of them with the help of an electric screwdriver, the other two using a pneumatic

3 A video of the complete demonstration is available at the following link: https://www.youtube.com/watch?v=qci5WAzPcqA. The output of the STSN is also used to instruct the worker on assembly procedures.

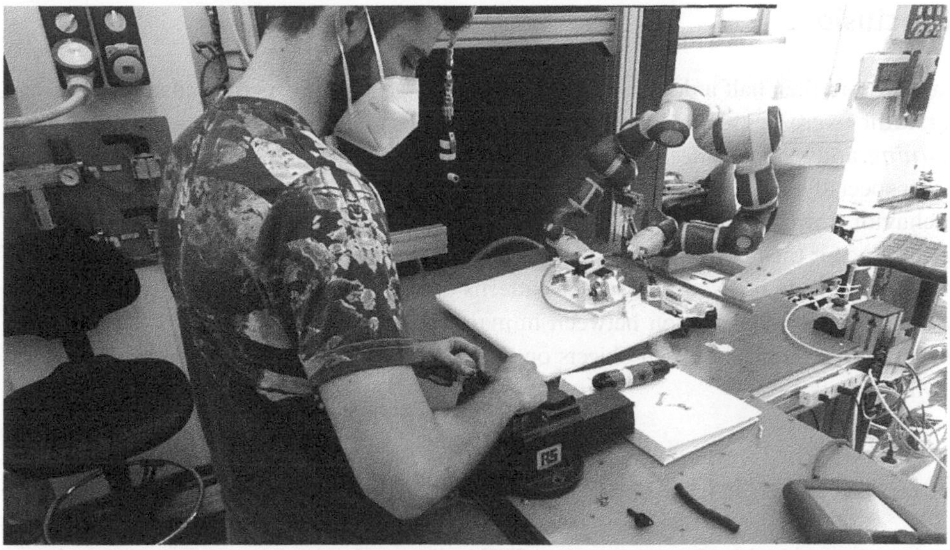

**Figure 18.7** Experimental setup adopted in the second demonstration.

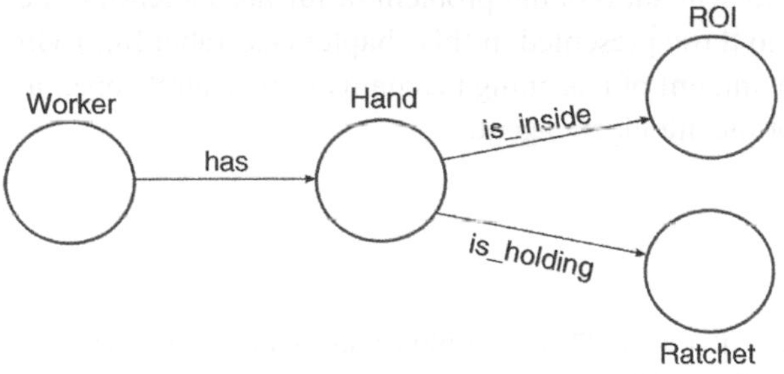


**Figure 18.8** Subgraph describing the tightening operation in a specific position.

ratchet. The ratchet is controlled by an electrical valve that enables the pressure according to the state of the assembly process. Figure 18.7 shows the experimental setup.

Object detection and human tracking are combined to understand the ongoing activity of the human operator and to synchronize the robot accordingly. Specifically, the demonstration was intended to test the capability of the STSN to correctly detect whether the tightening operation is performed at the right time and in the right place. To this end, the pattern in Figure 18.8 has to be found within the STSN. Notice that since air flow in the pneumatic ratchet is enabled by the valve, the condition in Figure 18.8 is also used to enable/disable the pressure, preventing the human to operate the ratchet where/when not needed.

When the robot completes the preassembly of the tube, it awaits for the human to tighten it using the air ratchet. As this operation introduces substantial vibration to the pallet containing all the parts, the robot has to wait for the human to finish before taking over with the following task.[4]

---

4 A video of the demonstration is available at the following link: http://y2u.be/g_sZjZCVx0w.

## 18.5 Conclusions

Since its dawn, more than half a decade ago, *Artificial Intelligence* has experienced several waves. While early studies were focused on logical reasoning, the most recent progresses are in the field of *machine learning*, and especially *deep learning*. In manufacturing environments, human–machines systems, and especially human–robot collaborative stations, has to be ready after begin installed. Learning behavior from specific experience might dramatically reduce their competitiveness by increasing the time for their deployment. This chapter was intended to brush up the semantic part of *artificial Intelligence* to be used to discover patterns between human, object, and activities to ultimately enhance the collaboration between humans and robots at the shop-floor. A method exploiting semantic relations between objects on the scene has been described and validated in relevant environments.

## 18.6 Future Research Challenges

The approach presented in this chapter, based on STSN, allows robots to reason about the environment in order to take conscious decisions. The output functions play the role of *oracles* capable of answering yes or no to simple questions, which are related to the presence of particular subgraphs in the STSN. On the one hand, future works will address the problem of further increasing the number of possible questions with respect to those presented in this chapter (see Table 18.1). On the other hand, the availability of a certain amount of reasoning mechanisms will surely open to new and more involved decision policies for the intelligent agent.

## References


1 Aei, M.J., Aksoy, E.E., Tamosiunaite, M. et al. (2013). Toward a library of manipulation actions based on semantic object-action relations. *2013 IEEE/RSJ International Conference on Intelligent Robots and Systems*, 4555–4562. IEEE.

2 Agarwal, K.K. (1983). Solving problems in robotics with semantic networks. *IEEE Transactions on Pattern Analysis and Machine Intelligence* 2: 213–217.

3 Aksoy, E.E., Abramov, A., Wörgötter, F., and Delle, B. (2010). Categorizing object-action relations from semantic scene graphs. *2010 IEEE International Conference on Robotics and Automation*, 398–405. IEEE.

4 Aksoy, E.E., Orha, A., and Wörgötter, F. (2017). Semantic decomposition and recognition of long and complex manipulation action sequences. *International Journal of Computer Vision* 122 (1): 84–115.

5 Andrews, P.B. (2002). *An Introduction to Mathematical Logic and Type Theory*, vol. 27. Springer Science & Business Media.

6 Blumenthal, S., Bruyninckx, H., Nowak, W., and Prassler, E. (2013). A scene graph based shared 3D world model for robotic applications. *2013 IEEE International Conference on Robotics and Automation*, 453–460. IEEE.

7 Farhadi, A., Hejrati, M., Sadeghi, M.A. et al. (2010). Every picture tells a story: generating sentences from images. In: *European Conference on Computer Vision*, Lecture Notes in Computer Science, vol. 6314 (ed. K. Daniilidis, P. Maragos, and N. Paragios), 15–29. Berlin, Heidelberg: Springer-Verlag.

8 Galindo, C., Saffiotti, A., Coradeschi, S. et al. (2005). Multi-hierarchical semantic maps for mobile robotics. *2005 IEEE/RSJ International Conference on Intelligent Robots and Systems*, 2278–2283. IEEE.

9 Johnso, J., Krishna, R., Stark, M. et al. (2015). Image retrieval using scene graphs. *Proceedings of the IEEE Conference on Computer Vision and Pattern Recognition*, 3668–3678.

10 Lehman, F. (1992). Semantic networks. *Computers & Mathematics with Applications* 23 (2–5): 1–50.

11 Messeri, C., Zanchettin, A.M., Rocco, P. et al. (2020). On the effects of leader-follower roles in dyadic human–robot synchronization. *IEEE Transactions on Cognitive and Developmental Systems*. https://doi.org/10.1109/TCDS.2020.2991864.

12 Pieropa, A., Ek, C.H., and Kjellström, H. (2013). Functional object descriptors for human activity modeling. *2013 IEEE International Conference on Robotics and Automation*, 1282–1289. IEEE.

13 Ramirez-Amaro, K., Beetz, M., and Cheng, G. (2014). Automatic segmentation and recognition of human activities from observation based on semantic reasoning. *2014 IEEE/RSJ International Conference on Intelligent Robots and Systems*, 5043–5048. IEEE.

14 Ross, T.J. (2005). *Fuzzy Logic with Engineering Applications*. Wiley.

15 Thulasirama, K. and Swamy, M.N.S. (2011). Graphs: Theory and Algorithms. Wiley.

16 Wächter, M., Schulz, S., Asfour, T. et al. (2013). Action sequence reproduction based on automatic segmentation and object-action complexes. *2013 13th IEEE-RAS International Conference on Humanoid Robots (Humanoids)*, 189–195. IEEE.

17 Winsto, P.H. (1992). *Artificial Intelligence*. Addison-Wesley.

18 Yao, B. and Fei-Fei, L. (2010). Modeling mutual context of object and human pose in human-object interaction activities. *2010 IEEE Computer Society Conference on Computer Vision and Pattern Recognition*, 17–24. IEEE.

19 Zanchettin, A.M., Marconi, M., Ongini, C. et al. (2020). A formal control architecture for collaborative robotics applications. *2020 IEEE International Conference on Human-Machine Systems (ICHMS)*, 1–4. IEEE.

20 Ziaeetabar, F., Aksoy, E.E., Wörgötter, F., and Tamosiunaite, M. (2017). Semantic analysis of manipulation actions using spatial relations. *2017 IEEE International Conference on Robotics and Automation (ICRA)*, 4612–4619. IEEE.

# 19

# To Be Trustworthy and To Trust: The New Frontier of Intelligent Systems

*Rino Falcone, Alessandro Sapienza, Filippo Cantucci, and Cristiano Castelfranchi*

*Trust Theory and Technology Group, Institute of Cognitive Sciences and Technologies, National Research Council of Italy, Rome, Italy*

## 19.1 Introduction

The more artificial intelligence systems (AIS) become the mediators of our "hybrid society" (mixed human and artificial), the more crucial the question of trust and its construction will be. The AIS are already playing (and increasingly will play) a mediating role in the various areas: (i) data acquisition, processing, and prediction; (ii) knowledge as institution, education, and opinion building; (iii) interaction with the physical and virtual environment and WEB interaction; (iv) human interaction in conflict, cooperation, organizations, and their management; (v) political participation and decisions, government; and again Human–Robot-Interaction, Robot–Robot interaction in team work; etc. The "passport" for this role certainly is the Trustworthiness of these intelligent and interactive devices but also on such base the Trust toward them. This already is a very central and growing challenge (as showed in this review), not always so explicit.

Trust is what stands behind such trendy issues as "reliability," "safety," "transparency," "accountability, " "explainability," and even "moral" guaranties in algorithms and AIS. Its nature is multidirectional: trust of humans in AIS; trust of Robots in humans, and in the other Robots; trust within distributed multiagent systems; etc.

However, this growing and strategic research domain has some problem since trust is not only a complex notion but also a phenomenon:

- multilayered (beliefs, expectations, feeling, disposition, decision, and act);
- multidimensional (not only skills, competence, means but also intentionality, disposition, sociality, honesty, etc.);
- with multiple sources and trust in sources (not just learning and direct experience, but reasoning, reputation, etc.);
- with a complex dynamics and adjustment.

Trust also plays a central role in not only "networks of dependence," where it is not enough to establish who is able to do what and who can be counted on to achieve one's goals but also how much the potential partner of X, on which X depends, can be willing, available, and reliable in doing something for X. And possibly in exchange for what, that is, by verifying its dependence on X for some other goal, and, reciprocally, the trustworthiness of X which it perceives. In this sense, it is interesting to verify that more than the objective trustworthiness of each agent, what counts in

*Handbook of Human-Machine Systems*, First Edition. Edited by Giancarlo Fortino, David Kaber, Andreas Nürnberger, and David Mendonça.

the networks of dependence (increased with the concept of trust) is the trust that others attribute to their respective potential partners in collaborations.

This domain should become more analytical and articulated by explicitly modeling all these crucial dimensions and do not confuse, for example trustworthiness and trust, or probability and trust, trust of X toward Y or of Y toward X. We stress in our review all the precious ideas and models and also the limits to be overcome in the near future.

## 19.2 Background

The topic of trust has fascinated scholars in the most varied fields: from sociology to psychology, from economics to neuroscience. However, only recently, since distributed artificial intelligence (DAI) and multiagent systems (MAS) have become the main paradigm of AI and the issues closest to interaction have become a central element to be explored, the idea has been established that the attitude of trust should be modeled and also implemented in artificial systems.

Among the initiatives to be mentioned is certainly the "Workshop on Trust" which accompanied the main international conference on MAS (from AGENTS-1998, to AAMAS-2021) and which allowed the establishment of a community of reference on this issue. There are also works of fundamental importance that must be indicated [3, 14, 19, 20, 25, 26, 28, 32, 33, 38]. These works, together with many other publications and experiments, have made it possible to understand the meaning of the operationalization of the concept of trust even though this same concept presented aspects that were not entirely obvious from a theoretical point of view. At the same time, its practical application in complex domains, such as those of multiagent interaction or in Human–Robot-Interaction, has allowed to highlight issues of particular importance for the same theoretical reflection of the concept of trust.

## 19.3 Basic Definitions

As we have said, trust is an object of study of primary importance in the sociological and philosophical field. Already the British philosopher Locke [23] argued that "trust is the bond of society: the vinculum societatis." But the most relevant characterizations, very briefly, come from a couple of outstanding authors.

Luhmann [24], for whom "trust is nothing more than a mechanism for reducing complexity," that is, it allows you to operate in the social sphere without having to evaluate all the reliability criteria from time to time with which we relate to others. This evaluation would involve such a repetitive and constant commitment that it would exhaust us to the point of being forced to argue that "Without trust we would not even be able to get up in the morning: an indeterminate anguish, a paralyzing panic would assail us …" [24].

Furthermore, Gambetta [13], according to which "trust is the subjective probability through which an individual, A, expects another individual, B, to carry out a given action on which its own well-being depends." This definition includes all the basic concepts that trust brings with it, from the fact that it is a social relationship, to the fact that an expectation is involved; that there is a dependence to obtain one's own purpose (benefit), and that this may be successful based on someone else's actions. Our only criticism of this definition is that it does not analytically investigate the reasons underlying the so-called "subjective probability" and which, in our opinion, these reasons must enter in the social reasoning that leads to an attitude of trust.

Another relevant definition [27] considers "trust as the decision to make oneself vulnerable": a really relevant element in the trust conceptualization. In fact, there can be no trust if there is no risk factor, a possibility of failure on the part of the trustee.

Finally, Hardin [16] establishes the sense of trust by arguing that "I trust you because I believe it is in your interest to take my interests into account in a seriously relevant way." In other words, the author considers trust as "encapsulated interest" (although just focused on the disposition of the trustee not on competence/ability). The abstract expectation of the trustor is not sufficient: it must be founded in the concern/care/reference of the trustee with respect to the interests of the trustor (I think that you are rational, and therefore, if you do my interests, it is because it is your interest to keep account of my interests). With this concept of "embedded interest," Hardin gets near to the notion of "social adoption of purpose," i.e. the notion to which we refer and also the core component for any form of prosociality: from exchange to cooperation, from altruism to caring.

But providing a definition of trust also in light of the operationalization that one wants to achieve in order to transfer it to artificial systems is something much more complex. In this sense, the concept must be interpreted as our attempt at a sociocognitive approach that considers the state and mental attitudes of the interlocutors, the recursive and dynamic phenomena that trust brings with it, and the fact that it is both a mental and pragmatic process.

## 19.4 State-of-the-Art

In this section, we present a systematic review of the state-of-the-art by providing a broad overview of the existing work on trust in intelligent systems.

### 19.4.1 Trust in Different Domains

In particular, we investigate three macro domains where trust has a crucial impact: Internet of Things ($\mathcal{I}$), Multiagent Systems ($\mathcal{M}$), Human–Machine-Interaction ($\mathcal{H}$). Of course, while there are sometimes even strong overlaps between the considered domains, such a categorization process allowed us to identify the specific lines of research in each area, highlighting substantial differences.

It is worth underlining that the notion of trust is intrinsically defined in the domain of MAS. In fact, the very notion of agent is strictly linked to the concepts of task, collaboration, teamwork, autonomy, and delegation: all basic elements to which the concept of trust refers.

Conversely, trust has had a very different development in the internet of things (IoT) context. Indeed, this domain did not initially require the use of trust, since it initially considered the interaction of even very simple devices. It seemed completely useless to refer to such a complex and difficult to implement concept. Nevertheless, although not foreseen, the notion of trust emerged at a later time as a necessity for the purpose of providing reliable services and for the management of cooperation.

Trust is a critical issue even in Human–Machine-Interaction: given the increasing complexity, trust is a key factor for maximizing acceptability, reliability, and effectiveness of artificial entities. In addition, it arises the need to evaluate human's trustworthiness, for instance in joint tasks, where the actors depend on each other's effort to achieve a shared goal.

### 19.4.2 Selected Articles

The research has been conducted by making use of the following sources: IEEExplore, Google Scholar, Science Direct, and ACM. After a first phase concerning contributions retrieval, the selected articles were further reduced based on the following criteria: *valuable contribution*, including both computational model and real or simulated implementation; *recent paper*, being published in 2011 or after; *relevance*, the paper must be relevant for the trust domain (high impact factor, number of citations, etc.); *accessibility*, the article should be accessible via one of previously mentioned portals. Overall, we obtained a total of 22 papers:

- ($\mathcal{I}$): [1, 2, 5–7, 10, 12, 18, 35];
- ($\mathcal{M}$): [11, 15, 22, 29, 31, 39];
- ($\mathcal{H}$): [8, 9, 17, 21, 30, 34, 37].

### 19.4.3 Differences in the Use of Trust

Our analysis is theoretically inspired by the sociocognitive model of trust of [4]. Based on this grounded and solid theory, we start analyzing the above contributions according to two main characteristics:

1. The actors involved in this relationship: indeed, trust can involve different kinds of individuals, which can be *human*, *machine*, or generically an *agent*. Trustor and trustee can independently belong to one of these categories.
2. The model's perspective: whether the model considers the point of view of the trustor, i.e. it investigates how the trustor analyzes the trustee's *trustworthiness*, or if it considers how the trustee assesses the trustor's level of *trust*.

Figure 19.1 summarizes and provides a schematic representation of these concepts.

Then, Table 19.1 shows the results of the analysis we conducted, on the basis of these two concepts. As a first noteworthy finding, this investigation highlights that the use of H2M trust models is almost an exclusive prerogative of the human–machine interface (HMI) domain, having very limited development in the other domains.

Furthermore, we observed a complete absence of models analyzing the M2H trust, namely, the human reasoning process about how to appear trustworthy toward an artificial entity acting as trustor. This can be traced back to a lower interest in this area in such models or to the scarce diffusion of these scenarios. Remarkably, M2H trustworthiness is captured in the HMI field.

It is worth underlining, as a limitation, the presence of H2H trustworthiness scenarios in MAS. Here, the device is not considered as a trustee, but just as a simple instrument/intermediary managed by the human trustor with respect to a human trustee.

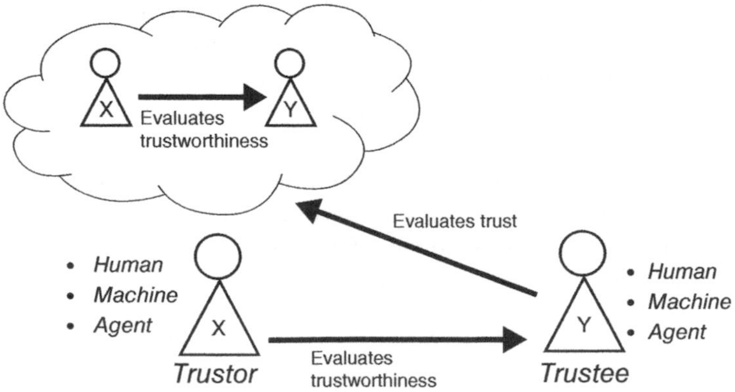


**Figure 19.1** Trust relationships and actors involved.

**Table 19.1** Considered perspective, as regards the trust relationship.

| Relationship – perspective | Contributions |
|---|---|
| M2M – trustworthiness | ($\mathcal{I}$): [1, 2, 5, 7, 12, 18, 35] |
| | ($\mathcal{M}$): [29] |
| H2M – trustworthiness | ($\mathcal{I}$): [6] |
| | ($\mathcal{M}$): [15, 29] |
| H2M – trust | ($\mathcal{I}$): [10] |
| | ($\mathcal{H}$): [8, 9, 17, 21, 30, 37] |
| H2H – trustworthiness | ($\mathcal{M}$): [31, 39] |
| M2H – trustworthiness | ($\mathcal{H}$): [34] |
| A2A – trustworthiness | ($\mathcal{M}$): [11, 12] |

Besides these considerations, we would also like to underline that even the trustee could assess the trustworthiness of the trustor (effectively repeating the A2A scheme in the opposite direction). This is, for example the case of [36], which propose a bidirectional model of trust for the Social Internet of Things, in which the trustee also assesses whether the trustor is trustworthy, deciding on the basis of this whether to collaborate with it or not. Such a characteristic is in line with the concept of "networks of dependence" introduced in Section 19.1.

### 19.4.4 Approaches to Model Trust

Therefore, we evaluated the approach exploited to model trust. In particular, we classified the contributions into three categories: *statistical/probabilistic*, *cognitive-oriented*, and *pseudo-cognitive*.

The category *statistical/probabilistic* includes models that are mainly based on metrics relating to agent performance, quantitative assessments of previous interactional experiences (without any reference to the cognitive mediations of these assessments).

On the contrary, *cognitive-oriented* models are based on mental attribution (explicit mental representations), such as belief, goals, and other motivational representations. In this case, trust is the result of the composition of these basic ingredients that account for a composite mental architecture and of the processes that derive from it.

At last, we classified as *pseudo-cognitive* those works that make an attempt at cognitive modeling, while being concretely implemented as data based. We report in Table 19.2 the classification of the contributions:

Most of the cognitive models fall into the HMI domain, while most of the statistical/probabilistic ones belong to the IoT domain. This result can be traced back to the characteristics of these domains and the use they make of trust. As previously seen in Table 19.1, the HMI domain usually deals with H2M trust models in one-to-one relationships. In these cases, the device acting as trustee must evaluate how much the trustor trusts it and/or what to do to stimulate such trust. Within this framework, it is essential to refer to cognitive models. On the other hand, as previously mentioned, in the IoT domain, the interaction models did not initially include trust, but this was introduced at a later time. The reference to simpler models could be a symptom of an incomplete maturation of the concept of trust in this sector.

Regrettably, some contributions would have the possibility of articulating trust in cognitive terms, given that they deal with situation in which even the trustee is cognitive, but they limit the analysis

**Table 19.2** Classification of approaches to modeling trust.

| Approach | Contributions |
|---|---|
| *Cognitive-oriented* | ($\mathcal{I}$): [10] |
| | ($\mathcal{M}$): [11, 39] |
| | ($\mathcal{H}$): [8, 9, 30, 34] |
| *Pseudo-cognitive* | ($\mathcal{I}$): [2] |
| | ($\mathcal{H}$): [37] |
| *Statistical/probabilistic* | ($\mathcal{I}$): [1, 5–7, 12, 18, 35] |
| | ($\mathcal{M}$): [15, 22, 29, 31] |
| | ($\mathcal{H}$): [17, 21] |

to performance-based dimensions. Conversely, some contributions try to forcibly grasp cognitive aspects, relying however solely on data related to performance or competence. This is the case, for instance, of some works in the IoT field, which make a misleading attempt to attribute intentionality to devices evidently unstructured in order to correspond to characteristics of this type.

### 19.4.5 Sources of Trust

A further articulation of trust models concerns the ways in which information relevant to trust is found: direct experience, reputation/recommendation, and mechanisms of generalization of knowledge (groups, categories, and stereotypes). Table 19.3 takes into account this characterization. In MAS and IoT, given the specific domain characteristics (high number of devices, dynamic environment, tasks requiring the collaboration of many devices, limited computational, and energy capabilities), the role of direct experience is strongly reduced. The need to evaluate the largest number of entities elicits the widespread use of information channels allowing for knowledge-sharing and generalization. This does not apply to HMI, which refers only to direct experience.

### 19.4.6 Different Computational Models of Trust

Of course, the computational models differ on the specific trust *dimensions* they consider. Tables 19.4–19.6 highlight the dimensions used in the analyzed works for the IoT, MAS, and HMI domains, respectively.

**Table 19.3** Trust information source (D = direct experience; R = recommendation, reputation; C = categorization, groups, stereotype).

| Source | Contributions |
|---|---|
| D | ($\mathcal{I}$): [10, 35] |
| | ($\mathcal{H}$): [8, 9, 17, 21, 30, 34, 37] |
| D-R | ($\mathcal{I}$): [2, 5, 7] |
| | ($\mathcal{M}$): [15, 29, 39] |
| D-R-C | ($\mathcal{I}$): [1, 6, 12, 18] |
| | ($\mathcal{M}$): [11, 22, 31] |

**Table 19.4** Trust dimensions in IoT.

| Contribution | Dimensions | Willingness | Socio-cognitive dimensions |
|---|---|---|---|
| Ba-hutair et al. [1] | Owner perspective (social relations, locality attributes), device perspective (reputation), service perspective (reliability), perspective significance, confidence | | |
| Bao and Chen [2] | Honesty, cooperativeness, community-interest | Honesty, cooperativeness | Honesty, cooperativeness |
| Chen et al. [5] | Domain attributes (packet forwarding ration etc.) | Semantically inconsistent | |
| Chen et al. [6] | User satisfaction, friendship, social contact, community of interest | Indistinguishable from competence | |
| Chen et al. [7] | Performance | It identifies fault and malicious behaviors | Willingness |
| Falcone and Sapienza [10] | Efficiency, autonomy, control (feedback/explainability, intervention) | Positive willingness taken for granted | Autonomy, control (feedback/explainability, intervention) |
| Fortino et al. [12] | Reliability, distance, helpfulness | Indistinguishable from competence | |
| Jayasinghe et al. [18] | Knowledge (cowork, colocation, cooperativeness, frequency, duration, reward, mutuality, centrality, community of interest), experience | Cooperativeness | Cooperativeness |
| Wang et al. [35] | Data collection behavior, communication behavior | Semantically inconsistent | |

**Table 19.5** Trust dimensions in MAS.

| Contribution | Dimensions | Willingness | Sociocognitive dimensions |
|---|---|---|---|
| Falcone et al. [11] | Competence, willingness, certainty about the belief, certainty about the source, and plausibility | Willingness | Willingness, certainty about the belief, certainty about the source, and plausibility |
| Guo et al. [15] | Competence | | |
| Liu et al. [22] | Performance | | |
| Messina et al. [29] | Reliability | Indistinguishable from competence | |
| Ruan et al. [31] | Impression, confidence | Indistinguishable from competence | |
| Zhong et al. [39] | Competence, integrity, context | Integrity | Integrity |

**Table 19.6** Trust dimensions in HMI.

| Contribution | Dimensions | Willingness | Socio-cognitive dimensions |
|---|---|---|---|
| Chen et al. [8] | Performance | The robot may intentionally change its performance to modulate human trust | The robot may intentionally change its performance to modulate human trust |
| Edmonds et al. [9] | Competence, explainability | Explainability | Explainability |
| Hu et al. [17] | Performance, cumulative trust, expectation bias, nationality, gender | | Expectation bias |
| Lee et al. [21] | Non verbal behaviors | | |
| Nikolaidis et al. [30] | Performance, adaptability | Adaptability | Adaptability |
| Vinanzi et al. [34] | Human action, human belief | Maliciousness | Human belief, maliciousness |
| Xu and Dudek [37] | Competence, intervention, direct feedback | Positive willingness taken for granted | Adaptability |

It is worth underlining that trust should not be reduced to an epistemic representation, (prevision; subjective probability; strength of the belief about performance; etc.). Indeed, the core of trust can be divided into its two fundamental dimensions: competence and willingness. Competence models skills and the actual capacity of the trustee, while willingness accounts for intentional aspect, disposition, honesty, etc. Additionally, the trustee may possess cognitive and social interaction skills (theory of mind). Therefore, although the specific dimensions vary according to the application domain, it is important to understand that they always refer to these aforementioned components of trust.

## 19.5 Future Research Challenges

The development of AI is providing systems that are widely evolved in their operational and collaborative capabilities and, at the same time, significantly autonomous in their operation. These features, in order to be fully utilized, will require the need for trustworthy interoperability between the various components, be they artificial or human systems. This leads to a growing demand for implementable and realistic models of the attitude of trust. Since humans are also involved in this interaction between mixed systems (either in the potential role of trustor or trustee), it is all the more important to standardize trust/trustworthiness models to those that have always been in vogue in human–human collaboration. In this regard, a number of perspectives can be indicated for future developments.

A first consideration arises from the fact that trust is always oriented toward obtaining a "task" on the part of the trustor. Therefore, it is important to consider the task, even in and abstract or in the affective dimension. Moreover, it should also be properly identified and separated from the "context" in which it has to be realized (context that can condition meaning and perspective of the task).

It is also important to underline that trust trivially corresponds to the evaluation of the trustworthiness of the trustee, only if we refer to the "perceived" evaluation by the trustor rather than the "objective" evaluation of the trustworthiness. But trust is not just a state of mind (with the consequent cognitive evaluation) but also an action (the practical action of trusting and the relationship that arises from it). Then, in this case, the trust must take into account other factors that lead to action such as the acceptance of any risk of fail, and so on. Properly modeling this trust/trustworthiness relationship can be of paramount importance.

As a third point, given the growing role that machine learning is taking on, it is pivotal to consider the possible risks of distorting the mechanisms for acquiring trust, which are not always trivially replaceable with learning strategies: in particular, inferences based on analogical reasoning, by category/class/group, or even reasoning on transitivity phenomena.

The fourth point concerns explainability: as the complexity of artificial systems (and their autonomy) grows, it will increasingly represent a precondition for trusting these systems. However, to really be effective and understandable, it will have to develop in the social-cognitive direction. In fact, the artificial system must be able to provide explanations (spontaneously or upon request) in terms of the goals it wants to achieve and how it intends (intended to) achieve them. Which standards/values these explanations refer to. What priorities did it want to pursue, and so on. In practice, the system should pursue an action model (and consequent explanation) based on the interpretation of the interlocutor's mind (mind-oriented). This is human "understanding/explaining" of behavior.

Last but not least, an important reflection on the future of these systems that involve trust, that of users toward them, must focus on a concept of transparency at a deeper level, That is, on the awareness by users of the real interests and values that are being pursued (and in favor of whom) when using these systems. To avoid manipulation and deception, it will be necessary that also the scientific community operating in this sector considers to address this problem. A problem of a substantially ethical nature.

## References


1 Ba-hutair, M.N., Bouguettaya, A., and Neiat, A.G. (2021). Multi-perspective trust management framework for crowdsourced iot services. *IEEE Transactions on Services Computing* 15 (4): 2396–2409.

2 Bao, F. and Chen, I.-R. (2012). Dynamic trust management for Internet of Things applications. *Proceedings of the 2012 International Workshop on Self-Aware Internet of Things*, 1–6.

3 Castelfranchi, C. and Falcone, R. (1998). Principles of trust for MAS: cognitive anatomy, social importance, and quantification. *Proceedings International Conference on Multi Agent Systems (Cat. No. 98EX160)*, 72–79. IEEE.

4 Castelfranchi, C. and Falcone, R. (2010). *Trust Theory: A Socio-Cognitive and Computational Model*, vol. 18. Wiley.

5 Chen, D., Chang, G., Sun, D. et al. (2011). TRM-IoT: A trust management model based on fuzzy reputation for Internet of Things. *Computer Science and Information Systems* 8 (4): 1207–1228.

6 Chen, R., Guo, J., and Bao, F. (2014). Trust management for SOA-based IoT and its application to service composition. *IEEE Transactions on Services Computing* 9 (3): 482–495.

7 Chen, J., Tian, Z., Cui, X. et al. (2019). Trust architecture and reputation evaluation for Internet of Things. *Journal of Ambient Intelligence and Humanized Computing* 10 (8): 3099–3107.

**8** Chen, M., Nikolaidis, S., Soh, H. et al. (2020). Trust-aware decision making for human–robot collaboration: model learning and planning. *ACM Transactions on Human–Robot Interaction (THRI)* 9 (2): 1–23.

**9** Edmonds, M., Gao, F., Liu, H. et al. (2019). A tale of two explanations: enhancing human trust by explaining robot behavior. *Science Robotics* 4 (37): https://doi.org/10.1126/scirobotics.aay4663.

**10** Falcone, R. and Sapienza, A. (2018). On the users' acceptance of IoT systems: a theoretical approach. *Information* 9 (3): 53.

**11** Falcone, R., Sapienza, A., and Castelfranchi, C. (2015). The relevance of categories for trusting information sources. *ACM Transactions on Internet Technology (TOIT)* 15 (4): 1–21.

**12** Fortino, G., Messina, F., Rosaci, D., and Sarné, G.M.L. (2018). Using trust and local reputation for group formation in the cloud of things. *Future Generation Computer Systems* 89: 804–815.

**13** Gambetta, D. (1988). *Trust: Making and Breaking Cooperative Relations*, 213–238. Oxford: Basil Blackwell.

**14** Golbeck, J.A. (2005). Computing and applying trust in web-based social networks, Doctoral thesis. College Park, MD: University of Maryland.

**15** Guo, G., Zhang, J., and Yorke-Smith, N. (2016). A novel recommendation model regularized with user trust and item ratings. *IEEE Transactions on Knowledge and Data Engineering* 28 (7): 1607–1620.

**16** Hardin, R. (2002). *Trust and Trustworthiness*. Russell Sage Foundation.

**17** Hu, W.-L., Akash, K., Reid, T., and Jain, N. (2018). Computational modeling of the dynamics of human trust during human–machine interactions. *IEEE Transactions on Human–Machine Systems* 49 (6): 485–497.

**18** Jayasinghe, U., Lee, G.M., Um, T.-W., and Shi, Q. (2018). Machine learning based trust computational model for IoT services. *IEEE Transactions on Sustainable Computing* 4 (1): 39–52.

**19** Jonker, C.M. and Treur, J. (1999). Formal analysis of models for the dynamics of trust based on experiences. *European workshop on modeling autonomous agents in a multi-agent world*, 221–231. Springer.

**20** Josang, A., Hayward, R., and Pope, S. (2006). Trust network analysis with subjective logic. *Conference Proceedings of the 29th Australasian Computer Science Conference (ACSW 2006)*, 85–94. Australian Computer Society.

**21** Lee, J.J., Knox, B., Baumann, J. et al. (2013). Computationally modeling interpersonal trust. *Frontiers in Psychology* 4: 893.

**22** Liu, X., Datta, A., and Rzadca, K. (2013). Trust beyond reputation: a computational trust model based on stereotypes. *Electronic Commerce Research and Applications* 12 (1): 24–39.

**23** Locke, J. (1991). *A Letter Concerning Toleration*. New York: Routledge.

**24** Luhmann, N. (1968). Vertrauen: ein mechanismus der reduktion sozialer komplexität.

**25** Marsh, S.P. (1994). Formalising trust as a computational concept.

**26** Massa, P. and Avesani, P. (2007). Trust-aware recommender systems. *Proceedings of the 2007 ACM Conference on Recommender Systems*, 17–24.

**27** Mayer, R.C., Davis, J.H., and Schoorman, F.D. (1995). An integrative model of organizational trust. *Academy of Management Review* 20 (3): 709–734.

**28** McKnight, D.H. and Chervany, N.L. (2001). Conceptualizing trust: a typology and e-commerce customer relationships model. *Proceedings of the 34th Annual Hawaii International Conference on System Sciences*, 10. IEEE.

**29** Messina, F., Pappalardo, G., Rosaci, D. et al. (2016). A trust-aware, self-organizing system for large-scale federations of utility computing infrastructures. *Future Generation Computer Systems* 56: 77–94.

**30** Nikolaidis, S., Kuznetsov, A., Hsu, D., and Srinivasa, S. (2016). Formalizing human–robot mutual adaptation: a bounded memory model. *2016 11th ACM/IEEE International Conference on Human–Robot Interaction (HRI)*, 75–82. IEEE.

**31** Ruan, Y., Zhang, P., Alfantoukh, L., and Durresi, A. (2017). Measurement theory-based trust management framework for online social communities. *ACM Transactions on Internet Technology (TOIT)* 17 (2): 1–24.

**32** Sabater, J. and Sierra, C. (2001). REGRET: Reputation in gregarious societies. *Proceedings of the 5th International Conference on Autonomous Agents*, 194–195.

**33** Teacy, W.T.L., Patel, J., Jennings, N.R., and Luck, M. (2006). TRAVOS: Trust and reputation in the context of inaccurate information sources. *Autonomous Agents and Multi-Agent Systems* 12 (2): 183–198.

**34** Vinanzi, S., Patacchiola, M., Chella, A., and Cangelosi, A. (2019). Would a robot trust you? Developmental robotics model of trust and theory of mind. *Philosophical Transactions of the Royal Society B* 374 (1771): 20180032.

**35** Wang, T., Luo, H., Jia, W. et al. (2019). MTES: An intelligent trust evaluation scheme in sensor-cloud-enabled industrial Internet of Things. *IEEE Transactions on Industrial Informatics* 16 (3): 2054–2062.

**36** Wei, L., Yang, Y., Wu, J. et al. (2022). A bidirectional trust model for service delegation in social Internet of Things. *Future Internet* 14 (5): 135.

**37** Xu, A. and Dudek, G. (2015). OPTIMo: Online probabilistic trust inference model for asymmetric human–robot collaborations. *2015 10th ACM/IEEE International Conference on Human–Robot Interaction (HRI)*, 221–228. IEEE.

**38** Yu, B. and Singh, M.P. (2002). An evidential model of distributed reputation management. *Proceedings of the 1st International Joint Conference on Autonomous Agents and Multiagent Systems: Part 1*, 294–301.

**39** Zhong, Y., Bhargava, B., Lu, Y., and Angin, P. (2014). A computational dynamic trust model for user authorization. *IEEE Transactions on Dependable and Secure Computing* 12 (1): 1–15.

# 20

## Decoding Humans' and Virtual Agents' Emotional Expressions

*Terry Amorese*[1], *Gennaro Cordasco*[1], *Marialucia Cuciniello*[1], *Olga Shevaleva*[1], *Stefano Marrone*[1], *Carl Vogel*[2], *and Anna Esposito*[1]

[1] *Department of Psychology, Università della Campania "L. Vanvitelli", Caserta, Italy*
[2] *Trinity Centre for Computing and Language Studies, School of Computer Science and Statistics, Trinity College Dublin, The University of Dublin, Dublin, Ireland*

## 20.1 Introduction

Conversational technologies, such as Virtual Agents, are able to improve users' mental well-being and lifestyle, providing assistance and companionship. Key aspects of humans' interactional exchange, and consequently of human–machine interaction, are emotions. The design of a virtual assistant should consider its ability to convey emotional expressions. In order to smooth the interaction between humans and assistive technologies, it is necessary to furnish them with the ability to recognize and react appropriately to human emotions and with the ability to appropriately express emotions, considering that these skills impact user attitudes and behavior positively [9]. Numerous are the benefits and possible applications of these conversational technologies within the psychological field, especially when associated with specific psychotherapeutic technique [13]. For instance, it is possible to exploit them as diagnostic tools for monitoring and treating mental ill symptoms, decreasing clinicians' workload [15], to encourage users adopting healthy behaviors [7], to detect the presence of depressive symptoms monitoring the conversation with the user [4], or as mental health tools with the aim of providing support to people leaving with schizophrenia [10], phobias [3], depression [18], and autism [2]. Seniors could benefit from assistive technologies as well, since these systems are able to increase their independence, provide assistance, entertainment, company, and in general improve user's quality of life by promoting a healthy and active aging. Human capacities in interpreting and decoding emotions as well as in emotional expression are as crucial as the abilities of artificial agents. However, emotion recognition processes are complex and might be anticipated to have interactions with properties of the emotion decoder and of the emoting entity: the age or the gender of the person who must decode emotional expressions may matter, and also features of the face to be interpreted (for example, age, gender, typology) may influence judgments. For this reason, the present investigation aims at assessing these effects on participants' recognition scores of facial emotional expressions: (i) participant's age and gender, decoding static and dynamic facial emotional expressions; (ii) age and gender of the entity expressing an emotion, according to its type as static or dynamic; (iii) emotional expression by entities that are synthetic, virtual agents, or human beings.

*Handbook of Human-Machine Systems*, First Edition. Edited by Giancarlo Fortino, David Kaber, Andreas Nürnberger, and David Mendonça.

## 20.2 Related Work

As already highlighted, emotion recognition processes often interact both with properties of the emotion decoder and of the emoting entity. In this section, the previous studies investigating the same factor of interest for our work will be briefly reported (and summarized in Table 20.1). Differences between men and women in emotion interpretation are a widely investigated issue;

**Table 20.1** Comparison table of related work.

| Authors and year | Investigated factor influencing emotion decoding | Type of task | Main findings |
|---|---|---|---|
| Rigon et al. [20] | Participants' gender | Recognition of static and dynamic facial expressions | Females significantly surpassed males, in particular within the dynamic task |
| Hoffmann et al. [8] | Participants' gender | Recognition of static emotional expressions with distinct levels of intensity | Females more accurate than males in recognizing subtle facial displays of emotions |
| Lambrecht et al. [14] | Participants' gender | Recognition of dynamic emotional expressions with different sensory modalities (auditory, visual, audio-visual) | Females were more accurate than males only in recognition of emotional prosody |
| Man and Hills [16] | Gender of the face | Eye-tracking analysis indicated of scanning behaviors when processing own- and other-gender faces | Participants' longer fixations when viewing own-gender faces |
| Wolff et al. [21] | Gender of the face | Event-related potentials (ERP) measurement during a recognition memory experiment | Participants remembered faces of their respective own gender more accurately compared with other-gender faces |
| Isaacowitz et al. [11] | Participants' age | Recognition task of lexical stimuli and facial expressions | Seniors less accurate at identifying emotions than young adults |
| Richter et al. [19] | Participants' age | Recognition of dynamic facial expressions | Young participants more accurate at identifying emotions than older adults |
| Anastasi, and Rhodes [1] | Age of the face | Recognition of static emotional expressions | Participants better decoded faces of their respective age compared with differently aged faces |
| Joyal et al. [12] | Typology of face (human vs. synthetic) | Recognition of dynamic facial expressions conveyed by humans and virtual agents | Absence of differences in the recognition of emotions expressed by virtual agents and humans |
| Paetzel et al. [17] | Typology of face (human vs. synthetic) | Recognition of dynamic facial expressions conveyed ab agent characterized by different degrees of embodiment | Human emotional expressions better decoded than synthetic ones |

some studies highlight greater ability to accurately recognize emotion expression among women than among men [20]. Other studies have shown that the gender effect may be mediated by other factors such as stimulus intensity, highlighting that greater accuracy among women applies primarily to subtle expression of emotion [8]. Former research demonstrated the influence of the modality of stimulus presentation and the sensory channel involved: in particular, women demonstrate greater accuracy than men in emotional prosody interpretation [14]. Concerning the influence of the facial expression decoder's gender, some have proposed an effect known as "Own Gender Bias" [21], suggesting that people are quicker and more accurate in interpreting emotion expression of faces with their own gender compared to faces and emotion expression in faces of the other gender [16]. Aging, as well, has effects on emotion interpretation abilities and seniors' tendency to show a decreased ability to accurately interpret specific emotions is also a widely investigated topic [11, 19]. Some have suggested that the "Own Age Bias" is a robust effect in which people recognize more accurately facial expressions and emotions expressed by age-peers than those expressed by people of distinct age groups [1].

An ulterior variable affecting face recognition is the typology of face, human or artificial (virtual agent), conveying the emotional expression. Studies conducted to so far reached discordant results, bringing out two main trends: on the one hand is supported the absence of significant differences in the recognition of emotions expressed by virtual agents and humans [12], on the other hand studies highlighted that people better recognize human emotional expressions than synthetic ones [17].

## 20.3 Materials and Methodology

### 20.3.1 Participants

Following authorization of the project design by the research ethics committee of the Department of Psychology at the Università degli Studi della Campania "Luigi Vanvitelli" (protocol number 25/2017), 270 healthy participants were recruited, and each allocated to one of six groups (as described in Table 20.2). The "synthetic decoding task" relied upon virtual agents to express

**Table 20.2** Description of participants allocated to each experimental condition.

| Participants features | | | |
|---|---|---|---|
| | Age | | |
| Task | Young | Middle-age | Senior |
| Synthetic decoding | 25F/20M: $n = 45$<br>min age: 22 yr<br>max age: 35 yr<br>mean age: 27.67<br>SD: 2.75 | 23F/22M: $n = 45$<br>min age: 40 yr<br>max age: 55 yr<br>mean age: 49.76<br>SD: 3.95 | 25F/20M: $n = 45$<br>min age: 65 yr<br>mean age: 66 yr<br>SD: 1.41 |
| Naturalistic decoding | 23F/22M: $n = 45$<br>min age: 22 yr<br>max age: 35 yr<br>mean age: 30<br>SD: 2.82 | 25F/20M: $n = 45$<br>min age: 40 yr<br>max age: 55 yr<br>mean age: 50.22<br>SD: 4.73 | 23F/22M: $n = 45$<br>min age: 65 yr<br>mean age: 72.04 yr<br>SD: 5.50 |

emotions, while the "naturalistic decoding task" used pictures and videos of humans in popular movies expressing emotions (derived from the AFEW and SFEW databases). Participants were involved using online social networks and e-mails; they voluntarily joined the study and read and agreed to an informed consent formulated according to the Italian and European laws about privacy and data protection.

### 20.3.2 Stimuli

The synthetic decoding task involved participants being shown pictures and video segments of female and male virtual agents with varying age (young, middle-aged, and old) expressing disgust, anger, sadness, fear, happiness, surprise, and neutrality. In collaboration with Paphus Solutions Inc., the software system Daz3D was used to develop the agents; this allows emotion pose pre-sets. For each emotion, the expression morph from Daz3D was set with 100% magnitude. A video clip for each agent was developed, then to get every agent talk, audio files were extracted from video clips of the AFEW database [5], and embed within each agent video clip. Experts in the study of emotional interaction and human–machine communication provided qualitative assessment of each agent and emotion; stimulus acceptance required unanimity. A total of 90 virtual agents were selected. Six agents were used within the trial session (three static pictures and three dynamic videos), and the remaining 84 (42 static images and 42 dynamic) in the experimental session of this study.

The naturalistic task involved participants being shown pictures and video clips depicting female and male actors with varying age (young, middle-aged, and older) expressing disgust, anger, sadness, fear, happiness, surprise, and neutrality. Pictures were taken from the Static Facial Expressions in the Wild (SFEW) database and videos, from the Acted Facial Expressions in the Wild (AFEW) database [6]. The AFEW dataset contains dynamic facial expressions extracted from movies approximating naturalistic environments with focus on emotional faces with varied head poses. The age of faces ranges from 1 to 70 years. Static images in SFEW are selected frames of AFEW videos. SFEW contains 700 emotional faces expressing anger, disgust, fear, happiness, sadness, surprise, and neutrality. Emotion category labels were assigned by two annotators, independently. Our experiment uses 3 static pictures and 3 dynamic video clips for the trial session, and 42 static faces and 42 dynamic videos distributed across the three age groups and seven emotion categories in the experimental session. To obtain an equal number of male and female, seven additional face stimuli were used: (i) disgust expressed by one older female and one young male face, (ii) sadness expressed by one older female face, (iii) neutrality expressed by one older female face, (iv) fear expressed by two female faces, one middle-aged and the other, older, (v) surprise expressed by one older female. These stimuli were obtained from pictures available on the Internet.

Figure 20.1 shows representative images used in the synthetic and the naturalistic tasks.

### 20.3.3 Tools and Procedures

The naturalistic and the synthetic experiments were constructed using Lab.js, a free, open, online experiment development system. The experiments were exported to Just Another Tool for Online Studies (JATOS), a free server for hosting online experiments. This system supports generation of URLS that participants can use to access the experiment and which researchers may use to collect the results. Each volunteer who agreed to participate in the research was provided with an appropriate URL to access using a laptop. On accessing the URL, participants were invited to consent to a personal data processing form. Information about their degree of experience with

**Figure 20.1** Representative stimuli of the synthetic (on the top) and the naturalistic (below) decoding tasks.

technology was collected from consenting participants. They were provided through the system with the instructions for the experiment, followed by a trial session (classification of 3 static images and 3 videos) and by an experimental session (42 static images and 42 videos). Stimuli were randomized without replacement in both the trial and experimental phases. Participants applied a single emotion label to each stimulus; the options were disgust, anger, sadness, fear, happiness, surprise, neutrality, or "other." The last label was for use when participants felt none of the fixed choices were appropriate. Because the images were selected with a strong association to emotion categories, we interpret the selection of "other" as an "incorrect" response indicating that the participant was not able to correctly decode the portrayed emotion.

## 20.4 Descriptive Statistics

In the following tables we report, for both the synthetic and naturalistic experiment, the aggregated decoding accuracy as a percentage, with reference to the emotion categories presented to the participant aged groups (Tables 20.3 and 20.4). In addition, Table 20.5 provides confusion matrices of decoding accuracy as a percentage, for each emotion category.

**Table 20.3** Decoding accuracy (in %) for each differently aged group and for each emotional category.

| | Decoding accuracy of *synthetic* faces in % | | | | | | |
|---|---|---|---|---|---|---|---|
| | **Disgust** | **Anger** | **Sadness** | **Fear** | **Happiness** | **Surprise** | **Neutrality** |
| Young | 41.1 | 82.6 | 56.1 | 34.8 | 72.2 | 50.6 | 66.3 |
| Middle Aged | 42 | 73.3 | 46.5 | 26.1 | 63 | 37.8 | 47 |
| Seniors | 29.4 | 67.4 | 38.5 | 16.5 | 69.6 | 25.7 | 49.8 |

**Table 20.4** Decoding accuracy (in %) for each differently aged group and for each emotional category.

| | Decoding accuracy of *naturalistic* faces in % | | | | | | |
|---|---|---|---|---|---|---|---|
| | **Disgust** | **Anger** | **Sadness** | **Fear** | **Happiness** | **Surprise** | **Neutrality** |
| Young | 25.7 | 66.9 | 53.1 | 38.9 | 54.1 | 43.5 | 43.3 |
| Middle Aged | 23.9 | 73 | 51.7 | 33 | 64.1 | 49.1 | 37.9 |
| Seniors | 24.3 | 73.7 | 51.7 | 38.3 | 69.1 | 30.4 | 39.3 |

**Table 20.5** Confusion matrices of participants decoding accuracy (in %) for each emotional category.

| | **Disgust** | **Anger** | **Sadness** | **Fear** | **Happiness** | **Surprise** | **Neutrality** | **Other Emotion** |
|---|---|---|---|---|---|---|---|---|
| | | | | *Synthetic (%)* | | | | |
| Disgust | 37.5 | 46.3 | 6.5 | 3 | 0 | 0.9 | 3 | 2.8 |
| Anger | 12.4 | 74.1 | 3.7 | 3.8 | 0.4 | 2.4 | 1.7 | 1.4 |
| Sadness | 11.8 | 5.7 | 46.9 | 5.7 | 1.1 | 4.3 | 16.7 | 7.8 |
| Fear | 4.4 | 4.3 | 12.6 | 25.9 | 5.6 | 29.6 | 10.4 | 7.1 |
| Happiness | 0.7 | 0.7 | 0.7 | 0.7 | 68.3 | 5.9 | 16.2 | 6.8 |
| Surprise | 5 | 3.2 | 15.4 | 14.7 | 2.8 | 37.6 | 15.3 | 5.9 |
| Neutral | 3.2 | 4.6 | 13 | 2.2 | 3.5 | 7.8 | 54.3 | 11.4 |
| | | | | *Naturalistic (%)* | | | | |
| Disgust | 24.6 | 20.1 | 13.1 | 3.1 | 3.9 | 4.8 | 14.6 | 15.6 |
| Anger | 8.3 | 70.9 | 4.7 | 3.1 | 0.9 | 3.4 | 3 | 5.7 |
| Sadness | 4.2 | 5.4 | 52.2 | 4.9 | 1.5 | 4.6 | 13.8 | 13.4 |
| Fear | 3.4 | 4.2 | 12.5 | 36.7 | 0.6 | 17.1 | 10.1 | 154 |
| Happiness | 1.5 | 2.6 | 3.3 | 2.3 | 62.4 | 6.9 | 8.9 | 12 |
| Surprise | 3.2 | 8 | 7.8 | 15.4 | 6.2 | 41 | 8.1 | 10.1 |
| Neutral | 1.2 | 5.1 | 18.5 | 4 | 7 | 5.6 | 40.1 | 18.4 |

## 20.5 Data Analysis and Results

Hither data are profiled and analyzed.

Data acquired from young, middle-aged, and senior participants who responded to synthetic and naturalistic facial expressions, were analyzed separately for each task with the aim of investigating how age, gender, and the type of stimuli (static vs. dynamic), affected humans' ability to interpret emotional faces and whether there are differences among the three age groups of participants. ANOVA repeated measures analyses were conducted for each emotion category. Participants' age group and gender were studied as between-subjects factors, and age, gender, and type of stimuli as within-subject factors. The significance level $\alpha < 0.05$ was adopted. Bonferroni's post-hoc tests were used to assess differences in means. A further analysis was performed independently from the age, the gender, and the type of the faces. Recognition scores obtained from all stimuli's age, gender, and type were added together for each emotional category. Repeated measures ANOVA were conducted, attending to participants' gender and age groups as between-subject variables, and total decoding scores of the proposed emotional category as within-subject variables. The significance level was, again, $\alpha < 0.05$, with Bonferroni's post-hoc tests to assess differences in means. Results of these analyses are depicted in Tables 20.6 and 20.7, and in Figures 20.2 and 20.3.

Tables 20.6 and 20.7 show, respectively, factors affecting participants' decoding accuracy of synthetic and naturalistic emotional faces (participants' gender and age, and stimuli's age, gender, and typology). Figures 20.2 and 20.3 depict for each emotional category mean recognition scores of emotional expressions of virtual agents (synthetic) and real humans (naturalistic). Means ($Y$-axis)

**Table 20.6** Summary of factors affecting participants' decoding accuracy of synthetic emotional faces.

| | **Effects of participants' gender** | **Effects of participants' age** | **Age of stimuli effect** | **Gender of stimuli effect** | **Type of stimuli effect** |
|---|---|---|---|---|---|
| Disgust | No significant effects | Seniors less accurate with respect to young and middle aged | Old faces more accurately decoded than young and middle-aged ones | Female faces more accurately decoded | Dynamic faces more accurately decoded than static ones |
| Anger | No significant effects | Seniors less accurate with respect to young | Old faces less accurately decoded than young and middle-aged ones | Male faces more accurately decoded than female ones | No significant effects |
| Sadness | No significant effects | Seniors less accurate with respect to young | Young faces are worse decoded compared to middle-aged and old ones | No significant effects | Dynamic faces better recognized compared to static ones |
| Fear | No significant effects | Seniors less accurate with respect to young and middle-aged | Middle-aged faces more accurately decoded than young and old ones | Female faces more accurately decoded | Dynamic faces more accurately decoded compared to static ones |
| Happiness | No significant effects | No significant effects | Middle-aged faces more accurately decoded with respect to young and old ones | Female faces more accurately decoded | No significant effects |
| Surprise | No significant effects | Seniors less accurate with respect to young and middle-aged | Old faces less accurately decoded than young and middle-aged ones | Female faces more accurately decoded | Static faces more accurately decoded than dynamic ones |
| Neutrality | Males provide higher accuracy compared to females | Young less accurate with respect to middle-aged and seniors | Old faces less accurately decoded than young and middle-aged ones | Male faces more accurately decoded compared to female ones | Static faces better decoded compared to dynamic ones |

**Table 20.7** Summary of factors affecting participants' decoding accuracy of naturalistic emotional faces.

| | **Effects of participants' gender** | **Effects of participants' age** | **Age of stimuli effect** | **Gender of stimuli effect** | **Type of stimuli effect** |
|---|---|---|---|---|---|
| Disgust | No significant effects | No significant effects | Middle-aged faces better decoded than young and old ones | Female faces more accurately decoded | Static faces better decoded compared to dynamic ones |
| Anger | No significant effects | Seniors more accurate than young | Young faces better decoded than middle-aged and old ones | Female faces more accurately decoded | Dynamic faces more accurately decoded than static ones |
| Sadness | No significant effects | No significant effects | Old faces less accurately decoded compared to young and middle-aged ones | Female faces more accurately decoded | Dynamic faces worse decoded compared to static ones |
| Fear | No significant effects | No significant effects | Old faces less accurately decoded compared to young and middle-aged ones | Female faces more accurately decoded | Dynamic faces better decoded compared to static ones |
| Happiness | No significant effects | Young less accurate than middle-aged and seniors | Young faces worse decoded than middle-aged and old ones | Female faces more accurately decoded | No significant effects |
| Surprise | No significant effects | Seniors less accurate than young and middle-aged | Middle-aged faces worse decoded than young and old ones. | Male faces are better decoded compared to female ones. | Dynamic faces more accurately decoded compared to static ones. |
| Neutrality | No significant effects | No significant effects | Young faces less accurately decoded than middle-aged and old ones | No significant effects | Dynamic faces better decoded compared to static ones |

are shown for each stimulus (old female and male static and dynamic faces, middle-aged female and male static and dynamic faces, young female and male static and dynamic faces) comparing recognition scores of seniors, middle-aged, and young participants. For each chart, the $Y$-axis conveys the mean score (which ranges from 0 to 1 – 0 if the participant did not correctly decode the stimulus and 1 if the participant correctly decoded it). For each figure, the black and white chart, which appears at the bottom-right, provides a summary of the results, aggregating, for each emotional category, the mean scores obtained from all the 12 stimuli (the scoring range, in this case, vary between 0 and 12).

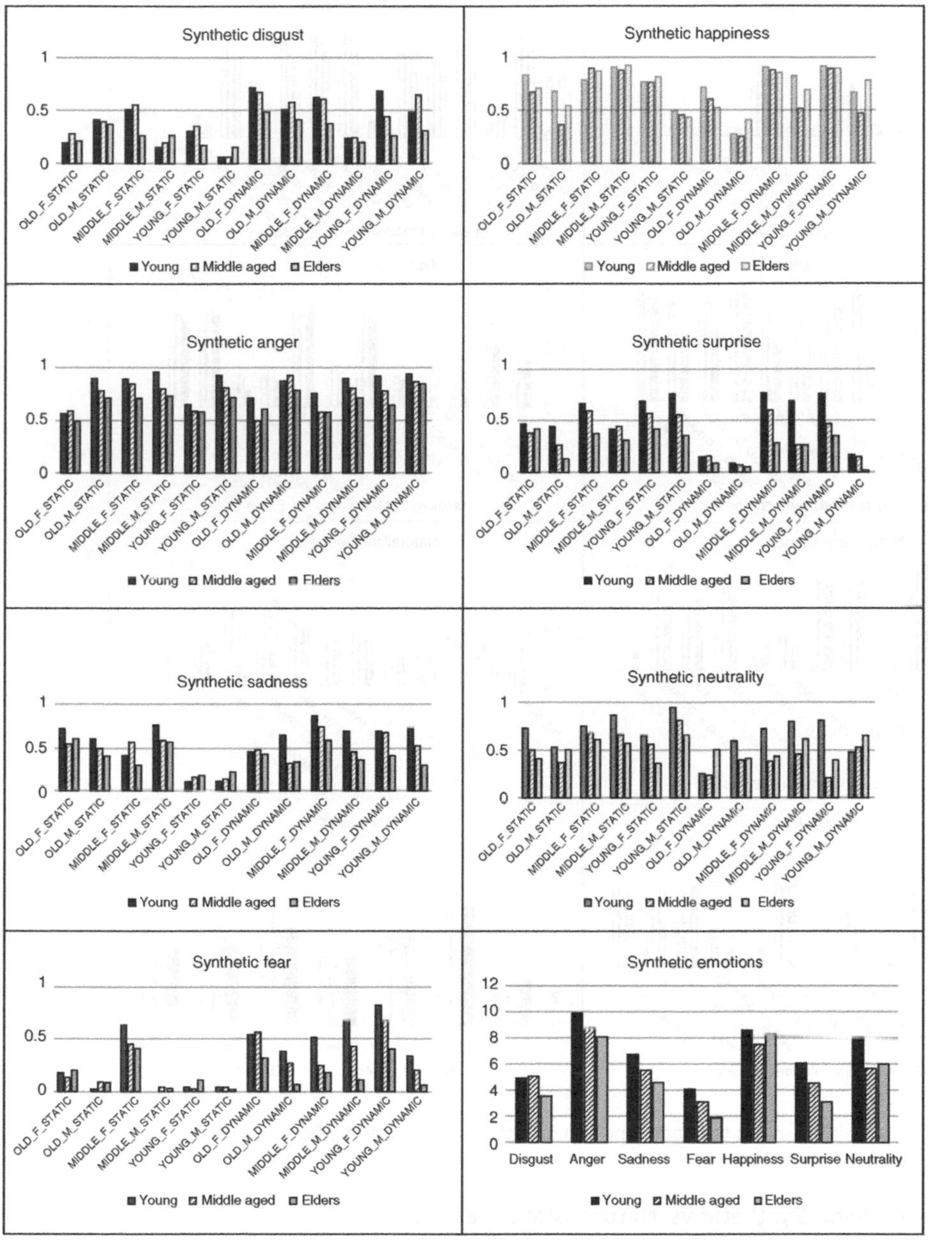


**Figure 20.2** Recognition scores for emotion categories expressed by virtual agents (synthetic); means are showed for each stimulus.

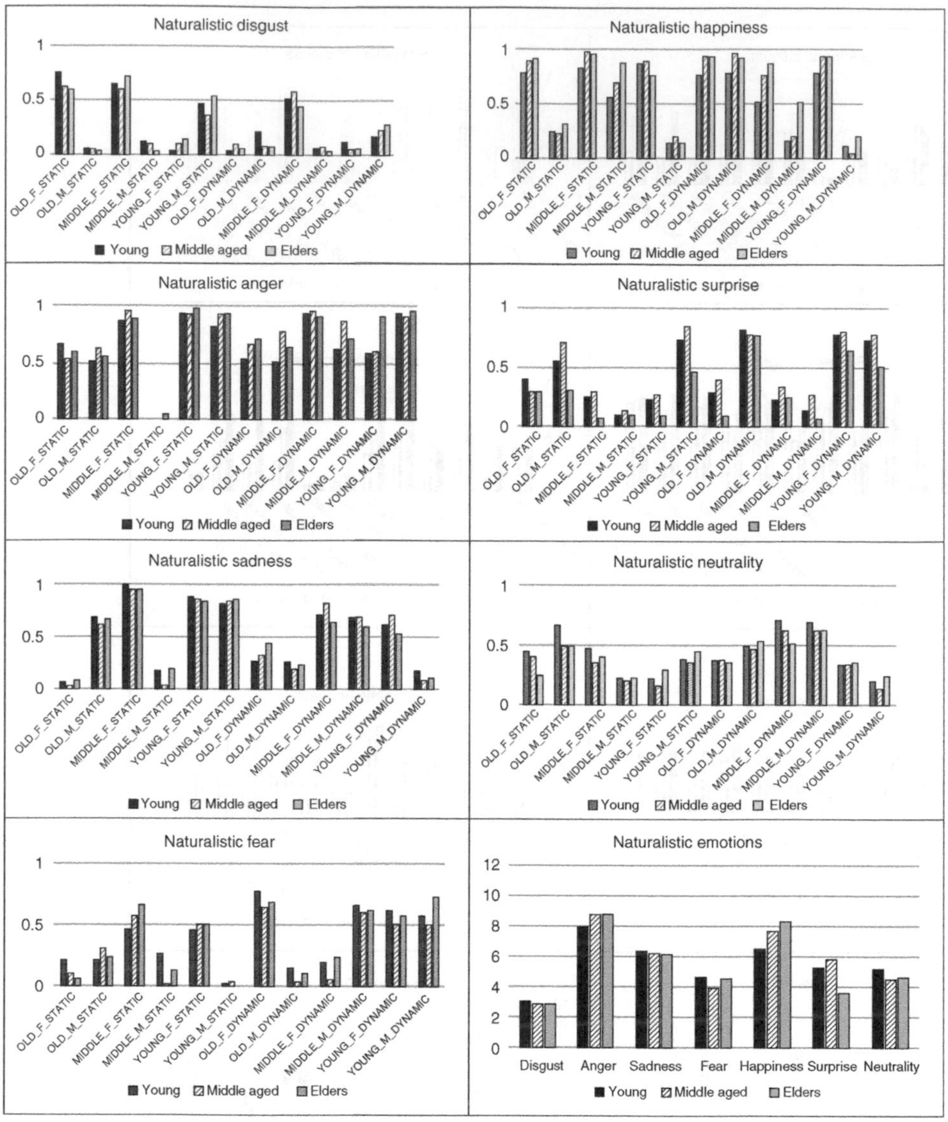


**Figure 20.3** Recognition scores for each emotion categories expressed by human faces (naturalistic); means are showed for each stimulus.

### 20.5.1 Comparison Synthetic vs. Naturalistic Experiment

To evaluate if there are differences in peoples' capacity to interpret synthetic and naturalistic emotional expressions, a further data elaboration was performed. Single analysis was performed for each age group, comparing young, middle-aged, and seniors who saw synthetic emotional expressions with young, middle-aged, and seniors who saw naturalistic emotional expressions, respectively. For each age group, ANOVA repeated measures analyses were conducted for each emotion category considering participants' group (synthetic and naturalistic) and gender as between-subject factors, and age, gender, and stimulus type (static and dynamic) as within-subject factors. The significance level adopted was $\alpha < 0.05$; Bonferroni's post-hoc tests were used to analyze differences in means. Table 20.8 shows main effects from the analysis.

**Table 20.8** Comparisons between synthetic and naturalistic faces for each age group.

| | | Effects of participants' group |
|---|---|---|
| Disgust | Young participants | Synthetic faces more accurately decoded than naturalistic ones |
| | Middle-aged participants | Synthetic faces more accurately decoded than naturalistic ones |
| | Senior participants | No significant effects |
| Anger | Young participants | Synthetic faces more accurately decoded than naturalistic ones |
| | Middle-aged participants | No significant effects |
| | Senior participants | No significant effects |
| Sadness | Young participants | No significant effects |
| | Middle-aged participants | No significant effects |
| | Senior participants | Naturalistic faces more accurately decoded than synthetic ones |
| Fear | Young participants | No significant effects |
| | Middle-aged participants | Naturalistic faces more accurately decoded than synthetic ones |
| | Senior participants | Naturalistic faces more accurately decoded than synthetic ones |
| Happiness | Young participants | No significant effects |
| | Middle-aged participants | No significant effects |
| | Senior participants | No significant effects |
| Surprise | Young participants | Synthetic faces more accurately decoded than naturalistic ones |
| | Middle-aged participants | Naturalistic faces more accurately decoded than synthetic ones |
| | Senior participants | No significant effects |
| Neutrality | Young participants | Synthetic faces more accurately decoded than naturalistic ones |
| | Middle-aged participants | Synthetic faces more accurately decoded than naturalistic ones |
| | Senior participants | Synthetic faces more accurately decoded than naturalistic ones |

## 20.6 Discussion and Conclusions

A study exploring how different participant age groups (young, middle-aged, and seniors) interpret static and dynamic facial emotional expressions conveyed by virtual agents and human beings of the same age group range. Effects of gender of participants and the emotional faces were also investigated factors. Participants completed an emotion recognition task involving emotions expressed by humans and synthetic agents. Target emotion categories were disgust, anger, fear, sadness, happiness, surprise, and neutrality. For both the synthetic and the naturalistic experiments, participants' age and the age, gender, and stimulus type interact with the way people decode expression of emotion, albeit a distinct manner according to the experimental condition (synthetic or naturalistic faces) and the emotional category considered. Concerning the synthetic experiment, namely emotions conveyed by virtual agents, participants' gender affected recognition accuracy of neutral facial expressions, with male participants showing better performances compared to female ones. Participants' age affected results, as well. Data showed that while decoding disgust, anger, sadness, fear, surprise, and neutrality among older participants, on average, demonstrated worse recognition performance compared to participants belonging to younger groups made up of participants aged between 40 and 55 years and those between 22 and 35 years. Even the age of the face expressing emotions had an impact on the study; anger, surprise, and neutrality were less properly decoded when expressed by older faces than by middle-aged and young faces, while disgust on the contrary was recognized better when expressed by older faces. Fear and happiness were better recognized when expressed by middle-aged faces, and sadness was interpreted with less accuracy when displayed on young faces. Concerning the effects of faces' gender, disgust, fear, happiness, and surprise were interpreted with greater accuracy when expressed by female faces. Anger and neutrality were interpreted with greater accuracy when expressed by male faces. Lastly, even the typology of the face (static or dynamic) administered had an impact on study's results, highlighting that disgust, sadness, and fear were interpreted with greater accuracy when presented with dynamic video; surprise and sadness obtained greater accuracy when interpreted through static pictures. Concerning the naturalistic experiment, namely emotions conveyed by human faces, even in this case participants' age affected results. More specifically, data showed that older participants decoded surprise any less compared to the younger groups, while when decoding anger and happiness, older participants demonstrated greater recognition accuracy compared to participants in younger groups. The age of the face conveying emotions had an impact on the study as well; disgust was better decoded when expressed by middle-aged faces, while surprise, if conveyed by middle-aged faces, was less accurately recognized; anger was better decoded when displayed by young faces, while happiness and neutrality, on the contrary, were worse decoded when conveyed by younger faces. Sadness and fear were worse decoded on old faces. As regards as the effects of faces' gender, disgust, anger, sadness, fear, and happiness, were better recognized when expressed by female faces, while surprise was met with greater accuracy when expressed by male faces. Again, the typology of the showed face (static or dynamic) had an impact: anger, surprise, and neutrality were more accurately interpreted when conveyed through dynamic video clips, while disgust and sadness were better recognized when conveyed through static pictures. Interesting information is provided by confusion matrices of participants' decoding percentage accuracy for each category of emotion for both the synthetic and naturalistic experiment. Confusion matrices contain the overall percentages of emotion identification and the percentage of time each emotion was confused with others. This information could be useful to evaluate the quality of the stimuli used, in particular for the synthetic experiment, since the dataset has not been previously validated. For disgust, both synthetic and naturalistic faces were confused mostly with anger, and anger was confused mostly with disgust. As regards as sadness, naturalistic faces were mostly confused with neutrality or identified as other emotion, synthetic ones were mostly confused with disgust and neutrality. Concerning fear, naturalistic faces were confused mostly with sadness, surprise, neutrality, or identified as other emotion. Synthetic facial expressions were confused mostly with sadness, surprise, and neutrality. For happiness, naturalistic facial expressions were confused mostly with neutrality or identified as "other emotion," while synthetic faces were confused mostly with neutrality. For surprise, naturalistic stimuli were mostly confused with anger, fear, neutrality, or identified as other emotion. Synthetic faces instead, were confused with sadness, fear, and neutrality. Concerning neutrality, naturalistic faces were confused with sadness, surprise, or identified as other emotions, and synthetic ones were confused mostly with sadness or identified as other emotion. The effects of several factors (participants' gender and age, the age, the gender, and the type of stimulus administered) on emotion interpretation accuracy have been studied. Concerning participants' gender, even though in this study seems not to have had a strong effect on results, previous studies highlighted that gender of the emotion interpreter is a relevant factor. Participants' age had a significant impact, in particular as regards to the recognition of emotions conveyed by the virtual agents, as we found that senior participants on average showed lower interpretation accuracy compared to participants belonging to differently aged groups made up of middle-aged subjects between 40 and 55 years and young between 22 and 35 years. This research highlighted that the differences among age groups of participants are stronger as regards the synthetic experiment, while the differently aged groups required to decode human faces (naturalistic experiment) did not significantly differ from each other for the majority of the emotional categories considered; moreover, anger and happiness, surprisingly, were more accurately decoded by senior participants compared to young and middle-aged ones. These two aspects outline the possibility that seniors' difficulty in emotion recognition were due to the nonhuman appearance of the faces expressing them. As regards as the age of the face expressing emotion, concerning the synthetic experiment, results showed lower accuracy in interpreting emotions of young faces than older ones in the case sadness; middle-aged faces were interpreted with greater accuracy when expressing fear and happiness compared to young and older faces. Older faces were interpreted with lower accuracy compared to younger ones when recognizing anger, surprise, and neutrality and interpreted with greater accuracy in the case of disgust. For the naturalistic, experiment was observed that young faces were better decoded than older ones in the case of anger, but worse decoded when considering happiness and neutrality; middle-aged faces were better decoded when expressing disgust compared to young and old faces, while in the case of surprise, middle-aged faces were worse decoded. Older faces were interpreted with lower accuracy compared to younger ones when recognizing sadness and fear. Our results seem to suggest that not everyone is affected in the same way by the phenomenon of the "Own Age Bias" [1]; actually, data seem to disconfirm the presence of this facilitation effect in particular with young subject. In fact, the only significant interaction between participants' age and the age of the shown faces were observed concerning synthetic fear and surprise with young participants' worse performances when decoding their peers' facial expressions, and naturalistic happiness with young participants better at decoding older faces than ones belonging to their age groups. Middle-aged and old participants instead worse decoded young faces showing better performances decoding older faces. This could suggest that young are less sensitive to the OAB, while older participants could be more affected by it. As regards to the gender of faces to be categorized, within both the synthetic and naturalistic, experiments emerged that for the substantial majority of emotional categories, female faces were better decoded compared to male ones. We did not observe significant interactions between participants' gender and the gender of the decoded faces: this means that our results cannot confirm the "Own Gender Bias" effect [14, 21]. Concerning the type of stimuli administered, the synthetic experiment highlighted that dynamic emotional expressions were better decoded compared to static ones in the case of disgust, sadness, and fear, while static facial expressions were better decoded than dynamic ones in the case of surprise and neutrality. As regards to the naturalistic experiment, dynamic emotional expressions were better decoded compared to static ones in the case of anger, fear, surprise, and neutrality, while static facial expressions were better decoded than dynamic ones in the case of disgust and sadness. These heterogeneous results outline that even the effect of dynamic and static emotional expressions depend on the emotional category to be decoded. Conclusively, we observed that concerning both the synthetic and naturalistic experiment, the emotional categories interpreted with greater accuracy were happiness and anger, followed by neutrality, sadness, and surprise. Disgust and fear elicited lower classification accuracy. On the whole, our results highlight that differences in the recognition of synthetic and naturalistic emotional expressions depend on the emotional category considered; for instance, the groups of participants which showed synthetic faces that displayed higher decoding accuracy percentage of disgust, anger, happiness, and neutrality, while the groups of participants which showed naturalistic faces that displayed higher decoding accuracy percentage of sadness, fear, and surprise. We hope that the present work increases knowledge in the field of human–machine interaction, through the development of differently aged virtual agents with robustly varied physical features. We tried to develop an extensive dataset of virtual agents expressing emotions and to provide insights which could be helpful in the design of future virtual assistants. Nevertheless, emotions are a complex process, consisting of thoughts, actions, communication, and physiological activation, and it follows that even trying to make virtual agents, and therefore synthetic and nonhuman faces, able to express them accurately turns out to be a complex task. A possibility consists in exploiting software as for instance Daz3D, which provides emotion and poses pre-sets for most emotions allowing also to adjust the intensity of the emotional expressions. Another possibility is represented by the Facial Action Coding System (FACS), a procedure used by Ekman and Friesen (1978) which allows a standardized encoding of action units (AUs), namely the muscular and mimic micro- movements characterizing a specific emotion; referring to the FACS. It is possible to manipulate the action units of a synthetic faces in order to obtain specific emotional expressions.

## Acknowledgment

This work received funding from Horizon 2020 research and innovation programs EMPATHIC (N. 769872) and MENHIR (N. 823907), from the project SIROBOTICS which received funding from Ministero dell'Istruzione, dell'Università, e della Ricerca (MIUR), PNR 2015-2020, Decreto Direttoriale 1735, 13 July 2017, and from the project ANDROIDS that received funding from Università della Campania "Luigi Vanvitelli" inside the program V:ALERE 2019, funded with D.R. 906 del 4/10/2019, prot. n. 157264, 17 October 2019.

## References

1 Anastasi, J.S. and Rhodes, M.G. (2006). Evidence for an own-age bias in face recognition. *North American Journal of Psychology* 8 (2): 237–252.

2 Bernardini, S., Porayska-Pomsta, K., and Sampath, H. (2013). Designing an intelligent virtual agent for social communication in autism. *Proceedings of the Ninth AAAI Conference on Artificial Intelligence and Interactive Digital Entertainment*, Boston, Massachusetts USA, pp. 9–15. PKP Publishing Services Network.

3 Brinkman, W.P., van der Mast, C.A.P.G., and de Vliegher, D. (2008). Virtual reality exposure therapy for social phobia: a pilot study in evoking fear in a virtual world. *Proceedings of HCI2008 Workshop – HCI for Technology Enhanced Learning*. Liverpool, UK (September 2008).

4 Delahunty, F., Wood, I.D., and Arcan, M. (2018). First insights on a passive major depressive disorder prediction system with incorporated conversational chatbot. In: *26th AIAI Irish Conference on Artificial Intelligence and Cognitive Science*, vol. 2259, 327–338. AICS.

5 Dhall, A., Goecke, R., Lucey, S., and Gedeon, T. (2011). Acted facial expressions in the wild database. Australian National University, Canberra, Australia, *Technical Report TR-CS-11*, 2, 1.

6 Dhall, A., Goecke, R., Lucey, S., and Gedeon, T. (2011). Static facial expressions in tough conditions: data, evaluation protocol and benchmark. *1st IEEE International Workshop on Benchmarking Facial Image Analysis Technologies BeFIT, ICCV2011*, Barcelona, Spain (06–13 November 2011): IEEE.

7 Gardiner, P.M., McCue, K.D., Negash, L.M. et al. (2017). Engaging women with an embodied conversational agent to deliver mindfulness and lifestyle recommendations: a feasibility randomized control trial. *Patient Education and Counseling* 100 (9): 1720–1729.

8 Hoffmann, H., Kessler, H., Eppel, T. et al. (2010). Expression intensity, gender, and facial emotion recognition: women recognize only subtle facial emotions better than men. *Acta Psychologica* 135 (3): 278–283.

9 Hortensius, R., Hekele, F., and Cross, E.S. (2018). The perception of emotion in artificial agents. *IEEE Transactions on Cognitive and Developmental Systems* 10 (4): 852–864.

10 Huckvale, M., Leff, J., & Williams, G. (2013). Avatar therapy: an audio-visual dialogue system for treating auditory hallucinations. *INTERSPEECH*, Lyon, France (25–29 August 2013). pp. 392–396, ISCA.

11 Isaacowitz, D.M., Löckenhoff, C.E., Lane, R.D. et al. (2007). Age differences in recognition of emotion in lexical stimuli and facial expressions. *Psychology and Aging* 22 (1): 147.

12 Joyal, C.C., Jacob, L., Cigna, M.H. et al. (2014). Virtual faces expressing emotions: an initial concomitant and construct validity study. *Frontiers in Human Neuroscience* 8 (787).

13 Kamita, T., Ito, T., Matsumoto, A. et al. (2019). A chatbot system for mental healthcare based on SAT counseling method. *Mobile Information Systems* 2019 (2): 1–11.

14 Lambrecht, L., Kreifelts, B., and Wildgruber, D. (2014). Gender differences in emotion recognition: impact of sensory modality and emotional category. *Cognition & Emotion* 28 (3): 452–469.

15 Lovejoy, C.A. (2019). Technology and mental health: the role of artificial intelligence. *European Psychiatry* 55: 1–3.

16 Man, T.W. and Hills, P.J. (2016). Eye-tracking the own-gender bias in face recognition: other-gender faces are viewed differently to own-gender faces. *Visual Cognition* 24 (9–10): 447–458.

17 Paetzel, M., Varni, G., Hupont, I. et al. (2018). The attribution of emotional state – how embodiment features and social traits affect the perception of an artificial agent. *27th IEEE International Symposium on Robot and Human Interactive Communication (RO-MAN)*, Nanjing, China (27–31 August 2018). pp. 495–502: IEEE.

18 Pérez Díaz de Cerio, D., Valenzuela González, J. L., Ruiz Boqué, S. et al. (2011). Help4Mood: a computational distributed system to support the treatment of patients with major depression. In COST IC1004: cooperative radio communications for green smart environments. https://www.research.ed.ac.uk/en/projects/help4mooda-computational-distributed-system-to-support-the-treatm/publications/

19 Richter, D., Dietzel, C., and Kunzmann, U. (2011). Age differences in emotion recognition: the task matters. *The Journals of Gerontology. Series B, Psychological Sciences and Social Sciences* 66 (1): 48–55.

20 Rigon, A., Turkstra, L., Mutlu, B., and Duff, M. (2016). The female advantage: sex as a possible protective factor against emotion recognition impairment following traumatic brain injury. *Cognitive, Affective, & Behavioral Neuroscience* 16 (5): 866–875.

21 Wolff, N., Kemter, K., Schweinberger, S.R., and Wiese, H. (2014). What drives social in-group biases in face recognition memory? ERP evidence from the own-gender bias. *Social Cognitive and Affective Neuroscience* 9 (5): 580–590.

# 21

# Intelligent Computational Edge: From Pervasive Computing and Internet of Things to Computing Continuum

*Radmila Juric*

*Independent Researcher London, UK*

## 21.1 Introduction

We have come a long way since the publication of a famous paper in The Scientific American in 1991 [100]. Mark Weiser's vision still captures our attention, and there are no papers which focus on pervasiveness and ubiquity of modern computing, which do not cite Weiser's famous sentences. He talked about technologies which weave themselves into the fabric of everyday life and computers becoming and invisible part of our lives: "People will use them unconsciously to accomplish everyday tasks." Weiser envisaged computations on small and wearable devices which change their role according to environments or circumstances, i.e. *contexts*, in which they happen to be. He emphasized that the real power of wearable devices would not come solely from them: it is their interaction which enables ubiquitous computing and creates pervasiveness and thus he hoped for transparent linking of wireless and wired networks. At the same time, Weiser worries about *social issues* when computers find their way invisibly into our lives, being capable of sensing people around them, intercepting messages, and introducing possibilities for "making totalitarianism seem like sheerest anarchy." He asked if a person's badge at work and invisible computers could fall into the hands of corporate superiors, overzealous governments, and marketing firms? His answer to security and privacy was the CMU computer which aimed to have privacy safeguards as in the real world "with ethical conventions applied regardless of settings." Weiser also said that ubiquity in computing may mean securing that machines fit human environments "instead of forcing humans to enter theirs."

Two years later, in 1993, Weiser's publication in Communications of ACM [101] elaborated on the role of computer science in ubiquitous computing, with remarks that the evaluation of ubiquitous computing and technologies will not choose our next step. It will be "the analysis of psychologists, anthropologists, application developers, artists and customers, who would find what does or does not work, in this ubiquitous world" and thus enable "cross disciplinary fertilization and learning."

No wonder that this text, written 30 years ago still captures our imagination.

When reading the same article in 2021, we could see the modern computational world potentially adhering to excerpts of Weiser's vision. We might use different vocabulary, have different hardware/software technologies/applications compared to 1991, but we still carry forward the same goal, and experience environments, where computational power, interwoven into our everyday lives, is treated as *normal*.

However, the question of having an ideal world of ubiquity in computing, as envisaged by Weiser, is still open. Have we achieved what he outlined in his visions, and have we created a living world

*Handbook of Human-Machine Systems*, First Edition. Edited by Giancarlo Fortino, David Kaber, Andreas Nürnberger, and David Mendonça.

which secures that machines fit human environments and not the other way around? Have we managed to make a symbiosis of machine and humans for sharing intelligence and augment it, at the same time? Does ubiquity fulfill our expectations? Could we identify where Weiser went wrong when he looked at ubiquitous computing with optimism? These questions cannot be addressed without looking at our journey in the computational world from Weiser's article to current times.

## 21.2 The Journey of Pervasive Computing

After Weiser's publications, it took us 10 years to start talking about pervasiveness and ubiquity in computing [6, 10, 75, 77]. We had visions and challenges, where pervasive computing became the paradigm of the twenty-first century. We were all engaged in context and situation awareness [25, 49], ambient intelligence [39], self-tuning, and adaptable software applications [52], but felt that we were still lagging behind Weiser's vision [73].

Twenty years on, we tried to articulate "next-generation research directions" [23] by asking "What's next Ubicomp" [3], as our infatuation with Weiser's vision was still going strong. We hoped for creating a new computational world to serve humanity [4, 31] and make the vision of ubiquitous connectivity real [96]. In 2017, the same idea was revisited, and we asked again "how far are we from making Weiser's vision our reality [29]"? This question is still difficult to answer.

The pathway toward pervasiveness and ubiquity in computing has taken unexpected turns since 1990, which was difficult to predict, and the answer to the question above cannot be straightforward. The advances in technologies in general impacted our world and the dominance of software and its applications in it is undisputable. However, was this sufficient to assume that we are close to achieving Weiser's visions?

We could analyze the current situation in ubiquitous computing by following ideas which created cyber physical spaces [50, 51]. We could also look at the journey from the Internet of computers to the Internet of Things (IoT) [59] and its explosion to the Internet of Everything (IoE) [16], with applications across domains. The history and current challenges in the IoT world might give answers to some questions we may have regarding Weiser's vision because the IoT may come very close to creating a ubiquitous world where devices and human cohabit.

However, future trends and prospects of the IoT stumbled upon problems. The first is the lack of new computational paradigms suitable for constantly changeable, dynamic, and heterogenous environments where the IoT operates. There is no widely accepted paradigm on the horizon. The second problem collates increasing worries about efficiency of cloud computing. Research communities and academia started looking at serverless computing and possibilities of deploying edge/fog/dust computing where we could address the dynamics, uncertainty, and constant changes dictated by pervasiveness in computing. This is not all. At the same time, we witnessed the explosion of wearable computing and robotics [37], sensing technologies, new human–machine interfaces, and unlimited applications of the IoT in many disciplines: from automated cars, vessels and unmanned flying objects to medical devices, cyborgs, and bio-machine intelligent systems. Our computational world is becoming complicated. It creates opportunities for having computing for human experience, augmenting human and machine intelligence, moving toward augmented cognition and cognitive engineering. This leads to the Internet-of-Materials (IoM), shape changing computing particles, and developing self-sustainable and energy self-harvesting computational materials. In this conundrum of innovations and new technologies, we aim to deploy predictive and learning technologies, which shape the current AI, hoping that it will bring more computational intelligence.

Has the paragraph above convinced us that we are not far from reaching Weiser's vision? Are we finally there?

There is one aspect of modern computing worthwhile exploring because it may create more intelligence in our interconnected world and come close to the Weiser's vision. Edge computing [40] could be converted into the powerful computational edge and enrich ubiquitous computing. It could be enhanced by computational models based on semantic and predictive technologies, which might enable dynamic intelligence at the computational edge, where humans reside. This is exactly what we wish to achieve when talking about the IoT. Therefore, if we really wish to talk about creating a new world as Weiser imagined 30 years ago, we need to look at the evolution and status of the IoT, as our best bet, and define which role an intelligent computational edge may play in it.

## 21.3 The Power of the IoT

The convergence between wireless technologies and portability/mobility of computers has changed our perception of who oversees computations in the twenty-first century. The pervasiveness of computational spaces has completely changed the way we run business, manage education, deliver healthcare, enhance manufacturing and engineering, govern, and manage our lives. The explosion of computationally powerful handheld devices and domination of sensory and wireless technologies required the development of computational solutions which started blurring the barriers between physical items and software artifacts [87, 89]. Communications, connections, and computations are thus interwoven, ad-hoc, spontaneous, and personalized. Software applications are self-configured, self-tuned, and adaptable to demands and adjustable to the contexts and situations in which they happen to reside [43, 90, 91].

This journey, starting 20 years ago, took us toward the IoT [27] and the IoE [17], and it did seem, at that time, that Weiser's vision was kept alive. However, the field of IoT has become too large to understand all advances and what the future holds. The IoT also spans disciplines of engineering, communications, business, computer science, and have been spreading across numerous applications. It is almost impossible to give a short overview of the current advances in and applications of the IoT because innovations in the field are scattered across various disciplines and they appear as we speak. The obvious example, which shows the scale of the problem, is that we have no commonly accepted definition of the IoT [36]. We do not have standardized software architectures for supporting software applications for (in) the IoT. There are no common software architectural styles for creating and managing instances of the IoT. There are publications in the format of *surveys,* and they range from 2011 [9] until today [55]. Are we still surveying the advances in the IoT? Probably, because these publications might be the only sources of information which touches an ongoing evolution of the IoT phenomenon.

It is interesting that in 2013, we had an attempt to associate context awareness in computing with the IoT [67], because of our success in the development of context aware software applications since the early 2000. The IoT has some resemblance to context awareness in computer science and as such could use computational models and definitions of *context* for extracting meaning from sensory data and interweave the notion of mobility with any instance of the IoT [46]. However, the published surveys of the status of and advances in the IoT unfortunately do not focus enough on computational models which run the IoT. They are more concerned with IoT technologies, communication theories, data storage, sensory information, and engineered devices, than on any aspect of software design, architectures, and computational models for the IoT. We can read about IoT-enabling technologies and applications [32], topics and trends [102], technologies and challenges [85], potentials and societal role [8], and open research issues [20]. They all reiterate similar problems and the following two problems dominate: (i) fragmentations of some of the standards used in IoT, and (ii) the diversity of deployed technologies. One of the best analyses on the status of the IoT is given in Ref. [84] from 2018. We do not know if its overview of the IoT field is still valid.

In the field of 5G-IoT, we focus on augmented reality, self-driven vehicles, e-Health, and smart environments in general, and claim that the IoT lives upon seamless connectivity between heterogeneous networks, and plug and play technologies [19, 66]. This might be in line with Weiser's vision. The statement *Connections and not things will change the world*" [28] may confirm CISCO's motto from 2012 that "relevant and valuable connections ***and not things*** will change the world."

Currently, the IoT/IoE stretch much further toward Internet-of-Vehicles (IoV) [21], Internet of Medical Things (IoMT) [14, 104], Internet of Robotic Things [65, 92] (IoRT), to Internet of Nano Things (IoNT) [62], and Internet of Materials (IoM) [5]. However, from the perspective of computer science, there are a few visible problems with the current and further advances in this field.

### 21.3.1 Inherent Problems with the IoT

Without advances in computer science and software engineering, none of these advances in technologies, which triggered ubiquity/pervasiveness, and thus the existence of the IoT, would be feasible. Computational models are essential in creating not only pervasive spaces but also enabling their dynamics and constant changes. We know that computational models conceptualize a variety of problem domains, model facts collected through data, reason upon the collected semantic from the problem domain, and make conclusions. They conceptualize human expectations and preferences; model uncertainties, predictions, and create inference using logical and predictive reasoning. In the third decade of the twenty-first century, we have created *programmable spaces,* inherently pervasive, enhanced with computational intelligence.

As in any fast-moving technologies, the world of IoT has been facing numerous challenges. Most of them are triggered by heterogeneities of hardware/software constituent parts of the IoT, ranging from physical items, software artifacts, and platforms to semantic heterogeneities, often triggered by software applications and the semantic of data and its conceptual models. Thus, achieving interoperability is a must for a smooth functioning of any IoT. There are also issues, such as (cyber) security and privacy. However, from the computer science point of view, there are more problems neglected in IoT research, related to the configuration, management, and manipulation of the IoT. They require expertise of computer scientists to create viable models, but they do not exist. We have an abundance of computational spaces, in which we merge their pervasiveness with either new or tested computational models, if we wish to make them contextually viable [22, 58, 88], and thus formal computational models for IoT are long overdue.

Regardless of having powerful hand-held, wearable, wireless, and sensory-geared devices, without computational models, which exploit the semantic of the context where the IoT could be configured, there would be no IoT and its applications across domains of interest. We need computational models to enable the existence of IoT with interwoven, ad-hoc, spontaneous, and personalized computations and communications. Considering that we have formalized computational models for pervasive spaces [87], it is a pity not to have a consensus on the computations and software technologies which would deliver what we expect from the IoT. Current configurations of IoT are sporadic, application-specific, with unsophisticated use of existing software technologies.

The second problem is related to an incorrect perception of the IoT. This is a highly dynamic pervasive spaces, inherently changeable. Computer scientists tend to address the changeable nature of any computational space, by looking at their instances and understanding how changes impact them. The same applies to the IoT and thus it would be difficult to imagine that one instance of IoT would be long lived. Instead of talking about IoT in general, it is more natural to focus on instances of IoTs, which may change their constituent parts whenever necessary [22, 45]. In our world of ad-hoc computing, and constantly changing environments, it is reasonable to think about the semantic of IoT's constituent parts, as we usually do in computer science, which could be manipulated through a computer program, in order to create an instance of the IoT [22, 87] The time when computer programs, specifically designed for a particular application, could have a long life has gone. The dynamic of pervasive computational spaces needs new computational model(s), which can address changes by looking at instances of the IoT.

## 21.4 IoT: The Journey from Cloud to Edge

In the last five years, the edge-computing paradigm has captured our full attention and established itself as a cornerstone of modern computational capabilities [78]. It has been heavily promoted by CISCO enterprise network solution [18], the foundation of the open edge computing consortium [64] and Gartner's strategic road map for Edge Computing [34]. We have all been aware of the pitfalls of clouds and cloud computing for some time, and the most frequently mentioned problems are in high latency and bandwidth issues. Therefore, it has been obvious that we need a new computational paradigm. This particularly applies to the domain of IoT, with interconnected devices, possibly equipped or surrounded with sensors and in charge of humans, who depend on them.

It has not been unusual to read something like "Save IoT from the Cloud" [106], considering that the level of centralization of data storage and services secured and delivered by cloud computing could not be the only answer to advances in the IoT. Computer scientists still remember the price paid for centralized solutions in software developments from the 1970, 1980s, and 1990s, particularly in database management. Regardless of the perfectionism of the transactional processing, using relational data base management systems, which were inherently centralized in the late 1980s and early 1990s, we did learn the lesson from the centralization. Thus, we opened doors to "decentralized" data processing through either heavy distribution of data and computations or encouraging event-driven, context-, and situation-aware computing. This was all feasible due to advances in software and communication technologies and powerful hardware which was constantly improving. However, today, when we generate data as we live, while sensory technologies are inevitably surrounding us, and we take mobile and wireless technologies as "normal" in our everyday life, it is almost impossible to believe that our modern data processing will survive with cloud computing in mind.

It is no surprise that decentralization of the clouds, initially triggered by location awareness and promoted through Fog Computing [15, 63, 98] had an inevitable and instant appeal for the IoT. It happened again that CISCO had an important say in promoting the Fog Computing [2], but we can read in academic papers about emerging coexistence of Edge/Fog/Clouds [83], focusing on Edge promises [86] despite its challenges [56], and relating fog and edge computing paradigms as a promising area for mobile and wireless computing, pervasiveness of our computational spaces and the IoT [105].

At the same time, in 2009, a couple of years before we talked about Fog computing, the Carnegie Melon University defined "cloudlets" in mobile computing [80], and proposed the idea of decentralized and scattered microservices, positioned between the clouds and computational devices, at the edges of computer networks. Initially, this was a fantastic idea. We read: "bring the cloud to the mobile user" [99], "cloudlets are the leading edge of mobile-cloud convergence" [81], "follow me cloud" [95], but there were doubts such as: "are cloudlets necessary" [33]? Suddenly, ideas of edge computing appeared again, to address the lack of cloud computing sustainability. Also, cloudlets as microservices are not free from clouds, and they do not guarantee the power of localized computing. Edge computing has a chance to remedy the problem.

Obviously, it has been difficult in computer science to expect that any computational paradigm will be long lived, particularly at times with advances in technologies and science at an unprecedented level. We tend to focus on every single innovation created by these advances. This was an opportunity for mobile edge computing to gain its momentum [1, 41, 74, 94]. Mobility is a sine qua non in the twenty-first century and in in 2020, we focused on taxonomy, challenges, and future of mobile edge computing [70], its symbiosis with Fog and Cloudlets [26] and possibilities of opening edge computing for ubiquitous AI [11, 54], which could take us to Edge Intelligence. Having a well-accepted edge-computing paradigm with technologies and computational power at the network edges, would justify questions like "we can squeeze deep learning into mobile devices" [53] or talking about "edge analytics in the IoT" [82]. Does this mean that we are at the brink of achieving Edge Intelligence? What exactly would this mean for current computing paradigms? What would the meaning of "intelligence" be? Whichever answer to these questions we may have, the IoT/IoE might be a driving force for achieving the edge intelligence.

## 21.5 Toward Intelligent Computational Edge

There is a subtle difference between achieving Edge Intelligence, as appeared in the literature, and potentially different directions of creating intelligence for the IoT environments by talking about Intelligent Computational Edge. The emphasis is on "computations" which should happen at the edges of networks and create Intelligent Edge. This could move us further away from clouds and toward a decentralization of computing for the sake of the IoE/IoT, without paying any significant price for eliminating services clouds offer. Publications which talk about Edge Intelligence appeared in parallel with the general writing about the Edge [69] and most of them are triggered using predictive and learning technologies in the Edge Computing Paradigm [57, 103]. The authors urge to integrate the popular paradigm with the current AI and thus talk about Edge Intelligence which is in [24] divided into (i) AI for edge, and (ii) intelligence-enabled edge computing which is *AI performed on the Edge*. It goes without saying that all authors assume that "AI" means using ML algorithms and deep learning, to create intelligence.

Obviously, this division in (i) and (ii) above exists for two reasons. First, we know that the complete process of defining and training algorithms in ML, while building what we call AI models, is difficult to secure within the current edge computing paradigm. Second, we currently do not consider creating computational intelligence outside our obsession of using learning and predictive technologies because we thrive in fast, cheap, and efficient processing of excessive amounts of data and claim that we create predictive inference, i.e. AI.

However, there are calls for creating AI-enabled IoT devices [60] and cooperative edge computing where AI and edge are subject to complementary integration [35]. This solution focuses on clouds, because IoT generated data are classified as "private" and thus kept isolated at the edge. The authors claim that it secures privacy preserving transfer learning, as opposed to manipulating public data which is transferred to clouds and processed there using AI. This is a rather unnatural data categorization into private and public. The same authors claim that they create localized AI which seems inexplicable. Why would the idea that the data created solely by the IoT define local intelligence? Does local intelligence differ from global in this case?

There is another, similarly unjustifiable idea in Ref. [42] of "dispersing unlabeled raw data across the edge nodes" and preparing it for AI models trained on clouds. Apart from engineering localized feature extractions to "understand" the local data, there is no other benefit. How would this feature engineering affect the global AI algorithms running on the cloud? Which type of intelligence would we develop at the edges?

An interesting step forward has been found in Ref. [72]. It converges humans, things, and AI to create edge intelligence. This work is triggered by research on augmenting human abilities through technologies or medicine [71, 76] and looking at the IoT for augmenting humans [68]. The idea of involving humans in managing intelligence in Edge computing has not been taken by researchers, although computational edge, within the IoT and cyber physical spaces, is often in the hands of humans and software as a service is tailored mostly for humans. In pervasiveness, where it is difficult to distinguish between cyber and physical, we should not exclude humans from supplying vital intelligence. This can improve machine intelligence, which lags behind our expectations, in spite of claiming the success of the current AI in real life. No one discusses this problem. We are slow in adopting human intervention to increase computational intelligence. There is one exception [38]. Content recommendations on mobile software-defined edge, depending on edge caching, uses human-like hybrid caching, based on reinforcement learning, and secures the increase of cache hit ratio by 20%.

## 21.6 Is Computing Continuum the Answer?

One of the tangible attempts to talk about seamlessly combining resources/services on a pathway from the edge to the cloud appeared in 2019 [97]. The idea is to mimic the fluid ecosystem in which services are federated and orchestrated on demand, with emphasis on real-time reaction to unexpected situations in data processing, including, their sizes, rates, location, and similar. This was particularly important in data-driven applications and therefore the term "computing in the continuum" was appropriate, according to the authors. A year later, the term "computing continuum" was solely reserved for edge to cloud integration for data-driven workflows [61]. The authors still see edge resources as NOT being capable of supporting data-intensive computing and therefore edge computing must rely on cloud services. However, the authors propose the use of federation for infrastructure and programming services and thus creating workflows which could deal with "unexpected" situations. There is an overlapping between the ideas in Refs. ([61, 97] and the latter has been applied to the case study of managing a tsunami early warning system. The authors of [97] also carry the notion of "ecosystem" when talking about computing continuum, which seamlessly combine resources and services at the cloud, and then "in-transit," along the data path from the edge to the cloud [79]. In Ref. [12], the cloud-edge continuum works on the principle of the orchestration of operations between edges and the cloud, where context awareness helps in deciding where to store data and run computations.

These publications are rather new, with no follow-ups, but this does not stop us from promoting new paradigms, such as cognitive computing continuum [30]. The provision of services for the dynamic IoTs is geared toward distributed, opportunistic, self-managed collaboration of devices within the IoT, which may reside outside the data centers/clouds. The word cognition applies to devices, which make decisions autonomously, based on the data sensed from their environments.

## 21.7 Do We Have More Questions than Answers?

If we wish to debate the content of the previous sections, then the first question is obvious: "How close are we to creating Intelligent Computational Edge?" This is still difficult to answer, but if we wish to guess, there are possibly more reasons for answering NO than YES. Why?

First, revisiting the definition of AI is needed. Are current AI algorithms based on statistics really the same AI as envisaged 50+ years ago? Are statistical algorithms which shape current AI, exactly what brings our computers close to the human level of intelligence?

Second, empowering edge with computations to create intelligence does not necessarily mean using predictive and learning technologies. What about other software technologies used to interpret the meaning and exploit the computable semantic of the surrounding world? They may not need excessive computational power and data storages.

Third, what about new computational models for edge computing paradigm? They are nonexistent. We are obsessed with technical issues, communications, and device interoperation, but this is only one part of the story. Where are generic software architectures for fitting the bill in Edge Computing and in creating intelligence?

Fourth, research in the IoT and Edge computing is reserved for researchers who shy away from the principles of software development. Intelligent edge must come as a product of computational models, geared by computer scientists. We do not have either models or computer scientists leading this research.

There is also a set of concerns in understanding the role of intelligent computational edge related to the IoT. We must ask again "Are we finally very close to making Weiser's vision a reality in 2022?" Table 21.1 clearly shows that our journey toward Weiser's vision has not ended. In the left column of the table, we list the essence of Weiser's vision [100]. In the middle column, we outline current situations in computing regarding the visions. The right column gives an insight on future works which might fulfill Weiser's vision and thus lead to intelligent computational edge.

Therefore, how do we answer his questions in 2022? Are we going to repeat ourselves as we did in the last three decades? One option is to learn from the past computational models, add an understanding of the nature of the IoT and its applications and their impact on the computational edge. Do we need a shift in thinking in 2022? Probably. This shift in thinking might require:

(1) Looking at the instances and slices of time (moments?) in which computations happen and removing total centralization of data and computations (are the clouds out?)
(2) Using software technologies for managing semantics and creating environments enabling the reasoning upon the semantics and make decisions based on the reasoning?
(3) Creating computationally independent Edge, to enable (1) and (2) above.
(4) Using clouds to secure computational continuum in cases where computational edge needs a natural extension of its computing, but specific for the problem domain.
(5) Initiating new ways of creating and designing devices with computational power. We need intelligent engineering with computer scientist as team members, for the design of devices which would support intelligent edge.
(6) Considering logic inference in decision-making on where and how to compute for creating an intelligent computational edge without being dependent on algorithms which shape the current AI.

**Table 21.1** Are we close to making Weiser's vision a reality in 2022.

| | | |
|---|---|---|
| Computers will become invisible part of our lives | We are not there yet, but we are moving toward computational materials and new era of human machine interfaces | Focusing on design challenges of computational devices which should fit around computations (and not the other way around) |
| People will use computers unconsciously to accomplish everyday tasks | This is debatable because human–machine interactions and human input are essential in bringing more intelligence in modern computational spaces | Addressing (i) moving computing to the "edge" and (ii) using the semantic from human interactions to add intelligence. How far do we go in eliminating humans' "consciousness"? |
| Computations will be on small and wearable devices | We talk about a range of smart wearables, but they may store a limited number/types of comp. models. Size does matter (still) | Considering semantic mediation on deciding on comp. across the range of possibilities between the edge and clouds |
| Small devices will change their role according to environments or circumstance | Software contextualization has existed since the early 2000, but contextualization is nonexistent when designing devices | Rethinking distinction between hardware/software. Is this important? Will contextualized software be enough in future? |
| Wearable devices will become powerful | This is true, but computations on most of wearables still depend on cloud infrastructures | Perceiving power of new era of devices. Should we have comp. paradigms with ternary and quantum computing included? |
| The power of wearables will also come from interactions | This is true: interactions are essential in any comp. space | New generations of Internet of Everything are our reality |
| Transparent linking of wireless/wired networks is needed | Wireless technologies dominate our computational world | |

## 21.8 What Would our Vision Be?

We could have various visions for the future of intelligent computational edge. In Ref. [13], the authors acknowledge "a gap of approaches supporting the engineering of dynamic, heterogeneous environments," such as the IoT, and co-ordination of managing the complex task of providing services. Their proposal to integrate the aggregate computing and opportunistic IoT service models results in engineering "Edge of Things" applications. This is a novel idea. We would like to add to this proposal another option, which uses semantic mediation based on reasoning and the first-order logic, for deciding on the best configuration of Computational Edges. This mediation must consider the context in which an instance of the IoT exists and use the semantic of that contest for making decision on (i) where computations should reside, and (ii) which data they should use. It would generate computing continuum, based on the mediation, for accommodating algorithms, from current AI at the computational edge, and spread it in the space between edges and clouds.

Figure 21.1 illustrates the idea of mediations on the best possible configuration of computations. It shows only software artifacts or components making a software architectural style for mediations. It excludes hardware components for one reason. If we wish to push forward the development of formal computational models for edge computing, we must start the conceptualization using software components.

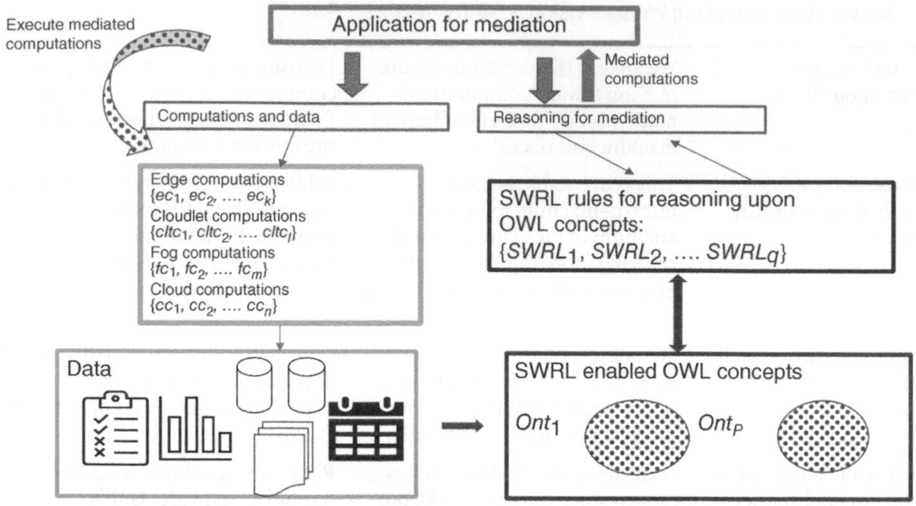


**Figure 21.1** Software architecture for mediation through reasoning.

In the left part of the figure, computations and data across edge, fog, cloudlets, and clouds (**{$ec_1$, $ec_2$,... $ec_k$}, {$cltc_1$, $cltc_2$,... $cltc_l$} {$fc_1$,$fc_2$,...$fc_m$}** and **{$cc_1$, $cc_2$,... $cc_n$}**) are described with definitions of data and their types for this spectrum of computations. We allow any type of data from tabular data, originating in sensor technologies and socially generated data, to highly structured databases and data resulting from analytics.

The left part of the Figure 21.1 contains the semantic for creating ontological concepts to enable reasoning upon "which computation and which data is the most suitable in any moment when decision is needed." The right side of the Figure 21.1 takes data about and from our computations in the left part of the figure and generates ontological concepts which would enable reasoning. The mediation, based on reasoning, judges how far we go in empowering the computational edge and how fog/cloudlets/clouds help in creating intelligence. Consequently, we may create a powerful and changeable computing continuum. Figure 21.1 is feasible to implement by deploying component-based software architectures with technologies and tools, as illustrated in Refs. [45, 46, 87, 90].

The idea of mediation in computer science is rather old. It was exploited 30 years ago when the predecessor of client server technologies, based on middleware, used mediation for (i) resolving heterogeneities in software and (ii) addressing semantic interoperability in databases developed through the 1980s and 1990. However, the mediation was short lived in the 1990s for two reasons. Client server computing took off and enabled service-oriented software development, which addressed the problem of heterogeneity [47]. Second reason is that we did not have a computational model to the supported mediations. Without logic inference, it was impossible to mediate about anything in the 1990s. It took 10+ years to create software technologies which enabled logic reasoning. Semantic web technologies based on first-order logic can run reasoning upon abstract, but computable concepts [43, 87, 89, 91]. If we merge the idea of mediation with logic inference, we could address problems in configurations of instances of the IoT and thus create an infrastructure for computational continuum. Would this be the way forward toward an intelligent Edge Computing? There are attempts to use semantic matching combined with taxonomy clustering to improve the effectiveness of publish/subscribe model for communication in IoT [7]. The interest of merging semantic matching and mediation in configuration of the IoT is triggered using semantic web technologies, and computational models based on SWRL-enabled OWL ontologies across problem domains [44, 48, 87]. At this moment, there is nothing else on offer in either computer science or communication theories or predictive technologies which could take us forward to fully functional instances of the IoT. Looking at semantic mediation, when creating a computational continuum and intelligent computational edge, might be what we desperately need: a new computational paradigm. Well, this can be just an idea or a vision, but without visions, the people would perish [93].

## References


1 Abbas, N., Zhang, Y., Taherkordi, A., and Skeie, T. (2018). Mobile edge computing: a survey. *IEEE Internet of Things Journal* 5 (1): 450–465.

2 Abdelshkour, M. (2015). IoT. From Cloud to Fog Computing, CISCO Blogs. https://blogs.cisco.com/perspectives/iot-from-cloud-to-fog-computing (accessed 17 February 2023).

3 Abowd, G.D. (2012). What next, ubicomp? Celebrating an intellectual disappearing act. In: *Proceedings of ACM Conference on Ubiquitous Computing (UbiComp 12)*, 31–40. Association for Computing Machinery https://doi.org/10.1145/2370216.2370222.

4 Abowd, G.D. (2016). Beyond Weiser: from ubiquitous to collective computing. *Computer* 49 (1): 17–23.

5 Abowd, G.D. (2020). The internet of materials: a vision for computational materials. *IEEE Pervasive Computing* 19 (2): 56–62.

6 Abowd, G.D. and Mynatt, E.D. (2000). Charting past, present, and future research in ubiquitous computing. *ACM Transactions on Computer-Human Interaction* 7 (2000): 29–58.

7 Alhakbani, A., Hassan, M.M., Ykhlef, M., and Fortino, G. (2019). An efficient event matching system for semantic smart data in the Internet of Things (IoT) environment. *Future Generation Computer Systems* 95: 163–174.

8 Atzori, L., Iera, A., and Morabito, G. (2017). Understanding the Internet of Things: definition, potentials, and societal role of a fast-evolving paradigm. *Ad Hoc Networks* 56: 122–140.

9 Bandyopadhyay, D. and Sen, J. (2011). Internet of Things: applications and challenges in technology and standardization. *Wireless Personal Communications* 58 (1): 49–69.

10 Bell, G. and Dourish, P. (2007). Yesterday's tomorrows: notes on ubiquitous computing's dominant vision. *Personal and Ubiquitous Computing* 11 (2): 133–143.

11 Bernardi, K.M.L. (2021). Keynote: edge intelligence – emerging solutions and open challenges. In: *2021 IEEE International Conference on Pervasive Computing and Communications Workshops and other Affiliated Events (PerCom Workshops)*, Kassel, Germany (22–26 March 2021), 160. https://doi.org/10.1109/PerComWorkshops51409.2021.9431071. IEEE.

12 Carvalho, L.I., da Silva, D.M.A., and Sofia, R.C. (2020). Leveraging context-awareness to better support the IoT cloud-edge continuum. In: *2020 Fifth International Conference on Fog and Mobile Edge Computing (FMEC)*, Paris, Francepp (20–23 April 2020), 356–359. IEEE.

13 Casadei, R., Fortino, G., Pianini, D. et al. (2019). A development approach for collective opportunistic Edge-of-Things services. *Information Sciences* 498 (2019): 154–169.

14 Chatterjee, R., Maitra, T., Islam, S.K.H. et al. (2019). A novel machine learning based feature selection for motor imagery EEG signal classification in Internet of medical things environment. *Future Generation Computer Systems* 98: 419–434.

15 Cisco (2015). Fog Computing and the Internet of Things: Extend the Cloud to Where the Things Are, White paper, Google Scholar.

**16** CISCO (2013). About IEEE Internet of Things (IoT) initiative. https://www.cisco.com/c/dam/en_us/about/business-insights/docs/ioe-value-at-stake-public-sector-analysis-faq.pdf (accessed 17 February 2023).

**17** CISCO (2012). Point of view the Internet of Everything. https://www.cisco.com/c/dam/global/en_my/assets/ciscoinnovate/pdfs/IoE.pdf (accessed 17 February 2023).

**18** CISCO (2023). What is edge computing. https://www.cisco.com/c/en/us/solutions/enterprise-networks/edge-computing.html (accessed 17 February 2023).

**19** CISCO point of View (2013). The Internet of Everything. https://www.cisco.com/c/dam/en_us/about/business-insights/docs/ioe-value-index-faq.pdf (accessed 17 February 2023).

**20** Čolaković, A. and Hadžialić, M. (2018). Internet of Things (IoT): a review of enabling technologies, challenges, and open research issues. *Computer Networks* 144: 17–39.

**21** Contreras-Castillo, J., Zeadally, S., and Guerrero-Ibañez, J. (2018). Internet of Vehicles: architecture, protocols, and security. *IEEE Internet of Things Journal* 5 (5): 3701–3709.

**22** Da Silva, D.M.A. and Sofia, R.C. (2020). A discussion on context-awareness to better support the IoT cloud/edge continuum. *IEEE Access* 8: 193686–193694.

**23** Davies, N. (2012). Twenty years on. *IEEE Pervasive Computing* 11 (1): 2–4.

**24** Deng, S., Zhao, H., Fang, J. et al. (2020). Edge intelligence: the confluence of edge computing and artificial intelligence. *IEEE Internet of Things Journal* 7 (8): 7457–7469.

**25** Dey, A.K. (2001). Understanding and using context. *Personal and Ubiquitous Computing* 5 (1): 4–7.

**26** Dolui, K. and Datta, S.K. (2017). Comparison of edge computing implementations: fog computing, cloudlet and mobile edge computing. *Global Internet of Things Summit (GIoTS)* 2017: 1–6.

**27** Dorsemaine, B., Gaulier, J. P., Wary J. P., and Kheir, K. (2015). Internet of Things: a definition & taxonomy. *2015 9th International Conference on Next Generation Mobile Applications, Services and Technologies*, Cambridge, UK (09–11 September 2015): IEEE.

**28** Eavans, D. (2013). Why connections (not things) will change the world. CISCO BLOGS. https://blogs.cisco.com/digital/why-connections-not-things-will-change-the-world.

**29** Ebling, M.R. and Want, R. (2017). Satya revisits "Pervasive computing: vision and challenges". *IEEE Pervasive Computing* 16 (3): 20–23.

**30** Ferrer, J., Becker, S., Schmidt, F. et al. (2021). Towards a cognitive compute continuum: an architecture for ad-hoc self-managed swarms. In: *2021 IEEE/ACM 21st International Symposium on Cluster, Cloud and Internet Computing (CCGrid), 2021*, 634–641. IEEE.

**31** Ferscha, A. (2012). 20 Years past Weiser: what's next? *IEEE Pervasive Computing* 11 (1): 52–61.

**32** Fuqaha, A., Guizani, M., Mohammadi, M. et al. (2015). Internet of things: a survey on enabling technologies, protocols, and applications. *IEEE Communication Surveys and Tutorials* 17 (4): 2347–2376.

**33** Gao, Y., Hu, W., Ha, K. et al. (2015). Are cloudlets necessary? Oct 2015 CMU-CS-15-139 at. http://reports-archive.adm.cs.cmu.edu/anon/2015/CMU-CS-15-139.pdf (accessed 17 February 2023).

**34** GARTNER (2020). Strategic road map for edge computing. https://www.gartner.com/en/documents/3992656/2021-strategic-roadmap-for-edge-computing (accessed 17 February 2023).

**35** Gong, C., Lin, F., Gong, X., and Lu, Y. (2020). Intelligent cooperative edge computing in Internet of Things. *IEEE Internet of Things Journal* 7 (10): 9372–9382.

**36** Goumagias, N., Whalley, J., Dilaver, O., and Cunningham, J. (2021). Making sense of the internet of things: a critical review of internet of things definitions between 2005 and 2019. *Internet Research* 31 (5): 1583–1610.

**37** Gravina, R. and Fortino, G. (2020). Wearable body sensor networks: state-of-the-art and research directions. *IEEE Sensors Journal* 21 (11): 12511–12522.

**38** Hao, Y., Li, M., Wu, D. et al. (2020). Human-like hybrid caching in software-defined edge cloud. *IEEE Internet of Things Journal* 7 (7): 5806–5815.

**39** Hristova, A., Bernardos, M., and Casar, J.R. (2008). Context-aware services for ambient assisted living: a case-study. In: *First International Symposium on Applied Sciences on Biomedical and Communication Technologies*, Aalborg, Denmark (25–28 October 2008), 1–5. IEEE.

**40** Huh, J. and Seo, Y. (2019). Understanding edge computing: engineering evolution with artificial intelligence. *IEEE Access* 7: 164229–164245.

**41** Jararweh, Y., Doulat, A., AlQudah, O. et al. (2016). The future of mobile cloud computing: integrating cloudlets and mobile edge computing. In: *23rd International Conference on Telecommunications (ICT)*, Thessaloniki, Greece (16–18 May 2016), 1–5. IEEE.

**42** Jin, H., Jia, J., and Zhou, Z. (2020). Boosting edge intelligence with collaborative cross-edge analytics. *IEEE Internet of Things Journal* 8 (4): 2444–2458.

**43** Juric, R. (2012). Editorial on pervasive healthcare, transactions of the SDPS. *Journal of Integrated Design and Process Science* 16 (1): 1–3.

**44** Juric, R. (2016). Could semantic web technologies create new computational models outside semantic web. *Proceedings of the 21st SDPS 2016 Conference* (December 2016).

**45** Juric, R. (2019). Semantic model for creating an instance of the IoT. *Proceedings of the IEEE CyberScieTech Conference*, Fukuoka, Japan (05–08 August 2019): IEEE.

**46** Juric, R. and Madland, O. (2020). Semantic framework for creating an instance of the IoE in urban transport: a study of traffic management with driverless vehicles. *IEEE International Conference on Human-Machine Systems (ICHMS)* 2020: 1–8.

**47** Juric, R., Kuljis J., and Paul, R. (2004). Software architecture to support interoperability in multiple database systems. *Proceedings of the 22nd International Conference on Software Engineering*, IASTEDInnsbruck, Austria (17–19 February 2004): IEEE.

**48** Kataria, P. (2011). Resolving semantic conflicts through ontological layering. PhD thesis University of Westminster, London, UK.

**49** Kataria, P., Juric, R., and Madani, K. (2007). Go-CID: generic ontology for context aware, interoperable and data sharing applications. In: *Proceedings of the 11th IASTED Conf. on Software Engineering Applications*, Cambridge, SEA '07, ACTA Press, USA, 439–444.

**50** Khaitan, S.K. and McCalley, J.D. (2015). Design techniques and applications of cyberphysical systems: a survey. *IEEE Systems Journal* 9 (2): 350–365.

**51** Kim, K. and Kumar, P.R. (2012). Cyber–physical systems: a perspective at the centennial. *Proceedings of the IEEE* 100 (Special Centennial Issue): 1287–1308.

**52** Kramer, J. and Magee, J. (2009). A rigorous architectural approach to adaptive software Engineering. *Journal of Computer Science and Technology* 24: 183–188.

**53** Lane, N.D., Bhattacharya, S., Mathur, A. et al. (2017). Squeezing deep learning into mobile and embedded devices. *IEEE Pervasive Computing* 16 (3): 82–88.

**54** Leung, V.C.M., Wang, X., Jamalipour, A. et al. (2021). IEEE access special section editorial: edge computing and networking. for ubiquitous AI. *IEEE Access* 9: 90933–90936.

**55** Lohiya, R. and Thakkar, A. (2021). Application domains, evaluation data sets, and research challenges of IoT: a systematic review. *IEEE Internet of Things* 8 (11): 8774–8798.

**56** Lopez, P.G., Montresor, A., Epema, D. et al. (2015). Edge centric computing: vision and challenges. *SIGCOMM Computer Communication Review* 45 (5): 37–42.

**57** Mahdavinejad, M.S., Rezvan, M., Barekatain, P. et al. Machine learning for internet of things data analysis: a survey. *Digital Communications and Networks* 4 (3): 161–175.

**58** Manaligod, H.J.T., Diño, M.J.S., and Ghose, S. (2019). Context computing for internet of things. *Journal of Ambient Intelligence and Humanized Computing* 11: 1361–1363.

**59** Mattern, F. and Floerkemeier, J.D. (2010). From the internet of computers to the internet of things. In: *From Active Data Management to Event-Based Systems and More. LNCS*, vol. 6462 (ed. K. Sachs, I. Petrov, and P. Guerrero). Berlin, Heidelberg: Springer.

**60** Merenda, M., Porcaro, C., and Iero, D. (2020). Edge machine learning for AI-enabled IoT devices: a review. *Sensors* 20: 2533.

**61** Milojicic, D. (2020). The edge-to-cloud continuum. *Computer* 53 (11): 16–25.

**62** Miraz, M.H., Ali, M.S., Excell, P.S., and Picking, R. (2015). A review on internet of things, internet of everything and internet of nano things. In: *2015 Internet Technologies and Applications (ITA)*, Wrexham, UK (8–11 September 2015), 219–224. IEEE.

**63** Mukherjee, M., Shu, L., and Wang, D. (2018). Survey of fog computing: fundamental, network applications, and research challenges. *IEEE Communication Surveys and Tutorials* 20 (3): 1826–1857. third quarter 2018.

**64** Open Edge Computing (2018). Open Edge Computing Initiative. http://openedgecomputing.org/ (accessed 17 February 2023).

**65** Ovidiu, V., Roy, B., Marco, O. et al. (2010). Internet of robotic things intelligent connectivity and platforms. *Frontiers in Robotics and AI* 7 (0): 104.

**66** Painuly, P., Sharma, S., and Matta, P. (2021). Future trends and challenges in next generation smart application of 5G-IoT. In: *2021 5th International Conference on Computing Methodologies and Communication*, Erode, India (08–10 April 2021), 354–357. IEEE.

**67** Perera, C., Zaslavsky, A., Christen, P., and Georgakopoulos, D. (2014). Context aware computing for the internet of things: a survey. *IEEE Communication Surveys and Tutorials* 16 (1): 414–454.

**68** Pirmagomedov, R. and Koucheryavy, Y. (2021). IoT technologies for augmented human: a survey. *Internet of Things* 14 (2021): 100120.

**69** Portelli, K. and Anagnostopoulos, C. (2017). Leveraging edge computing through collaborative machine learning. In: *5th International Conference on Future Internet of Things and Cloud Workshop*, Prague, Czech Republic (21–23 August 2017), 164–169. IEEE.

**70** Qadir, J., Sainz-De-Abajo, B., Khan, A. et al. (2020). Towards mobile edge computing: taxonomy, challenges, applications and future realms. *IEEE Access* 8: 189129–189162.

**71** Raisamo, R., Rakkolainen, I., Majaranta, P. et al. (2019). Human augmentation: past, present and future. *International Journal of Human-Computer Studies* 131: 131–143.

**72** Rausch, T. and Dustdar, S. (2019). Edge intelligence: the convergence of humans, things, and AI. In: *2019 IEEE International Conference on Cloud Engineering (IC2E)*, Prague, Czech Republic (24–27 June 2019), 86–96. IEEE.

**73** Rogers, Y. (2006). Moving on from Weiser's vision of calm computing: engaging ubicomp experiences. In: *Proceedings of 8th International Conference, Ubiquitous Computing (UbiComp 06)*, Orange County, CA, USA (17–21 September 2006), 404–421. Springer Berlin Heidelberg.

**74** Sabella, D., Vaillant, D., Kuure, P. et al. (2016). Mobile-edge computing architecture: the role of MEC in the internet of things. *IEEE Consumer Electronics Magazine* 5 (4): 84–91.

**75** Saha, D. and Mukherjee, A. (2003). Pervasive computing: a paradigm for the 21st century. *Computer* 36 (3): 25–31.

**76** Saracco, R. (2018). Disruptive technologies in human augmentation impacting beyond 2040. Blog at IEEE Future Directions. https://cmte.ieee.org/futuredirections/2018/04/29/disruptive-technologies-in-human-augmentation-impacting-beyond-2040-v/ (accessed 17 February 2023).

**77** Satyanarayanan, M. (2001). Pervasive computing: vision and challenges. *IEEE Personal Communications* 8 (4): 10–17.
**78** Satyanarayanan, M. (2017). The emergence of edge computing. *Computer* 50 (1): 30–39.
**79** Satyanarayanan, M. and Davies, N. (2019, 2019). Augmenting cognition through edge computing. *Computer* 52 (7): 37–46.
**80** Satyanarayanan, M., Bahl, P., Caceres, R., and Davies, N. (2009). The case for VM-based cloudlets in mobile computing. *IEEE Pervasive Computing* 8 (4): 14–23.
**81** Satyanarayanan, M., Chen, Z., Ha, K. et al. (2014). Cloudlets: at the leading edge of mobile-cloud convergence. In: *6th International Conference on Mobile Computing, Applications and Services 2014*, 1–9. IEEE.
**82** Satyanarayanan, M., Simoens, P., Xiao, Y. et al. (2015). Edge analytics in the internet of things. *IEEE Pervasive Computing* 14 (2): 24–31.
**83** Seal, A., and Mukherjee, A. (2018). On the emerging coexistence of edge, fog and cloud comp. paradigms, in real-time internets-of-every things which operate in the big-squared data space. *SoutheastCon 2018*, St. Petersburg, FL, USA (19–22 April 2018). pp. 1–9: IEEE.
**84** Shafique, K., Khawaja, B.A., Sabir, F. et al. (2020). Internet of Things (IoT) for next-generation smart systems: a review of current challenges, future trends and prospects for emerging 5G-IoT scenarios. *IEEE Access* 8: 23022–23040.
**85** Shah, S.H. and Yaqoob, I. (2016). A survey: Internet of Things (IOT) technologies, applications and challenges. In: *IEEE Smart Energy Grid Engineering Conference*, Oshawa, ON, Canada (21–24 August 2016), 381–385. IEEE.
**86** Shi, W. and Dustdar, D. (2016). The promise of edge computing. *Computer* 49 (5): 78–81.
**87** Shojanoori, R. (2013). Towards formalisation of situation-specific computations in pervasive computing environments. PhD thesis. University of Westminster, London, UK.
**88** Shojanoori, R. and Juric, R. (2013). Semantic remote patient monitoring system. *Tele-Medicine and e-Health Journal* 19 (2): 129–136.
**89** Shojanoori, R. Juric, R., and Lohi, M. (2010). Reasoning and decision making in managing pervasive computational spaces. *17th Automated Reasoning Workshop*, University of Westminster, 30–31 March.
**90** Shojanoori, R., Juric, R., and Lohi, M. (2012). Computationally significant semantics in pervasive healthcare. *Journal of Integrated Design and Process Science*, IOS Press 16: 43–62.
**91** Shojanoori, R., Juric, R., Lohi, M., and Terstyanszky, G. (2014). ASeCS: assistive self-care software architectures for delivering service in care homes. *2014 47th Hawaii International Conference on System Sciences*, Waikoloa, HI, USA (06–09 January 2014). IEEE.
**92** Simoens, P., Dragone, M., and Saffiotti, A. (2018). The Internet of Robotic Things: a review of concept, added value and applications. *International Journal of Advanced Robotic Systems* 15: 1–11.
**93** Stirling, B. (2002). Without vision, the people perish. *Speech Given at CRA Conference on Grand Research Challenges in Computer Science and Engineering*, Warrenton, Virginia (June 23): Computing Research Association – CRA.
**94** Sun, X. and Ansari, N. (2016). EdgeIoT: mobile edge computing for the internet of things. *IEEE Communications Magazine* 54 (12): 22–29.
**95** Taleb, T., Ksentini, A., and Frangoudis, P.A. (2019). Follow-me cloud: when cloud services follow mobile users. *IEEE Transactions on Cloud Computing* 7 (2): 369–382. 1 April–June 2019.
**96** Talia, V., Hessar, M., Kellog, K. et al. (2017). LoRaBackscatter: enabling the vision of ubiquitous computing. *ACM Interactive, Mobile, Wearable Ubiquitous Technology* 1 (3): 1–24.

**97** Thomert, B., Renart, D., Zamani, E.G. et al. (2019). Towards a computing continuum: enabling edge-to-cloud integration for data-driven workflows, International Journal on The. *International Journal of High Performance Computing Applications* 33 (6): 1159–1174.

**98** Vaquero, L.M. and Rodero-Merino, L. (2014). Finding your way in the fog: towards a comprehensive definition of fog computing. *ACM SIGCOMM Computer Communication Review* 44 (5): 27–32.

**99** Verbelen, T., Simoens, P., De Turck, F., and Dhoedt, B. (2012). Cloudlets: bringing the cloud to the mobile user. In: *Third ACM Workshop on Mobile Cloud Computing and Services*, –29, 36. ACM.

**100** Weiser, M. (1991). The computer for the 21st century. *Scientific American* 265 (3): 78–89.

**101** Weiser, M. (1993). Some computer science issues in ubiquitous computing. *Communications of the ACM* 36 (7): 75–84.

**102** Whitmore, A., Agarwal, A., and Da Xu, L. (2015). The internet of things – a survey of topics and trends. *Information Systems Frontiers*, Springer US 17 (2): 261–274.

**103** Wolf, M. (2019). Machine learning + distributed IoT = edge intelligence. In: *2019 IEEE 39th International Conference on Distributed Comp. Systems (ICDCS)*, Dallas, TX, USA (07–10 July 2019), 1715–1719. IEEE.

**104** Yaacoub, J.P.A., Noura, M., Noura, H.N. et al. (2020). Securing internet of medical things systems: limitations, issues and recommendations. *Future Generation Computer Systems* 105: 581–606.

**105** Yousefpour, A., Fung, C., Nguyenc, T. et al. (2019). All one needs to know about fog computing and related edge computing paradigms: a complete survey. *Journal of Systems Architecture* 98: 289–330.

**106** Zhang, B., Mor, N., Kolb, J. et al. (2015). The cloud is not enough: saving IoT from the cloud. In: *Proceedings of the 7th USENIX Conference on Hot Topics in Cloud Computing (HotCloud)*, Santa Clara CA (6–7 July 2015)., 21–28.

# 22

# Implementing Context Awareness in Autonomous Vehicles

*Federico Faruffini[1,2], Alessandro Correa-Victorino[1], and Marie-Hélène Abel[1]*

[1] *Heudiasyc Laboratory, University of Technology of Compiègne, Compiègne, France*
[2] *DIBRIS, University of Genoa, Genoa, Italy*

## 22.1 Introduction

Many autonomous driving models exist nowadays, and some of them are fully capable of performing safe global navigation avoiding obstacles on their path. However, a problem which is still present to our day is the big difference between a person and an autonomous car in the way they drive, as this relies on many factors. One of the most important is the implicit information about the situation that a human driver naturally considers while driving, while autonomous vehicles don't. The totality of this implicit pieces of information specific to the driving scenario is the contextual information. In this chapter, we are going to illustrate how the context of navigation can be used to reduce the gap between a robotic driver and a human one, by fully adapting its driving style and choices to the situation. In particular, we will show an approach we developed, based on modeling the context and using it in the control loop of the autonomous car to modify its standard behavior.

Before to proceed, let us make a few examples to give the reader an idea of the scenarios which are possible to encode into the context of navigation. Our first example regards an autonomous car transporting a pregnant woman. In such a situation, for example, a human driver would probably take smoother turns, accelerate slowly, and when possible take safer roads. In this scenario, it is important to know the state of the pregnancy and how many weeks the pregnancy has lasted so far, as we know there are specific weeks in which it is more dangerous to a pregnant woman to be on a car or drive it. These and many other information can be stored in the context of navigation to let the car understand them.

Another example is the one of objects which are being carried in our car: a human driver would care about their size, positioning in the vehicle, properties (is it at risk of melting, or fragile?) and would decide on how to adapt his driving style to it. For instance, in the case of a heavy package on the upper luggage rack, the driver would avoid steering to fast as it could cause instability problems.

The structure of this chapter is the following: at first, we are going to discuss some background information on ontologies and autonomous driving in Section 22.2, then in Section 22.2.3, we will give a formal definition of the context of navigation. Later, in Section 22.3, we will present the state-of-the-art studies on related fields. Then, we will proceed with Section 22.4, in which we show our method to build the context of navigation, reason over it and use it to suggest to the control loop how to operate. We will also see some tests at the end of the section. Finally, in Section 22.5, we will draft our conclusions, and in Section 22.6, we will discuss the future research challenges for this study field.

*Handbook of Human-Machine Systems*, First Edition. Edited by Giancarlo Fortino, David Kaber, Andreas Nürnberger, and David Mendonça.

## 22.2 Background

In this section, we are going to recall some topics which will be useful to the reader to understand our implementation strategies.

### 22.2.1 Ontologies

The first point we'd like to discuss is that of ontologies. According to Studer et al. [9], an ontology is "a formal, explicit specification of a shared conceptualization." It is a tool to represent data in a domain of discourse in such a way that it is both understandable by humans and computers. Ontologies, differently from standard relational databases, have a really interesting property to our scope, as they allow for reasoning on their data to infer new knowledge over the existing one. Another difference from databases is the way data are stored in ontologies: instead of tuples, ontologies use triples. The structure of a triple is *Subject-Predicate-Object*, for instance

*Mark isOwnerOf RedCar*
*Mark hasAge 43*

The information stored in an ontology make up the so-called "knowledge graph." The standard language for ontology definition is OWL,[1] the Web Ontology Language, and it allows for complex triple structures. It defines classes for the instances in our triple store and properties for them. In the first example, *Mark* is an instance of the *Person* class, while *RedCar* could be an instance of a *Car* class. This latter class could be in turn a child class to a more generic *Vehicle* class. The link between *Mark* and *RedCar* is *isOwnerOf*, which is an object property (class to class). In the second example, *hasAge* is a data property, as *43* is just a value and not an object. With restrictions over the classes and properties, we shape our ontology and a first simple reasoning. One of the ways it is possible to obtain a more complex reasoning over an ontology is the Semantic Web Rule Language (SWRL) by Horrocks et al. [3]. SWRL lets the programmer define inference rules as follows: one or more boolean variables are considered as antecedent, one as a consequent: if all the ones in the antecedent are true, then the consequent is true in turn. An example of SWRL rule is the following:

$$\mathit{EgoVehicle}(?v) \wedge \mathit{hasPassenger}(?v, ?p) \wedge \mathit{Person}(?p) \wedge$$
$$\mathit{hasLocalRoadDrivingPreference}(?p, ?\mathit{pref}) \rightarrow$$
$$\mathit{hasLocalRoadDrivingStyle}(?v, ?\mathit{pref})$$

This rule lets the car infer that it must take the preferred driving style of the one passenger onboard. SWRL rule consequents can be used as antecedents in other rules so that a multilayered structure is created for a more deep reasoning in our ontology.

### 22.2.2 Autonomous Driving

Starting in 2004, the Defense Advanced Research Projects Agency (DARPA) of the USA held three major competitions for autonomous cars [10, 11]. Since then, this field has seen a lot of interest by the scientific community and many autonomous vehicle models currently exist. Much of them

1 https://www.w3.org/OWL/.

are based on sensors (internal – endoceptive, external – exteroceptive) like GPS systems in order to navigate. Some of such models suffer from sensor problems, as temporary disconnection or sensor failures. Another kind of autonomous vehicle model is based on Visual Servoing (VS), meaning the car drives itself by using a frontal camera. This approach was proven to be more stable than standard sensor-based ones. Since we based our solution on an existing one which relies on Visual Servoing, we are now going to illustrate how it operates. Such an approach is called the Image-based Dynamic Window Approach (IDWA) [7], and it combines VS to drive the car with the Dynamic Window Approach to perform obstacle avoidance.

In Figure 22.1, we show how the way the car is driven in the center of the lane by IDWA. The model computes the limits of the lane (continuous line delimiting the right lane) in order to compute the center of the lane (continuous line in the center of the right lane). Then, the position of the car is computed, and the control needed to get to the center (if there is some position error) is computed.

When an obstacle is perceived, the control is given to the DWA (dynamic window approach) module, which computes the best couple of tangential and rotational velocities $(v, w)$ to overcome it safely and comfortably. This is achieved by finding the best couple which optimized the following cost function:

$$IDWA(v, w) = \alpha \cdot heading(v, w) + \beta \cdot dist(v, w) + \gamma \cdot velocity(v) \tag{22.1}$$

where $\alpha$, $\beta$, and $\gamma$ are real-valued parameters to be properly tuned. The *heading* function aims at keeping the car in the center of the lane, the *dist* function is used to avoid obstacles and the *velocity* function's objective is to keep the car's speed close to a desired setpoint.

### 22.2.3 Basic Definitions

A formal definition of the context of navigation was given in [2]:

> The navigation context is any information that can be used to characterize the situation of navigation over a given period of time. Here, navigation is a movement considered relevant to the interaction between a driver and an application, including the driver and the applications themselves.

The context of navigation has two main components: the static context and the dynamic context. The static context comprehends all those information which don't change with respect to the

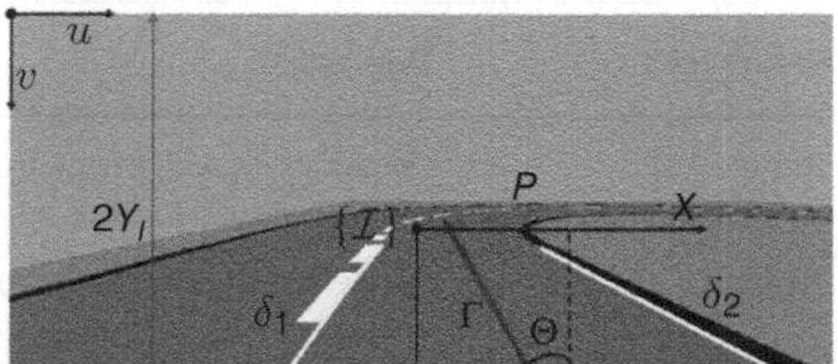


**Figure 22.1** IDWA visual servoing in [7].

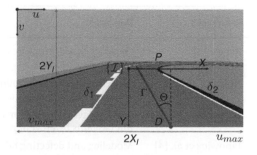

current navigation. Instances can be the preferences of the passengers, their health situation, the type of carried load and its property, etc. The dynamic context contains the information which may vary during the navigation, as the position of obstacles, other vehicles, state of traffic lights, temperature of the engine, and fuel in the tank. Given its modular nature, the context of navigation can be easily implemented for different applications through the use of an ontology.

## 22.3 Related Works

As we decided to use ontologies to our scopes, we will now see some of the most interesting studies on ontologies applied to the vehicle navigation.

Regele [8] proposed an ontology-based structure to model the topology of the road, in order to let the autonomous car understand it. Each road segment is labeled to allow the car to understand which of the lanes are available for it to navigate and which cannot be used. Also, with the same labels the car understands the concept of conflicting/merging lanes and is enabled to use traffic rules in them in a safe way. One of the key points of this approach is the low computational power required in real time by the car, as it can only be given information on the lanes around itself and not the full structure, to reason over in real time. Xiong et al. [12] proposed to divide the space surrounding the ego vehicle and label the portions, for instance *Follower, Follower's Follower, Leader, NearSide Follower*. This way it is easier to model reasoning, for instance when the car has to deal with overtaking a slower vehicle.

Many ontology-based solutions can be found in ADAS (Advanced Driving Assistance Systems), and some of them consider some external information to aid the driver. In the case of Zhao et al. [13] the authors studied a model for a safer ride by helping the driver in uncontrolled intersections and by preventing him to exceed the speed limit. Since the car's perception is sensor-based, it is important to model and detect failures in them. The (Sensor, Observation, Sample, and Actuator) SOSA ontology proposed by Janowicz et al. [4] can be used to deal with this problem.

A very interesting study is the one by Armand et al. [1]. proposed an ontology to let the car reason in a way which is extremely similar to the one of a human driver. This is important as this way the rules are also easier to be implemented, tested, and debugged. These works are resumed in a comparative way in Table 22.1.

**Table 22.1** Related works comparison table.

| References | Description |
|---|---|
| Regele [8] | Ontology-based structure to model the topology of the road and lanes. |
| Xiong et al. [12] | Modeling the space surrounding the ego vehicle and label the portions to overtaking maneuvers. |
| Zhao et al. [14] | Ontology-based model for a safer ride in uncontrolled intersections by preventing excessive speed. |
| Janowicz et al. [4] | Modeling and detecting failures in perception. |
| Armand et al. [1] | Ontology for reasoning as a human driver. |

## 22.4 Implementation and Tests

In this section, we are going to illustrate how our structure works in more detail. At first, we are going to provide an example of the context of navigation modeling using an ontology and SWRL. Later in this section, we are going to see our solution to implement a context-aware control loop rule called Image-and-Context-based Dynamic Window Approach (ICDWA).

### 22.4.1 Implementing the Context of Navigation

In Section 22.2, we gave an overview of the semantic tools we can use to model the context of navigation, which is ontologies and the Semantic Web Rule Language. We will now see how simple it is to use them to create a modular structure to store information over the context of navigation and reason over it. From the definition of the context of navigation [2], we can understand how much information can be considered part of it: for the sake of brevity, we are just going to show a small example of it. Also, the complexity of debugging ontologies is known in the literature by Lambrix [5], and a modular approach is often seen as a good solution to avoid needing big debugging operations.

The main purpose of our ontology structure is to reason and give a real time suggestion of maximum speed $v$ and yaw rate $w$ depending on the situation. The control loop rule will take these suggestions in its optimization function to find the best $(v, w)$ for the car.

Let us take the following scenario as our example. We have an autonomous car with a sick passenger called Mark, who is going to the hospital. Fortunately, the situation is not an emergency, so the car must stick to the traffic rules as usual. As the passenger is sick and nauseated, we want the car to adapt its driving behavior to this situation, to avoid worsening the man's condition. To complicate this scenario, let us assume we have different paths to the destination, with different features as speed bumps, heavy traffic, and so on.

How can we model the context in this case? Of course, we are going to need the triples to store data about our passenger and his condition:

*Mark isOwnerOf RedCar*
*RedCar a EgoVehicle*
*Mark hasAge 43*
*Mark hasPassengerState Sick*
*Mark hasPassengerState Nauseated*
*RedCar hasPassenger Mark*
*RedCar hasCurrentFuel 10.4*

Also, we can have some rules to support the reasoning. We can now show just a couple of them to understand how they are written:

*EgoVehicle(?v) ∧ hasPassenger(?v, ?p) ∧ Person(?p) ∧ hasPassengerState(?p, Sick) →*
*hasSickPassenger(?v, True)*
*EgoVehicle(?v) ∧ hasSickPassenger(?v, ?p) →*
*hasDrivingStyle(?v, Sick_Passenger_DrivingStyle)*
*EgoVehicle(?v) ∧ hasDrivingStyle(?v, Sick_Passenger_DrivingStyle) →*
*hasSuggestedMaxSpeed(?v, 40)*

So with these three rules we created a reasoning stack that brings the suggested speed of the car to a lower value, which is 40 km/h to not worsen the passenger's nausea. As we can see, with just a simple structure like this one we get the required suggestion to be sent to the control loop. A similar but slightly more complex structure can be created for the $w$ suggestion.

### 22.4.2 Control Loop Rule

Here, we will present our solution for a control loop rule able to adapt to the situation. It is based on the IDWA [7] algorithm we presented in Section 22.2.2 and implements context awareness. Its full name is ICDWA – the Image and Context-based Dynamic Window Approach. So how does the interaction between context and control loop work? As we said in Section 22.4, our ontology in real time gets us a suggestion of maximum values of speed $v$ and yaw rate $w$. We can add a component to the cost function in (22.1), a new component called *context* to take the ontology suggestions into account, and we obtain

$$IDWA(v, w) = \alpha \cdot heading(v, w) + \beta \cdot dist(v, w) + \gamma \cdot velocity(v) + \delta \cdot context(v, w) \tag{22.2}$$

which is the objective function for ICDWA. Let us now discuss the *context* component. First of all, $\delta \in \mathbb{R}$ is a parameter to be tuned with the others in order to assign weight to this component. Second, we can say that since $v$ and $w$ are not fully related, we can split the component into two subcomponents and then add those to get its value:

$$context(v, w) = \epsilon \cdot (context_v(v) + context_w(w)) \tag{22.3}$$

Here, $\epsilon \in [0, 1]$ is a parameter which we will discuss later on. Let us now consider $context_v$: what is the behavior we want from it? Given a suggestion of maximum speed $v_{MAX}$, we want it to generate a high cost if $v \geq v_{MAX}$, a lower one, otherwise. Since we will find the best values $(v, w)$ from (22.2) through gradient descent, we need it to be continuous, derivable, and convex. If we define

$$x = v - v_{CN} \tag{22.4}$$

we can then use the following implementation for $context_v$:

$$context_v(v) = \begin{cases} \sigma(x), & \text{if } x \leq 0 \\ \frac{1}{2} + \frac{1}{4}x, & \text{otherwise} \end{cases} \tag{22.5}$$

where the $\sigma$ function is the sigmoid function. Our $context_v$ component as defined in (22.5) has a smoothed ramp-like behavior, which increases as long as we don't follow the ontology's suggestions.

We previously hinted at the parameter $\epsilon$ in (22.3). Why to use another gain for the component, and not just one containing both $\delta$ and $\epsilon$ in it? We decided to do so for an easier model: let us see why we need $\epsilon$ and why we need these parameters to be separated. Let us now assume to have a very old passenger in our car, who prefers it to be driven at a very low speed to feel safer on board. Now, is it always correct to follow this desire? Probably, if we have a low-traffic situation there won't be any issues in following it. However, if we have a high-traffic scenario, if we decide to slow down the car we could worsen the traffic situation, and that is not acceptable. By real time reasoning, we can compute the optimal value of $\epsilon$ so that we can follow the suggestions only when it is possible ($\epsilon = 1$) and ignore them otherwise ($\epsilon = 0$). Now, if we consider also the full range $[0, 1]$, we can have a mixed behavior, in which we try to adapt to the desires of the passenger while keeping in account the traffic situation. The value of $\epsilon$ is computed in real time by a specific part of the ontology.

To finish, why do we need to separate $\delta$ and $\epsilon$? The reason lies in their nature: $\delta$ is tuned in laboratory, and then kept constant throughout the navigation, while $\epsilon$ can change at any instant.

**Figure 22.2** The simulation of ICDWA in SCANeR Studio

### 22.4.3 Simulations

The Image-and-Context-based Dynamic Window Approach was eventually tested in a professional simulator for the automative industry and academics, called SCANeR Studio.[2] Java is the native language of most of the software implementations of ontologies; however, SCANeR doesn't have a Java interface, so we decided to test our solution with Python code. The Python3 library we used is called owlready2, developed in [6].

We will now present the results we obtained with a particular test. The scenario we chose is the one we can see in Figure 22.2, in which the car starts from a speed of 0 km/h and needs to proceed in a road with three obstacles to be overcome, staying in the center of the lane when possible. The maximum speed for the car was set to 10 km/h for this test.

In Figure 22.3, we can see the behavior of the longitudinal speed for an autonomous car with and without context awareness, and see the differences in its behavior. The solid line, with $\epsilon = 0$, is the one in which we don't consider the contextual suggestions at all, resulting in a pure IDWA control. We can see clearly the pattern that the speed of the car follows for the three obstacles. The dark dashed line represents the situation in which we assign the weights $\delta = 0.75$ and $\epsilon = 1$ to the context component. In this case, the speed limit is set to the same as before, but as we can see the car keeps a little below it, as we instructed it through the cost function in (22.5). Finally, the higher line

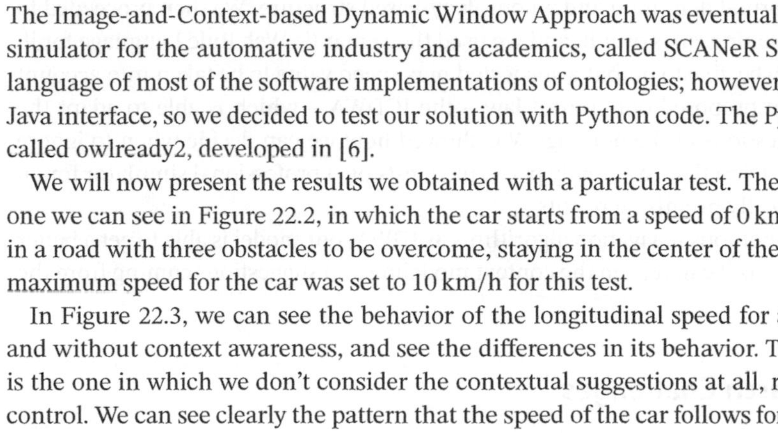

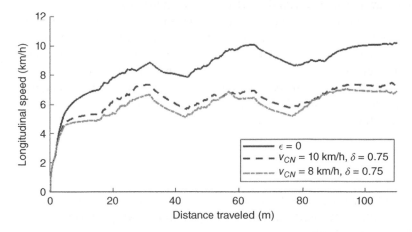


**Figure 22.3** The speed profile of the autonomous car with ICDWA.

2 https://www.avsimulation.com/scaner-studio/.

represents the same situation with a lower value of suggested speed $v_{CN}$, which was set to $8km/h$. We can see how the car keeps a speed which is even lower than the previous test and respects again the suggestions. This was a simple simulation, but it showed promising results.

We performed other tests, varying the values of the parameters and the max speed. All of them were successful (the vehicle did not crash into an obstacle or go off the road) and led to different car behaviors. It was clear the problem now is to find a way to set the four parameters in the cost function of ICDWA to optimize the performance. Also, the $\epsilon$ parameter was for the moment chosen before runtime, but it must be computed in real time to be effective.

## 22.5 Conclusions

In this chapter, we presented a new context-aware control loop called ICDWA – the Image-and-Context-based Dynamic Window Approach. We proposed a way to structure the context of navigation by giving it a formal definition and an ontology-based structure. We then proceeded to study the way to build reasoning rules over it, and we used the Semantic Web Rule Language for it. We shaped our ontology to be able to output a suggested max speed value to be taken into account by the controller. We then proposed our control law – the ICDWA – which is able to adapt the car's behavior to the suggestions of the ontology. We showed how we can decide when to ignore such suggestions and how to do that. We finally performed tests on a professional simulator for an automotive which led to really promising results.

Compared to other autonomous navigation algorithms as IDWA, our model is able to get a better adaptation to the situation, as it can rely on the context modeling and suggestions coming from the ontology in real time.

## 22.6 Future Research Challenges

Even if the proposed structure was proven to have a good performance, many more challenges are still open. In future works, the automated tuning of $\alpha, \beta\gamma, and\ \delta$ will be studied, as well as the computation for the $\epsilon$ parameter. Also, the control loop rule is to be expanded with the real-time suggestion of the maximum yaw rate $w$, and with the jerk computation for $v$ too.

On the other hand, the context of navigation we proposed in our examples is small if compared to what it could be: future works will focus on expanding it with many more information. Some of the latter are the integration of a trajectory planner, traffic rules, obstacle trajectory predictor, and many more. Also, a way to input data into the ontology is needed, and it must not take too long for the users, so this will be another interesting part of future studies. Since many data about the potential passengers will be collected and stored, it is important to consider security aspects as well as data ethics in early stages of the project.

## References


1 Armand, A., Filliat, D., and Ibañez-Guzman, J. (2014). Ontology-based context awareness for driving assistance systems. *2014 IEEE Intelligent Vehicles Symposium Proceedings*, 227–233. https://doi.org/10.1109/IVS.2014.6856509.

2 Faruffini, F., Correa-Victorino, A., and Abel, M.-H. (2021). Towards a semantic model of the context of navigation. In: *Information and Knowledge Systems. Digital Technologies, Artificial*

*Intelligence and Decision Making* (ed. I. Saad, C. Rosenthal-Sabroux, F. Gargouri, and P.-E. Arduin), 168–183. Cham: Springer International Publishing. ISBN 978-3-030-85977-0.

3 Horrocks, I., Patel-Schneider, P.F., Boley, H. et al. (2004). SWRL: A semantic web rule language combining OWL and RuleML. W3C Member Submission, 21 May 2004. http://www.w3.org/Submission/SWRL/.

4 Janowicz, K., Haller, A., Cox, S.J.D. et al. (2018). SOSA: A lightweight ontology for sensors, observations, samples, and actuators. *CoRR*, abs/1805.09979. http://arxiv.org/abs/1805.09979.

5 Lambrix, P. (2020). Completing and debugging ontologies: state of the art and challenges.

6 Lamy, J.-B. (2017). Owlready: Ontology-oriented programming in python with automatic classification and high level constructs for biomedical ontologies. *Artificial Intelligence in Medicine* 80: 11–28. https://doi.org/10.1016/j.artmed.2017.07.002.

7 Lima, D. and Victorino, A. (2016). A hybrid controller for vision-based navigation of autonomous vehicles in urban environments. *IEEE Transactions on Intelligent Transportation Systems* 17 (8): 2310–2323. https://doi.org/10.1109/TITS.2016.2519329.

8 Regele, R. (2008). Using ontology-based traffic models for more efficient decision making of autonomous vehicles. *4th International Conference on Autonomic and Autonomous Systems (ICAS 2008)*, Gosier, Guadeloupe (16–21 March 2008), 94–99. IEEE Computer Society. https://doi.org/10.1109/ICAS.2008.10.

9 Studer, R., Benjamins, V.R., and Fensel, D. (1998). Knowledge engineering: principles and methods. *Data & Knowledge Engineering* 25 (1): 161–197. https://doi.org/https://doi.org/10.1016/S0169-023X(97)00056-6.

10 Thrun, S. (2006). Winning the DARPA grand challenge. In: *Machine Learning: ECML 2006* (ed. J. Furnkranz, T. Scheffer, and M. Spiliopoulou), 4. Berlin, Heidelberg: Springer-Verlag. ISBN 978-3-540-46056-5.

11 Thrun, S., Montemerlo, M., Dahlkamp, H. et al. (2006). Stanley: the robot that won the DARPA Grand Challenge. *Journal of Field Robotics* 23: 661–692.

12 Xiong, Z., Dixit, V.V., and Waller, S.T. (2016). The development of an ontology for driving context modeling and reasoning. *2016 IEEE 19th International Conference on Intelligent Transportation Systems (ITSC)*, 13–18. https://doi.org/10.1109/ITSC.2016.7795524.

13 Zhao, L., Ichise, R., Mita, S., and Sasaki, Y. (2015). Core ontologies for safe autonomous driving. *International Semantic Web Conference (Posters & Demos)*, volume 1486 of *CEUR Workshop Proceedings* (ed. S. Villata, J.Z. Pan, and M. Dragoni). CEUR-WS.org.

14 ZhaoLihua, L., Ichise, R., Yoshikawa, T. et al. (2015). Ontology-based decision making on uncontrolled intersections and narrow roads. *2015 IEEE Intelligent Vehicles Symposium, IV 2015*, Seoul, South Korea (June 28 – July 1, 2015), 83–88. IEEE. https://doi.org/10.1109/IVS.2015.7225667.

# 23

# The Augmented Workforce: A Systematic Review of Operator Assistance Systems

*Elisa Roth, Mirco Moencks, and Thomas Bohné*

*Department of Engineering, Institute for Manufacturing, University of Cambridge, Cambridge, UK*

## 23.1 Introduction

Advances in manufacturing technologies, shortening product life cycles, and high product variability are changing the nature of work in industry. Despite ongoing strides toward automation, human workers are expected to remain essential on shop floors. What is more, the operation and maintenance of increasingly complex technologies impose new challenges for manufacturing workers [22]. Yet, the current workforce often lacks the skills to excel in future production systems [2]. This gives rise to an interesting and important question: *How can technologies augment – rather than replace – the set of skills that enable humans to thrive in the production industry?* Operator Assistance Systems (OAS) could be a potential solution: they promise to close the gap between operational demands and workers' capabilities [19, 23]. OAS are systems that interact with operators to augment their cognitive or physical abilities while performing industrial tasks [18]. Examples for OAS include augmented reality headsets, in situ projectors, mobile devices, wearable devices, and desktop setups (see Figure 23.1).

OAS research can be characterized by (i) their *applied industrial research* nature, (ii) *cyber-physical integration*, (iii) *sociotechnical* considerations such as ergonomics and privacy, (iv) *suitability* for harsh industrial environments, and (v) their potential to *transform the nature of work*. However, research on OAS is highly fragmented and heterogeneous [9]. This fragmentation has resulted in a lack of context and connection among contributions, which are constraining academic discourse and research impact. A structured overview of the current state in OAS-related topics is currently missing. This review, therefore, contributes a systematic map of the intellectual territory around OAS to create a systematic foundation for future OAS research. The following research question is addressed: *What are the main empirical approaches, application areas, system capabilities, hardware, user interfaces, and future directions for OAS research?*

*Handbook of Human-Machine Systems*, First Edition. Edited by Giancarlo Fortino, David Kaber, Andreas Nürnberger, and David Mendonça.

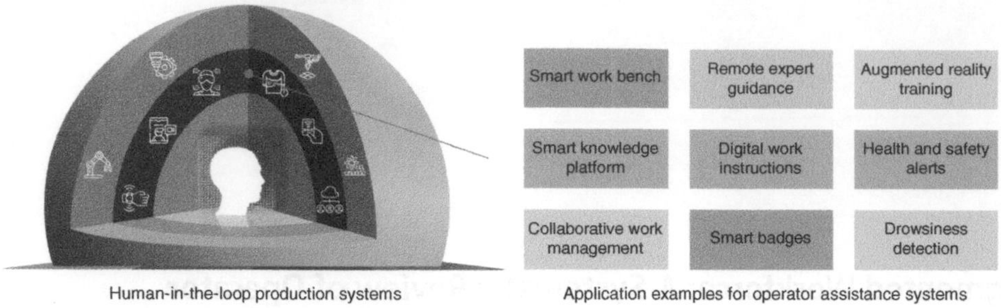


**Figure 23.1** Industrial human–machine systems: Examples of operator assistance systems.

## 23.2 Background

Assistance systems have been reviewed and conceptualized from different perspectives. Despite an increasing interest in OAS, a systematic review of the field is missing. Early work in conceptualizing assistance systems has been done by Wandke [27], providing a taxonomy of technology-agnostic assistance capabilities. The elaborations on system adaption and initiation classifications add value to the field. Beyond this, Bertram et al. [4] provide an overview of nine assistance systems for manual workstations. Their contribution can be seen in discussing application scenarios in assembly and deriving design requirements. Hold and Sihn [14] propose a taxonomy for digital assistance systems, providing a differentiation of user interfaces and task domains. The Operator 4.0 taxonomy introduced by Romero et al. [24] is gaining increasing consideration in industry, depicting future technology-assisted work styles. The field has also been shaped by Pacaux-Lemoine et al. [20]'s work on human–machine cooperation principles, by Cimini et al. [6] proposing a human-in-the-loop manufacturing control architecture, by Kaasinen et al. [15] shifting worker empowerment into the focus of discussion, and by Pinzone et al. [21] establishing a wider framework for social sustainability in cyber-physical production systems (CPPS). While these studies make important contributions, they do not synthesize capabilities, meta-information, and challenges around OAS research. This is, however, crucial when advancing theory building within emerging research domains and motivates our systematic review.

### 23.2.1 Definitions

Wandke [27] refers to assistance as giving access to functions performed by interactive devices that would otherwise not be accessible. Marks et al. [16] classify assistance systems along the lower to medium levels of the 10 Levels of Automation of Decision and Action Selection. In general, the level of assistance should be adequate to the intended use and context [14]. In information systems research, adequate refers to get the right information to the right people at the right time, amount, and format. Assistance systems support workers by providing, processing, or collecting information [24]. OAS in industry has been characterized from intelligent, smart, flexible, digital, knowledge-based, interactive, to cognitive. Since the attributes vary among studies, this review refrains from overly restricting the concept definition. Synthesizing the above, the following definition is introduced: ***Operator Assistance Systems*** *collect, process, and disseminate information to assist workers with industrial tasks. In doing so, OAS provide the right information to the right people, at the right time, in the right amount and in the right format. As a result, interactive computing devices provide additional functions which would otherwise not be accessible to the operator.*

## 23.3 State of the Art

We systematically reviewed 201 papers published between 2005 and 2020 to depict the field's development and most relevant contributions. The review methodology follows [7] and is depicted in Figure 23.2. The search string can be seen in Figure 23.3. A meta-analysis systemizes contribution types, application areas, and empirical parameters. The review further elaborates on nine key capabilities of OAS: five assistance capabilities (task guidance, knowledge management, monitoring, communication, and decision-making), and four meta-capabilities (configuration flexibility, interoperability, content authoring, and initiation). We further systemize the state of the art in hardware and interfaces identified within use cases.

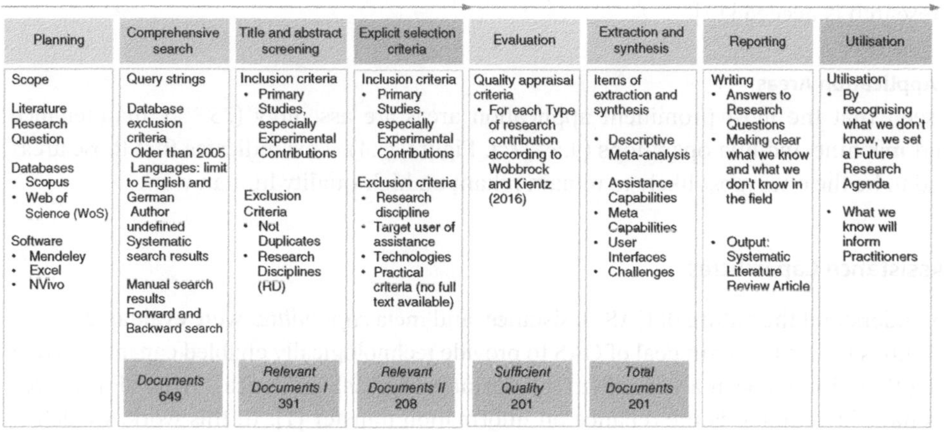

Planning
Comprehensive search
Title and abstract screening
Explicit selection criteria
Evaluation
Extraction and synthesis
Reporting
Utilisation
Scope
Literature Research Question
Databases • Scopus • Web of Science (WoS)
Software • Mendeley • Excel • NVivo
Query strings
Database exclusion criteria Older than 2005 Languages: limit to English and German Author undefined Systematic search results
Manual search results
Forward and Backward search
Inclusion criteria • Primary Studies, especially Experimental Contributions
Exclusion Criteria • Not Duplicates • Research Disciplines (HD)
Inclusion criteria • Primary Studies, especially Experimental Contributions
Exclusion criteria • Research discipline • Target user of assistance • Technologies • Practical criteria (no full text available)
Quality appraisal criteria • For each Type of research contribution according to Wobbrock and Kientz (2016)
Items of extraction and synthesis • Descriptive Meta-analysis • Assistance Capabilities • Meta Capabilities • User Interfaces • Challenges
Writing • Answers to Research Questions • Making clear what we know and what we don't know in the field • Output: Systematic Literature Review Article
Utilisation • By recognising what we don't know, we set a Future Research Agenda • What we know will inform Practitioners
Documents 649
Relevant Documents I 391
Relevant Documents II 208
Sufficient Quality 201
Total Documents 201


**Figure 23.2** Systematic review protocol building on [7].

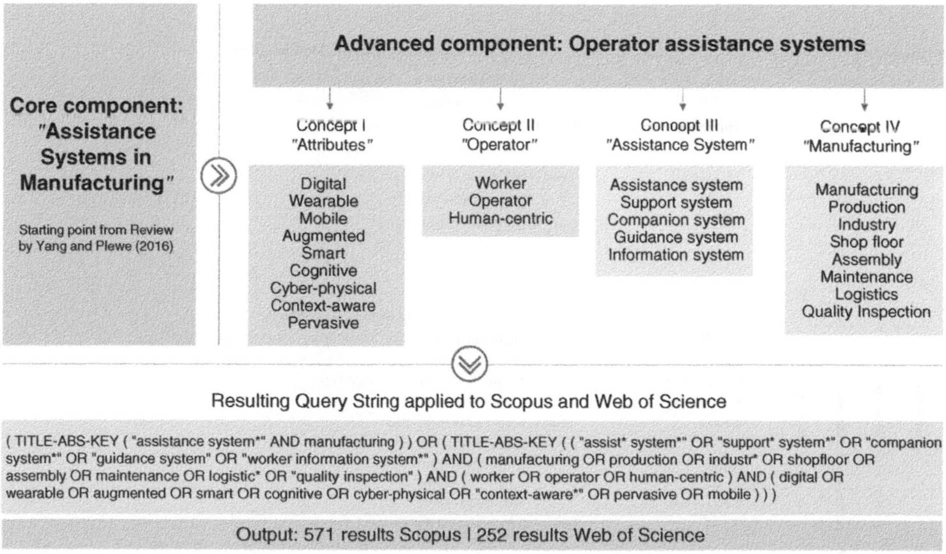


**Figure 23.3** Systematic derivation of the literature search strings, building on the screening of a related review paper [28].

### 23.3.1 Empirical Considerations

Our review examined empirical practices in OAS research (cf. Figure 23.4). Laboratory and field experiments can help to gain generalizable insights for system improvement. However, the average sample sizes of laboratory experiments ($n = 20$) and proof-of-concept studies ($n = 9$) tend to be small (cf. Figure 23.4). In total, only few field experiments and longitudinal studies have been conducted ($n = 9$). This could be explained by the challenge of conducting experiments during daily operations. Constructs and variables such as Time to Completion (TTC, $n = 34$), Error Rate (ER, $n = 28$), and NASA-Task Load Index (TLX, $n = 15$) prevail as dominant evaluation criteria. Measuring human performance with TTC and error rates (ER) has proven to be a valid indicator for efficiency. However, this does not apply for the overall effectiveness and human-centricity of OAS. To identify whether OAS can increase the performance of the wider production system, more empirical research is needed [17].

#### 23.3.1.1 Application Areas

It can be seen that the most prominent application areas are assembly (35.3%), maintenance (10.4%), and machine and line operations (9.5%) (cf. Figure 23.4). This indicates that those areas are expected to be the ones most likely to remain reliant on high-quality human work.

### 23.3.2 Assistance Capabilities

In order to understand the nature of OAS, assistance, and meta *capabilities* were evaluated. Assistance capabilities reflect the main goal of OAS to provide technologically enabled capabilities that would have otherwise not been accessible to the operator (e.g. task guidance). What all reviewed capabilities have in common is the reliance on information transfer [1]. In this work, we define *meta capabilities* as capabilities which (i) are required to run in the background of an OAS infrastructure, or (ii) define the underlying design or principles of OAS, thus enabling and facilitating the assistance capabilities outlined in the chapter 23.3.2. In contrast to meta-capabilities, assistance

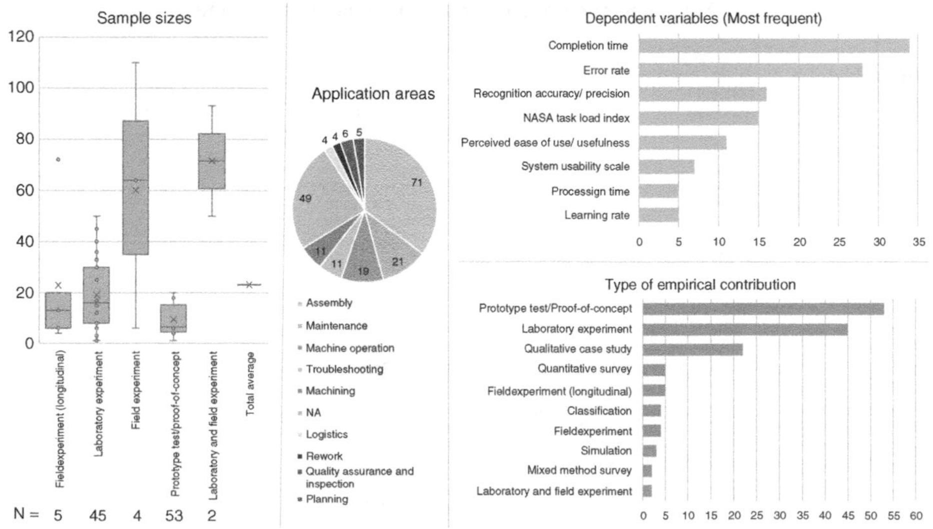


**Figure 23.4** Overview of empirical approaches including sample sizes, experimental design, dependent variables, and types of empirical contribution.

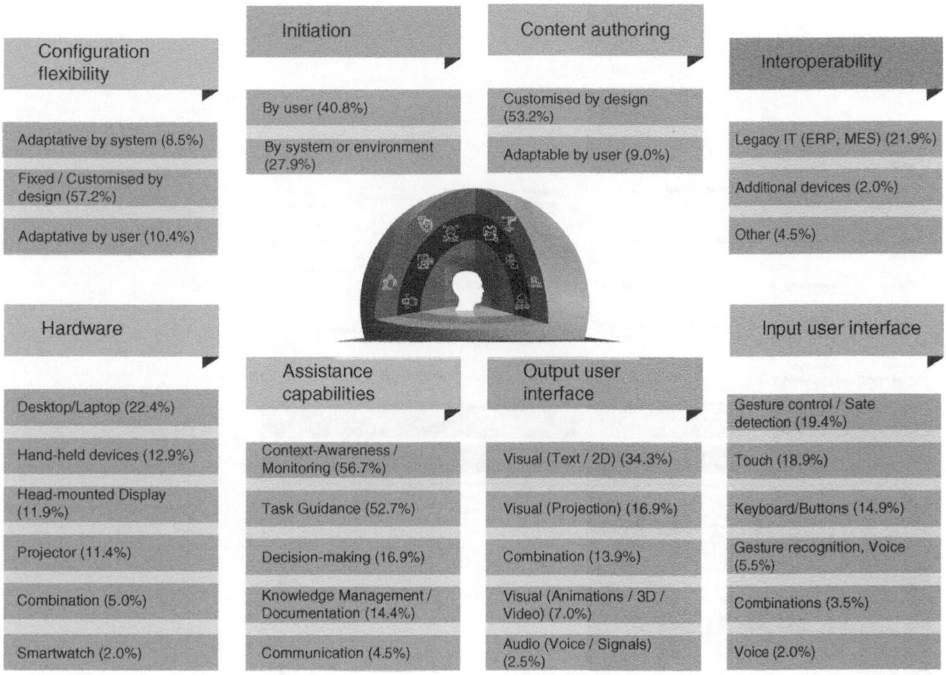


**Figure 23.5** System map: assistance and meta-capabilities. The relative values represent the occurrence of subthemes out of the 201 reviewed papers. Capabilities and subthemes are not mutually exclusive.

capabilities are directly accessible by the operator and have the potential to add direct value to the current task. The review of 201 publications revealed five types of assistance capabilities: *Task guidance, Communication, Knowledge Management, Monitoring, and Decision-making.* The meta-capabilities identified are *Interoperability, Initiation, Content Authoring, and Configuration Flexibility.* A hierarchical map of assistance and meta-capabilities that have been coded within the review process is depicted in Figure 23.5. An additional structured overview of the identified capabilities, features, and characteristics of OAS is provided in Figure 23.6.

#### 23.3.2.1 Task Guidance

Task guidance can be considered as an essential assistance feature (52.7%). Task guidance has traditionally been realized by paper manuals, human supervision, or by assembly principles such as Poka Yoke. For more complex tasks, however, applying these mechanisms is not always feasible. Paper manuals and digital task guidance typically include detailed work instructions to indicate which task has to be executed in which order. Within the review, we identified four objectives of task guidance: (i) Quality-assured execution of work, (ii) Training, (iii) Health and safety, and (iv) Performance improvement. To date, quality assurance of work execution dominates use cases.

#### 23.3.2.2 Knowledge Management

Knowledge management on the shop floor enabled by OAS is a rather novel and a less-researched topic (14.4%) than task guidance (cf. Figure 23.5). However, since several reviewed studies revealed that operators spend up to 25% of their work time to get relevant information, operational knowledge management is considered to be of increasing importance in the future. In the literature, the main subjects of knowledge management are characterized as (i) *factual*, (ii) *procedural*,

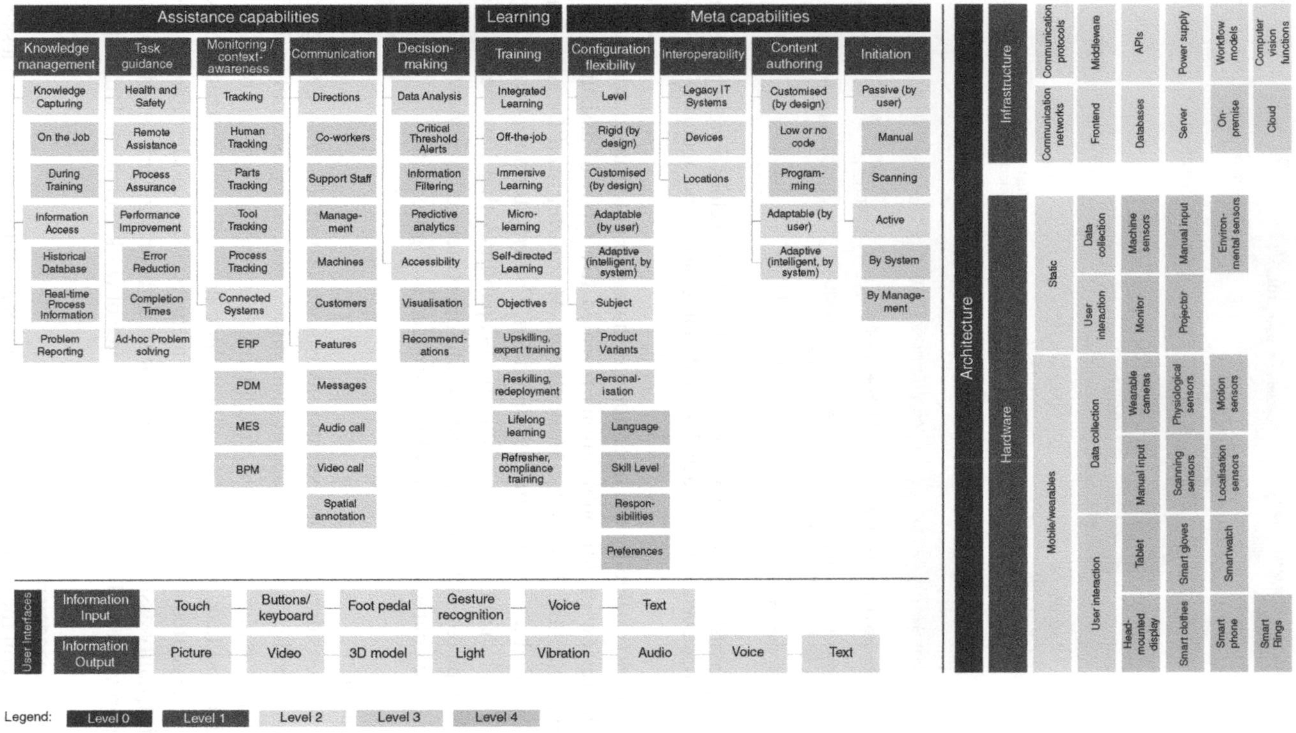


**Figure 23.6** Structured overview of OAS derived within the systematic review.

and (iii) *conceptual* knowledge. The main challenges of knowledge management facilitated by OAS can be characterized as the (i) application of knowledge, (ii) identification of existing knowledge, (iii) safeguarding, and (iv) creation of transparency about existing knowledge [22]. It follows that the advance of OAS might be an opportunity to store and make use of knowledge, thus transforming factories into adaptive and knowledge-based platforms. Storing knowledge is relying on capturing and contextualizing information beforehand. OAS offer novel functions such as on-the-go recording which may transform tacit expert knowledge into accessible, explicit knowledge [22].

#### 23.3.2.3 Monitoring

*Context-aware monitoring* capabilities have been identified as another key capability in the OAS literature (56.7%). In the future, effective OAS are expected to have additional sensing capabilities, connected data and information sources, and analytical capabilities [14]. Context-awareness enables both humans and systems to adapt resources to the requirements of the situation, thus enabling human–machine cooperation [20]. For OAS to respond adequately to the context, multimodal data need to be taken into account [11]. These data encompass human behavior (e.g. motions, vital data), parts, tools (e.g. tool tracking), products (e.g. target/actual comparison), machines (e.g. log files), and business processes (e.g. order status) [9].

#### 23.3.2.4 Communication

Within the context of OAS, communication can be defined as the mutual information exchange between subjects, either between humans or humans and machines. Communication features are an fundamental part for effective work processes that require collaboration in real time. This especially applies during remote work, for example maintenance, where information asymmetry may exist between the after sales team and field technicians. Thus, the capability to request information from different stakeholders, including machines, is critical [6]. Given the high complexity of most working environments, it seems unlikely that OAS will be able to provide adequate assistance in all possible contexts. Therefore, the ability to proactively request information from coworkers, help desk employees, or supervisors via OAS should be integrated. A study comparing the usage frequency and usability of tablet instructions and expert calls found that expert calls are preferred in situations characterized by time pressure [26]. On-site technicians might particularly benefit from video calls or AR guidance.

#### 23.3.2.5 Decision-Making

A common objective of decision support systems (DSS) is to automate tasks related to the decision-making process and to provide its user with a set of possible solutions regarding their problems [3]. This requires a system's capability of reasoning about the situation under uncertain conditions. This in turn requires a knowledge base of historical events and trends. Aligned with the ten levels of automation [16], the decision has to be selected, accepted, or modified by the human [3]. In doing so, the cognitive load and human failure should be reduced. Decision-making assistance is closely intertwined with monitoring capabilities. This goes beyond alerts and context-sensitive instructions by particularly fostering the support of exception handling and troubleshooting. Decision-making support has been long applied in operative control scenarios like aviation or nuclear power generation. However, due to a lack of data and unknown economic viability, decision-making assistance in manufacturing is not yet widespread (16.9%, cf. Figure 23.5).

### 23.3.3 Meta-capabilities

#### 23.3.3.1 Configuration Flexibility

For OAS to be effective in constantly changing production environments, they should be easily configurable for (i) *operator experience and needs* and (ii) *product and process requirements*. According to [27], there are four different configuration types for assistance: (i) *Fixed* ("one-size-fits-all" approach), (ii) *customized* (designed for a specific group or context), (iii) *adaptable* (users to adjust the system to their needs), and (iv) *adaptive* (autonomously adjust themselves to the context). Several reviewed publications emphasize the need for adaptive, easily configurable OAS. Yet, it can be seen that only 8.5% of use cases addressed adaptive features, most of them still in an early stage (cf. 23.5). A total of 10.4% studies presented technical approaches which enable a manual configuration by users. However, this is mostly limited to adjusting parameters such as font size, language, or task sequence. A total of 57.2% studies encompassed fixed or customized systems which can only be adjusted by developers, mostly requiring programming skills. In summary, the current level of configuration flexibility remains low, based on high customization costs.

#### 23.3.3.2 Interoperability

For OAS to add value to connected production environments, interoperability is a key requirement [22]. Interoperability refers to two or more systems being able to exchange and use information among each other. OAS need to be compatible in terms of *(i) software and hardware modules, (ii) communication protocols, (iii) concept definitions and semantics. and (iv) organizational information exchange practices.* Not ensuring a sufficient level of OAS interoperability may result in additional, resource-intensive integration efforts. In general, a minimum of technical interoperability should be ensured by providing well-defined *application programming interfaces* (APIs) for each system module. In the organizational context, interoperability can be assumed when operators from different departments can communicate and exchange information in real time. Despite the need for systems to support a wide range of technologies and platforms, interoperability has been explicitly addressed in less than 29% of the reviewed studies (see Figure 23.5).

#### 23.3.3.3 Content Authoring

For the efficient applicability of OAS, a simple content creation process appears to be necessary. To that end, Bertram et al. [4] propose an automatic authoring process as a mandatory design requirement. Some OAS already provide system-specific graphical editor tools to upload previously generated information. Yet, the authoring process still requires high manual efforts which need to be repeated for every process change. Especially for AR, programming skills are required to develop applications which are spatially well referenced. Two main approaches exist to overcome manual authoring challenges: (i) **Programming by Demonstration** (PbD) [5], and (ii) **Creation from Construction Data** [10]. With PbD, an expert executes a task while the OAS records and simultaneously translates the task into instructions [5]. Through creation from construction data, the generation of instructions is based on computer-aided manufacturing and design data enhanced with safety information or compression methods [10].

#### 23.3.3.4 Initiation

As opposed to automated systems, the decision-making authority of whether to act upon the input of an OAS should remain with the operator [16]. OAS can nevertheless be distinguished by two initiation mechanisms. **Passive** systems require an initiation by the user, whereas **active** systems recognize if they should provide assistance or not [27]. Active assistance can create conflicts between process requirements and individual worker needs. For example, instructions for the next step are provided only if the previous step has been performed which might annoy experienced workers. For passive OAS to foster behavioral changes, the user needs to be aware of three things [27]: *(i) there exists a system that can offer support, (ii) the system can be used in case assistance that is needed in certain situations, and (iii) it is possible to prompt the system to get the right support.* One approach was identified that combines active and passive assistance: based on a known user state the system continuously adapts assistance. However, users can manually change the level of assistance if needed. In current research, passive systems still dominate (40.8%), despite a trend toward automatic initiation is visible (27.9%), see Figure 23.5.

#### 23.3.3.5 Hardware

Desktop setups (22.4%) were found to be the most frequently used devices for OAS, followed by handheld devices (HHDs, 12.9%) including tablets and smartphones (cf. Figure 23.5). The low costs and high availability of HHDs are particularly attractive. Simultaneously, head-mounted displays (HMD, 11.9%), in situ projectors (11.5%), and combinations of devices (5.0%) are gaining traction in OAS research. In field studies, the acceptance of HHDs appeared to be higher than the one for wearables such as smartwatches or HMDs. This may be partly be explained by the widespread adoption of HHDs in the consumer space. However, several studies indicate a trend toward hands-free interaction in the future [8]. Further, for harsh or dangerous environments, the choice of adequate OAS is highly limited for functional and compliance reasons. For moderate- and low-risk environments; however, consumer devices are often considered sufficient, contributing to the rising trend of **Bring Your Own Device** policies.

#### 23.3.3.6 User Interfaces

The review found that visual approaches make up more than 60% of user interface (UI) output modalities. Nevertheless, multimodal feedback is common, too (13.9%). Audio emerges as a prominent complementary output. Haptic feedback remains the exception to date (1%). Among UI inputs, gesture control and context tracking have been addressed most frequently (19.4%), followed by touch screens (18.9%). Physical input (buttons, keyboards, etc.) have been used in 14.9% of references. Several studies state that robust physical interfaces will continue to play an important role in industry.

## 23.4 Future Research Directions

In order to guide future research, current challenges and action areas have been identified in Table 23.1. Key directions for future research are outlined below:

### 23.4.1 Empirical Evidence

The slow adoption of OAS is still one of the most pressing challenge as shown in the low number of studies in real industrial environments. Therefore, more empirical research is needed on the impact of OAS in different industrial contexts [12], while taking legacy architectures and organizational conditions into account. This presents many opportunities to contribute important empirical research. Particularly valuable would be large-scale and longitudinal experimental studies, as well as qualitative and mixed method studies uncovering the on-the-job realities of implementing, using, and managing OAS in industry.

**Table 23.1** Summary of the most relevant current research issues around OAS identified within the review of 201 publications.

| Class | Category | Challenge 1 | Challenge 2 | Challenge 3 |
|---|---|---|---|---|
| **Meta-analysis** | **Empirical** | Few field studies, small sample sizes, and sampling bias | Industrial relevance of OAS research, Economic effectiveness | Technology acceptance |
| **Assistance capabilities** | **Task Guidance** | Differences in training and execution assistance | Effectiveness of predetermined task guidance | Integrated learning within daily operations |
| | **Knowledge management** | Usability of knowledge capturing and processing | Integration into daily processes | Consistent information handling strategies |
| | **Monitoring** | Increased dependency on technology | Predictive assistance capabilities | Algorithms for improved context-awareness |
| | **Communication** | Change of current workflows and processes | Effectiveness of human communication versus assistance features | Situational applicability of communication features |
| | **Decision-making** | How to secure processes against failure of DSS | Trust in DSS | DSS under small data conditions |
| **Meta-capabilities** | **Configuration flexibility** | Integration of multiple information sources | State-based graphs, user models, and ontologies | Self-service for enhanced scalability |
| | **Interoperability** | Cross-platform solutions | Industry-specific SDKs and APIs | Robust, reliable IT Architecture |
| | **Content authoring** | Automatic sensing, labeling, and analytics; data integration | 3D scanning, quality of 3D representation, object registration | Workflow modeling for modular instruction creation |
| | **Initiation** | Preferences and attitudes toward initiation mechanisms | Conflicts between skill development and error prevention with active assistance | Tracking approaches for active assistance |
| **Technologies** | **Hardware** | Wearing comfort, ergonomics | Robustness in harsh environments, wireless network connections | Field of view and resolution of HMDs |
| | **User Interface Output** | Standardization and Customizability | Effects on cognitive load and performance of output modalities | Development and evaluation mental models, visualization, and nudging techniques for industrial UIs |
| | **User Interface Input** | Standardization | Recognition models and transfer learning approaches | Vital-sensor-based inputs, especially BCIs |

### 23.4.2 Collaborative Research

Rapid technological advances make it difficult to capture all relevant developments across the wide spectrum of OAS technologies. Moreover, many developments around OAS are happening in the private sector, which is often not published in academic outlets. For future scientific progress of OAS, this makes close collaboration between research institutions, manufacturers, and technology providers particularly important to ensure breadth, depth, and topicality of research.

### 23.4.3 Systemic Approaches

In human–machine research, the system boundaries are usually drawn around the individual interacting with the technology. To realize the improvements and value-added on a production system or organizational level, it is however important to view OAS in their larger context [19]. For example, a time efficiency gain through using OAS at one workstation is of limited value if it leads to a bottleneck at the next workstation. Similarly, efficiency gains have to be interpreted with care, if they lead to a decrease in human factors, e.g. autonomy or variety of tasks [13], which may in turn have negative implications for operators' wages. In the future, more research is hence required around optimizing objectives for systemic, human-centric approaches on an organizational level.

### 23.4.4 Technology-Mediated Learning

The review showed that human factors are at the center of augmented work. Learning, mediated by OAS, can be seen as another key direction for future research. It will be important to explore the dual role of assistance for task execution and training, integrated into daily operations [25]. In the future, a value-add is likely to be creating solutions that integrate personalized, adaptive, on-demand assistance capabilities to empower the workforce [15]. Another key research focus on OAS has to be how, and to what extent, flexible industrial up- and reskilling can be achieved to prepare the workforce for a fast changing industrial future.

## 23.5 Conclusion

OAS is a growing field in human–machine systems research. This is driven by the increasing industrial skills gap and the resulting need for industrial organizations to support both their existing and prospective workforce. This review identified the most relevant **empirical considerations, application areas, system capabilities, and research challenges** around OAS as a foundation to build on for future research. In doing so, the review aims at sharpening the picture around OAS by structuring a previously fragmented field. The five identified assistance capabilities such as task guidance, monitoring, decision-making, knowledge management, and communication were discussed in detail. In addition, this review sheds light on the four meta-capabilities such as configuration flexibility, initiation, interoperability, and content authoring, as well as hardware and user interfaces. In addition to continuous technological improvements, future research in the human–machine systems community is encouraged to focus on larger empirical studies of OAS in industrial rather than laboratory environments.

## References


1 Aehnelt, M. and Bader, S. (2015). From information assistance to cognitive automation: a smart assembly use case. In: *Agents and Artificial Intelligence, ICAART 2015, Lecture Notes in Computer Science*, vol. 9494 (ed. B. Duval, J. van den Herik, S. Loiseau, and J. Filipe), 207–222. Cham: Springer.

2 Arndt, A. and Anderl, R. (2016). Employee data model for flexible and intelligent assistance systems in smart factories. *Advances in Intelligent Systems and Computing* 490: 503–515.

3 Belkadi, F., Dhuieb, M., Aguado, J. et al. (2020). Intelligent assistant system as a context-aware decision-making support for the workers of the future. *Computers & Industrial Engineering* 139: 105732.

4 Bertram, P., Birtel, M., Quint, F., and Ruskowski, M. (2018). Intelligent manual working station through assistive systems. *IFAC-PapersOnLine* 51 (11): 170–175.

5 Bhattacharya, B. and Winer, E. (2019). Augmented reality via expert demonstration authoring (AREDA). *Computers in Industry* 105: 61–79.

6 Cimini, C., Pirola, F., Pinto, R., and Cavalieri, S. (2020). A human-in-the-loop manufacturing control architecture for the next generation of production systems. *Journal of Manufacturing Systems* 54: 258–271.

7 Denyer, D. and Tranfield, D. (2009). Producing a systematic review. In: *The Sage Handbook of Organizational Research Methods* (ed. D.A. Buchanan and A. Bryman), 671–689. Sage Publications Ltd.

8 Egger, J. and Masood, T. (2020). Augmented reality in support of intelligent manufacturing–a systematic literature review. *Computers & Industrial Engineering* 140: 106195.

9 Fellmann, M., Robert, S., Büttner, S. et al. (2017). Towards a framework for assistance systems to support work processes in smart factories. *International Cross-Domain Conference for Machine Learning and Knowledge Extraction*, 59–68. Springer.

10 Geng, J., Zhang, S., and Yang, B. (2015). A publishing method of lightweight three-dimensional assembly instruction for complex products. *Journal of Computing and Information Science in Engineering* 15 (3): 031004 (12 pages).

11 Gollan, B., Haslgruebler, M., Ferscha, A., and Heftberger, J. (2018). Making sense: experiences with multi-sensor fusion in industrial assistance systems. *Proceedings of the 5th International Conference on Physiological Computing Systems*, 64–74.

12 Hannola, L., Lacueva-Pérez, F., Pretto, P. et al. (2020). Assessing the impact of socio-technical interventions on shop floor work practices. *International Journal of Computer Integrated Manufacturing* 33 (6): 550–571.

13 Heinrich, P. and Richter, A. (2015). Captured and structured practices of workers and contexts of organizations. *Project Report - FACTS4WORKERS: Worker-Centric Workplaces in Smart Factories*, 1.

14 Hold, P. and Sihn, W. (2016). Towards a model to identify the need and the economic efficiency of digital assistance systems in cyber-physical assembly systems. *2016 1st International Workshop on Cyber-Physical Production Systems (CPPS)*, 1–4. IEEE.

15 Kaasinen, E., Schmalfuß, F., Özturk, C. et al. (2020). Empowering and engaging industrial workers with operator 4.0 solutions. *Computers & Industrial Engineering* 139: 105678.

16 Marks, P., Müller, T., Vögeli, D. et al. (2018). Agent design patterns for assistance systems in various domains - a survey. *IEEE International Conference on Automation Science and Engineering*, volume 2018-August, 168–173.

**17** Moencks, M., Roth, E., and Bohné, T. (2020). Cyber-physical operator assistance systems in industry: cross-hierarchical perspectives on augmenting human abilities. *IEEE International Conference on Industrial Engineering and Engineering Management*, 419–423. IEEE.

**18** Moencks, M., Roth, E., Bohné, T., and Kristensson, P.O. (2022). Augmented workforce: contextual, cross-hierarchical enquiries on human-technology integration in industry. *Computers & Industrial Engineering* 165: 107822.

**19** Moencks, M., Roth, E., Bohné, T. et al. (2022). Augmented workforce canvas: a management tool for guiding human-centric, value-driven human-technology integration in industry. *Computers & Industrial Engineering* 163: 107803.

**20** Pacaux-Lemoine, M.-P., Trentesaux, D., Rey, G.Z., and Millot, P. (2017). Designing intelligent manufacturing systems through human–machine Cooperation principles: a human-centered approach. *Computers & Industrial Engineering* 111: 581–595.

**21** Pinzone, M., Albe, F., Orlandelli, D. et al. (2020). A framework for operative and social sustainability functionalities in human-centric cyber-physical production systems. *Computers & Industrial Engineering* 139: 105132.

**22** Prinz, C., Kreimeier, D., and Kuhlenkötter, B. (2017). Implementation of a learning environment for an Industrie 4.0 assistance system to improve the overall equipment effectiveness. *Procedia Manufacturing* 9: 159–166.

**23** Romero, D., Bernus, P., Noran, O. et al. (2016). The operator 4.0: human cyber-physical systems & adaptive automation towards human–automation symbiosis work systems. *IFIP International Conference on Advances in Production Management Systems*, 677–686. Springer.

**24** Romero, D., Stahre, J., Wuest, T. et al. (2016). Towards an operator 4.0 typology: a human-centric perspective on the fourth industrial revolution technologies. *Proceedings of the International Conference on Computers and Industrial Engineering (CIE46)*, Tianjin, China, 29–31.

**25** Roth, E. and Moencks, M. (2021). Technology-mediated learning in industry: solution space, implementation, evaluation. *2021 IEEE International Conference on Industrial Engineering and Engineering Management (IEEM)*, 1480–1484.

**26** Vernim, S. and Reinhart, G. (2016). Usage frequency and user-friendliness of mobile devices in assembly. *Procedia CIRP*, Volume 57, 510–515.

**27** Wandke, H. (2005). Assistance in human–machine interaction: a conceptual framework and a proposal for a taxonomy. *Theoretical Issues in Ergonomics Science* 6 (2): 129–155.

**28** Yang, X. and Plewe, D.A. (2016). Assistance systems in manufacturing: a systematic review. In: *Advances in Ergonomics of Manufacturing: Managing the Enterprise of the Future, Advances in Intelligent Systems and Computing*, vol. 490 (ed. C. Schlick and S. Trzcieliński), 279–289. Cham: Springer.

# 24

# Cognitive Performance Modeling

*Maryam Zahabi and Junho Park*

*Wm Michael Barnes '64 Department of Industrial and Systems Engineering, Texas A&M University, College Station, TX, USA*

## 24.1 Introduction

Cognitive performance models (CPM) are computational models that represent humans' performance as they interact with interfaces and provide information on user intentions and information processing. These models can analyze the tasks in high detail, predict operator task performance and cognitive workload, and identify serial and parallel operations.

Use of CPM provides several advantages compared to conducting human subject experiments. These advantages include (i) quantification and prediction of human behavior in natural tasks based on human information processing models; (ii) the model generation does not require human subject involvement and therefore can save time and cost in early stages of interface design and evaluation process; (iii) these computational models can be easily modified and do not require the analyst to have substantial programming background [43]; and (iv) the method is nonobtrusive as compared to physiological measures of workload [45].

The CPM approach has been applied in different human factors applications, including the analysis of aerospace systems [33], augmented cognition [11], computer systems [37], human-artificial intelligent (AI)-robot teaming [10], perception and performance [4], surface transportation [40], and user testing and evaluation [32]. Furthermore, a number of reviews have been conducted on CPM approaches for understanding design patterns [34], decision-making process [28], cognitive architecture [23], application of CPM in aviation safety [26], and error prediction [27]. However, there has been no comprehensive review on application of CPM approaches for understanding human–system interaction (HSI), which is the main focus of this chapter.

## 24.2 Background

Early models were used to quantify HSI in military applications during World War II [28]. These models included Fitts' law [12], Hick and Hyman's selective response model [15], and the signal detection model [38]. The Command Language Grammar developed by Moran [31] could be considered as the first human–computer interaction (HCI) model [1]. The top-down approach decomposed the tasks and gave a conceptual view of the interface during the design process.

*Handbook of Human-Machine Systems*, First Edition. Edited by Giancarlo Fortino, David Kaber, Andreas Nürnberger, and David Mendonça.

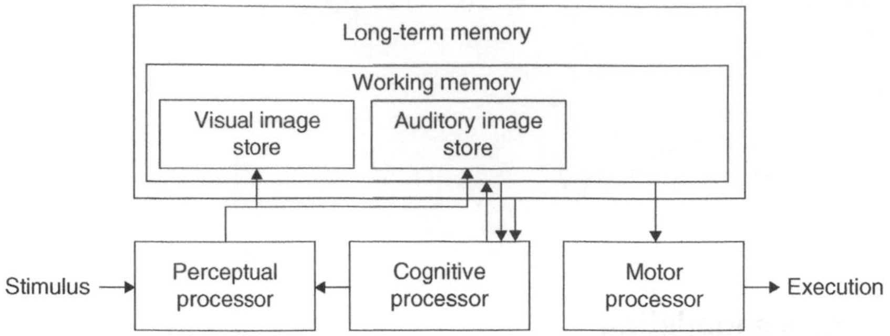


**Figure 24.1** Model Human-Processor. Source: Modified from Card et al. [8].

However, it mainly focused on modeling human motor activities and did not include perceptual and cognitive operators.

A basic architecture of human performance model is illustrated in Figure 24.1 [8]. After the initial models, various CPMs emerged applying cognitive science theory [34]. These models included Goals, Operators, Methods, and Selection (GOMS) rules [7], Adaptive Control of Thought-Rational (ACT-R) [2], Executive-Process Interactive Control (EPIC) [21], State, Operator, and Result (SOAR) [25], and Queuing Network-Model Human Processor (QN-MHP) [30].

These CPMs have been extended for specific purposes, especially GOMS and ACT-R models, as illustrated in Figure 24.2. Although the original GOMS models only supported serial activities, this limitation was resolved in later models such as the Critical Path Model-GOMS method. In addition, some variants of keystroke-level models (KLM) were developed for assessing HSI in touchscreen (i.e. touch-level model, TLM) and gesture-based interfaces (i.e. gesture-level model, GLM). Other variants of these models were generated for cockpit evaluation, reliability analysis, and modeling of social interactions (e.g. Enhanced-GOMS Language [13], GOMS-Human Reliability Analysis [5], sociotechnical GOMS [42]). ACT-R models have also been advanced for specific applications such as image processing and analyzing mobile applications, or by integration with other models and different programming languages. However, there have not been many advances in the applications of other methods such as QN-MHP, EPIC, or SOAR.

## 24.3 State-of-the-Art

In this review, we provided a general description of CPMs with their capabilities and limitations to further identify the challenges associated with their use and provide directions for future research. Modeling using the GOMS method starts with constructing a hierarchical structure of goals from top-level goals and is processed until the unit tasks or subgoal levels cannot be further decomposed [41]. To achieve a goal at the unit-task level, methods (or interactive routines) are required to specify what operators need to be executed to perform a specific action. GOMS method is based on the Model Human Processor (MHP) theory [8]. Goals are symbolic structures that establish the state to be achieved. Operators are fundamental perceptual, motor, or cognitive acts whose execution is needed to change any aspect of the user's mental state or affect the task environment. Methods describe a procedure for a goal. Finally, selection rules are required if more than one method is available for a user to accomplish the goal. There are numerous extensions of GOMS, including KLMs [6], Cognitive-Perceptual-Motor GOMS [16], Goals, Operators, Methods, and Selection Language (GOMSL) [17], Natural Goals, Operators, Methods, and Selection Language

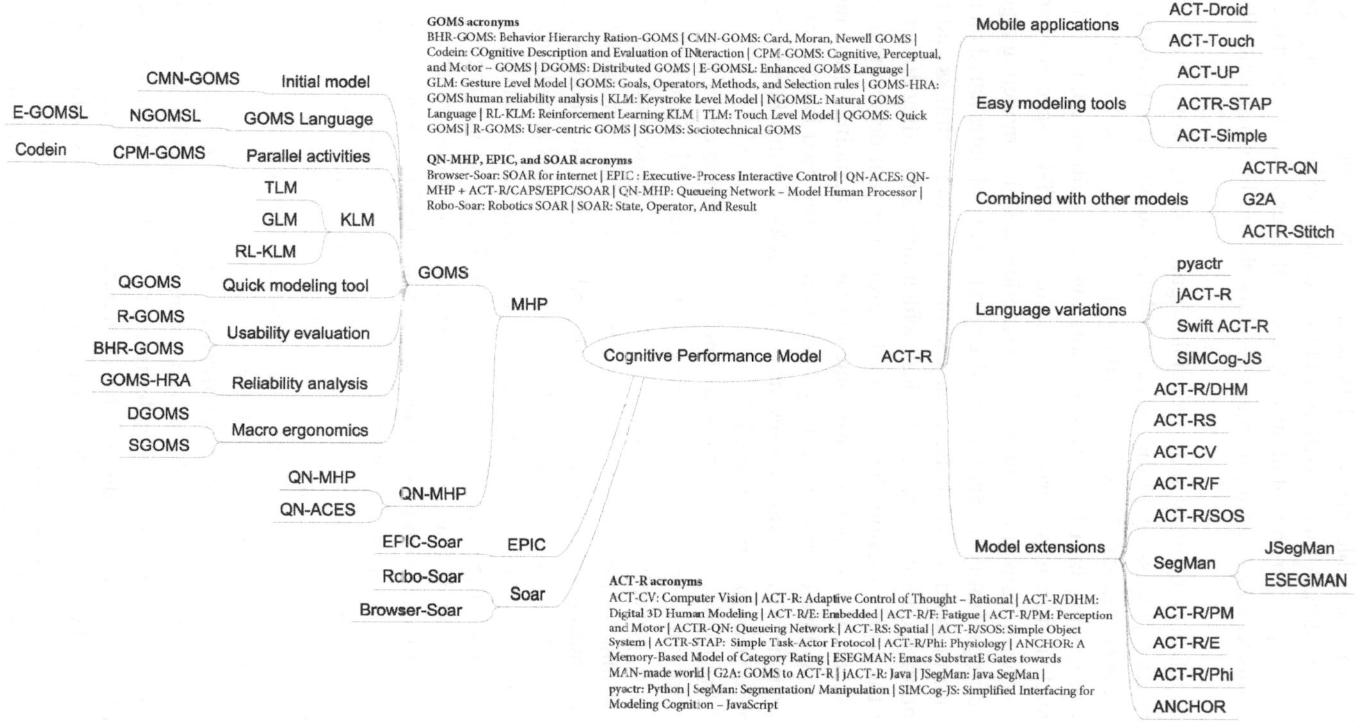
Cognitive Performance Model
MHP
GOMS
Initial model
CMN-GOMS
GOMS Language
E-GOMSL
NGOMSL
Parallel activities
Codein
CPM-GOMS
KLM
TLM
GLM
RL-KLM
Quick modeling tool
QGOMS
Usability evaluation
R-GOMS
BHR-GOMS
Reliability analysis
GOMS-HRA
Macro ergonomics
DGOMS
SGOMS
QN-MHP
QN-MHP
QN-ACES
EPIC
EPIC-Soar
Soar
Robo-Soar
Browser-Soar
ACT-R
Mobile applications
ACT-Droid
ACT-Touch
Easy modeling tools
ACT-UP
ACTR-STAP
ACT-Simple
Combined with other models
ACTR-QN
G2A
ACTR-Stitch
Language variations
pyactr
jACT-R
Swift ACT-R
SIMCog-JS
Model extensions
ACT-R/DHM
ACT-RS
ACT-CV
ACT-R/F
ACT-R/SOS
SegMan
JSegMan
ESEGMAN
ACT-R/PM
ACT-R/E
ACT-R/Phi
ANCHOR
GOMS acronyms
BHR-GOMS: Behavior Hierarchy Ration-GOMS | CMN-GOMS: Card, Moran, Newell GOMS | Codein: COgnitive Description and Evaluation of INteraction | CPM-GOMS: Cognitive, Perceptual, and Motor – GOMS | DGOMS: Distributed GOMS | E-GOMSL: Enhanced GOMS Language | GLM: Gesture Level Model | GOMS: Goals, Operators, Methods, and Selection rules | GOMS-HRA: GOMS human reliability analysis | KLM: Keystroke Level Model | NGOMSL: Natural GOMS Language | RL-KLM: Reinforcement Learning KLM | TLM: Touch Level Model | QGOMS: Quick GOMS | R-GOMS: User-centric GOMS | SGOMS: Sociotechnical GOMS
QN-MHP, EPIC, and SOAR acronyms
Browser-Soar: SOAR for internet | EPIC : Executive-Process Interactive Control | QN-ACES: QN-MHP + ACT-R/CAPS/EPIC/SOAR | QN-MHP: Queueing Network – Model Human Processor | Robo-Soar: Robotics SOAR | SOAR: State, Operator, And Result
ACT-R acronyms
ACT-CV: Computer Vision | ACT-R: Adaptive Control of Thought – Rational | ACT-R/DHM: Digital 3D Human Modeling | ACT-R/E: Embedded | ACT-R/F: Fatigue | ACT-R/PM: Perception and Motor | ACTR-QN: Queueing Network | ACT-RS: Spatial | ACT-R/SOS: Simple Object System | ACTR-STAP: Simple Task-Actor Protocol | ACT-R/Phi: Physiology | ANCHOR: A Memory-Based Model of Category Rating | ESEGMAN: Emacs SubstratE Gates towards MAN-made world | G2A: GOMS to ACT-R | jACT-R: Java | JSegMan: Java SegMan | pyactr: Python | SegMan: Segmentation/ Manipulation | SIMCog-JS: Simplified Interfacing for Modeling Cognition – JavaScript

**Figure 24.2** Major CPMs and their extensions.

(NGOMSL) [18], and Enhanced GOMSL [13]. KLM is a method that predicts task completion time for experts to accomplish a routine task without errors. CPM-GOMS is an advanced method in that it can model parallel processes. NGOMSL is a high-level (natural language) syntax for GOMS representation. GOMSL is an executable form of NGOMSL and a computationally realized version of MHP, which is a basis of GOMS. Although GOMS is a fast and easy model to develop and includes all processes to access task performance, it mainly represents the behavior of expert users without errors, and is deterministic. Also, adding mental operators should be consistent following the rules in [20].

ACT-R provides models of elementary and irreducible cognitive and perceptual operations that enable human information processing. In theory, each task that humans can perform consists of a series of these discrete operations [3]. ACT-R's primary time unit is 50 ms which can describe human information processing in a fine-grained resolution. In addition, ACT-R can generate essential outcomes such as time to perform a task and accuracy. ACT-R's specific characteristics include connection between human cognition and perception, detailed modeling algorithm for memory process including memory storage/update/decay/retrieval estimates based on mathematical equations, and use of standard symbolic variables. In this method, chunks and production rules are discrete, and their operations are syntactical, which means that they do not refer to the semantic content of the representations but only to the properties that deem them appropriate for calculations. However, ACT-R models have some limitations, including (i) the models only allow serial access of cognitive operators, (ii) they have been mainly used in academic research, and (iii) it takes a long time to model (at least several days to weeks of using the system) and takes months to years to become an expert in its use [35].

EPIC is a general framework, represented as a simulation modeling environment, in which models of human performance in specific tasks may be constructed [21]. Since EPIC was mainly developed for modeling perception and motor functions [39], it influenced the development of ACT-R/Perceptual and Motor and SOAR that combined detailed perceptual and motor components into their models [34]. Similar to ACT-R and SOAR, EPIC models encompass a production-rule system (a "cognitive processor") that provides procedural knowledge. "Perceptual processors" also process different sensory information including visual, tactile, and auditory information. The outcomes of the perceptual processors are delivered to working memory. There are two types of working memory that are not related to the sensory-motor information: one is to store current goals and steps to reach those goals (i.e. "control store"), and the other is a general working memory for miscellaneous information. Similar to ACT-R, modeling work of EPIC is complex, and therefore, it has been mainly used for academic research. Also, the model does not consider changes in human behavior as a result of learning a system. For example, users may perform tasks in a serial manner at the beginning, while they can perform the same tasks in parallel once they learn the system and change their interaction style.

SOAR is a functional model to understand cognitive mechanisms as a basis of intelligent human behavior [25]. Also, it is an architecture for human cognition expressed in the form of a production system. SOAR can represent extensive and complex rule sets. Its primary use is in artificial intelligence (AI) and cognitive modeling. In addition, it has been combined with EPIC's perceptual-motor processors. AI agents in SOAR can be developed based on different types of knowledge, whether programmed or learned by the system. In addition, in SOAR, cognitive tasks can be processed in parallel, which is the main distinction between this model and models such as ACT-R and CPM-GOMS.

Lastly, QN-MHP is a computational cognitive architecture that integrates the mathematical framework of queuing network theory with MHP [30]. Based on a network structure of 20 process

**Table 24.1** Comparison of cognitive performance models.

| Feature | GOMS | ACT-R | EPIC | SOAR | QN-MHP |
|---|---|---|---|---|---|
| Capability | Estimate task performance and cognitive workload | Estimate task performance and cognitive workload, outcomes similar to neurological data | Estimate task performance, cognitive workload | Estimate task performance, cognitive workload | Estimate task performance, cognitive workload |
| Characteristics | Fast and easy modeling, can see the detailed codes | Integration of perception, cognition, and motor functions, detailed modeling of memory, symbolic language | Detailed perception and motion algorithm | Multiple problem spaces, unlimited working access | Based on human brain structure and functions, use of queuing theory, real-time visualization |
| Limitations | Modeling of skilled user behavior, deterministic operator time | Serial cognitive process, mainly used in academia, complex modeling | Does not consider human learning capabilities, mainly used in academia, complex modeling | Not subject to forgetting, learning is tied to impasse, complex modeling | Not publicly available[a)] |
| Major application | Human–computer interaction | Memory, attention, education | Visual search, auditory tasks | Expert system, Autonomous agents | Surface Transportation |
| Language or Tool | Cogulator | CogTool, Common Lisp, Python, Java | Common Lisp, C++ | C, Java | ProModel, Matlab, Eclipse |

a) The model can be accessed by contacting the model authors.

units (e.g. visual recognition server, phonological loop server, or sensorimotor integration server), different cortical areas of human brain and corresponding functional modules of human information acquisition, processing, and implementation are simulated. Because of this "brain-like" structure, QN-MHP can visualize internal information flows during the simulation of related activities. However, its inability to generate or model complex cognition such as language comprehension or problem-solving requires creating new rules rather than only using the rules preprogrammed by a model developer [29]. In addition, QN-MHP codes and software application for creating these models are not publicly available. A comparison of these models is provided in Table 24.1.

## 24.4 Current Research Issues

Some of the developed models (e.g. SOAR and EPIC) are difficult to use for practitioners or experts in different domains even though there are several documents explaining the methods in detail (e.g. [19]). There were a few cases of using CPMs in the military domain such as Air Force [24], or Office of Naval Research [22]. This was mainly possible because the authors of these models (i.e. SOAR and EPIC) were engaged in those projects. Although all of the models argue that they can be used to evaluate human performance while interacting with a commercially available product or service such as mobile phones, in-vehicle displays, or vehicles, applying CPM to commercial applications still seems far away [44]. Finding, learning, and applying models in other commercial domains still demand practitioners to consider the merits of using models in their work.

Another issue with CPMs is model validation. Some of these models have been found to be inadequate or outdated after conducting validation studies [1]. This issue and the limitation above regarding the difficulty of using these models could be why so many model extensions in the family tree are not currently used. In addition, without validation, use of these models in commercial applications is not justifiable.

Finally, moderator effects have not been included in the current models. The models assume a fixed set of parameters and do not reflect users' interaction style change in the middle of the task (e.g. serial to parallel task performance). Although a few studies investigated the effects of stress, fatigue, sleep deprivation, drugs, or emotions on human performance, they did not implement how the model mechanism could change as a result of these effects [14]. Also, group behavior modeling has not been incorporated in these models (e.g. drones, ground weapon systems, or robots).

## 24.5 Future Research Directions Dealing with the Current Issues

In order to enhance the use of CPM approaches in future, we recommend the following steps:

1. A technical group which has the expertise and authority to manage models is needed (e.g. Human Performance Modeling-Management Group [HPM-MG]). HPM-MG includes steps for model development and releases and protocols for model verification, validation, and accreditation (VVA) [36]. In HPM-MG, a simplified version of the VVA process should be established and applied to the models. In the verification stage, researchers first propose a new methodology with possible data. This is what current studies are doing. Next, in the validation stage, the researchers need to validate the model with additional data and compare with other models. One of the possible ways for validation is using a genetic algorithm to automate the model fitting

work [34]. Finally, the researchers should develop a user-friendly interface (e.g. graphical user interface), manual, and tutorials for practitioners in the accreditation stage. HPM-MG oversees each stage and finally accredits the model. Furthermore, this process can improve the transparency and reproducibility of the model. A common repository or portal can also be provided to researchers to share each model's latest status to avoid redundant work or using outdated information.

2. A user-friendly modeling interface is needed. CogTool is one of the examples which enables modeling without coding. However, it is mainly used for webpage usability analysis, and the tool needs to be updated. The latest version on Github is from 2014 (https://github.com/cogtool/cogtool). Cogulator is another CPM interface, which requires coding and does not allow loops (https://cogulator.io/). Distract-R is a GUI-based model for driving (https://www.cs.drexel.edu/~salvucci/cog/distract-r/). However, the model has specific routes and can only model dial-pad based secondary task devices.
3. Analysts who are interested in using CPM but are not familiar with modeling work should refer to Figure 24.1 and Table 24.1 first to decide the appropriate model and its extension. Then, they need to select and use a GUI-based tool. Finally, once they develop a particular model and if need additional functions, they can look into a coding-based approach that enables more detailed functionalities. For example, an analyst can implement or modify specific arguments of a function in the original code.
4. Dynamic parameter adjustment or mechanism of calculation is required for users' skill development and changes in performance due to external stimulus (e.g. fatigue or stress) in the middle of the task. For example, Cognitive Jack (CoJACK) project enabled an agent to learn knowledge from the environment and generate new behaviors [34]. Recently, ACT-R/phi has been developed to model moderators of cognition and combined that with human physiology. This is a more straightforward way as some of the physiological modulating processes entail bottom-up effects on cognitive processes [9].

## References


1 Al Seraj, M.S., Pastel, R., and Al-Hasan, Md. (2018). A survey on user modeling in HCI. *Computer Applications: An International Journal (CAIJ)* 5 (1): 1–8.

2 Anderson, J.R. (1993). *Rules of the Mind*, 319p. Hillsdale, NJ: Lawrence Erlbaum Associates, Inc.

3 Anderson, J.R., Matessa, M., and Lebiere, C. (1997). ACT-R: a theory of higher level cognition and its relation to visual attention. *Human–Computer Interaction* 12 (4): 439–462.

4 Bolkhovsky, J., Ritter, F.E., Chon, K.H., and Qin, M. (2018). Performance trends during sleep deprivation.

5 Boring, R.L. and Rasmussen, M. (2016). GOMS-HRA: a method for treating subtasks in dynamic human reliability analysis. *Proceedings of the 2016 European Safety and Reliability Conference*, 956–963.

6 Card, S.K., Moran, T.P., and Newell, A. (1980). The keystroke-level model for user performance time with interactive systems. *Communications of the ACM* 23 (7): 396–410.

7 Card, S.K., Moran, T.P., and Newell, A. (1983). *The Psychology of Human–Computer Interaction.* Hillsdale, NJ: Lawrence Erlbaum Associates, Inc.

8 Card, S., Moran, T., and Newell, A. (1986). The model human processor: an engineering model of human performance. In: *Handbook of Perception and Human Performance, Cognitive Processes and Performance*, vol. 2 (ed. K.R. Boff, L. Kaufman, and J.P. Thomas), 1–35. Wiley.

9 Dancy, C.L. (2019). A hybrid cognitive architecture with primal affect and physiology. *IEEE Transactions on Affective Computing* 12 (2): 318–328.

10 Dudzik, K.A.T. (2019). Cognitive modeling as a method for agent development in artificial intelligence. PhD thesis. Carleton University.

11 Fincham, J.M. (2005). Cognitive modeling and fMRI: an integrated approach toward understanding mechanisms of complex skill performance. PhD thesis. Carnegie Mellon University.

12 Fitts, P.M. (1954). The information capacity of the human motor system in controlling the amplitude of movement. *Journal of Experimental Psychology* 47 (6): 381.

13 Gil, G.-H. (2010). An accessible cognitive modeling tool for evaluation of human–automation interaction in the systems design process. PhD thesis. North Carolina State University.

14 Gunzelmann, G. and Gluck, K.A. (2008). Approaches to modeling the effects of fatigue on cognitive performance. *Proceedings of the 17th Conference on Behavior Representation in Modeling and Simulation*, 136–145. Citeseer.

15 Hick, W.E. (1952). On the rate of gain of information. *Quarterly Journal of Experimental Psychology* 4 (1): 11–26.

16 John, B.E. and Gray, W.D. (1995). CPM-GOMS: an analysis method for tasks with parallel activities. *Conference Companion on Human Factors in Computing Systems*, 393–394.

17 Kieras, D.E. (1988). Towards a practical GOMS model methodology for user interface design. In: *Handbook of Human–Computer Interaction*, 135–157. Elsevier.

18 Kieras, D. (1994). *A Guide to GOMS Task Analysis*. University of Michigan.

19 Kieras, D.E. (1999). *A Guide to GOMS Model Usability Evaluation Using GOMSL and GLEAN3*, 313. University of Michigan.

20 Kieras, D. (2001). *Using the Keystroke-Level Model to Estimate Execution Times*, 555. University of Michigan.

21 Kieras, D.E. and Meyer, D.E. (1995). Predicting human performance in dual-task tracking and decision making with computational models using the epic architecture. *Proceedings of the 1st International Symposium on Command and Control Research and Technology*, June 1995. Washington, DC: National Defense University, Citeseer.

22 Kieras, D.E. and Wakefield, G.H. (2016). Extending and Applying the Epic Architecture for Human Cognition and Performance: Auditory and Spatial Components. *Technical report*. FR-11/ONR-EPIC-17. University of Michigan Division of Research Development Ann Arbor United States. https://apps.dtic.mil/sti/pdfs/ADA535789.pdf.

23 Kotseruba, I. and Tsotsos, J.K. (2020). 40 years of cognitive architectures: core cognitive abilities and practical applications. *Artificial Intelligence Review* 53 (1): 17–94.

24 Laird, J.E. and Nielsen, E. (1994). Coordinated behavior of computer generated forces in TacAir-SOAR. *AD-A280* 63 (1001): 57.

25 Laird, J., Hucka, M., Huffman, S., and Rosenbloom, P. (1991). An analysis of SOAR as an integrated architecture. *ACM SIGART Bulletin* 2 (4): 98–103.

26 Leiden, K. and Best, B. (2005). *A Cross-Model Comparison of Human Performance Modeling Tools Applied to Aviation Safety*. Boulder, CO: Micro Analysis & Design, Inc.

27 Leiden, K., Laughery, K.R., Keller, J. et al. (2001). A review of human performance models for the prediction of human error. *Ann Arbor* 1001: 48105.

28 Li, N., Huang, J., and Feng, Y. (2020). Human performance modeling and its uncertainty factors affecting decision making: a survey. *Soft Computing* 24 (4): 2851–2871.

29 Liu, Y. (2009). QN-ACES: integrating queuing network and ACT-R, CAPS, EPIC, and SOAR architectures for multitask cognitive modeling. *International Journal of Human–Computer Interaction* 25 (6): 554–581.

30 Liu, Y., Feyen, R., and Tsimhoni, O. (2006). Queuing Network-Model Human Processor (QN-MHP) a computational architecture for multitask performance in human–machine systems. *ACM Transactions on Computer–Human Interaction (TOCHI)* 13 (1): 37–70.

31 Moran, T.P. (1981). The command language grammar: a representation for the user interface of interactive computer systems. *International Journal of Man-Machine Studies* 15 (1): 3–50.

32 Oyewole, S.A., Farde, A.M., Haight, J.M., and Okareh, O.T. (2011). Evaluation of complex and dynamic safety tasks in human learning using the ACT-R and SOAR skill acquisition theories. *Computers in Human Behavior* 27 (5): 1984–1995.

33 Redding, R.E. (1992). Cognitive Task Analysis of Prioritization in Air Traffic Control.

34 Ritter, F.E., Tehranchi, F., Dancy, C.L., and Kase, S.E. (2020). Some futures for cognitive modeling and architectures: design patterns for including better interaction with the world, moderators, and improved model to data fits (and so can you). *Computational and Mathematical Organization Theory* 26 (3): 278–306.

35 Salvucci, D.D. and Lee, F.J. (2003). Simple cognitive modeling in a complex cognitive architecture. *Proceedings of the SIGCHI Conference on Human Factors in Computing Systems*, 265–272.

36 Sanders, P. (1996). DoD Modeling and Simulation (M&S) Verification, Validation, and Accreditation (VV&A). *Technical Report*. NSN 7540-01-280-5500. Office of the Under Secretary of Defense for Acquisition and Technology. https://apps.dtic.mil/sti/pdfs/ADA315867.pdf.

37 St. Amant, R., Horton, T.E., and Ritter, F.E. (2004). Model-based evaluation of cell phone menu interaction. *Proceedings of the SIGCHI Conference on Human Factors in Computing Systems*, 343–350.

38 Swets, J.A. (1964). *Signal Detection and Recognition in Human Observers: Contemporary Readings*. Wiley.

39 Taatgen, N. and Anderson, J.R. (2010). The past, present, and future of cognitive architectures. *Topics in Cognitive Science* 2 (4): 693–704.

40 Tsimhoni, O. and Reed, M.P. (2007). The virtual driver: integrating task planning and cognitive simulation with human movement models. *SAE Transactions* 116: 1525–1531.

41 Van Rijn, H., Johnson, A., and Taatgen, N. (2011). Cognitive user modeling. In: *Handbook of Human Factors in Web Design*, (eds. A. Johnson, R. Proctor), 527–542. CRC Press.

42 West, R.L. and Nagy, G. (2000). Situating GOMS models within complex, sociotechnical systems. *Proceedings of the Annual Meeting of the Cognitive Science Society*, volume 22.

43 Wiendahl, M., Wierling, P.S., Nielsen, J. et al. (2008). High throughput screening for the design and optimization of chromatographic processes–miniaturization, automation and parallelization of breakthrough and elution studies. *Chemical Engineering & Technology: Industrial Chemistry-Plant Equipment-Process Engineering-Biotechnology* 31 (6): 893–903.

44 Wilson, M.D., Boag, R.J., and Strickland, L. (2019). All models are wrong, some are useful, but are they reproducible? Commentary on Lee et al.(2019). *Computational Brain & Behavior* 2 (3): 239–241.

45 Zahabi, M., White, M.M., Zhang, W. et al. (2019). Application of cognitive task performance modeling for assessing usability of transradial prostheses. *IEEE Transactions on Human–Machine Systems* 49 (4): 381–387.

# 25

# Advanced Driver Assistance Systems: Transparency and Driver Performance Effects

*Yulin Deng[1] and David B. Kaber[2]*

[1] *Cepheid Human Factors and Engineering Team, Sunnyvale, CA, USA*
[2] *University of Florida, Department of Industrial and Systems Engineering, Gainesville, FL, USA*

## 25.1 Introduction

In the past few years, there has been a dramatic increase in the number and type of automated vehicles. Increasingly powerful automation systems have been developed, and semiautonomous features are now available in both luxury and less expensive vehicle models [6].

To date, few commercial vehicle models have integrated "conditional driving automation" (or SAE Level 3 capabilities), which do not require drivers to monitor the roadway environment at all times. While vehicle automation is gaining increasing popularity, some researchers have pointed out potential "pitfalls" of automation exposure. Degraded hazard negotiation performance with automated driving has been widely reported (including documentation of Tesla vehicle accidents in newspapers).

Previous studies have also suggested that operators might experience vehicle control performance degradation after exposure to automation [5, 25].

With these issues in mind, there is a need to explore effective methods by which to mitigate driver performance degradations resulting from automation. One potential method is to increase the level of automation transparency for the driver. "Automation transparency," by definition, is "the degree to the extent which the inner workings or logic of the automated systems are known to human operators to assist their understanding about the system" [24]. Generally, automation transparency tends to afford operators with understanding and the capability to predict automation system states and, thus, improve performance. Systems with higher levels of automation transparency support greater levels of information sharing with operators [28].

The objective of this research was to explore the effectiveness of using high-level automation transparency as a remedy for potential driving performance degradation. A driving simulation study was conducted, comparing driver performance under low (baseline)- and high-level automation transparency conditions, which were manipulated by varying the presence of audio information on vehicle automation system states. It was expected that introducing higher-level automation transparency would result in superior hazard negotiation performance, as indicated by shorter hazard reaction times and longer time-to-collision (in the event of an accident). The latter measure was used to evaluate the criticality of the hazard negotiation at the point at which drivers initiated

*Handbook of Human-Machine Systems*, First Edition. Edited by Giancarlo Fortino, David Kaber, Andreas Nürnberger, and David Mendonça.

a hazard avoidance maneuver. Higher-level automation transparency was also expected to lead to superior manual vehicle control performance, after driver exposure to automation.

## 25.2 Background

### 25.2.1 Context

Many of today's commercial vehicles have advanced driver assistance systems (ADAS), typically including adaptive cruise control (ACC) and/or lane keeping assistance (LKA) systems [25], which, if used independently, these systems represent SAE Level 1 automation ("driver assistance"). ACC manages the longitudinal speed of a vehicle and automatically maintains a constant safe headway to a lead vehicle. LKA provides steering inputs and maintains the vehicle in the center of a detected lane.

A small number of vehicle models have incorporated both functions to make them capable of partial driving automation [25], reaching SAE Level 2 automation. With both Level 1 and Level 2 vehicle automation, drivers are required to supervise these systems and monitor the driving environment to take over vehicle control when necessary [21]. Integration of LKS and ACC enables automatic lateral and longitudinal vehicle control, which has become a market trend in recent years. However, only a limited number of commercial vehicle models can provide such automation, and these combinations of systems require drivers to stay attentive at all times, supervise the vehicle's actions during use, and takeover control of the vehicle when necessary.

Recent years have seen an increasing number of crashes involving automated vehicles, as more automated vehicles are put on public roadways [23]. Several recent accidents involving automated vehicles have gained national attention, including a Tesla Model 3 accident in Delray Beach, Florida on March 1, 2019, and a Tesla Model S accident near Williston, Florida on May 7, 2016. Related to this, researchers pointed out two major sources of uncertainty in the safety of automated vehicles. Schoettle and Sivak [23] observed that automated vehicles are driven mainly in limited and less demanding driving conditions, and Blanco et al. [2] argued that automated vehicles have relatively low public exposure. These circumstances led to a lack of clarity on how automated vehicles will operate under other congested roadway conditions.

In general, the accident evidence indicates the need for further understanding of the safety implications of vehicle automation. The existing research also suggests that it is necessary to explore effective methods to improve driver engagement with ADAS in potentially hazardous driving conditions. Among the available literature, the majority of studies concentrate on driver performance under noncritical driving conditions rather than hazardous conditions. Therefore, it is worthwhile to further examine the effectiveness of driver's use of higher levels of vehicle automation under both noncritical and hazardous conditions. In addition, only a limited number of studies have considered the impact of automation transparency on driver performance [10, 18]. As there may be a positive influence of vehicle automation transparency on the driver's performance, it is also worthwhile to examine such capabilities for hazardous driving conditions.

### 25.2.2 Basic Definition

As stated above, "automation transparency" is the degree "to which the inner workings or logic of the automated systems are known to human operators to assist their understanding about the system" [24]. This definition is relevant to the definition of the experimental conditions for the present research.

## 25.3 Related Work

A number of researchers have observed deteriorated driver hazard negotiation with ADAS, and a few theories have been provided regarding the underlying cause (Table 25.1).

One potential solution to negative effects of ADAS exposure on driver's critical task performance is automation transparency. In general, automation transparency tends to afford users with

**Table 25.1** Studies on effects of ADAS exposure on driver critical task performance.

| Author | Study summary |
|---|---|
| Gold et al. [8] | Drivers are less attentive and prone to distraction with highly automation driving systems. They observed longer reaction time to hazards during highly automated driving, as compared to manual driving. |
| Rudin-Brown et al. [20] | By comparing driver reaction time to safety-critical events under manual driving and ACC, they found drivers using ACC took longer to react to lead vehicle brake lights, and they were more likely to crash. According to the authors, although ACC partially freed-up driver cognitive or attentional resources, such resources were used for "other purposes" instead of hazard avoidance, like secondary task performance. |
| Schleicher and Gelau [22] | Reported delayed responses to hazards with cruise control or ACC, as compared to manual driving. The authors observed that drivers took some time to notice a situation that posed driving demands beyond the automation capabilities as well as the need to intervene and handle the issue. They explained that drivers paid reduced attention to signs or cues that required adaptation of speed because speed was expected to be controlled by the automated system (ACC). |
| Young and Stanton [30] | Lower mental workload in automated driving could lead to a rapid increase in mental demand when drivers were put in a hazardous situation requiring control intervention; thus, driver hazard negotiation performance would be deteriorated under automated driving. The authors speculated that drivers under automated driving conditions would have difficulty coping with and avoiding collisions due to mental underload. |
| Parasuraman, et al. [19] | Human use of automation consistently applied to decision-making functions for extended periods may lead to operator manual skill decay. They also suggested that the impact of cognitive performance degradations might be elevated in the case of automation failure, for example, when human drivers are required to take over vehicle control and negotiate hazardous conditions following automation failure. |
| Merat et al. [15] | Conducted simulator study to compare driving performance in manual and highly automated driving (SAE Level 2). Results showed that in the absence of secondary tasks, driver's responses to critical incidents under automated driving conditions were similar to manual control. However, in the presence of secondary tasks, when driver's attentional resources were partially diverted from primary driving, drivers exhibited degraded response performance to critical incidents under automated driving conditions. |
| Deng and Kaber [5] | Compared driver's hazard negotiation performance under ACC and manual driving with short exposure to automation (the first hazard exposure occurred at ~5 minutes of driving). Drivers were informed of the possibility of hazard occurrence to support demonstration of full performance potential. Superior hazard reaction performance with ACC was observed as compared to manual driving. |
| McClumpha [14] | Conducted a survey with civil pilots regarding their attitude toward automation, and the majority of pilots reported erosion of flying performance by automation. |
| Vlakveld [26] | Drivers may lose practical skills in the absence of active driving over time. |

**Table 25.2** Studies on potential of automation transparency as solution to negative effects of ADAS exposure.

| Author | Study summary |
|---|---|
| Westin et al. [28] | Systems with higher levels of automation transparency support greater levels of information sharing with operators, and consequently, further ensure operator awareness of system states for effective decision-making. |
| Mercado et al. [16] | Compared unmanned vehicle operator performance under different levels of automation transparency and found that operator performance increased as a function of transparency level. |
| Yang et al. [29] | Transparent automation enhances operator performance as a result of supporting proper operator situation awareness (SA) on system states. |
| De Waard et al. [27] | System functionality needed to be communicated clearly to operators in highly automated situations. |
| Chen et al. [4] | Providing additional automation state information to operators can substantially increase cognitive workload. |
| Naujoks et al. [18] | Conducted a driving simulator study to examine the effect of automated system speech output on driver performance. Results revealed that communicating upcoming automated maneuvers by speech decreased driver workload and interaction with nondriving-related tasks, leading to overall performance improvements. |
| Koo et al. [10] | Presented drivers with auto-braking functions (SAE Level 1 vehicle automation) to examine how verbalized messages on automation state influenced performance. Results revealed that providing information on "what" automated actions are being performed (e.g. "The car is braking") and "why" actions are occurring (e.g. "Obstacle ahead") produced the safest driving performance. The authors concluded that verbalized "what" and "how" messages, accompanying a car's autonomous action, resulted in safe performance, specifically less road edge excursions. They attributed this finding to improved driver SA. However, they also observed that drivers expressed negative attitudes in postdriving questionnaires when the "how" and "why" information was provided. |

understanding and the capability to predict automation system states and, thus, can improve overall system performance (Table 25.2).

Consequently, there is a need to determine an appropriate amount of information that mitigates "mental underload," which Young and Stanton [30] associated with vehicle automation, and at the same time does not overload operators and pose a detriment to driver hazard negotiation.

## 25.4 Method

In this section, we detail an empirical study to assess the impact of higher-level ADAS exposure on driver performance in hazard negotiation. We also detail an automation transparency manipulation to assess the utility of auditory messages on SAE Level 2 vehicle automation state for mitigating potential operator over-reliance on the automation and negative performance outcomes in hazard exposure (Figure 25.1).

| SAE level | Name | Description |
|---|---|---|
| Level 0 | No automation | Manual driving |
| Level 1 | Driver assistance | Automation system performs sustained execution of either lateral or longitudinal vehicle motion control. |
| Level 2 | Partial automation | Automation system performs sustained execution of both steering and acceleration/deceleration. Drivers must remain engaged and monitor the environment at all times. |
| Level 3 | Conditional automation | Drivers are not required to monitor the environment at all time, but must respond appropriately to a request to intervene in automated control. |
| Level 4 | High automation | Vehicle is capable of performing all driving functions under some driving modes (under some geographic areas, roadway types, weather conditions, etc.). Drivers are not required to respond appropriately to a request to intervene. |
| Level 5 | Full automation | Vehicle is capable of performing all driving functions under all driving modes. |

**Figure 25.1** SAE level of driving automation (Note. SAE level of driving automation. SAE, Copyright 2016 by SAE International).

### 25.4.1 Apparatus

Driving Simulator: We used the North Carolina State University Driving Simulator, which integrates Forum8s UC-win/Road driving simulation software (FORUM8 Co., Ltd, Tokyo, Japan) with a Moog 6-degree-offreedom hexapod (1000 Kg capacity) for full motion simulation. The setup also includes a roadway environment visualization frame comprising six 55-in. UDHD monitors arranged to surround a driver in the simulator cab. The displays provide a 315-degree field of view (FOV) of the driving environment (see Figure 25.2). The full-motion simulator also integrates a surround-sound audio speaker system for driver auditory feedback.

Drivers interact with the simulator through cab controls, including a modular steering-wheel unit and a modular accelerator and brake pedal.

**Figure 25.2** Driving simulator motion platform and visualization frame.

**Figure 25.3** Driving simulator partial vehicle cab.

The driver's ownship was simulated as a coupe at 5.01 m in length and 2.22 m in width. The simulated vehicle was similar to a Toyota Echo 1300 CC model with automatic transmission. The maximum brake force was 9800N, and the minimum turning radius was 9.8°. The simulated vehicle wheels provided a rolling resistance of 137.2N. The steering wheel had a resistance factor of 3 (Figure 25.3).

### 25.4.2 Participants

Twenty-four (24) participants were recruited for the study. All drivers had valid driver's licenses and 20/20 vision (either natural or with corrective lenses) at the time of experiment participation. All participants were middle-aged drivers (30–45 years). This specific age group was selected because prior research has indicated that they are more likely to use vehicle automation technologies as compared with other age groups [32].

### 25.4.3 Experiment Design

This experiment followed a 2*2*2 between-within subjects design. Both the level of (vehicle) automation (LOA) and automation transparency represented between-subject variables. The settings of the LOA variable included SAE Level 1 (active ACC) and SAE Level 2 (active ACC + LKA) automation. The automation transparency manipulation included two levels: (1) a baseline condition providing no additional information on the state of automation; and (2) high-level automation transparency with supporting audio information on system states. The duration of automation exposure served as a within-subjects factor with two levels including "short" and "long." (More detail will be provided on these duration settings.)

Level of automation: The Level 1 type of automation (ACC) maintained a constant headway between the driver's ownship and a leading vehicle. It also maintained a constant longitudinal speed when the lead vehicle was absent. In this study, the ACC was set at 105 km/h (approximately 65 mph), and the headway distance was set at 160 ft, which is a frequently used headway setting by ACC users [7]. The Level 2 type of automation (ACC + LKA) provided the same ACC functions along with a lane-keeping function. The vehicle automation maintained the lateral position of the driver's ownship in a selected lane with less than +/−1.37 ft of deviation about a virtual center line. Half of the participants drove with Level 1 automation and half drove with Level 2.

Automation transparency: The high automation transparency condition provided drivers with information of vehicle status through audio messages. The message content included a vehicle's actions as well as reasoning for actions. This approach was based on Koo et al. [10] research identifying such a combination to be most effective for improving driver safety performance. Examples of audio messages included: "the car is decelerating due to slow traffic" and "the car is turning due to a curve."

All messages were presented at the time of action. The other half of participants experienced the baseline condition and did not receive any audio information on system status.

Duration of automation exposure: Each participant completed 10 experiment trials, and two hazards occurred during the experiments with one in the fifth driving trial and one in the tenth driving trial.

Consequently, each participant experienced two durations of automation exposure prior to encountering a roadway hazard. The first level of exposure included five driving trials, which was approximately 50 minutes of driving, in total. The second level of exposure included 10 driving trials, taking approximately 100 minutes.

### 25.4.4 Tasks

The driving simulator presented a rural highway with two lanes on each side of the highway and light traffic on the road (Level of Service C).

Drivers were instructed to control their vehicle in the lateral direction and drive in the right lane of the freeway at all times.

Two types of hazard events were presented during the experiment. The first type of hazard involved an abrupt lane incursion by a leading vehicle. The second type of hazard involved sudden braking by a leading vehicle. One instance of each type of hazard took place during the experiment. The order of the two types of hazards was randomized.

As indicated by prior literature, driving skill is a reliable indicator of a driver's maximum performance capability [11]. To ensure that drivers achieved their full potential, experimenters informed drivers of the possibility of hazard occurrences prior to experiment trials. However, the order and timing of hazards were not revealed to prevent driver's advance preparation for the hazard events.

After the completion of hazard negotiation, drivers were exposed to a 2-minute manual drive, during which they were assessed on their lane keeping and speed maintenance capabilities. Performance during this period of observation at the close of the fifth test trial was compared with the performance of drivers in same observation period at the close of the tenth test trial.

### 25.4.5 Dependent Variables

#### 25.4.5.1 Hazard Negotiation Performance

Hazard negotiation performance was measured in terms of driver's reaction time and time-to-collision. Hazard reaction time has been shown to be an effective indicator of driver hazard negotiation performance (e.g. Refs. [8, 20]).

In the present study, hazard reaction time was recorded from when the vehicle posing a hazard initiated an offensive maneuver until the time at which a participant driver initiated a conscious hazard avoidance maneuver. The criteria for identifying a hazard avoidance maneuver included a driver depressing the simulator brake pedal [12]. If drivers did not press the brake pedal before their ownship crashed into the lead vehicle, the hazard reaction time was recorded from when the vehicle posing a hazard initiated an offensive movement until the time at which the vehicles crashed.

Time-to-collision was calculated as the distance gap between the driver's ownship and a lead vehicle divided by the relative speed when a participant driver initiated a conscious hazard avoidance maneuver [12]. This measure was used to evaluate the criticality of the hazard event at the point at which drivers begin their hazard avoidance maneuver. If drivers did not press the simulator brake pedal before their ownship crashed into the lead vehicle, the time to collision would be zero.

#### 25.4.5.2 Vehicle Control Performance

Post-automation exposure: Lane deviation and speed deviation data were also collected to assess vehicle control performance after automation exposure. Lane deviation was defined as the average absolute deviation of the center of the vehicle from the center of an intended driving lane during a performance observation period. This measure has been extensively used to assess driver vehicle control performance [13, 17, 31]. In a recent study of vehicle automation and driver performance, Mok et al. [17] used lane deviation to assess driver's performance after taking over a fully automated vehicle. In their study, lane deviation was measured during a two-minute manual driving period immediately following a transition of vehicle control. A similar approach was adopted in the present study. The observation period for assessing lane deviation was a two-minute segment of road following the completion of hazard negotiation, where drivers took over the control of the vehicle. Speed deviation was measured during the same observation period. The speed deviation value was calculated as the average absolute deviation of actual vehicle speed from the posted speed limit.

### 25.4.6 Procedure

Drivers consented to participate in the study and completed a brief demographic questionnaire. They subsequently completed a training session for familiarization in use of the simulator controls. The training included two phases. The first phase assessed whether participant speed control and lane maintenance met established criteria. All participants were required to maintain 1 mph or less speed deviation and 1.37 ft or less lane deviation, on average [9]. In the second training session, participants learned to use the driving systems to which they were assigned (Level 1 or 2) and to negotiate hazards.

To minimize participant fatigue and reduce any effect on experiment results, a fatigue questionnaire was administered prior to any test trials and between every trial. The questionnaire included 14 items, all contributing to a fatigue scale developed by Chalder et al. [3]. The scale assessed both physical and mental fatigue symptoms, and a fatigue score of 3 represented absence of fatigue for a participant.

Following the training sessions, participants completed the test trials.

Between trials, they took brief breaks and completed the fatigue scale.

At the completion of all experiment trials, participants who experienced high-level automation transparency would complete a posttrial usability questionnaire on their experience with the audio information they were provided while driving. Finally, they filled-out a payment form and were escorted out of the lab. See Figure 25.4 for a detailed schematic of the study design.

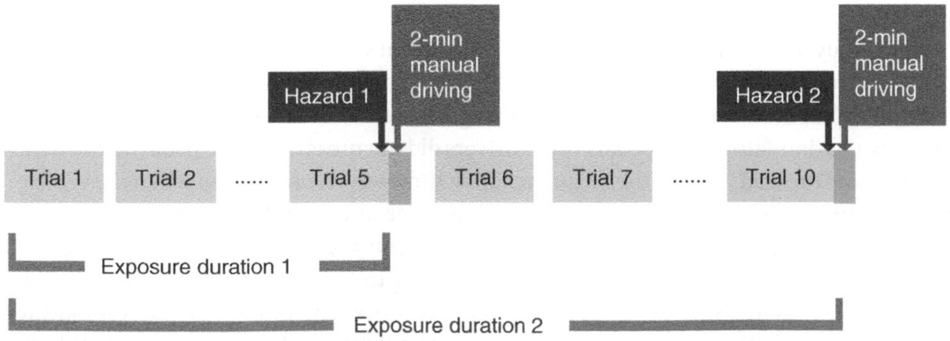


**Figure 25.4** Duration of driver exposure to automation.

## 25.5 Results

This section presents the results on driver hazard negotiation performance as well as manual driving performance following the ADAS failures. We also present results from the usability questionnaire, administered after all test trials.

### 25.5.1 Hazard Reaction Performance

Automation transparency had a significant effect on driver's hazard reaction time ($F$ (1,46) = 7.9262, $p$ = 0.0110, $1 - \beta$ = 0.7614). High-level automation transparency produced faster hazard reaction responses than the baseline condition (see Figure 25.5). No significant effects of level of automation ($F$ (1,46) = 0.3227, $p$ = 0.5767, $1 - \beta$ = 0.050) or duration of automation exposure ($F$ (1,46) = 0.1382, $p$ = 0.7142, $1 - \beta$ = 0.0533) were observed. That is, the functional differences in SAE Level 1 and Level 2 automation were not revealed in hazard response times and driver responses did not vary between the fifth and tenth test trials.

Automation transparency ($F$ (1,46) = 7.2628, $p$ = 0.0143, $1 - \beta$ = 0.7247) had a significant effect on time-to-collision in driver hazard negotiation. Higher-level automation transparency produced longer time-to-collision than the baseline condition (see Figure 25.6). No significant effect was found for duration of automation exposure ($F$ (1,46) = 0.0001, $p$ = 0.9940, $1 - \beta$ = 0.0500). The level of automation ($F$ (1,46) = 4.4129, $p$ = 0.0492, $1 - \beta$ = 0.5136) had a marginally significant effect on time-to-collision (see Figure 25.7).

### 25.5.2 Posthazard Manual Driving Performance

In the manual driving performance period following hazard exposure, the level of vehicle automation had a significant effect on driver performance with SAE Level 2 producing higher speed

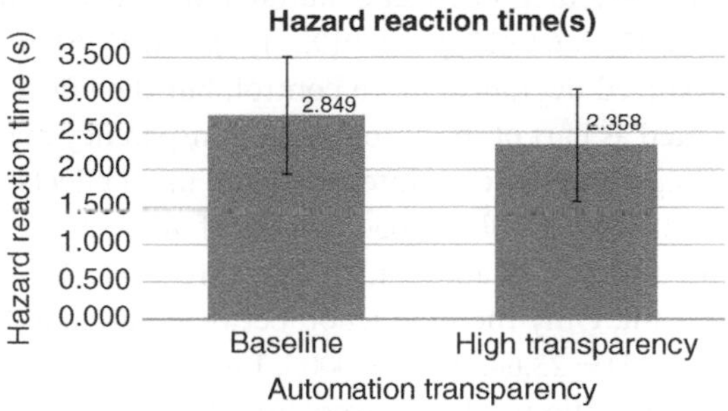


**Figure 25.5** Effect of automation transparency on reaction time.

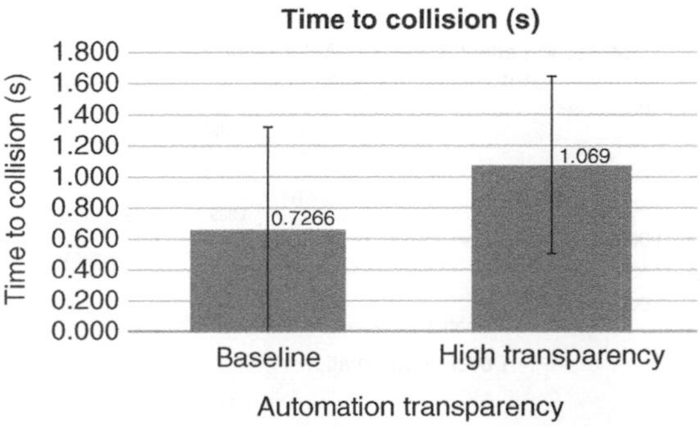


**Figure 25.6** Effect of automation transparency on time to collision.

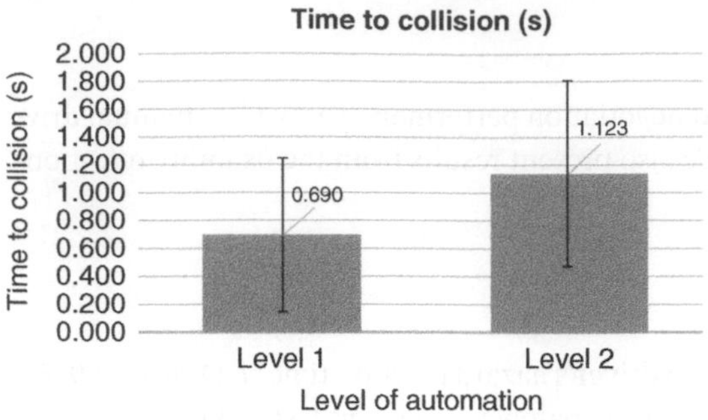


**Figure 25.7** Effect of level of automation on time-to-collision.

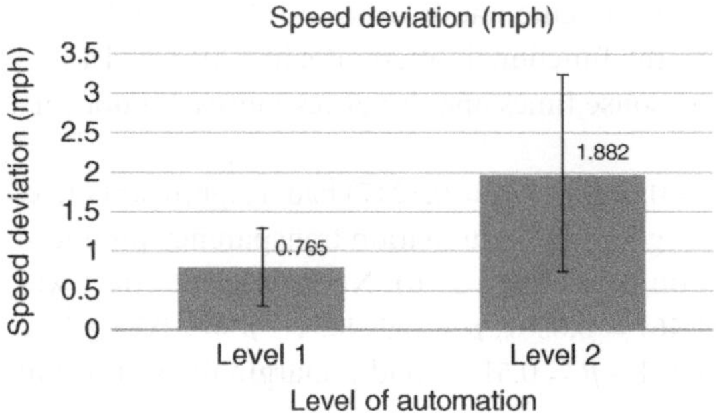


**Figure 25.8** Effect of level of automation on speed deviation.

deviations than Level 1 ($F$ (1,47) = 24.7709, $p < 0.0001$, $1-\beta > 0.999$; see Figure 25.8). No significant effect was identified for the automation transparency manipulation ($F$ (1,47) = 0.1465, $p$ = 0.7064, $1-\beta$ = 0.100) or duration of driver exposure to automation ($F$ (1,47) = 0.0135, $p$ = 0.9089, $1-\beta$ = 0.0685).

The interaction effect of automation transparency and level of automation was also significant ($F$ (1,47) = 6.9817, $p$ = 0.0192, $1-\beta$ = 0.6576) in driver performance. Higher level of automation produced degraded speed control, but the effect was mitigated when audio messages were presented as part of the automation transparency manipulation (see Figure 25.9).

Regarding lane maintenance, the main effects of automation transparency ($F$ (1,47) = 0.0372, $p$ = 0.8493, $1-\beta$ = 0.0503), level of automation ($F$ (1,47) = 0.3590, $p$ = 0.5565, $1-\beta$ = 0.1427), and duration of automation exposure ($F$ (1,47) = 0.0052, $p$ = 0.943, $1-\beta$ = 0.0505) were not significant. Only the interaction between automation transparency and level of vehicle automation ($F$ (1,47) = 23.6452, $p$ = 0.0005, $1-\beta$ = 0.9810) was significant. Automation transparency reduced lane deviations when drivers used Level 2 automation, but the effect of automation transparency

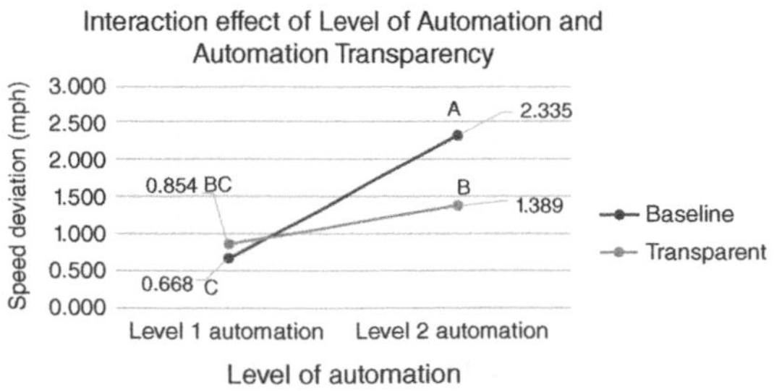


**Figure 25.9** Interaction effect of level of automation and automation transparency on speed deviation.

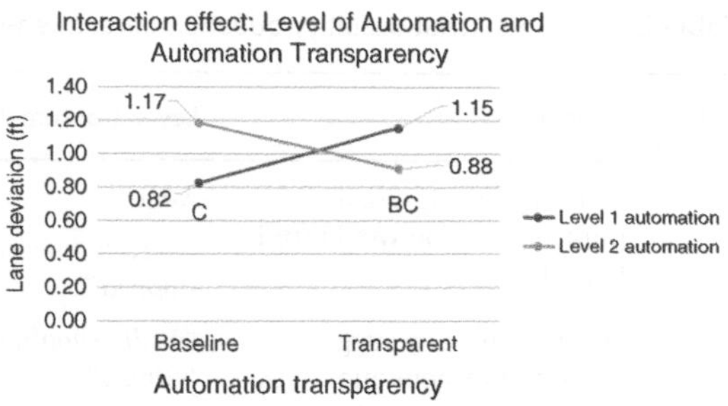


**Figure 25.10** Interaction effect on lane deviation: duration of exposure and automation transparency.

was reversed for Level 1 automation. Figure 25.10 presents this interaction effect, which is further addressed in the discussion section.

### 25.5.3 Posttesting Usability Questionnaire

Participants who drove with high-level automation transparency were asked to complete a usability questionnaire after all test trials were complete. Among the participants, six drivers used Level 1 automation and six drove with Level 2 automation. The overall score for each automation usability question, as well as the average score for Level 1 and 2 automation are presented in Figure 25.11.

Overall, participants found the audio messages and automation system states to be helpful. They indicated that the messages promoted comprehension of system states and helped them stay alert. Results suggested drivers were likely to use such audio messages, if they were provided in commercial vehicles. It is worth noting that drivers under Level 2 automation found the audio messages to be more helpful than Level 1. They also indicated being more likely to use such messages if they were provided in commercial vehicles.

In addition to the scores for questions, participants were also asked to respond to open-ended automation usability questions with concerns or recommendations. All comments from participants are presented in Table 25.3. In the majority of cases, drivers didn't have additional concerns or suggestions regarding the automation transparency manipulation.

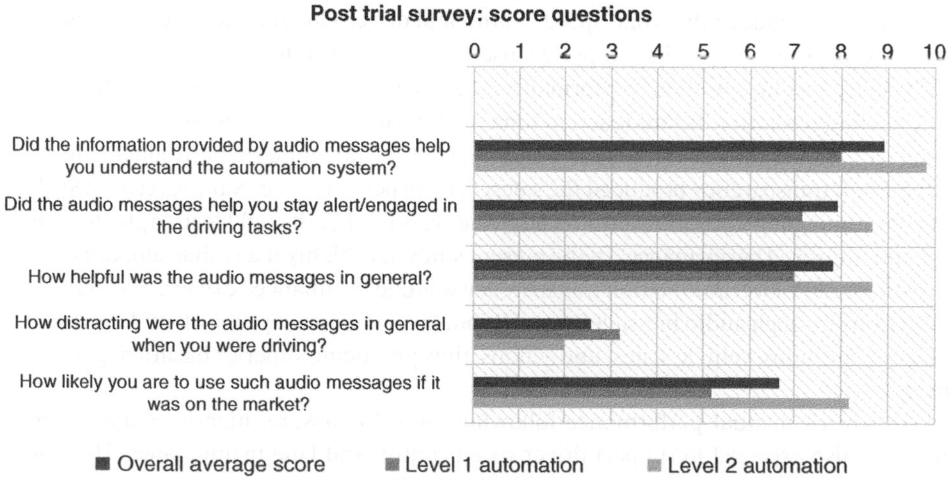


**Figure 25.11** Post-trial survey: question scores.

**Table 25.3** Posttrial usability questionnaire: open-ended question responses.

| No. | Question | Level 1 automation response | Level 2 automation response |
|---|---|---|---|
| 1 | Is there any additional information you would find helpful? | *None*<br>*"Need to know if vehicle has stopped"* | *"Numeric speed information"* |
| 2 | Do you have any suggestions/recommendations you would like to share? | *"Audio should sound more like human"* | *"Need more human-like audio"* |
| 3 | Do you have any concerns you would like to share? | *"Audio message was helpful in the beginning but annoying beyond that"* | *None* |

## 25.6 Discussion

Results of the experiment indicated no differences in driver's hazard negotiation performance with the different levels of vehicle automation, including comparison of SAE Levels 1 and 2. This finding may have been due to the simple simulated roadway conditions and ease of vehicle lateral control tasks. Drivers under Level 2 automation did exhibit higher time-to-collision, but this effect was marginal, and the statistical power was low. Having noted these outcomes, the level of vehicle automation proceeding the driver's manual performance period did have an influence on speed control. As expected, Level 2 automation led to worse driver performance than Level 1. The expectation that higher level of automation would produce higher lane deviations, however, was not supported. Comparable lane maintenance performance was observed under the two levels of automation. Therefore, results provided some evidence of postautomation exposure driving skill decay with higher-level automation, but this evidence was not as strong as expected. The level of vehicle automation was also involved in an interaction with automation transparency in influence on driver speed control as well as lane maintenance performance. Level 2 automation without transparency produced the worst speed control and driver lane maintenance outcomes.

In general, the experiment results supported use of high-level automation transparency to enhance driver hazard negotiation performance. Findings included high-level automation transparency leading to shorter hazard reaction times and greater time-to-collision.

These results are in line with observations by Koo et al. [10], who found that introducing higher levels of automation transparency produced the safest driving performance. Naujoks et al. [18] also argued that communicating upcoming automated maneuvers by speech could lead to greater drive engagement and improved performance. In the present study, it is highly likely that superior driver performance under high-level automation transparency was due to enhanced driver understanding of vehicle functions through audio messages. In addition, the audio message may have kept drivers alert to roadway conditions, vehicle states, and actions, thus producing superior hazard negotiation performance.

In regard to driver's manual performance following hazard exposure, high-level automation transparency was also expected to support driver speed control and lane maintenance. However, the main effect of automation transparency was not significant for either response measure. As mentioned above, results revealed a significant interaction effect of level of automation and automation transparency on driver's performance with high-level automation transparency reducing speed deviations but only for Level 2 automation. For lane maintenance, automation transparency produced lower deviations than the baseline condition, but this effect was reversed with Level 1 automation. It should also be noted that the duration of automation exposure was not influential on any response measures. This finding could be attributed to the relatively short and discontinuous exposure of drivers to automation during the experiment.

To further understand these observations on the automation transparency manipulation, driver's attitudes toward automation transparency were investigated through the posttrial questionnaire.

According to the survey results, drivers under Level 1 and Level 2 automation considered audio messages on automation states and actions to be useful. However, when asked, "how likely you are to use such audio messages, if available on the market?" drivers under Level 1 automation gave a mean rating of 5.17/10, while drivers under Level 2 automation gave a mean rating of 8.17/10. It is possible that participants, who drove with ACC only found the audio messages redundant and "annoying," because Level 1 automation involved simpler automated functions. In fact, one participant who drove with ACC mentioned that the messages were helpful at the beginning of the experiment but "annoying" beyond that time. Therefore, it appears that the complexity of vehicle automation could have a significant influence on driver's perceptions of the usefulness of automation transparency. Although automation transparency had a positive effect for use of Level 2 automation, the same effect was not observed for Level 1 automation likely due to the simplicity of the automation and negative driver attitudes. Related to this inference, Koo et al. [10] also found drivers under Level 1 automation to have negative emotional responses when they were presented with both "how" and "why" information about automated vehicle behavior, even though the information proved to improve driving performance.

Based on the above findings, it appears that automation transparency has some utility for supporting driver performance with ADAS. However, additional investigation is necessary to determine an optimal amount of information or most appropriate time at which to present automation states and actions to users. There also appears to be a need to ensure that all audio messaging is "human like" and that information is provided on vehicle speed along with automation states.

## 25.7 Conclusion

In conclusion, this study considered how the introduction of ADAS in commercial vehicles may lead to changes in driver behavior, particularly in negotiating roadway hazards. The approach of applying high-level automation transparency, including information on automation states and functions was also considered for offsetting any negative effects of ADAS on driver performance, such as overreliance, loss of SA, and reduced vehicle control. In addition to a literature review, we conducted a driving simulation experiment to quantify the effect of SAE levels of vehicle automation on driver's hazard reactions and vehicle control performance as well as the influence of automation transparency on the same situation responses.

The experiment results indicated use of high-level automation transparency to support driver's performance with ADAS, including hazard negotiation. Participants who used transparent automation (i.e. audio messages providing information on automation states and actions) demonstrated superior hazard negotiation performance. Automation transparency also appeared to enhance speed control and lane maintenance under SAE Level 2 automation. Posttrial surveys revealed that drivers, especially the ones using Level 2 automation, found automation transparency to be most useful, and they were likely to use such a method if it were available in the commercial market.

In addition, findings revealed some performance degradation associated with automated driving preceding periods of manual control that followed roadway hazard negotiation. The higher the level of vehicle automation before manual takeover, the greater the speed control and lane deviations during manual driving. These results have implications for ADAS design by automotive manufacturers.

The current research is one of the first driving simulation studies on effects of automation transparency on driver performance. This study can also provide a basis for enhancing the design of information systems in automated vehicles.

## 25.8 Future Research

Due to the scope of this study, only drivers aged between 30 and 45 years were included in the sample. Drivers from other age groups (e.g. elderly or younger drivers) might exhibit different adaptive control behaviors (braking, steering) when vehicle automation is active. Their attitudes toward automation transparency features may also differ. Therefore, it is necessary for future research to include drivers from different age groups.

As another limitation, the roadway condition presented in the simulator experiment was a rural freeway with clear weather, and only two types of hazard events. Real-life roadway conditions are significantly more complicated, and current automated driving systems are highly susceptible to such complexity (e.g. rain, unclear lane markers, and pedestrians). To obtain further insights into driver behavior with automated driving, and achieve more accurate crash prediction analysis, it is recommended for future studies that a large variety of environmental conditions and hazard scenarios be investigated.

In addition to the study sample and simulation design issues, the duration of exposure to automated driving was relatively short. The exposure was also interrupted by rest breaks between test trials to mitigate fatigue effects. In real-life cases, it is common for drivers to experience longer and continuous exposure to automation. Sleep deprivation and intoxication would also be expected to lead to greater impact of automation use on performance. Future studies should also consider investigating a broader set of exposure durations, in order to identify potential skill decay associated with each level of automation.

Further investigation into the use of automation transparency is also warranted. For example, additional visual messaging could be provided with similar content as audio messages. This method may ensure reliability of messaging but could lead to additional driver visual distraction. It would also be interesting to assess the impact of transparency on driver trust in automation. Future investigations could ensure similar levels of engagement across levels of vehicle automation and assess trust outcomes using subjective ratings scales [1].

## References

1 Bagheri, N. and Jamieson, G.A. (2004). Considering subjective trust and monitoring behavior in assessing automation-induced "complacency". In: *Human Performance, Situation Awareness, and Automation: Current Research and Trends*, vol. 1, 54–59. Psychology Press.

2 Blanco, M., Atwood, J., Russell, S.M. et al. (2016). *Automated Vehicle Crash Rate Comparison Using Naturalistic Data*. Virginia Tech Transportation Institute.

**3** Chalder, T., Berelowitz, G., Pawlikowska, T., and Watts, L. (1993). Development of a fatigue scale. *Journal of Psychosomatic Research* 37 (2): 147–153.

**4** Chen, J.Y., Procci, K., Boyce, M., et al. (2014). *Situation awareness-based agent transparency*. Army Research Lab, Aberdeen Proving Ground (MD), Human Research and Engineering Directorate.

**5** Deng, Y. and Kaber, D. (2018). Effect of vehicle control format on driver performance and attention allocation under adaptive cruise control. In: *Proceedings of the Human Factors and Ergonomics Society Annual Meeting*, September (Vol. 62, No. 1, pp. 1510–1514). Sage CA: Los Angeles, CA. SAGE Publications.

**6** Dikmen, M. and Burns, C.M. (2016). Autonomous driving in the real world: experiences with tesla autopilot and summon. In: *Proceedings of the 8th International Conference on Automotive User Interfaces and Interactive Vehicular Applications*, October, 225–228. Association for Computing Machinery.

**7** Eichelberger, A.H. and McCartt, A.T. (2016). Toyota drivers' experiences with dynamic radar cruise control, pre-collision system, and lane-keeping assist. *Journal of Safety Research* 56: 67–73.

**8** Gold, C., Damböck, D., Lorenz, L., and Bengler, K. (2013). "Take over!" How long does it take to get the driver back into the loop? In: *Proceedings of the Human Factors and Ergonomics Society Annual Meeting*, September (Vol. 57, No. 1, pp. 1938–1942). Sage CA: Los Angeles, CA. Sage Publications.

**9** Horrey, W.J. and Wickens, C.D. (2006). Examining the impact of cell phone conversations on driving using meta-analytic techniques. *Human Factors* 48 (1): 196–205.

**10** Koo, J., Kwac, J., Ju, W. et al. (2015). Why did my car just do that? Explaining semi-autonomous driving actions to improve driver understanding, trust, and performance. *International Journal on Interactive Design and Manufacturing (IJIDeM)* 9 (4): 269–275.

**11** Lajunen, T. and Summala, H. (1995). Driving experience, personality, and skill and safety-motive dimensions in drivers' self-assessments. *Personality and Individual Differences* 19 (3): 307–318.

**12** Louw, T., Markkula, G., Boer, E. et al. (2017). Coming back into the loop: drivers' perceptual-motor performance in critical events after automated driving. *Accident Analysis & Prevention* 108: 9–18.

**13** Ma, R. and Kaber, D.B. (2005). Situation awareness and workload in driving while using adaptive cruise control and a cell phone. *International Journal of Industrial Ergonomics* 35 (10): 939–953.

**14** McClumpha, A.J., James, M., Green, R.G., and Belyavin, A.J. (1991). Pilots' attitudes to cockpit automation. In: *Proceedings of the Human Factors Society Annual Meeting*, September (Vol. 35, No. 2, pp. 107–111). Sage CA: Los Angeles, CA. SAGE Publications.

**15** Merat, N., Jamson, A.H., Lai, F.C., and Carsten, O. (2012). Highly automated driving, secondary task performance, and driver state. *Human Factors* 54 (5): 762–771.

**16** Mercado, J.E., Rupp, M.A., Chen, J.Y. et al. (2016). Intelligent agent transparency in human–agent teaming for Multi- UxV management. *Human Factors* 58 (3): 401–415.

**17** Mok, B.K.J., Johns, M., Lee, K.J. et al. (2015). Timing of unstructured transitions of control in automated driving. In: *2015 IEEE Intelligent Vehicles Symposium (IV)*, June, 1167–1172. IEEE.

**18** Naujoks, F., Forster, Y., Wiedemann, K., and Neukum, A. (2016). Speech improves human-automation cooperation in automated driving. *Mensch und Computer 2016–Workshop*.

**19** Parasuraman, R., Sheridan, T.B., and Wickens, C.D. (2000). A model for types and levels of human interaction with automation. *IEEE Transactions on Systems, Man, and Cybernetics-Part A: Systems and Humans* 30 (3): 286–297.

**20** Rudin-Brown, C.M., Parker, H.A., and Malisia, A.R. (2003). Behavioral adaptation to adaptive cruise control. In: *Proceedings of the Human Factors and Ergonomics Society Annual Meeting*, October (Vol. 47, No. 16, pp. 1850–1854). Sage CA: Los Angeles, CA: SAGE Publications.

**21** SAE (2016). U.S. Department of Transportation's New Policy on Automated Vehicles Adopts SAE International's Levels of Automation for Defining Driving Automation in On-Road Motor Vehicles. Retrieved January 24, 2017, from https://www.sae.org/news/3544/.

**22** Schleicher, S. and Gelau, C. (2011). The influence of Cruise Control and Adaptive Cruise Control on driving behaviour–A driving simulator study. *Accident Analysis & Prevention* 43 (3): 1134–1139.

**23** Schoettle, B. and Sivak, M. (2015). *A Preliminary Analysis of Real-World Crashes Involving Self-driving Vehicles. University of Michigan Transportation Research Institute.*

**24** Seong, Y. and Bisantz, A.M. (2008). The impact of cognitive feedback on judgment performance and trust with decision aids. *International Journal of Industrial Ergonomics* 38 (7–8): 608–625.

**25** Smith, B.W. and Svensson, J., (2015). Automated and autonomous driving: regulation under uncertainty.

**26** Vlakveld, W.P., (2016). Transition of control in highly automated vehicles: a literature review.

**27** de Waard, D., van der Hulst, M., Hoedemaeker, M., and Brookhuis, K.A. (1999). Driver behavior in an emergency situation in the Automated Highway System. *Transportation Human Factors* 1 (1): 67–82.

**28** Westin, C., Borst, C., and Hilburn, B. (2016). Automation transparency and personalized decision support: air traffic controller interaction with a resolution advisory system. *IFAC-Papers Online* 49 (19): 201–206.

**29** Yang, X.J., Unhelkar, V.V., Li, K., and Shah, J.A. (2017). Evaluating effects of user experience and system transparency on trust in automation. In: *2017 12th ACM/IEEE International Conference on Human-Robot Interaction (HRI)*, March, 408–416. IEEE.

**30** Young, M.S. and Stanton, N.A. (1997). Automotive automation: investigating the impact on drivers' mental workload.

**31** Zahabi, M., Machado, P., Pankok, C. Jr., et al. (2017). The role of driver age in performance and attention allocation effects of roadway sign count, format and familiarity. *Applied Ergonomics* 63: 17–30.

**32** Zmud, J.P. and Sener, I.N. (2017). Towards an understanding of the travel behavior impact of autonomous vehicles. *Transportation Research Procedia* 25: 2500–2519.

# 26

# RGB-D Based Human Action Recognition: From Handcrafted to Deep Learning

*Bangli Liu*[1] *and Honghai Liu*[2]

[1] *School of Computer Science and Informatics, Faculty of Computing, Engineering, and Media, De Montfort University, Leicester, England, UK*
[2] *School of Computing, Faculty of Technology, University of Portsmouth, Portsmouth, England, UK*

## 26.1 Introduction

The task of action recognition systems is to automatically identify the human behaviors in a video stream or a still image. Human action recognition has wide applications, such as assistant robots [4], virtual reality, human–robot interaction, surveillance. Most of the early research focus on activity recognition from RGB images. However, this kind of methods is sensitive to illumination, and their performance is not robust due to the absence of 3D information. Fortunately, these shortcomings can be largely alleviated by the cost-effective RGB-D sensors which provide extra depth and 3D skeleton information. As a consequence, more and more algorithms based on RGB-D data have been developed, which reveals a promising future direction for human action recognition. Recently, inspired by the remarkable success of deep learning techniques in image categorization tasks [27], approaches based on the deep learning which aims to learn high-level representations directly from training data have been adopted for action recognition.

This chapter conducts a comprehensive review of human action recognition using RGB-D data, including handcrafted and deep learning-based approaches. Moreover, it summaries challenges as well as promising future directions in human action recognition. The structure of this chapter is organized as follows: Section 26.2 introduces RGB-D Sensors and 3D Data. Sections 26.3 and 26.4 presents a review of the handcrafted and deep learning-based human action recognition, respectively. Section 26.5 provides an overall discussion of different methods. Section 26.6 reviews the most commonly used RGB-D based human action datasets. Section 26.7 concludes the chapter and discusses the future directions.

## 26.2 RGB-D Sensors and 3D Data

The task of vision-based human action recognition is to identify the human behaviors from the scene observed by an acquisition system. The cost-effective RGB-D sensors such as Microsoft Kinect and ASUS Xtion provide extra 3D structure of the scene. Compared to traditional RGB cameras, the third dimension (depth) of users provided by the Kinect sensor makes computer vision tasks such

*Handbook of Human-Machine Systems*, First Edition. Edited by Giancarlo Fortino, David Kaber, Andreas Nürnberger, and David Mendonça.

as body language understanding much easier. With its excellence and low cost, Kinect sensors' impact has extended far beyond the gaming industry.

Each pixel in a depth map captured by RGB-D sensors stores the corresponding distance with respect to the sensor. Structured light or time-of-flight technology is used to estimate the depth information. Microsoft Kinect SDK and OpenNI SDK are developed for providing human skeleton joints. Therefore, a single Kinect sensor can simultaneously provide a RGB image, a depth map, and 3D skeleton information of human subjects. Compared to traditional RGB cameras which have high sensibility to color and light conditions, the Kinect sensors have the robustness to illumination changes as well as the capability to work in complete darkness. In addition, the depth information indeed facilitates the subtraction of objects of interest from the background. Due to these benefits, a lot of methods based on RGB-D data have been proposed, which reveals a promising future direction for human action recognition.

## 26.3 Human Action Recognition via Handcrafted Methods

The advent of low-cost RGB-D sensors, providing extra-depth images and 3D skeleton information, has significantly boosted the development of human action recognition. Based on the data modality used, three categories: skeleton-based, depth-based, and hybrid feature-based methods will be discussed.

### 26.3.1 Skeleton-Based Methods

In [16], joints' 3D movement was described by projecting skeleton sequences onto three 2D projections. The final action classification was conducted based on these trajectory descriptors. In [44], angles between connected body parts were selected as movement features and then similarities between each angle pair with temporal information were used to represent actions. A modified histogram of oriented gradients, i.e. HOG, was utilized to capture the posture information around each joint over the time. Guo et al. [17] encoded motion trajectories of body parts to a gradient variation-based sparse histogram and applied a support vector machine for action recognition. Some research applied joint information such as locations, angles, and geometric relationships to build effective representations of actions [30, 37, 40, 70]. In [70], the histogram of 3D joint locations, i.e. HOJ3D, was used to depict human postures which were then clustered into $K$ clusters using $K$-means. These $K$ clusters representing the prototypical poses of actions were considered as observation symbols in a hidden Markov model to explain motion features in the time domain. Instead of using all skeleton joints' movement, Eweiwi et al. [14] tried to extract joints that contain apparent movement (including their locations, velocity, and movement normals) by partial least squares. Vemulapalli et al. [61] encoded 3D geometry features of actions which consist of body parts' rotations and translations in Lie group.

Compared with single person action, the feature space of human interaction has more variations in subject appearance, scale, viewpoint, interacting motion patterns, etc., due to multiple persons involved. Moreover, diverse interacting motion patterns make human interaction recognition more challenging. Some human interaction recognition algorithms utilize features of joint pairs to describe interaction [22, 34, 76]. Yun et al. [76] extracted different features of skeleton joints, such as distance, joint movement between consecutive frames, and the geometric relation. To reduce the irrelevant frames, interaction sequences were depicted by a bag of body-pose via multiple instance learning. Interactive body part pairs are distinct among different interactions, thus, the activities between two persons were described as the motion and spatial relations between informative body parts in [22].

Some researchers addressed interaction recognition via individual action recognition [2, 3]. For example, in [3], each player's action in a computing game was trained and classified separately, and the interaction between players was identified through the combination probability of each player's actions. Unlike the methods mentioned above, Coppola et al. [8] created a multivariate Gaussian distribution model to obtain the distribution of interaction categories with the help of physical proximity features in social interaction environment.

### 26.3.2 Depth-Based Methods

With the help of depth information, it is easy to extract human bodies from the background. Furthermore, depth information is invariant to the change of lighting conditions, thus stable and rich information could be provided for describing human shape or motion. Some researchers [5, 28, 75] proposed to extract action features by projecting the depth information onto three 2D orthogonal planes which are corresponding to three different views: front, side, and top. For example, Li et al. [28] utilized postures represented by selected informative points of the body silhouette from the three planes for action classification. The bi-gram maximum likelihood decoding algorithm was employed to reduce the computational complexity. In [75], depth maps sequences were stacked to create Depth Motion Maps, i.e. DMMs, from which HOGs were calculated to describe actions. The concatenation of HOGs was the input of a linear support vector machine for action classification. To reduce the computation cost caused by the computation of HOGs in [5, 75] used the concatenation of DMMs from three viewpoints as the final representation. Human body shape was reflected in detail from different viewpoints in these DMMs.

Oreifej and Liu [45] proposed Histogram of Oriented 4D, i.e. HON4D to describe actions, where depth sequences were represented via spatiotemporal cells. HON4D counting surface normals in each cell depicts the change of human shape and motion. Slama et al. [53] modeled sequence features as subspaces lying on Grassmann manifold, where the geometric and dynamic information of human body were computed. Alternatively, some scholars proposed to extract concise features from interest areas on depth images. As these features can depict actions' local characters, they are robust to occlusions or clutter. In [31], a context-based depth descriptor was constructed using the spatial relation between joints with discriminate motion.

### 26.3.3 Hybrid Feature-Based Methods

It is believed that information coming from different modalities such as skeleton, color, and depth can complement each other [46, 64, 65, 74]. For example, the depth or RGB information can reflect the appearance or texture information surrounding the skeleton joints while the movement of joints can describe the motion information.

Movement information from depth images and skeleton joints was normally combined to construct hybrid features in [20, 23, 46, 48, 64, 65]. Wang et al. [64, 65] interpreted body movement by the relative positions of joint pairs. Meanwhile, they used local occupancy pattern features which were obtained by projecting cloud points in the spatial grid around each joint to describe the depth appearance around joints. In [23], the skeleton information was used to segment the human body into different body parts, which were treated as geometrical structure guidance for the depth maps to improve the recognition performance in complex backgrounds. Raman and Maybank [46] developed a two-level hierarchical Hidden Markov method to model the 3D joint positions of a human skeleton and the local depth image pattern around these joint positions. Yang and Tian [74] proposed to calculate EigenJoints which combine the difference of postures, motion, and offset information of joints. The EigenJoints were chosen via accumulated motion energy in depth sequences. Some methods also included RGB information [26, 57] for action representation.

In [26], an united space was built to enable information from RGB and depth channel can be shared. The united space can help reduce noise and improve the recognition accuracy.

Some researchers thought that focusing on the area of interest could help to improve the action recognition performance. For example, bounding boxes were proposed to restrict the area of interest in [15]. By doing this, the redundant or less informative data could be removed. For joints in each bounding box, their distances and depth difference were extracted to describe the local relations. Bounding boxes were also used to indicate where interaction happens between persons in [60], from which shape and movement features of joints were explored to select key time frames for interaction representation. Xia et al. [71] combined the posture, motion information, and local appearance feature in RGB images and depth images. They studied interaction from a robot-centric view instead of the conditional third-person view. Appearance and motion properties were extracted directly from body parts in [1] and [72]. Alazrai et al. [1] proposed to reflect body parts' semantic meaning during interacting using movement profile and appearance of the corresponding bounding box. In [59], human interactions were described via a comprehensive feature descriptor which consists of spatial and temporal features from skeleton, RGB, and depth images, respectively.

Contextual information is a vital factor for recognizing human activity, especially for those during human interaction, human–object interaction [42]. The relationship between activities and backgrounds and features from a specific object with which a person interacting could support valuable context for action recognition. In [42], constraints based on depth value were used to improve the accuracy of objects detection. Apart from extracting appearance features by HOG for each individual, the spatiotemporal contextual attributes were encoded by relative distances, velocity, or time order. Additionally, the depth-based environment description was considered for representing different scenes and thus makes the recognition more precisely. A dual assignment K-means clustering algorithm that exploits the correlation between actions and scenes was proposed in [24].

## 26.4 Human Action Recognition via Deep Learning Methods

Motivated by the great achievements of deep learning techniques in computer vision, more and more researchers have applied deep learning for human activity recognition. According to the applied deep learning structure type, the research reviewed in this section are categorized into three groups: convolutional neural network (CNN) based, recurrent neural network (RNN) based, and graph convolutional neural network (GCN) based methods.

### 26.4.1 CNN-Based Methods

Inspired by the remarkable success of CNN in image categorization tasks [27], CNN-based methods which aim to obtain representations directly from input color images have been adopted for action recognition. Although depth sequences captured by RGB-D devices contain rich motion information, they cannot be directly input to the CNN models, since CNN is initially utilized in 2D space with powerful capacity of extracting spatial information from still images. To enable and learn representation from depth sequences, some researchers [66, 67] proposed to convert the manually extracted features from depth images to texture images by some predefined encoding method. The texture images can then be input to CNN architectures for high-level feature learning and classification. For example, in [66], both the posture and motion feature in depth sequences were extracted by building different kinds of dynamic depth images. The spatialtemporal information was encoded into images using bidirectional rank pooling. These image-based representations enable existing CNN models being used for depth-based action recognition. To overcome the limitations of skeleton data, such as a poor tolerance to self-occlusion and noise, Crabbe et al. [9]

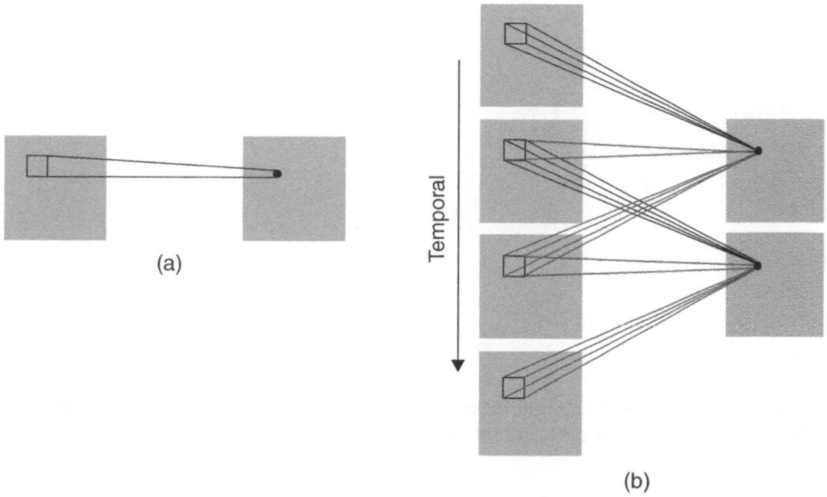


**Figure 26.1** (a) 2D convolution and (b) 3D convolution [21]. In (b) the size of the convolution kernel in the temporal dimension is 3 and the sets of connections are color-coded so that the shared weights are in the same color. In 3D convolution, the same 3D kernel is applied to overlapping 3D cubes in the input video to extract motion features.

proposed to estimate skeleton-free body poses from depth sequences by mapping depth silhouettes of a human body to a pose space through the CNN.

Another straightforward solution to apply CNN for action recognition is to perform 3D convolutions on action sequences [19, 21, 69, 78]. The 3D convolution is able to explore both spatial and temporal information. Figure 26.1 shows the comparison between 2D and 3D convolutions. Wu et al. [69] proposed to apply a 3D convolutional neural networks (3DCNN) to learn spatial and temporal information from RGB and depth videos. They proved that the fusion of multimodal information could result in a better performance over unimodal ones due to the complementary relation among different data channels. Liu et al. [33] applied a 3DCNN structure to extract high-level features from depth sequences. The temporal information was inferred from depth sequences by introducing the 3D filters which take the temporal dimension into account. They also proposed JointVector to calculate low-level features such as joints' position and angle information. The classification results of support vector machine (SVM) using both kinds of features were fused for the final action recognition.

Instead of the later fusion of results from each separate CNN model with individual modality input, Wang et al. [68] proposed to extract action information from RGB and depth channels, which were integrated as one entity via a scene flow to action map (SFAM). Different variants of SFAM could encode effective spatial and temporal dynamics and enable the direct action recognition from two data modalities without a score fusion later. Apart from the fusion of different types of features from multiple modalities, some hybrid neural networks combining CNN and RNN were also designed to deal with the spatial and temporal information in an end-to-end network [43]. Before an RNN, individual images were input into CNN to learn frame-level texture features, which encoded the temporal relation in the memory.

### 26.4.2 RNN-Based Methods

As an alternative solution to CNN, RNN could effectively model the temporal information. Most of RNN-based methods were trying to identify action categories with skeleton joint sequences. Figure 26.2 shows that different geometric features of joints or body parts were extracted as the

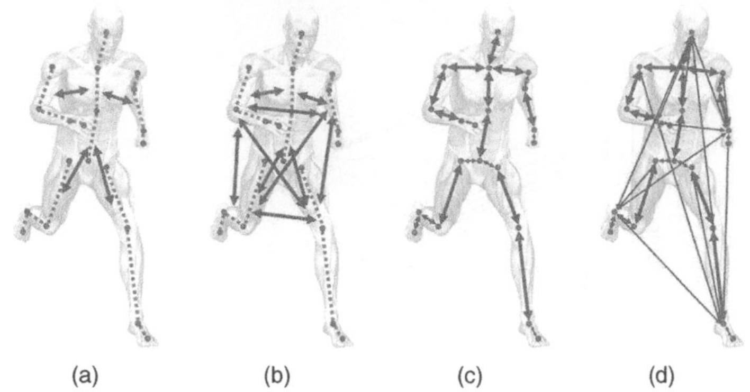


**Figure 26.2** Evolution of geometric relation modeling for RNN-based action recognition [80]. (a) Relations between adjacent parts, (b) relations among all parts, (c) relations between adjacent joints, and (d) relations among all joints.

RNN input [47, 79, 83]. In [12], an individual RNN was created for each human body part to extract features which were fused for action classification. However, the relationship between nonadjacent body parts that could be useful to depict the dynamic characteristics of actions was not considered in this approach. Alternatively, Shi and Kim [51] investigated a privileged information-based RNN framework for depth-based action recognition. Skeleton joints provided during training were considered as a type of privileged information to achieve a better estimation of network parameters. Apart from the temporal dependency, Wang and Wang [62] proposed to use a spatial RNN structure to model skeleton joints' spatial dependency. To address the view variation challenge in human action recognition, Zhang et al. [81] proposed a self-regulated adaptation scheme to learn the proper viewpoints and transformed skeleton data to the learned viewpoints. The adaptive view scheme was embedded to CNN and RNN to demonstrate its effectiveness.

Due to the gradient vanishing problem, most of the RNN methods lack the ability to process long-term temporal dependency. One of the RNN's variants named the long short-term memory (LSTM) [18] is proposed to ease the gradient vanishing problem. It utilizes a gating mechanism to control the temporal memory length in an action sequence. Zhang et al. [80] proposed three-layer LSTM architectures to take different geometric features of skeleton. The output of each architecture was fused using a smoothed score fusion method for final action classification. CNN and LSTM were jointly utilized for action recognition in [43], where the output of CNN was served as the input of LSTM. A two-stage training procedure was further developed, which first trains the CNN and then trains the combined network.

It is agreed that discriminative action information could be helpful in improving the recognition performance [10, 52, 54]. Different attention mechanisms were developed to extract informative spatial and temporal features for action recognition. As shown in Figure 26.3, Song et al. [54] proposed a spatial attention and a temporal attention to assign adaptive attention to each skeleton joint and each frame, respectively. They also leveraged the produced temporal attention for action detection in action videos. Si et al. [52] proposed an attention-enhanced graph convolutional LSTM network (AGC-LSTM) to obtain both spatial and temporal action data. It can also explore the co-occurrence relationship between two domains. An attention mechanism was applied to enhance informative joints, which can help to extract discriminative spatial features.

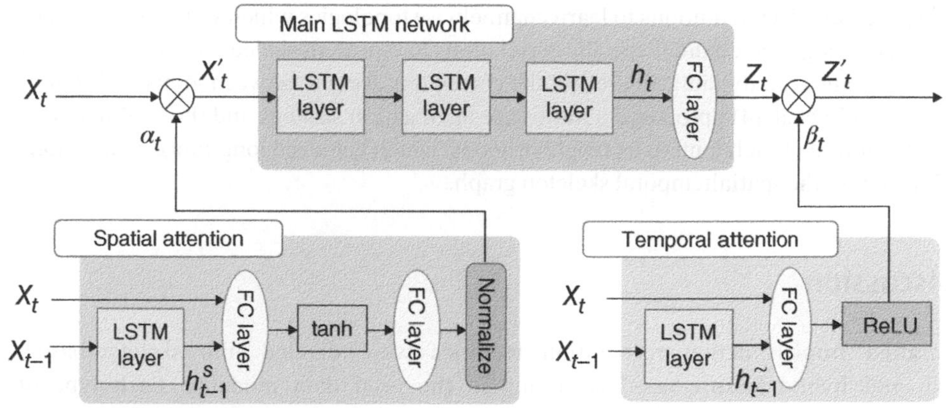


**Figure 26.3** Structure of spatiotemporal attention-based LSTM [54].

### 26.4.3 GCN-Based Methods

Early CNNs are only implemented on structured data (regular or Euclidean), while skeleton joint sequences have underlying graph structures which are non-Euclidean. To enable conduct convolution operations on skeleton joint sequences, researchers introduced GCNs to learn features from skeleton graphs with nodes represented by skeleton joints. For example, Yan et al. [73] constructed a spatiotemporal graph of a skeleton sequence using joints' coordinates and estimation confidences as graph nodes. The skeleton graph was input to the proposed Spatial-Temporal Graph Convolutional Networks (ST-GCN) to extract spatial and temporal features of action sequences. The undirected spatiotemporal graph well perseveres both the connectivity of body structure and temporal variation.

To explore more joint dependencies via skeleton graphs, Li et al. [29] proposed a A-link inference module to adaptively extract action-specific latent and higher-order dependencies from skeleton graphs. Shi et al. [50] used a directed acyclic graph to describe the correlation between skeleton joints and bones which were considered as vertexes and edges in a graph, as shown in Fig. 26.4.

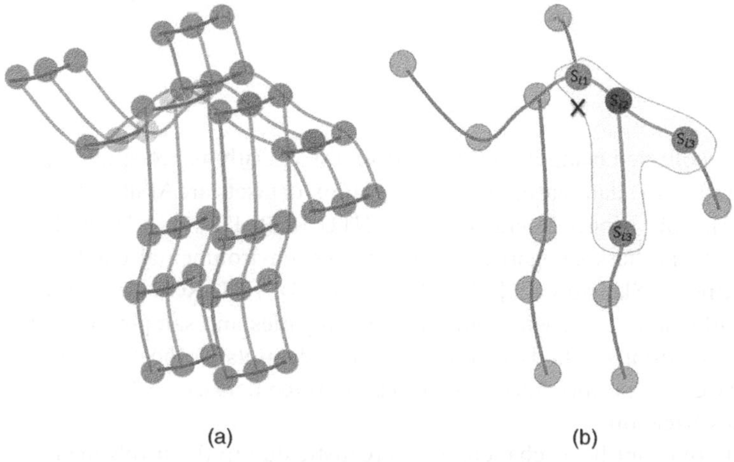


**Figure 26.4** Constructed spatiotemporal skeleton graph [50]. (a) Illustration of the spatiotemporal graph. (b) Illustration of the mapping strategy. Different colors denote different subsets.

Chen et al. [6] used graph convolutions to learn channelwise topologies which were modeled via a shared skeleton topology and channel-specific correlations to represent skeleton data. The learned channelwise topologies can dynamically reflect the correlation weight between joints in different action sequences. Liu et al. [41] proposed a multiscale aggregation strategy and the G3D to disentangle the contribution of each joint to its neighborhoods, which achieved long-range connections between joints across the spatialtemporal skeleton graph.

## 26.5 Discussion

The handcrafted human action recognition methods were divided into skeleton-based, depth-based, and hybrid feature-based according to the used data modality. Each type of methods has its advantages and limitations. Although depth images have the outstanding capability to describe appearance information, they might suffer from holes where depth data is missing. Skeleton joints are compact and straightforward to depict the motion properties of actions; however, the limitation of the skeletal feature is lacking its surrounding information which could be useful when modeling human–object interaction. In addition, the skeleton tracking output from RGB-D sensors is not very reliable when human body parts are occluded or the subject is not in an upright position facing sensors. The combination of features from different modalities has the potential to improve the recognition performance by overcoming the respective weakness. Apart from the single person's actions, some researchers proposed methods to recognize more complex activity like human interaction. Currently, most of the proposed methods only used the distance between body parts to depict the interdependent relation between interactive persons. Although the distance property is useful, it might not be competent to describe underlying relations. Thus, one direction of future research may be designing effective approaches toward the semantic interpretation of activities.

Different from the handcrafted methods which manually design feature extraction, deep learning methods conduct the feature extraction work automatically via neural networks. Thus, different kinds of network structures proposed for action recognition. Three popular structures: CNNs, RNNs and LSTM, and GCNs, were discussed. To achieve a more comprehensive representation of actions, hybrid models which combine these structures are becoming more and more popular.

## 26.6 RGB-D Datasets

Different types of datasets were collected using RGB-D sensors to test algorithms' recognition performance. The commonly used RGB-D data-based action recognition datasets are MSR-Action3D [28], MSRDailyActivity3D [64], SBU Kinect Interaction [76], NTU RGB+D [47], NTU-RGB+D 120 [39] (with increased variety in class categories, camera views, environmental conditions, and human subjects), and Kinetics-Skeleton [25]. The NTU-RGB+D, NTU-RGB+D 120, and Kinetics-Skeleton have relatively larger scale with more action categories and sample numbers. Most of recently proposed deep learning methods are tested on these datasets for the performance comparison. Table 26.1 compares the performance of methods on three datasets: NTU RGB+D, NTU-RGB+D 120, and Kinetics-Skeleton.

Most of the existing datasets may not be as challenging as realistic due to the involvement of constantly clustered or clean backgrounds. Moreover, most of the datasets provided only manually trimmed activity segments, which only contain one activity inside. This configuration does

**Table 26.1** Comparison of action recognition performance (mAP) on the NTU RGB-D, NTU RGB-D 120, Kinetics-Skeleton dataset. X-Sub: Cross-Subject, X-View: Cross-View, X-Set: Cross-Setup.

| Methods | Year | Type | NTU RGB-D | | NTU RGB-D 120 | | Kinetics-Skeleton |
|---|---|---|---|---|---|---|---|
| | | | X-Sub | X-View | X-Sub | X-Set | |
| [36] | 2017 | CNN + Skeleton | 80.03 | 87.21 | — | — | — |
| [32] | 2018 | CNN + Skeleton | 91.71 | 95.26 | — | — | — |
| GCA-LSTM [38] | 2018 | LSTM + Skeleton | 76.10 | 84.00 | — | — | — |
| [63] | 2018 | RNN + Skeleton | 79.50 | 87.60 | — | — | — |
| [58] | 2018 | GCN + Skeleton | 83.50 | 89.80 | — | — | — |
| PoseC3D [13] | 2021 | Convnet + Skeleton | 94.1 | 97.1 | 86.9 | 90.3 | 47.4 |
| CTR-GCN [6] | 2021 | GCN + Skeleton | 92.4 | 96.8 | 88.9 | 90.6 | — |
| ST-GCN [73] | 2018 | GCN + Skeleton | 81.5 | 88.3 | — | — | 30.7 |
| AGC-LSTM [52] | 2019 | GCN + Skeleton | 89.2 | 95.0 | — | — | — |
| GCA-LSTM [35] | 2017 | LSTM + Skeleton | 76.1 | 84.0 | — | — | — |
| MS-G3D [41] | 2020 | GCN + Skeleton | 91.5 | 96.2 | 86.9 | 88.4 | 38.0 |
| AS-GCN [29] | 2019 | GCN + Skeleton | 86.8 | 94.2 | 78.3 | 79.8 | 34.8 |
| Shift GCN [7] | 2020 | GCN + Skeleton | 90.7 | 96.5 | 85.9 | 87.6 | — |
| VPN [11] | 2020 | ConvNets + RGB + pose | 95.5 | 98.0 | 86.3 | 87.8 | — |
| MS-AAGCN [50] | 2020 | GCN + Skeleton | 90.0 | 96.2 | — | — | 37.8 |
| DGNN [49] | 2019 | GCN + Skeleton | 89.9 | 96.1 | — | — | 36.9 |
| SGN [82] | 2020 | SGN + Skeleton | 89.0 | 94.5 | 79.2 | 81.5 | — |
| 3s RA-GCN [55] | 2020 | GCN + Skeleton | 87.3 | 93.6 | 81.1 | 82.7 | — |
| Skeletal GNN [77] | 2021 | GNN + Skeleton | 91.6 | 96.7 | 87.5 | 89.2 | — |
| EfficientGCN-B4 [56] | 2022 | GCN + Skeleton | 92.1 | 96.1 | 88.7 | 89.1 | — |

not mimic practical scenarios where activities are performed continuously. Therefore, it is hard to guarantee the action recognition performance of the proposed methods when applying them to real world. Therefore, the wild dataset without any constraints, where subjects acting actions naturally in the realistic environment, is imperative and promising for the future research.

## 26.7 Conclusion and Future Directions

In this chapter, RGB-D data-based human action recognition methods have been reviewed, including handcrafted feature extraction from different data modality and different deep neural network structures for action recognition. Most of the existing action recognition methods have achieved good recognition performance on pretrimmed datasets which were collected in constrained environment, such as NTU RGB-D and NTU RGB-D 120. While the performance on the Kinetics-Skeleton dataset which is close to practical human action scenarios, still has a big space to be improved. Human action recognition remains great challenges such as variations in viewpoints, occlusions, and online performance. Thus, the following directions can be considered for future research: (i) to develop view-invariant algorithms to tackle the realistic view variance issue; (ii) to effectively fuse multimodal data (e.g. skeleton, RGB, depth) or multimodel (CNN, RNN, GCN) to build robust human action recognition; and (iii) to develop algorithms with online adaption that can simultaneously detect and identify actions in practical scenarios.

## References


1 Alazrai, R., Mowafi, Y., and Lee, C.S.L. (2015). Anatomical-plane-based representation for human–human interactions analysis. *Pattern Recognition* 48 (8): 2346–2363.

2 Bloom, V., Argyriou, V., and Makris, D. (2014). G3Di: a gaming interaction dataset with a real time detection and evaluation framework. *ECCV Workshop*, 698–712.

3 Bloom, V., Argyriou, V., and Makris, D. (2016). Hierarchical transfer learning for online recognition of compound actions. *Computer Vision and Image Understanding* 144: 62–72.

4 Cai, H., Fang, Y., Ju, Z. et al. (2019). Sensing-enhanced therapy system for assessing children with autism spectrum disorders: a feasibility study. *IEEE Sensors Journal* 19 (4): 1508–1518.

5 Chen, C., Liu, K., and Kehtarnavaz, N. (2013). Real-time human action recognition based on depth motion maps. *Journal of Real-Time Image Processing* 12: 155–163.

6 Chen, Y., Zhang, Z., Yuan, C. et al. (2021). Channel-wise topology refinement graph convolution for skeleton-based action recognition. *Proceedings of the IEEE/CVF International Conference on Computer Vision*, 13359–13368.

7 Cheng, K., Zhang, Y., He, X. et al. (2020). Skeleton-based action recognition with shift graph convolutional network. *Proceedings of the IEEE/CVF Conference on Computer Vision and Pattern Recognition*, 183–192.

8 Coppola, C., Faria, D.R., Nunes, U., and Bellotto, N. (2016). Social activity recognition based on probabilistic merging of skeleton features with proximity priors from RGB-D data. *IROS*, 5055–5061.

9 Crabbe, B., Paiement, A., Hannuna, S., and Mirmehdi, M. (2015). Skeleton-free body pose estimation from depth images for movement analysis. *ICCV Workshops*, 70–78.

10 Dai, C., Liu, X., and Lai, J. (2020). Human action recognition using two-stream attention based LSTM networks. *Applied Soft Computing* 86: 105820.

11 Das, S., Sharma, S., Dai, R. et al. (2020). VPN: learning video-pose embedding for activities of daily living. *European Conference on Computer Vision*, 72–90. Springer.

12 Du, Y., Fu, Y., and Wang, L. (2016). Representation learning of temporal dynamics for skeleton-based action recognition. *IEEE Transactions on Image Processing* 25 (7): 3010–3022.

13 Duan, H., Zhao, Y., Chen, K. et al. (2021). Revisiting skeleton-based action recognition. *arXiv preprint arXiv:2104.13586*.

14 Eweiwi, A., Cheema, M.S., Bauckhage, C., and Gall, J. (2015). Efficient pose-based action recognition. In: *Computer Vision – ACCV 2014. ACCV 2014, Lecture Notes in Computer Science*, vol. 9007, 428–443. Cham: Springer.

15 Gori, I., Aggarwal, J.K., Matthies, L., and Ryoo, M.S. (2017). Multi-type activity recognition from a robot's viewpoint. *Proceedings International Joint Conference on Artificial Intelligence*, 4849–4853.

16 Gowayyed, M.A., Torki, M., Hussein, M.E., and El-Saban, M. (2013). Histogram of oriented displacements (HOD): describing trajectories of human joints for action recognition. *Proceedings of the International Joint Conference on Artificial Intelligence*, 1351–1357.

17 Guo, Y., Li, Y., and Shao, Z. (2018). DSRF: a flexible trajectory descriptor for articulated human action recognition. *Pattern Recognition* 76: 137–148.

**18** Hochreiter, S. and Schmidhuber, J.U. (1997). Long short-term memory. *Neural Computation* 9 (8): 1735–1780.

**19** Ijjina, E.P. and Chalavadi, K.M. (2017). Human action recognition in RGB-D videos using motion sequence information and deep learning. *Pattern Recognition* 72: 504–516.

**20** Jalal, A., Kim, Y.-H., Kim, Y.-J. et al. (2017). Robust human activity recognition from depth video using spatiotemporal multi-fused features. *Pattern Recognition* 61: 295–308.

**21** Ji, S., Xu, W., Yang, M., and Yu, K. (2012). 3D convolutional neural networks for human action recognition. *IEEE Transactions on Pattern Analysis and Machine Intelligence* 35 (1): 221–231.

**22** Ji, Y., Cheng, H., Zheng, Y., and Li, H. (2015). Learning contrastive feature distribution model for interaction recognition. *Journal of Visual Communication and Image Representation* 33: 340–349.

**23** Ji, X., Cheng, J., Feng, W., and Tao, D. (2018). Skeleton embedded motion body partition for human action recognition using depth sequences. *Signal Processing* 143: 56–68.

**24** Jones, S. and Shao, L. (2014). Unsupervised spectral dual assignment clustering of human actions in context. *CVPR*, 604–611.

**25** Kay, W., Carreira, J., Simonyan, K. et al. (2017). The kinetics human action video dataset. *arXiv preprint arXiv:1705.06950.*

**26** Kong, Y. and Fu, Y. (2015). Bilinear heterogeneous information machine for RGB-D action recognition. *CVPR*, 1054–1062.

**27** Krizhevsky, A., Sutskever, I., and Hinton, G.E. (2012). ImageNet classification with deep convolutional neural networks. *NIPS*, 1097–1105.

**28** Li, W., Zhang, Z., and Liu, Z. (2010). Action recognition based on a bag of 3D points. *CVPRW*, 9–14.

**29** Li, M., Chen, S., Chen, X. et al. (2019). Actional-structural graph convolutional networks for skeleton-based action recognition. *Proceedings of the IEEE/CVF Conference on Computer Vision and Pattern Recognition*, 3595–3603.

**30** Lillo, I., Niebles, J.C., and Soto, A. (2017). Sparse composition of body poses and atomic actions for human activity recognition in RGB-D videos. *Image and Vision Computing* 59: 63–75.

**31** Liu, M. and Liu, H. (2016). Depth context: a new descriptor for human activity recognition by using sole depth sequences. *Neurocomputing* 175: 747–758.

**32** Liu, M. and Yuan, J. (2018). Recognizing human actions as the evolution of pose estimation maps. *CVPR*, 1159–1168.

**33** Liu, Z., Zhang, C., and Tian, Y. (2016). 3D-based deep convolutional neural network for action recognition with depth sequences. *Image and Vision Computing* 55: 93–100.

**34** Liu, B., Cai, H., Ji, X., and Liu, H. (2017). Human–human interaction recognition based on spatial and motion trend feature. *ICIP*, 4547–4551.

**35** Liu, J., Wang, G., Duan, L.-Y. et al. (2017). Skeleton-based human action recognition with global context-aware attention LSTM networks. *IEEE Transactions on Image Processing* 27 (4): 1586–1599.

**36** Liu, M., Liu, H., and Chen, C. (2017). Enhanced skeleton visualization for view invariant human action recognition. *Pattern Recognition* 68: 346–362.

**37** Liu, B., Ju, Z., and Liu, H. (2018). A structured multi-feature representation for recognizing human action and interaction. *Neurocomputing* 318: 287–296.

**38** Liu, J., Wang, G., Duan, L.-Y. et al. (2018). Skeleton-based human action recognition with global context-aware attention LSTM networks. *IEEE Transactions on Image Processing* 27 (4): 1586–1599.

**39** Liu, J., Shahroudy, A., Perez, M. et al. (2019). NTU RGB+D 120: a large-scale benchmark for 3D human activity understanding. *IEEE Transactions on Pattern Analysis and Machine Intelligence* 42 (10): 2684–2701.

**40** Liu, B., Cai, H., Ju, Z., and Liu, H. (2020). Multi-stage adaptive regression for online activity recognition. *Pattern Recognition* 98: 107053.

**41** Liu, Z., Zhang, H., Chen, Z. et al. (2020). Disentangling and unifying graph convolutions for skeleton-based action recognition. *Proceedings of the IEEE/CVF Conference on Computer Vision and Pattern Recognition*, 143–152.

**42** Ni, B., Pei, Y., Moulin, P., and Yan, S. (2013). Multilevel depth and image fusion for human activity detection. *IEEE Transactions on Cybernetics* 43 (5): 1383–1394.

**43** Nú nez, J.C., Cabido, R., Pantrigo, J.J. et al. (2018). Convolutional neural networks and long short-term memory for skeleton-based human activity and hand gesture recognition. *Pattern Recognition* 76: 80–94.

**44** Ohn-Bar, E. and Trivedi, M.M. (2013). Joint angles similarities and HOG2 for action recognition. *CVPRW*, 465–470.

**45** Oreifej, O. and Liu, Z. (2013). HON4D: histogram of oriented 4D normals for activity recognition from depth sequences. *CVPR*, 716–723.

**46** Raman, N. and Maybank, S.J. (2016). Activity recognition using a supervised non-parametric hierarchical HMM. *Neurocomputing* 199: 163–177.

**47** Shahroudy, A., Liu, J., Ng, T.-T., and Wang, G. (2016). NTU RGB+d: a large scale dataset for 3D human activity analysis. *CVPR*, 1010–1019.

**48** Shahroudy, A., Ng, T.-T., Yang, Q., and Wang, G. (2016). Multimodal multipart learning for action recognition in depth videos. *IEEE Transactions on Pattern Analysis and Machine Intelligence* 38 (10): 2123–2129.

**49** Shi, L., Zhang, Y., Cheng, J., and Lu, H. (2019). Skeleton-based action recognition with directed graph neural networks. *Proceedings of the IEEE/CVF Conference on Computer Vision and Pattern Recognition*, 7912–7921.

**50** Shi, L., Zhang, Y., Cheng, J., and Lu, H. (2020). Skeleton-based action recognition with multi-stream adaptive graph convolutional networks. *IEEE Transactions on Image Processing* 29: 9532–9545.

**51** Shi, Z. and Kim, T.-K. (2017). Learning and refining of privileged information-based RNNs for action recognition from depth sequences. *CVPR*, 3461–3470.

**52** Si, C., Chen, W., Wang, W. et al. (2019). An attention enhanced graph convolutional LSTM network for skeleton-based action recognition. *Proceedings of the IEEE/CVF Conference on Computer Vision and Pattern Recognition*, 1227–1236.

**53** Slama, R., Wannous, H., and Daoudi, M. (2014). Grassmannian representation of motion depth for 3D human gesture and action recognition. *ICPR*, 3499–3504.

**54** Song, S., Lan, C., Xing, J. et al. (2018). Spatio-temporal attention-based LSTM networks for 3D action recognition and detection. *IEEE Transactions on Image Processing* 27 (7): 3459–3471.

**55** Song, Y.-F., Zhang, Z., Shan, C., and Wang, L. (2020). Richly activated graph convolutional network for robust skeleton-based action recognition. *IEEE Transactions on Circuits and Systems for Video Technology* 31 (5): 1915–1925.

**56** Song, Y.-F., Zhang, Z., Shan, C., and Wang, L. (2022). Constructing stronger and faster baselines for skeleton-based action recognition. *IEEE Transactions on Pattern Analysis and Machine Intelligence* 45 (2): 1474–1488.

**57** Sung, J., Ponce, C., Selman, B., and Saxena, A. (2012). Unstructured human activity detection from RGBD images. *ICRA*, 842–849.

**58** Tang, Y., Tian, Y., Lu, J. et al. (2018). Deep progressive reinforcement learning for skeleton-based action recognition. *Proceedings of the IEEE Conference on Computer Vision and Pattern Recognition*, 5323–5332.

**59** Trabelsi, R., Varadarajan, J., Pei, Y. et al. (2017). Robust multi-modal cues for dyadic human interaction recognition. *Proceedings of the Workshop on Multimodal Understanding of Social, Affective and Subjective Attributes*, 47–53.

**60** van Gemeren, C., Tan, R.T., Poppe, R., and Veltkamp, R.C. (2014). Dyadic interaction detection from pose and flow. In: *Human Behavior Understanding, Lecture Notes in Computer Science*, vol. 8749 (ed. H.S. Park, A.A. Salah, Y.J. Lee et al.), 101–115. Cham: Springer.

**61** Vemulapalli, R., Arrate, F., and Chellappa, R. (2014). Human action recognition by representing 3D skeletons as points in a lie group. *CVPR*, 588–595.

**62** Wang, H. and Wang, L. (2017). Modeling temporal dynamics and spatial configurations of actions using two-stream recurrent neural networks. *CVPR*, 499–508.

**63** Wang, H. and Wang, L. (2018). Beyond joints: learning representations from primitive geometries for skeleton-based action recognition and detection. *IEEE Transactions on Image Processing* 27 (9): 4382–4394.

**64** Wang, J., Liu, Z., Wu, Y., and Yuan, J. (2012). Mining actionlet ensemble for action recognition with depth cameras. *CVPR*, 1290–1297.

**65** Wang, J., Liu, Z., Wu, Y., and Yuan, J. (2014). Learning actionlet ensemble for 3D human action recognition. *IEEE Transactions on Pattern Analysis and Machine Intelligence* 36 (5): 914–927.

**66** Wang, P., Li, W., Liu, S. et al. (2016). Large-scale isolated gesture recognition using convolutional neural networks. *International Conference on Pattern Recognition (ICPR)*, 7–12.

**67** Wang, P., Li, W., Gao, Z. et al. (2016). Action recognition from depth maps using deep convolutional neural networks. *EEE Transactions on Human-Machine Systems* 46 (4): 498–509.

**68** Wang, P., Li, W., Gao, Z. et al. (2017). Scene flow to action map: a new representation for RGB-D based action recognition with convolutional neural networks. *CVPR*, 595–604.

**69** Wu, D., Pigou, L., Kindermans, P.-J. et al. (2016). Deep dynamic neural networks for multimodal gesture segmentation and recognition. *IEEE Transactions on Pattern Analysis and Machine Intelligence* 38 (8): 1583–1597.

**70** Xia, L., Chen, C.-C., and Aggarwal, J.K. (2012). View invariant human action recognition using histograms of 3D joints. *CVPRW*, 20–27.

**71** Xia, L., Gori, I., Aggarwal, J.K., and Ryoo, M.S. (2015). Robot-centric activity recognition from first-person RGB-D videos. *WACV*, 357–364.

**72** Xu, N., Liu, A., Nie, W. et al. (2015). Multi-modal & multi-view & interactive benchmark dataset for human action recognition. *Proceedings of the ACM International Conference Multimedia*, 1195–1198.

**73** Yan, S., Xiong, Y., and Lin, D. (2018). Spatial temporal graph convolutional networks for skeleton-based action recognition. *32nd AAAI Conference on Artificial Intelligence.*

**74** Yang, X. and Tian, Y.L. (2014). Effective 3D action recognition using eigenjoints. *Journal of Visual Communication and Image Representation* 25 (1): 2–11.

**75** Yang, X., Zhang, C., and Tian, Y.L. (2012). Recognizing actions using depth motion maps-based histograms of oriented gradients. *Proceedings of the ACM International Conference Multimedia*, 1057–1060.

**76** Yun, K., Honorio, J., Chattopadhyay, D. et al. (2012). Two-person interaction detection using body-pose features and multiple instance learning. *CVPRW*, 28–35.

**77** Zeng, A., Sun, X., Yang, L. et al. (2021). Learning skeletal graph neural networks for hard 3D pose estimation. *Proceedings of the IEEE/CVF International Conference on Computer Vision*, 11436–11445.

**78** Zhang, L., Zhu, G., Shen, P. et al. (2017). Learning spatiotemporal features using 3DCNN and convolutional LSTM for gesture recognition. *CVPR*, 3120–3128.

**79** Zhang, S., Liu, X., and Xiao, J. (2017). On geometric features for skeleton-based action recognition using multilayer LSTM networks. *WACV*, 148–157.

**80** Zhang, S., Yang, Y., Xiao, J. et al. (2018). Fusing geometric features for skeleton-based action recognition using multilayer LSTM networks. *IEEE Transactions on Multimedia* 20 (9): 2330–2343.

**81** Zhang, P., Lan, C., Xing, J. et al. (2019). View adaptive neural networks for high performance skeleton-based human action recognition. *IEEE Transactions on Pattern Analysis and Machine Intelligence* 41 (8): 1963–1978.

**82** Zhang, P., Lan, C., Zeng, W. et al. (2020). Semantics-guided neural networks for efficient skeleton-based human action recognition. *Proceedings of the IEEE/CVF Conference on Computer Vision and Pattern Recognition*, 1112–1121.

**83** Zhu, W., Lan, C., Xing, J. et al. (2016). Co-occurrence feature learning for skeleton based action recognition using regularized deep LSTM networks. *AAAI*, 3697–3703. ISBN 9781577357605.

# 27

# Hybrid Intelligence: Augmenting Employees' Decision-Making with AI-Based Applications

*Ina Heine, Thomas Hellebrandt, Louis Huebser, and Marcos Padrón*

*Organizational Development, Laboratory for Machine Tools and Production Engineering, RWTH Aachen University, Aachen, NRW, Germany*

## 27.1 Introduction

Increasing demands in the work context such as faster response times in customer interactions lead to higher work-related stress and possibly to negative health conditions [18]. Recent advancements in the field of artificial intelligence (AI) include promising approaches for supporting employees in dealing with large datasets and decision-making. For instance, in the medical context deep learning (DL) algorithms have shown across various studies to be beneficial in identifying pathology using medical imaging [2]. However, the usage of such augmenting decision-support-systems in practice remains rather limited [27]. One of the main reasons for this gap between research findings and their practical applicability is poor contextual fit [29]. To address this gap, we present the participatory design and development of an AI-based application. In Section 27.2, we provide an overview of this chapter's background in terms of theoretical context and basic definitions. Section 27.3 summarizes related work before in the Section 27.4, we present the technical part of this chapter in terms of a use case. Sections 27.5 and 27.6 provide our conclusion and an outlook on future research challenges, respectively.

## 27.2 Background

In the first part of this section, an overview of the theoretical context focusing on decision-making, human strengths, and machine capabilities is given. The following second part provides the most relevant basic definitions for this chapter. These are the following: (i) work-related stress, (ii) AI-based applications, and (iii) human-centered design approach.

### 27.2.1 Context

The decision-making process has been subject to research since many decades, and it has been shown consistently that there is a significant gap between the rational or normative decision-making process and what is observed in naturalistic decision-making [10]. For instance, instead of identifying and weighing all possible alternatives in a decision situation, humans rely on heuristics and cognitive schemata that develop based on similar previous situations [8].

*Handbook of Human-Machine Systems*, First Edition. Edited by Giancarlo Fortino, David Kaber, Andreas Nürnberger, and David Mendonça.

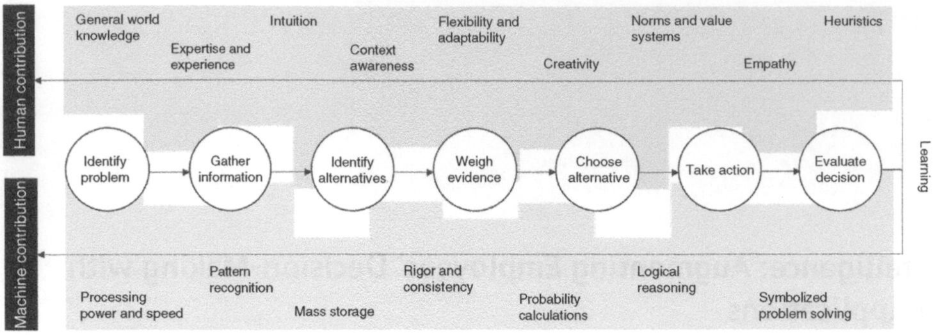


**Figure 27.1** Hybrid Intelligence decision-making process.

Depending on the person's level of expertise, this ability can be very powerful in high-stakes situations like firefighting that require immediate action [15].

However, there are also many challenging routine decision contexts in which stakes are rather low in terms of both possible losses and time-pressure, but information load is high. In customer service, this type of decision context is common for instance when managing complaints. In such contexts, we expect that following a rational decision-making process, which includes gathering evidence for the respective alternatives, is beneficial for making the "right" decision. We also expect that by using Hybrid Intelligence (i.e. a combination of human and AI) within the entire decision-making process superior performance is achieved. In addition, we assume that augmenting this decision-making process with AI-based applications can reduce employees' work-related stress, if designed and developed under their participation.

Figure 27.1 shows the sequence of steps for normative decision-making processes based on the DECIDE model by Guo Guo [11] and the "close-loop" view by Gonzalez Gonzalez [10]. First, the (decision) problem needs to be identified. Then information is gathered to identify possible alternatives and weigh their evidence (e.g. in terms of their probability of success). Based on this, one of the alternatives is chosen and the respective action taken. Lastly (and often with some delay), the decision is evaluated in terms of outcomes and learning takes place. In addition, Figure 27.1 summarizes the hybrid and complementary capabilities both human and machine can contribute to achieve superior decision performance.

While humans are known to be capable of dealing with complex and uncertain situations due to their general world knowledge, experience, intuition, context awareness, flexibility and adaptability, creativity, norms and value systems, empathy, and the use of heuristics, machines are very powerful in more narrowly defined contexts. This can be explained by their strengths in processing power and speed, pattern recognition, mass storage, rigor and consistency, probability calculations, logical reasoning, and symbolized problem-solving [3, 7, 12, 25, 30].

### 27.2.2 Basic Definitions

The chapter's most relevant constructs that require a formal basic definition are briefly defined in the following:

(1) Work-related stress refers to negative strains on an individual's mental and physical health as a reaction to adverse and noxious aspects of work content, work organization, and work environment [19]. In the past two decades, work-related stress has even been further exacerbated by digital technologies and the inability of an individual to deal with those in a healthy way [9].

(2) AI describes computer science applications that aim to exhibit intelligent behavior to perform human-like functions and tasks [22]. To achieve this, certain core capabilities are required in varying proportions: sense (e.g. structure patterns in large data sets), comprehend (e.g. recognize ambiguous and contradictory information), act (e.g. support situational decisions based on relative importance), and learn (e.g. learn from experience) [17].
(3) With respect to AI applications, key requirements are the human-centered design of robust, trustworthy AI systems that people understand, and that behave appropriately in a social context [24]. In order to meet these requirements different human-centered design approaches (e.g. [14]) have become established in industrial context. In general, such approaches cover four main operational steps: (i) understand and specify the context of use, (ii) specify the usage requirements, (iii) develop design solution, and (iv) evaluate the design against the requirements.

## 27.3 Related Work

Call centers represent an important point of business interaction and thus have a key function in customer satisfaction. Recent work in the field of AI applications for similar business operations has been published with different foci. The majority of work has centered on leveraging the large amounts of data collected in recent years for improved service quality and operational planning. Such is the case for AI-assisted performance evaluation and quality analysis of customer dialogs [13, 21], predictive modeling of performance of call centers [20, 26], and call arrival forecasting for resource allocation and workforce scheduling [1, 4]. A more recent and commercially available approach concerns the intelligent routing and pairing of customers to the most suitable call agent based on historical data [23]. Related work is summarized in Table 27.1.

**Table 27.1** Overview of a selection of cases of AI applications in call centers.

| Authors | Use case objective | Development approach |
|---|---|---|
| Valle et al. (2012) [26] | Performance prediction model for call center agents | Performance estimation based on classification of performance indicator attributes of individual call center agents |
| Hsu et al. (2016) [13] | Performance evaluation of call center agents | Performance evaluation based on selected attributes and management performance evaluation metrics as output labels |
| Mehrbod et al. (2018) [23] | Routing and pairing of customers to call center agents | Routing and pairing based on customer demographics, agent information, and historical call center interaction data |
| Li et al. (2019) [20] | Performance prediction model for call centers | Performance prediction model trained on a developed simulation model for service quality |
| Aattouri et al. (2021) [1] | Call arrival forecasting for resource allocation | Incoming call flow estimation based on answered and unanswered calls |
| Albrecht et al. (2021) [4] | Scheduling of call center agents | Intradaily call arrival's forecasting based on customer support and complaints queue data |
| Liu et al. (2021) [21] | Service quality improvement through customer dialog analysis | Dialog classification based on key utterance labels |

While related work addresses operative performance and quality improvement through AI, none of the approaches targets efficiency improvement and the associated stress reduction of the task. Much of the recent research takes an analytical approach based on available data and state-of-the-art AI methods, while not explicitly involving personnel in the development process to tailor the application to the users' needs.

## 27.4 Technical Part of the Chapter

### 27.4.1 Description of the Use Case

In order to develop AI applications that deliver value in the form of monetary added value while reducing the cognitive load on employees, a thorough understanding of the company's business model and processes is essential.

#### 27.4.1.1 Business Model

The company featured in this use case is a call center service provider for original equipment manufacturers (OEMs) in the telecommunications, media, and technology sectors. Claims and support requests from the OEM's customers are directly rerouted to the company's call center (see Figure 27.2). The company employs more than 50 people, about half of whom work in the call center providing support for different product lines. The present case concerns a product family of a single OEM. Claims and support requests (tickets) are either forwarded via e-mail or via phone call. Such claims may concern, for example, network problems of Wi-Fi-enabled products or blinking LEDs on hardware indicating different failure modes. The company generates its revenue per customer ticket served and therefore aims to maximize the rate of solved tickets. Furthermore, the company offers its services in several languages, which places additional demands on the agents' qualification profile.

#### 27.4.1.2 Process

The process for resolving a ticket submitted either by phone or by e-mail comprises essentially the same steps. The call center agent receives the customer's request, transfers basic information such as customer name and number into the company's ticket management system and subsequently investigates the request. In doing so, the agent takes into account the contact history, if available, and an internally compiled FAQ catalog. In addition, all agents have undergone a three-month technical qualification program. After identifying a feasible solution, the agent responds directly to the customer by e-mail or telephone. For this purpose, either pre-formulated answers from the FAQ catalog, own pre-formulated text modules or individual answers are provided in the response.

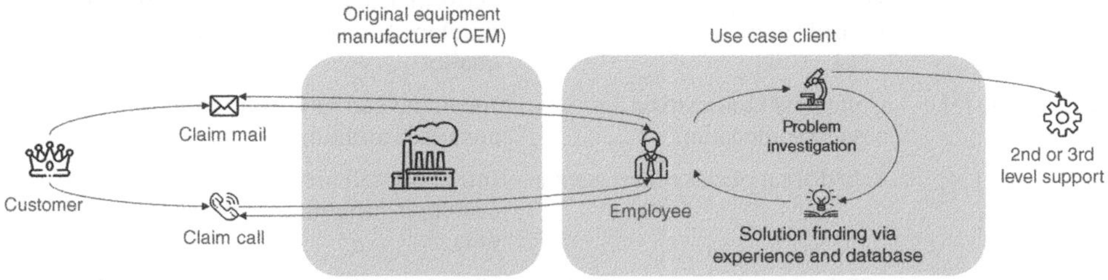


**Figure 27.2** Business model of the use case company.

If no feasible solution is found, the enquiry is forwarded to the internal second-level or third-level support, depending on the technical difficulty and depth of the enquiry.

#### 27.4.1.3 Use Case Objectives

In consultation with the company, the following goals were set for the defined use case: (i) faster response to requests/tickets per day, (ii) reduction of agent qualification time, (iii) reduction of agent cognitive load, and (iv) increase of agent trust. Objectives (i) and (ii) are mainly technical in nature and of financial interest, while objectives (iii) and (iv) are strongly influenced by the agent during the development phase when involved from the initial idea to implementation.

### 27.4.2 Description of the Envisioned Solution

To preserve the agent's decision space, the agent can overrule the intended solution design at any time. At its core, natural language processing is facilitated to classify the e-mail text into different class IDs. Such classification algorithms include the GPT-3 model [5], which can be modified to perform classification tasks, or any other classification algorithm that is still being worked on in the context of this use case. Prior to the classification step, the e-mail text is preprocessed by, for example, lowercasing, and filtering e-mail headers. Furthermore, additional preprocessing steps can be performed such as byte-pair encoded tokenization [28], which is currently being evaluated as a preprocessing alternative in the context of this use case. A matching table converts the predicted class ID to the corresponding ID within the FAQ catalog. In doing so, changes in the FAQ catalog lead to a recompilation of the matching table and not to a complete retraining of the system. Regarding data availability for model training, the company has an extensive database, which contains all e-mails, contact history, and the solution proposed to the customer by the agent encoded by the corresponding FAQ ID. Figure 27.3 presents the overall concept with its reengineered business process flow.

Although the company offers its services in a variety of languages, German is the main language for which most of the data are accessible. Therefore, commercially available translation algorithms are used such that classification is always done in German and translated back when needed. The focus of the application lies on e-mails as the primary channel. The possibility of live transcription of telephone conversations and using the same model on it, initially trained on an e-mail corpus, will be explored at a later stage.

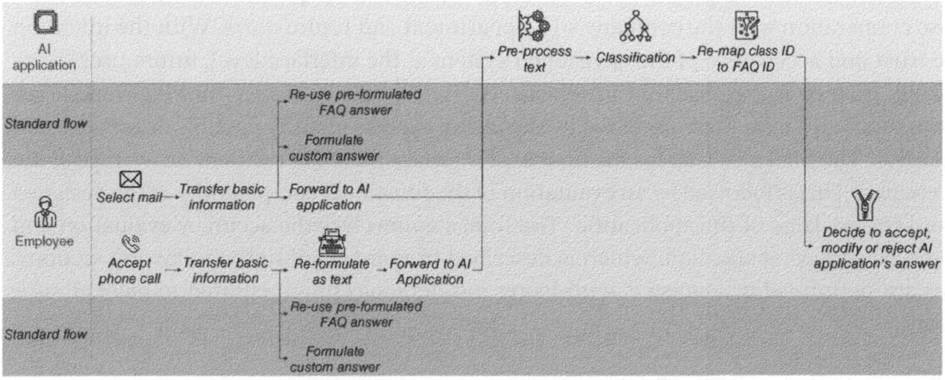


**Figure 27.3** Concept of the envisioned system.

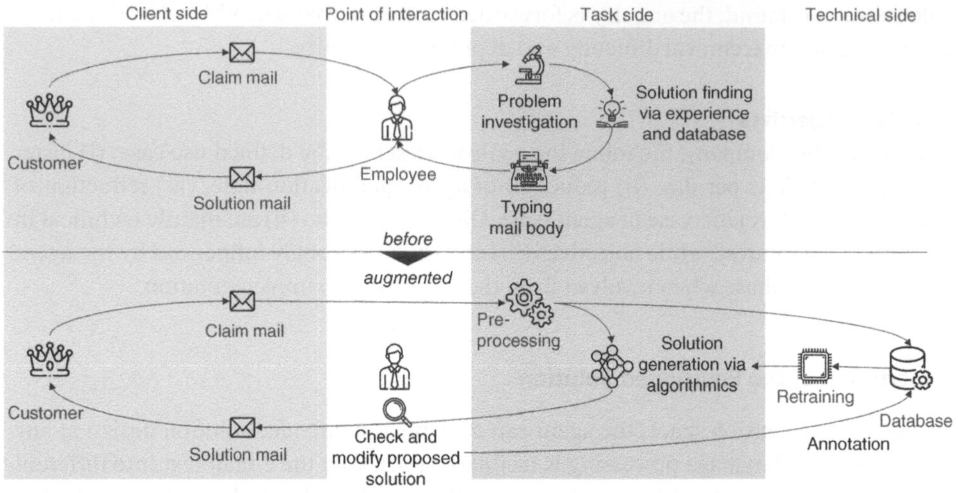


**Figure 27.4** Reengineered process flow.

The envisioned system does not replace any agent, but serves as a tool to provide preformulated e-mails for standard and frequent queries. Alternatively, the system supports by providing an initial guess for more complex queries, on which an agent can build its solution-finding process. In the end, the entire system requires a final decision from the agent to either override or accept the proposed solution. Thereby, the envisioned system reduces an agent's stress mainly by reducing his backlog of tickets and by providing valuable hints during the solution finding process. Figure 27.4 shows that, even though our system's concept supports problem investigation and solution ideation, the call agent still remains the central point of interaction within the process flow.

## 27.4.3 Development Approach of AI Application

### 27.4.3.1 Development Process

The development process is based on the human-centered approach as proposed in the ISO 9241-210 standard. First, multiple workshops with management and employees were conducted to understand and specify the context of use. Second, process analysis including time studies and cognitive walkthroughs within a typical day of a call center agent was carried out to specify usage requirements. Current work in progress deals with the iterative development of the technical solution in close cooperation with the company's IT-department and future users. With the intention to increase trust and acceptance of the envisioned system at the interface level, future users were asked to design their own graphical user interfaces (GUI) in a series of design thinking workshops. The different mock-ups were then discussed by the future users to identify possible drawbacks and missing features. The final mock-up for the final user interface therefore contains an average of the mock-ups created. This is followed by an evaluation of the functional compatibility of the designed frontend and the backend of the application. The final step involves the accuracy evaluation and testing of the developed application, which is described in more detail in the following sections. These steps are performed in sequence, with loops and iterations often required to meet all user requirements.

### 27.4.3.2 Process Analysis and Time Study

In order to evaluate the effectiveness of the AI augmented system in production as well as to estimate possible levers during the development process, a process analysis and time study was

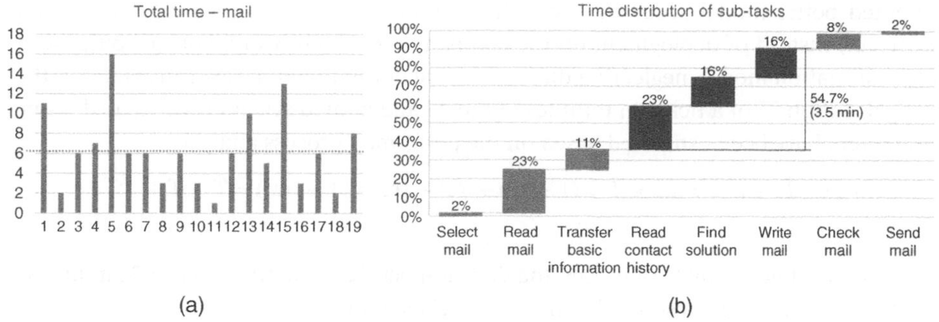


**Figure 27.5** Process analysis and time study. (a) Excerpt from the ticket processing sample. (b) Average time distribution of sub-tasks for ticket processing.

conducted in advance. A typical process flow of an agent to process a ticket consists of eight subtasks, shown in Figure 27.5. The subtasks "4-Read contact history," "5-Find solution," and "6-Write Mail" constitute the main areas of intervention by the AI-model. Currently, these subtasks account for 54.7% of the overall processing duration and may be significantly reduced by employing the AI augmented system. The overall average processing duration per ticket amounts to 6.32 minutes.

#### 27.4.3.3 Development and Deployment Data

Input data for the use case is represented by unstructured e-mail texts, whereas the output data are defined by categorical IDs (from the internally compiled FAQ). Development data currently comprises about 6000 data points. Before the first deployment, the target amount of data to train the entire system is at least 100,000 data points to ensure reliable accuracy. In order to account for changing characteristics between training and deployment data, monthly retraining is planned for at least the first two quarters to assess and determine future retraining and redeployment cycles during model operation.

#### 27.4.3.4 System Testing and Deployment

The initial implementation of the system will take place in a separate testbed within the company's systems. The separate instance will allow testing of all technical interfaces such as data retrieval, GUI functionality, and processing time of the application to ensure smooth operation. Additionally, it will ensure that the functionalities of the GUI can be operated by the model and the backend. In the first phase, only the system administrators and second- and third-level support users will have access to the system to evaluate its accuracy using redirected real operational data. In addition to conventional algorithmic accuracy metrics, the plausibility of the system output is evaluated from a business perspective and compared to the data collected during the process analysis. In a second phase, controlled experiments will be conducted with a sample of users to determine trust and acceptance characteristics of the system, such as an application-specific accuracy threshold and consequent measures, e.g. opt for hiding a system output if a certain accuracy level is not reached. The planned experiments and a subsequently developed user training to improve the understanding of the generation of system output complete the test phase of the system.

#### 27.4.3.5 Development Infrastructure and Development Cost Monitoring

The infrastructure for deployment depends on the availability of hardware, the amount of data, and the computational effort required. To ensure an appropriate trade-off between increase in ticket-processing efficiency and technology-related costs, an evaluation is performed before each iteration within the model architecture to determine whether the cost savings resulting from an estimated better model accuracy justify the additional cost of Software/Platform as a Service (SaaS/PaaS) instead of deployment on the company's local hardware. For this purpose, a simplified cost estimation model, neglecting direct software development costs, is used. First, the new processing duration $T^*$ of a ticket in minutes of the AI augmented system is calculated. Time and ratio parameters have been estimated based on the performed process analysis:

$$T^* = [(1 - r_m) * \hat{T}] + [r_m * acc * \hat{T} * (1 - r_T) + T_r] + [r_m * (1 - acc) * \hat{T} + T_r]$$

where

$\hat{T}$ : Current time estimate of processing duration per ticket in minutes (=6.32 minutes)
$r_m$ : Share of all tickets resolved by the AI model (=50%)
$acc$ : (Estimated) model classification accuracy
$T^*$ : Overall system's processing duration with AI-model inplace

The calculation of $T^*$ comprises three components given by each summand of $T^*$: (i) time taken to process a ticket without AI, (ii) time taken to process a ticket given the AI model's prediction is true, and (iii) time taken to reprocess a ticket by the agent, given the AI model's prediction was false. For simplification, secondary effects such as loss of trust due to repeated high error rates of the AI model are not considered. Shorter computational run-times lead to overall reduced $T^*$. A higher classification accuracy of the AI-model reduces the amount of an agent's intervention and rework, and therefore, reduces $T^*$. The ratio $r_m$ is fixed, as only a fixed subset of tickets within the use case will be processed by the AI-augmented system. In general, the use of an AI-model only is beneficial above the isochronal line, given in Figure 27.6.

Second, the per minute costs $C$ of using SaaS/PaaS are calculated. Finally, the excess return to assess the profitability of switching to SaaS/PaaS is determined:

$$C = \frac{1}{T^*} * r_m * c * T_r$$

$$P = 1 - \frac{(C + \frac{W^*}{60}) * T^*}{\frac{W^*}{60} * \hat{T}} - E[RoI]$$

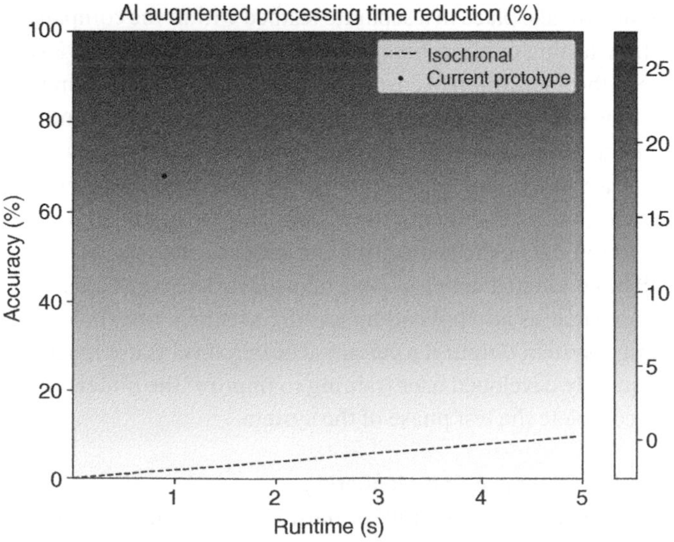


**Figure 27.6** Time reduction by employing the AI-augmented system.

where

| | | |
|---|---|---|
| $r_T$ | : | Proportion of reducible time on $\hat{T}$ by deploying the AI model (=54.7%) |
| $T_r$ | : | Runtime of the AI model in minutes |
| $c$ | : | SaaS baseline costs by service provider per minute (=0.0075 €/min) |
| $C$ | : | Realized SaaS costs of the system per minute |
| $W^*$ | : | Hourly wage including social spendings of 21% (=14.52 €/h) |
| $E[RoI]$ | : | Targeted Return on Invest as benchmark against capital markets (=10%) |
| $P$ | : | Profitability |

A switch toward deployment on SaaS/PaaS is only justifiable if the profitability is positive, whereas an on-premise solution does not cause any additional costs as long as $T^*$ is above the isochronal line, given in Figure 27.6, by outperforming the current processing duration $\hat{T}$. Whether switching to SaaS/PaaS deployment is profitable, mainly depends on the excess outperformance of the AI-model. Thereby, the above profitability calculation evaluates if enough excess outperformance is generated to compensate SaaS/PaaS costs. Nonetheless, even if profitability for SaaS/PaaS is given, a local deployment might still be a considerable option if the model is small enough to run locally as no excess outperformance is needed to compensate SaaS/PaaS costs. A low profitability in turn indicates that either the classification accuracy is too low or the computational run-time is too high in order to generate excess outperformance, such that a local deployment is more cost-effective assuming that the model is small enough to run locally and lies above the isochronal line given in Figure 27.6.

A first naive prototype approach with byte-pair-encoded tokenization in combination with a Naïve Bayes Classifier reaches an accuracy of around 70% with a runtime of slightly under one second. Even though a SaaS/PaaS deployment would be feasible as depicted in Figure 27.7, the current prototype is small enough to run on local non graphics processing unit (GPU)-supported hardware.

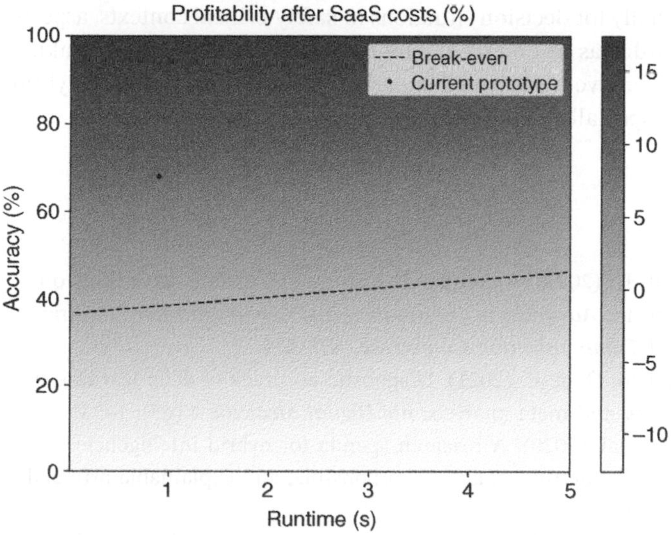


**Figure 27.7** Profitability for switching to SaaS/PaaS.

## 27.5 Conclusions

With the objective of reducing work-related stress and improving decision-making, this chapter presents the human-centered development of an AI-based application. Based on the defined projects goals, there is a thorough understanding of the business context and the identified user requirements, and therefore the technical solution is currently under iterative development. The proposed AI application is intended to augment call center agents in handling customer queries and claims by suggesting a solution generated by a natural language processing classification algorithm. Current work in process concerns the improvement of the model's level of accuracy to conduct further user studies for performance evaluation and tailor the application as specified by the human-centered design approach.

## 27.6 Future Research Challenges

Further research and development of the proposed technical solution will address the trade-off between profitability by saving time in processing a customer ticket and technology-related costs due to specialized hardware required for further model improvements. In addition, the effect of different accuracy levels on employees' trust in machine decisions requires consideration as very high accuracy might lead to overconfidence (i.e. automation bias), while low accuracy might result in a decreased acceptance level [6, 16]. Once an acceptable accuracy level of 85% is achieved, the AI application and its interface will be integrated with the backend and tested with future users.

With regard to the Hybrid Intelligence concept, this use case exemplifies how human and machine capabilities can be combined to achieve superior performance in customer service. However, in its current version, the AI application's contribution to the decision-making process is mainly targeted toward proposing responses for customer queries. Thus, human–machine interaction is not continuous along the entire decision-making process, leading to limited collaboration and information exchange. Considering the vision of truly joint human–machine decision-making, there is a need to elaborate on the synergistic potential across the entire process and its related costs as well as ethical implications. Especially for decision situations in safety-critical contexts, aspects such as profitability analysis are regarded as secondary, if joint human–machine decision-making enables superior performance. Thus, for leveraging and demonstrating the full potential of Hybrid Intelligence, future research should especially focus on safety-critical decision contexts.

## References

**1** Aattouri, I., Rida, M., and Mouncif, H. (2021). A comparative study of learning algorithms on a call flow entering of a call center. In: *Advances in Information and Communication*, K. Arai vol. 2 of *Future of Information and Communication Conference*, 507–519.

**2** Aggarwal, R., Sounderajah, V., Martin, G. et al. (2021). Diagnostic accuracy of deep learning in medical imaging: a systematic review and meta-analysis. *npj Digital Medicine* 4 (65): 1–23.

**3** Akata, Z., Balliet, D., De Rijke, M. et al. (2020). A research agenda for hybrid intelligence: augmenting human intellect with collaborative, adaptive, responsible, and explainable artificial intelligence. *Computer* 53 (08): 18–28.

**4** Albrecht, T., Rausch, T.M., and Derra, N.D. (2021). Call me maybe: methods and practical implementation of artificial intelligence in call center arrivals' forecasting. *Journal of Business Research* 123: 267–278.

5 Brown, T.B., Mann, B., Ryder, N. et al. (2020). Language models are few-shot learners.

6 Buçinca, Z., Malaya, M.B., and Gajos, K.Z. (2021). To trust or to think: cognitive forcing functions can reduce overreliance on AI in AI-assisted decision-making. *Proceedings of the ACM on Human–Computer Interaction* 5 (CSCW1): 1–21.

7 Dellermann, D., Ebel, P., Söllner, M., and Leimeister, J.M. (2019). Hybrid intelligence. *Business & Information Systems Engineering* 61 (5): 637–643.

8 Ehrlinger, J., Readinger, W., and Kim, B. (2016). Decision-making and cognitive biases. *Encyclopedia of Mental Health* 12 (3): 83–87.

9 Gimpel, H. and Schmied, F. (2019). Risks and side effects of digitalization. *Proceedings of the 27th ECIS*, Stockholm and Uppsala, Sweden (8–14 June 2019), 1–15.

10 Gonzalez, C. (2017). Decision-making: a cognitive science perspective. *The Oxford handbook of cognitive science* 1: 1–27.

11 Guo, K.L. (2020). DECIDE: A decision-making model for more effective decision making by health care managers. *The Health Care Manager* 39 (3): 133–141.

12 Hemmer, P., Schemmer, M., Vössing, M., and Kühl, N. (2021). Human-AI complementarity in hybrid intelligence systems: a structured literature review. *PACIS 2021 Proceedings.*

13 Hsu, H., Chen, T., Chan, W., and Chang, J. (2016). Performance evaluation of call center agents by neural networks. *2016 30th International Conference on Advanced Information Networking and Applications Workshops (WAINA)*, 964–968.

14 ISO 9241-210 (2019). *Ergonomics of human–system interaction –part 210: human-centred design for interactive systems.* International Organization for Standardization.

15 Klein, G. (2008). Naturalistic decision making. *Human Factors* 50 (3): 456–460.

16 Kocielnik, R., Amershi, S., and Bennett, P.N. (2019). Will you accept an imperfect AI? Exploring designs for adjusting end-user expectations of AI systems. *Proceedings of the 2019 CHI Conference on Human Factors in Computing Systems*, CHI '19, 1–14, New York, NY, USA: Association for Computing Machinery.

17 Kolbjørnsrud, V., Thomas, R.J., and Amico, R. (2016). The promise of artificial intelligence: redefining management in the workforce of the future. *Accenture Institute for High Performance Research Report May, 2016.*

18 Kubicek, B., Paškvan, M., and Korunka, C. (2015). Development and validation of an instrument for assessing job demands arising from accelerated change: the intensification of job demands scale (IDS). *European Journal of Work and Organizational Psychology* 24 (6): 898–913.

19 Levi, L. and Levi, I. (2000). Guidance on work-related stress. *Office for Official Publications of the European Communities, Luxembourg.*

20 Li, S., Wang, Q., and Koole, G. (2019). Predicting call center performance with machine learning. In: *Advances in Service Science*, Springer Proceedings in Business and Economics (ed. H. Yang and R. Qiu), 193–199. Cham: Springer.

21 Liu, Y., Cao, B., Ma, K., and Fan, J. (2021). Improving the classification of call center service dialogue with key utterences. *Wireless Networks* 27: 1–12.

22 Lunze, J. (2016). *Artificial Intelligence for Engineers.* De Gruyter Oldenbourg.

23 Mehrbod, N., Grilo, A., and Zutshi, A. (2018). Caller-agent pairing in call centers using machine learning techniques with imbalanced data. *2018 IEEE ICE/ITMC*, 1–6.

24 Shneiderman, B. (2020). Bridging the gap between ethics and practice: guidelines for reliable, safe, and trustworthy human-centered AI systems. *ACM TIIS* 10 (4): 1–31.

25 Tan, S., Adebayo, J., Inkpen, K., and Kamar, E. (2018). Investigating human+ machine complementarity for recidivism predictions. *arXiv preprint arXiv:1808.09123.*

**26** Valle, M.A., Varas, S., and Ruz, G.A. (2012). Job performance prediction in a call center using a naive bayes classifier. *Expert Systems with Applications* 39 (11): 9939–9945.

**27** Walsh, S., de Jong, E., van Timmeren, J.E. et al. (2019). Decision support systems in oncology. *JCO Clinical Cancer Informatics* 3: 1–9.

**28** Wang, C., Cho, K., and Gu, J. (2020). Neural machine translation with byte-level subwords. *Proceedings of the AAAI Conference on AI*, Volume 34, 9154–9160.

**29** Yang, Q., Steinfeld, A., and Zimmerman, J. (2019). Unremarkable AI: fitting intelligent decision support into critical, clinical decision-making processes. *Proceedings of the 2019 CHI Conference on Human Factors in Computing Systems*, 1–11.

**30** Zheng, N., Liu, Z., Ren, P. et al. (2017). Hybrid-augmented intelligence: collaboration and cognition. *Frontiers of Information Technology & Electronic Engineering* 18 (2): 153–179.

# 28

## Human Factors in Driving

*Birsen Donmez[1], Dengbo He[2,3], and Holland M. Vasquez[1]*

[1] *Department of Mechanical and Industrial Engineering, University of Toronto, Toronto, ON, Canada*
[2] *Intelligent Transportation Thrust, Systems Hub, Hong Kong University of Science and Technology (Guangzhou), Guangzhou, China*
[3] *Department of Civil and Environmental Engineering, Hong Kong University of Science and Technology, Hong Kong SAR, China*

## 28.1 Introduction

Road transport is the main form of mobility in many parts of the world both for people and goods. However, this type of transportation is also a relatively risky one, with a large variability in the capabilities and training of its operators, i.e. human drivers. It is estimated that 36,096 people were killed in motor vehicle collisions on US roadways during 2019 [37] and 94% of motor vehicle collisions are attributed to driver factors [50].

The human factors that contribute to crashes are varied. Lack of skill is an issue. For example, novice drivers, who also tend to be young, fixate their eyes less on roadway areas that are indicative of risk [43]. Drivers also engage in risky behaviors intentionally, knowingly, or unknowingly about the risks. Intentional behaviors can be explained by factors such as personality, attitudes toward the behavior, and perceived social norms [1].

There are also limitations to human information processing abilities, as impressive as they are. Attention, a limited resource for humans, is arguably the biggest limiting factor when it comes to driving. The task of driving is mainly visual in perception and manual in control. A crash can occur if the driver is not looking at the road (e.g. due to a distraction source such as their phone) or fails to see a hazard even if looking at the road. In addition to the general limitations that humans have, our information processing abilities may degrade transiently or permanently. Fatigue and driving under the influence of alcohol and other drugs are major safety issues that can have short and long-term effects on our perceptual, cognitive, and motor-control abilities [52]. With the increase in the older driving population in many parts of the world, aging and chronic medical conditions are also big concerns that can lead to permanent degradation in driver abilities [42].

While human capabilities change at the pace of evolution, the task of driving is changing rapidly in our lifetimes. Infotainment, carried-in technologies, and the associated need for connectivity are some of the ways driving has been changing. While these technologies raise concerns regarding driver distraction, there are also smart vehicle and traffic technologies that are being developed which can help enhance safety. For example, a driver state detection system can warn drivers based on long eyes off-road times [24]. Vehicles are also becoming highly automated; some of the implementations of automation are good, some not so good at this stage [30].

Research in driving human factors is vast, including but not limited to studies of antecedent causes of risky behaviors, the effects of these behaviors on driving performance and crash outcomes,

*Handbook of Human-Machine Systems*, First Edition. Edited by Giancarlo Fortino, David Kaber, Andreas Nürnberger, and David Mendonça.

driver training and licensure, driver distraction, driver fatigue, novice and older drivers, vehicle automation, and advanced driver assistance systems. In this chapter, we present the state of the art in driving human factors, including research methodologies and relevant findings, with a focus on driver interactions with technology, including in-vehicle technologies, vehicle automation, and driver monitoring. We also discuss research challenges.

## 28.2 Research Methodologies

A variety of methods are used to research human factors in driving, including crash data analysis, surveys, driving simulator experiments, on-road/instrumented vehicle studies, and naturalistic driving studies (see Figure 28.1 for an illustration).

Crash data analysis are conducted on police-reported crashes. This type of analysis can inform how different driver factors affect crash risk and severity. There are national and local databases that are shared with researchers for this purpose (e.g. Fatality Analysis Reporting System (FARS) [16]). While crash data provide insights into risk factors, it can suffer from missing or incomplete data (e.g. a detailed account of what the driver was doing before a crash).

Subjective means of data collection, such as surveys, interviews, focus groups, and questionnaires, can help researchers understand driver opinions and antecedent causes of driver behavior, and also test design ideas early in the design stage (e.g. design of an in-vehicle interface). Social desirability and recall biases are some of the limitations associated with subjective data collection.

Driving simulators enable researchers to create controlled and repeatable conditions to investigate causality [49]. The participants can be placed in risky driving situations with no such actual

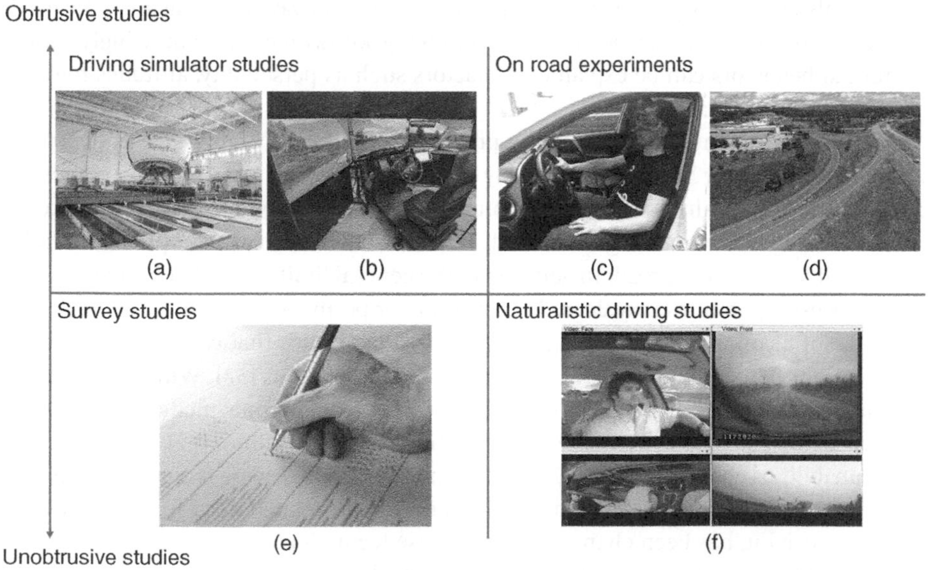


**Figure 28.1** Strategies for human factors research in driving applications. (a) National Advanced Driving Simulator: motion based. (b) Human Factors and Applied Statistics Laboratory driving simulator: fixed based. (c) Instrumented driver and vehicle. (d) Virginia smart road. (e) A paper-based survey. (f) Camera views from a naturalistic driving study. (a) Photo Credit: University of Iowa. (b, c) Photo Credit: Human Factors and Applied Statistics Laboratory, University of Toronto. (d, f) Photo Credit: The Virginia Tech Transportation Institute. (e) Photo Credit: oodluz/Adobe Stock.

risk. Simulators also enable researchers to test systems that do not yet exist in the real world. But simulators are not appropriate for all questions. For example, if one wants to study driver attention to vulnerable road users, real-world data would be more appropriate as simulators lack the required resolution and also the perceived social pressures from other road users [49]. Also, simulator findings are highly dependent on the particular conditions tested by the researchers and may not generalize to road conditions that have not been tested.

On-road studies, for example, those performed via instrumented vehicles, enable semicontrolled experiments to be conducted in the real world. An experimenter is generally present in the vehicle with the participant, and the participant may be outfitted with sensors such as eye-trackers. Compared to simulators, it is not possible to control environmental and traffic conditions in on-road studies unless the data are collected in a closed-test track. The resulting variability introduces issues with statistical power while overcoming the generalizability issues found in simulator studies. In general, lack of control increases the required sample size for a research study.

The highest level of ecological validity is achieved through naturalistic studies where drivers' own vehicles are instrumented with data collection equipment. For example, the Strategic Highway Research Program 2 (SHRP2) conducted in the US [57] collected data from about 3000 drivers as they drove their own vehicles for a year. Naturalistic studies provide very rich data but also are very costly to run and have significant data storage and processing requirements (e.g. manual coding of video data). Each of these methods has inherent strengths and weaknesses, with tradeoffs between precision and realism. Overall, they are used as complementary tools to address complex problems related to driving human factors.

## 28.3 In-Vehicle Electronic Devices

With the rapid development of microelectronic and high-speed network, vehicles have become increasingly intelligent – they serve not only our mobility needs but are also a hub of entertainment and information. Recent years have witnessed a number of new infotainment devices and new human machine interface (HMI) solutions being deployed in vehicles, both for input (e.g. gesture control in BMW) and output (e.g. Augmented Reality Head Up Display in Mercedes Benz). There have also been significant advances in smartphone and wearable technologies which are widely available to the consumers and are brought into the vehicle. While these built-in and carried-in devices can enhance safety, productivity, and satisfaction of the vehicle user, they may also increase crash risk by causing distraction.

### 28.3.1 Distraction

The largest naturalistic driving study to date, SHRP2 [57], which collected data from about 3000 drivers as they drove their own vehicles for a year, revealed that handheld cellphone use is at about 6.4% and in-vehicle device use is at about 3.5% in terms of prevalence [13]. This data also showed that drivers are far from always being in an attentive state but are rather inattentive about 50% of the time, and when drivers are engaged in a distraction that takes their eyes-off the road (e.g. dialing on a handheld cellphone), their crash risk can increase by up to 12-folds.

Distraction can be voluntary (i.e. intentional engagement in nondriving tasks). For example, drivers may choose to initiate a phone call while driving. Distraction can also be involuntary due to the drivers' inability to suppress or disengage from an attention capture, such as a ringing phone [5]. It may also be habitual, for example, drivers may check for notifications on their phone out of habit without conscious intention [19]. The different reasons for distraction can inform appropriate distraction mitigation strategies. For example, function lockouts (e.g. "Do not disturb mode" or "Driving mode") can be useful to reduce involuntary distractions [45] but may not be accepted for voluntary distraction engagement as was the case in Funkhouser and Sayer [17] with participants overriding cellphone blocker technology. For voluntary engagement, behavioral modification may be needed. For example, parental normative feedback has been shown to be effective in reducing distraction engagement among teenagers [35].

Distraction can also be minimized through the design of device interfaces. For example, auditory interaction may be used in place of visual interaction to minimize eyes off-road time. Both the International Organization for Standardization (ISO) and the National Highway Traffic Safety Administration (NHTSA) released guidelines to inform the design of in-vehicle devices [25, 38].

### 28.3.2 Interaction Modality

According to the Multiple Resource Model by Wickens [64], while humans rely on different channels to process information, tasks that share the same channels are more likely to conflict with each other. As stated earlier, driving is mainly a visual–manual task and relies heavily on vision [51]. Thus, vehicle manufacturers and researchers have explored a variety of design ideas to optimize the manner in which visual information is presented in vehicles, through traditional in-vehicle devices, as well as novel display systems, such as heads-up display (HUD, Figure 28.2) and ambient lighting systems. Novel human–machine interaction technologies that rely less on visual perception and impose less interference with manual operation of the vehicle have also been investigated and/or adopted in vehicles, for example, vibrating steering wheel and seats, and voice assistants. In this section, we briefly review emerging in-vehicle technologies with different modalities. It should be noted that although we group the technologies under three main modalities (i.e. visual and manual, audio and vocal, and haptic), a system can fall in more than one of these groups. For example, a touchscreen display (visual–manual) may provide audio and haptic feedback when touched.

#### 28.3.2.1 Visual and Manual Modalities

Vehicle manufacturers have traditionally adopted the visual modality to present information to drivers, first in analog and then increasingly in digital form, and mainly on the dashboard (e.g. speedometer) and center console (e.g. GPS). With advances in technology, the type and amount

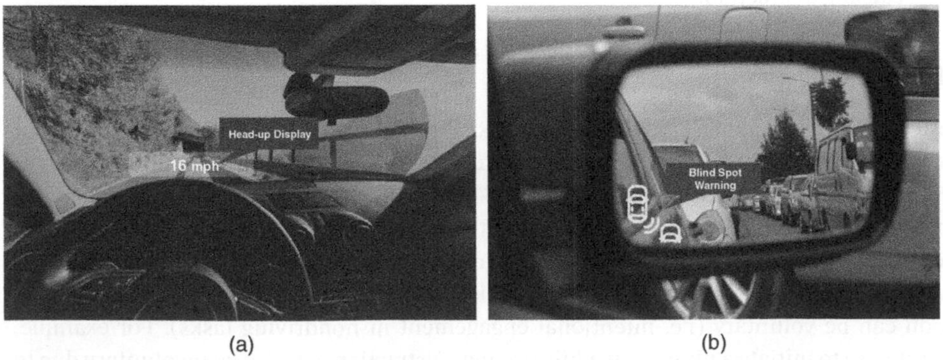


**Figure 28.2** Heads up displays depicting (a) vehicle speed and (b) blindspot warning. Source: Riccardo/Pexels; Stan/Pexels.

of information that can be presented have increased (e.g. streaming rear-view video) as well as the options of positioning (e.g. blind spot warning on mirrors, speed, and navigation information on HUDs). Positioning information closer to the roadway through a HUD rather than on the center console can shorten the response time to urgent events (e.g. a message of engine overheating) and reduce mental workload [31]. It is however important to consider the risk of visual clutter in the forward view when designing the content of HUDs.

Another common trend adopted in recent years is the replacement of physical buttons with large touchscreens. This switch has cost-cutting advantages to vehicle manufacturers as updates to controls can be performed with no additional hardware costs. Touchscreens also have some advantages to users: Bhise [2] lists a number of them, including (i) the input device also being used as the output device, (ii) the reduction in hand and eye movement to locate and grasp the buttons, (iii) the reduction in activation times (as touch inputs do not require finger bending and grasping motions), and (iv) the removal of input device (thus space saving). The large in-vehicle touchscreens also make it possible to aggregate and prioritize critical and context-related information in an adaptive manner.

However, introducing a touchscreen display to the vehicle needs careful design consideration, as touchscreens can create larger visual demands on the driver compared to physical buttons. Physical buttons afford manual control with no visual engagement from the driver due to their feel, whereas the same type of tactile feedback is not inherently available in touchscreen controls. Feedback as a result of interactions is also necessary for touchscreens, especially in vehicles; otherwise, drivers will have to visually confirm their operations. So far, audio (e.g. 2016 Toyota RAV4) and tactile (e.g. Audi A6 2019) feedback has been adopted to overcome these limitations. Other potential issues with touchscreens include the touch area being obscured while being touched, and the difficulty of performing fine motor control with touchscreens. A simulator study has found that touch operations used in cellphones are more detrimental to driving performance compared to traditional physical buttons when drivers were required to input text while performing a lane keeping task [10]. To overcome the difficulty of fine control movements when using touchscreens, "swiping" operations have been adopted in mobile devices (e.g. iOS system and Android system). Research has also identified the benefits of "swiping" over "touching," with the former being considered as "less distracting" to the driver [40].

Another type of manual interaction technology being widely explored and adopted in vehicles in recent years (e.g. BMW 7 series) is gesture control. In-vehicle gesture control has the potential to reduce the visual and manual demands compared to conventional interfaces as it can remove the need for fine motor control, increasing driving safety and reducing the time required for input [55]. However, gesture-based interfaces still have various technological and design challenges, e.g. the meaningfulness of gesture vocabularies to a wide range of drivers.

#### 28.3.2.2 Auditory and Vocal Modalities

The auditory modality has traditionally been used to present warnings and navigation instructions given the omnidirectionality of auditory perception and our natural tendency to attend to loud and distinct sounds [65].

The development of natural language processing algorithms has made smarter in-vehicle voice control systems (VCS) possible, which allow users to fulfill relatively complex tasks without relying on visual/manual interactions but rather use auditory perception and vocal input. These systems are considered to be "less distracting" as they compete less for visual–manual attentional resources.

Although VCS can be less demanding, they are not demand-free. If not designed for vehicle use, they can even be as demanding as or more demanding than visual/manual systems. For example, Yager et al. [67] compared drivers' reaction times to a green light on the dashboard when they were required to input text through either Siri or Vlingo voice-to-text applications, or through manual text-entry on a handheld phone. These voice assistants are not designed specifically for in-vehicle use, though they are widely used by drivers. Regardless of the input method, reaction times were nearly twice slower than baseline performance, and driver gaze toward forward roadway significantly decreased. Drivers felt safer using the voice-to-text applications compared to manual text-entry, although there were no differences in performance metrics.

In an on-road study, Cooper et al. [9] compared the mental demands of simple auditory-vocal commands performed across multiple in-vehicle infotainment systems from vehicle model years 2012 and 2013. They concluded that common voice tasks are generally more demanding than natural conversations, listening to the radio, or listening to a book on tape. In another on-road study, Reimer et al. [46] showed that there is still high level of visual engagement during voice-controlled tasks, such as the use of a voice-command interface for entering addresses into a navigation system. This was particularly due to the lack of appropriate feedback from the systems.

Despite the advancements in natural language processing, accuracy issues still persist for VCS, which can lead to acceptance issues and disuse. Chakraborty [4] found that the perceived usefulness of VCS and perceived ease-of-use of VCS were significant predictors of attitude toward VCS, and the attitude toward technology was the main differentiator between drivers who used in-vehicle VCS frequently and those who did not. Through a wizard-of-oz approach in a driving simulator, Sokol et al. [53] found that the robustness of the VCS to background noise can increase user acceptance of the system.

Overall, audio/vocal systems are promising for in-vehicle applications, but do have their own limitations that need to be addressed (e.g. robustness to background noise, natural language processing ability).

#### 28.3.2.3 Haptic Modality

"Haptics refers to a type of human–computer interaction technology that encompasses tactile feedback or other bodily sensations to perform actions or processes on a computing device" [20]. Vibration is a type of haptic feedback commonly used in vehicles. For example, vibration warnings are widely adopted for lane keeping assistance systems. When the vehicle deviates from the lane, the steering wheel (e.g. 2019 Mazda 3) or the driver's seat (e.g. Safety Alert Seat in some Cadillac models) vibrate to warn the driver, simulating the effects of a rumble strip. Seat vibration has also been proposed for other safety events (e.g. rear traffic crossing) and for directional alerts [29]. In addition to vibration, researchers have explored feedback from gas and brake pedals to enhance eco-driving and driving safety [3, 41]. Haptic feedback has also been investigated in the context of driving automation as part of multimodal takeover requests (TORs) from the vehicle to the driver [7].

### 28.3.3 Wearable Devices

Advances in technology have increased the number of wearable devices that can be used while driving. Given that these devices are not specifically designed to be used while driving, they may create safety issues. For example, a simulator study has found that smart watches can be more visually and manually distracting compared to cellphones, when drivers were required to engage in a visual–manual non-driving task [18]. Head-mounted augmented reality (AR) devices superimpose virtual imagery onto the real world (e.g. Google Glass). AR devices may be able to reduce visual distractions when drivers are engaging in nondriving tasks, given that they can overlay the information on the front view. However, research shows that these displays may lead to driving performance decrements (e.g. for lane keeping and sign detection) [68].

It should be noted that, although some of the portable device manufacturers have considered the use of their products in driving situations (e.g. the "Driving Mode" or "Do Not Disturb" in smart phones), the focus for regulation and public education has been on cellphones but not on other carried-in devices, such as wearables. Thus, there is a risk of drivers inappropriately using wearable devices while driving, leading to an increased risk of distraction.

## 28.4 Vehicle Automation

The Society of Automotive Engineers (SAE) introduced a taxonomy of levels of driving automation in 2014, with revisions in 2016, 2018, and 2021 [26]. The SAE taxonomy of driving automation was created based on the level of sustained control; see Table 28.1 for the overview of this taxonomy and some relevant human factors considerations. Although this taxonomy has been criticized by many, for example due to some categories not being clear (e.g. [54]), it is very commonly used in academia, industry, and the media. Thus, we introduce the taxonomy here and refer to it in the rest of the chapter.

### 28.4.1 Driver Support Features

Driver support features, including SAE Level 0, Level 1, and Level 2 automation are currently available to consumers. The SAE Level 0 features are limited to providing warnings and momentary assistance, for example automatic emergency braking (AEB [56]) and rear cross-traffic alert (RCTA [63]). Systems that fall under Level 0 can be highly effective safety-wise. In 2020, the Insurance Institute for Highway Safety (IIHS) reported that the forward collision warning (FCW) systems equipped in trucks reduced crashes by 22%, while AEB reduced crashes by 12% [59]. In an earlier study, IIHS had reported that the Volvo's City Safety System, which has similar features, significantly reduced rear-end crashes [8]. The benefits of these safety features are also now recognized by auto insurance providers for premium reductions (e.g. Insurance Corporation of British Columbia). There are, however, concerns on negative driver adaptation, which may decrease the benefits of these safety systems. For example, drivers were found to adopt shorter headways with anti-lock brake systems (ABS) [48].

Many vehicles on the market now come with longitudinal and/or lateral control automation. For example adaptive cruise control (ACC) is a form of cruise control that can maintain a constant set speed, or keep a time headway with a lead vehicle if the lead vehicle is slower than the set speed. Lane keeping assist (LKA) controls steering and can center the vehicle in its lane. When either lateral or longitudinal control is activated, the automation is categorized as SAE Level 1; while when ACC and LKA are combined, the automation is labeled as SAE Level 2, for which drivers are still required to monitor the roadway and the automation at all times.

For SAE Level 2, drivers can fail to fulfill these monitoring requirements. There have been several highly publicized crashes that occurred due to drivers failing to properly monitor Level 2 automation, in particular by engaging in distractions. Monitoring a system while not actively engaged in the vehicle control task is a type of vigilance task. Human factors research is conclusive since World

**Table 28.1** Levels of driving automation.

| SAE Level | Explanation | State-of-the-art | Human factors considerations |
|---|---|---|---|
| Level 0 – no driving automation | Drivers perfrom all driving tasks, but the system can provide **warnings** and **momentary assistance** | Some functions have become mandatory in mass production vehicles | Driver adaptation [48]; modality of warnings |
| Level 1 – driver assistance | It features a single automated system, e.g. steering **OR** brake/acceleration support | Widely available in mass production vehicles | Trust and reliance; workload; distracted driving; situation awareness |
| Level 2 – partial driving automation | It can perform steering **AND** acceleration but requires drivers to monitor the roadway and the systems and be ready to take control at any time | Widely available in mass production vehicles | Quality of takeover process [14]; trust and reliance; situation awareness; mental model; workload; distracted driving |
| Level 3 – conditional driving automation | It can perform most driving tasks and does **NOT** require driver monitoring of the system, but the driver must takeover and drive when the system requests | Germany recently gave regulatory permission for the Mercedes Drive Pilot System, which is claimed to be a SAE Level 3 system and planned to work under 45 km/h on the autobahn, serving as a traffic jam assist [34] | Quality of takeover process [14]; trust and reliance; situation awareness; mental model; workload; distracted driving |
| Level 4 – high driving automation | It can perform all driving tasks and does not require the human to take over driving nor pay attention to the driving tasks **under specific conditions** | Automated taxis or shuttles are being tested within a constrained geography [62]; but this level of automation is far from mass production | User acceptance and trust [33]; AVs' interactions with other road agents [58]; motion sickness |
| Level 5 – full driving automation | It can perform all driving tasks and does not require the human to take over driving nor pay attention to the driving task **under all conditions** | Automated taxis or shuttles are being tested within a constrained geography [62]; but this level of automation is far from mass production | User acceptance and trust [33]; AVs' interactions with other road agents [58]; motion sickness |

War II that vigilance tasks are difficult, and decrements in performance are guaranteed for tasks that require sustained operator attention for a relatively long period of time [32]. Thus, Level 2 driving automation arguably makes the task of driving harder than it normally is. The failures of monitoring can also be attributed to drivers overrelying on these systems [28] while not knowing the system limitations [12].

If drivers are not engaged in distractions while maintaining the vigilance task of monitoring automation, they may slide into drowsiness and sleep, states that are also dangerous. The risks of distraction or drowsiness are also not uniform across different driver groups, which make the issue more complex. For example, novice drivers have been shown to engage in distractions with a Level 2 system more than experienced drivers [21].

To keep drivers in the loop and away from distractions and sleep, the Tesla Autopilot System, which is an SAE Level 2 system, used to provide warnings to drivers if they did not keep their hands on the steering wheel [61]. Instead of focusing on "manual engagement," the General Motors' Super Cruise, another SAE Level 2 system, is based on drivers' "visual engagement" – a warning is triggered if the driver's eyes are detected to be off-road for an extended period of time [24]. However, these warning systems have many limitations and require further development (e.g. drivers could trick the Tesla system by sticking an orange in the steering wheel, the General Motors system loses tracking under glare, and with polarized glasses).

### 28.4.2 Automated Driving Features

The remainder of the taxonomy is automated driving features, including SAE Levels 3, 4, and 5. These levels are still in the testing stage, with some Level 4 systems being used by the public but not available for consumer purchase.

Level 3 systems fall under automated driving systems in that they would not require driver monitoring, but the driver must takeover and drive when the system requests. Germany recently gave regulatory permission for the Mercedes Drive Pilot system, which is claimed to be a SAE Level 3 system and planned to work under 45 kph on the autobahn, serving as a traffic jam assist [34]. Overall, there are safety and regulatory issues regarding this level so the introduction of these systems to the traffic has not happened yet. One can imagine the terror a driver can experience if the automation requests the driver to takeover in an emergency situation when the driver was not monitoring the roadway (because they were not required to).

The idea of Level 3 automation has generated the concept of TORs, the system detecting a need for driver takeover and alerting the driver to do so [14]. One can imagine these takeovers to be scheduled ahead of time (e.g. approaching my exit on the highway at which point my automation won't be operational) or emergency (e.g. automation losing lane markings or a sensor failure). A large body of literature has already investigated TOR design and effectiveness for Level 3 systems. Research has also looked at its application to Level 2 systems. He et al. [22] found that although drivers performed well during takeover scenarios, they showed a tendency to overrely on the automation to tell them when to takeover. When surrounding traffic information was provided to the drivers in addition to TORs, this overreliance issue was rectified. Adding information on surrounding traffic kept drivers better engaged in monitoring and anticipating traffic conflicts, and also improved takeover performance.

A technical obstacle for SAE Level 3 and higher levels of automation is the weak reasoning capability of artificial intelligence [11]. For example, humans can anticipate hazards based on environmental cues while driving automation is not be able to. In a recent Tesla crash, several lead vehicles changed lanes due to a stopped firetruck in their lane. An attentive driver would have anticipated a potential conflict in their lane even if they did not yet see the truck. Yet, the Tesla autopilot system did not detect nor anticipate the stopped truck and sped up into it [60].

Level 4 automation, according to the taxonomy, does not require the driver to take over driving under limited conditions. Examples are automated taxis or shuttles that work within a constrained geography (e.g. [62]). Human factors research related to level 4 automation includes people's acceptance of and trust in such technology as riders and other road users. This type of research is generally hypothetical and survey-based with data collected from individuals who have not interacted with these types of vehicles [33]. However, further studies with actual users are now coming out as these vehicles are being tested on public roads [62].

Level 5 is the true self-driving automation – it will not require the human to take over driving and will drive the vehicle under all conditions. This is a very hard problem to solve and may not be reachable at least in our lifetimes. Even Waymo's previous CEO stated that "Level 5 is a bit of a myth" [15].

There is also research and development regarding how high levels of (SAE Level 4 or 5) driving automation should interact with other road users, for example, how they may communicate with pedestrians who would normally get visual cues from drivers regarding their intent (e.g. [58]).

## 28.5 Driver Monitoring Systems

According to NHTSA, in 2019, 3839 traffic fatalities were due to driver fatigue and inattention [37]. With the introduction of higher levels of automation, there is more than ever a need for driver monitoring systems (DMS) to be implemented in vehicles to fight distraction and drowsiness. The National Transportation Safety Board (NTSB) recommendations released in 2020 call for these systems [39]. European Union is ahead as they have taken steps to make DMS mandatory in new vehicles [47].

Driver monitoring can utilize four sources of information: (i) physiological-based, such as electrocardiogram (ECG) and galvanic skin response (GSR); (ii) eye tracking-based, such as blink rate and pupil diameter; (iii) performance-based, such as steering wheel input and vehicle speed; and (iv) subjective, such as the NASA task load index (NASA-TLX) or Karolinska Sleepiness Scale (KSS).

No single measure alone can provide sufficient information to estimate driver state, and each measure has its pros and cons [36]. For example, subjective measures are direct, but they may interfere with the driving task (if drivers are asked while driving) and do not provide a continuous assessment [36]. Driving-performance measures are much less intrusive but may not be sensitive to some driver states, such as detecting low-cognitive load levels [36], and may be significantly influenced by the driving-context (e.g. the steering wheel inputs are different on highways than in city traffic). Eye-tracking measures, such as the standard deviation of gaze position and the percentage of eyelid closure over the pupil over time (PERCLOS), are easily influenced by ambient light, which is difficult to control on the road. Physiological measures can be highly sensitive to different driver states, such as drowsiness and high workload, but most of the previous research used research-grade measures, which are too intrusive to be deployed in vehicles.

The use of these different measures generally in controlled conditions has led to relatively high detection accuracy in a variety of machine learning models. For example, using linear discriminant analysis (LDA) and based on 32-channel EEG, Kohlmorgen et al. [27] reached over 95% accuracy in estimating high cognitive load experienced by drivers while driving on a real highway. However, some of the machine learning models, such as LDA and support vector machines (SVM), do not consider the temporal correlations between nearby samples. Models such as Hidden Markov [44] and Hidden-Semi Markov Models [69], and Recurrent Neural Networks [66] may incorporate such additional information that can boost estimation accuracy.

Caution should also be exercised with respect to the generalizability of models that have utilized research-based data. First, the robustness of the sensors used to collect the relevant measures can be an issue when the data are collected on real roads as opposed to laboratory settings. Second, when training the models, data may be partitioned in two different ways: for within-subject data partition, the training and the test data come from the same group of drivers; for across-subjects data partition, the training and the test data come from different group of drivers. Many research studies suffer from sample size limitations and therefore, use within-subject data partition. In practice, this would correspond to requiring historical data from each driver in order to train detection models.

Finally, as stated earlier, some of the sensors used in relevant studies, particularly physiological sensors, are research-grade and thus are expensive and generally intrusive to the drivers. Recent technological developments have allowed for more affordable and less intrusive physiological sensors; however, their effectiveness is still not well known. For example, He et al. [23] investigated the application of EEG signals collected through a wearable consumer-level device, along with ECG signals and GSR signals to classify three levels of cognitive load among drivers and reached 79.4% accuracy. Further, carried-in devices, including wearables, also serve as sensors that can facilitate driver state estimation (e.g. daily routine and physiological data). Using the photoplethysmogram (PPG), GSR, skin temperature, acceleration, and rate of rotation collected through a wristband, Choi et al. [6] reached up to 84% accuracy in detecting drowsiness through SVM.

Overall, to date, we have not yet seen good implementations of DMS systems in production-level vehicles as different types of sensors have different issues associated with them. There are implementations based on vehicle measures such as steering wheel inputs (e.g. Attention Assist in Mercedes-Benz), as well as based on eye-tracking information (e.g. DMS in Lexus and Toyota). In general, these systems monitor drivers' operation of the vehicle (driving performance measures) or track drivers' eye and head movements (through machine vision) (e.g. Audi Pre sense and Toyota Safety). However, as mentioned previously, these measures may not work well in certain situations. For example, driving performance measures are sensitive to traffic situations, and machine vision measures may not work when drivers' face and eyes are blocked (e.g. by sunglasses). Overall, further research is still needed in this area to develop driver monitoring technologies by fusing multisource data, and by considering not just accuracy but also equity and privacy issues.

## 28.6 Conclusion

In this chapter, we have provided an overview of human factors in driving, with a focus on state-of-the-art advancements in technology, including devices that are carried-in or built-into the vehicle, higher levels of vehicle automation, and driver state monitoring.

There have indeed been significant advances in technology in all of these areas. However, there has also been much hype regarding vehicle automation technologies and the goal post for self-driving vehicles has continually been moving into the future. Some of what may be considered to be the more advanced technologies (e.g. SAE Level 2 automation) turned out to be dangerous in certain situations, and require further oversight from regulators.

Overall, systems that have considered human factors appropriately in their design (e.g. FCW systems) have proved to enhance safety. Human-centered system design should be used to enhance road users' understanding and interaction with vehicle technologies.

## References

1 Ajzen, I. (1991). The theory of planned behavior. *Organizational Behavior and Human Decision Processes* 50 (2): 179–211.

2 Bhise, V. (2019). *Ergonomics in the Automotive Design Process.* CRC Press.

3 Caliskan, U. and Patoglu, V. (2020). Efficacy of haptic pedal feel compensation on driving with regenerative braking. *IEEE Transactions on Haptics* 13 (1): 175–182.

4 Chakraborty, J. (2020). An exploration of predictors of adoption and use of in-vehicle voice control systems. MASc thesis. Toronto: University of Toronto.

5 Chen, H.-Y.W., Hoekstra-Atwood, L., and Donmez, B. (2018). Voluntary- and involuntary-distraction engagement: An exploratory study of individual differences. *Human Factors* 60 (4): 575–588.

6 Choi, M., Koo, G., Seo, M., and Kim, S.W. (2017). Wearable device-based system to monitor a driver's stress, fatigue, and drowsiness. *IEEE Transactions on Instrumentation and Measurement* 67 (3): 634–645.

7 Chu, D., Wang, R., Deng, Y. et al. (2020). Vibrotactile take-over requests in highly automated driving. *2020 4th CAA International Conference on Vehicular Control and Intelligence (CVCI)*, 695–700. IEEE.

8 Cicchino, J.B. (2016). Effectiveness of Volvo's city safety low-speed autonomous emergency braking system in reducing police-reported crash rates. Insurance Institute for Highway Safety.

9 Cooper, J.M., Ingebretsen, H., and Strayer, D.L. (2014). Mental workload of common voice-based vehicle interactions across six different vehicle systems. AAA Foundation for Traffic Safety. Report No. 01548553. https://trid.trb.org/view/1326372.

10 Crandall, J.M. and Chaparro, A. (2012). Driver distraction: Effects of text entry methods on driving performance. In: *Proceedings of the Human Factors and Ergonomics Society Annual Meeting*, vol. 56, 1693–1697. Sage, CA, Los Angeles, CA: SAGE Publications.

11 Cummings, M.L. (2021). Rethinking the maturity of artificial intelligence in safety-critical settings. *AI Magazine* 42 (1): 6–15.

12 DeGuzman, C.A. and Donmez, B. (2021). Knowledge of and trust in advanced driver assistance systems. *Accident Analysis & Prevention* 156: 106121.

13 Dingus, T.A., Guo, F., Lee, S. et al. (2016). Driver crash risk factors and prevalence evaluation using naturalistic driving data. *Proceedings of the National Academy of Sciences of the United States of America* 113 (10): 2636–2641.

14 Eriksson, A. and Stanton, N.A. (2017). Takeover time in highly automated vehicles: Noncritical transitions to and from manual control. *Human Factors* 59 (4): 689–705.

15 Experts Call Elon Musk's Level 5 Autonomy Claims Absurd. https://carbuzz.com/news/experts-call-elon-musks-level-5-autonomy-claims-absurd (last accessed December 2021).

16 Fatality Analysis Reporting System (FARS). https://www.nhtsa.gov/research-data/fatality-analysis-reporting-system-fars (last accessed January 2022).

17 Funkhouser, D. and Sayer, J.R. (2013). Cellphone Filter/Blocker Technology Field Test. *Report No. DOT HS 811 863.*

18 Giang, W.C.W., Hoekstra-Atwood, L., and Donmez, B. (2014). Driver engagement in notifications: A comparison of visual–manual interaction between smartwatches and smartphones. In: *Proceedings of the Human Factors and Ergonomics Society Annual Meeting*, vol. 58, 2161–2165. Los Angeles, CA: Sage Publications Sage CA.

19 Hansma, B.J., Marulanda, S., Chen, H.-Y.W., and Donmez, B. (2020). Role of habits in cell phone-related driver distractions. *Transportation Research Record* 2674 (12): 254–262.

20 Haptic Interface. https://www.techopedia.com/definition/3638/haptic-interface (last accessed December 2021).

21 He, D. and Donmez, B. (2019). Influence of driving experience on distraction engagement in automated vehicles. *Transportation Research Record* 2673 (9): 142–151.

**22** He, D., Kanaan, D., and Donmez, B. (2021). In-vehicle displays to support driver anticipation of traffic conflicts in automated vehicles. *Accident Analysis & Prevention* 149: 105842.

**23** He, D., Risteska, M., Donmez, B., and Chen, K. (2021). Driver cognitive load classification based on physiological data–Case study 7. In: *Intelligent Computing for Interactive System Design: Statistics, Digital Signal Processing, and Machine Learning in Practice*, 409–429.

**24** Innovating the Future of Driving. Again. https://www.cadillac.com/world-of-cadillac/innovation/super-cruise. (last accessed December 2021).

**25** ISO 15005:2017 (2017). *Road vehicles –Ergonomic aspects of transportation and control systems – Dialogue management principles and compliance procedures*. Geneva, CH: International Organization for Standardization.

**26** J3016_202104 (2018). SAE On-Road Automated Vehicle Standards Committee, 2021. Taxonomy and Definitions for Terms Related to Driving Automation Systems for On-Road Motor Vehicles (J3016_202104). 1–16.

**27** Kohlmorgen, J., Dornhege, G., Braun, M. et al. (2007). Improving human performance in a real operating environment through real-time mental workload detection. *Toward Brain-computer Interfacing* 409–422.

**28** Körber, M., Baseler, E., and Bengler, K. (2018). Introduction matters: Manipulating trust in automation and reliance in automated driving. *Applied Ergonomics* 66: 18–31.

**29** Krüger, M., Wiebel-Herboth, C.B., and Wersing, H. (2021). Tactile encoding of directions and temporal distances to safety hazards supports drivers in overtaking and intersection scenarios. *Transportation Research Part F: Traffic Psychology and Behaviour* 81: 201–222.

**30** Kyriakidis, M., de Winter, J.C.F., Stanton, N. et al. (2019). A human factors perspective on automated driving. *Theoretical Issues in Ergonomics Science* 20 (3): 223–249.

**31** Liu, Y.-C. and Wen, M.-H. (2004). Comparison of head-up display (HUD) vs. head-down display (HDD): Driving performance of commercial vehicle operators in Taiwan. *International Journal of Human-Computer Studies* 61 (5): 679–697.

**32** Mackworth, N.H. (1948). The breakdown of vigilance during prolonged visual search. *Quarterly Journal of Experimental Psychology* 1 (1): 6–21.

**33** Merat, N., Madigan, R., and Nordhoff, S. (2017). Human factors, user requirements, and user acceptance of ride-sharing in automated vehicles. *International Transport Forum Discussion Papers*, No. 2017/10. OECD Publishing.

**34** Mercedes Drive Pilot Level 3 Autonomous System to Launch in Germany. https://www.caranddriver.com/news/a38475565/mercedes-drive-pilot-autonomous-germany/ (last accessed December 2021).

**35** Merrikhpour, M. and Donmez, B. (2017). Designing feedback to mitigate teen distracted driving: A social norms approach. *Accident Analysis & Prevention* 104: 185–194.

**36** Miller, S. (2001). *Workload Measures*. Iowa City, United States: National Advanced Driving Simulator.

**37** National Center for Statistics and Analysis. Overview of Motor Vehicle Crashes in 2019. *Report DOT HS 813 060*. National Highway Traffic Safety Administration, 2020.

**38** National Highway Traffic Safety Administration (2012). Visual–manual NHTSA driver distraction guidelines for in-vehicle electronic devices (Report No. 2014-21991). Washington, DC: National Highway Traffic Safety Administration (NHTSA), Department of Transportation (DOT).

**39** Office of the Chairman (2021). Attention: Docket. *Report DOT-NHTSA-2020-0106*. National Highway Traffic Safety Administration.

**40** Ohn-Bar, E., Tran, C., and Trivedi, M. (2012). Hand gesture-based visual user interface for infotainment. *Proceedings of the 4th International Conference on Automotive User Interfaces and Interactive Vehicular Applications*, 111–115.

**41** Oswald, D., Vu, A., Williams, N. et al. (2021). Real-world efficacy of a haptic accelerator pedal-based eco-driving system. *2021 IEEE International Intelligent Transportation Systems Conference (ITSC)*, 1541–1546. IEEE.

**42** Owsley, C., McGwin, G. Jr., and Ball, K. (1998). Vision impairment, eye disease, and injurious motor vehicle crashes in the elderly. *Ophthalmic Epidemiology* 5 (2): 101–113.

**43** Pradhan, A.K., Hammel, K.R., DeRamus, R. et al. (2005). Using eye movements to evaluate effects of driver age on risk perception in a driving simulator. *Human Factors* 47 (4): 840–852.

**44** Rabiner, L. and Juang, B. An introduction to hidden Markov models. *IEEE ASSP Magazine* 3 (1): 4–16.

**45** Reagan, I.J. and Cicchino, J.B. (2020). Do not disturb while driving–use of cellphone blockers among adult drivers. *Safety Science* 128: 104753.

**46** Reimer, B., Mehler, B., Dobres, J., and Coughlin, J.F. (2013). The effects of a production level "voice-command" interface on driver behavior: Summary findings on reported workload, physiology, visual attention, and driving performance.

**47** Road safety: Commission welcomes agreement on new EU rules to help save lives. https://ec.europa.eu/commission/presscorner/detail/en/ip_19_1793 (last accessed January 2022).

**48** Sagberg, F., Fosser, S., and Sætermo, I.-A.F. (1997). An investigation of behavioural adaptation to airbags and antilock brakes among taxi drivers. *Accident Analysis & Prevention* 29 (3): 293–302.

**49** Shechtman, O., Classen, S., Awadzi, K., and Mann, W. (2009). Comparison of driving errors between on-the-road and simulated driving assessment: A validation study. *Traffic Injury Prevention* 10 (4): 379–385.

**50** Singh, S. (2015). Critical Reasons for Crashes Investigated in the National Motor Vehicle Crash Causation Survey. *Technical report* DOT HS 812 115. Washington, DC: National Center for Statistics and Analysis. https://trid.trb.org/view.aspx?id=1346216&source=post_page.

**51** Sivak, M. (1996). The information that drivers use: is it indeed 90% visual? *Perception* 25 (9): 1081–1089.

**52** Smiley, A. (2015). *Human Factors in Traffic Safety*, 550. Tucson, AZ: Lawyers and Judges Publishing.

**53** Sokol, N., Chen, E.Y., and Donmez, B. (2017). Voice-controlled in-vehicle systems: Effects of voice-recognition accuracy in the presence of background noise. *Driving Assessment Conference* 9. https://doi.org/10.17077/drivingassessment.1629.

**54** Stayton, E. and Stilgoe, J. (2020). It's time to rethink levels of automation for self-driving vehicles. Available at SSRN 3579386.

**55** Stecher, M., Michel, B., and Zimmermann, A. (2017). The benefit of touchless gesture control: An empirical evaluation of commercial vehicle-related use cases. *International Conference on Applied Human Factors and Ergonomics*, 383–394. Springer.

**56** Stop Right There–Automatic Emergency Braking Explained. https://www.motortrend.com/features/automatic-emergency-braking/ (last accessed December 2021).

**57** Strategic Highway Research Program 2. http://shrp2.transportation.org/pages/default.aspx (last accessed December 2021).

**58** Tabone, W., Lee, Y.M., Merat, N. et al. (2021). Towards future pedestrian-vehicle interactions: introducing theoretically-supported AR prototypes. *13th International Conference on Automotive User Interfaces and Interactive Vehicular Applications*, 209–218.

**59** Teoh, E.R. (2021). Effectiveness of front crash prevention systems in reducing large truck crash rates. *Traffic Injury Prevention* 22 (4): 284–289.

**60** Tesla car was on Autopilot when it hit a Culver City firetruck, NTSB finds. https://www.latimes.com/business/story/2019-09-03/tesla-was-on-autopilot-when-it-hit-culver-city-fire-truck-ntsb-finds (last accessed December 2021).

**61** Tesla starts using in-car camera for Autopilot driver monitoring. https://www.theverge.com/2021/5/27/22457430/tesla-in-car-camera-driver-monitoring-system. (last accessed March 2022).

**62** We're building the World's Most Experienced Driver. https://waymo.com (last accessed December 2021).

**63** What is a Rear Cross Traffic Alert? https://www.kia.com/dm/discover-kia/ask/what-is-a-rear-cross-traffic-alert.html (last accessed December 2021).

**64** Wickens, C.D. (2008). Multiple resources and mental workload. *Human Factors* 50 (3): 449–455.

**65** Wickens, C.D., Helton, W.S., Hollands, J.G., and Banbury, S. (2021). *Engineering Psychology and Human Performance*. Routledge.

**66** Williams, R.J. and Zipser, D. (1989). A learning algorithm for continually running fully recurrent neural networks. *Neural Computation* 1 (2): 270–280.

**67** Yager, C. (2013). An Evaluation of the Effectiveness of Voice-to-Text Programs at Reducing Incidences of Distracted Driving. *Technical report* SWUTC/13/600451-00011-1. Southwest Region University Transportation Center (US). https://rosap.ntl.bts.gov/view/dot/25912.

**68** Young, K.L., Stephens, A.N., Stephan, K.L., and Stuart, G.W. (2016). In the eye of the beholder: A simulator study of the impact of Google glass on driving performance. *Accident Analysis & Prevention* 86: 68–75.

**69** Yu, S.-Z. (2010). Hidden semi-Markov models. *Artificial Intelligence* 174 (2): 215–243.

# 29

# Wearable Computing Systems: State-of-the-Art and Research Challenges

*Giancarlo Fortino and Raffaele Gravina*

*Department of Informatics, Modeling, Electronics and Systems, University of Calabria, Rende Via P. Bucci, Italy*

## 29.1 Introduction

Gartner, Inc. [33] estimates that the global smart wearable computing systems (WCS) market will be worth more than USD 93 billion in 2022, with an increasing growth caused by the COVID-19. The industry and public sector are then pushing for innovative solutions with high levels of dependability and trustworthiness that can efficiently operate in increasingly complex scenarios.

Due to the new wave of wearable gadgetry hitting the ICT market, WCS [29] are emerging as a new computing platform with full capabilities to support diversified application domains. Wearables, which include both devices and body sensors, are networked cyberphysical objects that may offer enough power to support local computation and sensor-based information as well as some actuation [58].

The advancement of ubiquitous/pervasive computing and the development of wearable computers/devices lay the foundation for wearable computing. Steve Mann, father of the wearable computer, defined wearable computing as "the study or practice of inventing, designing, building, or using miniature body-borne computational and sensory devices" [62].

Wearable devices provide smart sensing, multimodal interfacing, and motoring capabilities in addition to wearability, data input, data recording, and communication. Potential applications of wearable devices include healthcare, wellness, consumer electronics, entertainment, sports, and so forth [58].

In this chapter, we aim to provide an overview of wearable computing devices and their history, categories, applications, and systems and future challenges. We will introduce the history of wearable devices and some remarkable wearable products in Section 29.2.1. In Section 29.2.2, we describe the various types of wearable devices available nowadays. To make the wearable devices connected and play a more significant role, the development of body sensor networks (BSNs) is essential. To some extent, the development of BSNs further boosts the general development of WCS. Therefore, Section 29.3 presents the basics and related challenges of BSNs in the context of the Signal Processing In-Node Environment-Body of Knowledge (SPINE-BoK). In Section 29.4, we describe the main application areas that WCS are or will be employed in. Section 29.5 discusses the research challenges and future perspectives. Section 29.6 concludes this chapter.

*Handbook of Human-Machine Systems*, First Edition. Edited by Giancarlo Fortino, David Kaber, Andreas Nürnberger, and David Mendonça.

## 29.2 Wearable Devices

### 29.2.1 A History of Wearables

In Figure 29.1, it is shown that a timeline of the historical appearance of the most important wearable devices. The earliest wearable device was the first wearable watch invented by Peter Henlein from Nuremberg in 1505 [94]. It is the oldest watch in the world that still works. The first wearable "computing" gadget was the abacus ring, a "smart ring" invented in the seventeenth century in China, which was able to perform mathematical calculation by moving beads along nine rows [61]. The very first wristwatch was created by the French watchmaker Breguet for the Queen of Naples [9] in 1812.

In 1957, the first "VR" visor/Head-Mounted Display named Telesphere was proposed in the Patent n. US2955156 entitled "STEREOSCOPIC TELEVISION APPARATUS FOR INDIVIDUAL USE" [41]. In 1968, the first "AR" visor was developed [84]. The so-called "The Sword of Damocles" was based on the superpositions of virtual images to the real scene, Stereo Vision, Beam splitter, Tethered to video source and power supply. As the inventors stated: "Our objective in this project has been to surround the user with displayed three-dimensional information. We can display objects which appear to be close to the user or which appear to be infinitely far away."

In the 1970s, the calculator watches, combining both the calculation and the timekeeping functions, were introduced by many important watch brands, such as Seiko, Casio, Pulsar, Timex. They can be regarded as "wearable computers" in the sense that they can be worn and they can do calculation and timekeeping.

In 1979, the Sony Walkman cassette player made music listening movable, allowing users to enjoy their favorite music when moving or doing fitness. A total of 50 million units sold and 186 million units sold 10 and 20 years after the launch, respectively. In the following years, mobile music listening went through several transitions, from cassette-based to CD-based, and then to MP3-based. Nowadays, mobile music listening is a built-in function of most smartphones.

The first successful wearable device in the medical area could be the hearing aids. Although the attempt to invent hearing aids for deaf people dated back to the seventeenth century, it was the creation of microprocessor in the 1970s that made the miniaturization of the hearing aid possible. The first commercial digital hearing aid was created by the Nicolet Corporation in 1987. It consists of a pocket processor that connected to a behind-the-ear transducer with a cord. Nowadays, hearing aids have been further miniaturized and can be conveniently fitted in the outer ear bowl or in the canal. The first wearable device in the fitness area was the smart shoes proposed by Adidas (Adidas Micropacer, 1984) and Puma (Puma RS Computer Shoe, 1985).

Wearable technology also extended its influence to the fashion industries. In 2004, using smart textiles and microelectronics, the CuteCircuit company introduced the KineticDress, which can

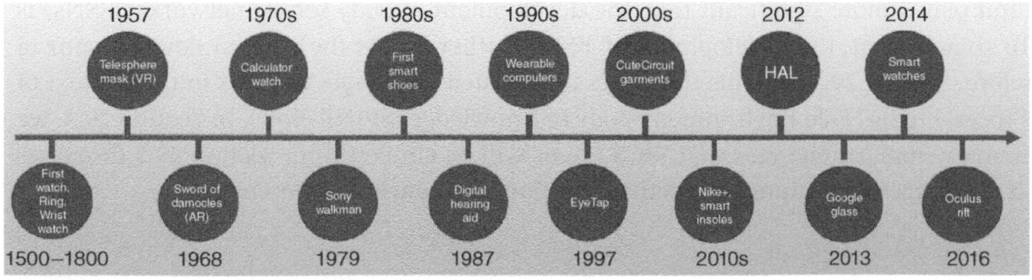


**Figure 29.1** Remarkable wearable devices in the history.

change its patterns following the wearer's movements. Later on, CuteCircuit created several other smart garments that can sense emotions, receive phone calls, or show images and texts through iOS programming.

Also in 2004, the American technology company GoPro introduced its first wearable action camera, the GoPro 35mm HERO. Such cameras are mostly used for outdoor sports or law enforcement. Attached to helmets, armbands, or clothes, they can provide a first-person perspective and allow continuous capture of actions, while keeping the users' hands and vision free.

In 2009, the Fitbit Tracker, a small gizmo clipped onto clothing, was released by the American consumer electronics company Fitbit. It is a representative of the emerging activity trackers since the early 2000s. Containing a 3D accelerometer, the Fitbit Tracker can measure your movements 24/7, and then calculate your steps taken, calories burnt, sleep quality, etc. After its first product, Fitbit has released over 10 products in the following years. The most recent product, Fitbit Alta HR [19], is a wristband with an OLED touchscreen. Except for tracking fitness-related metrics, many current activity trackers can be synced to smart devices wirelessly for long-term tracking and analysis.

Powered exoskeletons are types of robotic systems supporting the limb movements of their wearers with increased strength and endurance. They can expand the physical capabilities of able-bodied people, serve as assistive devices for disabled people, and be used for rehabilitation [99]. The Hybrid Assistive Limb (HAL) is a leader in the powered exoskeleton technology. Developed by the Tsukuba University and the robotics company Cyberdyne, the HAL suit was first released in 2012. Its two versions, the HAL-3 and HAL-5 can support leg function and full-body (legs, arms, and torso) function, respectively.

In 2013, the Google Glasses were released. They attracted great media attention and were one of the most remarkable wearable devices in recent years. Google Glass is an optical head-mounted display in the shape of eyeglasses, which (i) can deliver texts and notifications and be activated by voice commands; (ii) can take photos and record video with cameras on-board.

Although the development of smartwatches (wristwatches with functionalities except for timekeeping) started as early as 1970s, they have only begun gaining mass-market attention with the introduction of new models by Samsung, Sony, Apple, Razer, etc. in the 2010s. An essential feature of the new-generation smartwatches is their connection with other smart devices, especially smartphones. Through Bluetooth or Wi-Fi, connected smart devices can share resources and cooperate on tasks. Devices, apps, and services are forming an active ecosystem that serves a well-defined need.

Another increasingly popular wearable technology is virtual reality (VR). With the help of a VR headset (such as the Oculus Rift headset), a person can immerse in an artificial world that is comparable to real scenes. People can see, hear, and even interact with objects in this virtual world. The VR headsets have been applied in video games to provide more immersive gaming experience; been introduced to virtual surgery for surgical training; and been adopted for military training.

### 29.2.2 Sensor Types

Due to technological advancements in circuit design, micro electro-mechanical systems (MEMS) and signal processing, wearable sensors are becoming smaller and more computational powerful. Wearable sensors can now be used to measure many types of signals: physiological signals, motion, images, sounds, forces, and so forth. In this section, we introduce the main types of wearable sensors and some important research works that used such wearable sensors.

#### 29.2.2.1 Physiological Sensors

Since the world population is aging and the healthcare costs are increasing [72, 88], wearable health-monitoring systems (WHMS) recently became a popular research topic and even commercial systems. Physiological sensors are the basic components of WHMS. In Table 29.1, we list some significant physiological parameters commonly measured by wearable sensors: electrocardiogram (ECG), respiration rate, respiration flow, heart rate, blood pressure, body temperature, blood oxygen saturation ($SpO_2$), galvanic skin response (GSR)/electro-dermal activity (EDA), blood glucose, electromyogram (EMG), and electroencephalogram (EEG). We also summarize some significant research works employing some physiological sensors in Table 29.1. According to different physiological signals measured and different principles of measurement, the sensors can be worn on head [12, 55], on face [39, 46], in or behind ears [64, 103], on neck [46], on fingers [11, 46], on arms [102, 104], and so forth. They can be embedded into armband [56] or headband [55], integrated into clothes [65, 70], directly attached to skin [12], or implanted under skin [96].

Physiological sensors are mainly used for continuous vital sign monitoring. Many chronic diseases, such as cardiovascular diseases, respiratory diseases, hypertension, and diabetes, respectively require long-term monitoring of ECG, $SpO_2$, blood pressure, blood glucose as well as of other vital physiological signals. EEG reflects the electrical activity of the brain, thus is often measured to diagnose epilepsy, sleep disorder, coma, and other neural system diseases. Besides, many physiological signs are related to people's emotional states, thus are measured for emotion recognition. For instance, Katsis et al. [46] used facial EMG, ECG, respiration rate, and EDA to estimate the emotional state of car-racing drivers. Heart rate, body temperature, and EEG are also indicators of emotions [12, 56]. Since EMG is related to muscular activity, monitoring EMG is also a commonly used method for gesture recognition [102].

#### 29.2.2.2 Inertial Sensors

Inertial sensors, or inertial measurement units (IMUs), refer to the combinations of accelerometers, gyroscopes, and magnetometers. With the advances of sensor miniaturization and embedded processing, current IMUs are lightweight, low-cost, low-power, and can be easily embedded into wearable devices [10]. Inertial sensors measure accelerations and orientations, so they are often used for motion analysis and activity monitoring [59, 79], especially for gesture recognition [42, 102] and fall detection [75]. Inertial sensors are often combined with other types of sensors to achieve better task performance or to realize more complex functions. For instance, Zhang et al. [102] used accelerometers and EMG sensors to recognize Chinese Sign Language. Chen et al. [14] used inertial sensors and depth camera for human action recognition. Cao et al. [11] combined accelerometers, $SpO_2$ sensor, and respiratory airflow sensor for respiratory disease monitoring.

#### 29.2.2.3 Visual Sensors

Digital cameras can be embedded in smartphones, smartwatches, and other wearable consumer gadgets. These wearable visual lifeloggers (WVLs) [100] provide continuous recordings of the wearer's surroundings from the first-person perspective. Ozcan and Velipasalar [68] attached a Samsung Galaxy S4 smartphone to a person's waist. Using the onboard camera and accelerometer, they can reliably perform fall detection. Researchers are also trying to make RGB-D sensors wearable in order to assist visually impaired people. RGB-D sensors, such as Microsoft Kinect and ASUS Xtion, can provide range information that greatly facilitates target detection and recognition. Neto et al. [66] mounted a RGB-D sensor on top of the head of the wearer to perform face detection and recognition. Aladren et al. [1] used a RGB-D sensor hung in front of the wearer's chest to recognize paths and obstacles for navigation assistance.

**Table 29.1** Types of wearable sensors and some example research work using such sensors.

| Categories | Signals | Technical features | Positioning | Application focus |
|---|---|---|---|---|
| Physiological sensors | Electrocardiogram (ECG) | A three-lead ECG sensor [46] | Thorax [46] | Emotion recognition [46] |
| | | Noncontact capacitively coupled ECG sensing [65] | Electrodes embedded into T-shirt [65] | Continuous vital signs monitoring [65] |
| | Respiration rate | A Hall-effect respiration sensor [46] | Thorax [46] | Emotion recognition [46] |
| | Respiration flow | A hot-film flow sensor [11] | Upper body [11] | Respiratory diseases monitoring [11] |
| | Heart rate | Sensors embedded into armband and chest strap [56] | Upper arm and chest [56] | Emotion recognition [56] |
| | | Calculated through weak ear-ECG/PPG signals [103] | Behind two ears [103] | Hypertension control [103] |
| | Blood pressure | 24-h cuffless BP monitoring, calculated through pulse transit time (PTT) [104] | Upper arm [104] | Cardiovascular risk screening [104] |
| | | Calculated through weak ear-ECG/PPG signals [103] | Behind two ears [103] | Hypertension control [103] |
| | Body temperature | A temperature sensor embedded into armband [56] | Upper arm [56] | Emotion recognition [56] |
| | | Platinum Thermistor (PT100) [70] | At the armpit of a smart vest [70] | Continuous vital signs monitoring [70] |
| | Blood oxygen saturation | Reflectance pulse oximetry [71] | Wrist [71] | Continuous vital signs monitoring [71] |
| | | Transmittance pulse oximetry [11] | Finger [11] | Respiratory diseases monitoring [11] |
| | Electrodermal activity (EDA) | Electrodes attached to fingers [46] | Index and middle fingers [46] | |
| | | A EDA sensor embedded into armband [56] | Upper arm [56] | Emotion recognition [46, 56] |
| | | A dry Ag–AgCl electrode [70] | Thenar and hypothenar positions of palm [70] | Continuous vital signs monitoring [70] |
| | Blood glucose | Amperometric electrochemical sensor [96] | Implanted under the skin [96] | Continuous diabetic monitoring [96] |
| | Electromyogram (EMG) | Four EMG thin flexible sensors [46] | Frontalis and masseter muscles [46] | Emotion recognition [39, 46] |
| | | Six differential electrode pairs [39] | Left face [39] | |
| | | Five-channel surface EMG sensors [102] | Forearm [102] | Gesture recognition [102] |

*(Continued)*

**Table 29.1** (Continued)

| Categories | Signals | Technical features | Positioning | Application focus |
|---|---|---|---|---|
| | Electroencephalogram (EEG) | 19 wet electrodes [12] | Skull [12] | Emotion recognition [12] |
| | | Five dry electrodes embedded to a headband [55] | Forehead [55] | Sleep monitoring [55, 64] |
| | | Cloth electrodes attached on viscoelastic earplugs [64] | In ears [64] | |
| Inertial sensors | Acceleration | A 3-axis MEMS accelerometer [11, 102] | Upper body [11], Forearm [102] | Respiratory diseases monitoring [11] |
| | | Multiple three-axis accelerometers [42] | Limbs [42] | Gesture recognition [42, 102] |
| | Acceleration and orientation | Three-axis accelerometer, gyroscope, and magnetometer [75] | Waist [75] | Fall detection [75] |
| Visual sensors | Image and depth map | Microsoft Kinect, identify people through face recognition [66] | On top of head [66] | Aiding low-vision people [1, 66] |
| | | ASUS Xtion Pro live camera, path, and obstacle recognition [1] | In front of chest [1] | |
| | Image | Samsung Galaxy S4 smartphone camera [68] | Waist [68] | Fall detection [68] |
| Audio sensors | Throat sounds | Swallowing sound can be separated from respiration, speech etc. [82, 83] | Over laryngopharynx [82, 83] | Ingestive behavior monitoring [82, 83] |
| | | Eating, drinking, speaking, and laughing activities can be identified [98] | Lower neck [98] | Activity recognition [98] |
| | Environmental sounds | A total of 22 personal and social activities can be identified [101] | In front of chest [101] | Activity recognition [101] |
| Strain sensor | Strain | Jaw motions produce piezoelectric strain signals [82] | Below the outer ear [82] | Ingestive behavior monitoring [82] |
| Force sensor | Force | Five triaxial force sensors deployed on the shoe sole [57] | Under feet | Gait analysis [57] |
| RFID tag | RF signal | Different user motions result in different radio patterns [93] | Embedded to clothes [93] | Activity recognition [93] |

#### 29.2.2.4 Audio Sensors

Many personal and social activities can produce characteristic sounds, so using wearable audio sensors for activity monitoring could be an effective approach [79]. Zhan and Kuroda [101] used a wearable audio sensor mounted in front of chest to recognize environmental sounds (vacuum cleaner, washing machine, hair dryer, telephone ringing, etc.) and determine what kind of personal or social activity is taking place. Sazonov et al. [82, 83] employed throat microphone to identify swallowing events for ingestive behavior monitoring.

#### 29.2.2.5 Other Sensors

Except for the abovementioned physiological, inertial, visual, and audio sensors, other wearable sensors can be adopted depending on different application requirements. For instance, in [82], a piezoelectric strain sensor was attached below the outer ear to capture the motion of lower jaw in order to monitoring chewing events. In order to analyze gait variability, Liu et al. [57] constructed a wearable ground reaction force system with five tri-axial force sensors embedded in the shoe sole. Wang et al. [93] adopted wearable RFID tags for activity recognition. RFID tags and antennas were attached to specific body parts, so that different activities result in different radio patterns, which can differentiate these activities.

## 29.3 Body Sensor Networks-based Wearable Computing Systems

### 29.3.1 Body Sensor Networks

BSNs originated from existing sensor network technology and modern biomedical engineering. The term was first coined by Prof. Guang-Zhong Yang of Imperial College in the early 2000s [97]. A BSN is a network of wireless wearable sensor nodes managed by more capable coordinators (smartphones, tablets, PCs). Although the basic elements (sensors, communication protocols, and coordinators) of a BSN are available (already from a commercial point of view), developing BSN systems/applications remains a complex task that requires design methods based on effective and efficient programming approaches and data processing techniques [25]. BSNs involve wireless wearable physiological sensors applied to the human body for medical and nonmedical purposes. In particular, they allow for the continuous, unobtrusive measurement of body movements and physiological parameters, such as heart rate, muscular tension, skin conductivity, breathing rate, and volume, during the daily life of a user.

A key aspect of BSNs [36] is the use of programmable wearable devices so to enable in-node signal processing, a central computing method in advanced wireless sensor platforms through which data processing is carried out directly on the sensor node to preprocess data acquired from sensors, to fuse data coming from other sensor nodes, and, notably, to perform higher-level computation such as classification and decision-making. Furthermore, with the diffusion of personal handheld devices, BSN systems substituted desktop and laptop PCs with mobile network coordinators, so allowing for BSN mobile computing, a form of human–computer interaction by which a computer is expected to be transported during normal usage.

In more recent times, BSNs are exploiting the Cloud paradigm with the use of computing and storage (hardware and software) resources that are delivered as a service over a network (typically the Internet). Cloud computing entrusts remote services with a user's data, software, and computation.

This roadmap depicts a three-tier reference architecture of the BSN. The tiers communicate through wireless (or sometimes wired) channels [48]. The first tier represents the body sensor layer and includes a set of wearable sensor nodes. Each node is able to detect, sample, and process one or more physiological signals. The second tier is the personal area network layer and contains the personal coordinator device (often a smartphone) running the end-user applications. This tier is responsible for a number of functions providing a transparent interface to the BSN, to the user and to the upper tier. The third tier is the global network layer and comprises one or more remote servers or a Cloud computing platform. This tier usually provides services to medical personnel for off-line analysis of a patient's health status, real-time notification of life-critical events and abnormal conditions, and scientific and medical visualization of collected data. In addition, this tier can provide a web interface for the patient itself and/or relatives too.

Very heterogeneous information and diversified physiological signals can be transmitted, possibly after the application of sensor fusion techniques [37], by the sensor nodes to the coordinator device.

BSNs are usually arranged in a star network topology with the coordinator device acting as the center of the star and in charge of configuring the remote sensor nodes (which do not communicate among each other directly) and gathering the sensory information.

In terms of communication standards, the IEEE 802.15.4 [43] is widely adopted in the BSN domain. Indeed, it is intended to offer the fundamental lower-network layers (physical and MAC) of Wireless Personal Area Networks (WPANs) focusing on low-cost, low-speed ubiquitous communication between devices. The emphasis is on very low-cost communication of nearby devices with little to no underlying infrastructure. However, to enable direct communication between sensors and mobile devices, Bluetooth [8], a proprietary open wireless technology standard for exchanging data over short distances with high levels of security, is a better technological choice. Bluetooth is actually suitable only for BSN systems that do not require long battery life before recharging. This is because its power consumption profile is significantly higher compared with IEEE 802.15.4. Another factor hindering the use of conventional Bluetooth standard in the BSN domain is the limited number (seven) of slave devices (the sensors) that can be connected simultaneously to a master device (the mobile personal device). To overcome these limitations, Bluetooth released a newer, specifically designed version called Bluetooth Low Energy (BLE) [7]. One of the BLE design driving factors is the specific support for applications such as healthcare, sport, and fitness.

Several challenges have to be tackled during BSN systems development; a few remarkable ones are reported in the following:

- *Interference reduction*. BSNs use wireless connectivity for communications. The BSN system should be able to reduce/mitigate interference on the wireless link and increase the co-existence of wearable sensor nodes with other networked devices [49]. This is important to ensure that the functionalities of BSN nodes (and the whole BSN system) do not degrade due to the presence of other devices capable of possible interruption/interference in the data transmission.
- *Data validation and consistency*. Data collected from multiple sensor nodes need to be collected and analyzed seamlessly. BSN sensors are subject to inherent hardware, network, and communication failures that may result in erroneous gathered datasets [86]. It is crucial that the sensed data are validated, and data quality is maintained under control to reduce any noise in the data and identify possible weaknesses in the BSN system.
- *Heterogeneity and interoperability*. A BSN system should be capable of integrating various different sensors in terms of complexity, power efficiency, storage, and ease-of-use. Moreover, it should provide a common interface between the sensors and a storage service to facilitate remote storage and viewing of sensed data as well as access to external processing and networked analysis tools [24]. Finally, a BSN system should transfer data seamlessly across different standards to promote information exchange, plug-and-play device interaction, and uninterrupted connectivity [26].

- *Security and privacy*. Transmission of BSN data streams should be secured to prevent potential intruders [91]. Moreover, integrity of each assisted living's data has to be maintained with guarantee that data of different users are not mixed. Another key problem is to protect the privacy of personal data [50]. A BSN system should ensure that assisted livings' privacy is maintained even when data are being analyzed using an external tool.
- *Programming*. BSNs are usually programmed by using the low-level APIs provided by the adopted BSN sensor platforms (e.g. TinyOS and ZigBee). However, to enable a more rapid and effective prototyping, higher-level programming abstractions, offered by BSN middlewares and frameworks, are needed [25].
- *Systems methodology*. The development of BSNs should be driven by suitable methodologies dealing with all diversified requirements of BSN.
- *Wearability and deployment*. BSNs need to fulfill the important wearability requirement that would promote its effective deployment on the human body.
- *Collaborative behavior*. Next-generation BSNs should be able to cooperate in order to create opportunistic collaborative multiuser services [28, 52].
- *Interaction with environmental sensors and IoT devices*. BSNs need to interact with surrounding IoT systems in order to provide data to the dynamic environment in which they are situated [23].
- *Situational awareness*. BSNs should also be situation-aware in order to understand not only the context where they are located but also high-level information derived from the human-environment-driven situation [16, 47].

### 29.3.2 The SPINE Body-of-Knowledge

The SPINE-BoK [89] has been created over the last 15 years in the context of the open-source SPINE project and includes models, methods, algorithms, frameworks, tools, and systems for the systematic and full-fledged development of WCS based on BSNs.

SPINE covers many different application domains: Healthcare, Fitness, Sport, Factory, Transportation, Gaming, Social interactions, and Defense.

The SPINE project was originally established in 2006 at the Telecom Italia/Pirelli Wireless Sensor Networks Lab in Berkeley (CA). The founders were University of Calabria (G. Fortino), Telecom Italia/Pirelli WSN Lab (M. Sgroi), Telecom Italia Lab (F. Bellifemine), and University of Berkeley (A. Sangiovanni-Vincentelli). Since 2013, the project is fully driven and managed by the Prof. Fortino's research group at University of Calabria. Many R&D groups from Academia and Industry contributed to SPINE BoK, both with research contributions and with contribution to the open-source code.

In particular, the SPINE BoK includes the SPINE framework and related methodology (SPIME-DM), the SPINE extension frameworks (SPINE2, C-SPINE, A-SPINE, SPINE-*), the BodyCloud infrastructure and related methodology, the BodyEdge infrastructure, and a rich set of application-specific multisensor data fusion algorithms.

Overall, the SPINE research and dissemination activities produced 100+ papers, notably 40+ in top-level journals (e.g. IEEE-THMS, IEEE-SensorsJ, IEEE-IoTJ, IEEE-Network, IEEE-WCM, IEEE-TASE, INFFUS, FGCS, JNCA), 5000+ number of citations according to Google Scholar with an h-index=30, and five highly cited papers according to Web of Science.

#### 29.3.2.1 The SPINE Framework

SPINE (Signal Processing in Node Environment) is a software Framework for the design and fast prototyping of Wireless BSN applications. SPINE enables efficient implementations of signal processing algorithms for analysis and classification of sensor data through libraries of processing functionalities. It also embedded an application-level communication protocol.

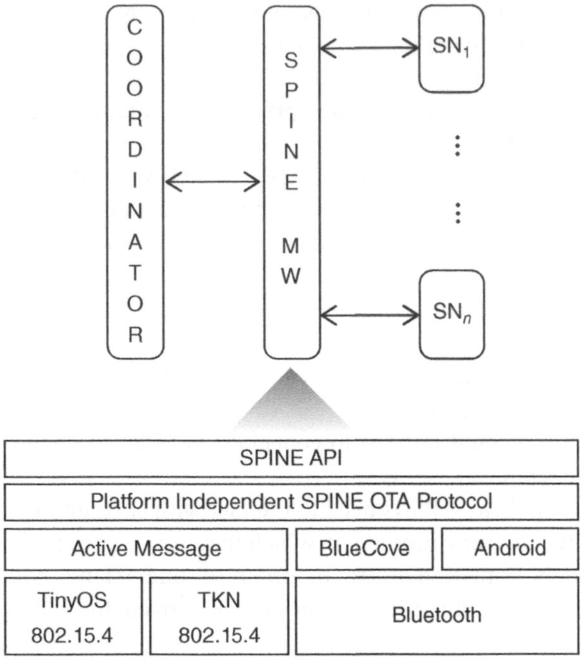


**Figure 29.2** The SPINE middleware architecture.

SPINE is organized in two interacting macro-components (see Figure 29.2), which are, respectively, implemented on commercially available sensor devices and on the personal coordinator (such as an Android smart-phone or tablet or a personal computer). Communication among these devices is wireless, using the Bluetooth 2.1 or IEEE 802.15.4 standards.

The high-level SPINE API (at coordinator level) allows for dynamic and flexible configuration of sensing and processing functionalities available at the sensor node level. Many biophysical sensors and signal processing functionalities are natively implemented and available to application developers; in addition, the SPINE framework has been carefully designed to allow for very easy integration of new, custom-defined sensor drivers, and processing functionalities.

SPINE supports the most popular TinyOS-enabled sensor platforms (mote): Shimmer (rev. 1.3 and 2R), TelosB/Tmote Sky, MicaZ. The following physical sensors are natively supported by SPINE (each one is generally available only on specific sensor platforms):

- Accelerometers and gyroscopes, force and pressure (for postural, gesture, and activity monitoring);
- ECG sensor (for cardiac monitoring);
- Electro-impedance-plethysmographic (EIP) sensor (for respiratory rhythm and volume);
- EMG sensor (for muscular activity);
- Photo-plethysmographic (PPG) sensor and SpO2 (pulse oximetry and blood oxygen saturation, for indirect measurement of heart rate and breathing);
- GSR sensor (e.g. for emotion recognition);
- Environmental temperature sensor;
- Humidity sensor;
- Light sensor.

The application developer, through the SPINE API available at the coordinator, can perform data collection of the raw signals from one or multiple available sensors (even simultaneously). It is possible to configure dynamically sensor parameters such as the sampling frequency (from less than 1 Hz up to about 200 Hz). Depending on the application needs, each sensor node can also be configured (through the SPINE API available at the coordinator) to perform simple preprocessing operations to user-selectable time windows of the sensor signals, for instance to reduce the amount of data the sensor nodes has to transmit over-the-air back to the coordinator. Specifically, SPINE provides native support for several general-purpose processing functions, including Average, Median and RMS; Max and Min; Amplitude; Variance and standard deviation; Zero-crossing; Entropy; and Cross-Axial Energy. In addition, SPINE also provides some dedicated functionalities which can be applied only on certain physical sensors that are available (e.g. pitch and roll features are based on accelerometer data).

As a middleware for the development of BSN applications, SPINE has been adopted to prototype several BSN research systems, including Physical rehabilitation assistant, Fall detector, Physical activity monitor [30, 34], Smart step-counter, Mental stress detector [4], ECG monitoring, Handshake detection system.

The Latest stable version (SPINE 1.3 release), source code and documentation are available for free download at our GitHub project https://spine.dimes.unical.it/spine.html.

#### 29.3.2.2 The BodyCloud Framework

BodyCloud [27] is an open platform for the integration of BSNs with a Cloud Platform-as-a-Service (PaaS) infrastructure, and it is currently based on Google App Engine. It has been developed to make the middleware layer fully distributed; it specifically supports remote sensory data storage, offline signal processing, and custom-defined algorithms via a plug-in mechanism. Its design and implementation choices allow BodyCloud to flexibly be tailored, in a very effective manner, for supporting a broad range of application domains, including m-Health, Building automation, and environmental monitoring.

The architecture, see Figure 29.3, consists of four main subsystems (or sides):

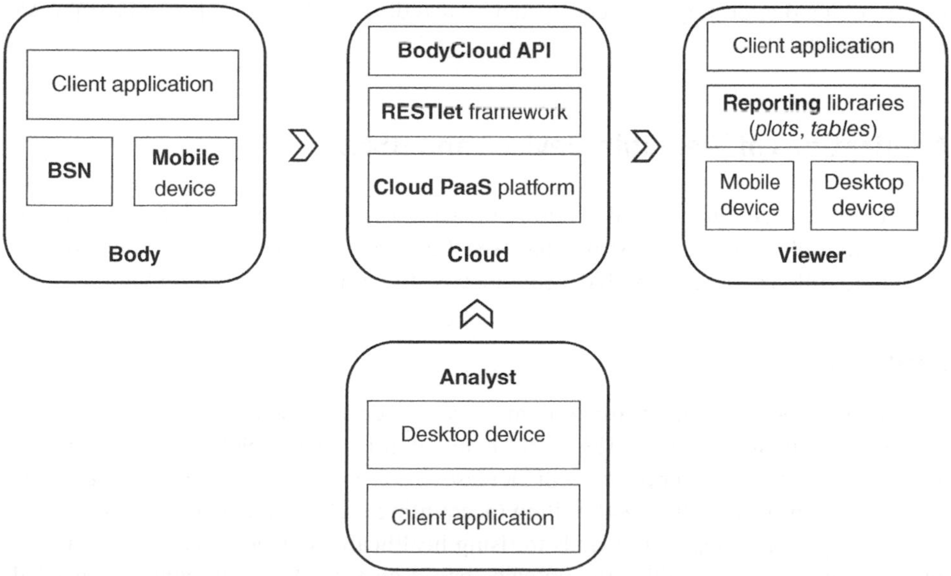


**Figure 29.3** The BodyCloud architecture.

Body, which is the system side that monitors the target environment, phenomenon, or assisted living by means of wireless networked sensors, and sends the collected data to the Cloud through a mobile coordinator device. In particular, BSN data acquisition is currently based on SPINE, and on the BMF for Building sensor networks. Data collected are then streamed up to the Cloud-side. In Android-SPINE communication of wearable sensors with the BAN coordinator is based on Bluetooth, while for the BMF the communication is based essentially on IEEE 802.15.4/Zigbee.

Cloud is the system side providing full support for specific applications through data collection, processing/analysis, and visualization. In particular, each specific application can be defined through the following programming abstractions: Group, Modality, Workflow/Node, and View. Such abstractions are supported by a RESTful web service (Server Servlet), implemented using the Restlet Framework, making the interaction with the Cloud-side fully based on HTTP methods (get, put, post, delete). The interactions are authenticated by the OAuth Verifier component based on OAuth 2.0. The Cloud-side is supported by the Google App Engine PaaS that provides the Datastore API, atop which the Persistence Layer managing the collected sensory data is built, and the Task Queue API, which enables asynchronous execution of tasks are triggered by requests.

Analyst is the side of the system that supports the development of new BodyCloud application services. In particular, users can create new BodyCloud services by defining the aforementioned entities: groups, modalities, workflows, and views. Each entity can be created with an HTTP PUT request to the corresponding Cloud-side resource, thus requiring only a simple HTTP client as Analyst-side supporting application. As the workflow requires new nodes to be developed, the Analyst-side also requires an appropriate development environment. Once developed, new nodes are also uploaded with a HTTP PUT request to the corresponding Cloud-side resource. A predefined set of nodes is typically available, depending on the adopted implementation of the Workflow Engine.

Viewer is the system side able to visualize the output produced by the data analysis through advanced graphical reporting facilities. The graphical view is automatically generated by applying the View specification to the data.

As a middleware for the development of Cloud-based community-based BSN systems, BodyCloud has been adopted to prototype several systems, including ECG-AAS [27], ACTIVITY-AAS [38], and REHAB-AAS [21].

## 29.4 Applications of Wearable Devices and BSNs

Wearable devices and systems are applied to many application scenarios, among which healthcare and fitness-related applications are most popular (see Table 29.2). Besides, in education, sports, entertainment, and military areas, wearable technology is attracting increasing attentions.

### 29.4.1 Healthcare

For decades, healthcare-related applications dominated the developments of wearable devices in both academic and industrial areas. The world population is aging rapidly. Estimated by the United Nations, the number of older people will increase to more than 2 billion (accounting 21.1% of the world population) in 2050 from 841 million (accounting 11.7% of the world population) in 2013 [17]. Increasing elderly population leads to rising healthcare demands. Except for building more hospitals, more efficient healthcare strategies based on wearable technology are needed to realize autonomous, proactive, and predictive clinical services [88]. For many age-related

**Table 29.2** Application areas of wearable devices and BSNs.

| Areas | | Typical studies/Products | Highlights/features |
|---|---|---|---|
| Healthcare | Cardiovascular disease | MyHeart project [40, 60] | Smart textile, embed ECG sensors to clothing |
| | | HeartToGo project [44] | 2-lead ECG sensors + 3-axis accelerometer + cellphone |
| | | Lin et al. [54] | Detect atrial fibrillation and provide automatic warning |
| | | Gravina and Fortino [35] | CDR detection from ECG signal |
| | Parkinson's disease | Salarian et al. [80] | Activity recording and analysis with three inertial sensors and a portable data logger |
| | | Bachlin et al. [5] | Detect freezing of gait symptom and provide audio feedback |
| | Respiratory disease | Cao et al. [11] | Use hot-film flow sensor, oximetry sensor, and accelerometer to measure respiratory airflow, $SpO_2$, and posture |
| | | Dieffenderfer et al. [18] | Asthma monitoring based on physiological and environmental parameters tracking |
| | | Oletic and Bilas [67] | Asthma monitoring based on respiratory sound analysis |
| | Diabetes | Medtronic's CGMS and Guardian systems [63] | Electrode needs to be inserted in tissue fluid |
| | Rehabilitation | Vitiello et al. [92] | Elbow exoskeleton, enable robot-in-charge, and patient-in-charge exercise modes |
| | | Pan et al. [69] | For balance rehabilitation with inertial sensors and fingertip skin stretch feedback |
| | | Patel et al. [74] | For quantitative assessment of rehabilitative movements with accelerometers |
| Fitness | Diet monitoring | Sazonov et al. [82, 83] | Detect swallowing and chewing through throat microphone and strain sensor |
| | | Yatani and Truong [98] | Detect eating and drinking activities with headset microphone |
| | | Päßler et al. [73] | Eating detection and food classification with ear-canal microphone |
| | | Sun et al. [90] | Dietary assessment with wearable camera |
| | Activity/fitness tracker | Randriambelonoro et al. [78] | Study on how fitness trackers influence wearers' lifestyle |
| Sports | | Seshadri et al. [85] | Survey on wearable devices used for sports |
| | | Li et al. [51] | Review on movement and physiologic sensors for sports performance measurement |
| Entertainment | | Chanel et al. [12] | Adapt game difficulty based on emotions assessed from physiological signals |
| | | Chu et al. [15] | Use pressure and inertial sensors embedded in trousers to measure player's movements during a dancing game |

chronic and degenerative diseases, such as cardiovascular diseases, Parkinson's disease, and diabetes, long-term home-based monitoring is quite essential. In the following, we introduce some representative research works using wearable technology to monitor these diseases.

#### 29.4.1.1 Cardiovascular Disease

The MyHeart project [40, 60] initiated in 2004 was supported by the European Commission. It was joined by 33 partners, including industrial partners such as Philips, Nokia, Vodafone, and Medtronic. This project aimed to fight cardiovascular diseases by prevention and early diagnosis. They developed smart textiles and embedded ECG sensors to clothing, so that patients wearing the smart clothes can be comfortably monitored anywhere. The HeartToGo project [44] developed a cellphone-based wearable platform for continuous ECG monitoring and recording. ECG signals measured by a two-lead ECG-sensing device were wirelessly transmitted to a cellphone and were analyzed real time to detect abnormal cardiovascular conditions. Lin et al. [54] developed a lightweight wireless ECG device equipped with automatic warning system. It can accurately detect atrial fibrillation and alert the wearer and remote healthcare personnel instantaneously, which greatly facilitates early medical intervention. Gravina and Fortino [35] focused on the detection of a particular heart activity called cardiac defense response (CDR). Frequent CDR activations can pose the patient to health risk and eventually develop into severe psychophysical disorders. Based on the extraction of specific features from ECG, they designed an automatic method to detect CDR and to understand the patient's mental status.

#### 29.4.1.2 Parkinson's Disease

Parkinson's disease is a long-term degenerative disorder of the central nervous system that mainly affects the patients' motor system. Therefore, monitoring the physical activities of the patients is the most essential. Salarian et al. [80] developed an ambulatory monitoring system for Parkinson's disease patients. This system consists of three inertial sensors attached to the trunk and shanks, and a portable data logger fixed to the waist. Sitting, standing, lying, and walking activities can be reliably detected and recorded, which enables quantitative analysis of motor functions of Parkinson's disease patients. Bachlin et al. [5] also used inertial sensors to measure the patients' movements. Their system can automatically detect freezing of gait symptom and provide audio feedback to the patients to help them resume walking.

#### 29.4.1.3 Respiratory Disease

Cao et al. [11] proposed a wireless portable monitoring system for respiratory diseases, incorporating a hot-film flow sensor, an oximetry sensor, and an accelerometer to measure the patients' respiratory airflow, $SpO_2$, and posture. These parameters can be transmitted via Bluetooth to a mobile phone or a PC for telemedicine. In order to continuously monitor asthma symptoms and environmental substances that affects asthma, Dieffenderfer et al. [18] developed a low-power wearable system consisting of a wristband, a chest patch, and a handheld spirometer. The system tracks physiological parameters, such as ECG, skin impedance, PPG, and lung function (forced expiratory volume, peak expiratory flow, and forced vital capacity). It also tracks environmental parameters, such as ozone exposure, ambient temperature, and humidity, which can affect the asthma patients' lung function. The work by Oletic and Bilas [67] also explored asthma monitoring, but they adopted a wearable audio sensor. The measured respiratory sounds were transmitted wirelessly to a smartphone, where wheeze detection is performed.

#### 29.4.1.4 Diabetes

To conduct continuous blood glucose monitoring, there are many commercially available products, such as the Medtronic's CGMS and Guardian systems [63]. A tiny electrode need to be inserted under the skin to measure glucose levels in tissue fluid. Measured information is then transmitted to a display device to remind the user whether the glucose level reaches limits.

#### 29.4.1.5 Rehabilitation

Robot-aided rehabilitation, especially the rehabilitation exoskeleton, is gradually being accepted by the therapist community. These wearable devices provide patients with more effective and stable rehabilitation process and reduce therapists' workload [76]. A powered elbow exoskeleton system for poststroke physical rehabilitation was developed by Vitiello et al. [92]. This system features double-shelled links, a four-degree-of-freedom passive mechanism, and an antagonistic compliant actuation system, which enables both robot-in-charge and patient-in-charge rehabilitation exercise. Pan et al. [69] focused on balance rehabilitation of poststroke patients. They used wearable inertial sensors to detect patients' body sway angles during balance rehabilitation exercise and provide fingertip skin stretch feedback to the patients through a portable sensory augmentation device. Their system can help the patients correct their postures and improve their balance. Except for directly providing rehabilitation exercises, wearable technologies provide researchers and clinicians with quantitative assessment tools of the rehabilitation process. Patel et al. [74] used accelerometers attached to a poststroke patient's hand, forearm, and upper arm to track his/her motor tasks. Then these information can be used to accurately estimate the quality of movement (functional ability scale), which provides valuable feedback to guide clinical interventions.

### 29.4.2 Fitness

Although fitness is often mixed with healthcare, here we separate fitness-related applications from healthcare-related applications, focusing on applications that engage people in physical activities or motivate people to adopt healthier lifestyle. More specifically, in this section, we focus on diet monitoring and activity/fitness trackers.

#### 29.4.2.1 Diet Monitoring

According to the *Global Status Report on Noncommunicable Diseases 2014* released by the World Health Organization (WHO), 11% of men and 15% of women aged 18 years and older were obese worldwide in 2014 [95]. Obesity increases the possibility of diabetes, hypertension, coronary heart disease, and other diseases. To prevent obesity, low-energy diet and regular exercise are encouraged [45]. Diet monitoring can be realized by wearing audio sensors, such as throat microphones [83], headset microphone [98], or ear-canal microphone [73], which can identify chewing and swallowing events and even detect food classes. Besides, wearable camera [90] and strain sensor [82] can be used to identify eating behaviors.

#### 29.4.2.2 Activity/Fitness Tracker

Activity/fitness trackers are devices or applications that track fitness-related metrics, such as the distance walked, calories consumption, and sleep quality. In fact, many current smartwatches and smartphone apps can be regarded as fitness trackers. Research has shown that wearing fitness trackers can make positive lifestyle changes for diabetic and obese people [78]. They become more aware of their inactivity and try to conduct a more active lifestyle; they are in fact more motivated to participate in activities and they feel stronger sense of social connections.

### 29.4.3 Sports

Athletes and professional sports teams are often interested in monitoring movements and workloads to improve athletic performance [85]. Wearable movement sensors (such as pedometers, accelerometers, gyroscopes, and GPS device) and physiological sensors (such as temperature sensor and heart rate sensor) enable real-time measurements of biomarkers and biovitals during training and competitive sports. These parameters can be analyzed to design more efficient training programs that maximize performance and minimize injury [51].

### 29.4.4 Entertainment

Wearable technology is offering new platforms and devices to make gaming more visually and physically engaging [77]. VR headsets can now be used with computer games and create environments that make wearers feel like they really are somewhere else. These VR headsets can offer 360° vision and sounds, enable the wearers to interact with what they see and make gaming more immersive.

Wearable technology can make gaming more emotionally engaging by monitoring player's emotional response and making adjustments accordingly. Chanel et al. [12] monitored Tetris game players' physiological signals (EEG, EDA, body temperature, and respiratory rate) and assessed their emotional states. Then the game difficulty was adapted to avoid boredom and to maintain the players' engagement in the game.

Using wearable sensors, game interface can be more intuitive and intelligent. In [15], textile pressure sensors and inertial sensors are embedded to the game player's trousers, belt, and socks to measure his/her movements during a dancing game. Then the player's dancing image were emerged as a virtual professional dancer in the game screen. The mixed reality presentation can increase the enjoyment of the game and trigger the player's lasting interest.

## 29.5 Challenges and Prospects

There is no doubt that networked wearable devices are becoming more ubiquitous in our life and this trend will continue. According to the report released by Forrester Research in 2017 [20], wearables were in the stage of piloting and early adoption from 2014 to 2016; they would have become mainstreaming from 2017 to 2019 and will move to business centrality from 2020 to 2024. People's attitudes toward wearable technology is becoming more positive [77], and more consumers are optimistic about the effects that wearables can bring to us. However, there are still some challenges need to be addressed by researchers to further boost the wearable technology [53].

### 29.5.1 Materials and Wearability

Wearable devices are mostly in direct contact with people's skin or even implanted into our body, so their size and biocompatibility to human tissues have to be carefully studied [88]. This requirement motivates synthesis of novel materials and technologies. Integrating sensing elements with textile is an approach that more and more researchers are adopting. Skin-mounted wearable sensor can be made with nanomaterials and polymers. Nanomaterials can serve as functional sensing elements due to their excellent electrical, mechanical, optical and chemical properties, and polymers can be employed as flexible support due to their flexibility, stretchability, human-friendliness, and durability [3].

### 29.5.2 Power Supply

Modern wearable sensors and systems should be able to operate for long periods, so there should be enough power capacity. However, the lightweight and high wearability requirements on the other hand limit the space for battery. For instance, the current wearable cameras on the market can last for a reasonable period when they are only used for capturing images at a moderate rate. However, when transferring of images or videos happens at the same time, the lifespan of the battery will be significantly reduced [100]. For BSNs/BANs, even more power supply is needed to collect, process, and transmit data [13].

### 29.5.3 Security and Privacy

Data collected by wearable devices relates to the wearers' locations, motions, health status, and other private information. Therefore, proper encryption and authentication mechanisms are essential factors that affect people' trust in wearable devices [72]. Besides, the reliance of sensors nodes on wireless protocols for communication also exposes users to data interception [88].

### 29.5.4 Communication

More efficient and smarter use of radio communication is crucial for extending the network lifetime with energy and bandwidth efficient approaches. An interesting approach for reducing the energy consumption is based on the use of adaptive radio scheduling schema employing reinforcement learning [87]. A recent study to achieve higher bandwidth utilization and connectivity consists of decentralized time-synchronized channel swapping, a novel MAC protocol in wireless networks [31].

### 29.5.5 Embedded Computing, Development Methodologies, and Edge AI

Deploying computing tasks in the wearable nodes is essential to fully exploit their hardware resource and therefore improve system performance. However, programming such wearable devices is often not trivial and the support of domain-specific frameworks and middleware can effectively help developers. SPINE2, for instance, by means of task-oriented programming, allows the implementation of fairly sophisticated signal-processing applications in the form of easy-to-implement embedded processes [6, 22, 32]. Supporting rigorous BSN system design is another relevant challenge that could be tackled with development methodologies that enable reliable systems, system efficiency, and true interoperability between different applications as well as between different implementation platforms. SPINE-DM is the only platform-based design methodology available in the BSN domain [25]. Finally, another important challenge is to apply Edge AI [2, 81] approaches for WCS development so that learning methods will be embedded directly in the wearable sensors/mobile coordinators/in-proximity environment and the DL/ML workflow will soon start at the micro edge.

## 29.6 Conclusions

This chapter reviewed the history of wearable sensors and computing systems and introduced the many wearable sensors used to measure different kinds of signals, such as physiological signals, movements, images, sounds, forces. The wearable computing technology is bringing innovations to healthcare and fitness, sports, entertainment, and many other industries. Although a wearable future is right around the corner, more efforts are needed to tackle open challenges, including the development of biocompatible materials, increased power supply, better security and privacy protection, reliable communication, stronger embedded computing ability, and novel system development methodologies including Edge AI frameworks.

## Acknowledgment

This work has been partially carried out under the framework of PRIN 2020 COMMON-WEARS (2020HCWWLP) and PRIN 2017 Fluidware (2017KRC7KT), financed by the Italian Ministry of Research.

## References

1 Aladren, A., Lopeznicolas, G., Puig, L., and Guerrero, J.J. (2016). Navigation assistance for the visually impaired using RGB-D sensor with range expansion. *IEEE Systems Journal* 10 (3): 922–932.

2 Aloi, G., Fortino, G., Gravina, R. et al. (2021). Simulation-driven platform for edge-based AAL systems. *IEEE Journal on Selected Areas in Communications* 39 (2): 446–462. https://doi.org/10.1109/JSAC.2020.3021544.

3 Amjadi, M., Kyung, K.-U., Park, I., and Sitti, M. (2016). Stretchable, skin-mountable, and wearable strain sensors and their potential applications: a review. *Advanced Functional Materials* 26 (11): 1678–1698.

4 Andreoli, A., Gravina, R., Giannantonio, R. et al. (2010). SPINE-HRV: a BSN-based toolkit for heart rate variability analysis in the time-domain. In: *Wearable and Autonomous Biomedical Devices and Systems for Smart Environment*, *Lecture Notes in Electrical Engineering*, vol. 75 (ed. A. Lay-Ekuakille and S.C. Mukhopadhyay), 369–389. Berlin, Heidelberg: Springer. ISBN 978-3-642-15687-8. https://doi.org/10.1007/978-3-642-15687-8_19.

5 Bachlin, M., Plotnik, M., Roggen, D. et al. (2010). Wearable assistant for Parkinson's disease patients with the freezing of gait symptom. *IEEE Transactions on Information Technology in Biomedicine* 14 (2): 436–446.

6 Bellifemine, F.L., Fortino, G., Guerrieri, A., and Giannantonio, R. (2009). Platform-independent development of collaborative wireless body sensor network applications: SPINE2. *Proceedings of the IEEE International Conference on Systems, Man and Cybernetics*, San Antonio, TX, USA (11–14 October 2009), 3144–3150. IEEE. https://doi.org/10.1109/ICSMC.2009.5346155.

7 Bluetooth Low Energy Website. https://www.bluetooth.com/what-is-bluetooth-technology/how-it-works/le-p2p (accessed July 2022).

8 Bluetooth Website. http://www.bluetooth.com (accessed July 2022).

9 Breguet. https://www.breguet.com/en/history/inventions/first-wristwatch (accessed July 2022).

10 Bruno, B., Mastrogiovanni, F., and Sgorbissa, A. (2015). Wearable inertial sensors: applications, challenges, and public test benches. *IEEE Robotics & Automation Magazine* 22 (3): 116–124.

11 Cao, Z., Zhu, R., and Que, R. (2012). A wireless portable system with microsensors for monitoring respiratory diseases. *IEEE Transactions on Biomedical Engineering* 59 (11): 3110–3116.

**12** Chanel, G., Rebetez, C., Betrancourt, M., and Pun, T. (2011). Emotion assessment from physiological signals for adaptation of game difficulty. *systems Man and Cybernetics* 41 (6): 1052–1063.

**13** Chen, M., Gonzalez, S., Vasilakos, A. et al. (2011). Body area networks: a survey. *Mobile Networks and Applications* 16 (2): 171–193.

**14** Chen, C., Jafari, R., and Kehtarnavaz, N. (2016). A real-time human action recognition system using depth and inertial sensor fusion. *IEEE Sensors Journal* 16 (3): 773–781.

**15** Chu, N.N.Y., Yang, C.-M., and Wu, C.-C. (2012). Game interface using digital textile sensors, accelerometer and gyroscope. *IEEE Transactions on Consumer Electronics* 58 (2): 184–189.

**16** D'Aniello, G., Gravina, R., Gaeta, M., and Fortino, G. (2022). Situation-aware sensor-based wearable computing systems: a reference architecture-driven review. *IEEE Sensors Journal* 22 (14): 13853–13863. https://doi.org/10.1109/JSEN.2022.3180902.

**17** Department of Economical and Social Affairs, United Nations (2013). World Population Aging. *Department of Economic and Social Affairs, United Nations. World population aging. Technical report.* https://www.un.org/en/development/desa/population/publications/pdf/ageing/WorldPopulationAgeing2013.pdf.

**18** Dieffenderfer, J., Goodell, H., Mills, S. et al. (2016). Low-power wearable systems for continuous monitoring of environment and health for chronic respiratory disease. *IEEE Journal of Biomedical and Health Informatics* 20 (5): 1251–1264.

**19** Fitbit, Inc. https://www.fitbit.com/shop/altahr (accessed July 2022).

**20** Forrester Research Inc. (2017). Deliver Digital Operational Excellence and Digital Customer Experience Innovation with Wearables. *Technical Report.* https://www.forrester.com/report/deliver-digital-operational-excellence-and-digital-customer-experience-innovation-with-wearables/RES103381.

**21** Fortino, G. and Gravina, R. (2014). Rehab-aaService: a cloud-based motor rehabilitation digital assistant. In: *Proceedings of the 8th International Conference on Pervasive Computing Technologies for Healthcare, PervasiveHealth 2014*, Oldenburg, Germany (20–23 May 2014) (ed. A. Hein, S. Boll, and F. Kohler), 305–308. ICST. https://doi.org/10.4108/icst.pervasivehealth.2014.255273.

**22** Fortino, G., Guerrieri, A., Bellifemine, F.L., and Giannantonio, R. (2009). SPINE2: developing BSN applications on heterogeneous sensor nodes. *IEEE 4th International Symposium on Industrial Embedded Systems, SIES 2009* (July 8–10 2009). Switzerland: Ecole Polytechnique Federale de Lausanne, 128–131. IEEE. https://doi.org/10.1109/SIES.2009.5196205.

**23** Fortino, G., Gravina, R., and Guerrieri, A. (2012). Agent-oriented integration of body sensor networks and building sensor networks. *Federated Conference on Computer Science and Information Systems (FedCSIS 2012)*, 1207–1214.

**24** Fortino, G., Pathan, M., and Di Fatta, G. (2012). BodyCloud: integration of cloud computing and body sensor networks. *4th IEEE International Conference on Cloud Computing Technology and Science Proceedings (CloudCom 2012)*, 851–856.

**25** Fortino, G., Giannantonio, R., Gravina, R. et al. (2013). Enabling effective programming and flexible management of efficient body sensor network applications. *IEEE Transactions on Human–Machine Systems* 43 (1): 115–133.

**26** Fortino, G., Di Fatta, G., Pathan, M., and Vasilakos, A.V. (2014). Cloud-assisted body area networks: state-of-the-art and future challenges. *Wireless Networks* 20 (7): 1925–1938.

**27** Fortino, G., Parisi, D., Pirrone, V., and Di Fatta, G. (2014). BodyCloud: a SaaS approach for community body sensor networks. *Future Generation Computer Systems* 35: 62–79. https://doi.org/10.1016/j.future.2013.12.015.

**28** Fortino, G., Galzarano, S., Gravina, R., and Li, W. (2015). A framework for collaborative computing and multi-sensor data fusion in body sensor networks. *Information Fusion* 22: 50–70. https://doi.org/10.1016/j.inffus.2014.03.005.

**29** Fortino, G., Gravina, R., and Galzarano, S. (2018). *Wearable Computing: From Modeling to Implementation of Wearable Systems based on Body Sensor Networks*. Wiley-IEEE Press.

**30** Fortino, G., Guzzo, A., Ianni, M. et al. (2021). Predicting activities of daily living via temporal point processes: approaches and experimental results. *Computers and Electrical Engineering* 96 (Part B): 107567. https://doi.org/10.1016/j.compeleceng.2021.107567.

**31** Galzarano, S., Fortino, G., and Liotta, A. (2014). A learning-based MAC for energy efficient wireless sensor networks. *7th International Conference on Internet and Distributed Computing Systems (IDCS 2014)*, 396–406.

**32** Galzarano, S., Giannantonio, R., Liotta, A., and Fortino, G. (2016). A task-oriented framework for networked wearable computing. *IEEE Transactions on Automation Science and Engineering* 13 (2): 621–638.

**33** Gartner, Inc. https://www.gartner.com/en/newsroom/press-releases/2021-01-11-gartner-forecasts-global-spending-on-wearable-devices-to-total-81-5-billion-in-2021 (accessed February 2021).

**34** Ghasemzadeh, H., Panuccio, P., Trovato, S. et al. (2014). Power-aware activity monitoring using distributed wearable sensors. *IEEE Transactions on Human–Machine Systems* 44 (4): 537–544. https://doi.org/10.1109/THMS.2014.2320277.

**35** Gravina, R. and Fortino, G. (2016). Automatic methods for the detection of accelerative cardiac defense response. *IEEE Transactions on Affective Computing* 7 (3): 286–298.

**36** Gravina, R. and Fortino, G. (2021). Wearable body sensor networks: state-of-the-art and research directions. *IEEE Sensors Journal* 21 (11): 12511–12522. https://doi.org/10.1109/JSEN.2020.3044447.

**37** Gravina, R., Alinia, P., Ghasemzadeh, H., and Fortino, G. (2017). Multi-sensor fusion in body sensor networks: state-of-the-art and research challenges. *Information Fusion* 35: 68–80.

**38** Gravina, R., Ma, C., Pace, P. et al. (2017). Cloud-based activity-aaservice cyber-physical framework for human activity monitoring in mobility. *Future Generation Computer Systems* 75: 158–171. https://doi.org/10.1016/j.future.2016.09.006.

**39** Gruebler, A. and Suzuki, K. (2014). Design of a wearable device for reading positive expressions from facial EMG signals. *IEEE Transactions on Affective Computing* 5 (3): 227–237.

**40** Habetha, J. (2006). The MyHeart project–fighting cardiovascular diseases by prevention and early diagnosis. *Proceedings of the 28th Annual International of the IEEE EMBS Conference*, 6746–6749.

**41** Heilig, M.L. (1957). *Stereoscopic Television Apparatus for Individual USE*. Patent No. US2955156. https://patentimages.storage.googleapis.com/81/df/f1/f6cc2106f8c7ab/US2955156.pdf (accessed July 2022).

**42** Hu, F., Hao, Q., Sun, Q. et al. (2016). Cyberphysical system with virtual reality for intelligent motion recognition and training. *IEEE Transactions on Systems, Man, and Cybernetics* 47 (2): 347–363.

**43** IEEE 802.15.4 Website. http://www.ieee802.org/15/pub/tg4.html (accessed July 2022).

**44** Jin, Z., Oresko, J., Huang, S., and Cheng, A.C. (2009). HeartToGo: a personalized medicine technology for cardiovascular disease prevention and detection. *Life Science Systems and Applications Workshop, 2009. LiSSA 2009. IEEE/NIH*, 80–83. IEEE.

**45** Kalantarian, H., Alshurafa, N., and Sarrafzadeh, M. (2017). A survey of diet monitoring technology. *IEEE Pervasive Computing* 16 (1): 57–65.

**46** Katsis, C.D., Katertsidis, N.S., Ganiatsas, G., and Fotiadis, D.I. (2008). Toward emotion recognition in car-racing drivers: a biosignal processing approach. *Systems Man and Cybernetics* 38 (3): 502–512.

**47** Korel, B.T. and Koo, S.G.M. (2007). Addressing context awareness techniques in body sensor networks. *21st International Conference on Advanced Information Networking and Applications Workshops*, 798–803.

**48** Kuryloski, P., Giani, A., Giannantonio, R. et al. (2009). DexterNet: an open platform for heterogeneous body sensor networks and its applications. *International Conference on Body Sensor Networks (BSN 2009)*. IEEE.

**49** Le, T.T.T. and Moh, S. (2015). Interference mitigation schemes for wireless body area sensor networks: a comparative survey. *Sensors* 15: 13805–13838.

**50** Li, M., Wenjing, L., and Kui, R. (2010). Data security and privacy in wireless body area networks. *Wireless Communications* 17 (1): 51–58.

**51** Li, R.T., Kling, S.R., Salata, M.J. et al. (2016). Wearable performance devices in sports medicine. *Sports Health: A Multidisciplinary Approach* 8 (1): 74–78.

**52** Li, Q., Gravina, R., Li, Y. et al. (2020). Multi-user activity recognition: challenges and opportunities. *Information Fusion* 63: 121–135. https://doi.org/10.1016/j.inffus.2020.06.004.

**53** Liang, T. and Yuan, Y.J. (2016). Wearable medical monitoring systems based on wireless networks: a review. *IEEE Sensors Journal* 16 (23): 8186–8199.

**54** Lin, C.-T., Chang, K.-C., Lin, C.-L. et al. (2010). An intelligent telecardiology system using a wearable and wireless ECG to detect atrial fibrillation. *IEEE Transactions on Information Technology in Biomedicine* 14 (3): 726–733.

**55** Lin, C.-T., Chuang, C.-H., Cao, Z. et al. (2017). Forehead EEG in support of future feasible personal healthcare solutions: sleep management, headache prevention, and depression treatment. *IEEE Access* 5: 10612–10621.

**56** Lisetti, C.L. and Nasoz, F. (2004). Using noninvasive wearable computers to recognize human emotions from physiological signals. *EURASIP Journal on Advances in Signal Processing* 2004 (11): 929414.

**57** Liu, T., Inoue, Y., and Shibata, K. (2010). A wearable ground reaction force sensor system and its application to the measurement of extrinsic gait variability. *Sensors* 10 (11): 10240–10255.

**58** Liu, P.X., Fortino, G., Yuce, M.R., and Chen, D. (2015). New SMCS technical committee on interactive and wearable computing and devices [society news]. *IEEE Systems, Man, and Cybernetics Magazine* 1 (3): 70–72.

**59** López-Nava, I.H. and Mu noz-Meléndez, A. (2016). Wearable inertial sensors for human motion analysis: a review. *IEEE Sensors Journal* 16 (22): 7821–7834.

**60** Luprano, J., Solà, J., Dasen, S. et al. (2006). Combination of body sensor networks and on-body signal processing algorithms: the practical case of MyHeart project. *Proceedings of the International Workshop on Wearable and Implantable Body Sensor Networks (BSN'06)*. IEEE.

**61** Mail Online. https://www.dailymail.co.uk/sciencetech/article-2584437/Is-wearable-computer-300-year-old-Chinese-abacus-ring-used-Qing-Dynasty-help-traders.html (accessed July 2022).

**62** Mann, S. Wearable computing. In: *The Encyclopedia of Human–Computer Interaction*, Chapter 23. Interaction Design Foundation.

**63** Medtronic, Inc. http://www.medtronic.com/us-en/index.html (accessed July 2022).

**64** Nakamura, T., Goverdovsky, V., Morrell, M.J., and Mandic, D.P. (2017). Automatic sleep monitoring using ear-EEG. *IEEE Journal of Translational Engineering in Health and Medicine* 5: 1–8.

**65** Nemati, E., Deen, M.J., and Mondal, T. (2012). A wireless wearable ECG sensor for long-term applications. *IEEE Communications Magazine* 50 (1): 36–43.

**66** Neto, L.B., Grijalva, F., Maike, V.R.M.L. et al. (2017). A Kinect-based wearable face recognition system to aid visually impaired users. *IEEE Transactions on Human–Machine Systems* 47 (1): 52–64.

**67** Oletic, D. and Bilas, V. (2016). Energy-efficient respiratory sounds sensing for personal mobile asthma monitoring. *IEEE Sensors Journal* 16 (23): 8295–8303.

**68** Ozcan, K. and Velipasalar, S. (2016). Wearable camera- and accelerometer-based fall detection on portable devices. *IEEE Embedded Systems Letters* 8 (1): 6–9.

**69** Pan, Y.-T., Yoon, H.U., and Hur, P. (2017). A portable sensory augmentation device for balance rehabilitation using fingertip skin stretch feedback. *IEEE Transactions on Neural Systems and Rehabilitation Engineering* 25 (1): 31–39.

**70** Pandian, P.S., Mohanavelu, K.S., Safeer, K.P. et al. (2008). Smart Vest: wearable multi-parameter remote physiological monitoring system. *Medical Engineering & Physics* 30 (4): 466–477.

**71** Pang, G. and Ma, C. (2014). A neo-reflective wrist pulse oximeter. *IEEE Access* 2: 1562–1567.

**72** Pantelopoulos, A. and Bourbakis, N.G. (2010). A survey on wearable sensor-based systems for health monitoring and prognosis. *IEEE Transactions on Systems, Man, and Cybernetics, Part C (Applications and Reviews)* 40 (1): 1–12.

**73** Päßler, S., Wolff, M., and Fischer, W.-J. (2012). Food intake monitoring: an acoustical approach to automated food intake activity detection and classification of consumed food. *Physiological Measurement* 33 (6): 1073.

**74** Patel, S., Hughes, R., Hester, T. et al. (2010). A novel approach to monitor rehabilitation outcomes in stroke survivors using wearable technology. *Proceedings of the IEEE* 98 (3): 450–461.

**75** Pierleoni, P., Belli, A., Palma, L. et al. (2015). A high reliability wearable device for elderly fall detection. *IEEE Sensors Journal* 15 (8): 4544–4553.

**76** Pons, J.L. (2010). Rehabilitation exoskeletal robotics. *IEEE Engineering in Medicine and Biology Magazine* 29 (3): 57–63.

**77** Price Waterhouse Coopers (2016). The Wearable Life 2.0: Connected Living in a Wearable World. *Technical Report*. https://www.pwc.com/ee/et/publications/pub/pwc-cis-wearables.pdf.

**78** Randriambelonoro, M., Chen, Y., and Pu, P. (2017). Can fitness trackers help diabetic and obese users make and sustain lifestyle changes? *Computer* 50 (3): 20–29.

**79** Reiss, A. (2014). Personalized mobile physical activity monitoring for everyday life. PhD thesis. Technical University of Kaiserslautern.

**80** Salarian, A., Russmann, H., Vingerhoets, F.J.G. et al. (2007). Ambulatory monitoring of physical activities in patients with Parkinson's disease. *IEEE Transactions on Biomedical Engineering* 54 (12): 2296–2299.

**81** Savaglio, C. and Fortino, G. (2021). A simulation-driven methodology for IoT data mining based on edge computing. *ACM Transactions on Internet Technology (TOIT)* 21 (2): Article No. 30, 1–22. https://doi.org/10.1145/3402444.

**82** Sazonov, E., Schuckers, S., Lopezmeyer, P. et al. (2008). Non-invasive monitoring of chewing and swallowing for objective quantification of ingestive behavior. *Physiological Measurement* 29 (5): 525–541.

**83** Sazonov, E.S., Makeyev, O., Schuckers, S. et al. (2010). Automatic detection of swallowing events by acoustical means for applications of monitoring of ingestive behavior. *IEEE Transactions on Biomedical Engineering* 57 (3): 626–633.

**84** Schmalstieg, D. and Höllerer, T. (2016). *Augmented Reality: Principles and Practice.* Addison-Wesley Professional.

**85** Seshadri, D.R., Drummond, C., Craker, J. et al. (2017). Wearable devices for sports. *IEEE Pulse* 8 (1): 38–43.

**86** Sha, K. and Shi, W. (2008). Consistency-driven data quality management of networked sensor systems. *Journal of Parallel and Distributed Computing* 68: 1207–1221.

**87** Smart, G., Deligiannis, N., Surace, R. et al. (2016). Decentralized time-synchronized channel swapping for ad hoc wireless networks. *IEEE Transactions on Vehicular Technology* 65 (10): 8538–8553.

**88** Soh, P.J., Vandenbosch, G.A.E., Mercuri, M., and Schreurs, D.M.M.-P. (2015). Wearable wireless health monitoring. *IEEE Microwave Magazine* 16 (4): 55–70.

**89** SPINE-BoK. https://projects.dimes.unical.it/spine-bok/ (accessed June 2022).

**90** Sun, M., Burke, L.E., Mao, Z.-H. et al. (2014). eButton: a wearable computer for health monitoring and personal assistance. *Design Automation Conference (DAC), 2014 51st ACM/EDAC/IEEE*, 1–6. IEEE.

**91** Tan, C.C., Wang, H., Zhong, S., and Li, Q. (2008). Body sensor network security: an identity-based cryptography approach. *1st ACM Conference on Wireless Network Security (WiSec'08)*, 148–153.

**92** Vitiello, N., Lenzi, T., Roccella, S. et al. (2013). NEUROExos: a powered elbow exoskeleton for physical rehabilitation. *IEEE Transactions on Robotics* 29 (1): 220–235.

**93** Wang, L., Gu, T., Tao, X., and Lu, J. (2017). Toward a wearable RFID system for real-time activity recognition using radio patterns. *IEEE Transactions on Mobile Computing* 16 (1): 228–242.

**94** Wikipedia, Watch 1505. https://en.wikipedia.org/wiki/Watch_1505 (accessed July 2022).

**95** World Health Organization (2014). *Global Status Report on Noncommunicable Diseases 2014*. Geneva: World Health Organization.

**96** Xiao, Z., Tan, X., Chen, X. et al. (2015). An implantable RFID sensor tag toward continuous glucose monitoring. *IEEE Journal of Biomedical and Health Informatics* 19 (3): 910–919.

**97** Yang, G.-Z. (ed.) (2006). *Body Sensor Networks.* Springer-Verlag.

**98** Yatani, K. and Truong, K.N. (2012). BodyScope: a wearable acoustic sensor for activity recognition. *Proceedings of the 2012 ACM Conference on Ubiquitous Computing*, 341–350. ACM.

**99** Young, A.J. and Ferris, D.P. (2017). State of the art and future directions for lower limb robotic exoskeletons. *IEEE Transactions on Neural Systems and Rehabilitation Engineering* 25 (2): 171–182.

**100** Zarepour, E., Hosseini, M., Kanhere, S.S. et al. (2017). Applications and challenges of wearable visual lifeloggers. *Computer* 50 (3): 60–69.

**101** Zhan, Y. and Kuroda, T. (2012). Wearable sensor-based human activity recognition from environmental background sounds. *Ambient Intelligence* 5 (1): 77–89.

**102** Zhang, X., Chen, X., Li, Y. et al. (2011). A framework for hand gesture recognition based on accelerometer and EMG sensors. *IEEE Transactions on Systems, Man, and Cybernetics-Part A: Systems and Humans* 41 (6): 1064–1076.

**103** Zhang, Q., Zeng, X., Hu, W., and Zhou, D. (2017). A machine learning-empowered system for long-term motion-tolerant wearable monitoring of blood pressure and heart rate with ear-ECG/PPG. *IEEE Access* 5: 10547–10561.

**104** Zheng, Y.-L., Yan, B.P., Zhang, Y.-T., and Poon, C.C.Y. (2014). An armband wearable device for overnight and cuff-less blood pressure measurement. *IEEE Transactions on Biomedical Engineering* 61 (7): 2179–2186.

# 30

# Multisensor Wearable Device for Monitoring Vital Signs and Physical Activity[1]

*Joshua Di Tocco[1*], Luigi Raiano[1*], Daniela lo Presti[1], Carlo Massaroni[1], Domenico Formica[2], and Emiliano Schena[1]*

[1] *Departmental Faculty of Engineering, Università Campus Bio-Medico di Roma, Rome, Italy*
[2] *School of Engineering, Newcastle University, Newcastle upon Tyne, UK*

## 30.1 Introduction

Wearable systems are an exciting opportunity to perform continuous and noninvasive monitoring of a variety of physiological parameters [23]. In addition, recent advances in fabrication techniques and transmission protocols are enabling the design of thin, comfortable, and robust wearables able to perform accurate estimation of physiological parameters [6]. In this scenario, wearables devoted to performing the measurement of two or more parameters (e.g., respiratory rate RR, heart rate, body temperature, and physical activities) are overcoming the main limitation of the systems able to measure only a single parameter at a time. An exciting challenge is to monitor physical activities and the related physiological changes which can provide a more complete picture of physiological mechanisms in different scenarios, ranging from elderly to clinical applications, to sport [14, 21]. In this chapter, we propose a wearable system designed to simultaneously monitor RR during physical activities. The principle of working the sensors used to instrument the wearable system is described. In addition, the system's feasibility has been evaluated in static condition, during walking and running.

## 30.2 Background

In this chapter, we proposed a multisensor approach for monitoring the health status of the body in terms of physiological and physical activities. The proposed multisensor wearable system embeds two modules based on piezoresistive sensors for monitoring RR and on a magneto-inertial measurements unit (M-IMU) for detecting joint angular velocities and accelerations.

### 30.2.1 Context

Physiological parameters are biomarkers of human health since any change in these functions could be a predictor of potential adverse conditions. In particular, RR is a crucial indicator of several

* Joshua Di Tocco and Luigi Raiano equally contributed
[1] Our chapter is chapter 30.

*Handbook of Human-Machine Systems*, First Edition. Edited by Giancarlo Fortino, David Kaber, Andreas Nürnberger, and David Mendonça.

pathological conditions affecting the cardiorespiratory system and stressors including emotional stress, physical effort, and exercise-induced fatigue [20]. Similarly, the analysis of human motion has served as a primary window into physical behavior, and by proxy, social function, psychology, and cognition. Joint angular velocities and accelerations are fundamental for analyzing movement tasks essential to daily life (e.g. walking and lifting) and sportive tasks (e.g. running and jump) [5].

### 30.2.2 Basic Definitions

Piezoresistive sensors can detect a mechanical deformation of the material structure by the change of their electrical resistance (ΔR). Their working principle can be summarized as follows (Equation (30.1)):

$$\frac{\Delta R}{R_0} = GF \cdot \epsilon \tag{30.1}$$

with $R_0$, the resistance in absence of strain, $\epsilon$ the strain, and GF is the gauge factor. Usually, GF is an important index of the sensor performance and high GF indicates high sensitivity [8]. Physiological activities can cause different body deformations or movements. For instance, chest movements induced by the breathing activity are bigger than the ones caused by the heart beating with consequent different ΔR caused by these two physiological activities. Therefore, material selection and structure optimization strategies have been investigated to improve this issue.

Generally, a piezoresistive sensor consists of a conductive layer combined with a stretchable substrate. The conductive element is often a metal component in the form of fiber, filament, or particle, while the stretchable material is an elastomeric yarn (e.g. nylon and spandex) to endow the sensor high elongation at break and fast recovery from high elongations [1, 8].

The M-IMUs integrate tri-axis orthogonally mounted sensors: an accelerometer which measures the linear accelerations, a gyroscope which measures the angular velocities, and a magnetometer which measures the magnetic field in the M-IMU coordinate systems [11].

Basically, an accelerometer can be represented by a mass ($m$) suspended by a spring with an elastic constant $k$. In case of an acceleration ($a$), $m$ moves from its initial position, and the spring is subjected to a displacement ($x$) [3] proportional to $a$, as described in Equation (30.2):

$$a = \frac{k \cdot x}{m} \tag{30.2}$$

Thanks to the advances of micro electromechanical systems (MEMS), miniaturized gyroscopes, and magnetometers have been also integrated into M-IMUs.

Gyroscopes consist of a vibrating element that, if subjected to a rotation, is also affected by a vibration in the direction orthogonal to the original one according to the Coriolis effect (Equation (30.3):

$$F_c = -2m(\omega \times v) \tag{30.3}$$

with $m$ the mass, $\omega$ the angular velocity of the object, $v$ the velocity of the object [7]. Similarly to the accelerometers, gyroscopes can measure $\omega$ since its rotation induces an additional vibration to m and so a displacement due to $F_c$.

The working principle of magnetometers exploit the Hall effect and the magneto-resistive effect. At the basis of both, there is the Lorentz force ($F_L$) expressed by (Equation (30.4)):

$$F_L = q(E + (v \times B)) \tag{30.4}$$

where $q$ is the charged particle, $E$ the electrical field, $v$ the velocity of $q$, and $B$ the magnetic field vector. The term $qE$ denotes the electric force and the term $qv \times B$ denotes the magnetic force [19].

Similarly, when B is applied perpendicularly to the surface of a conductor, charged particles of opposite sign of $q$ (electrons) move toward an edge of the conductor transversely to the current flow ($I$) producing a voltage ($V_h$) on the opposite faces of the conductor according to the Hall effect (Equation (30.5)):

$$V_h = \frac{IB}{nqd} \tag{30.5}$$

with $n$ the number of $q$ and $d$ the thickness of the conductor. Therefore, if the magnetometer changes orientation, also the magnetic field along the sensing axes changes [19].

Usually, magnetometers are integrated into M-IMUs to work together with the accelerometer for providing accurate estimation of an object orientation.

## 30.3 Related Work

With the advancement of technology, the number of interconnected devices for monitoring the human health has been growing dramatically empowered by the rapid proliferation of Internet of Things (IoT) in activities of daily living [4]. In this context, wearable devices are playing an increasingly important role in comfortable and long-term health monitoring. Recent research on wearable technologies and applications have led to a transition from single noninterconnected sensors to multisensor synchronous measurement environments [4]. Figure 30.1 shows an example of the multisensor system with the related architecture to support long-term and remote monitoring, data storage, and analysis. It is commonly known as a Body Sensors Network (BSN).

If on the one hand, such a change makes more complex the wearable network, since data from multiple and potentially heterogeneous sensors should be processed, fused together, streamed, and transmitted remotely, on the other hand, it allows a comprehensive monitoring of the human health [4, 15].

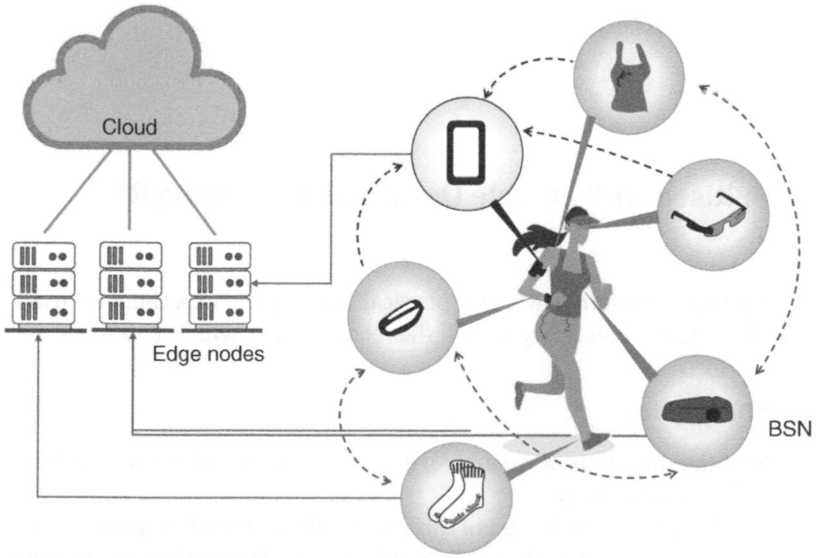


**Figure 30.1** Example of a BSN. Adapted from Freepik.com.

Detecting signals from multiple wearable systems often worn on different body segments can give more reliable information about the human health by leveraging complementary sources of information to characterize the human behavior and by enabling the implementation of strategies for artifact noise removal [9, 10]. For instance, as in the following use case, the development of multisensor wearable devices integrating piezoresistive sensors and M-IMUs has been proposed for the detection of activity and the continuous monitoring of a physiological parameter (i.e. RR) even under challenging conditions such as walking and running when motion artifacts occur [2, 12, 13, 18]. By exploiting data from M-IMUs, breathing unrelated movements can be discharged to reduce the motion influence on the RR measurement accuracy [12]. Investigating the influence of torso movements on the respiratory signals retrieved by multisensor wearable devices can optimize the design of wearable systems in terms of sensors number and position [13, 16]. Some studies proposed multiple sensors to be worn on thorax, on the abdomen, or on both to better assess the influence of sensors' number and position on the system performance. These studies are also useful to implement algorithms to automatically exclude the most motion-affected sensors and define the best subset of sensors for RR monitoring during physical activity [13].

| Author | Technology | Monitored Parameters |
|---|---|---|
| Di Tocco et al. [2] | Conductive textile sensor, M-IMU | RR[a], RP[b] |
| Li et al. [9] | ECG module, temperature sensor, motion sensor | ECG[c], HR[d], Body Temperature, Steps, distance |
| Lo Presti et al. [10] | FBG sensors | Neck FE[e], Neck AR[f], RR |
| Massaroni et al. [12] | Conductive textiles | RR |
| Massaroni et al. [13] | Conductive textiles, IMU | RR, Torso Rotation |
| Lo Presti et al. [16] | FBG | RR |
| Raiano et al. [18] | Conductive textiles, M-IMU | RR |

a) RR = Respiratory Rate
b) RP = Running Pace
c) ECG = Electrocardiography
d) HR = Heart Rate
e) FE = Flexion-Extension
f) AR = Axial Rotations

## 30.4 Case Study: Multisensor Wearable Device for Monitoring RR and Physical Activity

In this section, the modules used to monitor RR and physical activity, the experimental trials performed to test the modules, and the data analysis with the related results will be described.

### 30.4.1 Wearable Device Description

According to Figure 30.2(a), the multisensor wearable device is capable of retrieving both breathing-related activity and physical activity.

It has been already presented in [2], and in the rest of this paragraph, we report its main characteristics. Even though the device is characterized by two submodules, one dedicated for monitoring RR and the other one for monitoring the physical activity, they use a common Printed Circuit Board

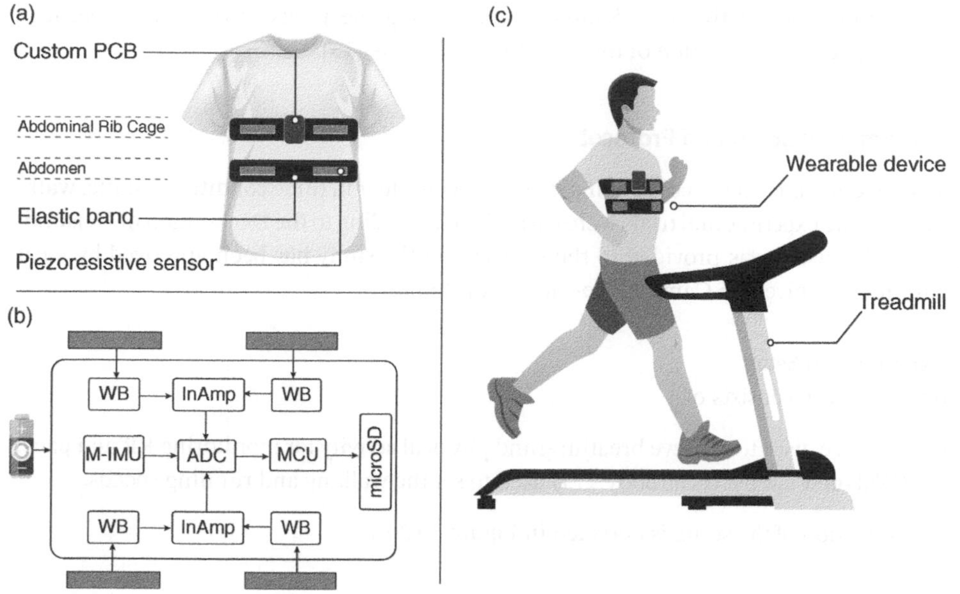


**Figure 30.2** (a) Wearable device architecture based on four piezoresistive sensors, two elastic bands, and a PCB. (b) Schematic representation of the custom designed PCB. (c) Overview of the experimental setup. Adapted from Freepik.com.

(PCB). It embeds a microcontroller unit (MCU, STM32F446 by STMicroelectronics Inc.) which is in charge of collecting the signals and store them into a microSD card with a sampling rate of 100 Hz. The entire device is battery-powered using a 3.7 V 750 mAh Li-Po battery which guarantees a continuous operation time of approximately eight hours. In addition, a custom TPU case has been 3D-printed for the PCB and battery placement.

#### 30.4.1.1 Module for the Estimation of RR

The RR is estimated from the output of four piezoresistive sensors stitched on two elastic bands, located on abdominal rib cage and abdomen pulmonary compartments. Each band includes two sensors, which are strained accordingly to the user's breathing activity, which determines the resistance variation of the sensors. In addition, the elastic bands are adaptable to the subjects' anthropometry with the integrated Velcro strips. The choice of locating four sensors on both sides of the user's is twofold: (i) it allows implementing a compartmental monitoring [22], and (ii) it guarantees a correct RR estimation in static, walking, and running trials [17].

The output of the piezoresistive sensors is collected by the PCB. It includes four Wheatstone Bridges (WBs) used for transducing the resistance of the sensors into a voltage, along with four instrumentation amplifiers (InAmp). Each signal is then digitized using a dedicated 12-bit Analog-to-Digital Converted (ADC) and finally collected by the embedded MCU.

#### 30.4.1.2 Module for the Estimation of Physical Activity

The physical activity is estimated on the basis of a M-IMU (LSM9Ds1 by STMicroelectronics Inc.) embedded in the PCB. The M-IMU allows recording inertial information of the user during physical activity, in terms of linear acceleration and angular velocity. According to Figure 30.2(b), given the specific orientation of the PCB, by analyzing the signal related to the $y$-axis of the embedded accelerometer in the frequency domain, it is possible to obtain information regarding the walking/running pace of the user. Similarly, considering the $y$-axis of the gyroscope, it is possible to estimate the torso rotation of the user during the task [13].

### 30.4.2 Experimental Setup and Protocol

The proposed system has been tested on a single healthy volunteer in three conditions: static, walking, and running. The experimental trials were carried out according to the Declaration of Helsinki. Written informed consent was provided to the subject and the study has been approved by local Ethics Committee of Universitá Campus Bio-Medico di Roma.

#### 30.4.2.1 Experimental Setup

The experimental setup consists of

- the wearable device, used to retrieve breathing and physical activity for monitoring RR and pace;
- a treadmill (Walker-View by TecnoBody s.r.l) used to set the walking and running speeds.

A graphical description of the setup is depicted in Figure 30.2(c).

#### 30.4.2.2 Experimental Protocol

The experimental protocol consists in three consecutive trials:

1. *Static trial* – The subject is asked to stand still and breathe for 1 min;
2. *Walking trial* – The subject is asked to walk on the treadmill at 3 $km \cdot h^{-1}$;
3. *Running trial* – The subject is asked to run on the treadmill at 12 $km \cdot h^{-1}$;

The duration of both the walking and the running trials is equal to 2 min.

### 30.4.3 Data Analysis

To extract from the collected data, the average RR and the average walking/running pace, data have been processed in MATLAB™ environment using a frequency-based method. First, a filtering stage consisting of a third-order Butterworth bandpass filter was implemented. Cutoff frequency bands of 0.05–2 Hz and 0.05–5 Hz were used for the respiratory signals and the M-IMU signals, respectively. Then, the average respiratory signal was calculated from the four piezoresistive sensors' signals. Finally, the Power Spectral Density (PSD) of the signals was computed using pwelch estimator. The average RR ($RR_{avg}$) was obtained by considering the maximum peak of the PSD performed on the respiratory signal and multiplying it by 60 (to obtain the RR in bpm –breaths per minute). On the other hand, the average pace ($RP_{avg}$) was obtained by considering the maximum peak of the PSD performed on the $Y$-axis of the accelerometer of the M-IMU (vertical direction) and multiplying it by 60.

### 30.4.4 Results

From the performed analysis, the volunteer showed an $RR_{avg}$ of ~11.5 bpm in the static trial, an $RR_{avg}$ of ~10.6 bpm in the walking trial and an $RR_{avg}$ of ~22.9 bpm in the running trial. Figure 30.3 shows the PSD plots obtained for the three trials. The small difference between the static trial and the walking trial compared to the running trial highlights how the RR is affected by the effort made by the volunteer in performing the selected tasks.

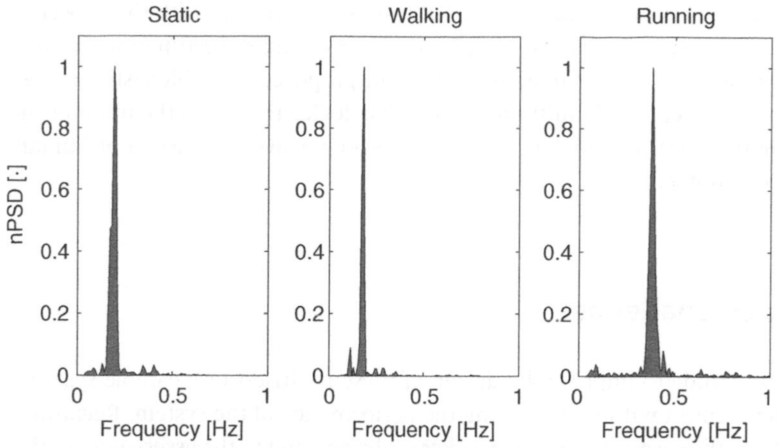


**Figure 30.3** Normalized PSD of the respiratory signal in the three trials.

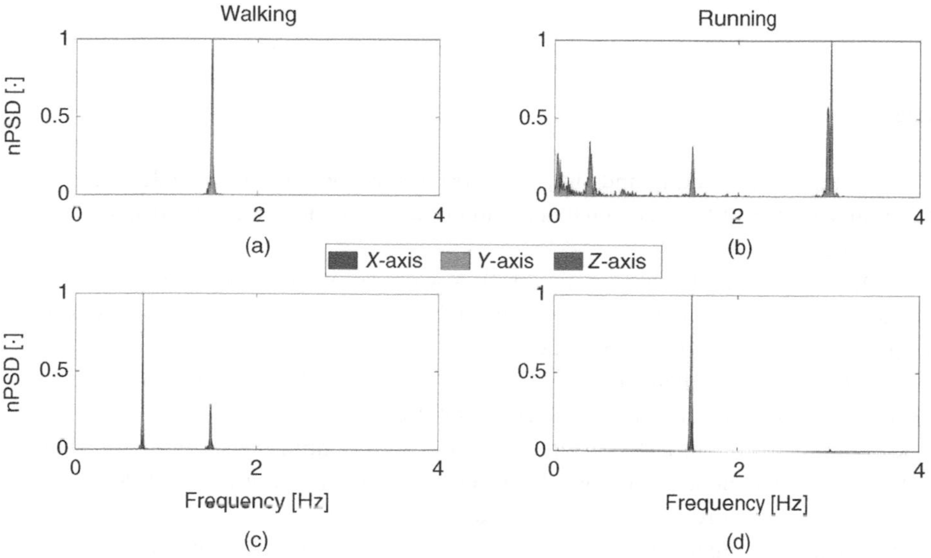


**Figure 30.4** Normalized PSD of the *Y*-Axis of the accelerometer in walking (a) and running (b) trials. Normalized PSD of all the gyroscope axes in walking (c) and running (d) trials.

Concerning the physical activity, the volunteer showed an $RP_{avg}$ of ~90.0 spm (steps per minute) for the walking trial and an $RP_{avg}$ of ~182.9 spm for the running trial. The PSD was not calculated for the static trial due to the absence of movement. Figure 30.4 shows the PSD plots obtained for the three trials.

## 30.5 Conclusions

The multisensor system described in this chapter is an example that fuses the measurement of a physiological parameter sensitive to a variety of stressors (i.e. RR) with the estimation of physical activity into a single wearable device. The wearable testing on a healthy volunteer in a realistic scenario considering three conditions revealed that the RR values were in-line with the expected results (during running RR increased in response to a physical stress), and the estimation was not adversely affected by the potential presence of motion artifact. The proposed wearable system represents a relevant first step in the research of multisensor wearable device that fuses the monitoring of physical activity and physiological parameters for more comprehensive knowledge of human response to exercise-induced fatigue.

## 30.6 Future Research Challenges

Future research challenges include to improve the design of these multisensor wearable systems to ensure wearer safety and comfort without impairing the performance of the system. Regarding the wearable system shown in the case study, future works will be devoted to the assessment of the accuracy of RR estimation and to the integration of sensors allowing a more comprehensive analysis of wearer response to the physical activity by measuring additional physiological parameters (e.g. heart rate).

## References


1 Amjadi, M., Kyung, K.-U., Park, I., and Sitti, M. (2016). Stretchable, skin-mountable, and wearable strain sensors and their potential applications: a review. *Advanced Functional Materials* 26 (11): 1678–1698.

2 Di Tocco, J., Massaroni, C., Raiano, L. et al. (2020). A wearable system for respiratory and pace monitoring in running activities: a feasibility study. *2020 IEEE International Workshop on Metrology for Industry 4.0 & IoT*, 44–48. IEEE.

3 Ferrero, R., Gandino, F., and Hemmatpour, M. (2019). Estimation of displacement for Internet of Things applications with Kalman filter. *Electronics* 8 (9): 985.

4 Gravina, R., Alinia, P., Ghasemzadeh, H., and Fortino, G. (2017). Multi-sensor fusion in body sensor networks: state-of-the-art and research challenges. *Information Fusion* 35: 68–80.

5 Homayounfar, S.Z. and Andrew, T.L. (2020). Wearable sensors for monitoring human motion: a review on mechanisms, materials, and challenges. *SLAS TECHNOLOGY: Translating Life Sciences Innovation* 25 (1): 9–24.

6 Imani, S., Bandodkar, A.J., Mohan, A.M.V. et al. (2016). A wearable chemical–electrophysiological hybrid biosensing system for real-time health and fitness monitoring. *Nature Communications* 7 (1): 1–7.

7 Jose, K.A., Suh, W.D., Xavier, P.B. et al. (2002). Surface acoustic wave MEMS gyroscope. *Wave Motion* 36 (4): 367–381.

8 Li, Y., Chen, W., and Lu, L. (2020). Wearable and biodegradable sensors for human health monitoring. *ACS Applied Bio Materials* 4 (1): 122–139.

9 Li, H., Sun, G., Li, Y., and Yang, R. (2021). Wearable wireless physiological monitoring system based on multi-sensor. *Electronics* 10 (9): 986.

10 Lo Presti, D., Carnevale, A., D'Abbraccio, J. et al. (2020). A multi-parametric wearable system to monitor neck movements and respiratory frequency of computer workers. *Sensors* 20 (2): 536.

11 Lopez-Nava, I.H. and Munoz-Melendez, A. (2016). Wearable inertial sensors for human motion analysis: a review. *IEEE Sensors Journal* 16 (22): 7821–7834.

**12** Massaroni, C., Di Tocco, J., Bravi, M. et al. (2019). Respiratory monitoring during physical activities with a multi-sensor smart garment and related algorithms. *IEEE Sensors Journal* 20 (4): 2173–2180.

**13** Massaroni, C., Di Tocco, J., Sabbadini, R. et al. (2020). Influence of torso movements on a multi-sensor garment for respiratory monitoring during walking and running activities. *2020 IEEE International Instrumentation and Measurement Technology Conference (I2MTC)*, 1–6. IEEE.

**14** Nicolò, A., Massaroni, C., Schena, E., and Sacchetti, M. (2020). The importance of respiratory rate monitoring: from healthcare to sport and exercise. *Sensors* 20 (21): 6396.

**15** Ometov, A., Shubina, V., Klus, L. et al. (2021). A survey on wearable technology: history, state-of-the-art and current challenges. *Computer Networks* 193: 108074.

**16** Presti, L., Massaroni, C., Saccomandi, P. et al. (2017). A wearable textile for respiratory monitoring: feasibility assessment and analysis of sensors position on system response. *Annual International Conference of the IEEE Engineering in Medicine and Biology Society. IEEE Engineering in Medicine and Biology Society. Annual International Conference*, volume 2017, 4423–4426.

**17** Raiano, L., Di Tocco, J., Massaroni, C. et al. (2020). A PCA-based method to select the number and the body location of piezoresistive sensors in a wearable system for respiratory monitoring. *IEEE Sensors Journal* 21 (5): 6847–6855.

**18** Raiano, L., Di Tocco, J., Massaroni, C. et al. (2021). Respiratory rate estimation during walking/running activities using principal components estimated from signals recorded by a smart garment embedding piezoresistive sensors. *2021 IEEE International Workshop on Metrology for Industry 4.0 & IoT (MetroInd4. 0&IoT)*, 544–549. IEEE.

**19** Ren, D., Wu, L., Yan, M. et al. (2009). Design and analyses of a MEMS based resonant magnetometer. *Sensors* 9 (9): 6951–6966.

**20** Seshadri, D.R., Li, R.T., Voos, J.E. et al. (2019). Wearable sensors for monitoring the physiological and biochemical profile of the athlete. *NPJ Digital Medicine* 2 (1): 1–16.

**21** Tatterson, A.J., Hahn, A.G., Martini, D.T., and Febbraio, M.A. (2000). Effects of heat stress on physiological responses and exercise performance in elite cyclists. *Journal of Science and Medicine in Sport* 3 (2): 186–193.

**22** Wilson, T.A. (1988). Mechanics of compartmental models of the chest wall. *Journal of Applied Physiology* 65 (5): 2261–2264.

**23** Yeo, J.C. and Lim, C.T. (2016). Emerging flexible and wearable physical sensing platforms for healthcare and biomedical applications. *Microsystems & Nanoengineering* 2 (1): 1–19.

# 31

# Integration of Machine Learning with Wearable Technologies

*Darius Nahavandi, Roohallah Alizadehsani, and Abbas Khosravi*

*Institute for Intelligent Systems Research and Innovation (IISRI), Deakin University, Waurn Ponds, VIC, Australia*

## 31.1 Introduction

Wearables are among the state-of-the-art technologies which can be used for data collection and processing needed in different applications. The wearables can help people to experience a better life. For example, some wearables can provide medical data which can be used for diagnosis and even treatment of some physiological problems. An essential requirement in developing wearable devices is their miniaturization. In addition, the capability of adding artificial intelligence algorithms can improve their performance in real-time medical cares. These devices can be used as contact interfaces for biochemical or electrophysiological signal collection.

Figure 31.1 [33] illustrates the processing cycle of wearables. The first step is data collection. The collected data (Figure 31.1) are preprocessed locally or in a cloud service. The collected data contain errors, duplicate information, or they may be even incomplete. To have acceptable quality, the data must be filtered and organized. Data filtering reduces processing time and improves the processing output which is beneficial since wearables storage capacity and computational power are limited.

The third step in Figure 31.1 is data transfer. Wearables apply data compression to reduce the amount of data transfer which in turn reduces the wearable power consumption during the transfer. Early wearables were only used as data collectors. The collected data were then postprocessed by connecting wearables to external computers. Today, wearables usually rely on computing paradigms such as cloud computing (Section 31.2.6), edge computing (Section 31.2.7), and fog computing to carry out the necessary data processing. Due to the centralized nature of cloud services and the increasing number of mobile devices like wearables, the bandwidth of cloud infrastructure will become a bottleneck leading to unacceptable lag time. Combining the edge and cloud computing reduces the lag time.

In the data processing step of Figure 31.1, machine learning methods are employed. Wearables data are mostly time series which are used for various tasks such as classification and forecasting. The patterns present in time-series data can be captured by deep learning (DL) methods (Section 31.2.4) such as CNN, multilayer perceptron multilayer perceptron (MLP), LSTM, gated recurrent unit (GRU), Bidirectional LSTM [17], etc.

*Handbook of Human-Machine Systems*, First Edition. Edited by Giancarlo Fortino, David Kaber, Andreas Nürnberger, and David Mendonça.

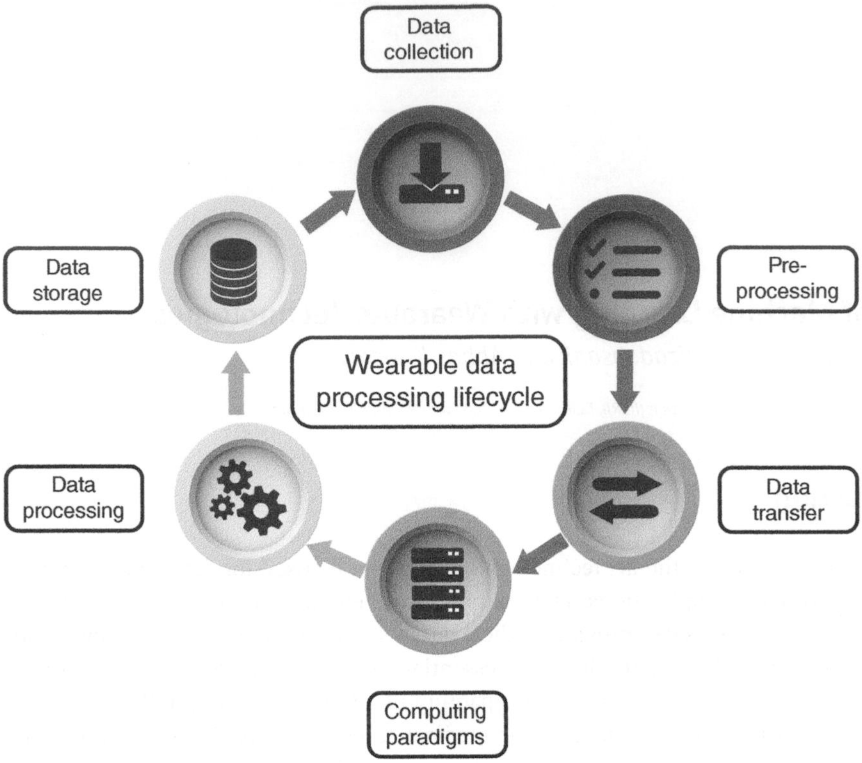


**Figure 31.1** Data processing life cycle of wearables.

## 31.2 Background

### 31.2.1 History of Wearables

As shown in Figure 31.2 (inspired by Ometov et al. [33]), wearables have been around longer than one can imagine. The earliest wearables are eyeglasses and pocket watch which predate the twentieth century. In the early twentieth century, the first-ever portable camera was invented by Julius Neubronner. The camera was attached to a pigeon, and it was probably used for aerial surveillance during the World War I. Portable radio communication and wristwatches with military applications also belong to early twentieth century. By the middle of the twentieth century, smartwatch and portable audio devices such as Sony Walkman were released. In the late twentieth century, augmented reality headset, location tracker, personal digital assistant, etc., were developed. At the beginning of the twenty-first century, wireless headset, activity tracker, Google Glass, etc., were released.

### 31.2.2 Supervised Learning

Supervised learning can handle both classification and regression problems. In classification, the job of the learner is to distinguish the class to which each input sample belongs Consider the example in Figure 31.3a. As can be seen the training samples represent pictures of cats and dogs. Each sample is accompanied with appropriate label (CAT or DOG). Given these data, the model must learn to distinguish dogs from cats. An example of supervised regression problem is also

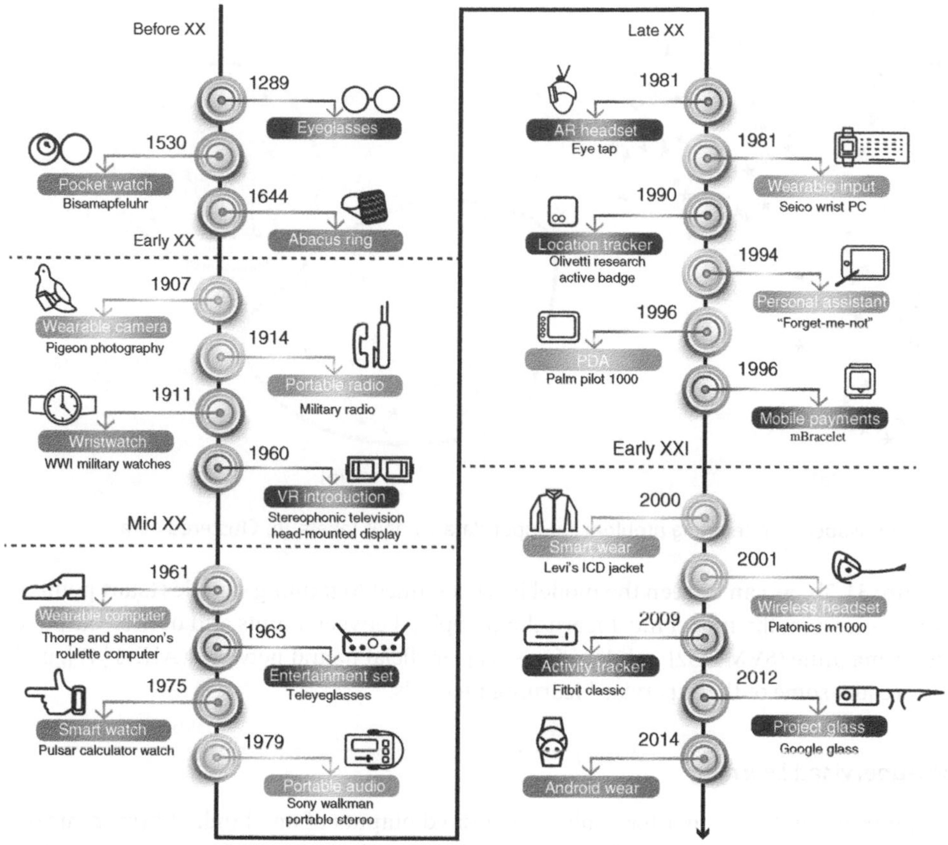


**Figure 31.2** Evolution of wearables through time.

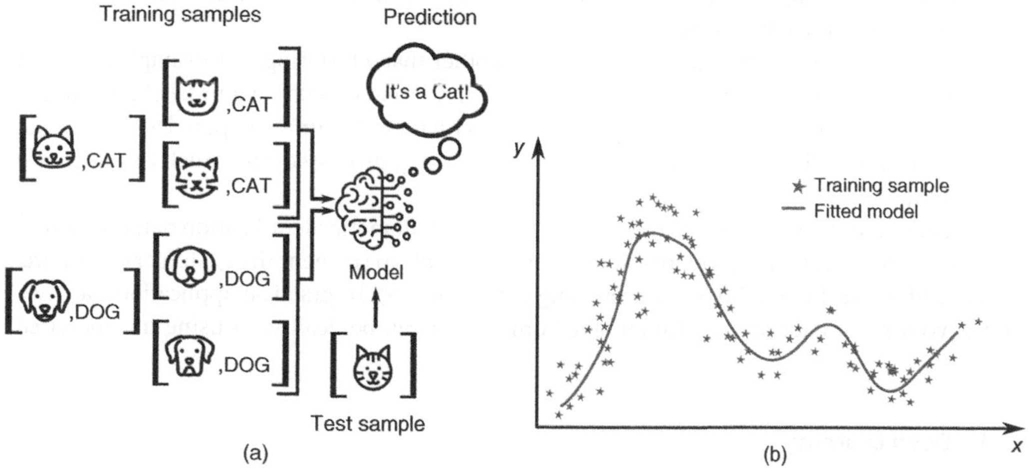


**Figure 31.3** Examples of supervised learning: (a) supervised classification problem: the model must learn to distinguish dogs from cats, (b) a supervised regression problem: the model must learn to predict appropriate $y$ values for input $x$ values.

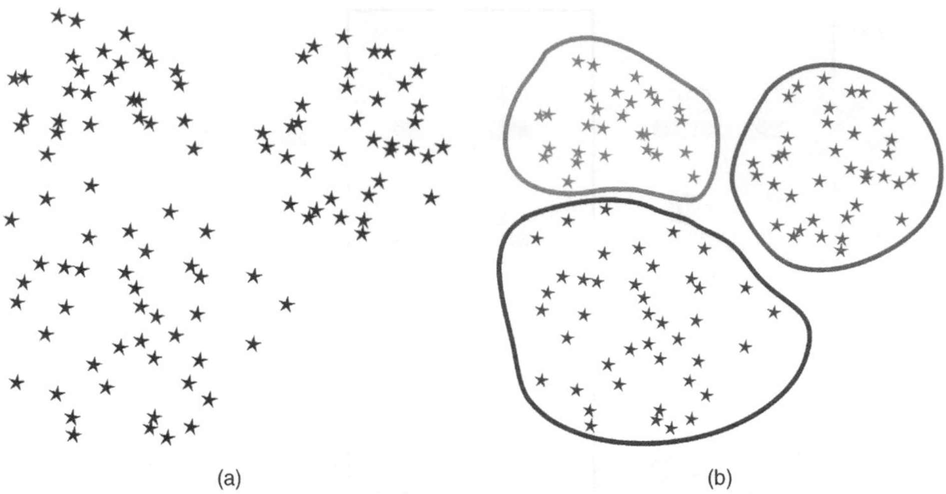


**Figure 31.4** An unsupervised learning problem: (a) Input data without labels, (b) Clustered data.

shown in Figure 31.3b. As can be seen the model has been fitted to training samples (start points). In supervised regression, the model must learn the mapping between inputs and desired outputs. Support vector machine (SVM) [32], random forest [7], artificial neural network (ANN) [47], and Naïve Bayes are just some of the supervised learning methods.

### 31.2.3 Unsupervised Learning

Sometimes the training data do not have labels or desired outputs of any kind. However, meaningful patterns may be present among the data. Unsupervised learning methods can be used to identify these patterns without reliance on any label or desired output. In Figure 31.4, an example of unsupervised learning is shown. In Figure 31.4a, the input data are not labeled. However, a clear pattern is present among the data. Using clustering approach, the data are clustered into three clusters which are shown in Figure 31.4b.

There are various unsupervised learning methods other than clustering. For example principal component analysis (PCA) can be used to reduce the dimension of data. In a nutshell, the aim of dimensionality reduction is the representation of data with fewer features compared to the original representation. After dimensionality reduction, the data can be processed with much less-intensive solutions [46].

Considering that unsupervised learning can be used for automatic identification of the structure of data, it can be useful for exploratory analysis. For example to segment the customers of a store, unsupervised clustering methods are promising candidates [6]. In practical applications, analyzing large volume of data may be tedious for humans but can be dealt with using unsupervised approaches.

### 31.2.4 Deep Learning

One of the relatively new fields in machine learning is deep learning which relies on convolutional neural networks (CNNs). The CNN performs dot product (convolution) between the input image and a special 2D array called a kernel [27]. The kernel size is usually smaller than the input image. The convolution of an image with a kernel is depicted in Figure 31.5. As can be seen, the kernel has

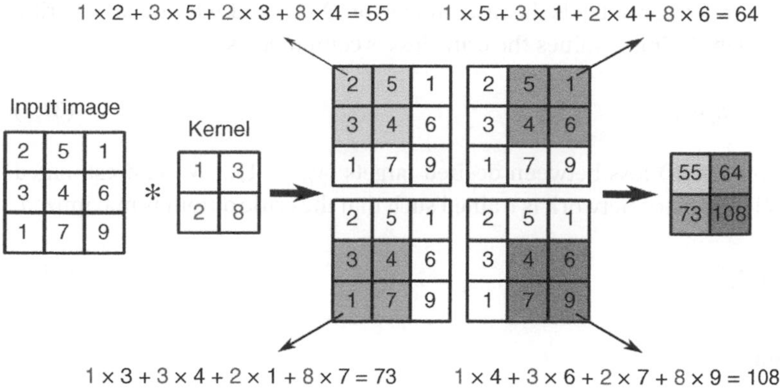


**Figure 31.5** Illustration of convolving a 3 × 3 image with a 2 × 2 kernel.

been applied four times on different patches of the input image. The four patches have the same dimension as the kernel. Applying the kernel to the image yields a new matrix called the feature map with values 55, 64, 73, 108. The computation of values in feature map is shown in Figure 31.5. In convolutional layers, after computing the feature map, it is passed through a nonlinearity such as ReLU.[1] Thanks to the convolutional layers, CNNs are able to extract important features from the input images.

### 31.2.5 Deep Deterministic Policy Gradient

Deep deterministic policy gradient (DDPG) [29] is a reinforcement learning (RL) approach that can perform learning in continuous state and action spaces. DDPG consists of actor neural networks ($\mu(s)$, $\mu'(s)$) and critic neural networks ($Q(s, a)$, $Q'(s, a)$). The actor network $\mu(s)$ selects appropriate action $a$ based on input state $s$. Critic network $Q(s, a)$ estimates the value of taking action $a$ in state $s$. In RL settings, the desired outputs for training actor and critic networks are not available, but it is still possible to achieve stable training for actor and critic networks. To this end, these networks are cloned as $\mu'(s)$ and $Q'(s, a)$ which are called target actor and target critic, respectively. The job of target networks is tracking the changes of their counterparts (i.e. $\mu(s)$ and $Q(s, a)$) very slowly during learning. To update $Q(s, a)$, the outputs of target networks are assumed to be the desired values. Since the parameters of target networks change very slowly, such assumption is valid and leads to stabilized training of actor and critic networks even though the actual true values for their training are not known.

The update rule of critic network is given in Figure 31.6. In this figure, $y_i$ is the desired target, $r_i$ is the reward for i-th training sample $(s_i, a_i, r_i, s_i')$, $d_i$ is a Boolean flag which specifies whether i-th

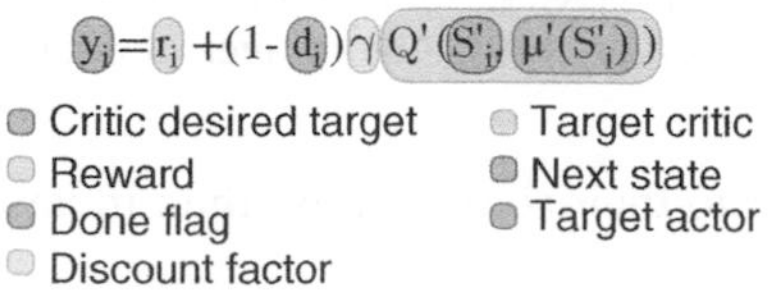


**Figure 31.6** DDPG critic target computation.

1 Rectified Linear Unit.

sample is the last sample of a rollout or not. $\gamma$ is the discount factor. $Q'(.,.)$ and $\mu'(.)$ are target critic and actor networks, respectively. Using $y_i$ values the critic loss is computed as

$$loss_Q = \frac{1}{N}\sum_{i=1}^{N}\left[y_i - Q(s_i, a_i)\right]^2, \tag{31.1}$$

which is mean squared error (MSE) loss between desired targets $\{y_i, i = 1, \ldots, N\}$ and estimated values $\{Q(s_i, a_i), i = 1, \ldots, N\}$. The actor network is trained such that the critic output is maximized,

$$loss_\mu = -\frac{1}{N}\sum_{i=1}^{N} Q(s_i, \mu(s_i)). \tag{31.2}$$

### 31.2.6 Cloud Computing

Cloud computing makes data storage and processing possible across a network of remote servers known as the "cloud." Therefore, cloud users are no longer bound to the storage and processing power of their personal devices. Data stored on cloud servers can be accessed from anywhere via the Internet regardless of the users locations and devices they use [43]. A schematic of a cloud service has been shown in Figure 31.7a. As can be seen, there are multiple centralized cloud servers which offer storage and processing services to the users (clients) over the Internet. The users may access these services via web browsers or mobile applications [15]. At first glance, cloud computing seems to be a good solution which meets the requirements of implementing a network of wearables. The centralized architecture of cloud computing is cost-effective but fails to provide the bandwidth required by vast number of IoT and mobile devices. Moreover, some of smart devices can operate without cloud computing. To avoid the back and forth data transfer between the devices and the cloud servers, edge computing can be used [15].

### 31.2.7 Edge Computing

Edge computing can alleviate the shortcoming of cloud computing by providing faster response time. In edge computing, connected devices (known as "edges") are able to process data closer to where they are generated. The processing can be done either within the devices (motors, pumps, etc.), or close to them leading to reduced data transfer between the devices and the could servers [39].

Edge computing utilizes a large, distributed network of much smaller data nodes (compared to cloud servers) to reduce latency. Therefore, the need to store and process large volume of data located in remote data centers is lifted [38].

Fog computing lies between edge devices and the cloud. Edge computing is the complement of cloud computing and works very closely with fog computing. The relation between cloud, fog, and edge computing has been depicted in Figure 31.7b. The number of edge devices and fog nodes is much higher than cloud servers. Therefore, local processing of data using fog and edge computing can significantly reduce the processing load on cloud servers. Using edge and fog computing also reduces data transfer traffic on the network connected to cloud servers [49]. Advantages of edge computing are summarized as below [38]:

- Data are processed faster since the processing is done closer to their source rather than in an external data center or cloud.
- Edge computing reduces the load on the cloud servers by performing a considerable amount of computations locally.
- Thanks to the lower latency of edge computing, applications can operate more efficiently and have a faster response time.

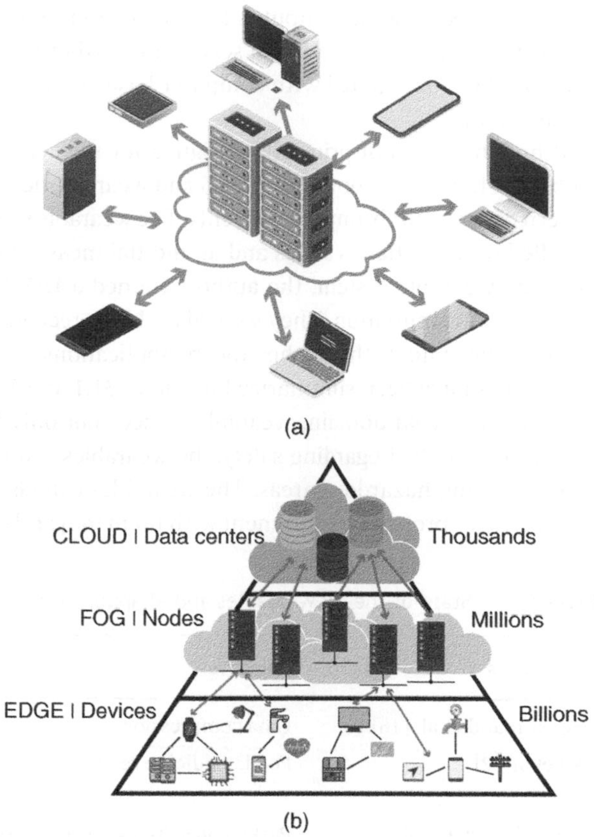


**Figure 31.7** Technologies used for wearables data storage and processing: (a) Illustration of cloud computing infrastructure, (b) The relation between cloud computing, fog computing, and edge computing.

Drawback of edge computing is the difficulty of keeping the balance between amount of local processing by edge devices and cloud processing done remotely. Depending on the situation, it may be more cost-effective to process data locally or remotely on the cloud servers [39].

## 31.3 State of the Art

Nowadays, wearable devices are used in various application domains. However, wearables play more important roles in medical and industrial domains. Wearables can improve the quality of healthcare services significantly. For example, vital signs of elderly people must be under constant supervision in order to take necessary actions, for example in case of heart attack or stroke. Moreover, wearable devices can be used to remind elderly people to take their medications on time. Wearable devices make noninvasive and cost-effective collection of biomedical signals such as blood pressure and electrocardiogram (ECG). However, due to limited battery capacity of wearables, it is necessary to reduce the data size before their transmission. Utilizing unsupervised learning is a promising approach to perform data compression [16].

Wearable devices can play major role in monitoring and treatment of chronic diseases. In [2], a recommendation system based on type-2 Fuzzy has been proposed for recommending appropriate food and medicine regiments based on patient's health condition. In this approach, data fed to the recommendation system were captured using wearable devices. As another example, in [8], patient's speech data were captured using smartwatch. K-means clustering was used to discover speech data patterns of patients suffering from Parkinson's disease (PD). The analysis of these data was performed on a fog computer. In case of observing unusual change in the speech patterns, the results were uploaded to a cloud service for further investigation of a clinician. Wearable devices have also been integrated with computer-based clinical decision support systems to track various diseases [48].

Although RL is not primarily designed for medical applications, it has been used in medical problems. In [53], the power of DDPG and wearable devices were combined to analyze the walking pattern of lower-limb amputee patients. The wearable system consisted of multiple pressure sensors installed in the patient's shoes and an inertial measurement unit (IMU). Using the data collected from the wearable system, the authors trained a DDPG agent to imitate the walking pattern of the patient in simulation. They were also able to recognize different walking modes of the patient. Some of the state-of-the-art healthcare applications of wearable devices in combination with AI approaches have been summarized in Tables 31.1 and 31.2.

In the industrial domain, wearable devices not only improve workers safety but also improve their productivity. Regarding safety, the wearables can track the workers position and warn them about entering hazardous areas. The wearables can also be used to make sure that workers have the necessary protective equipment with them [40] and comply with ergonomic regulations. Using

**Table 31.1** State-of-the-art wearables and AI applications in healthcare.

| References | Objective | Approach |
|---|---|---|
| Hooshmand et al. [16] | Data compression | Unsupervised learning |
| Ali et al. [2] | Food, medicine regiment | Type-2 fuzzy recommendation system |
| Borthakur et al. [8] | Parkinson's disease speech monitoring | K-means clustering, Fog/Cloud computing |
| Yin and Jha [48] | Disease monitoring | Wearable integration with clinical decision support systems |
| Zheng et al. [53] | Walking pattern imitation of lower-limb amputee patients | DDPG, IMU and pressure sensors |
| D'Haese et al. [11] | Prediction of viral symptoms | Rule-based approach |
| Klaynin et al. [19] | Cardiovascular diagnosis | Neural network, Electrocardiogram |
| Saini et al. [37] | Cardiovascular diagnosis | K-Nearest Neighbor, Electrocardiogram |
| Tripathy et al. [42] | Cardiovascular diagnosis | Support vector machine, Electrocardiogram |
| Gawande and Barhatte [13] | Cardiovascular diagnosis | Neural network, Electrocardiogram |
| Barhatte et al. [5] | Cardiovascular diagnosis | Support vector machine, Electrocardiogram |
| Debnath et al. [10] | Cardiovascular diagnosis | Neural network, Electrocardiogram |
| Sabeeha and Shiny [36] | Hypertrophic cardiomayopathy | Support vector machine, Electrocardiogram |

**Table 31.2** The rest of Table 31.1.

| References | Objective | Approach |
|---|---|---|
| Acharya et al. [1] | Cardiac abnormalities | Neural network, Electrocardiogram |
| Mohebbi et al. [31] | Diabetes diagnosis | Convolutional neural network, continuous glucose monitoring sensor |
| Hamdi et al. [14] | Diabetes diagnosis | Neural network, Continuous glucose monitoring sensor |
| Hamdi et al. [45] | Glycemic variability | Naïve Bayes,Continuous glucose monitoring sensor |
| Wang et al. [44] | Diabetes diagnosis | AdaBoost, Continuous glucose monitoring sensor |
| Reymann et al. [35] | Diabetes diagnosis | Support vector machine, Continuous glucose monitoring sensor |
| Zhao and He [51] | Alzheimer diagnosis | Support vector machine, Electroencephalography |
| Kim and Kim [18] | Alzheimer diagnosis | Neural network, Electroencephalography |
| Artuğ et al. [3] | Neuromuscular diagnosis | K-Nearest Neighbour, Electromyography |
| Baby et al. [4] | Parkinson's diagnosis | Naïve Bayes, accelerometer |
| Yu et al. [50] | Parkinson's diagnosis | Neural network, accelerometer |
| McGinnis et al. [30] | Depression diagnosis | K-Nearest Neighbour, accelerometer |

wearable devices such as IMUs, it is possible to monitor the postural patterns of workers during lifting/releasing loads and prevent work-related injuries due to inappropriate postures. To this end, in [9], workers were equipped with eight wireless IMUs to record their movement. A SVM was trained on captured kinematics parameters. The SVM was able to distinguish healthy and harmful postures of workers.

Regarding improving productivity by using wearables in industrial environments, the effect of using wearables for quality assurance in car assembly lines has been investigated [21]. This way, the routine checks which may be tedious and time-consuming are significantly shortened. Another example of using wearable in industrial domain is reported in [22]. Complexity of current assembly lines is beyond the capabilities of current robotic systems. Therefore, human element cannot be removed from the assembly lines. However, as reported in a case study in [22], wearables can assist the human operators during assembly. In this case study, the human operator had to connect plugs correctly. Such a process is prone to errors. To provide a fail-safe assembly routine, the human operator wore a device on his/her wrist that detects whether the plugs are connected properly or not. To this end, a CNN was trained on acoustic signals captured by a noise sensor during the assembly process.

In the Industry 4.0 paradigm [26], workers must be connected to cyber-physical systems (CPS). To this end, human activity recognition (HAR) is required which is realized based on acceleration

**Table 31.3** State-of-the-art wearables and AI applications in industry.

| References | Objective | Approach |
|---|---|---|
| Conforti et al. [9] | Healthy/harmful worker postures classification | SVM, eight IMUs |
| Kong et al. [21] | Efficient car assembly line quality assurance | Replacing paper-based workflow |
| Krenzer et al. [22] | Fail-safe assembly routine | CNN for acoustic signal capturing during assembly process, wrist-worn wearable |
| Zheng et al. [52] | Human activity recognition | Deep learning |
| Lara and Labrador [25] | HAR | Semi-supervised learning |
| Li et al. [28] | Secure home monitoring | Deep learning |

data collected by wearable sensors. DL has shown good performance in HAR problems [52]. Despite being powerful, DL models need huge amount of training data to reach their expected performance. Data collection capability of wearable devices is limited due to their battery constraints. Even if sufficient amount of training data is collected, their labeling requires considerable amount of time. Under such conditions, semisupervised learning is able to make use of limited amount of labeled samples and large amount of unlabeled ones to keep the labeling cost manageable. An example of using semisupervised learning is in HAR task [25]. The summary of some of the state-of-the-art industrial applications of wearable devices aided with AI approaches have been presented in Table 31.3.

## 31.4 Future Research Challenges

The motivation behind the development of wearables is the provision of specific services anytime, anywhere and to anyone. To realize such a goal, several challenges such as data storage and data processing, data anonymity, etc., must be addressed [12].

Constantly growing number of wearables demands faster connectivity (e.g. 5G). However, faster connections is only part of the solution. Traditionally, wearables data processing used to be done on centralized cloud servers. This approach faces two major problems: (i) data processing latency may be high; (ii) data transmission between wearables and cloud servers increases the network load. Edge computing can remedy this issue. However, as a wearable user moves from one geographical location to another, the services provided to the user must migrate from one Edge server to another. As the user gets farther away from the current Edge server, keeping the services on that server may lead to higher data transmission latency. On the other hand, migrating the services to another server puts some overhead on the network. Currently, ensuring efficient and seamless migration among Edge servers based on user location is still an open problem [33].

During data processing phase, heterogeneous data collected from different wearable devices can be combined to achieve higher-quality results. There are few works on disease diagnosis based on fusion of multimodal wearable data such as [20, 24, 34]. However, as pointed out in [33], there is still a huge research gap in this field which leaves many opportunities for future researches.

Wearable devices collect various data types such as users' locations, physical activity level, and biometric data. These data are considered sensitive so enforcing security and privacy of data collected by wearable devices is crucial. Data encryption can be employed to protect these data. However, given the limited processing power and battery capacity of wearable devices, running complex cryptographic operations on wearables is not practical. Therefore, devising lightweight cryptography methods suitable for execution on wearables is desirable.

In scenarios that connection availability is poor, mobile devices may rely on processing power of nearby mobile devices to perform their computations [41]. However, replacing mobile cloud computing by device-to-device (D2D) connectivity introduces a new challenge. The mobile devices must be able to use nearby devices for their computation efficiently without spending too much power on discovering suitable devices.

Without widespread user adoption, no matter how sophisticated and purposeful a wearable device is, it will be useless. Thus, it is necessary to provide precise and simple to follow instructions in order to ease the working process with wearables. Such requirement is especially important to encourage elderly individuals to use wearable devices. Gaining public trust is also a key factor. For example, in industrial domain, the workers might suspect that the data collected from the devices they are wearing will be used against them as a proof for dismissal [33]. They also may not feel comfortable to be under constant monitoring [23]. Therefore, improving user adoption is a key challenge.

## References


1 Acharya, U.R., Oh, S.L., Hagiwara, Y. et al. (2017). A deep convolutional neural network model to classify heartbeats. *Computers in Biology and Medicine* 89: 389–396.

2 Ali, F., Islam, S.M.R., Kwak, D. et al. (2018). Type-2 fuzzy ontology–aided recommendation systems for IoT–based healthcare. *Computer Communications* 119: 138–155.

3 Artuğ, N.T., Göker, I., Bolat, B. et al. (2014). Feature extraction and classification of neuro-muscular diseases using scanning EMG. *2014 IEEE International Symposium on Innovations in Intelligent Systems and Applications (INISTA) Proceedings*, 262–265. IEEE.

4 Baby, M.S., Saji, A.J., and Kumar, C.S. (2017). Parkinson's disease classification using wavelet transform based feature extraction of gait data. *2017 International Conference on Circuit, Power and Computing Technologies (ICCPCT)*, 1–6. IEEE.

5 Barhatte, A.S., Ghongade, R., and Thakare, A.S. (2015). QRS complex detection and arrhythmia classification using SVM. *2015 Communication, Control and Intelligent Systems (CCIS)*, 239–243. IEEE.

6 Barlow, H.B. (1989). Unsupervised learning. *Neural Computation* 1 (3): 295–311.

7 Biau, G. and Scornet, E. (2016). A random forest guided tour. *Test* 25 (2): 197–227.

8 Borthakur, D., Dubey, H., Constant, N. et al. (2017). Smart fog: fog computing framework for unsupervised clustering analytics in wearable Internet of Things. *2017 IEEE Global Conference on Signal and Information Processing (GlobalSIP)*, 472–476. IEEE.

9 Conforti, I., Mileti, I., Del Prete, Z., and Palermo, E. (2020). Measuring biomechanical risk in lifting load tasks through wearable system and machine-learning approach. *Sensors* 20 (6): 1557.

10 Debnath, T., Hasan, Md.M., and Biswas, T. (2016). Analysis of ECG signal and classification of heart abnormalities using artificial neural network. *2016 9th International Conference on Electrical and Computer Engineering (ICECE)*, 353–356. IEEE.

**11** D'Haese, P.-F., Finomore, V., Lesnik, D. et al. (2021). Prediction of viral symptoms using wearable technology and artificial intelligence: a pilot study in healthcare workers. *PLoS One* 16 (10): e0257997.

**12** Doukas, C. and Maglogiannis, I. (2011). Managing wearable sensor data through cloud computing. *2011 IEEE 3rd International Conference on Cloud Computing Technology and Science*, 440–445. IEEE.

**13** Gawande, N. and Barhatte, A. (2017). Heart diseases classification using convolutional neural network. *2017 2nd International Conference on Communication and Electronics Systems (ICCES)*, 17–20. IEEE.

**14** Hamdi, T., Ali, J.B., Fnaiech, N. et al. (2017). Artificial neural network for blood glucose level prediction. *2017 International Conference on Smart, Monitored and Controlled Cities (SM2C)*, 91–95. IEEE.

**15** Hayes, B. (2008). Cloud computing. *Communications of the ACM* 51 (7): 9–11.

**16** Hooshmand, M., Zordan, D., Melodia, T., and Rossi, M. (2017). SURF: subject-adaptive unsupervised ECG signal compression for wearable fitness monitors. *IEEE Access* 5: 19517–19535.

**17** Huang, Z., Xu, W., and Yu, K. (2015). Bidirectional LSTM-CRF models for sequence tagging. *arXiv preprint arXiv:1508.01991*.

**18** Kim, D. and Kim, K. (2018). Detection of early stage Alzheimer's disease using EEG relative power with deep neural network. *2018 40th Annual International Conference of the IEEE Engineering in Medicine and Biology Society (EMBC)*, 352–355. IEEE.

**19** Klaynin, P., Wongseree, W., Leelasantitham, A., and Kiattisin, S. (2013). An electrocardiogram classification method based on neural network. *The 6th 2013 Biomedical Engineering International Conference*, 1–4. IEEE.

**20** Klum, M., Urban, M., Tigges, T. et al. (2020). Wearable cardiorespiratory monitoring employing a multimodal digital patch stethoscope: estimation of ECG, PEP, LVET and respiration using a 55 mm single-lead ECG and phonocardiogram. *Sensors* 20 (7): 2033.

**21** Kong, X.T.R., Luo, H., Huang, G.Q., and Yang, X. (2019). Industrial wearable system: the human-centric empowering technology in industry 4.0. *Journal of Intelligent Manufacturing* 30 (8): 2853–2869.

**22** Krenzer, A., Stein, N., Griebel, M., and Flath, C. (2019). Augmented intelligence for quality control of manual assembly processes using industrial wearable systems. *ICIS*.

**23** Kritzler, M., Bäckman, M., Tenfält, A., and Michahelles, F. (2015). Wearable technology as a solution for workplace safety. *Proceedings of the 14th International Conference on Mobile and Ubiquitous Multimedia*, 213–217.

**24** Kumari, P., Mathew, L., and Syal, P. (2017). Increasing trend of wearables and multimodal interface for human activity monitoring: a review. *Biosensors and Bioelectronics* 90: 298–307.

**25** Lara, O.D. and Labrador, M.A. (2012). A survey on human activity recognition using wearable sensors. *IEEE Communication Surveys and Tutorials* 15 (3): 1192–1209.

**26** Lasi, H., Fettke, P., Kemper, H.-G. et al. (2014). Industry 4.0. *Business & Information Systems Engineering* 6 (4): 239–242.

**27** LeCun, Y., Kavukcuoglu, K., and Farabet, C. (2010). Convolutional networks and applications in vision. *Proceedings of 2010 IEEE International Symposium on Circuits and Systems*, 253–256. IEEE.

**28** Li, H., Ota, K., and Dong, M. (2018). Learning IoT in edge: deep learning for the Internet of Things with edge computing. *IEEE Network* 32 (1): 96–101.

**29** Lillicrap, T.P., Hunt, J.J., Pritzel, A. et al. (2015). Continuous control with deep reinforcement learning. *arXiv preprint arXiv:1509.02971*.

**30** McGinnis, R.S., McGinnis, E.W., Hruschak, J. et al. (2018). Wearable sensors and machine learning diagnose anxiety and depression in young children. *2018 IEEE EMBS International Conference on Biomedical & Health Informatics (BHI)*, 410–413. IEEE.

**31** Mohebbi, A., Aradottir, T.B., Johansen, A.R. et al. (2017). A deep learning approach to adherence detection for type 2 diabetics. *2017 39th Annual International Conference of the IEEE Engineering in Medicine and Biology Society (EMBC)*, 2896–2899. IEEE.

**32** Noble, W.S. (2006). What is a support vector machine? *Nature Biotechnology* 24 (12): 1565–1567.

**33** Ometov, A., Shubina, V., Klus, L. et al. (2021). A survey on wearable technology: history, state-of-the-art and current challenges. *Computer Networks* 193: 108074.

**34** Oung, Q.W., Hariharan, M., Lee, H.L. et al. (2015). Wearable multimodal sensors for evaluation of patients with Parkinson disease. *2015 IEEE International Conference on Control System, Computing and Engineering (ICCSCE)*, 269–274. IEEE.

**35** Reymann, M.P., Dorschky, E., Groh, B.H. et al. (2016). Blood glucose level prediction based on support vector regression using mobile platforms. *2016 38th Annual International Conference of the IEEE Engineering in Medicine and Biology Society (EMBC)*, 2990–2993. IEEE.

**36** Sabeeha, S. and Shiny, C. (2017). ECG-based heartbeat classification for disease diagnosis. *2017 International Conference on Computing Methodologies and Communication (ICCMC)*, 1113–1117. IEEE.

**37** Saini, R., Bindal, N., and Bansal, P. (2015). Classification of heart diseases from ECG signals using wavelet transform and KNN classifier. *International Conference on Computing, Communication & Automation*, 1208–1215. IEEE.

**38** Satyanarayanan, M. (2017). The emergence of edge computing. *Computer* 50 (1): 30–39.

**39** Shi, W., Cao, J., Zhang, Q. et al. (2016). Edge computing: vision and challenges. *IEEE Internet of Things Journal* 3: 637–646.

**40** Svertoka, E., Rusu-Casandra, A., and Marghescu, I. (2020). State-of-the-art of industrial wearables: a systematic review. *2020 13th International Conference on Communications (COMM)*, 411–415. IEEE.

**41** Ti, N.T. and Le, L.B. (2017). Computation offloading leveraging computing resources from edge cloud and mobile peers. *2017 IEEE International Conference on Communications (ICC)*, 1–6. IEEE.

**42** Tripathy, R.K., Sharma, L.N., and Dandapat, S. (2014). A new way of quantifying diagnostic information from multilead electrocardiogram for cardiac disease classification. *Healthcare Technology Letters* 1 (4): 98–103.

**43** Wang, L., Von Laszewski, G., Younge, A. et al. (2010). Cloud computing: a perspective study. *New Generation Computing* 28 (2): 137–146.

**44** Wang, Y., Liu, S., Chen, R. et al. (2017). A novel classification indicator of type 1 and type 2 diabetes in China. *Scientific Reports* 7 (1): 1–7.

**45** Wiley, M., Bunescu, R., Marling, C. et al. (2011). Automatic detection of excessive glycemic variability for diabetes management. *2011 10th International Conference on Machine Learning and Applications and Workshops*, volume 2, 148–154. IEEE.

**46** Wold, S., Esbensen, K., and Geladi, P. (1987). Principal component analysis. *Chemometrics and Intelligent Laboratory Systems* 2 (1–3): 37–52.

**47** Yegnanarayana, B. (2009). *Artificial Neural Networks*. PHI Learning Pvt. Ltd.

**48** Yin, H. and Jha, N.K. (2017). A health decision support system for disease diagnosis based on wearable medical sensors and machine learning ensembles. *IEEE Transactions on Multi-Scale Computing Systems* 3 (4): 228–241.

**49** Yousefpour, A., Fung, C., Nguyen, T. et al. (2018). All one needs to know about fog computing and related edge computing paradigms. *Journal of Systems Architecture* 98: 289–330.

**50** Yu, S., Chen, H., Brown, R., and Sherman, S. (2018). Motion sensor-based assessment on fall risk and Parkinson's disease severity: a deep multi-source multi-task learning (DMML) approach. *2018 IEEE International Conference on Healthcare Informatics (ICHI)*, 174–179. IEEE.

**51** Zhao, Y. and He, L. (2014). Deep learning in the EEG diagnosis of Alzheimer's disease. *Asian Conference on Computer Vision*, 340–353. Springer.

**52** Zheng, X., Wang, M., and Ordieres-Meré, J. (2018). Comparison of data preprocessing approaches for applying deep learning to human activity recognition in the context of industry 4.0. *Sensors* 18 (7): 2146.

**53** Zheng, J., Cao, H., Chen, D. et al. (2020). Designing deep reinforcement learning systems for musculoskeletal modeling and locomotion analysis using wearable sensor feedback. *IEEE Sensors Journal* 20 (16): 9274–9282.

# 32

## Gesture-Based Computing

*Gennaro Costagliola, Mattia De Rosa, and Vittorio Fuccella*

*Dipartimento di Informatica, Università di Salerno, Fisciano (SA), Italy*

## 32.1 Introduction

Gesturing is a nonverbal form of communication. In most cases, it is combined with verbal communication. In special cases, such as especially hearing disabilities, it can completely replace verbal communication.

In recent years, there has been a widespread use of gestures for input in electronic devices. Many applications of mobile devices (smartphones, tablets, smartwatches, etc.) support gesture-based interaction, but this is also possible on larger devices (touch video walls, touch tables, etc.); moreover, the use of gestures has been studied also without the use of touchscreens, without direct contact of the user with the device, and both with the whole body or with parts of it (besides fingers).

The hardware capabilities of touchscreen devices have improved over the years, for example in accuracy, pressure detection, and the number of simultaneously detectable points (multitouch). This has also affected the types of gesture interactions used, e.g. the common pinch-to-zoom iteration is only possible on multitouch devices.

While the use of a few gestures may be easily feasible from a software point of view and could also be supported directly by the device's OS, more complex gestural interactions involve the designer in two main challenges: the choice of the gesture set, and the recognition algorithm.

Gestures should be simple, easy to learn and remember. Often, end users want to improve their productivity through gesture interactions. The problem with complex gestures is that users might reject them or use them only occasionally in the case they are available as an additional interaction mode. Sometimes it is necessary to conduct gesture elicitation studies to find out the most natural gestures for users.

There are also problems specific to certain hardware–human combinations, for example with small devices, it can be difficult to touch the screen where desired since the user's fingers can hide the screen, obstructing visibility (occlusion problem), and compromising accuracy (fat finger problem), or with large displays the interaction can become uncomfortable and unnatural.

In addition to this human component, designers must also keep in mind hardware and software performance. Common questions are "how easy is it for the device to recognize the gesture performed?," "how long does the recognition or design process take?." Different devices and sensors have different precision, accuracy, and performance that need to be considered.

*Handbook of Human-Machine Systems*, First Edition. Edited by Giancarlo Fortino, David Kaber, Andreas Nürnberger, and David Mendonça.

For this reason, a lot of research has been done about gesture recognition algorithms, and also systems and techniques have been proposed to help developers in the design of a gesture set and the application that uses it, both for touchscreen and mid-air gestures.

Particularly in the latter case, not being limited to having to touch a screen, one can think of detecting meaningful expressions of movement by a human being, performed using fingers, hands, arms, head, lips, legs, or other parts/whole body. This can then be used, for example, to interact with devices in a more comfortable and natural way or to increase immersiveness when playing video games. The application fields are many, e.g. human–robot interaction (HRI), virtual reality, entertainment [19], sign language recognition, assistive technologies, medical domain [25, 70], etc. Hardware for recognizing such gestures can be of different types, with techniques based on computer vision, RF sensing, data gloves, electromyography, etc. [32, 42], both with wearable and nonwearable devices. It should also be noted that when there is no need for contact between the user's body and the device (shared between multiple people), it is possible to avoid potential vehicles of infection, which is relevant, for example in the context of the COVID-19 pandemic.

Furthermore, these types of interactions can be beneficial even when touch-based interactions may be unsatisfactory or inappropriate for the purpose. For example in wall-mounted displays, touch-based interaction may be inconvenient if there is a need to touch areas that are too far for users to reach [23] or because the screen may not be fully visible [55].

## 32.2 Background

### 32.2.1 History of the Development of Gesture-Based Computing

Communicating with the computer through gestures is a very natural form of input. Gestures, unlike the mouse, allow a *direct manipulation*. According to Shneiderman's definition, the characteristics of a direct manipulation interface include visibility of objects, incremental action, rapid feedback, reversibility, exploration, syntactic correctness of all actions, and replacing language with action. The first of such kind of interfaces we have a trace in the history of human-computer interaction is the *Sketchpad* system, developed by Ivan Southerland at Massachusetts Institute of Technology (MIT) in the early 1960s [56]. That system, as shown by its own inventor in a famous demo,[1] allowed the drawing and manipulation of objects and geometric shapes on a screen via a *lightpen*.

Later, gesture interfaces became popular with the advent of mobile computing in the 1980s, with the spread of the first pen-based pocket organizers and personal digital assistants. In the early 1990s, the research of Sears and Shneiderman [53] had already proved how touchscreen devices can be at least as effective as traditional workstations in a variety of situations. At the same time, the earliest systems based on mid-air gestures were being developed. One of the first systems described in the literature dates back to 1986 by Zimmerman et al. [75]. They proposed two different devices to capture hand-gestures to enable touchless interaction with a computer: the Z-Glove and the Data-Glove. Both gloves used sensors to measure finger flexion and provided two types of gestures: object manipulations and commands, which allow to grasp an object, rotate an object, or draw a line. The interface used a hand-shaped mobile icon to track user's hand. The Z-Glove employed an ultrasonic transmitter system controlled by a Commodore 64, while the Data-Glove employed a magnetic transmitter system controlled by an Apple Macintosh.

The 2007 release of Apple iPhone gave a tremendous boost to the spread of touch-based gestures, with finger-based actions such as swiping, flicking, tapping, and so on [38]. Some of these gestures are performed with multiple fingers, and therefore fall within the type of interaction allowed

1 https://www.youtube.com/watch?v=6orsmFndx_o

by multitouch devices. A few years earlier, in 2003 and 2004, there had been the first significant searches for gesture-based text entry interfaces, with the introduction of the technology that allows a user to type a word with a single gesture, the *ShapeWriter* text entry method for smartphones, which is a predecessor to the modern *Swype* keyboard.

### 32.2.2 Basic Definitions

In this context, we refer to a "touch" gesture as the path traced on a touch-sensitive surface by a finger or a stylus, and although less common, it is also possible to make gestures with indirect devices such as mouses or trackpads. Single-stroke gestures are those made through a single pointer, while multistroke gestures are those made through multiple pointers on multitouch-enabled hardware.

Lastly, we will refer to gestures not made on a touch-sensitive surface (or with mouse/trackpad) as "mid-air."

## 32.3 State of the Art

The problem of gesture recognition has been extensively investigated in the literature, with proposals for different methods depending on the type of gesture and hardware, sometimes proposing new hardware. These methods usually aim to maximize recognition accuracy, while paying attention to the required computational resources and response times. It is possible to highlight two main recognition strategies: one based on the use of classifiers of various kinds (such as feature-based statistical classifiers, Hidden Markov models (HMMs), neural networks) and the one based on matching algorithms, which calculate the similarity between two gestures. It is also possible to highlight a rather straightforward division between studies about recognition of touch and mid-air gestures.

In this context of touch gestures, it should be noted that a multistroke gesture recognition method can usually recognize also single-stroke gestures. The development of single-stroke recognizers has not ceased, since the use of these types of gestures can often be more effective both from the point of view of the user and the application designer, and algorithms designed for them can be more efficient.

Among the first works, we can remember Rubine [51], the first widely used gesture recognizer, a feature-based linear classifier. The various techniques used for gesture recognition include those based on HMMs [54], neural networks [13, 50, 69], feature-based statistical classifiers [26], or a combination of them [11].

Among the template-based matching algorithms, the "$-family" of gesture recognition algorithm has emerged. It started with $1 [68], an algorithm for unistroke gesture recognition, with a focus on simplicity and fast implementation, which compares points in the sampled strokes for each gesture and is scale and (optionally) rotation invariant. $1 has since been extended several times, e.g. for multistrokeand articulation-invariant recognition, culminating in $Q [65]. Other methods include PolyRec [20] which uses a nearest neighbor approach to recognize unistroke gestures with high accuracy [7] and requires a small number of samples for each class; and recognizers based on geometric [31, 60] functions.

Regarding the recognition of mid-air gestures, most approaches are based on computer vision-based techniques, RF, or sound-sensing, or other technologies generally based on wearable devices.

The computer vision approach is very common. It is based on a camera that captures user gestures and usually provides a contactless human–computer interaction. There is a lot of variety in this category regarding the types of cameras that can be used (e.g. monocular, fisheye, time-of-flight camera). However, there are several challenges with this technique, especially with respect to the environment surrounding the user (occlusions, lighting variations, or background issues). In addition, computational overhead is another issue. In general, vision-based gesture recognition approaches fall into two broad categories: methods based on more traditional two-dimensional (2D) images and those that additionally make use of 3D depth sensors.

The first proposed methods were based on 2D images and silhouette-based action recognition. Two main categories can be identified in this context. The first consists of extracting action descriptors from silhouette sequences and using conventional classifiers for recognition. In this context, action descriptors need to capture both spatial and temporal features of actions. One of the earliest works is that of Bobick and Davis [6]. The second category involves extracting features from each silhouette and explicitly modeling the dynamics of the action, e.g. using statistical models, graphs, or conditional random fields. Each silhouette needs to capture then the body shape and the possible local motion. For example, Davis and Tyagi [15] described the shape of a silhouette using moments and modeled the dynamics with continuous HMMs.

Cameras equipped with depth sensors such as the Microsoft Kinect [42] that have become popular in recent years allow to capture more information about the scene, so they generally allow the development of algorithms with higher accuracy than 2D systems. One of the first 3D methods is the one proposed by Li et al. [34], in which human gestures are recognized by sequences of depth maps. To reduce complexity, only a small fraction of relevant points for each posture are sampled, exploiting, for example the fact that the points on the silhouette contour are much more important than those on the inside. On a gaming gesture set, it halved the error rate compared to using 2D silhouette alone. Although most methods use cameras placed in the environment at some distance from the user, wearable cameras have also been proposed, e.g. Kim et al. [28] proposed Digits, a method that uses a wrist sensor based on a 2D camera that retrieves the full 3D model of the hand, so as not to require the use of data gloves or external cameras/sensors, obtaining an accuracy comparable to the use of a data glove-based method [17, 67]. Another example of a wearable device based method is CyclopsRing [10], which uses a fisheye 2D camera placed in a wearable ring. In addition, some methods are designed specifically for certain types of gestures, e.g. Pugeault and Bowden [47] have designed a method for recognizing the finger-spelling American Sign Language (ASL).

Another recent trend for implementing gesture recognition systems is the use of radio frequency (RF). One disadvantage of computer vision methods is that they are difficult to implement in larger environments, for example an entire house. RF-based approaches can instead work without line-of-sight (which is a requirement for computer vision methods) and can also be easily deployed since the required hardware is usually small. Some of these approaches take advantage of radar sensors or GSM signals [74], but most methods are Wi-Fi-based, which also has the advantage that the required hardware is widely deployed and inexpensive. The key idea is to analyze changes in wireless signals caused by human gestures. One of the first such approaches is WiSee [46], which enables detection and recognition of gestures performed within the home. Since wireless signals can pass through walls, there is no need for line-of-sight and only a few wireless sources are needed, with no user-worn sensors. A user study showed that WiSee with two wireless sources could classify nine body gestures with 94% accuracy. Among non-Wi-Fi methods, some approaches rely on radar sensors [73] or high-frequency chips like Google's Soli sensor (basically a miniature radar) [66].

Sound-based methods include the use speakers and microphones leveraging the Doppler effect [22] or even ultrasounds [48].

Other types of approaches are generally based on wearable devices, e.g. force sensitive resistors (FSRs) placed on the user's wrist [16]; data gloves of various kinds, e.g. in the case of [18] equipped with inertial and magnetic measurement units (IMMUs); electromyography (EMG) which measures electrical potentials generated by muscles [52, 72]; electrical impedance tomography (EIT) [71]; ambient light fluctuations [35]. Compared to computer vision, RF, and sound-based methods, these methods are generally limited to gestures involving only the hand or fingers, since it is usually not feasible to contemplate wearing sensors all over the body.

In addition, some approaches devote themselves to recognizing gestures independently of how their trace was detected, for example methods inspired by gesture recognizers on touch devices such as $3 [29] and Protractor3D [30].

In addition to methods for gesture recognition, tools for gesture-based application development have also been developed over the years. Most try to be a complete environment that supports the developer both in creating the set of gestures and in developing the application that uses them, although there are others with more specific functions. Some allow gesture recognition with a single built-in method, while others support multiple gesture recognizers.

GID (Gestural Interface Designer) [14] is the precursor of this type of tools. Quill [37] is one of the first tools for pen-based devices, preceding the spread of finger-based touch devices. Examples of tools for touch devices include RATA [44] which offers a wizard that does not require coding knowledge. PolyRec GDT [7] that allows to detect ambiguities and to automatically select the most representative gestures for each gesture class. Other tools do not deal exclusively with touch gestures, such as GestMan [39], which handles 2D/3D gestures and supports multiple gesture recognizers and gesture-sharing and collaborative experiments for gesture elicitation.

Although the touch-based interaction saw its first applications for information kiosks, touch gestures spread mainly thanks to mobile devices. On these devices, a frequent application is text entry. The current devices offer, in addition to the classic tapping-type interaction on the soft-keyboard, also the aforementioned Swipe keyboard. Moreover, almost all applications offer the possibility to operate through gestures. A very frequent operation is the scroll. Advanced applications, such as maps, offer pan, and zoom functions. A map is moved by simply touching the map and dragging the finger. Pinch gesture is instead used for zooming. The association of these gestures with their respective actions has become a de facto standard and even touchpads used with computers without touch screens support them. The touch-screen has evolved and by now many devices support a high number (> 2) of contact points and allow to detect the pressure, in order to allow advanced applications, such as the simulation of a piano keyboard and the collaborative work of multiple users on the same surface.

As for mid-air gestures, typical applications include the basic user operations, such as authentication, typing, and menu selection. authentication based on behavioral biometrics was experimented by Guerra Casanova et al. [21]. Specifically, the proposed technique allows user authentication through the recognition of a 3D gesture performed by moving the hand while grasping a mobile device with an embedded accelerometer. Menu interactions were experimented by Chattopadhyay and Bolchini [12] which proposed the use of simple directional movements to select commands from a touchless circular menu on large displays. The use of touchless menus is convenient in the automotive sector to avoid sources of distractions while driving. May et al. [41] proposed a hierarchical menu of three levels representing the main functions in a car. The prototypical system was realized using Leap Motion and tested with audio feedback. Markussen et al. [40] proposed Volture, a touchless implementation of Swipe. Volture projects users' movement onto a display and uses "pinch" as a gesture delimiter. That is the user moves a cursor over the first letter of the word they intend to enter, then perform a pinch gesture through index finger and thumb and drags the cursor through the letters of the word. Lastly, they stop pinching after the last letter.

A frequent application of gestures is sign language for communication for deaf people. Other aids for disabled people include the control of a wheelchair. Zeng et al. [70] developed such a prototypical system. Users with motor disabilities performed gestures with the fingers and were filmed by a camera mounted on the wheelchair.

Table 32.1 summarizes the characteristics of the different gesture recognition methods we discussed.

**Table 32.1** Gesture recognizer characteristics.

| Methods | Type | Recognized gestures | Approach |
|---|---|---|---|
| Kara and Stahovich [26], Sezgin and Davis [54], and Wu et al. [69] | Touch | Single-stroke | Statistical classifier, machine learning, multiple approaches |
| Vanderdonckt et al. [60] and Vatavu et al. [65] | Touch | Single-stroke | Template-based matching |
| Chang et al. [11], Cire et al. [13], and Rubine [51] | Touch | Multistroke | Statistical classifier, machine learning, multiple approaches |
| Fuccella and Costagliola [20], Kristensson and Zhai [31], and Wobbrock et al. [68] | Touch | Multistroke | Template-based matching |
| Chan et al. [10] and Kim et al. [28] | Mid-air | Hand | Computer vision: 2D camera on wrist/finger |
| Li et al. [34] | Mid-air | Body | Computer vision: depth camera |
| Pugeault and Bowden [47] | Mid-air | Hand | Computer vision: depth+2D camera |
| Bobick and Davis [6] and Davis and Tyagi [15] | Mid-air | Body | Computer vision: 2D Camera(s) |
| Dementyev and Paradiso [16] | Mid-air | Finger | Wearable (wrist): force sensitive resistors (FSRs) |
| Saponas et al. [52] | Mid-air | Finger | Wearable (upper forearm): Electromyography |
| Zhang and Harrison [71] | Mid-air | Hand | Wearable: Electrical Impedance Tomography (EIT) |
| Zhang et al. [72] | Mid-air | Hand | Wearable: EMG + 3D accelerometer (ACC) |
| Fang et al. [18] | Mid-air | Hand | Wearable (data glove): inertial and magnetic measurement units (IMMUs) |
| Li et al. [35] | Mid-air | Finger | Wearable: ambient light |
| Pu et al. [46] | Mid-air | Body | RF sensing: Wireless signals |
| Wang et al. [66] and Zhang et al. [73] | Mid-air | Hand | RF sensing: radar |
| Zhao et al. [74] | Mid-air | Hand | RF sensing: GSM signals |
| Gupta et al. [22] | Mid-air | Hand | Sound-sensing: speaker and microphone |
| Qifan et al. [48] | Mid-air | Hand | Sound-sensing: ultrasounds |

## 32.4 Future Research Challenges

Although the research on gestural interfaces has grown considerably over the years, there are still some challenges. In this section, we discuss current research issues and future research directions dealing with them.

### 32.4.1 Current Research Issues

Although, with the spread of mobile touch devices such as smartphones and tablets, interaction through simple gestures has been widely adopted and accepted by users, this has not yet happened in the case of other devices and scenarios. Whether they will be accepted by users on a large scale is yet to be verified, and may find resistance from people who have been operating differently for a large number of years.

Regarding mid-air gestures, a problem known in the literature and typical of this type of interaction is the lack of haptic feedback for the user.

Regarding gesture recognition, although current methods offer good performance, especially in the case of touch surfaces, 100% accuracy has not been achieved and can still be increased.

A crucial aspect for the successful use of gestures, both touch and mid-air, is getting the supported gestures right. For example, it may happen that gestures are not completely intuitive. Conducting elicitation studies can help solve this problem, but such studies are resource intensive and can still be problematic (e.g. selecting gestures that are too similar for accurate recognition). Allowing users to customize commands could be a solution, but such an operation can be both annoying for the user and may lead to legacy bias [5], which is the tendency of users to transfer gestures from existing technologies, which can lead to the use of familiar but not fully effective gestures, with the aggravation of making the system more difficult and tiring to use.

### 32.4.2 Future Research Directions Dealing with the Current Issues

Regarding the acceptance of the use of gestures in various situations and scenarios, research may investigate various strategies to accomplish this goal. For example, in some situations, proper training could be a solution to overcome this problem, but research has yet to completely understand how easily people can use these tools after becoming familiar with them in a guided context.

Regarding the feedback for mid-air gestures, research may go in different directions, such as studying wearable devices capable of providing such feedback, or using the body as an input surface by exploiting the principle of proprioception.

Regarding recognition accuracy, research will probably go in the direction of using artificial intelligence to improve accuracy, also exploiting information about the context in which the gesture is performed (e.g. previous gestures, interaction history of that user, application state). While for touch surfaces the hardware has reached a high level of maturity, in the other cases, the research will focus also on the use of new and more efficient hardware.

Regarding the choice of the right gestures, there are already systems that help to perform elicitation studies, and that warn about the presence of too similar gestures, in order to avoid recognition issues. The research may, in fact, go in the direction of the development of intelligent systems capable of enabling such operations without the need for the developer's intervention.

## Acknowledgment

This work was partially supported by grants from the University of Salerno (grant numbers: 300392FRB20COSTA, 300392FRB21COSTA).

## References

1 Anthony, L. and Wobbrock, J.O. (2010). A lightweight multistroke recognizer for user interface prototypes. *Proceedings of Graphics Interface 2010, GI '10*, 245–252. Toronto, Ontario, Canada: Canadian Information Processing Society. ISBN: 978-1-56881-712-5. http://dl.acm.org/citation.cfm?id=1839214.1839258 (accessed 24 February 2023).

**2** Anthony, L. and Wobbrock, J.O. (2012). $N-Protractor: a fast and accurate multistroke recognizer. *Proceedings of Graphics Interface 2012, GI '12*, 117–120. Canada: Canadian Information Processing Society. ISBN: 9781450314206.

**3** Anthony, L., Vatavu, R.-D., and Wobbrock, J.O. (2013). Understanding the consistency of users' pen and finger stroke gesture articulation. *Proceedings of Graphics Interface 2013, GI '13*, 87–94. Toronto, Ontario, Canada: Canadian Information Processing Society. ISBN: 978-1-4822-1680-6. http://dl.acm.org/citation.cfm?id=2532129.2532145 (accessed 24 February 2023).

**4** Ashbrook, D. and Starner, T. (2010). MAGIC: a motion gesture design tool. *Proceedings of the SIGCHI Conference on Human Factors in Computing Systems*, 2159–2168.

**5** Beşevli, C., Buruk, O.T., Erkaya, M., and Özcan, O. (2018). Investigating the effects of legacy bias: user elicited gestures from the end users perspective. *Proceedings of the 2018 ACM Conference Companion Publication on Designing Interactive Systems*, 277–281.

**6** Bobick, A.F. and Davis, J.W. (2001). The recognition of human movement using temporal templates. *IEEE Transactions on Pattern Analysis and Machine Intelligence* 23 (3): 257–267. https://doi.org/10.1109/34.910878.

**7** Bufano, R., Costagliola, G., De Rosa, M., and Fuccella, V. (2021). PolyRec gesture design tool: a tool for fast prototyping of gesture-based mobile applications. *Software: Practice and Experience* 52 (2): 594–618. https://doi.org/10.1002/spe.3024.

**8** Caputo, F.M., Prebianca, P., Carcangiu, A. et al. (2017). A 3 cent recognizer: simple and effective retrieval and classification of mid-air gestures from single 3D traces. *Proceedings of the Conference on Smart Tools and Applications in Computer Graphics, STAG '17*, 9–15. Goslar, DEU: Eurographics Association. https://doi.org/10.2312/stag.20171221.

**9** Casiez, G., Roussel, N., and Vogel, D. (2012). 1 filter: a simple speed-based low-pass filter for noisy input in interactive systems. *Proceedings of the SIGCHI Conference on Human Factors in Computing Systems, CHI '12*, 2527–2530. New York, NY, USA: Association for Computing Machinery. ISBN: 9781450310154. https://doi.org/10.1145/2207676.2208639.

**10** Chan, L., Chen, Y.-L., Hsieh, C.-H. et al. (2015). CyclopsRing: enabling whole-hand and context-aware interactions through a fisheye ring. *Proceedings of the 28th Annual ACM Symposium on User Interface Software & Technology*, UIST '15, 549–556, New York, NY, USA. Association for Computing Machinery. ISBN 9781450337793. https://doi.org/10.1145/2807442.2807450.

**11** Chang, S.H.-H., Plimmer, B., and Blagojevic, R. (2010). Rata.SSR: data mining for pertinent stroke recognizers. *Proceedings of the 7th Sketch-Based Interfaces and Modeling Symposium*, SBIM '10, 95–102. Goslar, DEU: Eurographics Association. ISBN 9783905674255.

**12** Chattopadhyay, D. and Bolchini, D. (2014). Touchless circular menus: toward an intuitive UI for touchless interactions with large displays. *Proceedings of the 2014 International Working Conference on Advanced Visual Interfaces*, 33–40.

**13** Cireşan, D.C., Meier, U., Gambardella, L.M., and Schmidhuber, J. (2010). Deep, big, simple neural nets for handwritten digit recognition. *Neural Computation* 22 (12): 3207–3220. https://doi.org/10.1162/NECO_a_00052.

**14** Dannenberg, R.B. and Amon, D. (1989). A gesture based user interface prototyping system. *Proceedings of the 2nd Annual ACM SIGGRAPH Symposium on User Interface Software and Technology*, 127–132.

**15** Davis, J.W. and Tyagi, A. (2006). Minimal-latency human action recognition using reliable-inference. *Image and Vision Computing* 24 (5): 455–472. https://doi.org/10.1016/j.imavis.2006.01.012.

**16** Dementyev, A. and Paradiso, J.A. (2014). WristFlex: low-power gesture input with wrist-worn pressure sensors. *Proceedings of the 27th Annual ACM Symposium on User Interface Software and Technology*, 161–166.

**17** Dipietro, L., Sabatini, A.M., and Dario, P. (2003). Evaluation of an instrumented glove for hand-movement acquisition. *Journal of Rehabilitation Research and Development* 40 (2): 179–190.

**18** Fang, B., Sun, F., Liu, H., and Liu, C. (2018). 3D human gesture capturing and recognition by the IMMU-based data glove. *Neurocomputing* 277: 198–207.

**19** Freeman, W.T. and Weissman, C.D. (1995). Television control by hand gestures. *Proceedings of International Workshop on Automatic Face and Gesture Recognition*, 179–183.

**20** Fuccella, V. and Costagliola, G. (2015). Unistroke gesture recognition through polyline approximation and alignment. *Proceedings of the 33rd Annual ACM Conference on Human Factors in Computing Systems*, CHI '15, 3351–3354. New York, NY, USA: ACM. ISBN 978-1-4503-3145-6. https://doi.org/10.1145/2702123.2702505.

**21** Guerra-Casanova, J., Sánchez-Ávila, C., Bailador, G., and de Santos Sierra, A. (2012). Authentication in mobile devices through hand gesture recognition. *International Journal of Information Security* 11 (2): 65–83.

**22** Gupta, S., Morris, D., Patel, S., and Tan, D. (2012). SoundWave: using the Doppler effect to sense gestures. *Proceedings of the SIGCHI Conference on Human Factors in Computing Systems*, 1911–1914.

**23** Han, J.Y. (2005). Low-cost multi-touch sensing through frustrated total internal reflection. *Proceedings of the 18th Annual ACM Symposium on User Interface Software and Technology*, 115–118.

**24** Herold, J. and Stahovich, T.F. (2012). The 1 recognizer: a fast, accurate, and easy-to-implement handwritten gesture recognition technique. *Proceedings of the International Symposium on Sketch-Based Interfaces and Modeling, SBIM '12*, 39–46. Goslar, DEU: Eurographics Association. ISBN: 9783905674422.

**25** Jalaliniya, S., Smith, J., Sousa, M. et al. (2013). Touch-less interaction with medical images using hand & foot gestures. *Proceedings of the 2013 ACM Conference on Pervasive and Ubiquitous Computing Adjunct Publication*, 1265–1274.

**26** Kara, L.B. and Stahovich, T.F. (2004). Hierarchical parsing and recognition of hand-sketched diagrams. *Proceedings of the 17th Annual ACM Symposium on User Interface Software and Technology*, UIST '04, 13–22. New York, NY, USA: Association for Computing Machinery. ISBN 1581139578. https://doi.org/10.1145/1029632.1029636.

**27** Khandkar, S.H., Sohan, S.M., Sillito, J., and Maurer, F. (2010). Tool support for testing complex multi-touch gestures. *ACM International Conference on Interactive Tabletops and Surfaces, ITS '10*, 59–68. New York, NY, USA, Saarbrücken, Germany: ACM. ISBN: 978-1-4503-0399-6. http://doi.acm.org/10.1145/1936652.1936663.

**28** Kim, D., Hilliges, O., Izadi, S. et al. (2012). Digits: freehand 3D interactions anywhere using a wrist-worn gloveless sensor. *Proceedings of the 25th Annual ACM Symposium on User Interface Software and Technology*, 167–176.

**29** Kratz, S. and Rohs, M. (2010). A $3 gesture recognizer: simple gesture recognition for devices equipped with 3D acceleration sensors. *Proceedings of the 15th International Conference on Intelligent User Interfaces*, IUI '10, 341–344. New York, NY, USA: Association for Computing Machinery. ISBN 9781605585154. https://doi.org/10.1145/1719970.1720026.

**30** Kratz, S. and Rohs, M. (2011). Protractor3D: a closed-form solution to rotation-invariant 3D gestures. *Proceedings of the 16th International Conference on Intelligent User Interfaces*, IUI '11,

371–374. New York, NY, USA: Association for Computing Machinery. ISBN 9781450304191. https://doi.org/10.1145/1943403.1943468.

**31** Kristensson, P.-O. and Zhai, S. (2004). Shark$^2$: a large vocabulary shorthand writing system for pen-based computers. *Proceedings of the 17th Annual ACM Symposium on User Interface Software and Technology*, UIST '04, 43–52, New York, NY, USA: ACM. ISBN 1-58113-957-8. https://doi.org/10.1145/1029632.1029640.

**32** Leapmotion (2021). https://www.ultraleap.com (accessed 24 June 2021).

**33** Li, Y. (2010). Protractor: a fast and accurate gesture recognizer. *Proceedings of the SIGCHI Conference on Human Factors in Computing Systems, CHI '10*, 2169–2172. New York, NY, USA: ACM. ISBN: 978-1-60558-929-9. http://doi.acm.org/10.1145/1753326.1753654.

**34** Li, W., Zhang, Z., and Liu, Z. (2010). Action recognition based on a bag of 3D points. *2010 IEEE Computer Society Conference on Computer Vision and Pattern Recognition - Workshops*, 9–14. https://doi.org/10.1109/CVPRW.2010.5543273.

**35** Li, Y., Li, T., Patel, R.A. et al. (2018). Self-powered gesture recognition with ambient light. *Proceedings of the 31st Annual ACM Symposium on User Interface Software and Technology*, 595–608.

**36** Lü, H. and Li, Y. (2013). Gesture studio: authoring multi-touch interactions through demonstration and declaration. *Proceedings of the SIGCHI Conference on Human Factors in Computing Systems, CHI '13*, 257–266. New York, NY, USA, Paris, France: ACM. ISBN: 978-1-4503-1899-0. http://doi.acm.org/10.1145/2470654.2470690.

**37** Long, A.C. Jr. (2001). Quill: a gesture design tool for pen-based user interfaces. PhD thesis. Berkeley: University of California. AAI3044573.

**38** MacKenzie, I.S. (2013). *Human-Computer Interaction: An Empirical Research Perspective*, 1e. San Francisco, CA: Morgan Kaufmann Publishers Inc. ISBN 0124058655.

**39** Magrofuoco, N., Roselli, P., Vanderdonckt, J. et al. (2019). GestMan: a cloud-based tool for stroke-gesture datasets. *Proceedings of the ACM SIGCHI Symposium on Engineering Interactive Computing Systems*, EICS '19. New York, NY, USA: Association for Computing Machinery. ISBN 9781450367455. https://doi.org/10.1145/3319499.3328227.

**40** Markussen, A., Jakobsen, M.R., and Hornbæk, K. (2014). Vulture: a mid-air word-gesture keyboard. *Proceedings of the SIGCHI Conference on Human Factors in Computing Systems*, 1073–1082.

**41** May, K.R., Gable, T.M., and Walker, B.N. (2014). A multimodal air gesture interface for in vehicle menu navigation. *Adjunct Proceedings of the 6th International Conference on Automotive User Interfaces and Interactive Vehicular Applications*, 1–6.

**42** Microsoft Kinect (2021). https://developer.microsoft.com/it-it/windows/kinect/ (accessed 24 June 2021).

**43** Myers, C.S. and Rabiner, L.R. (1981). A comparative study of several dynamic time-warping algorithms for connected-word recognition. *Bell System Technical Journal* 60 (7): 1389–1409. https://doi.org/10.1002/j.1538-7305.1981.tb00272.x.

**44** Plimmer, B., Blagojevic, R., Chang, S. H.-H. et al. (2012). RATA: codeless generation of gesture recognizers. *The 26th BCS Conference on Human Computer Interaction 26*, 137–146.

**45** Poppinga, B., Sahami Shirazi, A., Henze, N. et al. (2014). Understanding shortcut gestures on mobile touch devices. *Proceedings of the 16th International Conference on Human-Computer Interaction with Mobile Devices & Services*, 173–182.

**46** Pu, Q., Gupta, S., Gollakota, S., and Patel, S. (2013). Whole-home gesture recognition using wireless signals. *Proceedings of the 19th Annual International Conference on Mobile Computing & Networking*, 27–38.

**47** Pugeault, N. and Bowden, R. (2011). Spelling it out: real-time ASL fingerspelling recognition. *2011 IEEE International Conference on Computer Vision Workshops (ICCV Workshops)*, 1114–1119. IEEE.

**48** Qifan, Y., Hao, T., Xuebing, Z. et al. (2014). Dolphin: ultrasonic-based gesture recognition on smartphone platform. *2014 IEEE 17th International Conference on Computational Science and Engineering*, 1461–1468. IEEE.

**49** Reaver, J., Stahovich, T.F., and Herold, J. (2011). How to make a quick$: using hierarchical clustering to improve the efficiency of the dollar recognizer. *Proceedings of the 8th Eurographics Symposium on Sketch-Based Interfaces and Modeling, SBIM '11*, 103–108. New York, NY, USA: Association for Computing Machinery. ISBN: 9781450309066. https://doi.org/10.1145/2021164.2021183.

**50** Roy, P., Ghosh, S., and Pal, U. (2018). A CNN based framework for unistroke numeral recognition in air-writing. *2018 16th International Conference on Frontiers in Handwriting Recognition (ICFHR)*, 404–409. https://doi.org/10.1109/ICFHR-2018.2018.00077.

**51** Rubine, D. (1991). Specifying gestures by example. *Proceedings of the 18th Annual Conference on Computer Graphics and Interactive Techniques*, SIGGRAPH '91, 329–337. New York, NY, USA: ACM. ISBN 0-89791-436-8. https://doi.org/10.1145/122718.122753.

**52** Saponas, T.S., Tan, D.S., Morris, D., and Balakrishnan, R. (2008). Demonstrating the feasibility of using forearm electromyography for muscle-computer interfaces. *Proceedings of the SIGCHI Conference on Human Factors in Computing Systems*, 515–524.

**53** Sears, A. and Shneiderman, B. (1991). High precision touchscreens: design strategies and comparisons with a mouse. *International Journal of Man–Machine Studies* 34 (4): 593–613.

**54** Sezgin, T.M. and Davis, R. (2005). HMM-based efficient sketch recognition. *Proceedings of the 10th International Conference on Intelligent User Interfaces*, IUI '05, 281–283, New York, NY, USA: Association for Computing Machinery. ISBN 1581138946. https://doi.org/10.1145/1040830.1040899.

**55** Shoemaker, G., Tang, A., and Booth, K.S. (2007). Shadow reaching: a new perspective on interaction for large displays. *Proceedings of the 20th Annual ACM Symposium on User Interface Software and Technology*, 53–56.

**56** Sutherland, I.E. (1964). Sketchpad a man-machine graphical communication system. *Simulation* 2 (5): R-3–R-20.

**57** Tappert, C.C. (1982). Cursive script recognition by elastic matching. *IBM Journal of Research and Development* 26 (6): 765–771. https://doi.org/10.1147/rd.266.0765.

**58** Taranta, E.M., Vargas, A.N., and LaViola, J.J. (2016). Streamlined and accurate gesture recognition with Penny Pincher. *Computers & Graphics* 55: 130–142. https://doi.org/10.1016/j.cag.2015.10.011.

**59** Taranta, E.M. II, Samiei, A., Maghoumi, M. et al. (2017s). Jackknife: a reliable recognizer with few samples and many modalities. *Proceedings of the 2017 CHI Conference on Human Factors in Computing Systems, CHI '17*, 5850–5861. New York, NY, USA: Association for Computing Machinery. ISBN: 9781450346559. https://doi.org/10.1145/3025453.3026002.

**60** Vanderdonckt, J., Roselli, P., and Pérez-Medina, J.L. (2018). !FTL, an articulation-invariant stroke gesture recognizer with controllable position, scale, and rotation invariances. *Proceedings of the 20th ACM International Conference on Multimodal Interaction*, ICMI '18, 125–134. New York, NY, USA: Association for Computing Machinery. ISBN 9781450356923. https://doi.org/10.1145/3242969.3243032.

**61** Vatavu, R.-D. (2012). 1F: one accessory feature design for gesture recognizers. *Proceedings of the 2012 ACM International Conference on Intelligent User Interfaces, IUI '12*, 297–300. New York,

NY, USA: Association for Computing Machinery. ISBN: 9781450310482. https://doi.org/10.1145/2166966.2167022.

**62** Vatavu, R.-D., Anthony, L., and Wobbrock, J.O. (2012). Gestures as point clouds: a $P recognizer for user interface prototypes. *Proceedings of the 14th ACM International Conference on Multimodal Interaction, ICMI '12*, 273–280. New York, NY, USA: ACM. ISBN: 978-1-4503-1467-1. http://doi.acm.org/10.1145/2388676.2388732.

**63** Vatavu, R.-D., Anthony, L., and Wobbrock, J.O. (2013). Relative accuracy measures for stroke gestures. *Proceedings of the 15th ACM on International Conference on Multimodal Interaction, ICMI '13*, 279–286. New York, NY, USA, Sydney, Australia: ACM. ISBN: 978-1-4503-2129-7. http://doi.acm.org/10.1145/2522848.2522875.

**64** Vatavu, R.-D. (2017). Improving gesture recognition accuracy on touch screens for users with low vision. *Proceedings of the 2017 CHI Conference on Human Factors in Computing Systems, CHI '17*, 4667–4679. New York, NY, USA: ACM. ISBN: 978-1-4503-4655-9. http://doi.acm.org/10.1145/3025453.3025941.

**65** Vatavu, R.-D., Anthony, L., and Wobbrock, J.O. (2018). $q: A super-quick, articulation-invariant stroke-gesture recognizer for low-resource devices. *Proceedings of the 20th International Conference on Human-Computer Interaction with Mobile Devices and Services*, MobileHCI '18, 23:1–23:12. New York, NY, USA: ACM. ISBN 978-1-4503-5898-9. https://doi.org/10.1145/3229434.3229465.

**66** Wang, S., Song, J., Lien, J. et al. (2016). Interacting with soli: exploring fine-grained dynamic gesture recognition in the radio-frequency spectrum. *Proceedings of the 29th Annual Symposium on User Interface Software and Technology*, 851–860.

**67** Wise, S., Gardner, W., Sabelman, E. et al. (1990). Evaluation of a fiber optic glove for se-automated goniometric measurements. *Journal of Rehabilitation Research and Development* 27 (4): 411–424.

**68** Wobbrock, J.O., Wilson, A.D., and Li, Y. (2007). Gestures without libraries, toolkits or training: a $1 recognizer for user interface prototypes. *Proceedings of the 20th Annual ACM Symposium on User Interface Software and Technology*, UIST '07, 159–168. New York, NY, USA: ACM. ISBN 978-1-59593-679-0. https://doi.org/10.1145/1294211.1294238.

**69** Wu, D., Pigou, L., Kindermans, P.-J. et al. (2016). Deep dynamic neural networks for multimodal gesture segmentation and recognition. *IEEE Transactions on Pattern Analysis and Machine Intelligence* 38 (8): 1583–1597. https://doi.org/10.1109/TPAMI.2016.2537340.

**70** Zeng, J., Sun, Y., and Wang, F. (2012). A natural hand gesture system for intelligent human–computer interaction and medical assistance. *2012 3rd Global Congress on Intelligent Systems*, 382–385. IEEE.

**71** Zhang, Y. and Harrison, C. (2015). Tomo: wearable, low-cost electrical impedance tomography for hand gesture recognition. *Proceedings of the 28th Annual ACM Symposium on User Interface Software & Technology*, 167–173.

**72** Zhang, X., Chen, X., Wang, W.-h. et al. (2009). Hand gesture recognition and virtual game control based on 3D accelerometer and EMG sensors. *Proceedings of the 14th International Conference on Intelligent User Interfaces*, 401–406.

**73** Zhang, Z., Tian, Z., and Zhou, M. (2018). Latern: Dynamic continuous hand gesture recognition using FMCW radar sensor. *IEEE Sensors Journal* 18 (8): 3278–3289.

**74** Zhao, C., Chen, K.-Y., Aumi, M.T.I. et al. (2014). SideSwipe: detecting in-air gestures around mobile devices using actual GSM signal. *Proceedings of the 27th Annual ACM Symposium on User Interface Software and Technology*, 527–534.

**75** Zimmerman, T.G., Lanier, J., Blanchard, C. et al. (1986). A hand gesture interface device. *ACM SIGCHI Bulletin* 18 (4): 189–192.

# 33

# EEG-based Affective Computing

*Xueliang Quan and Dongrui Wu*

*School of Artificial Intelligence and Automation, Huazhong University of Science and Technology, Wuhan, China*

## 33.1 Introduction

Affect reflects a person's current physical and psychological state and has important impact on the individual's cognition, communication, and decision-making capabilities [26]. The changes of affect are always accompanied with changes of individual psychological and physiological responses. Therefore, the changes of affect can be measured and simulated computationally [12, 46].

Affective computing is a pioneering and interdisciplinary research area, involving many disciplines such as psychology, cognitive science, and computer science. The purpose of affective computing is to study and develop theories, methods, and systems which can recognize, interpret, synthesize, and/or stimulate human emotions [26].

Common inputs of affective computing include video (facial expressions, gestures, etc.), audio, text, physiological signals, etc. [8, 42]. Different from facial expressions, electroencephalograms (EEGs) can better reflect the intrinsic emotional state of an individual and are difficult to fake. Therefore, EEG-based affective computing could be used in accident prevention, clinical diagnostics, and treatment, etc. [13]. For example, in transportation, a driver's anger, anxiety, and other negative emotions may affect his/her concentration and lead to traffic accidents. Wearable devices can effectively reduce accidents by monitoring the driver's emotional state in real time. With the development of 5G technology, deep learning and human–computer interaction, EEG-based affective computing has great application potentials in healthcare, entertainment, education, etc.

## 33.2 Background

Although computers have powerful logic computing capabilities, due to the lack of emotional intelligence, human–computer interactions are not as natural as human–human interactions. That is why affective computing research is attracting great research interests recently.

### 33.2.1 Brief History

In 1986, MIT Professor Marvin Minsky proposed that [22] "*the question is not whether intelligent machines can have any emotions, but whether machines can be intelligent without emotions,*"

*Handbook of Human-Machine Systems*, First Edition. Edited by Giancarlo Fortino, David Kaber, Andreas Nürnberger, and David Mendonça.

pointing out the importance of emotions for intelligent machines. In 1997, MIT Media Lab Professor Rosiland Picard formally defined the concept of affective computing in her monograph *Affective Computing* [26]: "*computing that relates to, arises from, or influences emotions.*" In 2010, IEEE Computational Intelligence Society, IEEE Computer Society and IEEE Systems, Man and Cybernetics Society jointly launched the *IEEE Transactions on Affective Computing*, a journal dedicated to the research of affective computing.

### 33.2.2 Emotion Theory

How people interpret the world affects our emotion reactions. However, how such different interpretations lead to different emotions is not clear yet. From the cognitive science perspective, Ortony, Clore, and Collins systematically studied the cognitive structures that underlie a wide range of different emotions [25]. They proposed three broad classes of emotions, i.e. reactions to events, agents, and objects, each corresponding to a different attentional focus.

### 33.2.3 Emotion Representation

Emotions can be represented both categorically (discretely) and numerically (continuously).

Ekman and Friesen [5] analyzed human facial expressions and identified six basic emotions: happiness, surprise, sadness, disgust, anger, and fear. They are the most popular categorical emotions in affective computing. Plutchik [27] extended them to eight major emotions: joy, trust, fear, sadness, surprise, disgust, anticipation, and anger.

Russell [29] utilized a 2D space of valence and arousal to represent emotions. Mehrabian [21] further added a third dimension, dominance, to distinguish emotions which are hard to be separated in the valence-arousal 2D representation, e.g. anger and fear.

### 33.2.4 EEG

EEG reflects the electrical activities on the scalp and can be collected noninvasively. Human emotion changes are usually accompanied by changes in EEG [8, 42]. Compared with other inputs in affective computing, such as facial expressions and voice signals, EEG can better reflect the intrinsic emotion state and are difficult to fake. Therefore, it is an important input in affective computing.

EEG consists of five typical frequency bands, reflecting different activities of the brain, as shown in Table 33.1. Zheng et al. [46] found stable patterns over time in EEG-based emotion recognition, e.g. positive emotions have higher $\beta$ and $\gamma$ band responses at the lateral temporal areas than negative

**Table 33.1** Frequency bands of EEG [32].

| Band | Frequency (Hz) | State |
|---|---|---|
| $\delta$ | $< 4$ | Adult slow-wave sleep |
| $\theta$ | $4 - 7$ | Drowsiness in teens and adults, idling |
| $\alpha$ | $8 - 15$ | Keeping eyes closed, relaxed, reflecting, coma |
| $\beta$ | $16 - 31$ | Relaxed but focused, excited, or anxious |
| $\gamma$ | $> 32$ | Active thinking, focus, high alert, anxious |

emotions; neutral emotions have relatively obvious $\alpha$ band responses at occipital and parietal lobes; negative emotions have higher $\gamma$ band responses in the prefrontal lobe, and significantly higher $\delta$ band responses at parietal and occipital lobes.

### 33.2.5 EEG-Based Emotion Recognition

The steps of EEG-based affective computing mainly include [2, 42]:

(1) Stimulate the subject to elicit a desired emotion state and collect the corresponding EEG signals. Stimulations include pictures, videos, music, etc. [12].
(2) Preprocess the collected EEG, including temporal and spatial filtering, denoising, artifact removal, resampling, etc.
(3) Extract and select features.
(4) Train emotion recognition models and test.

## 33.3 State-of-the-Art

Representative studies on EEG-based affective computing are summarized in Table 33.2.

### 33.3.1 Public Datasets

High-quality datasets are very important for the study of EEG-based affective computing. Among various such datasets, SEED (Shanghai Jiao Tong University (SJTU) Emotion EEG Dataset) series [42] and DEAP (Database for Emotion Analysis using Physical Signals) [8] may be the most popular two.

The SEED series were collected and released by Professor Bao-Liang Lu of Shanghai Jiaotong University, China. It includes three subsets: SEED, the first published dataset for three-category emotion recognition; SEED-IV, a dataset for four-category emotion classification based on EEG signals and eye movements; and SEED-VIG, a dataset for EEG-based vigilance estimation.

DEAP, a dataset including EEG, physiological, and video signals for emotion analysis, was collected and published by the Queen Mary University of London. A total of 40 emotional videos were evaluated in the 3D space based on dominance, valance, and arousal. While the 32 subjects were watching the videos, their EEG and other physiological signals (electrooculogram, electromyogram, galvanic skin response, respiration, etc.) were recorded.

### 33.3.2 EEG Feature Extraction

EEG signals are multichannel time series, whose features can be extracted in the time domain, frequency domain, and time-frequency domain [7]. Discrete wavelet transform [23] features can also be extracted from EEG.

Duan et al. [4] proposed differential entropy features, which are very effective in EEG-based emotion recognition:

$$\begin{aligned} h(X) &= -\int_{-\infty}^{+\infty} \frac{1}{\sqrt{2\pi\sigma^2}} e^{-\frac{(x-\mu)^2}{2\sigma^2}} \log_2 \left( \frac{1}{\sqrt{2\pi\sigma^2}} e^{-\frac{(x-\mu)^2}{2\sigma^2}} \right) \mathrm{d}x \\ &= \frac{1}{2} \log_2 \left( 2\pi e \sigma^2 \right), \end{aligned}$$

where the variable $x$ follows the Gaussian distribution $N(\mu, \sigma^2)$.

**Table 33.2** Representative studies on EEG-based affective computing.

| Research questions | References | Brief introduction |
|---|---|---|
| Public datasets | Koelstra et al. [8] | DEAP dataset |
| | Zheng and Lu [42] | SEED dataset |
| Feature extraction | Jenke et al. [7] | Time domain, frequency domain and time-frequency domain features |
| | Mohammadi et al. [23] | Discrete wavelet transform features |
| | Duan et al. [4] | Differential entropy features |
| | Moon et al. [24] | Brain connectivity features |
| Feature fusion | Zheng et al. [44] | EEG and eye movements |
| | Guo et al. [6] | EEG, eye movements, and eye image |
| Algorithms | Zheng and Lu [43] | Transductive parameter transfer |
| | Zhang et al. [38] | Individual similarity |
| | Li et al. [11] | Style transfer mapping |
| | Wu and Parsons [33] | Active class selection |
| | Wu et al. [34] | Transfer learning and active class selection |
| | Zhang et al. [39] | Variational pathway reasoning |
| | Ma et al. [19] | Multi-modal residual LSTM network |
| | Zheng et al. [45] | Bimodal deep auto-encoder |
| | Liu et al. [14] | Deep canonical correlation analysis |
| | Rayatdoost et al. [28] | Cross-modal encoder |
| | Du et al. [3] | Multiview depth generative framework |
| | Li et al. [9] | Deep adaptation network |
| | Luo et al. [18] | WGAN-based domain adaptation |
| | Li et al. [10] | Bi-hemispheres domain adversarial network |
| | Zhao et al. [41] | Hypergraph learning framework |
| | Song et al. [30] | Instance adaptive graph |
| | Song et al. [31] | Dynamical graph convolutional network |

The same environment may elicit different emotions for males and females, resulting in different neural patterns [36]. Therefore, different feature extraction approaches may be designed for different genders.

Additionally, different brain regions may also contribute differently in emotion recognition. Moon et al. [24] considered brain connectivity features which can effectively capture asymmetric brain activity patterns and combined them with the power spectral density features as the input to a convolutional neural network classifier.

### 33.3.3 Feature Fusion

In addition to EEG, other physiological signals also contain useful information about emotions, and thus may be combined with EEG for better emotion classification [17, 45].

For example, in positive/negative/neutral emotion classification, EEG is better at distinguishing between positive and negative emotions, whereas eye movements are better at distinguishing neutral and negative emotions. Thus, Zheng et al. [44] fused the features of EEG and eye movements for emotion recognition, and Guo et al. [6] further integrated eye image information.

Additionally, many researchers also used deep learning for emotion recognition based on multimodal physiological signals, as introduced in the next section.

### 33.3.4 Affective Computing Algorithms

Many machine learning algorithms have been used for EEG-based affect recognition. This subsection introduces some representative ones, i.e. transfer learning, active learning, and deep learning.

#### 33.3.4.1 Transfer Learning

Transfer learning deals with the scenario where the training and test data are not independent identically distributed, which is very suitable for handling individual differences in EEG-based emotion recognition. Specifically, transfer learning uses the source domain (data or knowledge from existing subjects) to facilitate the learning in the target domain (a new subject). Wu et al. [35] comprehensively reviewed the latest applications of transfer learning approaches in EEG-based brain-computer interfaces since 2016, including affective brain–computer interfaces.

Zheng and Lu [43] compared the performance of several transfer learning approaches, including transductive parameter transfer (TPT), kernel principal component analysis, and transfer component analysis (TCA) on the SEED dataset. They demonstrated that TPT outperformed the other two. Zhang et al. [38] proposed a transfer learning approach based on individual similarity for EEG-based affective computing. Specifically, it measures the similarities between individuals via maximum mean discrepancy (MMD) and utilizes transfer AdaBoost to train the model. Li et al. [11] applied style transfer mapping (STM) for EEG emotion recognition with multiple source domains. STM reduces the data distribution gap between different domains via mapping the target domain to the transformed source domain. In this way, the model learned from the source subjects is more likely to perform well for the target subject.

#### 33.3.4.2 Active Learning

Active learning selects a small amount of the most useful unlabeled samples from a large pool to label. Then a better model will be trained using the small amount of labeled data [20, 33, 34]. As data labeling is time-consuming and expensive in affective computing, active learning is very suitable for it.

Wu and Parsons [33] applied active class selection to arousal classification from multiple physiological signals and achieved better results than uniform sampling. Wu et al. [34] also proposed an approach that combines transfer learning and active class selection, which achieved higher arousal classification accuracy from multiple physiological signals, than using either approach alone.

#### 33.3.4.3 Deep Learning

Deep learning can be used in various stages of EEG-based affective computing, e.g. feature representation, multi-modality fusion, and deep transfer learning.

***Feature Representation*** Research has shown that emotion change may lead to the change of EEG and other physiological signals [39, 46]. Deep learning can automatically learn EEG feature representations, which may be more convenient and effective than manually extracted features.

For example, Zhang et al. [39] proposed a heuristic variational pathway reasoning approach for this purpose.

***Multimodality Fusion*** Different modalities of physiological signals may be better at indicating different emotions. Thus, fusion of different physiological signals may result in more accurate and more robust affective computing. Ma et al. [19] proposed a multimodal residual LSTM network, which includes both temporal shortcut paths by LSTM and spatial shortcut paths by residual networks. It can effectively learn high-level emotion representations. Zheng et al. [45] further used a bimodal deep auto-encoder to extract emotion features of EEG and eye movements, improving the classification accuracy. Liu et al. [14] introduced deep canonical correlation analysis for emotion classification based on EEG and eye movement signals. Rayatdoost et al. [28] designed a cross-modal encoder to jointly learn the features extracted from EEG, electromyogram and electrooculogram.

To cope with missing modality and label scarcity, Du et al. [3] proposed a multiview depth generative framework, which can simultaneously learn the emotion representations of different modalities and assess the importance of each modality. It uses semisupervised learning to overcome label scarcity, and latent variable to represent the missing modality.

***Deep Transfer Learning*** Inspired by TCA, Long et al. [16] proposed deep adaptation network (DAN), whose task-specific layers are embedded with multikernel MMD to reduce the domain distribution difference. Li et al. [9] utilized DAN to EEG-based affective computing and achieved better performance than traditional transfer learning approaches.

In recent years, adversarial networks are gaining popularity in transfer learning. Luo et al. [18] proposed a domain adaptation approach based on the Wasserstein generative adversarial network to handle domain shift in EEG-based cross-subject emotion classification. Inspired by the asymmetry between the brain's left and right hemispheres, Li et al. [10] proposed bi-hemispheres domain adversarial neural network to map the EEG data of each hemisphere into a separate discriminative feature space, where emotions can be classified more easily.

In addition, graph neural network has also been introduced into EEG emotion recognition. Zhao et al. [41] used the hypergraph learning framework to build a personalized emotion recognition model to investigate the relationship between personality on emotional behaviors. Song et al. proposed instance adaptive graph [30] and dynamical graph convolutional neural networks [31] to tackle individual differences and characterize the dynamic relationships among different EEG regions.

## 33.4 Challenges and Future Directions

Although many advances have been made in EEG-based affective computing, there are still several challenges demanding future research:

1. *EEG feature extraction, selection, and fusion.* There are many different approaches for EEG feature extraction. How to efficiently extract appropriate features and effectively fuse them for emotion recognition deserves future research.
2. *Nonstationarity and individual differences of EEG signals.* Since there are physical and psychological differences between different individuals, the same stimulus may induce dramatically different emotions for different subjects. Even for the same subject, the EEG responses to

the same stimulus may vary over time due to its nonstationarity. To effectively cope with non-stationarity and individual differences of EEG signals, a personalized and adaptive emotion recognition model should be constructed. This requires the integration of various sophisticated machine learning approaches, e.g. active learning, transfer learning, incremental learning.

3. *Security.* Recent studies [15, 37, 40] have shown that EEG-based brain–computer interfaces are assailable to adversarial attacks, e.g. a tiny deliberately designed perturbation to EEG signals can significantly change the classification output of a brain–computer interface. These attacks should also exist in EEG-based affective computing. It is important to investigate the vulnerability of such systems and develop defense strategies to make them more secure and robust.
4. *Privacy.* As EEG signals contain rich private information, such as health and mental states, it is necessary to develop privacy-preserving affective computing systems [1]. Especially, in transfer learning, one subject's EEG data may not be used directly by another subject.

## Acknowledgment

This work was supported by the Technology Innovation Project of Hubei Province of China (2019AEA171).

## References

**1** Agarwal, A., Dowsley, R., McKinney, N.D. et al. (2019). Protecting privacy of users in brain-computer interface applications. *IEEE Transactions on Neural Systems and Rehabilitation Engineering* 27 (8): 1546–1555.

**2** Alarcao, S.M. and Fonseca, M.J. (2019). Emotions recognition using EEG signals: a survey. *IEEE Transactions on Affective Computing* 10 (3): 374–393.

**3** Du, C., Du, C., Wang, H. et al. (2018). Semi-supervised deep generative modelling of incomplete multi-modality emotional data. *Proceedings of the 26th ACM International Conference on Multimedia*, 108–116, Seoul, South Korea.

**4** Duan, R.-N., Zhu, J.-Y., and Lu, B.-L. (2013). Differential entropy feature for EEG-based emotion classification. *Proceedings of the 6th International IEEE Conference on Neural Engineering*, 81–84.

**5** Ekman, P. and Friesen, W.V. (1971). Constants across cultures in the face and emotion. *Journal of Personality and Social Psychology* 17: 124–129.

**6** Guo, J., Zhou, R., Zhao, L., and Lu, B.-L. (2019). Multimodal emotion recognition from eye image, eye movement and EEG using deep neural networks. *Proceedings of the 41st Annual International Conference of the IEEE Engineering in Medicine and Biology Society*, 3071–3074, Berlin, Germany.

**7** Jenke, R., Peer, A., and Buss, M. (2014). Feature extraction and selection for emotion recognition from EEG. *IEEE Transactions on Affective Computing* 5 (3): 327–339.

**8** Koelstra, S., Muhl, C., Soleymani, M. et al. (2012). DEAP: a database for emotion analysis; using physiological signals. *IEEE Transactions on Affective Computing* 3 (1): 18–31.

**9** Li, H., Jin, Y.-M., Zheng, W.-L., and Lu, B.-L. (2018). Cross-subject emotion recognition using deep adaptation networks. *Proceedings of the International Conference on Neural Information Processing*, 403–413, Siem Reap, Cambodia.

**10** Li, Y., Zheng, W., Cui, Z. et al. (2018). A novel neural network model based on cerebral hemispheric asymmetry for EEG emotion recognition. *Proceedings of the 27th International Joint Conference on Artificial Intelligence*, 1561–1567, Stockholm, Sweden.

**11** Li, J., Qiu, S., Shen, Y.-Y. et al. (2019). Multisource transfer learning for cross-subject EEG emotion recognition. *IEEE Transactions on Cybernetics* 50 (7): 3281–3293.

**12** Lin, Y.-P., Wang, C.-H., Jung, T.-P. et al. (2010). EEG-based emotion recognition in music listening. *IEEE Transactions on Biomedical Engineering* 57 (7): 1798–1806.

**13** Liu, Y., Sourina, O., and Nguyen, M.K. (2011). Real-time EEG-based emotion recognition and its applications. *Transactions on Computational Science* 12: 256–277.

**14** Liu, W., Qiu, J.-L., Zheng, W.-L., and Lu, B.-L. (2019). Multimodal emotion recognition using deep canonical correlation analysis. *arXiv preprint arXiv:1908.05349*.

**15** Liu, Z., Meng, L., Zhang, X. et al. (2021). Universal adversarial perturbations for CNN classifiers in EEG-based BCIs. *Journal of Neural Engineering* 8: 0460a4.

**16** Long, M., Cao, Y., Wang, J., and Jordan, M. (2015). Learning transferable features with deep adaptation networks. *Proceedings of the International Conference on Machine Learning*, 97–105, Lille, France.

**17** Lu, Y.-F., Zheng, W.-L., Li, B.-B., and Lu, B.-L. (2015). Combining eye movements and EEG to enhance emotion recognition. *Proceedings of the International Joint Conference on Artificial Intelligence*, Buenos Aires, Argentina.

**18** Luo, Y., Zhang, S.-Y., Zheng, W.-L., and Lu, B.-L. (2018). WGAN domain adaptation for EEG-based emotion recognition. *Proceedings of the International Conference on Neural Information Processing*, 275–286, Siem Reap, Cambodia.

**19** Ma, J., Tang, H., Zheng, W.-L., and Lu, B.-L. (2019). Emotion recognition using multimodal residual LSTM network. *Proceedings of the 27th ACM International Conference on Multimedia*, 176–183, New York City, NY.

**20** Marathe, A.R., Lawhern, V.J., Wu, D. et al. (2016). Improved neural signal classification in a rapid serial visual presentation task using active learning. *IEEE Transactions on Neural Systems and Rehabilitation Engineering* 24 (3): 333–343.

**21** Mehrabian, A. (1996). Pleasure-arousal-dominance: a general framework for describing and measuring individual differences in temperament. *Current Psychology* 14 (4): 261–292.

**22** Minsky, M. (1986). *The Society of Mind*. Simon and Schuster.

**23** Mohammadi, Z., Frounchi, J., and Amiri, M. (2017). Wavelet-based emotion recognition system using EEG signal. *Neural Computing and Applications* 28 (8): 1985–1990.

**24** Moon, S.-E., Jang, S., and Lee, J.-S. (2018). Convolutional neural network approach for EEG-based emotion recognition using brain connectivity and its spatial information. *Proceedings of the IEEE International Conference on Acoustics, Speech and Signal Processing*, 2556–2560, Calgary, Canada.

**25** Ortony, A., Clore, G.L., and Collins, A. (1990). *The Cognitive Structure of Emotions*. Cambridge University Press.

**26** Picard, R.W. (1997). *Affective Computing*. MIT Press.

**27** Plutchik, R. (2003). *Emotions and Life: Perspectives from Psychology, Biology, and Evolution*. American Psychological Association.

**28** Rayatdoost, S., Rudrauf, D., and Soleymani, M. (2020). Expression-guided EEG representation learning for emotion recognition. *Proceedings of the IEEE International Conference on Acoustics, Speech and Signal Processing*, 3222–3226, Barcelona, Spain.

**29** Russell, J.A. (1980). A circumplex model of affect. *Journal of Personality and Social Psychology* 39 (6): 1161.

**30** Song, T., Liu, S., Zheng, W., and Cui, Z. (2020). Instance-adaptive graph for EEG emotion recognition. *Proceedings of the 34th AAAI Conference on Artificial Intelligence*, 2701–2708, New York City, NY.

**31** Song, T., Zheng, W., Song, P., and Cui, Z. (2020). EEG emotion recognition using dynamical graph convolutional neural networks. *IEEE Transactions on Affective Computing* 11 (3): 532–541.

**32** Wikipedia (2021. Electroencephalography. https://en.wikipedia.org/wiki/Electroencephalography (accessed 7 February 2023).

**33** Wu, D. and Parsons, T.D. (2011). Active class selection for arousal classification. *Proceedings of the 4th International Conference on Affective Computing and Intelligent Interaction*, volume 2, 132–141, Memphis, TN.

**34** Wu, D., Lance, B.J., and Parsons, T.D. (2013). Collaborative filtering for brain-computer interaction using transfer learning and active class selection. *PLoS One* 8 (2): e56624.

**35** Wu, D., Xu, Y., and Lu, B.-L. (2020). Transfer learning for EEG-based brain-computer interfaces: a review of progress made since 2016. *IEEE Transactions on Cognitive and Developmental Systems* 14 (1): 4–19.

**36** Yan, X., Zheng, W.-L., Liu, W., and Lu, B.-L. (2017). Identifying gender differences in multimodal emotion recognition using bimodal deep autoencoder. *Proceedings of the 24th International Conference on Neural Information Processing*, 533–542, Guangzhou, China.

**37** Zhang, X. and Wu, D. (2019). On the vulnerability of CNN classifiers in EEG-based BCIs. *IEEE Transactions on Neural Systems and Rehabilitation Engineering* 27 (5): 814–825.

**38** Zhang, X., Liang, W., Ding, T. et al. (2019). Individual similarity guided transfer modeling for EEG-based emotion recognition. *Proceedings of the IEEE International Conference on Bioinformatics and Biomedicine*, 1156–1161, San Diego, CA.

**39** Zhang, T., Cui, Z., Xu, C. et al. (2020). Variational pathway reasoning for EEG emotion recognition. *Proceedings of the 34th AAAI Conference on Artificial Intelligence*, 2709–2716, New York City, NY.

**40** Zhang, X., Wu, D., Ding, L. et al. (2021). Tiny noise, big mistakes: adversarial perturbations induce errors in brain-computer interface spellers. *National Science Review* 8(4): https://doi.org/10.1093/nsr/nwaa233.

**41** Zhao, S., Ding, G., Han, J., and Gao, Y. (2018). Personality-aware personalized emotion recognition from physiological signals. *Proceedings of the 27th International Joint Conference on Artificial Intelligence*, 1660–1667, Stockholm, Sweden.

**42** Zheng, W.-L. and Lu, B.-L. (2015). Investigating critical frequency bands and channels for EEG-based emotion recognition with deep neural networks. *IEEE Transactions on Autonomous Mental Development* 7 (3): 162–175.

**43** Zheng, W.-L. and Lu, B.-L. (2016). Personalizing EEG-based affective models with transfer learning. *Proceedings of the 25th International Joint Conference on Artificial Intelligence*, 2732–2739, New York, NY.

**44** Zheng, W.-L., Dong, B.-N., and Lu, B.-L. (2014). Multimodal emotion recognition using EEG and eye tracking data. *Proceedings of the International Conference of the IEEE Engineering in Medicine and Biology Society*, Chicago, IL.

**45** Zheng, W.-L., Liu, W., Lu, Y. et al. (2019). EmotionMeter: a multimodal framework for recognizing human emotions. *IEEE Transactions on Cybernetics* 49 (3): 1110–1122.

**46** Zheng, W.-L., Zhu, J.-Y., and Lu, B.-L. (2019). Identifying stable patterns over time for emotion recognition from EEG. *IEEE Transactions on Affective Computing* 10 (3): 417–429.

# 34

# Security of Human Machine Systems

*Francesco Flammini[1], Emanuele Bellini[2], Maria Stella De Biase[2], and Stefano Marrone[2]*

[1] School of Innovation, Design, and Engineering, Mälardalen University, Eskilstuna, Sweden
[2] Dipartimento di Matematica e Fisica, Universitá degli Studi della Campania "Luigi Vanvitelli", Caserta, Italy

## 34.1 Introduction

It is a matter of fact that a relevant amount of failures in sociotechnical systems is originated by human faults (see e.g. reference [7]). Those failures can be due to wrong interactions and misuse through badly engineered Human Machine Interfaces (HMI), lack of training, maintenance mistakes such as incorrect repair interventions, as well as all deliberate, intentional, and malicious actions such as sabotage, hacking, identity thefts. Furthermore, the modern paradigm of cyber-physical systems (CPS) actually include humans in the control loop, especially at the top level of the pyramid, where data need to be visualized and analyzed and important management decisions must be taken (see, e.g. reference [31]). One of the issues to be addressed in such a context is that all information provided to control room operators should be visualized in such a way to be correct, timely, easily interpretable, and to represent a reasonable cognitive load, rather than overwhelming operators with huge amounts of useless alerts and nuisance alarms. The situation is even more critical if we consider modern applications of autonomous vehicles such as self-driving cars, where the DMI (driver–machine interface) represents a critical component holding the responsibility not to distract the driver and at the same time providing essential information to ensure driving safety. Therefore, human factors and usability play a role of paramount importance in the development of secure HMI, and that means systematic and structured approaches are needed that cross several disciplines (sociology, psychology, interaction design, ergonomics, engineering, computer science, etc.), possibly enriched with model-bases analysis and quantitative evaluations. In this chapter, we present a survey of those topics by briefly reviewing the state-of-the-art in secure human–machine systems (HMS) and by providing some pointers to open challenges and future directions.

The chapter is structured as follows: Section 34.2.1 provides an historical retrospective on HMS, while Section 34.2.2 and Section 34.2.3 summarize foundations of security theory and describe a reference model to address security in HMS, respectively. Section 34.3 provides the state-of-the-art using a systematic methodology (described in Section 34.3.1), and highlighting most relevant research trends (Section 34.3.2). Finally, Section 34.4 draws conclusions and provides some hints about future research challenges.

*Handbook of Human-Machine Systems*, First Edition. Edited by Giancarlo Fortino, David Kaber, Andreas Nürnberger, and David Mendonça.

## 34.2 Background

In this section, an historical retrospective on HMS and on the study of HMS security is given, trying to formalize a reference model used in the rest of this chapter.

### 34.2.1 An Historical Retrospective

According to Scopus, the oldest paper resulting with the search phrase "human-machine systems" is [1] appeared on the Journal of Heredity in 1916. Even if the point of view of this chapter is far from this age, some words of G.W. Crile are to report: "On the basis man's claim to a superior place among animals depends less upon *different reactions* than upon a *greater number* of reactions as compared with the reactions of 'lower animals'." Starting from these words, we may say that modern HMSs further expand this set of reactions, giving to humans many other possibilities to interact with their environment.

In more recent times (1985), the work appeared in [30] makes a review of the scientific English literature, finding three different ages in HMS.

Era A (1940–55): characterized by the proliferation of many studies oriented to measure the effect of automation on human activities. The studies published all along this era are mainly conducted on empirical basis without, according to Sheridan, defining theories on the inner mechanisms in the interaction between human and machines. The majority of the studies were commissioned by or conducted in military or industrial settings (e.g. Detroit's automobile manufacturers as General Motors, Ford, and Chrysler).

Era B (1955–70): during this era, all the engineering techniques that have been tuned and refined on system engineering and control all along the World War II, were applied to human factor. Many studies proposed models of human operators with the aim of demonstrating a man-plus-control invariance principle. In this period, the theory of probability started to be applied to the characterization of these human models: "probabilistic information processor" is one of the first of these models [11], wherein the knowledge of a human operator is explicitly modeled into a probabilistic model then computed by a computer. Era B also have seen the raising of some keystone journals as IEEE's Transactions on Human Factors in Electronics, shortly afterward changed to Transactions on Man–Machine Systems, and then Transactions on Systems, Man, and Cybernetics. In summary, Era B determined the HMS topics to move from an empirical body of knowledge to a quantitative discipline.

Era C: the advent of computer has impacted on this field of study, too. Due to the increasing of the computational power, computer application moved from basic calculations to real-time simulation of aircraft, nuclear power plants, and other environments where human operators can be trained to evaluate performance and also stressful conditions. Another classical research application of computer was "expert systems," developed with the final aim to automate the human decisional process, from drug therapy, to drilling of oil wells, to configuring computer systems. Cognition engineering is just another one of the research trends of the HMS in few words: "to develop products and services that provide actionable insights into specific human behaviors.[1]"

The schema that best represents HMS up to this point is reported in Figure 34.1.

A recent paper [26] describes humans and machines have four different functions: *sensory processing*, *perception and working memory*, *decision-making*, and *response selection*, for humans, and *information acquisition*, *information analysis*, *decision and action selection*, *action implementation*, for machines. From a global perspective, the level of how much the control of the task to perform is distributed between the human and the machine can be described according to the ten levels of

1 https://cognitionengineering.com/

automation reported in reference [29]. These levels of automation span from Level 1 – the human operator does the task and turns it over to the computer to implement – to Level 10 – the computer does the action if it decides it should be done: humans are informed under the decision of the computer itself.

Modern advanced applications of HMS are in the cooperation and coexistence of human and machine in accomplishing complex and/or critical tasks, e.g. cooperative robots (cobots), computer-intermediated movement of robotic arms and legs, autonomous computer-assisted vehicles. In this context, security plays a crucial role since in this modern, interconnected world, interaction between human and machine is more and more frequently intermediated by open communication networks and complex user interfaces.

### 34.2.2 Foundations of Security Theory

The theoretical framework of security is derived from the dependability theory proposed by Laprie [19] is in reference [3]. In this work, the classical security definition as a triad of integrity, confidentiality, and availability is done and, according to such a framework, the classical dichotomy between human and machines in HMS is explored under the security aspects. Avižienis et al. consider both the cases of security problems: (i) caused by faults occurred in machines, impacting on the human operators, and (ii) human errors causing failures of machines. It was stated that the HMS represents a hard challenge for security and dependability: "the problems of complex human-machine interactions (including user interfaces) remain a challenge that is becoming very critical – the means to improve their dependability and security need to be identified and incorporated."

### 34.2.3 A Reference Model

In this subsection, we want to provide a general schema for HMS that will guide the research. To be as general as possible, while embracing the modern applications of HMS, we modified the schema presented in Figure 34.1 with a new one, depicted in Figure 34.2.

Regarding the previous one, this schema reflects better the complexity of modern human–machine interactions, since it overcomes the classical settings where a human totally controls over the machine whose only aim is to act mechanical operations without playing any role in the cognitive and decisional process.

A complete survey of the papers detailing each research contributions in the field of security in HMS is out of the scope of this chapter. Instead, a discussion on the major trends and on the living challenges in this field will be described.

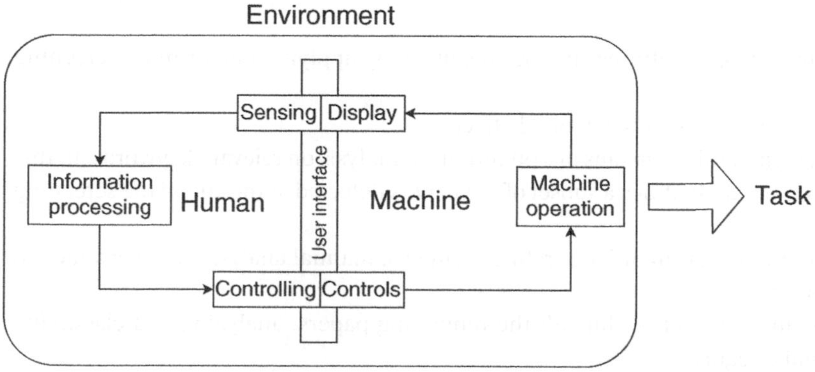


**Figure 34.1** Classical HMS Schema (inspired by Whitfield [32]).

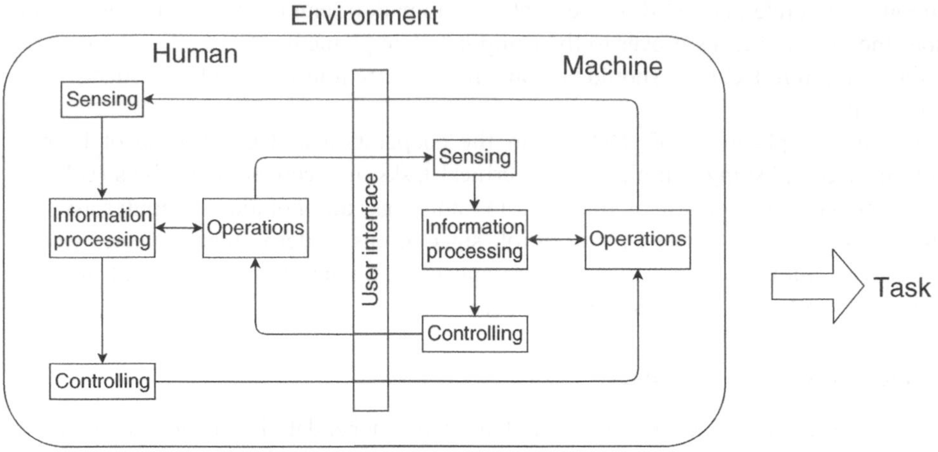


**Figure 34.2** HMS reference schema.

## 34.3 State of the Art

### 34.3.1 Survey Methodology

This section analyses articles, conference papers and reviews in accordance with the PRISMA 2020 guidelines [24] through a search in digital databases. The investigation includes publications, from 2011 to 2021, that analyzing the connections between HMSs and security issues, from the perspective of Security Challenge.

PRISMA stands for Preferred Reporting Items for Systematic reviews and Meta-Analysis, and it is a systematic process. PRISMA 2020, that replaces the 2009 statement, provides a checklist and a flow diagram useful for structuring an exhaustive and transparent report. The checklist contains the main sections that must be addressed in the review; instead, the flow diagram helps to describe the four research phases: identification of the sources, screening of bibliographic material, eligibility and inclusion of the most pertinent articles.

It is important to underline that, for the sake of the space, a complete, exhaustive execution of the PRISMA methodology is out of the scope of this chapter. This methodology is used here to highlight the major research trends in this field. To this aim, the following process is defined:

- Identification – whose aim is to choose the starting database and to define the initial query with relevant keywords;
- Screening – that is in charge of refining the first result set by applying one or more screening criteria;
- Eligibility – that, in our approach, has a twofold effect:
  (a) to define the research trends by means of a quantitative analysis on relevant keywords. In this way, each research trend identifies a subset of the papers detected at the end of the screening phase;
  (b) to filter each of these subsets in order to refine them by a manual analysis of the abstract, to avoid false positives;
- Inclusion – which is in charge of reading all the remaining papers, analyzing and classifying them into a set of final categories.

More in concrete, this work covers the phases from Identification to Eligibility (a), reaching the result of identifying the research trends.

***Identification*** As this chapter presents a lightweight review of the papers, we focus our attention on the Scopus bibliographic database[2]. Scopus not only furnish a large bibliography but also provides optimized analytical tools to enrich the research work with advanced analysis in graphical format, making so the research workflow more efficient and effective. Other relevant bibliographic databases are the ACM Guide to Computing Literature, IEEE Xplore is a digital library that collects publications in the field of computer science, electrical engineering, and electronics [33], DBPL computer science bibliography [20] and Web of Science[3], currently maintained by Clarivate that provides access to multiple databases with comprehensive citation for different academic disciplines. They will be considered in further publications. To motivate the choice of Scopus, two considerations are due (i) Scopus is a wide-spread database that is taken into high consideration from scholars and practitioners; (ii) Scopus is highly integrated with the Scival tool that makes powerful quantitative and trend analyses feasible and easy to accomplish. To start the analysis, some keyword groups are considered. The phrase is built by considering at least one term per group in the paper title, abstract, or keyword list. Such groups are

- "security" group: security, privacy, confidentiality, availability, integrity;
- "human" group: human, user, operator, driver;
- "machine" group: machine, system, computer;
- "interaction" group: interaction, interface, hms, ui, hmi.

Hence, the Scopus search phrase is *TITLE-ABS-KEY((security OR privacy OR confidentiality OR availability OR integrity) AND ((human OR user OR operator OR driver) AND (machine OR system OR computer) AND (interaction OR interface) OR (hms) OR (ui) OR (dmi))).*

***Screening*** as the second phase of the followed approach is oriented to limit the number of the papers previously selected, further searching criteria are here reported: (i) year, only papers related to the period 2011–2022 are considered; (ii) language, only papers in English; (iii) subject area, papers are limited to belong to the Computer Science area; (iv) source type, only journal and conference proceeding papers are considered.

***Eligibility (a)*** To match the objective of this phase, which is to define the hottest research trend using a quantitative analysis, the Scival tool has been used. SciVal is an analysis tool linked to the Scopus database, useful to visualize the Scopus research performance, and allows identifying and analyzing research trends. In this work, SciVal was used to analyze trends in the HMS security landscape over the past few years, extrapolating near future scenarios. After applying Scival-powered analysis, three main research trends are detected and deepened in next phase using traditional PRISMA tasks.

First, Figure 34.3 shows the growing trend of the entire research topic by plotting year per year, the number of the published paper.

Inside this panorama, all the keyphrases reported in Scopus for each article can be automatically computed and analyzed in Scival that, by means of a word cloud diagram, is able to visually report growing and declining trends. In Figure 34.4, such a diagram is reported for the considered dataset,

2 https://www.scopus.com/
3 https://access.clarivate.com/

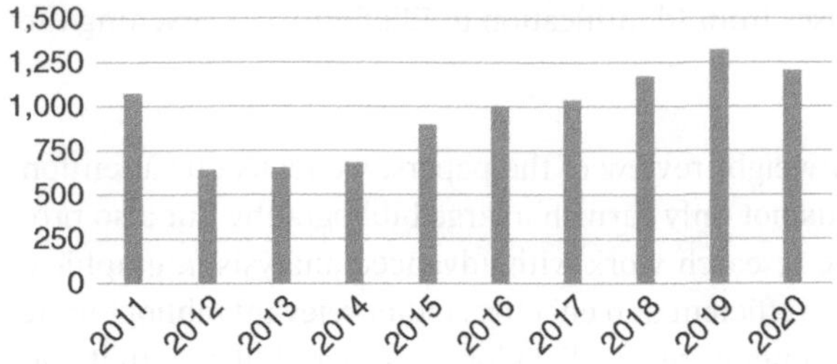


**Figure 34.3** Whole dataset publication per year.

**Figure 34.4** Keyphrase word cloud.

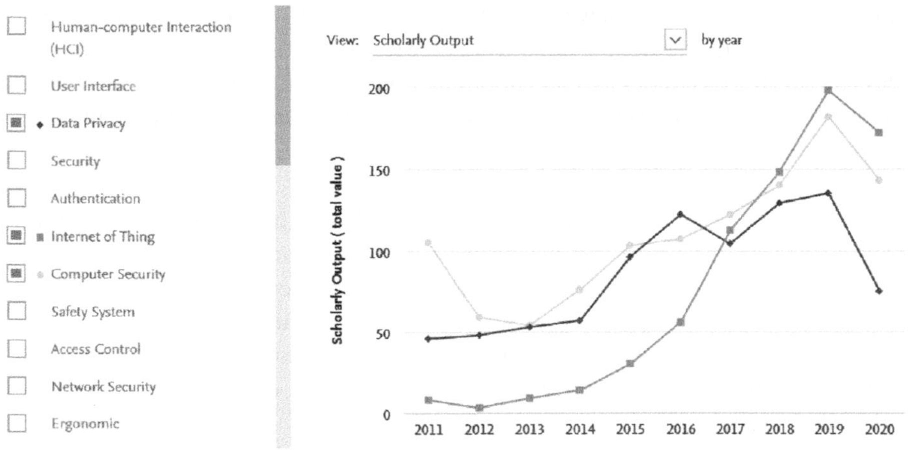


**Figure 34.5** Keyphrases trends (publication per year).

both highlighting declining (in light gray) and growing keyphrases (in dark gray): the analysis is computed by considering the number of the published papers per year. A more analytical picture (word cloud) is reported in Figure 34.5, where the first three trends emerged.

Such trends are (i) Data Privacy, (ii) Internet of Things, and (iii) Computer Security in order of intensity, which are discussed and detailed in Section 34.3.2.

### 34.3.2 Research Trends

For each selected trendy keyphrase, four of the most cited papers are identified and discussed in each paragraph to present a first excerpt of relevant research.

***Data Privacy*** is, according to Scival, the most relevant growing trend in the considered dataset. The selected paper for this keyphrase are

- in reference [18], a method of improving the effectiveness of recommender systems is presented with trade-offs between recommendation performance and data privacy;
- in reference [14], the perception of data privacy by Internet user in approaching to websites is presented;
- in reference [17], the impact of the presenting privacy concerns in the choice of apps permissions in the Android OS has been determined;
- in reference [27], the problem of data privacy is dealt with in the research area of facial recognition, which enables a more natural way to HMI. Encryption is here used to match with both the requirements.

***Internet of Things*** is a technical research topic: in Scopus, considering the same years, research areas, and source type, there are more than 74,000 papers selected just querying "Internet of Things" in paper's title, abstract, or keyword. Limiting the dataset of Eligibility(a) to the considered keyphrase detects 706 papers. Among these papers:

- in the comprehensive survey [21], the impact of IoT on HMI is presented, with a special focus on data privacy;
- in reference [12], the impact of different levels of IoT on mobile health, assisted living, e-medicine, implants, and early warning systems are presented. Aspects dealing with human interfaces are also covered;
- in reference [13], a mechanism is proposed supporting rights delegation and sophisticated customizations in access control by means of IoT;
- reference [2] is another highly cited paper dealing with access control in medical sensor network by means of IoT infrastructures.

***Computer Security*** is a vertical aspect highly affected by human factor; in particular, a critical role is played by authentication which is still the weak link in security.[4] Constraining the dataset with this keyphrase limits the number of the papers to 155; among the most cited papers in this group:

- in reference [6], the authors evaluated over 20-years of approaches to replace password-based authentication mechanisms with other proposals, from biometric-based to token-based. The authors define a concrete evaluation framework, showing the limit of many proposals. The problem is still topical, since it is quite hard to solve technically.
- authors of reference [9] improve existing remote authentication schemes based on low-cost mobile devices in telemedicine applications.
- in reference [4], authors provide a method for multimodal behavioral biometric data (e.g. keyboard usage patterns, and mouse interactions) for authentication purposes.
- in reference [16], a system based on a Secure Anonymized Information Linkage (SAIL) Gateway is introduced and adopted to allow proper trade-offs between usability and data privacy.

4 In a widespread report, IBM stated that human error is the main cause of 95% of cyber-security breaches – https://essextec.com/wp-content/uploads/2015/09/IBM-2015-Cyber-Security-Intelligence-Index_FULL-REPORT.pdf.

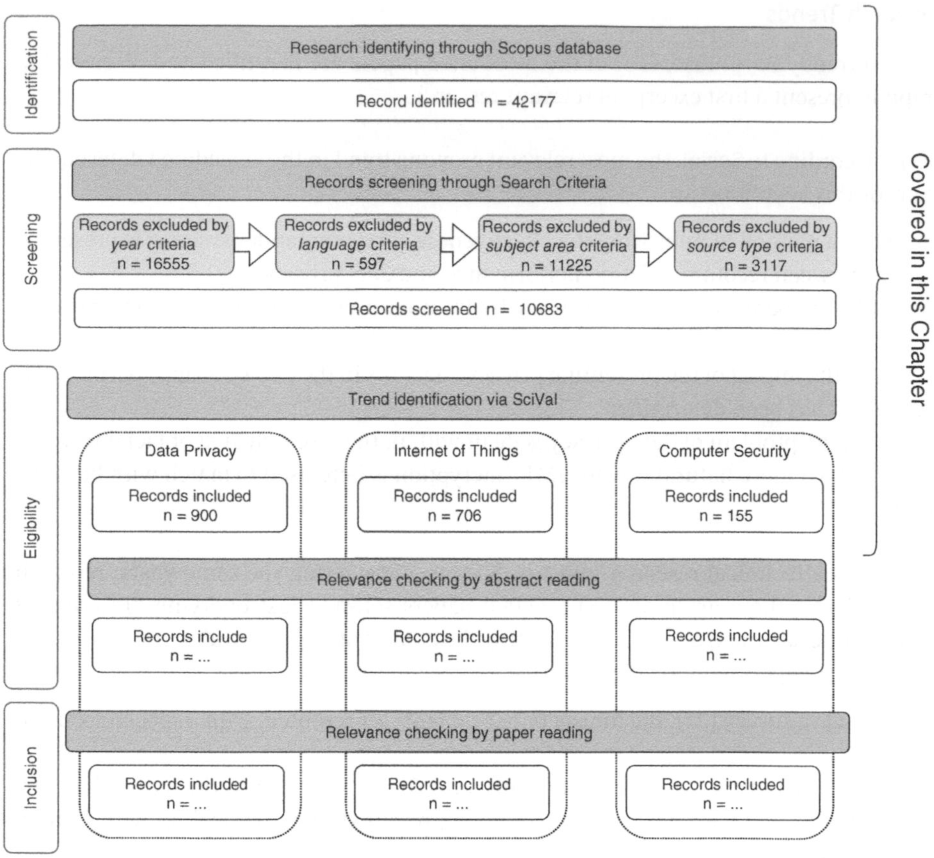


**Figure 34.6** Overview of the literature review.

The analysis conducted in this chapter must be considered as first, preliminary discussion about a research area that is wide as well as HMS that are pervasive in our everyday life. The great number of the considered papers after the first phase (i.e. 42177) is a result of a query quite constrained, revealing a huge research panorama. Figure 34.6 summarizes the followed approach also reporting the number of the paper selected/discarded at each stage. Table 34.1, summarizes the literature contributions considered in this paper. Other surveys and screening activities could reduce this set, allowing a manual analysis of the contents and the consequent paper aggregation and clustering.

## 34.4 Conclusions and Future Research

In this chapter, we have addressed current research in the field of secure HMS, with a focus on data privacy, the Internet of Things, and – more in general – computer security (i.e. availability, confidentiality, and integrity).

In particular, the data privacy trend in HMS includes both personal data as well as data collected from sensors/devices (e.g. video) that may refer to a person for recognition, or even to monitor health status (e.g. in personalized healthcare). The trade-off between application performance and privacy preservation is an open challenge and requires the introduction of a privacy-by-design approach in HMS. In this respect, emerging technologies as homophobic

**Table 34.1** List of all cited papers

| Cited papers list | | |
|---|---|---|
| **Keyphrase** | **Topic** | **References** |
| Data Privacy | Trade-offs between recommendation performance and data privacy. | Knijnenburg et al. [18] |
| | Perception of data privacy by Internet user. | Hong and Thong [14] |
| | Impact of the presenting privacy concerns in the choice of apps permissions. | Kelley et al. [17] |
| | Use of encryption to address privacy concerns. | Rahulamathavan et al. [27] |
| Internet of Things | Impact of IoT on HMI. | Lin et al. [21] |
| | Impact of different levels of IoT on mobile health. | Farahani et al. [12] |
| | Mechanism to supporting rights delegation and customizations in access control by means of IoT. | Gusmeroli et al. [13] |
| | Access control mechanism in medical sensor network by means of IoT infrastructures. | Al-Turjman and Alturjman [2] |
| Computer Security | Approaches to replace password-based authentication mechanisms with other proposals, from biometric-based to token-based. | Bonneau et al. [6] |
| | How to improve existing remote authentication schemes based on low-cost mobile devices. | Chen et al. [9] |
| | Method for multimodal behavioral biometric data for authentication purposes. | Bailey et al. [4] |
| | System based on SAIL Gateway to allow proper trade-offs between usability and data privacy. | Jones et al. [16] |

encryption (see, e.g. reference [22]) and Federated Learning (see, e.g. reference [28]) represent a desirable direction to secure HMS while maintaining its utility and functionality.

The IoT trend is making HMS evolve toward a deeper fusion of the human-related aspects with the machine-related ones. Emerging paradigms as the Internet of Everything (IoE) (see, e.g. reference [5], Internet of Body (IoB) (see, e.g. reference [8]), or Internet of Brain (IoB) (see, e.g. reference [15]), amongst others, provide evidence of such a trend. In such a scenario, where humans are so intimately connected to machines, a security violation happening in the cyber-world could cause implications and impacts that are difficult to evaluate (e.g. brain hacking).

The computer security trend in HMS is mainly related to authentication issues, i.e. granting the authorization to access cyber-functionalities. The identity theft (e.g. Sybil attack, see reference [10]) is one of the most critical threats that can be mitigated with techniques based on biometrics (e.g. fingerprints, voice recognition, and gesture recognition such as signature style, up to the use of DNA). The challenge is to make these tools even more integrated into the HMS in order to secure friction-less interactions.

Moreover, from the results of the analysis, we have seen that the interest to secure HMS has grown substantially in the last few years, and therefore, it represents a quite active research area, especially in the fields of information fusion and effective visualization, adaptive interfaces, multimodal, and behavioral biometrics for user identification and access control. Being a cross-discipline research field, with many anthropological, sociological, physiological, and psychological aspects related to the complexity of human perception and cognition, it is difficult to develop reference to formal models and to perform quantitative evaluations as in other engineering disciplines. However, we believe that the use of structured and systematic approaches, including multiparadigm statistical modeling and simulation (see, e.g. reference [23]), represents a promising approach to manage complexity and criticality of HMS and to address the uncertainties related to imperfect models. That would be essential within future trustworthy autonomous systems, which will be required to detect and counteract evolving threats through intelligent behaviors based on learning and self-adaptation. Together with collaborative security approaches, one important paradigm that would need to be addressed by future research is the so-called "explainable security," with the aim of easing HMS certification against reference international standards (see, e.g. reference [25]).

## References


1 AA.VV. (1916). The Human Machine: A Mechanistic View of Life Which Conceives Man as Being Merely a Venus' Fly-Trap Many Times Multiplied-The Kinetic System for the Transformation of Energy - Origin and Function of the Emotions. *Journal of Heredity* 7 (11): 483–493. https://doi.org/10.1093/oxfordjournals.jhered.a110589.

2 Al-Turjman, F. and Alturjman, S. (2018). Context-sensitive access in Industrial Internet of Things (IIoT) healthcare applications. *IEEE Transactions on Industrial Informatics* 14 (6): 2736–2744. https://doi.org/10.1109/TII.2018.2808190.

3 Avižienis, A., Laprie, J.-C., Randell, B., and Landwehr, C. (2004). Basic concepts and taxonomy of dependable and secure computing. *IEEE Transactions on Dependable and Secure Computing* 1 (1): 11–33. https://doi.org/10.1109/TDSC.2004.2.

4 Bailey, K.O., Okolica, J.S., and Peterson, G.L. (2014). User identification and authentication using multi-modal behavioral biometrics. *Computers and Security* 43: 77–89. https://doi.org/10.1016/j.cose.2014.03.005.

5 Bellini, E., Bellini, P., Cenni, D. et al. (2021). An IOE and big multimedia data approach for urban transport system resilience management in smart cities. *Sensors* 21 (2): https://doi.org/10.3390/s21020435.

6 Bonneau, J., Herley, C., Van Oorschot, P.C., and Stajano, F. (2012). The quest to replace passwords: a framework for comparative evaluation of web authentication schemes, 553–567. https://doi.org/10.1109/SP.2012.44.

7 Carayon, P. (2006). Human factors of complex sociotechnical systems. *Applied Ergonomics* 37 (4): 525–535. https://doi.org/10.1016/j.apergo.2006.04.011.

8 Celik, A., Salama, K.N., and Eltawil, A.M. (2021). The internet of bodies: a systematic survey on propagation characterization and channel modeling. *IEEE Internet of Things Journal* 9 (1): 321–345. https://doi.org/10.1109/JIOT.2021.3098028.

9 Chen, H.-M., Lo, J.-W., and Yeh, C.-K. (2012). An efficient and secure dynamic ID-based authentication scheme for telecare medical information systems. *Journal of Medical Systems* 36 (6): 3907–3915. https://doi.org/10.1007/s10916-012-9862-y.

10 Douceur J.R. (2002). The Sybil attack. In: *Peer-to-Peer Systems. IPTPS 2002, Lecture Notes in Computer Science*, vol. 2429 (ed. P. Druschel, F. Kaashoek, and A. Rowstron), 251–260. Springer. https://doi.org/10.1007/3-540-45748-8_24.

11 Edwards, W. (1963). Probabilistic information processing in command and control systems. esd-tdr-62-345. *Technical documentary report*. US Air Force, 86, 1–34.

12 Farahani, B., Firouzi, F., Chang, V. et al. (2018). Towards fog-driven IoT eHealth: promises and challenges of IoT in medicine and healthcare. *Future Generation Computer Systems* 78: 659–676. https://doi.org/10.1016/j.future.2017.04.036.

13 Gusmeroli, S., Piccione, S., and Rotondi, D. (2013). A capability-based security approach to manage access control in the Internet of Things. *Mathematical and Computer Modelling* 58 (5-6): 1189–1205. https://doi.org/10.1016/j.mcm.2013.02.006.

14 Hong, W. and Thong, J.Y.L. (2013). Internet privacy concerns: an integrated conceptualization and four empirical studies. *MIS Quarterly: Management Information Systems* 37 (1): 275–298. https://doi.org/10.25300/MISQ/2013/37.1.12.

15 Jingtao, Y., Li, Z., and Junlei, Q. (2019). Design of an internet of brain things network security system based on ICN. *IEEE Access* 7: 1694–1705. https://doi.org/10.1109/ACCESS.2018.2886571.

16 Jones, K.H., Ford, D.V., Jones, C. et al. (2014). A case study of the Secure Anonymous Information Linkage (SAIL) Gateway: a privacy-protecting remote access system for health-related research and evaluation. *Journal of Biomedical Informatics* 50: 196–204. https://doi.org/10.1016/j.jbi.2014.01.003.

17 Kelley, P.G., Cranor, L.F., and Sadeh, N. (2013). Privacy as part of the app decision-making process, 3393–3402. https://doi.org/10.1145/2470654.2466466.

18 Knijnenburg, B.P., Willemsen, M.C., Gantner, Z. et al. (2012). Explaining the user experience of recommender systems. *User Modeling and User-Adapted Interaction* 22 (4–5): 441–504. https://doi.org/10.1007/s11257-011-9118-4.

19 Laprie, J. (1985). Dependable computing and fault tolerance: concepts and terminology, 2–11.

20 Ley, M. (2009). Proceedings of the VLDB endowment. *Proceedings of the VLDB Endowment* 2 (2): 1493–1500. https://doi.org/10.14778/1687553.1687577.

21 Lin, J., Yu, W., Zhang, N. et al. (2017). A survey on Internet of Things: architecture, enabling technologies, security and privacy, and applications. *IEEE Internet of Things Journal* 4 (5): 1125–1142. https://doi.org/10.1109/JIOT.2017.2683200.

22 Marrone, S., Tortora, A., Bellini, A. et al. (2021). Development of a testbed for fully homomorphic encryption solutions. *2021 IEEE International Conference on Cyber Security and Resilience (CSR)*, 206–211. https://doi.org/10.1109/CSR51186.2021.9527988.

23 Moscato, F., Flammini, F., Di Lorenzo, G. et al. (2007). The software architecture of the OsMoSys multisolution framework. *Proceedings of the 2nd International Conference on Performance Evaluation Methodologies and Tools*, ValueTools '07.

24 Page, M.J., McKenzie, J.E., Bossuyt, P.M. et al. (2021). The PRISMA 2020 statement: an updated guideline for reporting systematic reviews. *BMJ* 372 (71): https://doi.org/10.1136/bmj.n71.

25 Pappaterra, M.J. and Flammini, F. (2019). A review of intelligent cybersecurity with bayesian networks. *2019 IEEE Conference on Systems, Man and Cybernetics (SMC)*, 445–452. https://doi.org/10.1109/SMC.2019.8913864.

26 Parasuraman, R., Sheridan, T.B., and Wickens, C.D. (2000). A model for types and levels of human interaction with automation. *IEEE Transactions on Systems, Man, and Cybernetics Part A: Systems and Humans* 30 (3): 286–297. https://doi.org/10.1109/3468.844354.

27 Rahulamathavan, Y., Phan, R.C.-W., Chambers, J.A., and Parish, D.J. (2013). Facial expression recognition in the encrypted domain based on local fisher discriminant analysis. *IEEE Transactions on Affective Computing* 4 (1): 83–92. https://doi.org/10.1109/T-AFFC.2012.33.

28 Rieke, N., Hancox, J., Li, W. et al. (2020). The future of digital health with federated learning. *npj Digital Medicine* 3 (1): 119. https://doi.org/10.1016/j.jbi.2014.01.003.

29 Verplank W.L. and Sheridan, T.B. (1978). *Human and Computer Control of Undersea Teleoperators*. MIT, Man-Machine Systems Laboratory. https://doi.org/10.21236/ADA057655.

**30** Sheridan, T.B. (1985). Forty-Five Years of Man-Machine Systems: History and Trends. Number 8, 1–9. https://doi.org/10.1016/b978-0-08-032566-8.50006-0.

**31** Tokody, D., Papp, J., Iantovics, L.B., and Flammini, F. (2019). *Complex, Resilient and Smart Systems*, 3–24. Cham: Springer International Publishing. ISBN 978-3-319-95597-1. https://doi.org/10.1007/978-3-319-95597-1_1.

**32** Whitfield, D. (1966). A review of: *"Man-Machine Engineering*." By A. CHAPANIS. (Belmont: Wadsworth and London: Tavistock, 1966.) [Pp. vii+134.] 21s. *Ergonomics* 9 (6): 537. https://doi.org/10.1080/00140136608964419.

**33** Wilde, M. (2016). IEEE xplore digital library. *The Charleston Advisor* 17 (4): 24–30. https://doi.org/10.5260/chara.17.4.24.

# 35

# Integrating Innovation: The Role of Standards in Promoting Responsible Development of Human–Machine Systems

*Zach McKinney[1], Martijn de Neeling[2], Luigi Bianchi[3], and Ricardo Chavarriaga[4,5]*

[1] *IEEE Standards Association, Piscataway, NJ, USA*
[2] *Department of Neurology, Amsterdam University Medical Centers (UMC), Amsterdam, Netherlands*
[3] *Department of Civil Engineering and Computer Science Engineering, "Tor Vergata" University of Rome, Rome, Italy*
[4] *Centre for Artificial Intelligence, School of Engineering, Zurich University of Applied Sciences ZHAW, Winterthur, Switzerland*
[5] *CLAIRE Office Switzerland, ZHAW digital, Zurich University of Applied Sciences Winterthur, Zürich, Switzerland*

## 35.1 Introduction to Standards in Human–Machine Systems

Human-Machine Systems (HMS) may be succinctly defined as "complex technical or social systems where human factors and tight human-machine interaction/coupling play a significant or indispensable role as an integral component [1]." Thus, maximizing the positive impact of HMS technologies while minimizing their risks and harms requires extensive coordination across a diverse array of disciplines, including human–machine interfacing (HMI) and interaction, assistive and information technologies, cognitive ergonomics, and human organizational interaction [2]. Given the deeply networked, interdependent nature of global IT infrastructures, supply chains, and scientific knowledge, the responsible development of effective HMS at scale requires a diverse and adaptive "technology governance toolbox" that can work at local, national, and global scales. This chapter outlines both the need and potential power of scientific and technical standards as a "soft law" instruments that complement binding regulations in guiding the responsible development and use of safe, effective, beneficial HMS on a global scale.

### 35.1.1 What Are Standards?

While the term "standards" may refer colloquially to a range of document types that describe widely recognized "best practices" in a given field, the formal meaning of *standards* as used in this chapter refers to official *consensus standards* developed and maintained by standards development organizations (SDOs) such that the Institute for Electrical and Electronics Engineers (IEEE) or the International Organization for Standardization (ISO), through a rigorous collaborative process. IEEE defines standards as "published documents that establish specifications and procedures designed to maximize the reliability of the materials, products, methods, and/or services people use every day. Standards address a range of issues, including but not limited to various protocols to help maximize product functionality and compatibility, facilitate interoperability, and support consumer safety and public health [3]." Similarly, the International Organization for Standardization (ISO) characterize standards as "formula[s] that [describe] the best way of doing something,"

*Handbook of Human-Machine Systems*, First Edition. Edited by Giancarlo Fortino, David Kaber, Andreas Nürnberger, and David Mendonça.

representing "the distilled wisdom of people with expertise in their subject matter and who know the needs of the organizations they represent – people such as manufacturers, sellers, buyers, customers, trade associations, users or regulators [4]." In addition to technical specifications and performance criteria, standards often specify the engineering and organizational *processes* by which technologies are designed, tested, and maintained.

While broad, these definitions provide insight into the far-reaching value and necessity of standards for supporting an ecosystem of safe, effective, reliable, and interoperable technologies, processes, and services. Due to the immense range of products, processes, and services they describe, standards affect a large and growing majority of the global population. To fulfil the needs and protect the rights of this immense diversity of "stakeholders" (i.e. all people and institutions with an interest in the development or application of a given technology), standards must be co-developed by a range of individuals with expertise and lived experience in diverse yet complementary fields – not only scientific and technical but also ethical, legal, cultural, and economic.

### 35.1.2 Standards in Context: Technology Governance, Best Practice, and Soft Law

Critically, standards themselves are not legally binding laws or regulations and do not include mechanisms for enforcement. Rather, they are informational resources intended for common reference by the developers, providers, and regulators of the goods, services, and processes they describe. Standards can, however, take on the force of law when governments and regulatory bodies require conformity to standards – typically in the context of safety-critical applications such as transportation, aeronautics, and medical devices. While laws and regulations can set firm guardrails against universally unacceptable practices and create general incentives favoring innovation, it is technical standards that offer the necessary specificity to enable interoperability and functional integration between diverse technologies.

Standards may thus be understood as one of several *soft law* instruments that complement national legal frameworks. The Organization for Economic Co-Operation and Development (OECD) defines soft law as "Co-operation based on instruments that are not legally binding, or whose binding force is somewhat 'weaker' than that of traditional law, such as codes of conduct, guidelines, roadmaps, peer reviews [5]." These instruments are numerous, ranging from published scientific consensus or guideline papers, industry white papers, policy recommendations, or general sets of "best practices" recognized by particular fields. In this vein, OECD has recently published recommendations that propose guiding legal principles in a variety of HMS-related domains, including Agile Regulatory Governance [6], Neurotechnology [7], and Artificial Intelligence [8].

Naturally, the relationships between standards, other soft law instruments, and laws present a complex web of complementarities, interdependencies, variations, and occasional conflicts between different scopes and legal jurisdictions (territories). For this reason, international *harmonization* between various standards and regional legal frameworks remains an ongoing challenge and barrier to adoption. Furthermore, standards must regularly adapt to reflect continually evolving technological capabilities and politico-economic realities.

By guiding a wide range of emerging technologies and applications, effective standards can serve as mechanisms of adaptive governance, thereby complementing existing legal frameworks, which are commonly based on antiquated sociotechnical realities and exceedingly slow to adapt. For this reason, OECD and others have called for a global technology governance approach that incorporates the use of "regulatory sandboxes" [9] to enable cross-sector collaboration and experimentation in creating guidelines and requirements to govern emerging technologies in different technological domains, application areas, and legal jurisdictions. In this way, standards are an essential tool in the "regulatory toolkit," toward fit-for-purpose and forward-looking legal and regulatory frameworks.

### 35.1.3 The Need for Standards in HMS

As outlined in the preceding chapters, the capabilities and potentialities of human–machine systems (HMS) are extensive and impressive, yet their impact remains limited by a host of ongoing challenges. These challenges may be summarized as issues of high system complexity, limited predictability, communication and coordination, balancing of risks and benefits, and achieving functional interoperability between a diversity of technologies, human users, organizations, and environments. While many HMS have achieved success in predictable, structured environments, the true potential power of HMS technologies lies in their application with a wider variety of users, in dynamic, unstructured environments. Addressing these demands continued technical innovation, creative implementation, and interdisciplinary collaboration between a wide range of academic, industry, and government players.

The gap between the current capabilities and ultimate potential of HMS demands the use of standard design methodologies and protocols that reduce variability in HMS design and usage, while preserving an optimal level of design freedom to facilitate product diversity and innovation. This difficult calibration between over- and under-constraint depends critically on both the maturity of the technology and the context of intended use, including economic and regulatory factors. In particular, operating environments (e.g. structured vs. unstructured) and risk-benefit ratios vary widely between pure research applications, consumer devices, medical devices, and industrial technologies. Inevitably, the optimal balance between standardization and innovation is both subjective and dynamic, shifting continuously with evolving technological capabilities, knowledge, and incentive landscapes.

Given the diversity and rapid advancement of HMS, achieving interoperability between various human-interfacing (HMI) technologies while maintaining product safety, effectiveness, and reliability remains a critical challenge. By codifying standard designs, methods, and performance criteria commonly recognized as "best practices" by a majority of stakeholders, standards can serve as powerful tools to reduce the uncertainty, risk, and costs associated with the development, validation, commercialization, and adoption of HMI technology. This enables researchers and developers of novel HMS to focus their efforts and resources on the novel and distinguishing aspects of their systems and approaches, while not having to "reinvent the wheel" for common elements and aspects of operation.

While standards have been developed and implemented to great effect in various technologically mature and large-scale fields such as automotive transportation, aeronautics, consumer electronics, and telecommunications – most notably, the IEEE 802 standards upon which the Internet and global telecommunications infrastructure based [10] – the level of standardization among emerging technologies varies widely. For instance, there remain relatively few standards in the field of neurotechnology, a key frontier of HMI technology – and thus HMS. From air traffic to web traffic to information flows in neuroprosthetic systems, standards are essential to governing and fostering innovation in HMS for industrial, consumer, and medical applications alike.

### 35.1.4 Benefits of Standards

As a versatile part of the technology governance toolbox, standards offer numerous benefits both to product quality and to research and innovation, which may be summarized in the following themes:

- Tools for improving quality and interoperability of emerging technology
- Lower development costs and risks (especially to start-ups and small and medium enterprises)
- Provide added technology/domain-specificity relative to regulations

- Democratic – reflect the expertise of diverse experts and the needs of various stakeholders, including tech developers, users, and regulators
- Applicable to the needs of technologies at different stages of maturity
- Voluntary conformity: flexible adoption relative to binding regulation
- Alignment of performance criteria across technologies and applications
- Tools for streamlining scientific and regulatory review processes [11]
- Enable both international harmonization and regionalized governance

To enable rather than limit innovation, effective standards for emerging technologies typically should not prescribe the granular details of system design or operation, but rather should identify the principles, processes, and performance criteria that ensure the quality of new technologies for their intended uses. However, standards *can* limit innovation, in cases where they prematurely bound the design space prior to a technology achieving satisfactory functionality. The balance between over- and under-standardization – and likewise between standardizing too soon vs. too late – is thus a delicate one, which can only be achieved through iterative engagement between technical experts and the prospective end users of both standards themselves and the technologies they describe. To support this balance, the essential characteristics for "what constitutes a good standard" are outlined in the following section.

### 35.1.5 What Makes an Effective Standard?

To promote a thriving innovation ecosystem, effective standards should possess a handful of key characteristics. First, they must be useful, by providing concrete, actionable guidance that improves product safety, performance, interoperability, and/or reliability (as applicable) in the intended uses. This focus on utility should remain central to a standard's development. Constraints on designs and methodologies should be limited primarily to ensuring product safety, quality, and reliability, including issues of traceability, as applicable.

Second, effective standards should be versatile in their applicability to a range of new and emerging technologies within a given class. Moreover, they should be modular and scalable, allowing (i) harmonization (consistency) between parallel and overlapping standards; (ii) complementarity of standards between related fields and technologies; (iii) expandability to include additional collateral standards to address emerging subclasses of technology, applications, and use cases. Above all, successful standards should be widely accessible to technology researchers and developers of all types and sizes.

Effective standards should seek to preserve the essential design freedoms of technology researchers and developers, while also establishing a sufficient level of interoperability to enable integration and meaningful contribution to the technical, scientific, clinical, or social ecosystem(s) in which they are applied. More concretely, this balance may be achieved through a principle of "mutually facilitative governance" – that effective standards should grant the greatest design freedom possible while ensuring the desired level of safety, functionality, and interoperability. Finally, effective standards should also be

- Adaptable: Standards must be updated as technology evolves – as typically required via prespecified expiration and re-review cycles.
- Modular: as a principle, standards should articulate the broadest set of principles applicable to the whole field of technology or applications to which they apply, with device- or application-specific requirements in dependent collateral ("child") standards, in a hierarchical structure.
- Suitable to technologies of different maturities/stages of development.
- Tailored to the operational needs of intended users and context of use.

## 35.2 The HMS Standards Landscape

The current standards landscape in Human–Machine Systems is as vast as the field itself, spanning a broad spectrum of domains, from human–machine interaction to cognitive, social, and organizational dynamics – thus including numerous transformational technologies such as robotics, artificial intelligence (AI), and human–machine interfacing (HMI). Rather than providing a comprehensive summary of standards across this entire scope of HMS, this chapter will focus on standards for medical devices and systems, which encompass a full range of technical and human factors – and thus highlight the key capabilities, potentialities, and challenges for standards in HMS. In this spirit, Table 35.1 identifies key HMS-related standards in the areas of medical devices, neurotechnology, and usability/human factors engineering, AI, and health informatics.

### 35.2.1 Standards in Neuroscience and Neurotechnology for Brain–Machine Interfaces

As the field of HMS encompasses such a broad array of disciplines, including human–machine and human organizational interactions, HMS design must consider the dynamics of human perception, behavior, physiology, and interaction with technological systems. By serving as literal human–machine interfaces, neurotechnologies provide an excellent example for the role of standards in promoting responsible innovation in emerging HMS-related technology. However, due to the technological diversity between different neural interface systems and the diversity of users and application scenarios, there is an enormous degree of variability in neuroscience and neurotechnology (NS/T) data, making it difficult to distill generalized knowledge from the body of literature. Accordingly, increased interoperability is needed, at both the data (*syntactic*), informational (*semantic*), and conceptual (*ontological*) levels. As a foundation for this interoperability, different neurotechnological systems and stakeholders must all operate using common terminology and information exchange standards. Despite numerous efforts to date, the need for further standardization of NS/T remains.

To illustrate the need and value of standards for HMS, this section highlights the work of two IEEE standards under current development, originating from the IEEE Industry Connection Activity on Neuro-technology for Brain–Machine Interfacing (NT-BMI) [12, 13] – namely, IEEE Standards Working Groups (SWG) P2731 (Unified Terminology for Brain–Computer Interfacing) and P2794 (Reporting Standard for in vivo Neural Interface Research). The scope and activities of these SWGs are detailed in the following sections, and the orientation of these IEEE standards and the NT-BMI activity within the broader landscape of neurotechnology standards and best practices is illustrated in Figure 35.1.

### 35.2.2 IEEE P2731 – Unified Terminology for BCI

Brain–computer interfaces (BCIs) (the core element of BMIs) represent a highly multidisciplinary field, encompassing a wide range of disciplines, such as neurology, engineering, psychology, computer science, robotics, and rehabilitation, to name a few. These disciplines all contribute to different perspectives, methods, and objectives that enrich the scientific discourse. However, this diversity poses practical challenges that the BCI field with respect to communicating scientific results because there is insufficient standardization of BCI ontology and terminology, BCI research methods, and resources (e.g. file formats and software environments) for sharing data among research groups. For example, performance assessments of BCI communication systems employ a

**Table 35.1** Overview of Key Standards in Medical HMSs.

| Standard number | Title | Scope of standard |
|---|---|---|
| *Usability and Human Factors Engineering* | | |
| ISO 9241-11 | Usability: Definitions and concepts | Defines "usability" and provides a framework for applying it to interactive systems (including built environments), products (including industrial and consumer products), and services (including technical and personal services). |
| ISO 9241-210 | Human-centered design (HCD) processes for interactive systems | Principles, requirements, and recommendations for HCD of computer-based human-interactive systems, including hardware and software considerations over full life cycle |
| ISO 9241-220 | Processes for enabling, executing, and assessing HCD in organizations | Elaborates on ISO 9241-210 by describing key processes that support required HCD activities, including the grouping of processes into *human-centered process categories* |
| ANSI/AAMI/IEC 62366-1:2015 | Medical devices – Part 1: Application of usability engineering (UE) to medical devices | • *Process* to analyze, develop, and evaluate *Medical Device Usability* relative to *Safety*<br>• Process to "assess and mitigate *Risks* associated with *Correct Use* and *Use Errors*."<br>• Part 2 describes methods for UE of medical devices, beyond safety-related aspects. |
| ANSI/AAMI HE75 | Human factors engineering – design of medical devices | General human factors engineering (HFE) principles, specific HFE principles geared toward certain user-interface attributes, and special applications of HFE (e.g. connectors, controls, visual displays, automation, software–user interfaces, hand tools, workstations, mobile medical devices, home health care devices). |
| IEEE 7000-2021 | IEEE Standard Model Process for addressing ethical concerns during system design | Values-based engineering process that complements traditional systems engineering;<br>Integrates ethical + functional req'ts to mitigate physical and ethical risks and increase innovation in design, development, and application of AI and other technical systems. |
| *Medical Devices (General)* | | |
| ANSI/AAMI/ISO 14971:2019 | Application of risk management to medical devices | • Specifies terminology, principles, and a process for risk management of medical devices, including software. Assists manufacturers to identify associated hazards; evaluate and control risks; and monitor the effectiveness of controls.<br>• Applies to device-associated risks including biocompatibility, data and systems security, electricity, radiation, and usability – for all phases of device life cycle.<br>• Applicable also to products not regulated as medical devices in some jurisdictions. |

**Table 35.1** (Continued)

| Standard number | Title | Scope of standard |
|---|---|---|
| ISO 13485:2016 | Medical devices – Quality management systems – Requirements for regulatory purposes | • Specifies quality management system requirements for organizations that provide medical devices, in conformance with applicable regulatory requirements.<br>• Applies to organizations involved in any stage of the medical device life-cycle, including design and development, production, distribution, or servicing. |
| ANSI/AAMI/ ES60601-1:2005 (IEC 60601-1: 2005, MOD) | Medical electrical equipment – Part 1: General requirements for basic safety and essential performance | • *Basic Safety* and *Essential Performance* of *Medical Electrical Equipment* and *Systems* used for alleviation of disease, injury, or disability.<br>• See also: Parts 1–2 (Electromagnetic compatibility), 1–6 (Usability), 1–9 (Environmentally conscious design), 1–10 (Physiologic closed-loop controllers) and 1–11 (Home healthcare) of this standard. |
| *Medical devices – Robotics, AI, Neurotechnology, and Health Informatics* | | |
| IEC 80601-2-78 Edition 1.0 2019-07 | Particular req'ts for basic safety and essential performance of medical robots for rehab, assessment, compensation, or alleviation | • Intended for medical robots that provide motor assistance or evaluation to patients with impaired movement functions.<br>• Does not apply to external limb prosthetic devices (use ISO 22523), electric wheelchairs (use ISO 7176), or personal care ROBOTS (use ISO 13482). |
| IEEE P3107/P3708[a)] | Human–robot interaction (HRI) | Defines Standard Terminology for HRI (P3107) and Recommended practice for design of human subject studies in HRI (P3108) |
| IEC 80601-2-26: 2019 | Particular requirements (req'ts) for basic safety and essential performance of EEG | • Applies to EEG intended for use in a range of healthcare environments.<br>• Does not cover other equipment used along with EEG, such as EEG data storage and retrieval devices, or non-EEG medical electrical equipment for patient monitoring. |
| ISO 14708-3 Second Ed. 2017-04 | Active implantable medical devices – Part 3: Implantable neurostimulators | • Applicable to active implantable medical devices intended for electrical stimulation of the central or peripheral nervous system.<br>• See also: ISO 14708 – Parts 2 (Cardiac pacemakers), 5 (Circulatory support devices), and 7 (cochlear implants) |
| ASNI/CTA-2060 | Attuned Container Format (ACF) for Consumer EEG Data | • Extensible storage format for simultaneous streams of multimodal time-series data.<br>• Minimal limitations on number of channels, sampling rates, or associated meta-data. |
| IEEE 2010-2012 (*under revision, 2022*) | Recommended practice for neurofeedback systems | • Recommendations to optimize quality of EEG-based biofeedback conveyed to users.<br>• *Original (2012) expires 2022 – under current revision* |
| IEEE 2801-2022 | Quality management of datasets for medical artificial intelligence | Best practice recommendations for quality management systems for data sets used for AI in medical devices (AIMD), to improve data quality and integrity. |

*(Continued)*

**Table 35.1** (Continued)

| Standard number | Title | Scope of standard |
|---|---|---|
| CEN ISO/IEEE 11073 | Health informatics | Extensive family of standards enabling communication between medical, health care, and wellness devices and computer systems, including automated patient data capture. |
| IEEE /UL P2933[a)] | Clinical IoT data and device Interoperability with TIPPSS | Framework for validating clinical Internet of Things (IoT) data, devices, and interop-erability based on principles of trust, identity, privacy, protection, safety, and security (TIPPSS). Includes wearable device interoperability with electronic health records. |
| IEEE (P)1752[a)] | Open mobile health (mHealth) | Defines standard representations of mHealth data of metadata, including sleep/physical activity (1752.1) and cardiovascular, respiratory, and metabolic measures (P1752.2). |
| IEEE P2795[a)] | Shared analytics across secure and unsecure networks | Establishes an overarching interoperability framework for using separate data analytic systems without users having shared access to the data within these systems. |

a) Standards working groups: standard currently in development

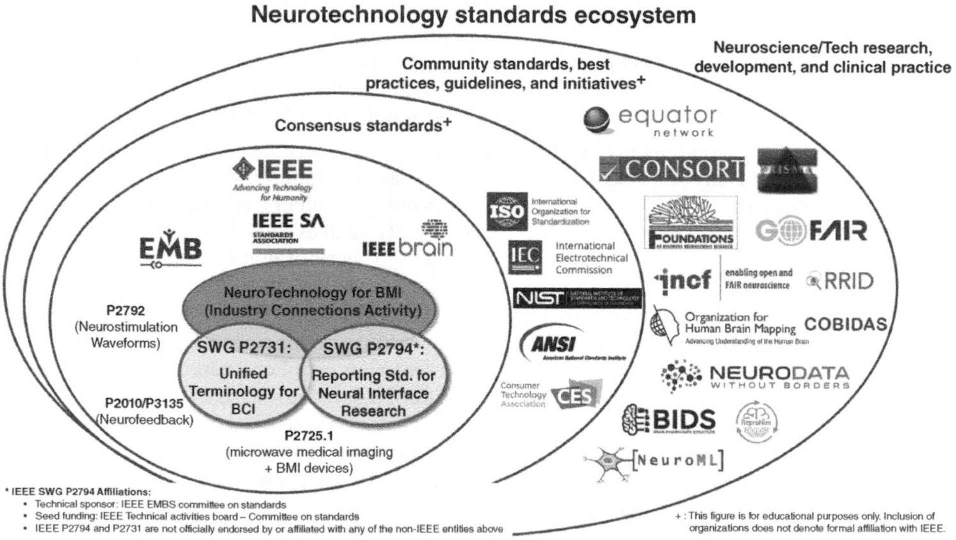


**Figure 35.1** Neuroscience and neurotechnology (NS/T) standards ecosystem.

variety of different metrics, such as accuracy, information transfer rate, and number of characters per minute – which limits the ability to compare the performance of different systems [14].

IEEE SWG P2731 started in 2019 to address these issues of inefficiency and heterogeneity of reporting and analyzing scientific literature in current BCI literature, including both surface electroencephalography (EEG)-based and implantable BCIs. The core aims of SWG P2731 are to define a standard BCI glossary, functional model, and data storage architecture. A key design precept of

SWG P2731 is that the standard must be minimally intrusive (burdensome) relative to the existing methods and tools, stakeholders in BCI research and development are deeply invested in their current platforms and would be prohibitively resistant to a dramatic paradigm shift imposed from the "top-down." Rather, the P2731 standard seeks to motivate conformity by providing a clear potential benefit that outweighs the costs, uncertainties, and challenges associated with adoption. The group has published a series of articles, summarized in Refs. [15, 16], that report its progress to date, including definitions of over 200 BCI Glossary terms, a preliminary functional model, and a multilevel data storage structure with practical examples. These elements are described in greater detail in the following sections.

#### 35.2.2.1 The BCI Glossary

IEEE SWG P2731 has been working on a standardized glossary for BCI research. To date, more than two hundred terms have been identified as critical for describing in a standardized way the BCI systems and their related aspects and domains (e.g. the neurophysiological characteristics of the neural signals recorded, the experimental paradigm, the application). Each term has been provided with a definition, with references to the current state of the art. The BCI glossary represents an iterative process, in which new terms will be added, revised, or removed as the field evolves. Separate competing definitions for the same term will be harmonized – for example by disambiguating terms like "trial," "run," and "session" that are used in various ways across research studies – so as to make all terms clear and easily understandable to stakeholders from every background [17]. Definitions for BCI paradigms are provided, such as "P300," "SSVEP" as well as modules that form a BCI system (e.g. "Transducer," "Control Interface,"). Together with the BCI Functional Model described in the next section, the glossary will provide an unambiguous way to characterize the vast majority of BCI systems.

#### 35.2.2.2 The BCI Functional Model

The definition of a Standard BCI Functional Model is a cornerstone for describing virtually any BCI system in a mutually intelligible manner that allows comparative benchmarking of system performance and design for interoperability. At present, IEEE P2731 SWG has recently published the initial version of the Functional Model illustrated in Figure 35.2 [15], which depicts the three main places in BCI systems where performance metrics are commonly computed, reflecting different points of view. Figure 35.2A describes the output of the entire system, representing the users, who are most interested in maximizing communication speed and accuracy. Meanwhile, informaticists are typically concerned with BCI performance as computed at the output of the classifier (Figure 35.2B); the machine-learning module responsible for recognizing specific brain signals of interest. Finally, neuroscientists and clinicians may be most interested in how users are able to modulate or adapt their brain activity (raw signals, Figure 35.1C) to control the system. Significantly, the BCI functional model can be adapted to any BCI paradigm or application, as detailed in Ref. [15].

#### 35.2.2.3 BCI Data Storage

In recent years, numerous datasets from different research fields have been shared in various ways, most recently via online data repositories. However, datasets in these repositories have used a variety of file formats and have included semantically different information, thus making the merging and aggregate analysis of datasets impossible. Further, metadata are often available only in separate (e.g. PDF) files, making automatic data extraction difficult or impossible. To overcome this problem, the Findable, Accessible, Interoperable, Reusable (FAIR) data principles [18] have been widely adopted as foundational by the global NS/T and neuroinformatics communities.

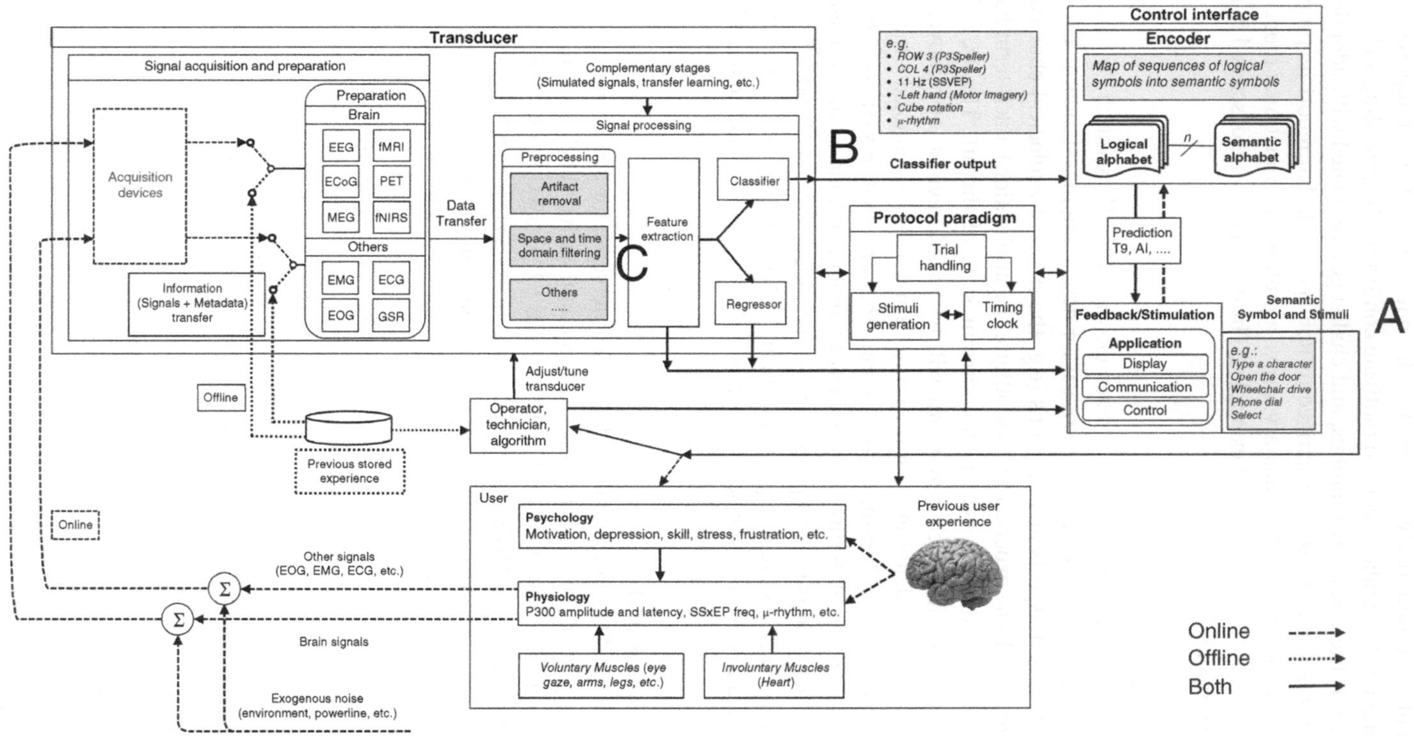


**Figure 35.2** Functional Model of a generic BCI system – draft version by IEEE SWG P2731. A, B, and C denote the most common places where metrics are computed, representing the points of view of (A) the user, (B) machine learning experts, and (C) neuroscientists. The Transducer is described in detail in [17], the Control Interface in [16], the Physiology in [18], and the Psychology in [19].

The problem of this multidisciplinary research field, however, is that there remains no standard vision for the essential information (technological and experimental details) to be stored. IEEE P2731 is working to overcome this problem by proposing a three-level semantic data structure [19]:

- **Level "0"** deals with the acquired data, regardless of the BCI paradigm. It should contain all information provided by the acquisition system, including system specifications, sensor locations, brain signals, events (e.g. stimulation events), sensor characteristics (e.g. dry vs. wet electrode), powerline noise frequency (e.g. 50 vs. 60 Hz), and a few more.
- **Level "1"** extends Level "0" by adding all the information that is needed to train a classifier. It is paradigm-specific so that different requirements exist according to different paradigms: for example, P300 experiments should include the number of iterations provided to the user, whereas SSVEP should include flickering frequencies used.
- **Level "2"** adds information about BCI feedback, including either the feedback rule or classifier output, in either free or copy mode tasks.

Significantly, the above schema are a purely *semantic* one, remaining agnostic to data file format (syntax). By integrating the BCI glossary, functional model, and information schema, IEEE P2731 is providing a foundation for *semantic interoperability* between BCI studies.

### 35.2.3 IEEE P2794 – Reporting Standard for *in vivo* Neural Interface Research (RSNIR)

Expanding the work of IEEE P2731 into the domain of human conceptual interoperability, the IEEE NT-BMI activity has also given rise to SWG P2794, which is developing a broader Reporting Standard for in vivo Neural Interface Research (RSNIR) in parallel. The purpose of this standard is to improve the transparency, interpretability, replicability, and meta-analyzability of NS/T research, including the integrated reporting of technical, clinical, and human factors across a full range of neural interfacing (NI) technologies, beyond traditional BCIs.

IEEE P2794 seeks to build on the FAIR Principles and on the high-level clinical reporting guidelines consolidated in the Enhancing QUAlity and Transparency Of health Research (EQUATOR) Network [20], which specify study design and reporting criteria for a variety of study types, including Randomized Controlled Trials (RCTs, CONSORT) [21], systematic reviews (PRISMA, [22]) and clinical trial protocols (SPIRIT, [23]). While these guidelines establish an excellent clinical reporting framework and include extensions for several technical areas such as web-based and mobile health interventions [24] and AI [25], they lack the technical specificity necessary to evaluate the effects of NI device characteristics, performance parameters, and neurocognitive factors on the safety, effectiveness, risks, and benefits of investigational devices/therapies in clinical and real-world applications. While several more technology-specific guidelines for data sharing and reporting have been developed for various NI subdomains as DBS, cochlear implants, EEG and magnetoencephalography (MEG) (see Table 35.2) – these guidelines vary in their attention to different technical, clinical, and cognitive aspects. The resulting patchwork of guidelines is not unified in a standard reporting framework and is thus insufficient to ensure interpretability, replicability, and meta-analysis across the diverse field of NS/T research. This lack of conceptual interoperability in turn limits innovation and translation of NS/T research into safe, effective, reliable, interoperable, and beneficial neurotechnologies.

To address this problem, IEEE P2794 (RSNIR) seeks to specify a minimum set of features that must be reported (including but not limited to peer-reviewed journal articles) to render any NI study fully transparent, interpretable, and replicable. SWG P2794 has published a preliminary set

**Table 35.2** Neurotechnology-specific reporting guidelines.

| | |
|---|---|
| EEG study schema [26] | • XML-based spec for packaging, sharing, and automated analysis of EEG and MEG data.<br>• Contains all necessary info to analyze EEG studies: task and paradigm descriptions, sensor locations, recording parameters, subject demographics (e.g. gender, age handedness, age.)<br>• Both human and machine-readable, based on user-centered design for usability. |
| Standard publication guidelines for DBS studies in Parkinson's disease (Guide4DBS-PD) [27] | Standard reporting guidelines for clinical studies of DBS for Parkinson's disease (PD).<br>Provide a minimal set of required data elements to facilitate interpretation and comparison of results across clinical studies. |
| Minimum reporting standards for adult cochlear implantation [28] | • Minimum standards for consistent reporting of adult cochlear implant outcomes.<br>• Intended to improve interpretability, comparison, and meta-analysis across studies. |
| Committee on best practice in Data analysis and sharing (COBIDAS) [29] | • Best practices for reproducible neuroimaging, data sharing, and reporting of MRI and M/EEG studies<br>• Includes COBIDAS-MRI (original) and COBIDAS-MEEG, for MEG and EEG data/studies. |
| Brain imaging data structure (BIDS) [30] | • Prescribes naming and organization of neuroimaging and electrophysiology data and metadata in a file system that facilitates collaboration, data validation, and software development.<br>• Addresses multiple NI modalities, including MRI (original)[31] and extensions for EEG [32], MEG[33], and intracranial electrophysiology (stereo EEG, electrocorticography, and DBS) [34]. |
| Neurodata without borders (NWB) [35] | • Standard for sharing, archiving, analyzing, and using a variety of experimental neurophysiology data, including intra-and extra-cellular electrophysiology, optical physiology, tracking, and stimulus data.<br>• Includes NWB file format and various software for data standardization and application programming. |

of minimum reporting requirements for implantable neural interfaces, which further outlines the need, approach, and initial recommendations of this working group [36]. In this work, the group divides NI research reporting elements into four categories:

1. Study aims and context: including descriptions of the type of study, intended application, technology tested, target neural pathway(s).
2. Experimental design and outcome measures: including descriptions of the animal/human subject, intervention, stimulus (if applicable), outcome, and statistics.
3. Neural interface device properties (hardware): including descriptions of the intended device service life, level of invasiveness, positioning procedure, device design, device fabrication materials and methodology, and electrical properties.
4. NI signal processing properties (software): including descriptions of target physiological signal, stimulus-waveform generation (if applicable), hardware conditioning and acquisition, signal processing, feature extraction, classification, and decision-making.

To develop RSNIR beyond these preliminary requirements and further in the human factors domain, IEEE P2794 is conducting a public survey to evaluate and integrate perspectives and experiences of all NS/T stakeholder types, including researchers, device developers, regulators, funding agencies, healthcare payers, clinicians, and end users. To participate or learn more about the NS/T Stakeholder Survey, visit [37].

By integrating diverse stakeholder perspectives in a reporting standard that spans technical, clinical, and human factors, IEEE P2794 aims to facilitate both the medical field's drive toward personalized ("precision") medicine and the need for rigorous neuroethical inquiry. Indeed, the need for more complete characterization of BCI users, including demographic, clinical, and cognitive aspects, is essential to tailor BCI design and performance to the needs of their users through a human/user-centered design (H/UCD) process [38, 39]. While H/UCD processes have been implemented in narrow use cases such as communication BCIs for people with locked-in syndrome [40], there remains insufficient standard criteria for capturing and reporting human factors in the design, development, and application of NI systems. By serving this need, IEEE P2794 aims to promote responsible innovation in neurotechnology, in line with consensus recommendations [7, 41] and initiatives such as IEEE Neuroethics Framework [42], International Neuroethics Society [43], and IEEE 7000 series standards [44].

## 35.3 Standards Development Process

To serve the needs of their users and the people they influence, standards must be developed in a highly inclusive manner, with extensive participation or input from all relevant experts and stakeholders. To remain useful through time, standards must evolve in step with technological innovation and the corresponding economic, legal, and societal context. To this end, standards – just as the technologies they govern – must be created and maintained through a rigorous collaborative process that covers their entire life cycle, from inception to drafting, approval, and adoption, and revision. Such a process is exemplified by the IEEE Standards Association's Standard Development Process [45], which is organized in the six stages outlined by Figure 35.3. Each of these steps is intended to adhere to IEEE's eight principles of standards development: direct participation, due process, broad consensus, balance of perspectives, broad openness, coherence, development, and transparency.

### 35.3.1 Who Can Participate in Standards Development?

In short, anyone with sufficient expertise or material interest in the topic (scope) of a given standard. While most SWGs are open to any individual who demonstrates sufficient knowledge and/or

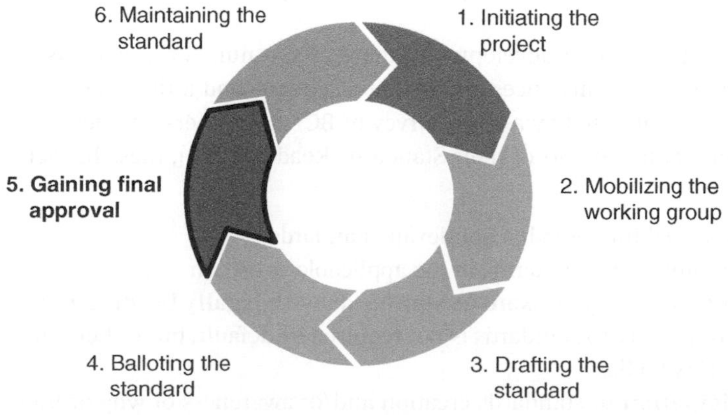


**Figure 35.3** IEEE standards development process [23].

interest in the technology(s), product(s), or process(es) at issue, some SWGs are *entity-based*, meaning that only business, research, regulatory, or advocacy organizations can participate.

### 35.3.2 Why Should I Participate in Standards Development?

The quality of standards depends on the breadth, diversity, and quality of participation in their creation. By participating in standards development, you have the opportunity both to learn from a variety of professional experts about the state-of-the-art practices in a given field, and to influence the designs and methods used by that field in the future!

### 35.3.3 How Can I get Involved in Standards Development?

**First, educate yourself** on existing standards, best practices, and related initiatives in your area(s) of interest, using public resources such as IEEE [46] or the International Neuroinformatics Coordinating Facility (INCF) [47], online webinars, and standards-related sessions and workshops at scientific conferences. **Next, join a standards working group (SWG)!** – For a representative list of active SWGs and other HMS standards-related projects, you may refer to IEEE Engineering in Medicine and Biology (EMB) Society's list of active standards-related projects [48] or search for an IEEE HMS Technical Committee [49].

## 35.4 Strategic Considerations and Discussion

### 35.4.1 Challenges to Development and Barriers to Adoption of Standards

While both the need and potential for standards to facilitate responsible innovation in HMS and emerging technologies are clear, there remain numerous challenges to their successful development and implementation. Central to these challenges are two delicate balances: first, the balance between standardizing a given technology *too early*, when the field has not yet achieved satisfactory functionality or reliability, and when imposed standards can inhibit innovation – versus *too late*, when existing designs and practices have become so widespread and deeply embedded that conforming to the standard is not practically or economically feasible. This challenge is commonly summarized as the Collingridge Dilemma [50]. Second, standards must balance between being *overly specific* (thus limiting design flexibility and innovation) and *overly general* (and thus of little practical use) in their degree of detail. Naturally, the optimal specificity increases with technological maturity.

Related to these core challenges to standard development, there exist a number of barriers to adoption resulting both from material circumstances and from perceptions and attitudes toward standards by prospective users. As highlighted by a large survey of BCI researchers and developers conducted by the NT-BMI activity in support of their Standards Roadmap [13], these barriers include the following:

- **Lack of awareness** about the availability or value of relevant standards
- **Lack of guidance on how to** implement standards in the applicable governance framework
- Resistance due to **conflation of voluntary consensus standards with legally binding regulations**: as noted previously, conformity to standards is not required by default, but rather must be imposed by legal and regulatory bodies
- **Lack of incentives for participation** in standards creation and/or awareness of why or how to participate – thus resulting in standards that are poorly suited to the needs of its prospective users

- **Lack of incentives to adopt** – e.g. when not required by any regulatory requirement or instrumental to success in a given field or market
- **Cost of access**: most standards are not free to access and the costs can be prohibitive for small and medium enterprises
- **Lack of harmonization** between standards and legal requirements in different technological areas or geographic jurisdictions
- **Mismatch between standards and technological maturity**

Naturally, attitudes toward standards were found to vary throughout the BCI domain: while many welcome standards as resources that lower regulatory uncertainty and provide concrete guidelines for technical interoperability or regulatory compliance, others (often in more research-oriented organizations) tended to regard *any* constraints on design or methodology as limits to creativity and innovation.

### 35.4.2 Strategies to Promote Standards Development and Adoption

On balance, the NT-BMI survey on attitudes toward BCI standardization [13] showed widespread awareness and receptivity to the need and *potential* value for further standardization in neurotechnology. Based on this survey and our additional experience in standards creation, we offer the following recommendations for promoting the development and adoption of standards in neurotech and other emerging HMS technologies:

- To maximize value to users, **standards development must be highly inclusive and participatory, including technical experts from all relevant fields and perspectives from all stakeholder types,** including future users of both the technology and the standard, regulators, funding entities, and policy makers.
- **Standards development should be an iterative process, employing principles of human-centered design** (see Table 35.1). In particular, their purpose and scope should first be defined to address well-characterized needs, and requirements should then be drafted, evaluated, and revised to best fulfil those needs, based on wide stakeholder feedback at all stages of development.
- To drive adoption, **standards should aim to offer functional and/or economic benefits greater than the costs and difficulty of adoption**. To this end, **standards must be sufficiently specific** to address real scientific, technical, or development challenges, **yet adaptable** enough to apply to a wide variety of technologies, processes, and services.
- To the extent possible, standards should be suitable and/or adaptable to the maturity level of the technologies to which they are applied, with greater specificity and prescriptiveness for more mature technologies
- **Emerging standards are encouraged to use open community development and open-access policies** to increase participation in their creation and to enable iterative revision and validation.
- **Regulatory bodies, funding agencies, and scientific publications should recognize and promote conformity to mature, well-validated standards.**

### 35.4.3 Final Perspective: On Innovation

In closing, we wish to emphasize that while this chapter has focused on standards as a means of promoting responsible innovation, technological innovation itself must not be conceived as a primary end unto itself, but rather as a toolbox for adaptively promoting human health and wellness. Critically, this higher aim of maximizing human well-being can only be achieved through coordinated responsible innovation between technological, legal, and cultural domains, on a shared foundation of social cohesion and mutual trust in institutions. This cross-disciplinary collaborative process is the essence of human-centered design, which we may extend to a broader concept of *human-centered (tech) governance*. In sum, by integrating diverse expertise and perspectives in a collaborative process, standards are an essential and indispensable instrument to fulfil IEEE's mission of "Advancing technology *for humanity*."

## Acknowledgements

This work has been supported by the IEEE Brain Initiative (via NT-BMI industry connections activity), IEEE EMB Committee on Standards, and IEEE Technical Activities Board Committee on Standards. Nevertheless, the views expressed herein are exclusively those of the authors and do not represent the official opinions or policy of their respective organizations. Ricardo Chavarriaga acknowledges the support of the DIZH Fellowship of "Digitalization Initiative of the Zurich Higher Education Institutions".

## References

1 International Federation of Automation and Control (IFAC). *Technical Committee on Human-Machine Systems (TC 4.5)*. https://tc.ifac-control.org/4/5/scope (accessed 29 January 2022).
2 IEEE SMC. *Transactions on Human-Machine Systems*. https://www.ieeesmc.org/publications/transactions-on-human-machine-systems (accessed 29 January 2022).
3 IEEE Standard Association (2023). *What Are Standards?*. https://standards.ieee.org/develop/develop-standards/overview.html (accessed 18 November 2021).
4 ISO Standards. *ISO Standards are Internationally Agreed by Experts*. https://www.iso.org/standards.html (accessed 18 November 2021).
5 Organisation for Economic Co-operation and Development (OECD). Soft law. https://www.oecd.org/gov/regulatory-policy/irc10.htm (accessed 29 January 2022).
6 Organisation for Economic Co-operation and Development (OECD), (July 2021). Recommendation OECD/LEGAL/0464. https://legalinstruments.oecd.org/en/instruments/OECD-LEGAL-0464 (accessed 17 November 2021).
7 Organisation for Economic Co-operation and Development (OECD), (2019). OECD-LEGAL-0457. Recommendation of the Council on Responsible Innovation in Neurotechnology. https://legalinstruments.oecd.org/en/instruments/OECD-LEGAL-0457 (accessed 31 January 2022).
8 Organisation for Economic Co-operation and Development (OECD), (May 2019). OECD-LEGAL-0449. Recommendation of the Council on Artificial Intelligence. https://legalinstruments.oecd.org/en/instruments/OECD-LEGAL-0449 (accessed 31 January 2022).
9 Attrey, A., Lesher, M., and Lomax, C. (2021). The role of sandboxes in promoting flexibility and innovation in the digital age. OECD, No. 2, https://goingdigital.oecd.org/toolkitnotes/the-role-of-sandboxes-in-promoting-flexibility-and-innovation-in-the-digital-age.pdf (accessed 29 January 2021).

**10** IEEE Standard Association (2023). IEEE 802. https://standards.ieee.org/featured/802/index.html (accessed 29 January 2022).

**11** US Food & Drug Administration (FDA) (2023). Recognized Consensus Standards Database. https://www.accessdata.fda.gov/scripts/cdrh/cfdocs/cfStandards/search.cfm (accessed 9 July 2022).

**12** R. Chavarriaga, C. Carey, J. Luis Contreras-Vidal, Z. Mckinney, and L. Bianchi, "Standardization of neurotechnology for brain-machine interfacing: state of the art and recommendations," *IEEE Open Journal of Engineering in Medicine and Biology*, vol. 2, pp. 71–73, 2021, doi: https://doi.org/10.1109/OJEMB.2021.3061328.

**13** IEEE Standards Association (2020). *Standards Roadmap: NeuroTechnologies for Brain-Machine Interfacing*. Piscataway, NJ, Industry Connections Report IC17-007, February 2020. https://standards.ieee.org/industry-connections/neurotechnologies-for-brain-machine-interfacing/ (accessed January 17 2022)

**14** P. Wierzgała, D. Zapała, G. M. Wojcik, and J. Masiak, "Most popular signal processing methods in motor-imagery BCI: a review and meta-analysis," *Frontiers in Neuroinformatics*, vol. 12, 2018, https://www.frontiersin.org/article/10.3389/fninf.2018.00078 (accessed 24 June 2022).

**15** C. Easttom, "BCI glossary and functional model by the IEEE P2731 working group," *Brain-Computer Interfaces*, vol. 8, no. 3, pp. 39–41, 2021, doi: https://doi.org/10.1080/2326263X.2021.1967659.

**16** C. Easttom Luigi Bianchi; Davide Valeriani *et al.*, "A functional model for unifying brain computer interface terminology," *IEEE Open Journal of Engineering in Medicine and Biology*, vol. 2, pp. 91–96, 2021, doi: https://doi.org/10.1109/OJEMB.2021.3057471.

**17** A. Antonietti, P. Balachandran, A. Hossaini, Y. Hu, and D. Valeriani, "The BCI Glossary: a first proposal for a community review," *Brain-Computer Interfaces*, vol. 8, no. 3, pp. 42–53, 2021, doi: https://doi.org/10.1080/2326263X.2021.1969789.

**18** M. D. Wilkinson, Michel Dumontier, IJsbrand Jan Aalbersberg *et al.*, "The FAIR Guiding Principles for scientific data management and stewardship," *Scientific Data*, vol. 3, no. 1, Art. no. 1, Mar. 2016, doi: https://doi.org/10.1038/sdata.2016.18.

**19** L. Bianchi, A. Antonietti, G. Bajwa, R. Ferrante, M. Mahmud, and P. Balachandran, "A functional BCI model by the IEEE P2731 working group: data storage and sharing," *Brain-Computer Interfaces*, vol. 8, no. 3, pp. 108–116, 2021, doi: https://doi.org/10.1080/2326263X.2021.1968632.

**20** Altman, D.G., Simera, I., Hoey, J. et al. (2008). EQUATOR: reporting guidelines for health research. *Open Medicine* 2 (2): e49–e50.

**21** K. F. Schulz, D. G. Altman, D. Moher, and CONSORT Group, "CONSORT 2010 Statement: updated guidelines for reporting parallel group randomised trials," *BMC Medincine*, vol. 8, p. 18, 2010, doi: https://doi.org/10.1186/1741-7015-8-18.

**22** M. J. Page, J. E. McKenzie, P. M. Bossuyt *et al.*, "The PRISMA 2020 statement: an updated guideline for reporting systematic reviews," *BMJ*, vol. 372, p. n71, 2021, doi: https://doi.org/10.1136/bmj.n71.

**23** A.-W. Chan Jennifer M. Tetzlaff, Douglas G. Altman, *et al.*, "SPIRIT 2013 statement: defining standard protocol items for clinical trials," *Annals of Internal Medicine*, vol. 158, no. 3, pp. 200–207, 2013, doi: https://doi.org/10.7326/0003-4819-158-3-201302050-00583.

**24** G. Eysenbach and CONSORT-EHEALTH Group, "CONSORT-EHEALTH: improving and standardizing evaluation reports of Web-based and mobile health interventions," *Journal of Medical Internet Research*, vol. 13, no. 4, p. e126, 2011, doi: https://doi.org/10.2196/jmir.1923.

**25** X. Liu, S. Cruz Rivera, D. Moher, M. J. Calvert, A. K. Denniston, and SPIRIT-AI and CONSORT-AI Working Group, "Reporting guidelines for clinical trial reports for interventions involving artificial intelligence: the CONSORT-AI extension," *Nature Medicine*, vol. 26, no. 9, pp. 1364–1374, 2020, doi: https://doi.org/10.1038/s41591-020-1034-x.

**26** EEG Study Schema (ESS) and related tools (2017). *EEG Study Schema (ESS) and related tools.* http://www.eegstudy.org/ (accessed 24 June 2022).

**27** J. L. Vitek, Kelly E. Lyons, Roy Bakay, *et al.*, "Standard guidelines for publication of deep brain stimulation studies in Parkinson's disease (Guide4DBS-PD)," *Journal of Movement Disorders*, vol. 25, no. 11, pp. 1530–1537, 2010, doi: https://doi.org/10.1002/mds.23151.

**28** O. F. Adunka, B. J. Gantz, C. Dunn, R. K. Gurgel, and C. A. Buchman, "Minimum reporting standards for adult cochlear implantation," *Otolaryngology--Head and Neck Surgery*, vol. 159, no. 2, pp. 215–219, 2018, doi: https://doi.org/10.1177/0194599818764329.

**29** C. Pernet Marta I. Garrido, Alexandre Gramfort *et al.*, "Issues and recommendations from the OHBM COBIDAS MEEG committee for reproducible EEG and MEG research," *Nature Neuroscience*, vol. 23, no. 12, pp. 1473–1483, Dec. 2020, doi: https://doi.org/10.1038/s41593-020-00709-0.

**30** Brain Imaging Data Structure (BIDS) 2022. *Brain Imaging Data Structure*, 15. https://bids.neuroimaging.io/index (accessed 4 July 2022).

**31** K. J. Gorgolewski Tibor Auer, Vince D. Calhoun *et al.*, "The brain imaging data structure, a format for organizing and describing outputs of neuroimaging experiments," *Scientific Data*, vol. 3, no. 1, Art. no. 1, Jun. 2016, doi: https://doi.org/10.1038/sdata.2016.44.

**32** C. R. Pernet Stefan Appelhoff, Krzysztof J. Gorgolewski, *et al.*, "EEG-BIDS, an extension to the brain imaging data structure for electro-encephalography," *Sci. Data*, vol. 6, no. 1, Art. no. 1, 2019, doi: https://doi.org/10.1038/s41597-019-0104-8.

**33** G. Niso Krzysztof J. Gorgolewski, Elizabeth Bock *et al.*, "MEG-BIDS, the brain imaging data structure extended to magnetoencephalography," *Scientific Data*, vol. 5, no. 1, Art. no. 1, 2018, doi: https://doi.org/10.1038/sdata.2018.110.

**34** C. Holdgraf Stefan Appelhoff, Stephan Bickel, *et al.*, "iEEG-BIDS, extending the Brain Imaging Data Structure specification to human intracranial electrophysiology," *Scientific Data*, vol. 6, no. 1, p. 102, 2019, doi: https://doi.org/10.1038/s41597-019-0105-7.

**35** J. L. Teeters Keith Godfrey, Rob Young *et al.*, "Neurodata without borders: creating a common data format for neurophysiology," *Neuron*, vol. 88, no. 4, pp. 629–634, 2015, doi: https://doi.org/10.1016/j.neuron.2015.10.025.

**36** C. D. Eiber Jean Delbeke, Jorge Cardoso *et al.*, "Preliminary minimum reporting requirements for in-vivo neural interface research: I. Implantable neural interfaces," *IEEE Open Journal of Engineering in Medicine and Biology*, vol. 2, pp. 74–83, 2021, doi: https://doi.org/10.1109/OJEMB.2021.3060919.

**37** IEEE Standards Association (2020). IEEE P2794 Standards Working Group – Reporting Standards for in vivo Neural Interface Research. https://sagroups.ieee.org/2794/ (accessed 17 January 2022).

**38** M. P. Branco, E. G. M. Pels, F. Nijboer, N. F. Ramsey, and M. J. Vansteensel, "Brain-Computer interfaces for communication: preferences of individuals with locked-in syndrome, caregivers and researchers," *Disability and Rehabilitation: Assistive Technology*, 1–11, 2021, doi: https://doi.org/10.1080/17483107.2021.1958932.

**39** J. E. Huggins, Dean Krusienski, Mariska J. Vansteensel *et al.*, "Workshops of the eighth international brain–computer interface meeting: BCIs: the next frontier," *Brain-Computer Interfaces*, vol. 9, no. 2, pp. 69–101, 2022, doi: https://doi.org/10.1080/2326263X.2021.2009654.

**40** A. Kübler Elisa M Holz, Angela Riccio, *et al.*, "The user-centered design as novel perspective for evaluating the usability of BCI-controlled applications," *PLoS One*, vol. 9, no. 12, p. e112392, 2014, doi: https://doi.org/10.1371/journal.pone.0112392.

**41** S. Goering, E. Klein, L. S. Sullivan, *et al.*, "Recommendations for responsible development and application of neurotechnologies," *Neuroethics*, pp. 1–22, 2021, doi: https://doi.org/10.1007/s12152-021-09468-6.

**42** IEEE Neuroethics Framework (2020). *The BRAIN Initiative*, January 11, 2020. https://www.braininitiative.org/2020/01/11/ieee-neuroethics-framework/ (accessed 23 October 2020).

**43** International Neuroethics Society (INS) https://www.neuroethicssociety.org/ (accessed 4 July 2022).

**44** K. Sookdeo (2023). IEEE 7000$^{TM}$ Projects | IEEE Ethics In Action in A/IS – IEEE SA. *Ethics In Action | Ethically Aligned Design*. https://ethicsinaction.ieee.org/p7000/ (accessed 4 July 2022).

**45** IEEE Standards Association (2023). Developing Standards. https://standards.ieee.org/develop/ (accessed 29 June 2022).

**46** IEEE Standards Association (2023). How to Get Involved. https://standards.ieee.org/participate/ (accessed 26 June 2022).

**47** International Neuroinformatics Coordinating Facility (2023). Standards and Best Practices organisation for open and FAIR neuroscience. https://www.incf.org/ (accessed 23 October 23, 2020).

**48** EMBS (2023). EMB Standards Working Groups, Projects, & Standards. https://www.embs.org/sc/emb-standards-working-groups-and-projects/ (accessed 25 June 2022).

**49** IEEE SMC (2023). Human Machine Systems Technical Committees. https://www.ieeesmc.org/technical-activities/human-machine-systems (accessed 25 June 2022).

**50** A. Genus and A. Stirling "Collingridge and the dilemma of control: Towards responsible and accountable innovation," Research Policy, vol. 47, no. 1. Elsevier BV, pp. 61–69, Feb. 2018. doi: https://doi.org/10.1016/j.respol.2017.09.012.

# 36

# Situation Awareness in Human-Machine Systems

*Giuseppe D'Aniello and Matteo Gaeta*

*Department of Information and Electrical Engineering and Applied Mathematics, University of Salerno, Fisciano (SA), Italy*

## 36.1 Introduction

A human-machine system (HMS) is a system wherein the goals and objectives are achieved through the integration of the functions of a human operator and a machine. The traditional role of humans in HMS is to perform direct manual control of elementary processes, via the observation of the state of the system. Nowadays, with the advances and increased sophistication of machines, computers, and automation, the role of humans shifts from a simple machine operator, to the role of supervisor of complex, capable, intelligent, and autonomous systems. However, despite the advances in technology, processes, and design of HMSs, the occurrence of critical human errors and accidents still remains a big challenge. The root cause of such accidents is the presence of humans in the loop of control. The reasons for such phenomenon are manifold. Technology alone is too often seen as a panacea to all issues, without considering the limitations of humans in terms of sensory, cognitive, and motor capabilities. Indeed, the more the system is automated, the more could be difficult for the operator to understand how the system works and acts, especially in unexpected and critical conditions. If the system is not well designed, the automation could bring the human out-of-the-loop of command and control of the system [13, 36]. Under these circumstances, the improper introduction of new technology could just worsen the situation. It can exacerbate human performance problems, reducing the human capabilities of making decisions and performing actions.

The solution to the out-of-the-loop syndrome, thus allowing an effective and correct interaction between humans and machines, is to support the situation awareness (SA) of the human operators by properly designing the HMS. From the point of view of the human operators, Situation Awareness (SA) is the capability of understanding what is happening in the environment at a specific moment and anticipating future evolutions to make coherent decisions and actions concerning their goals. We refer to this capability with the term "Human Situation Awareness" (HSA), to distinguish it from Computer Situation Awareness (CSA), which is the capability of systems and machines to process information for interpreting the situations, exhibiting situation-aware behaviors, and making decisions suitable for the current situation. This chapter provides an overview of state-of-the-art models, techniques, and approaches for supporting human situation awareness in HMS.

*Handbook of Human-Machine Systems*, First Edition. Edited by Giancarlo Fortino, David Kaber, Andreas Nürnberger, and David Mendonça.

## 36.2 Background

SA is a faceted concept encompassing many different elements ranging from cognitive mechanisms and decision-making processes to information processing and human factors. Figure 36.1 depicts a conceptual view of an HMS. In this system, the human operator interacts with the machine by processing the perceived information and taking decisions and actions to control the system. As it can be seen in the figure, the role of the human in the loop of control is critical. According to this perspective, and for this category of systems, the widely accepted definition of SA is the one proposed by Endsley [13]:

"*SA is the perception of the elements in the environment within a volume of time and space, the comprehension of their meaning, and the projection of their status in the near future*".

In this definition, we can identify three levels, depicted in Figure 36.1, that concur with the formation of the SA:

- **Level 1 SA – Perception**: perceiving the status of the elements in the environment. The elements to which you pay attention depend on the task to be performed. Although it may seem easy to perceive the elements related to a specific task, in many domains, it can be quite challenging just to detect all the needed data. Moreover, quite often the amount of data rapidly outpaces the capability of the operator to correctly perceive all of them.
- **Level 2 SA – Comprehension**: understanding what the data perceived at level 1 means in relation to the goals of the human. The elements of level 1 are synthesized and aggregated and then a goal-related meaning is associated with each piece of data. Understanding the meaning of the perceived data requires good knowledge and a good mental model in order to put together and interpret different pieces of information.
- **Level 3 SA – Projection**: predicting what the perceived elements will do in the future with respect to the goal. Level 3 SA depends on the correct understanding of the situation (level 2 SA) and on the knowledge about the dynamics of the system and the environment. Usually, such an operation is quite demanding, as it requires a good understanding of the domain, of the situation, and a great ability in the projection of the status of many elements in the future. Experience plays a major role in this level because it gives the ability to anticipate future situations and to be proactive with respect to them.

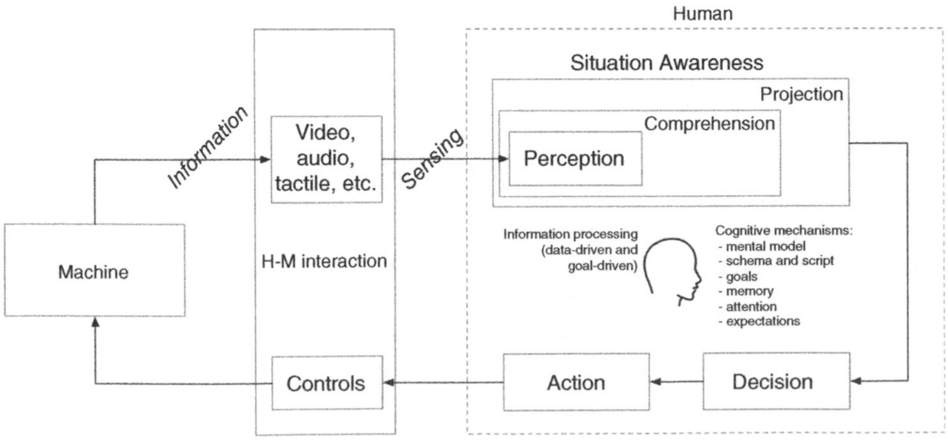


**Figure 36.1** Situation awareness in human–machine systems.

The SA is the product of several cognitive processes, and it is based on cognitive mechanisms depicted in Figure 36.1. In particular, from the point of view of the interaction with HMS, *mental models* are critical to achieving and maintaining SA. Mental models can be thought of as structures that model the behavior of the system, and in particular its interface, its possible states, its functions. Mental models are crucial to SA because they support people in the identification of the information to which pay attention and help in the creation of expectations about what could happen next. With poor or wrong mental models, a person has very few chances to understand and predict the situations. The design of the system interface influences the capability of developing and using the right mental model. More in general, a proper design of the system and its interface is fundamental for addressing the *SA demons*, i.e. a set of typical errors in SA [13] that causes a lack of SA. These demons include problems such as attentional tunneling, data overload, wrong mental models, human-out-of-the-loop syndrome, which works to undermine the human SA. The SA demons are due to the dynamic and complex interactions between system factors and human factors in the HMS. Computational approaches and techniques can be effective in reducing the effects of SA demons if they are founded on solid cognitive models capable of exploiting the characteristics and processes of human cognition and system factors. Such computational approaches should support the process of SA in all its phases – namely, the perception of the elements in the real environment, the understanding and the identification of the current situation, and finally, the prediction of future evolutions of the situation. In Section 36.3, we propose an overview of the main categories of approaches and techniques used to support SA in HMS.

## 36.3 State-of-the-Art

Figure 36.2 depicts a conceptual view of a generic situation-aware HMS system (SA-HMS), i.e. a system designed to support human SA. This conceptual view is based on the model of HMS described in Section 36.2.

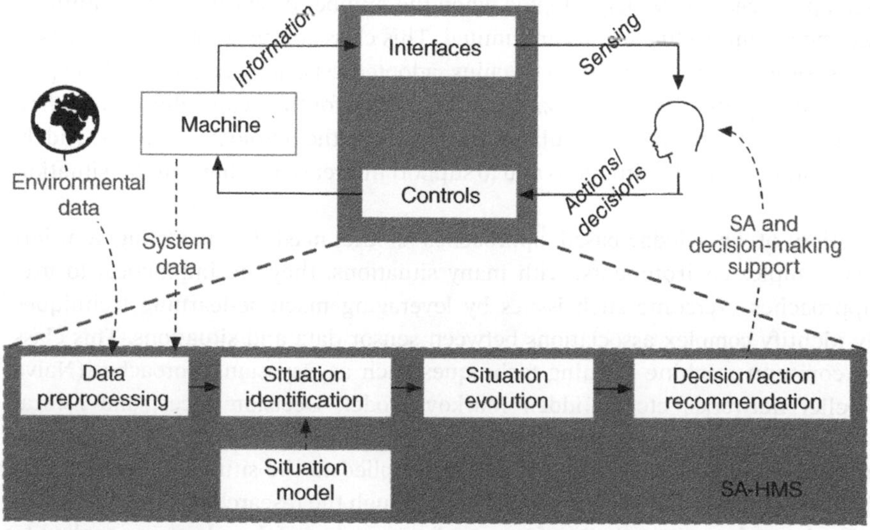


**Figure 36.2** Situation-aware HMS: a conceptual architecture.

The main capabilities of a SA-HMS are the following:

- **Data preprocessing**: the system gathers the data from the machine and from the environment and represents it according to a specific data model. The data are cleaned, standardized, and preprocessed to support the next phases.
- **Situation identification**: the data gathered by the system is processed by a situation identification technique to detect the current situation, with respect to a given situation model.
- **Situation model**: a model of the situation is useful to support the other functionalities of the system. It can be explicit or implicit.
- **Situation evolution**: tracking of the evolution of the situations to support the projection phase. The time dimension is crucial for many HMSs.
- **Decision-making and action support**: the decision-making support can be implemented by suggesting and executing the best decision or by proposing several alternatives to the user.

Using this conceptual architecture in what follows, we propose an overview of techniques and approaches for the two main capabilities of the SA-HMS: (i) situation identification techniques (with the related situation model); (ii) situation evolution. Lastly, we analyze real examples of SA-HMS in different application domains.

### 36.3.1 Situation Identification Techniques in HMS

Situation identification is one of the most important tasks in a SA-HMS system. From a computational perspective, a situation has been defined as a domain-relevant interpretation of data interesting to applications [42]. Table 36.1 reports some of the most common techniques for situation identification, proposing references to interesting works in the literature that implement such techniques. These are categorized into two main classes: (i) *knowledge-based approaches* relying on the representation of expert knowledge about the situations and on reasoning techniques to infer situations from data; (ii) *learning-based approaches* that exploit machine-learning techniques.

Knowledge-based approaches are widely adopted when the number of sensors and the number of relationships among the interesting events are limited. This class comprises approaches based on logic, such as first-order logic and situation calculus, adopted especially in the past in expert systems, and fuzzy logic, in particular using Fuzzy Cognitive Maps for their capability of modeling conceptual relations between concepts. Particularly important are the ontological models, widely adopted in many SA systems to model situations and to support inference mechanisms for situation identification.

The main limitation of knowledge-based approaches is the need for modeling a priori knowledge: in very complex environments, with many situations, they are impractical to use. Learning-based approaches overcome such issues by leveraging machine-learning techniques that automatically identify complex associations between sensor data and situations. This class includes the most common machine-learning techniques such as Bayesian approaches (Naive Bayes, Bayesian belief networks, etc.), Hidden Markov Model, Decision Trees, and Neural Networks.

Recently, some approaches of deep learning have been applied to the situation identification problem, especially for the ones based on image analysis, although the research in this sense is still at the beginning. Carrio et al. conducted a brief survey of approaches of deep learning applied to situation awareness in UAVs systems [5].

**Table 36.1** Summary of situation identification techniques.

| Techniques | | | References |
|---|---|---|---|
| Knowledge | Formal Logic | Situation calculus | [8] |
| | | Situation theory | [4] |
| | | S-DTT | [11] |
| | Evidence Theory | Dempster–Shafer theory | [23] |
| | | Context space theory | [2] |
| | Fuzzy logic | Fuzzy Sets | [44] |
| | | Fuzzy cognitive map | [18] |
| | Ontology | SAW Core | [26] |
| | | STO | [22] |
| | | GSO - SAW | [9] |
| Learning | Bayesian | Naive Bayes | [20] |
| | | Bayesian networks | [41] |
| | | Bayesian belief network | [31] |
| | Hidden Markov models | | [3] |
| | Decision trees | | [43] |
| | Support vector machines | | [19] |
| | Neural networks | | [45] |
| | Deep Learning | | [5, 40] |

### 36.3.2 Situation Evolution in HMS

Being able to anticipate the evolution of current situations is at the same time the most important and most difficult task in SA. Salfinger et al. proposed a concise overview of SA systems and frameworks with a specific focus on their support for the evolution of situations [32]. Stojanovic and Artikis analyzed the approaches based on Complex Event Processing supporting the prediction of future situations for activity recognition and social media observations [35]. Multientity Bayesian Networks have been applied for predictive situation awareness [29]. In [33], the authors proposed an approach for reasoning on incomplete data by means of Markov Logic Networks for predicting events and anomalies in maritime situation awareness. To handle uncertainty and vagueness in data, soft-computing approaches like Fuzzy logic has been investigated to support situation projection [18]. Lastly, Naderpour, Lu, and Zhang proposed a safety supervisor system based on neural networks and an expert system to support situation prediction [28].

### 36.3.3 Situation-Aware Human Machine-Systems

In this section, we briefly review a selection of recent Situation-aware Human-Machine Systems (SA-HMS) to provide an overview of different situation models, identification, and evolution approaches implemented in real systems in several domains.

Historically, systems for command and control centers gave a lot of attention to SA support. A situation awareness framework for traffic control centers based on ontologies is proposed in [1]. Furno et al. defined an agent-based framework leveraging ontological models of situations and fuzzy reasoning for the security control center of airports [15]. In [28], a system based on Bayesian networks for supporting SA in control centers of chemical plants is proposed. Using Complex Event Processing (CEP) for situation identification, Vlakhis et al. defined a situation-aware system for the supply chain management [38]. A manufacturing system, based on CEP, for handling disruptions based on SA is described in [12]. Lastly, a data-driven architecture using Kafka, Spark and Esper to support decisions in online surgery scheduling based on SA is described in [34].

A domain that traditionally attracted a lot of attention from SA practitioners is the maritime domain. Some recent works exploit deep learning to recognize vessels' trajectories, events, and situations from automatic identification system (AIS) data, radar, and satellite images [24, 25]. Unsupervised approaches have also been proposed, especially to support the identification of anomalous trajectories [27]. CEP has been used to identify situations involving vessels and their trajectories from AIS data [39]. An ontology-based framework for maritime SA with a bayesian belief network for situation identification is described in [37]. A SA system, namely GeMASS, for maritime SA based on discovering anomalous situations through a genetic algorithm for rule mining is proposed in [6].

Systems for crisis management (e.g. natural disasters, terroristic attacks, and plants incidents) benefit from the implementation of SA principles. In recent years, many systems exploit information published on social media to support crisis responder offering a global view of what is happening. In [21], a semantic clustering technique to analyze social media posts to offer an enhanced picture of the situation for crisis responders is proposed. Graf et al. proposed a machine-learning technique to identify situations by processing tweets related to disaster situations [17]. Lastly, a framework for crisis management based on a meta-model of situations and a CEP technique for situation identification is described in [14].

## 36.4 Discussion and Research Challenges

In Table 36.2, we compared the situation-aware HMSs analyzed in this chapter. From the analysis it emerged that all the systems implement at least a situation identification task, thus confirming that for an SA system, the capability of identifying situations is crucial. Knowledge-based approaches for situation identification were widely used in these systems, especially in the past. Ontologies and complex event processing (CEP) have been used to both explicitly model situations and identify situations because such approaches are effective ways of representing expert knowledge. However, the main drawback of these approaches is the large amount of time and effort required to model situations. Learning-based approaches are increasingly adopted. Such approaches do not have an explicit model of situations and thus they do not require experts to define situations. However, large (annotated) data sets are often needed to use these techniques, which are not always available. Furthermore, the techniques used to identify situations are often difficult to be interpreted by users, diminishing their SA. Hybrid approaches, bringing the advantages of knowledge-based and learning-based approaches, could be a valid solution to this issue, and they represent an interesting research direction in the field of SA systems.

The analysis also highlighted that most of the solutions are able to identify only expected and well-known situations, identified by the system to support the human operators. While this is certainly an important feature of SA-HMS, this is not sufficient. The real challenge is to have resilient systems able to identify and deal with unexpected situations. Unexpected situations and rare events lead to critical errors, with drastic effects on the human SA. Some techniques dealing with uncertain situations have been proposed in the literature, but these are still rarely implemented in real systems.

**Table 36.2** Summary of situation-aware human-machine systems.

| References | Situation Model | Situation Identification | Situation Evolution | Decision Support | Application Domain |
|---|---|---|---|---|---|
| [1] | Ontology | Ontology + Rules | Rules | Ontology based | Control centers (traffic) |
| [15] | Ontology | Fuzzy ontology | – | – | Airport security |
| [28] | Discrete Bayesian Network | Bayesian Network + FIS | FIS | If-Then Rules | Nuclear power plant |
| [38] | CEP | CEP | – | – | Supply Chain Mgmt. |
| [25] | – | Deep learning | – | – | Maritime |
| [24] | – | Deep learning | – | – | Maritime |
| [27] | – | Clustering | – | – | Maritime |
| [37] | Ontology | Bayesian belief network | – | – | Maritime |
| [6] | Rules | Rule mining | – | – | Maritime |
| [39] | Ontology | CEP | CEP | – | Maritime |
| [14] | Situation meta-model | CEP | CEP | – | Crisis mgmt. |
| [21] | – | Clustering | – | – | Crisis mgmt. |
| [17] | – | Machine learning | – | – | Crisis mgmt. |
| [12] | – | CEP | Machine learning | – | Manufacturing |
| [34] | – | CEP | Machine learning | optimization scheduling | Healthcare (surgery) |

In Table 36.2, it can be observed that most of the systems provide little or no support to situation evolution and decision support. Frequently, these phases are supported using rule-based and expert systems, which have the same limitations discussed above for knowledge-based situation identification techniques. Projection is a critical phase for SA, and the analyzed systems often delegate it to the human operators. A daunting research challenge is therefore the realization of approaches for tracking dynamically evolving situations and anticipating their future states, by providing human operators with a direct decision and action support.

An interesting emerging area of research that promises to bring the advantages of expert-based and learning-based approaches, and together supporting evolving situations by offering an explicit model of situations, is the Granular Situation Awareness [10, 16], i.e. the integration of the Granular Computing (GrC) paradigm with SA. GrC [7, 30] allows humans to analyze problems from different perspectives and different levels of detail. The concept of information granule enables the integration of expert-based and learning-based (also unsupervised) approaches. Consequently, granular structures can represent situations from different perspectives and evolvable granular structures that are inherently suitable to model evolving situations. A great advantage of this approach is that such models are directly interpretable by human operators. Lastly, GrC supports approximate reasoning and several paradigms for decision-making (like three-way decisions) providing a way to deal with uncertainty in data and actionable support to decision-making.

From the perspective of HMS, considering the advances in the level of automation and in artificial intelligence, the role of the systems is more and more those of a teammate of the human operator rather than a subordinate system. Intelligent systems and autonomous agents should have themselves their SA, allowing them to exhibit situation-aware behaviors and make intelligent decisions. Then, the SA of the systems should be shared with the humans in order to allow them to cooperate and act as a team. Therefore, models of shared and distributed SA have to be defined to realize novel SA-HMS. Research in the field of human-autonomy teaming and human-robot teaming, very fervent nowadays, in future cannot fail to take into account the fundamental role of SA to effectively support the interaction and cooperation between humans and intelligent agents and robots.

## 36.5 Conclusion

In this chapter, we discussed the important role of SA in HMS. An overview of the literature regarding the most relevant state-of-the-art approaches for situation identification and evolution in HMSs has been proposed. Some current research gaps emerged, in particular related to the lack of support for the SA projection phase, which is often delegated to the human operators with little or no support from the systems. Another research challenge is related to the human-out-of-the-loop problem and the need for humans and systems to work and cooperate as a team and develop team SA to effectively understand and predict what is happening in the environment. An interesting research direction to solve the aforementioned issues might rely on the adoption of hybrid (knowledge-based and learning-based) approaches to model and identify situations. In particular, granular computing has been identified as one of the promising information processing paradigms to support human SA in future HMS.

## References


1 Baumgartner, N., Mitsch, S., Muller, A., Retschitzegger, W. et al. (2014). A tour of BeAware - a situation awareness framework for control centers. *Information Fusion* 20: 155–173.

2 Boytsov, A., Zaslavsky, A., Eryilmaz, E., and Albayrak, S. (2015). Situation awareness meets ontologies: a context spaces case study. In: *Modeling and Using Context*, *Lecture Notes in Computer Science*, vol. 9405. *CONTEXT 2015: Proceedings of the 9th International and Interdisciplinary Conference* (ed. H. Christiansen, I. Stojanovic, and G. Papadopoulos), 3–17. Cham: Springer. https://doi.org/10.1007/978-3-319-25591-0_1.

3 Caelli, T., Mukerjee, J., McCabe, A., and Kirszenblat, D. (2021). The situation awareness window: a hidden Markov model for analyzing maritime surveillance missions. *The Journal of Defense Modeling and Simulation* 18 (3): 207–215. https://doi.org/10.1177/1548512920984370.

4 Canan, M., Sousa-Poza, A., and Kovacic, S.F. (2015). Semantic shift to pragmatic meaning in shared decision making: situation theory perspective. *International Journal of Design & Nature and Ecodynamics* 10: 267–278. https://doi.org/10.2495/DNE-V10-N3-267-278.

5 Carrio, A., Sampedro, C., Rodriguez-Ramos, A., and Campoy, P. (2017). A review of deep learning methods and applications for unmanned aerial vehicles. *Journal of Sensors* 2017: 3296874. https://doi.org/10.1155/2017/3296874.

6 Chen, C.-H., Khoo, L.P., Chong, Y.T., and Yin, X.F. (2014). Knowledge discovery using genetic algorithm for maritime situational awareness. *Expert Systems with Applications* 41 (6): 2742–2753. https://doi.org/10.1016/j.eswa.2013.09.042.

**7** Cheng, Y., Zhao, F., Zhang, Q., and Wang, G. (2021). A survey on granular computing and its uncertainty measure from the perspective of rough set theory. *Granular Computing* 6 (1): 3–17. https://doi.org/10.1007/s41066-019-00204-3.

**8** Claßen, J., Lakemeyer, G., and Zarrieß, B. (2019). Situation calculus meets description logics. In: *Description Logic, Theory Combination, and All That: Essays Dedicated to Franz Baader on the Occasion of His 60th Birthday* (ed. C. Lutz, U. Sattler, C. Tinelli et al.), 240–265. Cham: Springer International Publishing. ISBN 978-3-030-22102-7. https://doi.org/10.1007/978-3-030-22102-7_11.

**9** D'Aniello, G., Gaeta, A., Loia, V., and Orciuoli, F. (2016). Integrating GSO and SAW ontologies to enable situation awareness in green fleet management. *2016 IEEE International Multi-Disciplinary Conference on Cognitive Methods in Situation Awareness and Decision Support (CogSIMA)*, 138–144. https://doi.org/10.1109/COGSIMA.2016.7497801.

**10** D'Aniello, G., Gaeta, A., Loia, V., and Orciuoli, F. (2017). A granular computing framework for approximate reasoning in situation awareness. *Granular Computing* 2 (3): 141–158. https://doi.org/10.1007/s41066-016-0035-0.

**11** Dapoigny, R. and Barlatier, P. (2013). Formal foundations for situation awareness based on dependent type theory. *Information Fusion* 14 (1): 87–107. https://doi.org/10.1016/j.inffus.2012.02.006.

**12** Eirinakis, P., Kasapidis, G., Mourtos, I. et al. (2021). Situation-aware manufacturing systems for capturing and handling disruptions. *Journal of Manufacturing Systems* 58: 365–383. https://doi.org/10.1016/j.jmsy.2020.12.014.

**13** Endsley, M.R. (2011). *Designing for Situation Awareness: An Approach to User-Centered Design*, 2e. USA: CRC Press, Inc. ISBN 9781420063554.

**14** Fertier, A., Montarnal, A., Barthe-Delano, A.-M. et al. (2020). Real-time data exploitation supported by model- and event-driven architecture to enhance situation awareness, application to crisis management. *Enterprise Information Systems* 14 (6): 769–796. https://doi.org/10.1080/17517575.2019.1691268.

**15** Furno, D., Loia, V., and Veniero, M. (2010). A fuzzy cognitive situation awareness for airport security. *Control and Cybernetics* 39 (4): 960–982.

**16** Gaeta, A., Loia, V., and Orciuoli, F. (2021). A comprehensive model and computational methods to improve situation awareness in intelligence scenarios. *Applied Intelligence* 51 (9): 6585–6608.

**17** Graf, D., Retschitzegger, W., Schwinger, W. et al. (2018). Cross-domain informativeness classification for disaster situations. *Proceedings of the 10th International Conference on Management of Digital EcoSystems*, MEDES '18, 183–190. New York, NY, USA: Association for Computing Machinery. ISBN 9781450356220. https://doi.org/10.1145/3281375.3281385.

**18** Jones, R.E.T., Connors, E.S., Mossey, M.E. et al. (2011). Using fuzzy cognitive mapping techniques to model situation awareness for army infantry platoon leaders. *Computational and Mathematical Organization Theory* 17 (3): 272–295. https://doi.org/10.1007/s10588-011-9094-6.

**19** Kanda, T., Glas, D.F., Shiomi, M. et al. (2008). Who will be the customer? A social robot that anticipates people's behavior from their trajectories. *Proceedings of the 10th International Conference on Ubiquitous Computing*, UbiComp '08, 380–389. New York, NY, USA: Association for Computing Machinery. ISBN 9781605581361. https://doi.org/10.1145/1409635.1409686.

**20** Kasteren, T. and Krose, B. (2007). Bayesian activity recognition in residence for elders. *2007 3rd IET International Conference on Intelligent Environments*, 209–212. https://doi.org/10.1049/cp:20070370.

**21** Kingston, C., Nurse, J.R.C., Agrafiotis, I., and Milich, A.B. (2018). Using semantic clustering to support situation awareness on Twitter: the case of world views. *Human-centric Computing and Information Sciences* 8 (1): 22. https://doi.org/10.1186/s13673-018-0145-6.

**22** Kokar, M.M. and Endsley, M.R. (2012). Situation awareness and cognitive modeling. *IEEE Intelligent Systems* 27 (3): 91–96. https://doi.org/10.1109/MIS.2012.61.

**23** Li, Z.Y., Park, J.C., Lee, B., and Youn, H.Y. (2013). Situation awareness based on Dempster-Shafer theory and semantic similarity. *2013 IEEE 16th International Conference on Computational Science and Engineering*, 545–552. https://doi.org/10.1109/CSE.2013.87.

**24** Mantecón, T., Casals, D., Navarro-Corcuera, J.J. et al. (2019). Deep learning to enhance maritime situation awareness. *2019 20th International Radar Symposium (IRS)*, 1–8. https://doi.org/10.23919/IRS.2019.8768142.

**25** Marié, V., Béchar, I., and Bouchara, F. (2018). Real-time maritime situation awareness based on deep learning with dynamic anchors. *2018 15th IEEE International Conference on Advanced Video and Signal Based Surveillance (AVSS)*, 1–6. https://doi.org/10.1109/AVSS.2018.8639373.

**26** Matheus, C.J., Kokar, M.M., and Baclawski, K. (2003). A core ontology for situation awareness. *6th International Conference of Information Fusion, 2003. Proceedings of the*, volume 1, 545–552. https://doi.org/10.1109/ICIF.2003.177494.

**27** Murray, B. and Perera, L.P. (2020). Unsupervised trajectory anomaly detection for situation awareness in maritime navigation. Volume 6A: Ocean Engineering of *International Conference on Offshore Mechanics and Arctic Engineering*, 08 2020. https://doi.org/10.1115/OMAE2020-18281.

**28** Naderpour, M., Lu, J., and Zhang, G. (2014). An intelligent situation awareness support system for safety-critical environments. *Decision Support System* 59: 325–340. https://doi.org/10.1016/j.dss.2014.01.004.

**29** Park, C.Y., Laskey, K.B., Costa, P.C.G., and Matsumoto, S. (2013). Multi-entity Bayesian networks learning for hybrid variables in situation awareness. *Proceedings of the 16th International Conference on Information Fusion*, 1894–1901.

**30** Pedrycz, W. (2001). Granular computing: an introduction. *Proceedings Joint 9th IFSA World Congress and 20th NAFIPS International Conference (Cat. No. 01TH8569)*, volume 3, 1349–1354. https://doi.org/10.1109/NAFIPS.2001.943745.

**31** Rosario, C.R., Amaral, F.G., Kuffel, F.J.M. et al. (2022). Using Bayesian belief networks to improve distributed situation awareness in shift changeovers: a case study. *Expert Systems with Applications* 188: 116039. https://doi.org/10.1016/j.eswa.2021.116039.

**32** Salfinger, A., Retschitzegger, W., and Schwinger, W. (2013). Maintaining situation awareness over time–a survey on the evolution support of situation awareness systems. *2013 Conference on Technologies and Applications of Artificial Intelligence*, 274–281. https://doi.org/10.1109/TAAI.2013.62.

**33** Snidaro, L., Visentini, I., and Bryan, K. (2015). Fusing uncertain knowledge and evidence for maritime situational awareness via Markov Logic Networks. *Information Fusion* 21: 159–172. https://doi.org/10.1016/j.inffus.2013.03.004.

**34** Spangenberg, N., Augenstein, C., Franczyk, B., and Wilke, M. (2018). Implementation of a situation aware and real-time approach for decision support in online surgery scheduling. *2018 IEEE 31st International Symposium on Computer-Based Medical Systems (CBMS)*, 417–421. https://doi.org/10.1109/CBMS.2018.00079.

**35** Stojanovic, N. and Artikis, A. (2011). On complex event processing for real-time situational awareness. *Rule-Based Reasoning, Programming, and Applications*, 114–121.

**36** Turetta, F.M.S., Lima, F., and Ribeiro, R. (2021). When autonomy fails: the fallback pilot paradox and an innovative solution to unlock human intervention into autonomous systems. *Lecture Notes in Networks and Systems. Congress of the International Ergonomics Association.*

**37** Van den Broek, A.C., Neef, R.M., Hanckmann, P. et al. (2011). Improving maritime situational awareness by fusing sensor information and intelligence. *14th International Conference on Information Fusion.*

**38** Vlahakis, G., Apostolou, D., and Kopanaki, E. (2018). Enabling situation awareness with supply chain event management. *Expert Systems with Applications* 93: 86–103. https://doi.org/10.1016/j.eswa.2017.10.013.

**39** Vouros, G.A., Vlachou, A., Santipantakis, G. et al. (2018). Increasing maritime situation awareness via trajectory detection, enrichment and recognition of events. In: *Web and Wireless Geographical Information Systems*, W2GIS 2018. *Lecture Notes in Computer Science*, vol. 10819 (ed. M.R. Luaces and F. Karimipour), 130–140. Cham: Springer.

**40** Wang, Q., Bu, S., He, Z., and Dong, Z.Y. (2021). Toward the prediction level of situation awareness for electric power systems using CNN-LSTM network. *IEEE Transactions on Industrial Informatics* 17 (10): 6951–6961. https://doi.org/10.1109/TII.2020.3047607.

**41** Wiggers, P., Mertens, B., and Rothkrantz, L. (2011). Dynamic Bayesian networks for situational awareness in the presence of noisy data. *Proceedings of the 12th International Conference on Computer Systems and Technologies*, CompSysTech '11, 411–416. New York, NY, USA: Association for Computing Machinery. ISBN 9781450309172. https://doi.org/10.1145/2023607.2023676.

**42** Ye, J., Dobson, S., and McKeever, S. (2012). Situation identification techniques in pervasive computing: a review. *Pervasive and Mobile Computing* 8 (1): 36–66. https://doi.org/10.1016/j.pmcj.2011.01.004.

**43** Zhang, H., Kang, C., and Xiao, Y. (2021). Research on network security situation awareness based on the LSTM-DT model. *Sensors* 21 (14): 4788. https://doi.org/10.3390/s21144788.

**44** Zhao, J., Zhou, Y., and Shuo, L. (2012). A situation awareness model of system survivability based on variable fuzzy set. *Indonesian Journal of Electrical Engineering and Computer Science* 10 (8): 2239–2246. https://doi.org/10.11591/telkomnika.v10i8.1691.

**45** Zhu, Q. (2020). Research on road traffic situation awareness system based on image big data. *IEEE Intelligent Systems* 35 (1): 18–26. https://doi.org/10.1109/MIS.2019.2942836.

# 37

# Modeling, Analyzing, and Fostering the Adoption of New Technologies: The Case of Electric Vehicles

*Valentina Breschi[1], Chiara Ravazzi[2], Silvia Strada[3], Fabrizio Dabbene[2], and Mara Tanelli[2,3]*

[1]*Department of Electrical Engineering, Eindhoven University of Technology, Eindhoven, Netherlands*
[2]*Istituto di Elettronica e Ingegneria dell'Informazione e delle Telecomunicazioni - IEIIT, Centro Nazionale delle Ricerche, Torino, Italy*
[3]*Dipartimento di Elettronica, Informazione e Bioingegneria, Politecnico di Milano, Milano, Italy*

## 37.1 Introduction

The adoption of a new technology is always heavily dependent on the characteristics of the individuals who will be asked to adopt it, and the capability of encompassing the main drivers of adoption by explicating and capturing their specificity at individual level is key to succeed in spreading the technology massively. All the more so in those technological transitions linked to the environmental-related policies and goals which in Europe have been recently established within the framework of the "Green Deal" and the related Climate Law. The environmental transition, in facts, asks for major modifications of the living and working habits of individuals, all enabled by the adoption of the underlying technologies. In particular, in reaching climatic neutrality by 2050, mobility will for sure have a very important role, with road transport still being one the major green-house-gas producers.

To drive this change, it seems that electric vehicles (EVs) will need to take a significant share of the market, and recent governmental decisions in different countries are trying to shape the most effective incentive schemes to support this transition. The current adoption patterns of EVs, and of smart mobility services, however, show that the complexities in the social identities of the users, and the dynamic modifications that they experience over time, make it very complex to understand, and, most importantly, to govern a mass adoption of these new technologies [2, 16]. A promising framework for the analysis of the adoption mechanism is that of opinion dynamics, as it allows one to model the formation of beliefs, the aggregation of opinions, and follow their dynamic evolution in a hyperconnected society with a quantitative and rigorous approach, see [1, 9, 10, 14, 17].

In this chapter, we show how to model the adoption process of new technologies and how to foster it through the use of dedicated incentives, the effectiveness of which can be dynamically adjusted within a controlled application to the adoption of network model, using as a representative example the adoption of EVs. In order to model the individual characteristics, we work in a data-driven framework, where the users' suitability to adopting an EV is expressed in a quantitative fashion through the analysis of data representing anonymized private mobility patterns that are generated by vehicles equipped with insurance telematic e-Boxes in the urban area of Parma, see also [21]. Specifically, users are split into four classes according to a detailed

*Handbook of Human-Machine Systems*, First Edition. Edited by Giancarlo Fortino, David Kaber, Andreas Nürnberger, and David Mendonça.

analysis of their driving habits, with each class associated with an increasing suitability of the individuals to switching from their current Internal Combustion Engine (ICE) vehicle to an EV. Such suitability is quantitatively defined by considering which is the share of their daily trips that could be accommodated by an EV, assuming a single overnight recharge. The users are then connected in a network based on the proximity of their estimated homes (again derived by the analysis of their driving patterns), following the rationale that adoption is guided by homophily, i.e., with individuals being maximally influenced by those closest to them, who they recognize as representative examples, [12]. The proximity measure adopted in this work is data-based and grounded on physical distance, but the proposed framework allows one to employ notions of proximity that are described as a blend of quantitative and social measures. After the modeling of the adoption process, we show how to design different incentive policies that can be enacted to foster adoption and to quantitatively evaluate them within the proposed framework. In doing so, one can perform a detailed cost/benefit analysis at design time, tuning and comparing them before deployment. In this chapter, we first propose a novel, control-oriented framework that enacts these policies adjusting them in real time based on the reaction of the underlying adoption network. In this respect, we provide a full formalization of this control-over-network approach and practically prove its superiority to open-loop policy application.

The rest of the chapter is organized as follows: Section 37.2 illustrates the steps for modeling the adoption process, describing also the dataset used in this work to characterize the users' classes. Section 37.3 introduces the cascade model that describes the adoption mechanism and allows formulating the incentive schemes. Further, Section 37.4 presents the closed-loop formulation of the policy application, and Section 37.5 illustrates the obtained results comparing the cost/benefit analysis of both open- and closed-loop policies and analyzes their impact within the proposed framework.

## 37.2 Background

This section introduces the agent-based model used to build the networks on which the adoption process is modeled and analyzed. Further, we show how mobility patterns, measured on real vehicles, can be used as a basis to characterize the behaviors of the single individuals which informs the construction of the adoption network.

### 37.2.1 An Agent-based Model for EV Transition

By relying on the inkling that the relative popularity of EVs in the society can drive a shift of individual opinions on their adoption, we describe the EV-adoption process through a deterministic model of collective behavior, first introduced in [11]. In fact, this model is able to describe situations where individuals or agents have two alternatives, and the costs and/or benefits of each depend on how many other agents choose which alternative.

More formally, we consider the following mathematical framework. Let the set of real numbers and the set of nonnegative integers be denoted by $\mathbb{R}$ and $\mathbb{N}_0$, respectively. In order to take into account the effect of social contagion on the EV adoption mechanism, we consider a network that describes the social environment and captures the interactions of different individuals. The social environment is represented by an *undirected graph* $\mathcal{G} = (\mathcal{V}, \mathcal{E})$, where nodes in $\mathcal{V}$ identify the individuals and $\mathcal{E}$ the mutual influence among them. Each individual is endowed with two features $\{b_v, \alpha_v\}_{v \in \mathcal{V}}$, where $b_v \in \mathbb{R}^2$ is the base location of agent $v$, described in GPC coordinates, and $\alpha_v \in [0, 1]$ is a scalar representing the individual resistance to the transition to the EV. From base locations, we build the proximity network, which is defined as follows:

$$(v, w) \in \mathcal{E} \iff d(b_v, b_w) \leq D,$$

where $d(b_v, b_w)$ is the geodesic distance between the bases of the $v$-th and $w$-th agents, and $D$ denotes the maximum distance between base positions for two agents to be considered as *neighbors*. The structure of the graph is encoded in the adjacency matrix $A \in \{0,1\}^{\mathcal{V}\times\mathcal{V}}$, which is defined as follows: $A_{v,w} = 1$ if $(w, v) \in \mathcal{V}$, and 0 otherwise. We denote the *neighborhood* of a node $v \in \mathcal{V}$ by $\mathcal{N}_v = \{w \in \mathcal{V} : (w, v) \in \mathcal{E}\}$.

The variable $x_v(t) \in \{0, 1\}$ indicates whether the $v$-th agent adopts an EV ($x_v(t) = 1$) or not ($x_v(t) = 0$) at time $t \in \mathbb{N}_0$. Whenever an agent becomes an EV-adopter, its attitude toward EVs cannot further change. In this sense, the model is irreversible and implies that if there exists $t^\star$ such that $x_v(t^\star) = 1$, then $x_v(t) = 1$ for all $t \geq t^\star$. The dynamics starts at time $t = 0$ with an initial set of early adopters $S(0) = \{v \in \mathcal{V} : x_v(0) = 1\}$ and the opinion of each agent $v \in \mathcal{V}$ evolves as

$$x_v(t+1) = \begin{cases} 1 \text{ if } x_v(t) = 1 \textbf{ or } \frac{1}{|\mathcal{N}_v|} \sum_{w \in \mathcal{N}_v} x_w(t) \geq \alpha_v \\ 0 \text{ otherwise,} \end{cases} \tag{37.1a}$$

The term $\sum_{w \in \mathcal{N}_v} x_w(t)$ counts the number of neighbors of the $v$-th agent that have already adopted an EV at time $t$. Therefore, EV adoption over the network is driven by the relative popularity of this new technology among neighbors and takes into account the resistance of the agent based on its mobility habits. We denote the set of new EV-adopters at time $t$ as $S(t) = \{v \in \mathcal{V} : x_v(t-1) = 0$ and $x_v(t) = 1\}$, while $S^\star(t) := \cup_{\tau=0}^{t} S(\tau)$ denotes the total amount of EV-adopters in the network until time $t$, that are linked by the following:

$$S(t) = \left\{ v \in \mathcal{V} \backslash (\cup_{\tau=0}^{t-1} S(\tau)) : \frac{|S^\star(t) \cap \mathcal{N}_v|}{|\mathcal{N}_v|} \geq \alpha_v \right\}, \tag{37.1b}$$

where $v \in \mathcal{V} \backslash (\cup_{\tau=0}^{t-1} S(\tau))$ is the subset of nodes not yet adopters at time $t-1$, for $t \geq 1$. It should be noted that, since we consider an irreversible cascade model, the set of adopters $S_t^\star$ is non-decreasing, and the overall opinion dynamics converges in a finite number of steps to a final adopter set $\overline{S}^\star = \overline{S}^\star(S_0, \boldsymbol{\alpha})$.

In [20], the dynamics in (37.1a) is studied in general under deterministic topologies and for fixed values of thresholds. More precisely, the final set of adopters is characterized in terms of the so-called "cohesive" sets. We recall the following formal definition, introduced in [15] to answer the question of the existence of a finite set of early adopters able to trigger the cascading adoption in the entire network.

**Definition 37.1** ***[Cohesive set]*** Let us consider a graph $\mathcal{G} = (\mathcal{V}, \mathcal{E})$ and a set of thresholds $\{\alpha_v\}_{v\in\mathcal{V}}$. A set $\Omega \subseteq \mathcal{V}$ is said to be *cohesive* if for all $\omega \in \Omega$, it holds that $\frac{|\Omega \cap \mathcal{N}_\omega|}{|\mathcal{N}_\omega|} > 1 - \alpha_\omega$.

This definition characterizes the elements of the set of nodes whose relative number of neighbors not belonging to $\Omega$ is strictly less than their threshold. If $\Omega$ is a cohesive set, it follows that if $S_0 \cap \Omega = \emptyset$, then no agents in $\Omega$ can adopt the innovation. The following theorem relates the convergence properties of the diffusion process with the cohesive sets. The interested reader can refer to Lemma 2 in [1] for the details of the proof.

**Theorem 37.1** ***(Convergence)*** Given a network with seed set $S_0 \subset \mathcal{V}$, let $\Omega \subset \mathcal{V} \setminus S_0$ be the cohesive set of the complement of $S_0$ with maximal cardinality. Then, the set of final adopters is given by $\overline{S}^{\star} = \mathcal{V} \setminus \Omega$. ■

### 37.2.2 Calibration Based on Real Mobility Patterns

To have a deep understanding of the effect that policies promoting the adoption of electric vehicles can have on a network of individuals, it is of paramount importance to have a quantitative characterization of the individuals. Then it is pivotal to translate this characterization into parameters of the model considered in (37.1a), i.e., encoding the information in thresholds and connections. These elements are extracted from a dataset comprising information on the mobility patterns of 1000 vehicles, collected over a one-year period (from 1 September 2017 to 31 August 2018) from e-Boxes installed on ICE vehicles registered within the Italian province of Parma. Under the assumption that only the owner has access to the vehicle, the information embedded within the dataset allows us to get an insight on the mobility habits of the ICEs owners. We report the main rationale used for calibration, but the interested reader is referred to [21] a detailed analysis of the data.

We assume that the resistance to the transition toward EVs, encoded in the thresholds $\alpha_v$, are mainly due to mobility habits. Indeed, it is well known that one of the main obstacles to a mass adoption of EVs is the general lack of recharge stations. We quantitatively evaluate whenever a vehicle is repeatedly used in conditions that make the battery autonomy range to be exceeded. By considering those days in which the $v$-th vehicle is in use, here denoted as *active days*, we detect

- *eligible* days, namely the ones in which the driving range without recharge is exceeded[1] ;
- *critical* days, which are eligible days in which no stop characterizing the individual mobility habits would enable a proper recharge[2] of the vehicle.

By denoting the number of active, eligible, and critical days as $|\mathcal{A}_v|$, $|\mathcal{E}_v|$ and $|\mathcal{C}_v|$, we construct the *critical ratio* $CR_v \in [0, 1]$ for each agent $v \in \mathcal{V}$ as

$$CR_v = \frac{|\mathcal{E}_v| - |\mathcal{C}_v|}{|\mathcal{A}_v|}, \ \forall v \in \mathcal{V}, \tag{37.2a}$$

therefore, looking at the ratio between noncritical and active days. To better distinguish among the agents, this ratio is further normalized and projected onto the set $[0, 1]$ to construct our final indicator, the *electrification potential* ($\text{EP}_v$), which is defined as follows:

$$\text{EP}_v = 1 - 10 \tanh\left(\frac{CR_v - \min_{v \in \mathcal{V}} CR_v}{\max_{v \in \mathcal{V}} CR_v - \min_{v \in \mathcal{V}} CR_v}\right), \ \text{EP}_v \in [0, 1]. \tag{37.2b}$$

Since the higher the $\text{EP}_v$ is, the more the $v$-th agent would be suited for an immediate transition to an EV, we further distinguish between four classes of individuals:

- *not suited* (NS) agents, which are characterized by $\text{EP}_v < 0.67$;
- *mildly suited* (MS) agents, endowed with $\text{EP}_v \in [0.67, 0.83)$;
- *almost suited* (AS) agents, characterized by $\text{EP}_v \in [0.83, 1)$;
- *perfectly suited* (PS) agents, with $\text{EP}_v = 1$.

1 This is here conservatively regarded equal to 300 km.
2 We consider that stops lasting less than half an hour would not allow the driver to regain enough driving range to conclude its trip.

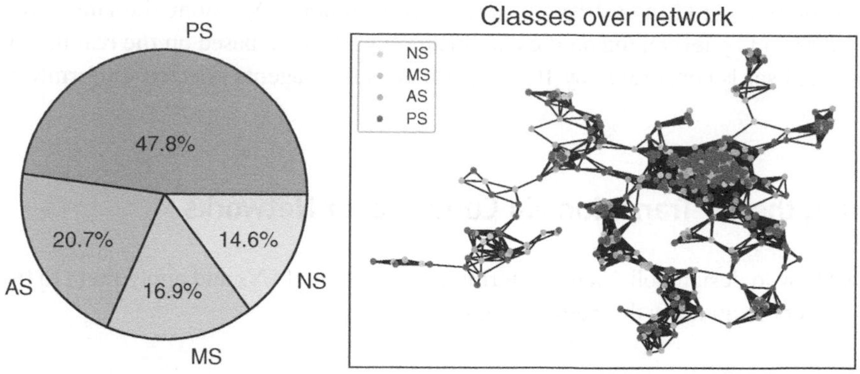


(a) Percentages of agents for each class

(b) Class shown over the proximity-based network

**Figure 37.1** Distribution of perfectly suited (PS), almost suited (AS), mildly suited (MS), and not suited (NS) agents over the community. Perfectly suited agents are spread over the network, yet the population is rather diverse.

This uneven characterization of the classes with respect to the constructed index allows us to account for the nonlinearity of the mapping used to obtain them. At the same time, it enables us to indirectly include other factors, such as the expense of buying an EV that can make them less appealing even when most of the trips throughout active days can generally be managed with an EV. The sizes of the different classes can be induced from the diagram in Figure 37.1(a), while their distribution over the network is shown in Figure 37.1(b). Clearly, the network is quite heterogeneous, with almost 50% of the agents being in principle suited to own an EV before any incentive policy is enacted. Note that the presence of these agents in almost all regions of the network is expected to enable a rather quick increase in the number of adopters.

- **(Network extraction)** The *base locations* $\{b_v\}_{v \in \mathcal{V}}$ are retrieved by focusing on overnight stops only. These positions are characterized as the average GPS location at which each vehicle stops for a fairly long time, namely at least 8 hours, in multiple occasions. The proximity network is built by connecting those agents whose base positions are within a radius $D = 3$ km[3]. Since the resulting network is characterized by some isolated communities, we then consider its largest connected component only so as to have a clearer picture of the effect that different policies have on the network, without biasing our analysis because of the complete isolation of some agents with respect to the main community. Based on this data processing steps, the network that will be always considered next is the one depicted in Figure 37.1(b).
- **(Calibration of the thresholds)** The thresholds $\{\alpha_v\}_{v \in \mathcal{V}}$ encode the resistance to the transition toward EVs based on the mobility habits. We use the pattern-based classification of individuals to calibrate these parameters according to the following distribution in order to take into account a sort of uncertainty:
  - $\alpha_v(0) \sim \mathcal{U}_{[0.55,0.95]}$, if the $v$-th agent is *not suited* to switch to an EV;
  - $\alpha_v(0) \sim \mathcal{U}_{[0.15,0.55]}$, if the $v$-th agent is *mildly suited* for a shift to an EV;
  - $\alpha_v(0) \sim \mathcal{U}_{[0.01,0.15]}$, when the $v$-th agent is *almost suited* for the transition to an EV;
  - $\alpha_v(0) \sim \mathcal{U}_{[0,0.01]}$, if the $v$-th agent is *perfectly suited* to shift to an EV.

3 This choice is coherent with the average dimension of a neighborhood in the city of Parma and the dimension of smaller cities and towns in its surrounding belt.

- **(Seed set)** The evolution of (37.1a) is driven by a set of early adopters $S_0$. Along the same rationale exploited in [6] and by leveraging on the classification performed based on the real mobility patterns, the seed set is constituted by $10_{\%}$ of perfectly suited agents selected uniformly at random.

## 37.3 Fostering the EV Transition via Control over Networks

This section shows how to design policies for fostering the adoption of EVs and apply them to the agents' network in order to quantify their effectiveness.

### 37.3.1 Related Work: A Perspective Analysis

In order to put our analysis into perspective, we formalize two different approaches that can be used to foster EV transition via control over networks. Let us denote the set of adopters at time $T$ induced by the diffusion process in (37.1a) with initial seed set $S_0$ and threshold values $\alpha = \{\alpha_v\}_{v\in\mathcal{V}}$ with $S^\star(T, S_0, \alpha)$.

**Problem 37.1** ***(Spread maximization via seed selection)*** Given $\mathcal{G} = (\mathcal{V}, \mathcal{E})$, $\{\alpha_v\}_{v\in\mathcal{V}}$, and $S_0 \in \mathcal{V}$, the spread maximization via seed selection selects the nodes by solving the following problem:

$$\max_{\mathcal{W}\in\mathcal{V}\setminus S_0 : |\mathcal{W}|\leq k} \mathbb{E}_\alpha \left[ |S^\star(T; S_0 \cup \mathcal{W}, \boldsymbol{\alpha})| \right]$$

**Problem 37.2** ***(Spread maximization via thresholds optimization)*** Given the graph $\mathcal{G} = (\mathcal{V}, \mathcal{E})$, the set of threshold $\{\alpha_v\}_{v\in\mathcal{V}}$, and the seed set $S_0 \in \mathcal{V}$, the spread maximization via threshold optimization adjust thresholds as follows:

$$\max_{\rho : \sum \rho_v \leq \overline{\rho}} \mathbb{E}_{S_0} \left[ |S^\star(T; S_0, (\mathbf{1} - \boldsymbol{\rho}) \cdot \boldsymbol{\alpha})| \right]$$

In the first approach (Problem 37.1), the design of the policies is based on the selection of a limited number (due for example to budget constraints) of agents in the network to be added in the seed set in order to maximize the diffusion of innovation. In the latter approach, the control acts, instead, by lowering the thresholds (in principle of all agents) to facilitate the spread of the innovation. It should be noticed that Problem 2 is more general and includes Problem 1 as a particular case if we add suitable constraints on variables, i.e., $\delta \in \{0, \alpha_v\}$ with $\|\delta\|_0 \leq k$, where $\|\cdot\|_0$ counts the number of nonzeros in $\delta$.

Regarding the computation of the solution for Problem 1, a possible approach is to compute, for all possible configurations of $\mathcal{W} \in \mathcal{V}\setminus S_0$ of $k$ elements, the number of adopters at time $T$:

1. If the time horizon is large enough to guarantee the convergence of the diffusion process, then one could leverage Theorem 37.1, as proposed in [18]. This approach requires solving a linear programming problem (LP). However, if the dimension of the network is large, retrieving the maximal cohesive set contained in the complement of $S_0$ becomes computationally demanding. Moreover, the number of configurations scales exponentially in the size of the network (the number of possible configurations is equal to $\binom{N-|S_0|}{k}$).
2. If the time horizon is not sufficiently large to guarantee convergence, then the final adopter set might not be reached and the computation must be performed by simulation.

To overcome the complexity that arises when looking for an exact solution of Problem 1, in [5], the cost function is approximated using Monte Carlo samples. With this approach, the evaluation of the cost function is proportional to the number of realizations $N_r$ considered in the Monte Carlo method and to the time-horizon $T$, i.e. $O(N_R T)$. Finally, to avoid a combinatorial search of the solution, a greedy heuristic can be used, and the agent selection can be carried out by choosing one node at a time, reducing significantly the computational complexity of the proposed solution with respect to the exact one.

Related to Problem 2 is the literature concerning optimal pricing cascade [7, 8]. In this body of research, the incentives are uniform, and the algorithms proposed are able to compute the optimal price $\rho^\star$ with a number of computations that is polynomial in the number of agents. Lim et al. [13] analyzes optimal pricing and seeding of cascades simultaneously in general finite networks showing that the structure of the network dramatically affects the optimal price.

The approach we present in Section 37.3.2 is related to the second family of methods with nonuniform weights $\rho$. More precisely, we consider a new model of irreversible cascade with time-varying thresholds, by modifying (37.1a) with the intent of making the associated dynamics directly dependent on an exogenous policy and to explicitly consider the heterogeneous response of individuals to the incentives.

### 37.3.2 A New Model for EV Transition with Incentive Policies

As previously introduced, we describe the spread of EVs over the network through an irreversible cascade model. As such, we assume that the advantages resulting from the use of an electric vehicle will convince the adopters not to resort back to traditional mobility solutions in the future. Still guided by the same rationale, here we consider the cascade model in (37.1a) with time-varying thresholds. More precisely, we consider the following dynamics for all $v \in \mathcal{V}$

$$x_v(t+1) = \begin{cases} 1, \text{ if } x_v(t) = 1 \textbf{ or } \frac{1}{|\mathcal{N}_v|} \sum_{w \in \mathcal{N}_v} x_w(t) \geq \alpha_v(t), & t = 0, 1 \ldots, T, \\ 0, \text{ otherwise} \end{cases} \quad (37.3)$$

whose evolution is still driven by a set of early adopters $S_0 = \{v \in \mathcal{V} \text{ s.t. } x_v(0) = 1\}$.

#### 37.3.2.1 Modeling Time-varying Thresholds

Among the variables that can be shaped by an external input, i.e. the actual states $x_v(t) \in \{0, 1\}$ and the (now time-varying) thresholds $\alpha_v(t)$, $v \in \mathcal{V}$, we assume the latter to be directly modified by the policy, while individual states cannot be directly controlled, although being fully accessible. This choice entails that the effect of social contagion is now modulated by the policy, as the number of adopters neighbor one must have to become an adopter is modified over time by the enacted policy. This new modeling paradigm allows us to fit the formulation to more practical scenarios, in which policy makers (*i*) often have only a rough idea of the inclination of each individual and (*ii*) opinions cannot be modified but indirectly (e.g., through advertising campaigns). Accordingly, the shaping effect of a policy is accounted for by considering a threshold dynamics driven by the following difference equation:

$$\alpha_v(t+1) = \alpha_v(t) + B_v u_v(t), \; t = 0, 1 \ldots, T, v \in \mathcal{V}, \quad (37.4)$$

where $B_v \in \mathbb{R}$ quantifies the policy's acceptance level of each agent $v \in \mathcal{V}$, thus indicating the actual impact of the policy $u_v(t) \in \mathbb{R}$ directed to the $v$-th agent.

#### 37.3.2.2 Calibration of the Model

In this new model, we have to calibrate the following parameters:

- **(Seed set)** The evolution of (37.3) is driven by a set of early adopters $S_0$, constituted by $10_{\%}$ of perfectly suited agents selected uniformly at random.
- **(Initial thresholds)** According to their meaning and based on the pattern-based classification introduced in Section 37.2.1, the initial values of the thresholds $\{\alpha_v(0)\}_{v\in\mathcal{V}}$ are randomly drawn from the class-based uniform distributions introduced in Section 37.2.1.
- **(Trust in the control policies)** Since the input $\{B_v\}_{v\in\mathcal{V}}$ embed insights on the individual resistance to benefit from the boosting policy, their values are decoupled from the EP-based classification presented in Section 37.2.1. In particular, we assume them to be drawn at random from a uniform distribution $\mathcal{U}_{[0,1]}$.

## 37.4 Boosting EV Adoption with Feedback

By leveraging on the features of the irreversible cascade model in (37.3) with thresholds dynamics described in (37.4), we aim at designing *feedback* policies to boost EV adoption over the network. This choice allows us to actively exploit updated information on the agents' opinion to tailor the incentive strategy to changes in their attitude toward EVs over time.

Most interestingly, we show how to do this in feedback via control over networks, which is per se a novel contribution in the scientific panorama. It will be proved that adjusting the policies in real time based on the evolution of the adoption patterns is key to optimize the trade-off between costs and benefits in terms of adoption maximization.

### 37.4.1 Formulation of the Optimal Control Problem

Under the assumption that we can access the values of the thresholds $\{\alpha_v(t)\}_{v\in\mathcal{V}}$ at all time instants $t \in [0, T-1]$, we search for a policy that allows us to increase the number of adopters with respect to that achieved when no incentive policy is enacted, without requiring excessive investments by the policy maker. To optimally attain such a combination of goals, we formulate the following quadratic program with time-varying cost.

**Problem 37.3** ***(Computation of feedback optimal control)***

$$\min_{\{U_v\}_{v\in\mathcal{V}}} \sum_{v\in\mathcal{V}} \left[ \sum_{t=0}^{T-1} \left( Q_v(t)(\alpha_v(t) - \overline{\alpha}_v)^2 + Ru_v^2(t) \right) + Q_v(T)(\alpha_v(T) - \overline{\alpha}_v)^2 \right] \tag{37.5a}$$

$$\text{s.t. } \alpha_v(t+1) = \alpha_v(t) + B_v u_v(t), \ \forall v \in \mathcal{V}, t = 0, \dots, T-1, \tag{37.5b}$$

where

- $U_v = \{u_v(t)\}_{t=0}^{T-1}$ is the sequence of incentives given to the $v$-th agent over the horizon $T$;
- $\overline{\alpha}_v \in [0, 1]$ represents the target threshold one aims at attaining;
- $R > 0$ is a parameter which penalizes the investment made by the policy maker uniformly over the agents and the horizon;
- $\{Q_v(t)\}_{t=0}^{T}$ with $v \in V$ are time-varying, nonnegative weights. They are driving the relative importance of mismatches between the desired and actual thresholds with respect to the policy maker's effort.

The target thresholds are indirectly embedding how much we aim the policy to contrast the initial aversion of agents toward EV adoption. In principle, one could select the constant target $\overline{\alpha}_v = 0$, so as to force the threshold to shrink to zero over time. However, such a choice induces individual opinions to be progressively invariant to the effects of social contagion and it is likely to lead to a waste of resources. Indeed, it is sufficient for $\alpha_v(t)$ to be equal to the percentage of neighbor adopters at time $t$ for the $v$-th agent to become an adopter. To leverage on this property of the considered model, without varying the target to be followed at each time step, we impose

$$\overline{\alpha}_v = \frac{1}{|\mathcal{N}_v|} \sum_{w \in \mathcal{N}_v} x_w(0), \ \forall v \in \mathcal{V}. \tag{37.5c}$$

The cost in (37.5a) is further dependent on the time-varying, nonnegative weights $\{Q_v(t)\}_{t=0}^{T}$, for $v \in \mathcal{V}$, driving the relative importance of mismatches between the desired and actual thresholds with respect to the policy maker's effort. Since we aim at designing efficient and effective policies, these last weights are selected as follows:

$$Q_v(t) = Q(1 - x_v(t)), \ \forall v \in \mathcal{V}, \tag{37.5d}$$

so that the contribution of the tracking objective vanishes whenever the $v$-th agent has turned into an adopter, with the tracking error being weighted by the constant, $Q$ otherwise. Note that, the problem in (37.5a) is separable over the agents so that the associated policies can be computed in parallel. At the same time, it must be pointed out that the incentive given to each agent is still indirectly influenced by the effect the policies have on the others, thanks to the dependence of the weights on the agent's opinion, which is governed by social contagion.

### 37.4.2 Derivation of the Optimal Policies

Among the alternative parameterizations of the policies, here we focus on

$$u_v(t) = K_v(t)(\alpha_v(t) - \overline{\alpha}_v), \ v \in \mathcal{V}, \tag{37.6}$$

where the gain $K_v(t) \in \mathbb{R}$ modulates the effect of the tracking error on the evolution of the thresholds. According to this choice, (37.5a) is a finite horizon linear quadratic regulation (LQR) problem [19]. Therefore, the gains $\{K_v(t)\}_{t=1}^{T}$ associated with the policy tailored for each agent $v \in \mathcal{V}$ can be explicitly computed by resorting to Bellman's equation [3]. To this end, let us initially reformulate the problem in (37.5a) as follows:

$$\underset{\{K_v\}_{v \in \mathcal{V}}}{\text{minimize}} \sum_{v \in \mathcal{V}} \left[ \sum_{t=0}^{T-1} \left( Q_v(t)\xi_v^2(t) + Ru_v^2(t) \right) + Q_v(T)\xi_v^2(T) \right] \tag{37.7a}$$

$$\text{s.t. } \xi_v(t+1) = \xi_v(t) + B_v u_v(t), \ \forall v \in \mathcal{V}, t = 0, \dots, T-1, \tag{37.7b}$$

$$u_v(t) = K_v(t)\xi_v(t), \ v \in \mathcal{V}, t = 0, \dots, T-1, \tag{37.7c}$$

where the evolution of the tracking error $\xi_v(t) = \alpha_v(t) - \overline{\alpha}_v$ can be straightforwardly obtained by manipulating (37.4). By splitting the problem over the agents, we can now solve $|\mathcal{V}|$ distinct LQR problems to design the optimal feedback policies. For each agent, let us define the *terminal cost* $J_v(T)$ as follows:

$$J_v(T) = P_v(T)\xi_v^2(T), \tag{37.8}$$

with $P_v(T) = Q_v(T)$. Moreover, let us introduce the *cost-to-go* at time $T-1$ as follows:

$$\begin{aligned} J_v(T-1) &= \min_{u_v(T-1)} \left[ Q_v(T-1)\xi_v^2(T-1) + Ru_v^2(T-1) + P_v(T)\xi^2(T) \right] \\ &= (Q_v(T-1) + P_v(T))\xi_v^2(T-1) \\ &\quad + \min_{u_v(T-1)} \left[ (R + P_v(T)B_v^2)u_v^2(T-1) + 2P_v(T)B_v\xi(T-1)u_v(T-1) \right] \end{aligned} \tag{37.9}$$

which is obtained by exploiting the definition of $P_v(T)$ and by manipulating the initial cost-to-go. By solving the minimization problem that characterizes (37.9), the optimal policy directed toward the $v$-th agent at time $t$ can be computed in closed form as

$$u_v^{\star}(T-1) = -\frac{P_v(T)B_v}{R + P_v(T)B_v^2}\xi_v(T-1) = K_v(T-1)\xi_v(T-1). \tag{37.10}$$

When replaced into (37.9), simple manipulations led to its equivalent expression

$$J_v(T-1) = P_v(T-1)\xi_v^2(T-1), \tag{37.11a}$$

where the matrix $P_v(T-1)$ can be recursively updated according to

$$P_v(T-1) = Q_v(T-1) + P_v(T) - \frac{(B_v P_v(T))^2}{R + P_v(T)B_v^2}. \tag{37.11b}$$

Similar manipulations can be propagated in time, leading to the following recursive formulas for the backward update of the matrices $P_v(t)$ and gains $K_v(t)$:

$$P_v(t) = Q_v(t) + P_v(t+1) - \frac{(B_v P_v(t+1))^2}{R + P_v(t+1)B_v^2}, \tag{37.12}$$

$$K_v(t) = -\frac{B_v P_v(t+1)}{R + P_v(t+1)B_v^2}, \tag{37.13}$$

for all $t \in [0, T]$ and $v \in \mathcal{V}$. The optimal policy for the $v$-th agent at $t$ is thus given by

$$u_v^{\star}(t) = K_v(\alpha_v(t) - \overline{\alpha}_v), \tag{37.14}$$

and it can be computed forward in time, given the optimal gain and the current threshold.

### 37.4.3 A Receding Horizon Strategy to Boost EV Adoption

As the weights on the tracking error in (37.5a) vary over time according to changes in the agents' opinion, the computation of the matrices $P_v(t)$ in (37.12) and the optimal control gains $K_v(t)$ in (37.13) has to be carried out iteratively. To this end, we exploit the same reasoning of model predictive control [4]. Therefore, at each time step $t = 0, \dots, T-1$, we proceed in a receding horizon fashion by performing the following steps:

1. Given the current opinions $\{x_v(t)\}_{v \in \mathcal{V}}$, the future inclination of each agent is predicted up to time $T$ via (37.1a), by exploiting the current thresholds $\{\alpha_v\}_{v \in \mathcal{V}}$.
2. The value of the weights is updated according to the predicted opinions from time $t+1$ up to time $T$.
3. The matrices $\{P_v(t)\}_{v \in \mathcal{V}}$ and the optimal gains $\{K_v(t)\}_{v \in \mathcal{V}}$ are then computed backward in time, from $T$ to $t$, through (37.12) and (37.13) with the updated weights.
4. The optimal policy to be applied at time $t$ based on the current tracking error is subsequently extracted, i.e. $u_v(t) = K_v(t)(\alpha_v(t) - \overline{\alpha}_v)$ for all $v \in \mathcal{V}$, while all the remaining optimal gains are discarded.
5. The one-step ahead value of the threshold to be used at time $t+1$ can finally be obtained via the dynamic equation in (37.4).

This procedure has to be carried out until the end of the horizon of interest.

## 37.5 Experimental Results

Let us consider an horizon of length $T = 10$ steps, each corresponding to 6 months, so as to look at a time span over which the opinion can actually evolve without being influenced by substantial changes in the EV technology. Over this finite horizon, the optimal receding horizon (RH) polices obtained as in Section 37.4 are assessed over 100 random choices of the seed set, the initial class-driven thresholds $\{\alpha_v(0)\}_{v\in\mathcal{V}}$, and the matrices $\{B_v\}_{v\in\mathcal{V}}$ in (37.4), defined as specified in Section 37.3.2, for three different tuning of the constant weights $R \in \mathbb{R}$ in (37.5a) and $Q \in \mathbb{R}$ in (37.5d). Specifically, we consider

- A first policy, denoted with the acronym $RH_1$, that is designed with $Q = R = 1$. As such, we do not attribute any priority to either tracking the reference thresholds and limiting the invested resources.
- A second strategy ($RH_2$) designed by setting $Q = 10^{-2}$ and $R = 1$. This tuning is expected to lead to policies that reduce the resources used by the policy maker at the price of a possible slower boost in the number of adopters.
- A third policy, here indicated as $RH_3$, obtained for $Q = 10^2$ and $R = 1$. Differently from $RH_2$, this choice the tracking objective, thus likely leading to a more consistent increase in the number of adopters at the price of a relevant use of resources.

These policies are further compared with the static benchmarks introduced in [6], where the threshold is kept constant over the entire horizon, i.e.

$$\tilde{\alpha}_v(t+1) = \tilde{\alpha}_v(t), \tag{37.15a}$$

with an initial value obtained according to the following static relationship:

$$\tilde{\alpha}_v(0) = \min\left\{\left(1 - \rho K_v B_v\right)\alpha_v(0), 1\right\}, \tag{37.15b}$$

where $\rho \in [0, 1]$ is a tunable parameter, here set to 0.3, $K_v$ is chosen based on the features of the considered policy and $\alpha_v(0)$ correspond to the initial threshold prior to the introduction of the policy. Note that, in this case, the opinion evolves according to the irreversible cascademodel with constant thresholds in (37.1). Specifically, the feedback policies are compared with the following:

- The behavior of the irreversible cascade model without incentives, i.e., the Free Evolution (F-E) obtained for $K_v = 0\ \forall v \in \mathcal{V}$.
- The performance attained via a *Flat* policy, designed by setting $K_v = 1$ independently from the features of the $v$-th node, for all $v \in \mathcal{V}$.
- The boost in EV adoption achieved with a *Connection-Based* (Co-B) strategy, where $K_v$ is chosen as the normalize degree of the node, i.e.

$$K_v = \frac{|\mathcal{N}_v| - \min_{w\in\mathcal{V}}|\mathcal{N}_w|}{\max_{w\in\mathcal{V}}|\mathcal{N}_w| - \min_{w\in\mathcal{V}}|\mathcal{N}_w|},\quad \forall v \in \mathcal{V}.$$

- The results are obtained by designing a class-based policy, where the incentive is given is directly linked to the individual electrification potential as follows:
  - $K_v = 1$, if the $v$-th node is *not suited* (NS) for the switch i to an EV;
  - $K_v = \frac{2}{3}$, if the agent is *mildly suited* (MS) for the transition;
  - $K_v = \frac{1}{3}$, if the agent is *almost suited* (AS) to perform the transition;
  - $K_v = 0$, if the agent is *perfectly suited* (PS).

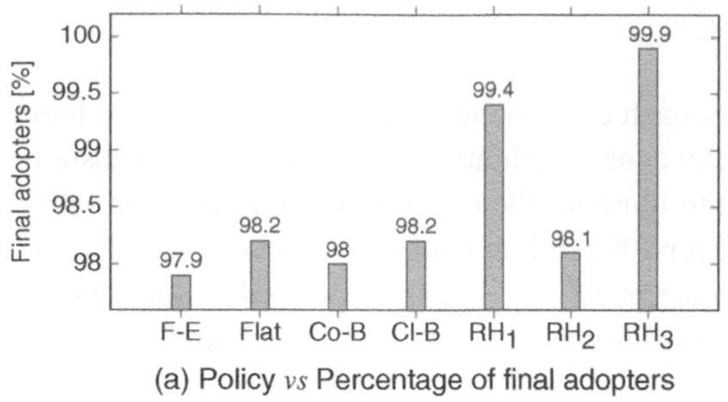


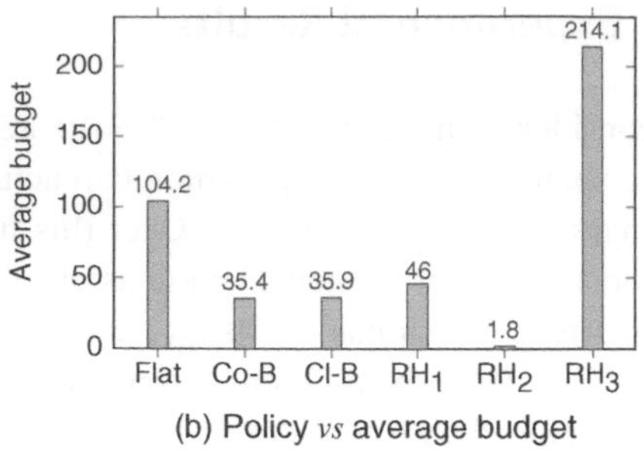


**Figure 37.2** Policy assessment: free evolution *vs* static and feedback policies with different tuning. We compare the flat, connection-based (Co-Based), class-based (Cl-Based), and three receding horizon policies for $R = 1$ and $Q = 1$ ($RH_1$), $Q = 10^{-2}$ ($RH_2$) and $Q = 100$ ($RH_3$).

Note that, differently from [6], both static and feedback policies are modulated by the individual acceptance $B_v$, where the latter influences the effect that the feature-based parameter $K_v$ has on the ultimate threshold obtained with static policies.

Figure 37.2(a) shows the percentage of final adopters achieved by social contagion only and via the use of both static and dynamic policies. Clearly, all optimal feedback strategies result in an increase in the number of final adopters, performing generally better than the connection-based policy and outperforming all the static strategies when the tracking error is properly weighted. It is thus of paramount importance to assess whether this improvement in the final adopters is linked to a marked difference in the costs of the different polices. To evaluate this additional feature, we measure the budget required by static and feedback policies, respectively, as follows:

$$C_{static} = \rho \sum_{v \in \mathcal{V} \setminus S_0} B_v K_v, \tag{37.16a}$$

$$C_{feedback} = \sum_{t=1}^{T} \sum_{v \in \mathcal{V}} u_v^{\star}(t), \tag{37.16b}$$

since static strategies rely on a single investment at the beginning of the horizon, while feedback policies require the investment to be carried out over time. As expected, by considering the average budgets over the 100 tests performed (see Figure 37.2(b)), we can conclude that , when increasing $R$, the average budget allocated by the policies is reduced, with $RH_1$ requiring a similar investment to the one required by connection-based and class-based static policies, while outperforming all of them in terms of percentage of final adopters. Note that, when heavily penalizing the control effort with respect to the tracking performance, as with $RH_2$, the reduction of overall expenditure is particularly marked, with this policy still outperforming at least one of the static strategies. As shown in Figure 37.3, $RH_1$ always outperforms flat policies in terms of budget, even when looking at the maximum investment required. Meanwhile, $RH_3$ is eventually characterized by a minimum average budget that is never smaller than the one required by the flat one, but considerably outperforms them all as it concerns the number of final adopters. Overall, these results show that a proper tuning of the weights for feedback policies allows us to attain improved performance in terms of

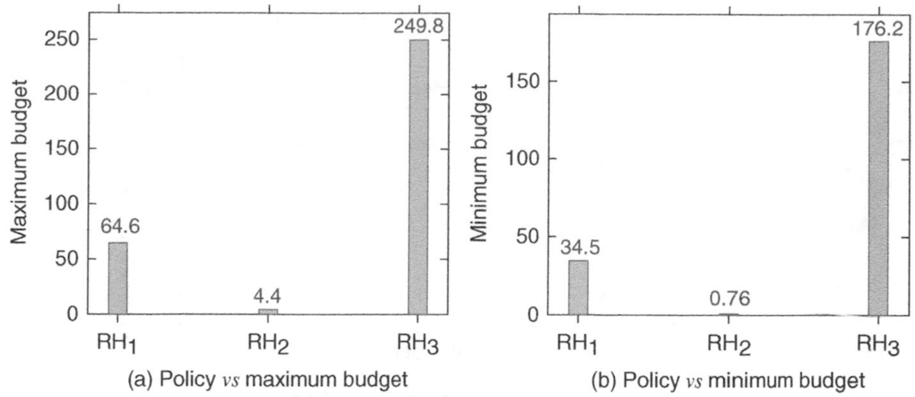


**Figure 37.3** Policy assessment: cost of the feedback policies with different tuning, obtained for $R = 1$ and $Q = 1$ ($RH_1$), $Q = 10^{-2}$ ($RH_2$) and $Q = 100$ ($RH_3$).

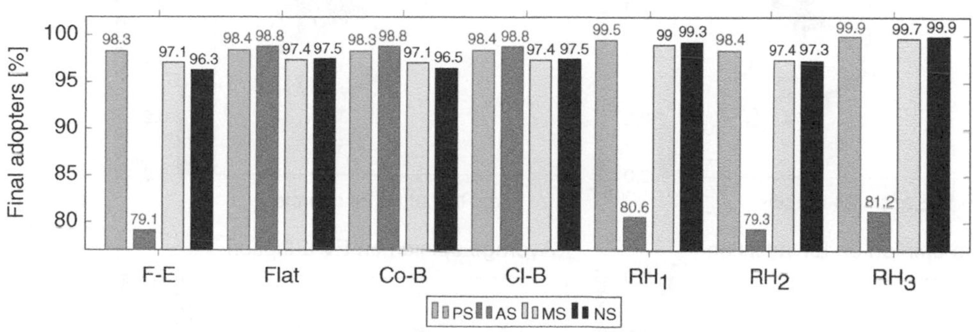


**Figure 37.4** Class-based policy assessment: free evolution *vs* static and feedback policies with different tuning. We compare the flat, connection-based (Co-Based), class-based (Cl-Based) and three receding horizon policies for $R = 1$ and $Q = 1$ ($RH_1$), $Q = 10^{-2}$ ($RH_2$) and $Q = 100$ ($RH_3$).

boosting with respect to *blind* static strategies, while containing the policy maker's effort despite the need for a (even small) incentive to be given to all agents that are not adopters (Figure 37.4).

When looking at the differences in boosting over the classes, static strategies generally lead to a fair number of final EV adopters over the considered classes. On the other hand, feedback policies tend to promote adoption mainly among perfectly, mildly, and not suited agents, while being less favorable to almost suited ones. As such, feedback policies seem to particularly favoring adoption over less-inclined agents, outperforming in this sense even the class-based strategy explicitly directed toward them. As a final comparison, Figure 37.5 juxtaposes the average opinions obtained when considering the free evolution of the irreversible cascade model and when applying the first optimal policy ($RH_1$), respectively. Even if the initial configuration is the same, the considered optimal strategy boosts adoption faster even in more peripheral regions of the network, resulting in a consistently higher number of adopters at the end of the considered estimation horizon.

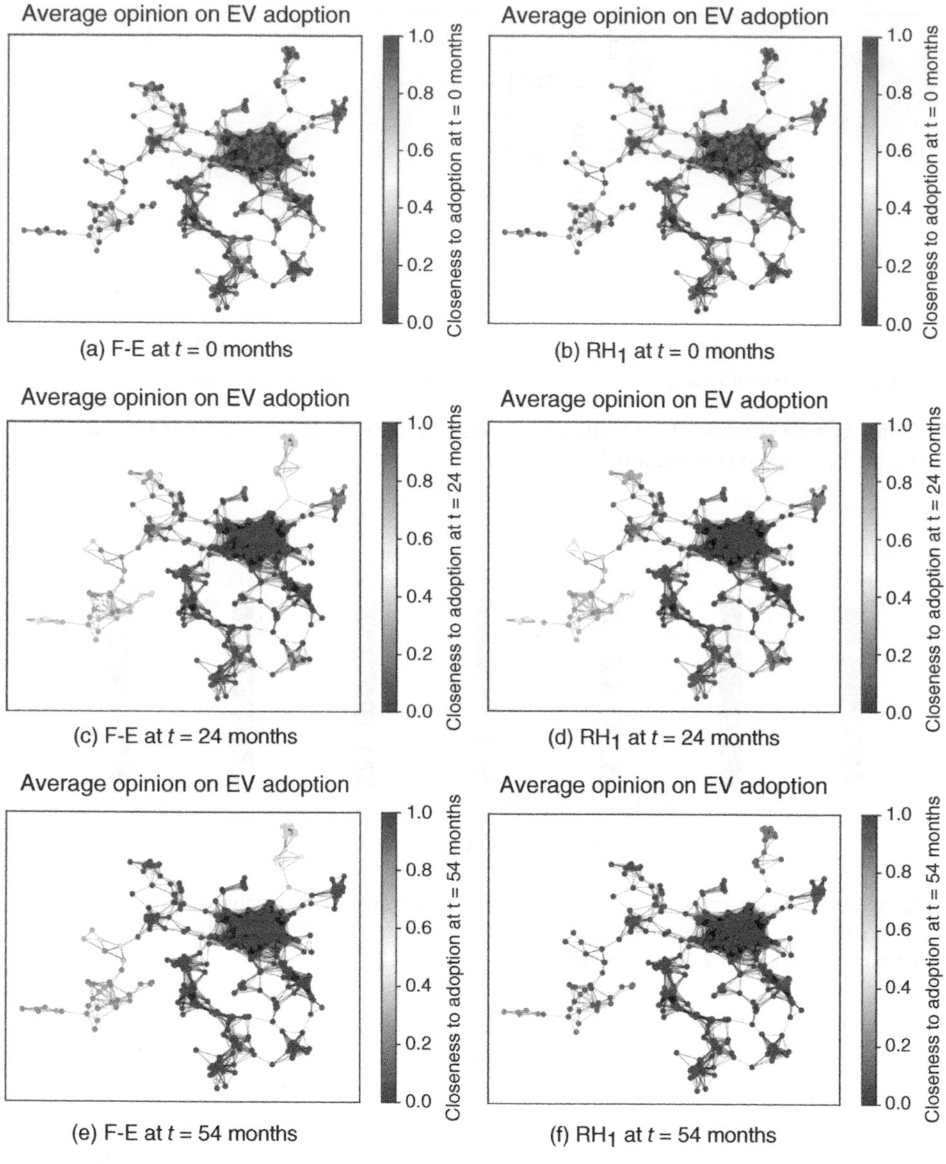


**Figure 37.5** A comparison over time between the average opinions of the nodes. Free evolution of the opinion dynamics *vs* forced one with $RH_1$.

## 37.6 Conclusions

In this chapter, we propose a novel approach to design feedback incentive policies for EV adoption, grounded on a data-based representation of agents' inclination and connections obtained from real mobility patterns. Differently from most existing static incentive strategies, the feedback one we propose does not rely on information on the initial configuration of the agents' opinion only, but it rather leverages a monitoring of the latter over time. As shown by our simulation tests, this eventually results in a more capillary adoption of EVs over the network with comparable resources allocation with respect to static policies, even if feedback polices require incentives to be distributed over time rather than once.

## 37.7 Future Research Challenges

From a technical standpoint, future work will formally analyze the properties of the irreversible cascade model with varying thresholds to have further insights on the features of both the proposed modeling and policy design rationale. As for the latter, the next step will involve introducing budget constraints and optimizing the use of limited resources. Further, we aim at testing the overall framework on different adoption problems.

## Acknowlegments

The work of M. Tanelli has been partially supported by the YOU-SHARE project, funded by Fondazione Cariplo.

## References


**1** Acemoglu, D., Ozdaglar, A., and Yildiz, E. (2011). Diffusion of innovations in social networks. *2011 50th IEEE Conference on Decision and Control and European Control Conference,* 2329–2334.

**2** Barr, S. and Prillwitz, J. (2014). A smarter choice? Exploring the behavior change agenda for environmentally sustainable mobility. *Environment and Planning C: Government and Policy* 32 (1): 1–19.

**3** Bertsekas, D.P. (2000). *Dynamic Programming and Optimal Control,* 2e. Athena Scientific. ISBN 1886529094.

**4** Borrelli, F., Bemporad, A., and Morari, M. (2017). *Predictive Control for Linear and Hybrid Systems,* 1e. Cambridge: Cambridge University Press.

**5** Breschi, V., Ravazzi, C., Strada, S. et al. (2021). Fostering the mass adoption of electrical vehicles: a network-based approach. *provisionally accepted to IEEE Transactions on Control of Network Systems* 9 (4): 1666–1678.

**6** Breschi, V., Tanelli, M., Ravazzi, C. et al. Designing effective policies to drive the adoption of electric vehicles: a data-informed approach. *2020 IEEE International Conference on Human-Machine Systems (ICHMS),* 1–4, 2020.

**7** Campbell, A. (2013). Word-of-mouth communication and percolation in social networks. *American Economic Review* 103 (6): 2466–2498. https://doi.org/10.1257/aer.103.6.2466.

**8** Candogan, O., Bimpikis, K., and Ozdaglar, A. (2012). Optimal pricing in networks with externalities. *Operations Research* 60 (4): 883–905. https://doi.org/10.1287/opre.1120.1066.

**9** Frasca, P., Ravazzi, C., Tempo, R., and Ishii, H. (2013). Gossips and prejudices: ergodic randomized dynamics in social networks. *IFAC Proceedings Volumes* 46 (27): 212–219.

**10** Friedkin, N.E., Proskurnikov, A.V., Tempo, R., and Parsegov, S.E. (2016). Network science on belief system dynamics under logic constraints. *Science* 354 (6310): 321–326.

**11** Granovetter, M. (1978). Threshold models of collective behavior. *The American Journal of Sociology* 83 (6): 1420–1443.

**12** Lévay, P.Z., Drossinos, Y., and Thiel, C. (2017). The effect of fiscal incentives on market penetration of electric vehicles: a pairwise comparison of total cost of ownership. *Energy Policy* 105: 524–533.

**13** Lim, Y., Ozdaglar, A., and Teytelboym, A. (2016). A simple model of cascades in networks. Working Paper.

**14** Lorenz, J. (2007). Continuous opinion dynamics under bounded confidence: a survey. *International Journal of Modern Physics C* 18 (12): 1819–1838.

**15** Morris, S. (2000). Contagion. *The Review of Economic Studies* 67 (1): 57–78. https://doi.org/10.1111/1467-937X.00121.

**16** Needell, Z.A., McNerney, J., Chang, M.T., and Trancik, J.E. (2016). Potential for widespread electrification of personal vehicle travel in the united states. *Nature Energy* 1 (9): 16112.

**17** Proskurnikov, A.V., Ravazzi, C., and Dabbene, F. (2018). Dynamics and structure of social networks from a systems and control viewpoint: a survey of Roberto Tempo's contributions. *Online Social Networks and Media* 7: 45–59.

**18** Rosa, D. and Giua, A. (2013). On the spread of innovation in social networks. *IFAC Proceedings Volumes* 46 (27): 322–327. 4th IFAC Workshop on Distributed Estimation and Control in Networked Systems (2013).

**19** Syrmos, V.L., Lewis, F.L., and Vrabie, D.L. (2012). *Optimal Control*, Wiley.

**20** Yildiz, E., Acemoglu, D., Ozdaglar, A., and Scaglione, A. (2011). Diffusions of innovations on deterministic topologies. *2011 IEEE International Conference on Acoustics, Speech and Signal Processing (ICASSP)*, 5800–5803. https://doi.org/10.1109/ICASSP.2011.5947679.

**21** Zinnari, F., Strada, S., Tanelli, M. et al. (2021). Electrification potential of fuel-based vehicles and optimal placing of charging infrastructure: a large-scale vehicle-telematics approach. *IEEE Transactions on Transportation Electrification*. https://doi.org/10.1109/TTE.2021.3114497.

# Index


## a

accuracy 12, 50, 86, 141, 161, 183, 227, 270, 284, 310, 326, 338, 376, 397, 413, 438
action classification 308
active BCI 12, 37
active learning 20, 86, 413
active mobility assistants 166
active systems 101, 159, 274, 287, 331, 404, 436
adaptation 20, 61, 73, 126, 141, 157, 170, 184, 223, 264, 293, 312, 339, 367, 412, 428
Advanced Driving Assistance Systems 260
Affective Computing 82, 192, 288, 368, 409, 429
Affective Interaction 29, 183
affective neurofeedback 16, 23
affective recognition 186
affective robot 181
agent architecture 81, 131
agent-based framework 131, 455
agent systems 72, 106, 139, 159, 213
agent transparency 105, 305
AI-augmented system 328
ambient intelligence 102, 115, 221, 242, 371
ANOVA 230, 401
artificial intelligence (AI) 73, 105, 125, 195, 321, 435
artificial social agents 83
assistance systems 63, 158, 260, 267, 291, 334
assistant robots 166, 307
assistant services 195
assistive technology/technologies 11, 21, 38, 44, 175, 225, 398, 448
athletes 364
augmented cognition 126, 242, 281
augmented perception 196
authority pathway for weapon engagement (APWE) 134
automated driving 109, 291, 341
automatic speech recognition (ASR) 119
automation transparency 111, 291
autonomous driving 109, 141, 257, 305
Autonomous Squad Member (ASM) 107
autonomous systems 72, 110, 178, 265, 428, 451
autonomous vehicles 137, 257, 306, 419

## b

battery autonomy 466
battery capacity 389
battery life 189, 356
BCI gateway 53
BCI4Kids program 35
belief–desire–intention (BDI) 106
big data 17, 72, 116, 136, 461
blockchain 193
body language 308
bounding boxes 310


*Handbook of Human-Machine Systems*, First Edition. Edited by Giancarlo Fortino, David Kaber, Andreas Nürnberger, and David Mendonça.

brain-controlled telepresence robot 64
brain-wearable devices 182

*c*
Case Management Model and Notation (CMMN) 99
case study 19, 29, 109, 247, 270, 345, 376, 391, 429, 458
central nervous system 12, 362
chat-based systems 115, 121, 238
Childes Corpus 85
Chinese Whispers 86
classification 17, 27, 36, 50, 119, 187, 194, 205, 217, 229, 251, 268, 308, 323, 345, 355, 383, 404, 411, 442, 467
cloud 141, 181, 222, 242, 309, 355, 375, 383, 406, 423
cloud-edge continuum 247
cloudlets 192, 245
Coactive System Model 106
cognitive computing continuum 183, 247
cognitive-oriented models 217
cognitive performance modeling 281
cognitive processor 284
cognitive stress 206
collaboration graphs 100
collective intelligence 143
Common Work Space 62
Companion system 156, 269
Companion technology 155
complex actions 206
computational edge 241
computational intelligence 19, 46, 75, 242, 410
computational models of trust 218
Computer-Mediated Interaction Modeling Language (CIMOL) 100
computer vision 203, 307, 396, 398
computing continuum 241
context-aware monitoring 273
context awareness 184, 243, 251, 257, 273, 322, 369
control 11, 23, 36, 49, 61, 73, 111, 115, 125, 142, 157, 166, 184, 193, 205, 219, 238, 257, 268, 282, 291, 312, 327, 333, 356, 377, 393, 398, 419, 436, 451, 463
control loop 257, 419
conversational technologies 225
convolutional neural network (CNN) 310
cooperative agents 62
cooperative multiagent architecture 131
cooperativeness 155, 219
COVID-19 51, 71, 96, 349, 398

*d*
data integration 188
data privacy 88, 424
dataset 29, 46, 52, 83, 116, 145, 160, 187, 202, 228, 253, 307, 321, 356, 406, 411, 423, 437, 456, 464
decision-making 38, 63, 73, 105, 125, 158, 170, 182, 248, 269, 281, 293, 321, 355, 409, 420, 442, 452
decision support systems 110, 273, 332, 390
deep learning 11, 117, 183, 199, 210, 246, 307, 321, 383, 409, 454
deep neural networks 11, 415
depressive disorder 25
depth cameras 168, 319
depth images 308
dialog systems 115
diffusion process 465
digitalization 71, 331, 446
distributed artificial intelligence 214
driver performance effects 292
driving 35, 61, 80, 109, 125, 141, 195, 246, 257, 287, 291, 333, 356, 401, 419, 464
driving simulator 294, 334

*e*
edge 13, 39, 76, 84, 99, 117, 126, 141, 156, 183, 193, 204, 213, 237, 241, 258, 268, 284, 294, 313, 322, 341, 349, 375, 383, 398, 413, 420, 431, 433, 452, 479

edge computing 141, 192, 199, 243, 370, 383
Edge Intelligence 246
Edge of Things 249
electric vehicles 463
electrocorticography (ECOG) 49
electroencephalography (EEG) 11, 23, 46, 49, 182
electromyography (EMG) 50, 400
embedded computing 365
emerging and disruptive technologies (EDTS) 125
emotional interactions 181
emotional stress 374
emotion expression 227
emotion recognition 156, 182, 225, 352, 410
empty nesters 189
emulated haptic feedback 64
encoder–decoder model 118
environmental transition 463
error rate 56, 270, 328, 400
exoskeletons 12, 351
expert system 59, 332, 420, 454
Explainable AI (XAI) 109

*f*

fall prevention 167
fatigue 13, 43, 76, 286, 298, 333, 374
feature extraction 28, 42, 53, 187, 247, 314, 393, 411, 442
feature fusion 412
feature selection 191, 200, 251
fog computing 242, 245, 285, 361, 383, 429
framework 36, 74, 105, 126, 142, 186, 193, 203, 217, 253, 268, 284, 312, 357, 393, 407, 412, 421, 432, 436, 455, 463
F1-score 56
functional intelligence 155
functional magnetic resonance imaging (fMRI) 11, 23, 74, 288, 442
functional near-infrared spectroscopy (fNIRS) 11, 24, 36
functional traits 12

*g*

Gaussian distribution model 309
gesture-based computing 397
gesture-based interfaces 282, 337
GPT 325
gravity compensation 169

*h*

handcrafted methods 120, 308
hand-object interaction 208
health monitoring 167, 181, 370, 375
heuristics 80, 321
hierarchical Hidden Markov 309
hospital 23, 35, 95, 165, 190, 261, 360
human action recognition 307, 352, 404
human activity recognition 310, 371, 391
human–agent teaming 72, 305
human Architecture Description Language (hADL) 99
human behavior 76, 85, 102, 129, 184, 205, 273, 281, 307, 376, 420
human-centered design (HCD) 129, 436
human-centered development 330
human-compatibility 158
human-engaged computing (HEC) 142
human factors 20, 47, 80, 102, 111, 126, 152, 199, 277, 281, 291, 331, 333, 404, 419, 431, 435, 452
human–human interaction (HHI) 83
human-in-the-loop (HITl) 142
human-in-the-loop cyber-physical systems (HiLCPSS) 142
human–machine combination 142
human–machine computing (HMC) 142
human–machine interface (HMI) 107, 158, 216
human–machine operating system (HMOS) 147

Human–Machine Social Systems (HMSS) 78
human–machine systems 61, 72, 95, 105, 173, 191, 200, 222, 268, 289, 367, 419, 431, 433, 452, 477
human–machine systems (HMS) 72, 419
human-machine team 82, 105
human–machine unit (HMU) 95
human multimodal behavior 91
human–object interaction 310
human-robot transparency model 106
human–swarm interaction 108
Human Systems Integration (HSI) 135
human–technology interaction 156
human tracking 209
hybrid BCI 12, 50
hybrid intelligence 321

*i*

IEEE P2731 17, 435
IEEE P7001 106
IMPACTS model 133
Industry 4.0 69, 71, 125, 380, 391
infrastructure 102, 137, 152, 222, 247, 327, 356, 383, 425, 431, 433, 478
integration 69, 81, 102, 112, 126, 143, 182, 246, 264, 267, 282, 292, 358, 380, 383, 415, 432, 434, 451
intelligent adaptive system (IAS) 126
intelligent collaboration 203
intelligent systems 81, 102, 105, 138, 201, 213, 242, 278, 383, 403, 458
intelligent transportation systems 198, 265, 346
intelligent vehicles 152, 193, 264, 305
interaction-centered design (ICD) 126
Internal Combustion Engine (ICE) 464
Internet of Everything 242, 427
Internet of Things (IoT) 152, 191, 215, 241, 380, 393, 424
Internet of Vehicles 198, 252
interoperability 220, 250, 271, 356, 431, 433
IoT Modeling notation 100

*k*

Kinect 167, 307, 352, 400
Know-How-to-Cooperate (KHC) 61
Know-How-to-Operate (KHO) 61
knowledge model 127

*l*

lane maintenance 298
laser range finders 168
linear discriminant analysis (LDA) 52, 342
logistic regression (LR) 50
long short-term memory 119, 312

*m*

machine learning (ML) 11, 45, 52, 84, 113, 116, 142, 191, 202, 210, 221, 251, 265, 278, 331, 342, 371, 383, 413, 457
magnetoencephalography (MEG) 23, 441
maneuverability improvement 167
maneuvering characteristics augmentation system (MCAS) 125
mental health 35, 122, 181, 225, 331
mental workload 13, 27, 293, 337
meta capabilities 270
Metaverse 71
methodology 103, 125, 151, 227, 269, 288, 357, 419, 442
methods 15, 27, 40, 50, 67, 76, 85, 109, 117, 128, 144, 162, 171, 184, 200, 205, 265, 274, 282, 291, 307, 324, 334, 355, 383, 399, 409, 431, 433, 458, 469
mid-air gesture 398
military 57, 71, 107, 134, 281, 351, 384, 420
ML training data 79
Mobile Collaboration Modeling (MCM) notation 99

mobile crowd sensing and computing (MCSC) 142
mobile robots 50
mobility assistance robots 165
modeling 16, 31, 83, 95, 123, 131, 143, 158, 175, 181, 200, 205, 214, 257, 276, 281, 312, 323, 349, 396, 400, 417, 428, 454, 463
motor imagery (MI) 49
multiagent systems 108, 139, 159, 213
multimodal communications 111
multimodal datasets 84
multimodal information 75, 181, 311
multimodal interaction 84, 407
multimodal reference resolution 84
multimodal sensory information 160
multimodal task description (MMTD) 85
multisensor 357, 373

***n***

Naïve Bayes 329, 386
naturalistic decoding 227
natural language 89, 109, 115, 143, 163, 204, 284, 325, 337
Natural language generation (NLG) 117
natural language processing 109, 116, 163, 325, 337
Natural language understanding (NLU) 117
neuroscience 18, 29, 45, 58, 74, 162, 214, 239, 435
nonverbal behavior 89, 220
North Atlantic Treaty Organization (NATO) 126

***o***

obstacle avoidance 64, 168, 193, 259
on-board 50, 351
ontologies 160, 251, 257, 276, 455
Operator Assistance Systems 268

***p***

passive BCI 12, 37
passive mobility assistants 166
path planning 170
P300-based BCI 16, 52
pediatric BCI 35
people-driven collaborative process (PDCP) 95
Pepper robot 90
performance prediction 323
personal digital assistants 115, 398
pervasive computing 152, 241, 349, 461
physical activity 18, 29, 165, 359, 373, 393, 438
physical disability 36
piezoresistive 373
posttraumatic stress disorder 25
power supply 189, 350
precision 14, 56, 144, 270, 335, 397, 443
prediction 21, 52, 108, 166, 188, 194, 213, 238, 244, 281, 304, 323, 385, 453
privacy 17, 71, 87, 101, 111, 121, 125, 189, 228, 241, 267, 343, 357, 393, 415, 423, 438
process analysis 326
prototype 66, 166, 185, 270, 328, 346, 359, 403
Python 51, 263

***r***

reactive BCI 12, 40
reasoning 80, 92, 105, 131, 155, 171, 186, 201, 203, 213, 244, 258, 273, 296, 322, 341, 412, 454, 472
recurrent neural network (RNN) 50, 119, 186, 310
respiratory rate 364, 373
robot signals 89
rollator 165
rule-based systems 116

***s***

safety 17, 62, 80, 125, 166, 189, 213, 268, 281, 292, 330, 333, 380, 390, 419, 431, 433, 455
self-confidence 185
self-explainability 155

sensitivity 14, 56, 374
sequence-to-sequence (Seq2Seq) 117
shared workspace 96, 158
signal processing 11, 28, 36, 317, 345, 349, 416, 442, 478
simulation 51, 106, 122, 150, 198, 263, 270, 284, 291, 323, 366, 390, 401, 420, 458, 468
simulation modeling 284
situation assessment 127
situation awareness (SA) 106, 126, 294, 451
situation awareness-based agent transparency (SAT) 106
smart garment 351, 381
smartphone 71, 184, 275, 335, 350, 397
social robots/robotics 75, 174, 181
Society 5.0 71
socio-affective factors 76
sociotechnical systems 125, 289, 419
software agents 130, 156
software development 95, 245, 328, 442
software engineering 98, 134, 244
spatiotemporal semantic network 207
specificity 56, 432, 433, 463
SPINE 190, 349
standards 17, 44, 86, 101, 126, 221, 244, 259, 345, 356, 428, 431, 433
support vector machine (SVM) 50, 308, 311, 342, 386, 455
survey 21, 40, 59, 73, 110, 116, 137, 153, 162, 165, 191, 202, 243, 270, 287, 293, 334, 367, 381, 394, 415, 419, 442, 454, 478
synthetic decoding 227

***t***

tactile devices 184
task guidance 269
task-oriented systems 117
taxonomy 19, 76, 246, 268, 339, 428
teamwork model 78
techniques 24, 42, 49, 74, 108, 133, 141, 162, 169, 193, 206, 253, 276, 305, 307, 331, 355, 373, 398, 420, 451
telepresence 63, 172
text-to-speech (TTS) 119
theory 58, 73, 92, 98, 111, 136, 162, 170, 210, 213, 268, 282, 343, 410, 419, 455
threats 133, 427
3D sensor 204
touch-based gesture 398
tracking 39, 50, 86, 122, 126, 174, 187, 200, 207, 226, 273, 288, 314, 341, 351, 387, 417, 442, 454, 471
trajectory planner 264
transfer learning 42, 117, 246, 276, 316, 412
transportation 16, 80, 137, 178, 195, 265, 281, 304, 333, 409, 432, 433, 478
trust 71, 86, 106, 125, 155, 190, 193, 213, 276, 304, 323, 340, 349, 393, 410, 428, 438, 470
trust model 126, 216
trust relationship 132, 216
trustworthiness 125, 155, 213, 349
trustworthy AI systems 323

***u***

ubiquitous computing 58, 241, 371, 405, 459
user-centered design (UCD) 129
user model 127, 161, 276, 287, 429

***v***

vehicle 50, 111, 125, 152, 193, 244, 257, 286, 291, 333, 398, 419, 458, 463
virtual agents 115, 225
virtual reality (VR) 17, 28, 89, 197, 351
visual-evoked potentials (VEP) 16
visual human–computer interactions 193
vital signs 373, 389
voice user experience (VUX) 118
VR headset 17, 351

### w

walking assistance 165
wearable 101, 142, 181, 241, 267, 335, 349, 373, 383, 398, 409, 438
wearable computing 183, 242, 349
wearable devices 182, 241, 267, 338, 349, 375, 383, 398, 409
wearables 146, 182, 249, 275, 339, 349, 373, 383
"what if" simulation 106
work-related stress 321

### x

XAI planning 111

### y

Youtube 85, 208, 398

IEEE Press Series on

## Human-Machine Systems

The IEEE Press Series on Human-Machine Systems is to publish leading-edge books that mainly cover the following topics integrated human/machine systems at multiple scales, including areas such as human/machine interaction; cognitive ergonomics and engineering; assistive/companion technologies; human/machine system modeling, testing and evaluation; and fundamental issues of measurement and modeling of human-centered phenomena in engineered systems. Our target audience includes human-machine systems professionals from academia, industry and government who are interested in enhancing their knowledge and perspectives in their areas of interest.

*Series Editor:*

**Giancarlo Fortino**
University of Calabria, Italy

1. *Handbook of Human-Machine Systems*
   **Edited by Giancarlo Fortino, David Kaber, Andreas Nürnberger, and David Mendonça**